American Heretic

American Heretic

Theodore Parker and Transcendentalism

Dean Grodzins

The University of North Carolina Press
Chapel Hill and London

Manufactured in the United States of America
Set in Janson with Van Dijck display
by Tseng Information Systems, Inc.

The paper in this book meets the guidelines
for permanence and durability of the Committee on
Production Guidelines for Book Longevity of the
Council on Library Resources.

Library of Congress Cataloging-in-Publication Data
Grodzins, Dean.
American heretic : Theodore Parker and transcendentalism /
Dean Grodzins.
p. cm.
Includes bibliographical references and index.
ISBN 0-8078-2710-X (alk. paper)
1. Parker, Theodore, 1810–1860.   2. Transcendentalism.
I. Title.
BX9869.P3 G76   2002
289.1′092—dc21
2002003832

06   05   04   03   02   5   4   3   2   1

To my father and mother

Contents

A section of photographs appears after page 294.

Preface

People loved Theodore Parker, or they hated him. He was a saint, a prophet, and a tribune—or an infidel, a fanatic, and a demagogue. Many believed, and some feared, that he was the most influential minister in mid-nineteenth-century America.

He pastored a "Congregational Society" that was the largest free church in the country and the largest church of any kind in Boston. In the 1850s, almost three thousand people went weekly to hear him preach (nearly 2 percent of the population of the city), and some 50,000 listened to him lecture every year, in lyceums from Maine to Illinois. Meanwhile, thousands more bought his published sermons and addresses, which he produced in a never-ending stream, and which found readers on both sides of the Atlantic. Scholars and thinkers took his work seriously, and even hostile critics respected his vast erudition; he seemed able to discourse learnedly on almost any topic and could read more than twenty languages.

Notable men and women, not a few of them controversial figures themselves, proudly counted him their friend and, in many cases, their pastor as well. William Lloyd Garrison regularly attended his services, as did many other abolitionists, while antislavery politicians, prominent among them Charles Sumner and Horace Mann, turned to Parker constantly for counsel. Wendell Phillips and Parker were close partners; in 1855, the two nearly went to prison together for trying to prevent the return to slavery of the fugitive Anthony Burns. Elizabeth Cady Stanton was for a time part of his congregation, as were other leading advocates of women's rights, including Julia Ward Howe, who credited Parker with encouraging her to become a writer. Louisa May Alcott considered Parker a decisive influence on her life and wrote warmly of her experiences with him and in his Society in her novel *Work* (in which he appears, thinly disguised, as the character Thomas Power). A generation of New England–born intellectuals, including Thomas Wentworth Higginson, Octavius Brooks Frothingham, Franklin Sanborn, and Caroline Healey Dall, regarded Parker as mentor.

Then there was Abraham Lincoln. A couple of Lincoln's old Springfield friends, most notably Billy Herndon, his law partner, political sidekick, and biographer (and himself a Parker enthusiast), claimed, after Lincoln's death, that Lincoln admired Parker's highly unorthodox theology. The claim was and is controversial, but Lincoln certainly read Parker. Lincoln's famous definition of democracy, as "government of the people, by the people, for the people," was inspired in part by one Parker developed: "government of all, by all, for all."

Parker's hold on others did not come from any animal magnetism. He was neither tall nor handsome; his big head was bald, and the features on his long face were plain. He did have piercing blue eyes, but in later life they often were hidden behind reading glasses; his voice was deep and resonant, but not especially strong (in large halls, the house had to sit very still to hear him). His impact came instead from the force of his complex personality, from the exciting power of his prose, and above all from the strength of his ideas and the appeal of his life story.

His ideas upset conventional thinking. In the first phase of Parker's career, up to 1846, when he was deeply involved in the Transcendentalist movement, he challenged how people thought about religious truth. In the second phase, when he was deeply involved in the events leading to the Civil War, he challenged how people thought about American democracy. I will deal with the second phase in a future book. Here, I explain how and why Parker became a heretic, and how heresy worked as religion for him and others. Politics is not, however, absent from this book. I track Parker's growing concern with political matters and close with him refining the epochal definition of democracy that Lincoln found so compelling.

I tell, too, the story of Parker's remarkable, strange rise from obscurity and poverty to fame, prosperity, and "martyrdom," and seek to explain the cultural context in which this story could occur and have widespread appeal. I look behind the public Parker; without some grasp of the hidden, inner man, the famous one cannot be understood. Parker had secrets so intimate that even his closest companions did not know them, yet he left a record of them on paper. This record is fragmentary and sometimes in code, but extraordinarily revealing nonetheless. Finally, I evoke Parker's world and provide a history of the relationships, ideas, and practices from which that world was made.

I am engaged in a work of recovery. First, I seek to recover Parker himself. Most Americans today, even many scholars, scarcely remember him—a fact that says more about the vagaries of reputation than about Parker himself. For nearly a century after his untimely death at age forty-nine, in 1860, interest in him remained high around the world. Two collected editions of his works were published, a fourteen-volume set in London and a fifteen-

x *Preface*

volume edition in Boston. Admirers in other countries, meanwhile, published his writings in translation. A collected *Werke* had appeared in Germany even before he died; afterward, a collected *Skrifter* came out in Sweden, and pamphlets in Japan. There were, as well, six English-language biographies (four American, two British), and others in French, German, and Dutch. The centennial of Parker's birth, in 1910, was marked by major celebrations. His life and works were treated in all the major literary histories.

Why the attention waned—and it began to wane around 1950—requires some explanation. When the American literary canon was reconceived restrictively in the mid-twentieth century, Parker, like many others, was unjustly dropped from it. At the same time, the rise of neo-Orthodoxy pushed his arch-liberal theology out of fashion. In recent years, the canon has expanded, and neo-Orthodoxy has ebbed, but no one has taken up Parker again. The resulting situation is odd. Books are written about Transcendentalism and antislavery, for example, that scarcely mention his name, although he was a major leader of both movements. Again, anthologies of American literature are published that include works by his mentors, co-workers, and protégés, but not by him. There is a great hole in our knowledge of the past, which I seek to fill.

Parker has been neglected lately, I suspect, because he held a view of the world that many today find alien. He was passionately religious, believed deeply in the existence of God and the immortality of the soul, without being theologically conservative. This perspective has been almost lost among contemporary intellectuals. It is something else I want to recover.

Doing so will change the way we think about Transcendentalism. It usually is discussed in the context of the so-called American Renaissance. The term "American Renaissance" was coined in 1878 by a New York clergyman, but it gained academic popularity only after the publication, in 1941, of F. O. Matthiessen's seminal *American Renaissance: Art and Expression in the Age of Emerson and Whitman*. Matthiessen justifiably placed Transcendentalism, the most important American intellectual movement of the nineteenth century, at the heart of the antebellum American literary awakening; yet he also seemed to imply, both with his title and his emphasis on Ralph Waldo Emerson, that Transcendentalism was a movement away from religion. After all, the original Italian Renaissance conventionally is identified as the birthplace of modern secular humanism, and the Protestant Reformation is portrayed, at least in some measure, as a reaction against the secularism of the Renaissance. Again, secularization seems to be the story if (as commonly happens) Parker's friend Emerson is taken as the representative Transcendentalist man. Emerson left the ministry to pursue a literary career, and theological themes moved from the foreground to the background of his work.

If the story of Transcendentalism is told from Parker's point of view, it looks very different. He never abandoned the ministry, and theology remained for him a central concern, even when he grew more political. Epochs in his life are marked by the preaching of sermons; as I will relate, his career was altered forever by the outraged reaction to a sermon he preached on 19 May 1841, *A Discourse on the Transient and Permanent in Christianity*. For Parker, Transcendentalism was at least as much a new Reformation as a new Renaissance. When readers close this book, then, I hope not only that they will feel they know Parker for the first time, but that they will look on his world, and on Transcendentalism, with fresh eyes.

My brother likes to say that I have been writing Theodore Parker's life in real time. I think he exaggerates, but this project has taken years, during which I inevitably accumulated many debts. If this book may be blamed on me alone, the credit for it must be shared.

It would never have been written had not two early teachers, Benson Bowditch and Jane Redlich Rabe, inspired me to become a historian. At Williams College, Charles Dew and Robert Volz called my attention to Parker and were unstinting with their help. At Harvard, Donald Fleming gave me encouragement and held me to high standards. I would not be the scholar I am today were it not for what I learned from him, and from Bernard Bailyn. David Hall deeply enriched my thinking about religion as lived experience. Conrad Wright taught me the fundamental lesson that I could never understand Transcendentalism without understanding the Unitarian context from which it emerged.

I always will be grateful to the Society of American Historians for awarding my doctoral dissertation, on which the first five chapters of this book are based, the 1994 Allan Nevins Prize; the kind words of John Higham, who presented me with the prize, I shall not forget. I am deeply grateful, too, to Harvard University, for awarding my dissertation the DeLancey K. Jay Prize, and to the Harvard History Department, for awarding it the Harold K. Gross Prize. I owe much to the Pew Program in Religion and American History at Yale (now the Center for the Advanced Study of Religion and American History), directed by Jon Butler and Harry Stout, for giving me a Faculty Fellowship in 1994–95, when I started to rework the dissertation into a book.

Some of the principal themes of this book I first developed in a paper presented at a conference on Transcendentalism sponsored by the Massachusetts Historical Society in 1997. The paper later was published as an article in *Transient and Permanent: The Transcendentalist Movement and Its Contexts*, edited by Charles Capper and Conrad E. Wright. I am grateful to the Massachusetts Historical Society, which published the volume, for allowing me to reproduce parts of this article in Chapter 10.

Various scholars have been extraordinarily generous in answering questions and making available to me the fruits of their own archival research. In this regard, I want to thank Sterling Delano, Philip F. Gura, Tim Jensen, David Johnson, and Guy Litton. Bruce Venarde helped me translate Parker's sometimes idiosyncratic Latin. I especially am indebted to Megan Marshall, who deepened my understanding of Elizabeth Palmer Peabody; Helen Deese, who led me to the treasures of Caroline Healey Dall's letters and diary; and Joel Myerson, who placed his impressive collection of manuscripts at my disposal. My greatest debt, however, is to Marc-Antoine Kaeser. He not only introduced me to the papers of Parker's friend, Edouard Desor, at the State Archives of Neuchâtel, Switzerland, but, with his partner, Milena Mile, he put me up while I was researching there in 1997.

The staffs of the various archives in which I worked were uniformly helpful. Those at the Andover-Harvard Theological Library, the Massachusetts Historical Society, and the Rare Book and Manuscript Department of the Boston Public Library have become my friends. But I particularly want to thank Alan Seaburg and Tim Driscoll, the former manuscript curators at Andover-Harvard, who bent rules to provide me with ideal working conditions.

My various research assistants have contributed more to this book than I suspect they know. I especially want to thank Karen Einstein and Alison Musgrave for their efforts. Naomi King, my assistant at Meadville/Lombard, provided valuable assistance in preparing the manuscript for publication. Seymour Shapiro photographed portraits for me, and David Kessler helped me with detective work.

My manuscript has benefited from the constructive criticism of others, who saved me from errors and helped clarify my thinking. For their care and acuity, I want to thank Charles Capper, Donald Fleming, and Barbara Packer, who examined every chapter, and Bernard Bailyn, Gary Collison, Conrad Wright, members of the 1995 Pew Fellows Conference at Yale, and members of the Religious History Colloquium at the Harvard Divinity School, who examined selected chapters.

My agent, William B. Goodman, believed in this book as much as I did. Lewis Bateman and his successor, Charles Grench, at the University of North Carolina Press showed unflagging interest in this project during its long gestation. Paula Wald, my project editor, Eric Schramm, my copy editor, and others on the staff of the press who helped see the manuscript through production deserve all praise for being efficient, informed, and considerate.

My aunt, Ethel Grodzins Romm, gave me much wise advice. My parents, Lee and Lulu A. Grodzins, gave me more help than I can ever repay. I happily and gratefully dedicate this book to them.

Note on Transcription

Parker's manuscripts are filled with older or British forms of certain words. When one of his manuscripts was published, the printer typically modernized or Americanized Parker's spelling. Because I quote from both manuscript and published sources, different spellings of the same word will sometimes appear (e.g., both "labour" and "labor").

Angle brackets (⟨ ⟩) indicate a deletion in the manuscript: "I came here against my ⟨will⟩, judgement ⟨& common sense⟩." Vertical lines (| |) indicate an interlining in the manuscript: "[I]t may be |said of this notion that there are no facts in history to support it| & but a few principles of Philosophy." Square brackets ([ ]) indicate either an editorial insertion or an expansion of an abbreviation or symbol (e.g., "Xty" becomes "[Christianity]" and "0" becomes "[nothing]"); in the latter case, the original abbreviation or symbol is provided in the note. Parker's underlining is indicated by italics, his double underlining by capitals, and his rare triple underlining by italicized capitals. A singular and unique instance of Parker double underlining a capitalized word is transcribed as underscored italicized capitals: "⟨My wife is a⟩ *DEVIL*."

Chapter One

This World of Joys
and Sorrows

"On the 24th of August, 1810, early on a hot, sweltering morning, I came into this world of joys and sorrows," wrote Theodore Parker forty-nine years later, shortly before his death. He first saw light in a hodge-podge farmhouse in "Kite's End," the southern district of Lexington, Massachusetts, a swampy village northeast of Boston that was home to a thousand people and half as many cows. He was the last of eleven children, with nine surviving sisters and brothers, ages four to twenty-five, most of them still living under the family roof. Theodore—"the gift of God"—was the child of his parents' old age. His father, John, was forty-nine, and his mother, Hannah Stearns, was a remarkable forty-six. His father's mother, the "Widow Pierce," still hale at seventy-nine, had a room of her own upstairs.[1]

Theodore later remembered the Parker farmhouse as a "cheerless shelter." It faced South, with two stories in front, one in back, a huge, central chimney made of bricks laid in clay, and massive oak beams protruding from the older, western part, which had been built by his grandfather's grandfather. The few large rooms were dark, for the windows were tiny. Theodore much preferred being outside, weather permitting. Among his earliest memories was a longing to see the winter gone, and the great snowbank out the front door melted, so that he need no longer be confined to the kitchen.[2]

Then came the first warm days of spring, "which brought the blue birds to their northern home, and tempted the bees to try short flights, in which they presently dropped on the straw my provident father had strewn for them over the snow about their hives." Finally the snow would melt, and the little blond boy in homespun brown petticoats would be allowed a free range. There was much to explore. Out the front door was a gentle slope down into the "Great Meadow," a grassy, spongy valley; in back the house was sheltered from the north winds by a steep, rocky hill. Theodore would delight in the smell of the damp earth, or sit in some dry spot and watch "the great yellow clouds of April" roll by. In May, the fruit trees would bloom—plum, peach, cherry, and apple—followed in June by the blossoming of a nearby grove of white locust. In his sisters' garden grew "crimson peony, daffodils, white and yellow narcissus, white and red roses," and nearby could be found the "handsomest flowering shrubs and plants of New England." The summer slowly passed to autumn, when the brilliant foliage came—"How red the maples were, how yellow the birches and the walnuts, and what richly tinted leaves did the chestnut shake down!" Too soon it grew cold, and the child was brought back indoors for the winter. The snows would pile as high as the top of the kitchen window, while he built corncob houses and hoped that his father or a brother would take him to the barn, "where the horse, the oxen and the cows were a perpetual pleasure," or that "sleighs full of cousins" would come to visit.[3]

Such joys cost little; they had to, for his family was not prosperous. His father's father, a farmer and wheelwright who had commanded the Lexington militia in the first battle of the Revolutionary War, had had a respectable property, but three years after his death in 1775, his widow, Lydia, had made a second marriage to one Ephraim Pierce, which, wrote Theodore, "both she and her children had bitter cause to repent." Her new husband was improvident and had nine children to support, while she had seven of her own. Soon, most of the estate was wasted, and they were all forced to live off what was left, her "widow's thirds." About 1784, her eldest son, John, had married Hannah Stearns, the daughter of a neighboring farmer, and "went back to the original homestead to take care of his mother, while he should support his handsome young wife and such family as might happen."[4]

A large family happened, and he did support them, mostly by building pumps and cider presses—"he was the only man about there that did that," recalled Theodore's orphaned nephew, Columbus Greene, who came to live with the family in 1819, when he was seven—and by repairing wagons, tools, and ploughs. Yet John Parker also "had lost a good deal of money and had debts on responsibilities for others that were not paid till near his death." He worked hard in his little shop, and while he taught his boys to be handy with wood, their big job was to run the farm. Theodore remembered that his father was "a skilful farmer; though, as he lived not on his own land, but on 'widow's thirds,' which his mother had only life estate in, he was debarred from making costly improvements in the way of buildings, fences and apple trees, which are long in returning profit to him that plants." Greene remembered that "the farm was run down and was running down." They did have a small orchard that produced fine peaches, and Greene recalled raising corn, potatoes, beans, other "vegetables," and apples. John let the boys sell what they grew "on commission," and later for themselves, sometimes as far off as the market in Boston. The women of the family took in sewing, and the Parkers "lived with rigid economy."[5]

"I HAVE often been praised for virtues which really belong to my mother and father," Theodore later wrote, "and if they were also mine, they must have come so easy under such training, that I should feel entitled to but small merit for possessing them." He remembered his parents as very different from one another, his father a figure of intellect and authority, his mother one of sentiment and love. The distinctions he drew between them sometimes appear as if he were determined that they had governed separate spheres. He asserts, for example, that although his mother "[l]oved Poetry . . . could repeat a good deal of Poetry—especially Ballads and religious Poems, Hymns, &c.," his father "did not like poetry"; but he also remembered that his father read Pope, Dryden, Milton, Shakespeare, John Trumbull, "Peter Pindar" (John Wolcot), and Abraham Cowley. Yet his parents did seem to have different outlooks and temperaments, and to relate differently to their youngest child. Theodore was emotionally close to his mother, as he was not with his father. Each had a distinct influence on his religious training.[6]

John Parker was "stout, able bodied," and " 'uncommon strong' "—"only one man in the town could surpass him in physical strength"; Theodore's own existence was evidence of his continued virility. He was a "thoughtful, reading man—not restless," with "all the manners of the neighborhood," who wore his hair tied in back (the old-fashioned way), and followed the "ancient Puritan custom" of seating his family at dinner by age. The adjective most often used to describe him was "silent"—an indication of his considerable reserved dignity. When he died in 1836, the minister recorded his name in the church records as "Mr. John Parker." In those days, at least in old-fashioned villages like Lexington, "Mister" was still an honorific reserved for gentlemen; it was seldom bestowed on a pump maker of yeoman stock and modest means. He clearly had the respect of his community—even though he was, by Theodore's admiring account, "fearless in the expression of opinion," and one of only five Federalists in the town. His neighbors often called on him to arbitrate disputes, administer estates, and serve as guardian for widows and orphans. The records of several estates that he administered survive, and they show that the trust in him was well placed. He also was respected at home. Greene remembered that his grandfather "kept good discipline in family— always used to read [aloud] in evening and with a wave of the [hand?] dismissed the children to bed at 8. Did not whip the children but they always obeyed him. . . . [He] had perfect government in his family and governed easily."[7]

John's formal schooling had ended at age fourteen, when the Revolution broke out, but he had gone on to educate himself. He had helped to found the small Lexington circulating library and in his spare moments he was usually with a book. He enjoyed reading history and travel (which is mostly what the library stocked), but was particularly "fond of Metaphysics—Psychology and all departments of *intellectual* and moral Philosophy." Greene did not think there was anyone in Lexington who had read so much as his grandfather. He needed only five hours sleep and would rise before the sun in the winter to study—a habit Theodore also acquired. There survives, as testimony to John Parker's painstaking efforts, a small, homemade book, dating from the 1790s, in which he carefully practiced his handwriting and worked out problems of applied mathematics, such as this one: "Passing by a Steeple I measure the Shadow and find it 45 Feet, at the same time my staff being 4 feet Length set up Perpendicular casteth a Shadow 18 inches in Length now I would know the Height of the Steeple?" The answer, he correctly calculated, is 120 feet. According to Theodore, in later life his father understood not only trigonometry, but algebra, plain and solid geometry, and logarithms.[8]

Theodore seems to have been in awe of his father. He sought his approval, but never his intimacy. The approval came sparingly enough, even though Theodore early established himself as the family's intellectual star. Greene recalled that although his grandfather enjoyed his son's conversation, he did so "quietly and in silence—He never boasted of it and never made remarks that would tend to make Theodore self-conscious or vain." Theodore never forgot the rare occasions when his father did praise him, even indirectly. Eight years after John Parker's death, his son delivered a lecture in Boston before a meeting of "men of colour" and was enthusiastically received as a "friend of mankind." He wrote in his journal that he had only been "so much gratified but once before," when he was a little boy at a public, oral examination in school: "One of the spectators—one of the general committee of the town asked my father—'Who was that fine boy who spoke up so smart'? My father said 'Oh that was one of *my* boys, the youngest.'! When my father told it at home—that John Muzzey [the eminent townsman] had asked so— I felt a deep Joy—not so much for my sake—as for the satisfaction it seemed to give my father."[9]

Although craving his father's sanction, Theodore did not, and perhaps could not, confide in him. "I don't think Theodore consulted his father much concerning his plans for education," recalled Greene. "He knew his father couldn't help him and so he laid his own plans and carried them out." When he decided to try to enter Harvard in 1830, he told his father nothing. Later, he courted Lydia Dodge Cabot for a year, yet his father knew nothing about her until Theodore announced to him that they were engaged.[10]

He recalled that his father's religion was more a matter of the head than the heart, and Greene confirms this portrait. John Parker was "a great reader of the Bible," owned a church pew, attended services regularly, gave his chil-

This World of Joys and Sorrows

dren religious instruction, and required them to say prayers and hymns before going to bed—but he was not deemed very pious by the high standards of New England. He did not have his children baptized until his wife insisted, nor, apparently, did he take communion. He led no family prayers and ceased saying grace at meals when Theodore was about ten. He was an *"independent thinker* in religion" who did not believe in eternal damnation, nor in "the grotesque miracles" of either Testament. Like most religious liberals of the time, he disliked equally the New Divinity Calvinism of Jonathan Edwards and the near-secular utilitarianism of William Paley's ethics. He was "very well read in English philosophy," "a powerful controversialist when engaged in argument," and "nice & acute in metaphysical analysis," but never passionate.[11]

Theodore did acquire one passion from his father—for learning. John Parker's example was the model for Theodore's own awesome self-education. A schoolmate recalled that Theodore was inclined to stay "at home in the chimney corner" with a book, and observed that this "disposition he inherited from his father, who very rarely went from home to visit his neighbors . . . but read books a good deal." With his father's quiet encouragement, he also early developed interests in botany, geology, and astronomy. The impression of his father's religious opinions, however, was not to be revealed for some time. Although John Parker rejected the "grotesque miracles" of the Bible, Theodore did not until years after he left home. Theodore's rationalistic habits of mind came from his father; his religion, as he often said, "was the inheritance my mother gave me."[12]

His mother, Hannah, was a slender woman of medium height, with fair hair turned grey, blue eyes, "and a singularly fresh and delicate complexion, more nervous than muscular." She would wear a workaday blue check dress until dinner was served at noon, but after the cooking, eating, and cleaning were over, would change into something prettier. A neighbor remembered her as a "very mild and amiable woman" with a "remarkable memory." Theodore confirms that she knew the Bible "thoroughly," as well as a great many ballads, hymns, and religious poems, and "knew by heart" many New England family histories, which she would tell to him. She was "imaginative, delicate-minded, poetic, . . . Fond of Literature," and "nice in her perceptions and judgements." Greene recalled fondly how she "used to lead us to bed with a light—and then came up to see that [we] were comfortable and tuck in the clothes and tell them [*sic*] to say their prayers."[13]

Hannah had certain strengths perhaps so taken for granted that they were never noted. Any woman, living before modern medicine and conveniences, who could survive eleven childbirths, the last when she was in her late forties, and who successfully could rear ten children on very little money, must have had extraordinary inner resources, a remarkable capacity for hard work, and a constitution of iron. Her health eventually did give way, however, and she died of overwork and consumption. Her life pattern was to be repeated by her youngest son.

They were emotionally very close. His first biographer speculates that because there was a gap of several years between him and his next older sibling, his sister Emily, he "had no playmate for a time but his mother." It certainly seems as if he was his mother's favorite. "As the youngest child," he recalled, "it may be supposed I was treated with uncommon indulgence, and probably received a good deal more than a tenth of the affection distributed. I remember often to have heard the neighbors say, 'Why, Miss Parker, you're spilin' your boy! . . .' To which she replied 'she hoped not,' and kissed my flaxen curls anew." [14]

Theodore often wrote that his mother took "great pains" with his religious education and that her religious opinions were undoctrinaire. She "cared little for such doctrines as *Trinity* &c. . . . [but saw] Religion as Love and good works." Elsewhere, he claimed that "the dark theology of the time seems not to have blackened her soul at all." In particular, he claimed that she instinctively denied the conception of God as wrathful: "To her the Deity was an Omnipresent Father, filling every point of space with His beautiful and loving presence." In turn, she taught him to "love and trust the dear God." And yet, a remark he made in a sermon in 1842 suggests a different story: "Perhaps there is no one of us, who believes the theology in which we were instructed by our mothers." [15]

What Hannah in fact taught him is difficult to say, for on this subject, more than any other, his memories seem to have been colored by his later religious opinions. The statement of one biographer about his theology, that his "mother's part in it was much greater than Kant's or Schelling's," is only partially true. [16] Although his piety was surely shaped in part by Hannah, his mature theology required that his fundamental religious knowledge be innate, so in his recollections he downplayed the importance of her actual theological opinions and instead showed her nurturing his natural instincts. This is her role in a recollection of Theodore's childhood that he related often as an adult and recorded most famously just before he died:

> When a little boy in petticoats in my fourth year, one fine day in spring, my father led me by the hand to a distant part of the farm, but soon sent me home alone. On the way I had to pass a little "pond-hole" then spreading its waters wide; a rhodora in full bloom—a rare flower in my neighborhood, and which grew only in that locality—attracted my attention and drew me to the spot. I saw a little spotted tortoise sunning himself in the shallow water at the root of the flaming shrub. I lifted the stick I had in my hand to strike the harmless reptile; for, though I had never killed any creature, yet I had seen other boys out of sport de-

This World of Joys and Sorrows

stroy birds, squirrels, and the like, and I felt a disposition to follow their wicked example. But all at once something checked my little arm, and a voice within me said, clear and loud, "It is wrong!" I held my uplifted stick in wonder at the new emotion—the consciousness of an involuntary but inward check upon my actions, till the tortoise and the rhodora both vanished from my sight. I hastened home and told the tale to my mother, and asked what was it that told me it was wrong? She wiped a tear from her eye with her apron, and taking me in her arms, said, "Some men call it conscience, but I prefer to call it the voice of God in the soul of man. If you listen and obey it, then it will speak clearer and clearer, and always guide you right; but if you turn a deaf ear or disobey, then it will fade out little by little, and leave you all in the dark and without a guide. Your life depends on heeding this little voice." ... I am sure no other event in my life has made so deep and lasting an impression on me.[17]

This story may well have happened as Theodore told it here. In another version, he adds that his mother would remind him of this incident whenever he later lost his temper or otherwise behaved badly—a detail that makes his ability to recall the event seem quite plausible. Besides, children do have such experiences. Yet Hannah sounds suspiciously like a Transcendentalist. It is unlikely she was anything of the sort.

She had been reared in a family devout in a traditionally Puritan way; her parents, both members of the Lexington Church, had baptized her ten brothers Asahel, Habakkuk, Nahum, Matthew, Ishmael, Noah, Hiram, Jeptha, Ammi, and Elisha. Hannah did not baptize her own children, however, until after Theodore was born. On 16 February 1812, the minister of the Lexington Church, Avery Williams, noted in the Church Record Book that he had baptized "Rebekah" Parker, one of Theodore's sisters, aged twelve, her mother "having been propounded for admission to the Church, and giving assent to the Covenant." The baptism was performed at the Parker house because the child was "dangerously sick"; she died two days later. The following Sunday, Hannah formally was admitted "to full Communion." The Sunday after that, she had Williams baptize her five youngest children, Isaac, Ruth, Hiram, Emily, and the one-and-a-half-year-old Theodore, who cried, "Oh, don't!" when the water was sprinkled on him. Finally, in May, Hannah persuaded her two older, unmarried daughters, Mary and Lydia, to get baptized. (Her only remaining children then were her daughter Hannah, who was married and living in Vermont, and her oldest son, John, who may also have been living away from home.)[18]

The significance of Hannah's actions can be perceived only against a backdrop of New England church history. In the original system of New England church polity, set up by Puritan immigrants in the 1630s, everyone was required to attend a church and to support it financially, but only a few worshipers were actual church members—allowed to take communion and have their children baptized. The test of membership was "visible sainthood," which required not only outward morality, but the ability to give an adequate account to the minister of an inward "work of grace." Most first-generation Puritans felt they could meet this standard, but those of later generations increasingly felt they could not (perhaps because the standard seems to have grown gradually more stringent).[19] Even those who led upright lives and went to meeting, if they were unable to give a "relation of grace," did not join the church. Their children remained unbaptized.

New England ministers, afraid these children and their descendants would be lost to the churches, gathered at a synod in 1662 and proclaimed the "Half-Way Covenant." Although communion remained restricted only to "full" church members, baptism was made an inclusive sacrament: all who had been baptized now were considered "half-way" members, who could in turn have their children baptized. This reform relieved parents of some of the pressure to become full members. Perhaps to prevent complacency, ministers soon began urging the half-way members of their congregations to "renew the covenant" before taking the sacraments. This was not a relation of grace, but more simply an affirmation of their commitment to the church. New Englanders came commonly to perform this ceremony just before they were to wed; it was understood that this permitted their future children to partake of the baptismal sacrament. Meanwhile, over the course of the eighteenth century, most churches, and all those with liberal tendencies, abandoned the distinction between full and half-way membership and made the Lord's Supper open to all.

The Lexington Church had marked liberal tendencies. No distinction was made between full and half-way members. When Hannah "assented to the Covenant" that winter day in 1812, she not only got her children baptized, she was "admitted to full Communion." But why had she not assented to the covenant already? She and her husband had been baptized, when infants, into the Lexington Church. They could have joined the church at any time, but did not—not even when they began having children in 1785. Yet they seem to have attended faithfully, for in 1794, when a pew auction was held to raise funds to build a new meetinghouse, John spent the considerable sum of fifty-seven dollars to buy one in the balcony, near the choir.[20]

Could Hannah have been religiously indifferent, until the illness of her child prompted her to experience an awakening in 1812? Columbus Greene later recalled that baptism was not widely practiced in Lexington and hinted that indifference was the cause. Or could Hannah have refrained from sacraments out of deference to her rationalistic husband? He pointedly did not assent to the covenant along with his wife. Neither of these explanations, however, accounts for Hannah's obvious concern to baptize all her children.

She probably held certain popular religious beliefs about baptism and communion. Puritan thinkers had rejected the "high," Catholic, view of the sacraments—that they actually imparted grace. Baptism and the Lord's Supper were regarded in Puritan theology merely as signs of faith. But these sacraments gained popular meanings they did not formally hold.[21] Puritan parents, out of concern for their children and a desire to bring them within the covenant of the church, came to regard baptism not merely as a sign of nurturing intent, but as a way actually to pass on grace to their children and to protect them spiritually. People holding such beliefs had approved of the Half-Way Covenant and tried to make baptism as widely available as possible. The Lord's Supper, on the other hand, came to be regarded by lay folk as necessarily restricted; only the truly pure could partake of it without danger of damning themselves and corrupting the church. This belief was so strong that even when, beginning in the 1690s, certain ministers opened communion to all, most lay people held back. The belief persisted even among Unitarians in the nineteenth century, many of whom remained reluctant to "approach the table" until they felt "ready." As a writer in the *Christian Examiner*, the principal Unitarian journal, complained in 1832:

> The peculiar awe, by which this ordinance is separated from every other ordinance of God's appointment; the habit of singling it out, and exalting it above every other mode of worship and means of grace; the singular dread, in the minds of many, of contracting some heinous and mysterious guilt by a wrong participation of it; . . . the very aspect, too, of many communicants, of constraint and almost of distress; the evident feeling which many of them have, that the *elements* are the solemn things in this commemoration, and that it becomes them to have a very special impression on their minds, at the moment when they take into their hands these elements,—all these things, are to our apprehension, proofs, that there is still on this subject a great deal of superstition among us.[22]

If Hannah Parker had held such popular, traditional beliefs, she might have hung back from being "admitted into full communion"—but why would she have waited so long to baptize her children? The Lexington church, with its liberal tendencies, had allowed anyone who affirmed the covenant to partake of both baptism and communion. Hannah must have felt that if she had joined the church for the sake of baptizing her children, she also would have had to partake of the Lord's Supper, which she felt unready to do. So she waited for years, until a desire to give spiritual help to her dying daughter prompted her to act.

The urgency with which she acted suggests that, despite Theodore's later denials, she believed enough in the Puritan "dark theology" to think God might damn eternally the souls of sinners. The story Theodore told many times in later life, that he wrestled with the doctrine of eternal damnation as a child, otherwise would be difficult to explain. He would recall the "many, many hours" that he had lain awake in bed, weeping and praying as he thought of Hell; "for years, say from 7 till 10, I said my prayers with much devotion I think & then continued to repeat 'Lord, forgive my sins,' till sleep came upon me." He recalled that he had first learned about Hell and the Devil from the *New England Primer*, which had been assigned to him in school against his father's wishes.[23]

What were his mother's wishes? Theodore recalled that it was she who had charge of the religious training of the children, and she who decided the religious reading of the family. She surely would have noticed her son's ordeal, and if she did not believe in eternal damnation, she would have tried to comfort him. Theodore claimed, however, that he saw his way through the crisis on his own, rejecting the doctrine as unnatural while still a boy (a claim that can be disputed). He portrays his mother as someone who did not care much for doctrine, but in light of her emotional religious temperament, she may have cast her undoctrinaire Christianity, with its strong folk beliefs, in an evangelical mold, and at the very least used the language of Hell for the unrighteous. Had she done so, she would have been keeping with the traditions of the Lexington Church.[24]

THE MEETINGHOUSE of the church, located about a mile north of the Parker farm, at the center of town alongside the road to Boston, was a two-storied, boxy building. Its big front doors opened out on the town common, where Theodore's father's father, Captain John, had commanded the little troop of militiamen who skirmished with British regulars in the dawn light of 19 April 1775, inaugurating the Revolutionary War. Theodore's father, who was fourteen on that "glorious morning," would tell how his father left in the middle of the night to answer the alarm that the "Red Coats" were coming, how his mother hid the family valuables in a tree trunk, how the family heard musket fire at daybreak, and how his mother sent him to a hill up behind a neighbor's farm to see if the British were heading their way (they were not). Many townspeople had such stories. Columbus Greene later remembered that on Sundays, in the dinner break between morning and afternoon services, he and Theodore would leave the meetinghouse and go over to nearby Dudley's tavern to "hear the old Revolutionary soldiers tell stories of the war." Relics of the war also abounded. John Parker kept as heirlooms two muskets, one that his father had used in the battle, the other that he was supposed to have captured from a drunken British soldier. John also had bought from the town the belfry shed, from which the alarm in 1775 had been rung. He had hauled it down to his farm, and, when Theodore and Columbus were growing up, used it as his woodworking shop.[25]

By that time, the Battle of Lexington, so-called, had grown into a political and religious event of mythic proportions. In 1799, the inhabitants of the town erected a monument on the common, about a hundred yards from the door of the meetinghouse and with an inscription written by the minister, which marked the spot as "Sacred to the Liberty and Rights of Mankind!!!" and commemorated the eight militiamen killed in the battle, including Theodore's distant cousin Jonas, as "[m]artyrs in the cause of God and their country," whose "[b]lood . . . was the Cement of the Union of these States, then Colonies," as it inspired their fellow citizens "to revenge" their death, "and at the Point of the Sword, to assert and defend their native Rights. They nobly dar'd to be free!!" In 1855, Theodore recalled the Sunday when, as a small boy, "my mother lifted me up . . . in her religious, patriotic arms, and held me while I read the first monumental line I ever saw: SACRED TO LIBERTY AND THE RIGHTS OF MANKIND."[26]

When he was eleven, Theodore witnessed the battle reenacted in front of the meetinghouse, with about twenty of the original participants taking part. His grandfather's role was taken by one of the substantial citizens of the town, Colonel William Monroe, who had been an orderly sergeant in the original. At the appropriate point, Monroe declaimed Captain Parker's famous order, "Don't fire unless fired upon; but if they mean to have a war, let it begin here!" and added, "For them is the *very words* Captain Parker said." It is unlikely that these were Captain Parker's words, but Theodore later asserted to the historian George Bancroft that they were "the family tradition of the day." When he was in his late teens, Theodore served as an ensign in his grandfather's militia company, although by that point the militia was a decadent institution (it was disbanded in 1832) and his duties were mostly clerical. In 1834, he watched as, with solemn ceremony and an oration by Edward Everett, the bodies of the eight militiamen who died in the battle were moved from the town graveyard and reinterred under the monument.[27]

Theodore later credited the influence of his Revolutionary War heritage on the moral part of his religious views. In 1855, when he was leading the resistance in Boston to the Fugitive Slave Law, he would write that

the Spirit of Liberty, the Love of Justice, was early fanned into a flame in my Boyish heart. That monument covers the bones of my own kinsfolk; it was their blood which reddened the long, green grass at Lexington. It is my own name which stands chiselled on that stone; the tall Captain who marshalled his fellow farmers and mechanics into stern array and spoke such brave and dangerous words as opened the War of

American Independence,—the last to leave the field,—was my father's father. I learned to read out of his Bible, and with a musket he that day captured from the foe, I learned also another religious lesson, that "REBELLION TO TYRANTS IS OBEDIENCE TO GOD."[28]

But his background left a deeper, less conscious influence. He grew up in a town where the common, the battle green, and the churchyard were the same space—a space dominated by a meetinghouse and marked by a monument that proclaimed it sacred. In such a place, was it not palpable that American liberty rested on a religious foundation? Was it not inevitable that when the mature Theodore, now a minister, set out to reform society, he should begin by trying to reform the church?[29]

THEODORE LATER had few kind things to say about the services at the meetinghouse. He recalled only their "notorious dulness [sic] . . . , their mechanical character, the poverty and insignificance of the sermons, the unnaturalness and uncertainty of the doctrines preached on the authority of a 'divine and infallible revelation,' the lifelessness of the public prayers, and the consequent heedlessness of the congregation." Although these criticisms, written in 1859, are in part aimed at his religious opponents at the time, an episode of his early life suggests that he was accurately recalling dissatisfaction.[30]

In 1830, after he left home, he spent a year teaching at a private school in Boston, during which time he "attended the preachings of Dr. Lyman Beecher, the most powerful Orthodox minister in New England," and "went through one of his protracted meetings." Theodore would later claim that when he was a boy the only minister he admired was William Ellery Channing, the foremost American Unitarian.[31] Why then did he bypass Channing and all the other Boston Unitarians to hear the leading New England evangelical, who spent much of his time attacking them? Theodore may have gone out of curiosity, but if so it was not idle curiosity. He attended Beecher's Hanover Street Church every Sunday for an entire year, and the revival meeting he "went through" lasted six days. Although he was not "converted," he seems to have been attracted to evangelicalism. His attraction can be understood only by looking back over the history of the Lexington Church.

It was organized in 1691, but its religious character was established later, largely by two ministers: John Hancock, who filled the Lexington pulpit from 1697 until his death in 1752, and Jonas Clarke, who filled it from 1755 until his death in 1805.[32] Through a tumultuous century of New England religious history, these two kept the Lexington Church at peace and in the process shaped the religious outlook of Theodore's parents and, indirectly, of Theodore himself.

Hancock was often called "Bishop Hancock," a sign of the respect in which he was held by his contemporaries. His personal authority in Lexington was considerable; as Nathaniel Appleton said, addressing the people of the town at Hancock's funeral: "[Y]ou your selves were so sensible of his Wisdom and Goodness, of his Capacity and Readiness to direct and advise you that, as I have understood, you seldom or never engaged in any important or difficult Affair, without consulting him upon it." In a traditional story, two farmers were on the verge of a lawsuit over a disputed property line when he intervened. He walked both farmers to the contested field and had each state his case. Then he instructed them where to drive the surveying stakes. Neither farmer appealed the decision.[33]

The greatest potential challenge to Hancock's authority came in the early 1740s, when he was in his seventies. A series of religious revivals, later named the Great Awakening, caused schisms in churches across New England, including neighboring Concord, and split the Puritan Standing Order of Massachusetts three ways. All three factions identified themselves with the New England Puritan tradition.[34]

Among the many groups of "New Lights," as the supporters of the Awakening called themselves, were the ministers who founded the "New Divinity" tradition in which Lyman Beecher was trained. They were mostly Yale-educated, pastored rural or small-town churches, and believed that they preserved the emotional Calvinist core of Puritanism. Like the Puritans, they preached that we were all born into sin, so that regardless of our efforts, in our hearts we hated God and justly deserved nothing but hellfire. God was merciful, however, and had sacrificed His Son, the Christ Jesus, to pay for our sins. A few souls, which God had chosen before the creation of the world, were thereby saved from eternal damnation. This salvation was wholly the work of divine grace; to suggest otherwise was to deny God's omnipotence. Truly saved persons first would feel acutely and unbearably aware of their own corruption, then realize with sudden elation that God loved them anyway. He would then regenerate them. This emotional "new birth" marked all true religious experience. The New Divinity men denounced certain other New England ministers as having abandoned Calvinism for the heresy of Arminianism, which they defined as the doctrine that you could work your way into Heaven without divine intervention.[35]

The opponents of the Awakening who have received the most historical attention were these so-called Arminians, led by mostly Harvard-trained ministers of wealthy churches in and around Boston; although not all Arminians were of the local elite, most of the local elite was Arminian. Arminians denounced the New Light innovations of mass revival meetings and itinerant preaching as "enthusiasm" at the expense of genuine morality and piety. Their emphasis was on the rational aspects of the Puritan heritage. Most Puritans had believed that although God was omnipotent and could redeem people arbitrarily, He had chosen instead to treat them as rational creatures and give them the terms of salvation in an infallible revelation, the Bible. By studying Scripture and human experience, mortals could identify the means God used to save people. Most Puritans held that God "prepared" a sinner for the on-slaught of grace; during preparation, the sinner, seemingly but not actually by his or her own efforts, struggled to be virtuous and pious and to engage in soul-searching.

The Arminians were trying to describe their own religious experience when they developed this idea of preparation and portrayed salvation as a gradual process brought about by human struggle, with divine assistance, against sin.[36] They thereby founded the tradition out of which the "liberal Christianity" of William Ellery Channing was to arise. The ministers who refined this tradition over the next decades were to be driven partly by con-troversy with the Calvinists, partly by Enlightenment ideas coming from England, and partly by the internal logic of their arguments. In the 1750s, they abandoned predestination and original sin, arguing that these doctrines made God, not humans, responsible for evil. In contrast, they emphasized God's benevolence, which led a few of them by the end of the century to abandon the idea of eternal damnation.

Hancock quietly objected to the excesses of the Awakening, but he was no Arminian. He believed strongly that people were "*born in Sin, and sold in Sin, and are in the Power of that Spirit that works in Children of Disobedience.*" He was among the many "Old Calvinists"—probably the majority of ministers in the 1740s—who saw themselves as the purest defenders of the Calvinist yet rationalist New England heritage. Hancock's specific objection to the revi-vals was that they encouraged "Divisions and Separations" in the church. "O what Caution and Wisdom should govern the Minds of Ministers in these dividing Times," he cautioned in 1748, "that they and their People may yet *take sweet counsel together, and walk to the House of God in Company.*" Rather than encourage ecclesiastical strife by condemning the Awakening, Hancock used his personal authority to harness and direct the new spirit. In 1741 and 1742, he "harvested" eighty new members for his church. At the same time, he did not denounce the Arminians; in 1747, for example, he attended the ordina-tion of Jonathan Mayhew, even though Mayhew was widely, and correctly, suspected of harboring Arminian tendencies.[37]

Hancock's example of "Old Calvinist" toleration was carried on by his grandson-in-law and successor, Jonas Clarke, whose influence over his con-gregation came to rival that of the "Bishop." Clarke became the undisputed leader of Lexington political opinion: he wrote the resolutions and instruc-tions given to the representatives of the town on every major issue from the Stamp Act in 1765 to Jay's Treaty in 1794. During the Revolution he was an ardent Whig and is generally credited with inspiring his parishioners' patriotism; it is his words that Theodore remembered reading on the Lexington monument.[38]

In religion, Clarke maintained an orthodox reputation, which is borne out in some of his surviving sermons. Yet he never engaged in theological disputes, and when he gave the Charge at ordinations—which he was reputed to have done more often than any other member of his generation—he usually told the new ministers that the "right of private judgment, in matters of Faith and Conscience, ought ever to be held sacred."[39]

Clarke's broad-church attitude was mixed with a vigorous piety, which inspired twenty-seven congregants to join the church in his first year. His sermons were noted not only for their length (sometimes three hours), but their emotionalism, in which he self-consciously imitated Hancock. Clarke, too, set great store by religious singing, by which he thought "the attention is roused, the passions are composed, the affections are engaged, the devotion is enlivened, and the whole soul is sweetly drawn forth in gratitude, and in most devout acknowledgements of praise of God." In 1766, he reformed the musical practices of the Lexington Church, when he persuaded the congregation to organize a choir, replace the literal New England Psalm book with the more poetic Tate and Brady version, and start using Isaac Watts's *Scriptural Hymns*. Similar reforms in other congregations frequently became the subject of fierce dispute. In Lexington, Clarke's influence was such that there was little dissent.[40]

Musical reform was often linked to religious liberalism, and Clarke did seem to have Arminian tendencies: his children and students all turned out liberal, as did many of his parishioners, like John Parker. In 1805, the year of his death, his son-in-law Henry Ware, a prominent liberal, was appointed Hollis Professor of Divinity at Harvard after a long debate. The appointment, along with that of Samuel Webber as president the following year, gave the liberals control of the university for the first time. This event was the opening of a twenty-year controversy between the liberals and orthodox, which was to end with the liberals forming the American Unitarian Association.

The most visible part of the controversy was not over the central issue of original sin, but over the secondary issue of the Trinity. Most liberals, because they did not believe sin was infinite, did not see the necessity of an infinite sacrifice to atone for it; God no longer needed to be crucified, so Christ no longer had to be God. Besides, they thought that if the Bible was read carefully and critically, the doctrine of the Trinity would be found unscriptural; as they read the New Testament, Jesus was portrayed as a superangelic being but not as God. This Christology became the focus of debate in 1815, when the orthodox minister Jedidiah Morse accused the liberals of secretly being "Unitarians"—that is, of thinking that Jesus was merely human. The liberals soon were stuck with the "Unitarian" label. In 1819, when Channing preached the sermon that became the liberal manifesto, he called it *Unitarian Christianity.*

The "Unitarian Controversy" raged throughout Theodore's boyhood, splitting many churches, but in Lexington all was quiet because, as Columbus Greene recalled, "Unitarian . . . ideas may be said to have prevailed." Clarke's immediate successor, Avery Williams—the minister who baptized Theodore—appears to have been another tolerant Calvinist; but liberal ideas had become so generally accepted that when Williams left after seven years and was replaced by Charles Briggs, a Unitarian, no schism occurred. Briggs was the minister during much of the childhood of both Theodore Parker and Columbus Greene; although most church members liked his "discreet & conciliatory deportment," both young men seemed disappointed in him as a religious teacher.[41]

Part of Briggs's problem was his feeble health, which often kept him from attending to his duties; the town historian notes that the "church records, kept by him, are not only meagre, but loose, and compare poorly with those of his predecessors." Worse, the religiousness of the town waned under his leadership. Greene, looking back on his childhood, could recall "no real depth of religious sentiment[,] no revivals, no love feasts. It was not the custom to have family prayers. The religious domestic customs of an older time seemed to have dyed [*sic*] out. It was not a universal custom to baptize children. Quite a proportion belonged to Church . . . but not many young persons."[42]

Briggs was himself worried about the growing apathy. "How many are there who do not value their religious privileges. . . !" he said in his only printed sermon. "How many who neglect the instructions of the sanctuary, the ordinances of religion, and all the means of personal holiness!" He called for people to attend worship "punctually" and "from right motives," to baptize their children and take communion, to promote the religious education of their children, and to be charitable. He did not seem to believe, however, that he could effect these changes; his basic argument was that while "the success of religion depends much on the ability . . . of those who dispense it . . . [,] it depends quite as much, nay more, on the disposition and character of those to whom it is preached." Apathy was more the fault of the congregation than the minister, and it was up to the congregation to improve itself. This passive outlook was not in the tradition of Hancock and Clarke, who had energetically sought to inspire devotion and piety.[43]

Theodore and his nephew probably picked up their discontent with Briggs from their elders. The older members of the Parker household had known his predecessors personally. Theodore's aged grandmother, Lydia Pierce, had been baptized by Hancock, had heard him preach during the Great Awakening, and had joined the church in 1756, a few years after Clarke was ordained.

This World of Joys and Sorrows

John and Hannah both had been baptized by Clarke,[44] and listened to his sermons for decades. Hannah's love of "ballads and psalms" matched Clarke's love of religious music.

Clarke, with his strong personality, long association with the community, tolerant Calvinism, and heartfelt piety, had been able to hold the allegiance of the spectrum of Lexington religious opinion, from liberal rationalists, like John Parker, to those who were devout but undoctrinaire, like Hannah, to those with orthodox sensibilities like John's mother, Lydia, who did not even use the Watts hymnbook. (Theodore remembered that "the original edition of the Puritan hymnbook . . . was much in her hands.") Briggs could not match Clarke's appeal. Although he excited no controversy, he stirred few hearts, and people drifted away from his church. During his ministry, the Baptists made their first inroads into the town, and had enough adherents by 1830 to form a congregation; the Church of Lexington was now merely one of two Lexington churches. Toward the end of Briggs's tenure, a group of Unitarians in the eastern part of town formed a church with Transcendentalist leanings. Emerson preached there on a supply basis from 1836 to 1838 (it was where he ended his ministerial career). The first regular minister was Karl Follen, a German who had been forced to flee Europe because of his religious and political radicalism.[45]

The Parker family felt the same pressures as the Lexington Church and split in a similar way. Both Theodore and his nephew wanted their religion to be deeply felt, like that of Hannah. They had not experienced enough religious feeling in the Unitarianism of Lexington and so were attracted to the fervor of the revivalists. Theodore, after he left Lexington to teach in Boston, attended Beecher's church and a six-day "protracted meeting"; Greene, who left Lexington a few years later to work in the Lowell mills, began attending a Baptist church, and also went to a "protracted meeting"—one that convened every evening for two weeks. Unlike his young uncle, he emerged a convert. He was ordained as a Baptist minister in 1840—just as Theodore was emerging as the major Transcendentalist minister.[46]

In 1834, when Greene first wrote to tell him that he had experienced "a change of heart," Theodore was studying for the Unitarian ministry at Harvard. He responded by congratulating his nephew for having "found religion, for which you were seeking," but added, "I do not suppose you mean to say that religion is some *one thing*, state or feeling, which comes to you in a *moment*, when you had no conception of such a thing before. But that it is, that Love to God, and good will to men, which gradually arises in the heart, and which goes on constantly increasing and shining, like the Lamp of the Just, more and more unto the perfect day." In Theodore's next letter, he wrote that although protracted meetings surely had awakened "many a careless thoughtless, worldly-minded, sensual man," they were for most people "too violent, and do more harm than good." He recalled his own experience with a protracted meeting a few years before: "I confess I derived much advantage from it, but it was too harsh a remedy for gentle souls." He urged Greene to read Henry Ware Jr.'s *On the Formation of the Christian Character* or *Life of the Savior*, which he thought were "excellent books."[47]

This suggestion indicates one reason why Theodore had not become an evangelical: he was drawn instead to a strain within the liberal tradition that was more suited to his temperament and more in keeping with his religious background. Although the liberals had drawn on the rationalism of the Puritan heritage, they had not wholly abandoned the "affections" to the orthodox. Instead, certain liberal ministers had cultivated a type of sensitive, emotional pietism that they united with their "reasonable" theology. These ministers, of whom the younger Ware was a prominent example, had an undoctrinaire religious fervor not unlike that of John Hancock and Jonas Clarke; Ware in fact was Clarke's grandson and Hancock's great-grandson. Ware had successfully cultivated a pietistic revival in his Boston church, as Charles Briggs had been unable to do in Lexington. Ware's revival was like the "harvests" of Hancock in the 1740s, and of Clarke in the 1750s, in that it was wholly free of the "violence" that Theodore thought marred the protracted meetings. For Theodore, a genuine spiritual awakening was not made in the midst of noise and crowds. Rather, genuine spirituality was, as he often claimed, "tranquil." Yet the young man seems to have been much less tranquil than fiercely ambitious, and his ambition may also have influenced his religious choices.[48]

AN IMPECUNIOUS young man in early-nineteenth-century New England had a clearly prescribed path for moving up in the world. The first step was to get an education, and here Theodore excelled. Everyone agreed there was not a scholar in Lexington who could keep up with him.[49]

He dated his ambition to a June day in his eighth year, when an old man he did not know overtook him going to school and walked with him a while. "[He] told me what it was possible for a bright boy to *do* & to *be*—what I might do & be. It had a great influence on me. I thought I 'might be somebody.'" His nephew Columbus Greene remembers him, some years later, advising a schoolmate to marry a certain girl, whom Theodore praised so highly that he was asked why he did not propose to her himself. "Oh she would not answer for a President's wife, but if I were to be a farmer I should not rest until I had made an effort to secure her." He may have been joking—but if so it was only a half-joke. Anyone who watched him study knew that he would not grow up to be a farmer.[50]

Under the influence of his studious father, John, the Parkers had become a reading family. Theodore recalled Sabbath evenings in summer, when as a small boy he sat on John's knee, being taught from the family bible, while

Hannah taught his youngest sister from "some sacred book" and his older siblings read "instructive" literature. Columbus Greene remembered winter nights when the dinner table would be moved before the fire and the men and boys would sit around it and read—John often reading aloud to the women, who would be sewing. In such an environment, Theodore came to love books. He could be found with one almost every free moment—early in the morning, late at night, during intermissions at school, even during summer "noonings," while the rest of the family napped. One neighbor recalled how Theodore would walk home from services on Sunday, so absorbed in some volume from the church library that he would stumble into a tree or a stone wall. When he was a young child, his parents would read each book he did, then examine him on its contents. He would not be allowed to read another until he "had satisfied the rigorous demands of father." Under this discipline, he developed the remarkable memory he had inherited from this mother. By age ten, he could repeat a poem hundreds of lines long after a single reading and had learned "whole volumes" of Pope, Milton, Cowley, and Dryden, as well as the New Testament. Greene recalled how Theodore once astonished a schoolmaster, who was a college man, by correcting his misquotation of a biblical verse.[51]

Theodore's parents also encouraged him to study nature. He "early learned the habits of all the plants . . . in the neighborhood" (except the mosses); by age ten he knew the names of all the woody shrubs and trees in Massachusetts, and about that time made a catalogue of all the "vegetable productions" on the farm. He also gathered every odd stone he could find from the rocky, boulder-strewn soil, and built a "rude chemical apparatus" to identify them. He would watch the sky as well, and once, with the sharp clear eyes of a twelve-year old, saw the crescent form of Venus. No one else could see it, and as his father was away on a trip, no one could explain it to him. He finally borrowed an astronomy book from the schoolmaster, "& found out the fact & its reason."[52]

Schoolmasters had become a part of Theodore's life in May 1816, when he was five and had begun to follow his brothers and sisters to the black-painted, hip-roofed schoolhouse, two miles away. Into its single, twenty-foot square room crowded forty to fifty students, ages five to twenty, and one young teacher. The two terms, summer and winter, were each no longer than fourteen weeks and could be as short as ten; the older children only attended in the winter, because in the summer they did farm work, as did Theodore himself after 1819. The basic curriculum consisted of arithmetic, grammar, history, and geography; groups of apt students, in which Theodore was always numbered, might also be taught geology, chemistry, natural philosophy, and rhetoric. The course varied, however, according to who the schoolmaster was that year, and as the position paid only $28 a term, not including board, it was hard to attract anyone good.[53] For a few winters, the teacher was a local farmer's son named John Hastings, whom Greene remembered as "an igno-ramus—no teaching, no discipline." Theodore, however, recalled that Hast-ings had given him the most severe disciplining he ever received, for firing a home-made pop gun in class.

John Parker was so dissatisfied with Hastings that in 1820 he persuaded a Brown University student, whose family he knew, to teach for two winters. This was William Hoar White, who later became a minister; he and his suc-cessor, another Brown student named George Fiske, "taught well" and "were respected." Theodore was always to remember them with affection and thirty years later dedicated a book to them, "with gratitude for early instruction received at their hands."[54]

The most important contribution that White and Fiske made to his educa-tion was to start him in classics. White, probably at John Parker's suggestion, began to tutor Theodore in classical Latin and the following winter in Bibli-cal Greek; Fiske continued these efforts for two more winters. John encour-aged his son by buying for him Smith's Latin Grammar and the *Historia Sacra*, while Theodore bought himself Young's Latin Dictionary, the first book he ever purchased, with money he had made by picking whortleberries and sell-ing them in Boston. He soon had worked his way through Virgil, Cicero's *Select Orations*, and Sallust. These texts were all required for the entrance examinations at the nearby "College at Cambridge," as Harvard was usually called, which suggests that Theodore was already thinking of going there—an optimistic but vain hope. His family could hardly afford the expense, which ran to over $400 a year.[55]

Theodore was not deterred by so mundane an obstacle, nor was his enthu-siasm dampened by the mediocre teachers who succeeded Fiske. The school-master in 1825–26 could teach Theodore no Latin, "[n]or anything else," so for five weeks Theodore reported to him his own studies on natural philoso-phy, astronomy, chemistry, and rhetoric. The teacher the next winter was no better, so Theodore got a copy of Colburn's *Algebra*, mastered the book in "20 days & a half," and quit the common school for good. The following year he attended a college preparatory school, the Lexington Academy. To afford the tuition he decided, against the urging of his sisters, not to take dancing les-sons, which were all the rage in his neighborhood. He never was to learn how to dance, but unfortunately the sacrifice was not worth the knowledge gained. The principal of the Lexington Academy taught him "nothing to speak of— except the pronunciation of Latin." After only ten or eleven weeks, in April 1827, Theodore left. He was sixteen years old, and his formal primary educa-tion was over.[56]

The following winter, he became a schoolmaster himself. At seventeen, he was several inches shorter than his father, and must have known he always

This World of Joys and Sorrows

would be, but he was stoutly built. Despite a few severe, acute bouts of illness as a child, he was now strong and active, if also rough and clumsy. He was "a raw boy, with clothes made by country tailors, coarse shoes, great hands, red lips, and blue eyes," his boyhood blond hair now darkened to brown. Transparently sincere, he was also visibly emotional. He recited poetry with feeling, wept easily, and struggled to control his volatile temper. He was remembered, too, for being "roguish," "arch," "apt," and "very quick for a reply." He was smarter than those around him and knew it. Greene recalled that he was "a perfect hector, taking neat satisfaction in making sport of what others might do & say." One evening, at a time when one of Theodore's older brothers was living at home because he was "out of business" (that is, he had no work), the fire burnt low, and the brother ordered Theodore outside to get brush. He probably was interrupted from reading and so only grudgingly complied; as he hurriedly brought the kindling in, he scattered branches and leaves on the floor and threw the rest into the fireplace in an "improper manner." His brother reprimanded him sharply and ordered him to pick up what he had dropped: "If you can not do better than that, I will keep you at it a month." "Then," replied Theodore, "*I* shall not be very likely to be *out of business*."[57]

He was young to be a teacher. According to one account, his former schoolmates were a little in awe of him when they found out about his new job. Despite meager pay, teaching was the usual way that college students like White and Fiske supported themselves during school vacations and that young men like Theodore tried to earn enough money to attend college. Many of them regarded it as a chore, but he seems to have enjoyed the work, although initially he was criticized for making "unreasonable" demands on his pupils and being too quick with the rod. He probably had trouble maintaining more gentle authority over the boys, some of whom were as large as he. With the girls, some of whom were his own age, there were surely other problems; he hinted at them in a story he later told about one recalcitrant boy whom he could not bear to ferule, because the lad looked too much like his pretty older sister.[58]

Theodore taught in common schools for four winters, first at Quincy, then at North Lexington, Concord, and Waltham.[59] In the summers he lived at home and worked for his father, while hiring himself out part-time as a farm laborer to earn more money. His self-education continued unabated. "When he taught school," recalled Greene, "he spent his evenings in study, & if away on an evening visit, he was in the habit of building a fire & studying till 2 or 3 in the morning to make up lost time." At Waltham, a young woman asked to be tutored in French; he began to learn the language in order to teach her.

The purpose of all this toil became clear on 23 August 1830, just before Theodore's twentieth birthday. He had secured the day off from his father, without telling him why he wanted it. That morning, he rose well before dawn and walked ten miles into Cambridge. Six o'clock found him with a group of about fifty other young men assembled on the portico of the South Dining Hall of Harvard College, being welcomed by President Josiah Quincy. After a short breakfast, they were tested orally in Latin. A midmorning recess followed. Then they were tested orally again, this time in Greek. A dinner break preceded oral tests in geography and written ones in arithmetic and algebra. By five in the afternoon, the examination was over. Each student was called up to a long table, where sat President Quincy and the faculty. Quincy informed Theodore that he was admitted into the freshman class. "How joyfully I went home," Theodore recalled years later, "and told my father—a-bed, but not yet asleep. . . . How joyfully I went to work again the next day!"[60]

John Parker had long been hoping that his prodigy of a son would go to college (why else would he have encouraged him to study Latin?), but he thought that Harvard was too expensive. His first reaction to his son's news is supposed to have been, "You know I cannot support you there." But Theodore had anticipated this objection. He told his father he would live at home, working on the farm until he turned twenty-one, as his brothers had done before him, and so fulfill his obligations to the family while avoiding paying college board. He would pay no tuition, either, because he would study on his own. He would keep up with his classmates, take examinations with them, and join them in their second year, after he had saved up enough money to pay all the fees himself. His father would have to pay nothing. John could hardly object to this plan, and Theodore went ahead with it.[61]

He had no trouble keeping up with the class of 1834. In one year, he finished three years of the college course, as well as reading "a good deal" of Latin, Greek, and mathematics that were not required. Meanwhile, he became preoccupied with making enough money to enroll in the college. Although he had promised his father he would work the farm until his twenty-first birthday, he in fact left Lexington for good a few months early, on 23 March 1831, because he had an offer to become assistant master of a school in Boston at a salary of fifteen dollars a month, plus board. Too conscientious not to worry about breaking his word, and knowing his premature departure would leave his father a hand short that spring, Theodore hired a laborer to fill his place until 24 August. John Parker at first rejected this arrangement—he wanted to pay the man's wages himself—but Theodore insisted on receiving no better treatment than the other boys in the family had received.

By this point, Theodore evidently had decided he was going to be a minister; John silently disapproved, as Greene reveals: "[I]t was understood that his father would be pleased to have him study law." John's preference may have resulted from his lack of fervent piety and his rationalistic tendencies, or it may have been simply a practical consideration. As a lawyer a man could become rich, but ministers were notoriously ill-paid, and their salaries increasingly uncertain. By 1830, the fall of the Standing Order of Massachusetts, the last establishment of public worship remaining in America, was inevitable. In 1833, it was abolished by the state constitutional convention. Ministers would no longer receive their salaries from taxation, but from less reliable voluntary contributions. There was, too, a growing sense that the ministry was beginning to lose influence and prestige, and that genius was leaving the temple, to haunt the senate, or the market.[62]

Theodore later admitted that a career in law and politics had held considerable attraction for him. He made "preliminary studies" in the law and could write to a friend as late as 1837 that he might have been more useful had he been a lawyer. Theodore loved to study, and the law was a learned profession; he had dreamed, too, of being a great orator. In 1835, he recalled to his fiancée how he would often miss his turning when steering the plow as a boy, because he was speaking before an imaginary senate. Yet he had doubts about legal ethics. Greene remembers that his young uncle worried about the "temptations" to which he would be exposed as a lawyer. Theodore himself remembered thinking that "the lawyer's moral tone was lower than the minister's": "I could not make up my mind to defend a cause I knew to be wrong, using all my efforts to lead judge or jury to a decision I thought unjust. A powerful and successful practitioner told me 'none could be a lawyer without doing so.'"[63]

The only other career he even fancied, much less considered, was a literary one. In 1836, while candidating for a pulpit, he could confess to a friend that "there is a pulse in my heart, that sometimes beats wildly for the stir and noise and tumult and dust of the Literary course." He not only loved to read poetry, but to write it. He had been doing so since he was eight, although he had shown none of his efforts to anyone until he submitted "The Starry Heavens," anonymously, to his schoolmaster, Fiske. Fiske, who had guessed the identity of the author, had told him that the only problem with the poem was that it was "too short." Encouraged, Theodore had written reams of juvenile verse, all of which (perhaps fortunately) have been lost. In 1831, he approached a bookseller with a thin quarto manuscript of "Poems by a Young Man"; the manuscript was rejected without even being opened—and years later, its author burnt it. Still, as late as 1838, after he was a settled minister in a parish, he privately planned to compose an epic four-book poem, about a first-century Greek's quest for truth, that would be the work of his life. He seems to have written no line of it. Despite periods of prodigious poetic output, he must have been aware that he would never be remembered for his verse.[64]

Meanwhile, the ministry had long been on his mind. "In my early boyhood," he recalled long afterward, "I *felt* I was to be a minister, and looked forward with eager longings for the work to which I still think my nature itself an 'effectual call.'" Perhaps this feeling explains why, when he was eleven, he began to study metaphysics, and why several years later, when he was at the Lexington Academy, in a bit of self-conscious humor he had performed the role of a Catholic priest in a school play. The ministry seemed a good fit not only because he was deeply pious, but because it would allow him to do the things that had most attracted him to law and to literature. Like a lawyer, he would be a public and learned figure, who could orate, study, and write; like a poet, he could write on the "highest" themes. No single moment can be identified when Theodore finally declared for the ministry, but in 1840, he recalled an incident from his boyhood that suggests how much he was tending toward the clerical profession even then. One Sabbath noon, when everyone else had left the meetinghouse for dinner, he slipped into the Lexington pulpit, "a place so sacred that I scarcely dared place my unholy feet therein," and there prayed for "wisdom—for the means of learning."[65]

He was still looking for those means in 1830, when he spent a busy but lonely year as an assistant at William Brown's school on Blossom Street in Boston; this was the year he attended Lyman Beecher's church. Theodore would teach for six to seven hours a day, and then, once he had learned to ignore the "incessant rattle" of the carriage wheels on the cobblestones outside his window, would study in his room for ten or twelve hours more. "[I]t makes my flesh creep," Theodore recalled many years later, "how I used to work, and how much I learned that year, and the four next." He was employed to teach Latin, Greek, mathematics, natural philosophy, and later French and Spanish—the latter he first had to learn. He also undertook to learn German, in which he made "rapid progress," and Hebrew, "but could get no tolerable grammar or dictionary." He read Virgil some twenty times, Horace nearly as many, all of Homer, and much of Xenophon, Demosthenes, and Aeschylus. Acquaintance with Francis Grund prompted him to study more mathematics, as did "the *sight* of Newton's *Principia*," which he could neither borrow nor afford to buy. He continued to study metaphysics and gave his first lecture, on Poland, to the Lyceum in Lexington.[66]

Despite these remarkable efforts, his college aspirations were slipping away. His salary was too low, and in the city he could save very little money. He thought he would do better with a school of his own and so left Boston in April 1832 for Watertown, a village of 1,600 people a few miles up the Charles River, where his mother's family, the Segurs, lived. He probably found out from them that a "flourishing" private school had just been closed by the departure of its master, a Mr. Wilder. Theodore leased Wilder's old schoolroom on the second floor above a former bakery that was now a storehouse; the

This World of Joys and Sorrows

place needed fixing up, so Theodore refloored it, added a wainscot, and built six desks. The building was owned by one Nathaniel Broad, who lived next door and with whose family Theodore boarded. It was in this house that he became acquainted with his future wife.[67]

For five dollars a quarter, Theodore offered his students a curriculum of Latin, Greek, French, Spanish, Algebra, "and such other sciences as are usually taught in country academies." These subjects would prepare boys for college, but he offered it to girls, too. He was a better teacher than before. Gone was the stern, teenage disciplinarian of the common schools. He was older now and a schoolmaster in his own right. Confident, he rarely resorted to corporal punishment. His new teaching style was relaxed and conversational. He liked his students and was popular with them. His school, and with it his finances, flourished. Beginning with two boys, in eighteen weeks he had twenty-four students, in a year thirty-five, and later fifty-four. In his two years at Watertown, despite having to meet living expenses and spending an extravagant $200 for books, he was able to save $150 for the future.[68]

The clearest indication of the kind of future he wanted is "History of the Jews," a 240-page manuscript that he wrote after school hours in the months following his arrival in Watertown. It was a religious textbook for young people, intended to supplement works about the New Testament, such as Henry Ware Jr.'s *Life of the Savior*. He found no publisher; he was probably grateful for this in later life, because the views he expressed in the book were so different from his mature opinions. It is, nonetheless, an impressive achievement for a largely self-educated twenty-one-year old. He covered Jewish history from Abraham to his own day, showed himself thoroughly acquainted not only with Scripture, but with Flavius Josephus, and he made use of Herodotus, the Babylonian Talmud, and German writers.[69]

He wanted to be a minister, obviously, but not merely a parish minister. He imagined becoming a renowned minister-scholar, a Reverend *Dr.* Parker, perhaps a professor at Harvard—or even more. In a letter he wrote to his fiancée in 1834, a few months before he entered the Harvard Divinity School, he made a revealing reference to the dean, John Gorham Palfrey, himself a poor boy who had made good: "Nothing is too much for young *ambition* to hope, no eminence too lofty for *his* vision; no obstacle too difficult for his exertions and no excellence unattainable. Patience, Perseverance, Prayer have done *something* already, and when we consider that sincere desires are never neglected, and real endeavors never unassisted, we need not *despair* of making some *approaches* at least to the eminence Mr. Palfrey now occupies. Would not this be truly delightful?"[70]

Unitarianism seems to have been an integral part of Parker's dream to get ahead—and understandably so. It was not just the religion of Lexington, but of Harvard and of the Boston elite. Orthodoxy, by contrast, was overwhelmingly the faith of the rural and laboring classes he aspired to leave.

"WHEN I RECALL the years of boyhood, youth, early manhood," said Parker in an 1858 sermon, "I am filled with a sense of sweetness, and wonder that such little things can make a mortal so exceeding rich! But I must confess that the chiefest of all my delights is still the religious. This is the lowest down, the inwardest of all; it is likewise the highest up." The remark is typical of his frequent public comments on his early years. He portrayed his childhood and youth as a happy time, and this happiness he linked to the nature of religious experience. Religion, he said in sermon after sermon, was intuitive, spontaneous, and above all joyful. Any child could know the truth, as he had done: "When a little boy, I used to hear ministers preach that the natural man did not love God; but I was sure the natural boy did. . . . [T]o my young experience, it seemed as natural for a man to worship God, to love God, to trust in him, and feel delight in him, as it was for my father's bees to get wax and honey from the yellow blossoms of the willow or the elm."[71]

He claimed that he based his theology on the organic religious experience of his happy childhood and youth, from which he learned that there was in each person an innate and completely sufficient "religious sentiment." He portrayed his religious development as a straightforward progression from joyful but uneducated belief to philosophical optimism.

This lyrical version of Parker's early religious and intellectual development is difficult to evaluate. Contemporary sources are few, and his own recollections are colored by his later opinions. Still, his story seems to have been more complex, and darker, than he later told it.

He admitted as much in a passage from his journal. He had gone up to Lexington, on a fall day in 1844, and visited the old Parker farm, now owned by one of his brothers. The old farmhouse had been torn down a few years earlier to make way for a new, more commodious one, but Parker could still find places where he had worked, "made verses," played with his sister, prayed. Revisiting these childhood scenes now gave him "pleasure," he observed, yet only a few years earlier his reaction had been very different. He would get "the heart ache only to see the place . . . a blight had come on it all. It seemed a spot in the forest—burnt and blasted by . . . fire."[72]

Theodore hinted at the nature of this "blight" in a sentimental poem he wrote when he was twenty-five, "My Childhood's Home." One stanza reads:

> My childhood's home! Oh, other sounds,
>   Than those of boyish pleasure,
> Have swelled and died beneath thy roof,
>   In many a tearful measure;

For broken is that golden tie,
   Which made our bosoms one,
The tear must glitter in his eye
   Whose race is not yet run.[73]

These lines refer to the series of deaths in his immediate family that began with his sister Rebecca when he was not yet two. Before his third birthday, his sister Ruth died at home. When he was five, his sister Hannah, the mother of Columbus Greene, died in Burlington, Vermont, after giving birth to another child, who also died. The following year, her husband, Samuel, married Theodore's oldest sister, Mary; two years later, Samuel died, and Mary took Greene, who was both her step-son and nephew, back to her father's house. Four years later, Theodore's grandmother, Lydia Pierce, died at a great old age. Five months after that, on 14 May 1822, Theodore's mother, Hannah, died; her youngest son was eleven. Over the next several years, Theodore's brother John and the husband of his sister Lydia also died. In the 1830s, consumption claimed his remaining sisters, who had reared him after his mother's death: Emily, his favorite, died while he was teaching school in Boston; Mary in 1833; and finally, in late 1837, Lydia. Theodore was left with only two brothers and his nephew Columbus Greene. With neither of the brothers was he especially close: Isaac was a stolid type who took over the family farm, while Hiram, a carpenter in Lowell, struggled unsuccessfully with intemperance. Theodore and his nephew, meanwhile, had less to say to one another after Greene became a Baptist minister and moved away to Vermont.[74]

The earliest of the family tragedies that Theodore remembered was that of Hannah. In the summer of 1846, when a lecture tour took him through Burlington, he visited his sister's grave and noted in his journal that he had last seen her when "she was flying to Burlington, to meet her husband—a Bankrupt & a runaway. She stopped at my father's—my older brother was conducting her. She came to my bedside—kissed me—then asleep. . . . I remember what sadness came . . . [to] our family when we heard of H[']s. death! First came a letter that the child was dead; then another that H was no more!" He remembered, too, what sadness came later. As he wrote to a friend in 1832, he had "felt, and keenly, the afflictive rod. . . . I have but two brothers, and as many sisters, who with myself alone remain of a family of 11 children—'The Lord giveth and taketh away' but we can but answer, 'blessed be the name of the Lord.' "[75]

Of all the deaths, that of his mother surely left the deepest wound. In later life, he went every spring to Lexington and gathered the first violets that grew on her unmarked grave,[76] but he never wrote about her death, despite all that he wrote about her. Could it have been too painful to mention? His reaction to his father's death in November 1836 provides an instructive comparison.

Theodore was away from home, a young minister candidating for a pulpit, when his fiancée sent him the news.

> After I read your letter, [he wrote in his reply,] . . . I could almost see his fathers of other days, the wife of his youth, and his children, and long separated friends pressing gloriously around him, to press him once more to their hearts. Their shout and song of welcome still ring in my ears! . . . [H]ow can I forbear lamenting now he is gone? But enough of this—we shall yet meet—and I will no longer weary your Soul with the bitterness of mine. He has gone, let *us* say no more about it, and now I entreat you to say nothing upon that subject in your letters nor when we meet. A thousand circumstances will bring it all up before me again and again; do not let us multiply them without need, nor foolishly turn away from them when they do occur naturally, for the valley of tears, if dwelt in, hath a poisonous influence upon the Soul, but if only occasionally passed through it is full of "healing waters" and fountains of Strength.[77]

Parker had learned how to keep his "Soul" from being "poisoned" by grief. First, he would force a path out of the "valley of tears" by pushing the grief from his mind and concentrating on other things. So, after the passage just quoted, he abruptly began to discuss current affairs.[78] Second, he would affirm the immortality of the soul.

In later life, Parker claimed that his knowledge of immortality, like his knowledge of God and of right, was innate and spontaneous. He portrayed it that way in his poem "My Childhood's Home." Yet here, the promptings of this innate sentiment, imagined as "a voice," come as a direct response to thoughts about the tragedies of his childhood:

> In vain I seek the ancient place
>   Of each remembered blessing;
> I meet no more the mother's kiss,
>   Nor sister's soft caressing.
> My childhood's home—"Oh seek no more,"
>   I hear a voice reply—
> "Thy friends have found a fairer shore,
> *Thy* home beyond the sky.["][79]

He later disclosed to a friend that he had discovered the "innate" knowledge of immortality only as one of his sisters lay dying. He had heard, he recalled, a minister preach that the only sufficient proof of immortality was the Resurrection of Jesus: "Boy as I was, I saw the folly of that to prove a universal proposition; but, boy as I was, I could not reason the matter out, and in default of understanding prove my immortality; so felt constrained to doubt, almost to deny it." This doubt caused him several weeks of "torment." Then his sister died, and "at the grave's mouth, as it closed in on [her] . . . , I could not doubt where my logic had failed me. Nature came in & completed her work." Yet "nature" seems to have been at the beck and call of his emotions: "If I had only Reason, which cares little about persons & deals more with *Ideas*, I should not think I suppose or care about meeting my friends in the next stage of life. But as I have Affections more powerful too than Reason, I cannot doubt that I shall see and know my friends in Heaven."[80] Most important, he would see and know his mother and sisters, as in this unpublished poem from 1839, found in his journal:

> . . . Oh I would die & go to other worlds,
> where old affection watches yet to bless
> as in its earlier days. There son & mother are
> & many sisters, all our hearts entwined in one.[81]

Linked to this faith in immortality came another: That God, like a loving parent, would not allow any real, lasting harm to come to him. All his sufferings were transient and partial, mere lessons to prepare him for his future state of eternal happiness. This simple theodicy, which would sustain Theodore through many trials, was also to turn him into a cosmic optimist. He later admitted he could not refute the arguments of a pessimist, but, because of his faith in God, he could never believe them.

Parker's early life did shape his religion, but not in the way he so often claimed. His religion was not a simple, natural affirmation of his happy religious experience; it was more a way of surviving tragic experience. William James once called him an "admirable example" of a "once born" or "healthy-minded" religious person, for whom happiness is "congenital and irreclaimable." Parker's mature writings often leave the impression that he was such a person. Yet he had another side. In his *Discourse of Matters Pertaining to Religion*, he devotes the opening chapter of the book to "the religious sentiment," the innate religious feeling that lay behind the universal phenomenon of worship. It is not happiness, he says, but a sense that we "are not sufficient for ourselves." Ralph Waldo Emerson, in his little book *Nature*, describes his own religious experience as ecstatic: "Crossing a bare common, in snow puddles, at twilight, under a clouded sky, without having in my thoughts any occurrence of special good fortune, I have enjoyed a perfect exhilaration. Almost I fear to think how glad I am." By contrast, Parker, in the *Discourse*, describes the "sense of dependence": "A few years ago, and we were not; a few years hence, and our bodies shall not be. A mystery is gathered about our little life. . . . Our schemes fail. Our plans miscarry. One after another our lights go out. Our realities prove dreams. Our hopes waste away. . . . We feel an irresistible tendency to refer all outward things and ourselves with them, to a power beyond us, sublime and mysterious, which we cannot measure, nor even comprehend." His religious experience had been shaped more by sorrows than by joys.[82]

Chapter Two

An Immense Change in My Opinions

In his mature writings, Parker denounced "the popular theology" for placing the authority of Scripture over reason. He may have been so vehement because he had once done it himself. When Parker came to Watertown in April 1832, wearing "homely and awkward dress, and carrying a small bundle," he believed the Bible to be the literal word of God, as he makes clear in "History of the Jews," which he wrote in May and June. He did not intend the book to be read primarily as a biblical commentary. He uses the Bible as his principal source only in the first thirteen chapters, and even in these, he leaves large parts of the Bible undiscussed. Because he begins his story with Abraham, he does not mention the Creation or the Flood, and because he is studying the Jews, he refers only tangentially to the New Testament.[1]

Although Parker does not use Jewish history as an excuse to write about the Bible, he does use the story of "the most remarkable People on the face of the Earth"[2] to illustrate a theological theme:

> We may ask what has enabled them, during many successive ages of hatred & persecution, to preserve their . . . national integrity, when other nations, under more favorable circumstances, have in a few . . . years been amnihilated [*sic*]. We answer, the same Providence who witnesses the fall of a Sparrow, & the destruction of a Kingdom; & whose operations are conspicuous in this History—Pilate, at the Judgement of Christ, pronounced himself innocent of his blood, but th impetuate [*sic*] Jews cried, "his blood be upon our heads, & our children's." A more dreadful denunciation was |never| pronounced, & fearfully have their own curses been visited upon them.[3]

Although Parker evidently thinks that the Jews are responsible for Jesus' death, he is not deliberately trying to spread anti-Semitism, for elsewhere in the book he strongly condemns the "hatred & persecution" of the Jews.

Rather, he is trying to use his subject to show how God "conspicuously" intervenes in human affairs. His "History of the Jews" is really about miracles.[4]

Parker accepts as literal truth all the miracle stories of the Old Testament that he discusses. He rejects any effort to explain them away, as when he denies that the parting of the Red Sea was the result of the natural action of tides. When he tells the story of how Joshua made the sun and moon stand still in his battle with the Amorites, a miracle that many commentators who argued for the infallibility of Scripture tried to explain away because it assumed that the sun circled the earth, he dismisses theories that the Jews actually witnessed a natural phenomenon involving "aerioul phosphori," or that the biblical chronicler, in this poetic passage (Joshua 10:12–14), was merely using a "daring style of oriental Metaphor," and comes down squarely for divine intervention. The "obvious purpose" of the miracle, he believes, "was to confound the superstition of the Canaanites, who paid especial veneration to the Sun & Moon. What than must have been their astonishment to find their *fanciful* deities thus promoting their destruction?"[5]

Most important, Parker thinks that the Bible itself is a miracle, written by God with little, if any, human mediation. He says that the Ten Commandments were inscribed on clay "by God's own finger," that the Mosaic Law was not produced by human action, and implies that the words of the prophets came directly from God, because the prophets were able to tell the Jews of the coming of the messiah "with sufficient minuteness & precision, one would suppose, to enable [the Jews] to distinguish him when he actually did appear." Because Parker believes that the language of Scripture was produced miraculously, he assumes that it cannot be interpreted as ordinary human language. He makes no attempt to place the words of any passage in the context of the time and place in which they were written.

Parker began to view the Bible more critically during his two years in Watertown, partly because he came under the influence of its Unitarian minister, Convers Francis. He paid Francis a call and introduced himself shortly after arriving in town. This was the proper thing for a new schoolmaster to do, especially as Francis had been active in the school committee. Yet Parker had more on his mind than a courtesy visit; the young scholar was looking for an intellectual mentor. "I long for books," he said to the older man, "and I long to know how to study."[6] The broad-faced, amiable Francis seemed in many ways the kind of man Parker dreamed of being. He was not only an able parish minister but had a deserved reputation for learning. In 1837, his abilities were recognized when Harvard awarded him a doctorate. As Parker one day would learn, however, Francis secretly yearned for greater honors than this.

Francis filled the role Parker asked of him. Parker later recalled how Fran-

An Immense Change

cis willingly had lent him books from his large private collection and checked out books for him from the Harvard College library, and how Francis's "devotion to letters" and "diligent study of the best thoughts and highest themes" offered an example that both "stimulated and encouraged" him, especially as Francis was a rare scholar who did not separate himself by learning from the people. His admiration for Francis was such that on 5 May 1833 he formally joined his church.[7]

Francis's influence on Parker was considerable, yet Francis was too intellectually diffident and ideologically tolerant to impose his opinions on anyone. In a sermon he preached in 1831 to an auxiliary of the American Unitarian Association, on "Enlightened Views of Religion," he was characteristically modest about his theme: "I certainly do not mean to say, that none but the theology which we deem to be true can be embraced by enlightened minds, nor even to *imply* the silly boast that we alone dwell on the mount of vision, around the foot of which others are wandering in darkness."[8] Willing to see value in other points of view, and recognizing Parker's ability for self-directed study, he simply exposed him to new opinions and let him find his own way. As a result, although Francis probably already held Transcendentalist views about religious inspiration when they first met, Parker took five more years to reach similar conclusions. His attitude toward Scripture changed more rapidly.

Francis exposed him to the ideas of the Unitarian biblical critics, such as Andrews Norton, whose view of the Bible had been widely accepted by Unitarians. Norton held that although the Bible contained Truth that had been miraculously revealed by God, the biblical writers had recorded the truth in their own words for specific audiences, so that their personal style, concerns, and even opinions appeared in what they had written. Many Unitarians, including Norton, thought that parts of the Bible were not miraculously revealed at all, but were merely human products — sacred history and literature. The Bible had to be examined with painstaking care to determine which parts had merely particular and not general significance. In 1813, Norton had used his introductory lectures in biblical criticism at Harvard to deride as the worst error of interpretation the idea that a scriptural passage could be interpreted literally, apart from its historical context.[9] Six years later, William Ellery Channing presented this idea as the consensus of religious liberalism in his famous sermon "Unitarian Christianity":

> The Bible is a book written for men, in the language of men, and . . . its meaning is to be sought in the same manner as that of other books. . . . Now all books . . . require in the reader . . . the constant exercise of reason; or their true import is only to be obtained by continual comparison and inference. . . . We profess not to know a book, which demands more

frequent exercise of reason than the Bible. . . . [We] feel it our bounden duty to exercise our reason upon it perpetually, to compare, to infer, to look beyond the letter to the spirit, to seek in the nature of the subject, and the aim of the writer, his true meaning; and in general, to make use of what is known for explaining what is difficult, and for discovering new truths.[10]

Norton and Channing believed that if the Bible was thus correctly interpreted, it would be found to support their own "liberal Christian" position—in other words, that the Trinity and original sin would be found to be unscriptural. This same belief had led a prominent Unitarian merchant, Samuel Dexter, in 1810 to endow the Dexter Lectureship (later Professorship) as the first American academic chair in biblical criticism, a position that Norton held for many years.[11] Convers Francis, who had graduated from the theological school in 1815, had early absorbed this view of Scripture.

Francis presented it in a series of sermons on the Old Testament that he preached to his Watertown congregation in early 1834, some of which Parker almost certainly heard. In one, on the "Creation of Man," Francis denies that the account in Genesis, in which Adam is made from dust, should be taken literally. Although the story contains in it the basic truth that we derive our existence from God, the form in which the truth is presented conforms to ancient taste and imagination. A Hebrew scribe, writing "in the midst of the childhood of our race," when reason was crude and ideas were sensual, could not have known what even modern science does not know—how humanity came to be. There was "nothing analogous" between flesh, blood, bones, and dust, so the former could not come from the latter. The idea was common, however, in the ancient world (the Greeks believed it), and it was probably recommended to the author of the story by the similarity of the Hebrew words for "man" and "earth," by our decaying into dust after death, and by the thought that people would be more humble if they believed they came from dust. Similarly, the account of the creation of Eve from Adam's rib is not literally true, but an allegorical moral lesson about the intimacy of the sexes and their mutual dependence. In another of these sermons, on the great longevity of the antediluvians and patriarchs, Francis suggests that the ages given in Scripture in fact refer to eras in which the person in question was the dominant figure. In a sermon on the Deluge, he takes the view of many geologists of the day, that although there had been a great flood, it could not have been universal, because otherwise no land plants could have survived it. The fossil fish found on most mountain peaks must have been left there by other, unrecorded floods.[12]

Besides absorbing these demythologizing interpretations of the Bible on Sundays, Parker also, with Francis's encouragement, took up biblical criticism. In February 1834, he wrote to his fiancée that "Mr. Francis" had come and lent him "the necessary books," so that he had "commenced the great study, the criticism of the New Testament." With "the little that has been yet explored of it," he added, "I am not only pleased but highly delighted."[13]

Within two years of Parker's writing his "History of the Jews," his view of the Bible had changed markedly. In the spring of 1834, in a letter to his fiancée, he was able to read critically the story of Saul speaking to the ghost of Samuel through the medium of the Witch of Endor (1 Samuel 20). Although this story seems to admit the existence of necromancy, Parker had retold it without comment in his "History." Now he opted for a naturalistic explanation. He did "not think *Saul* saw Samuel: the witch only *pretended* to see *him*, and gave the answers as if Samuel were actually present; it deserves notice besides that nothing new is told; nothing which Samuel had not declared while alive." Parker not only felt growing skepticism about particular miraculous events, but, more important, he had ceased to believe that the entire Bible was the literal word of God. He now doubted, for example, that all the Psalms of David breathed "the good and merciful spirit of the Lord"; some seemed to have a "revengeful Spirit" and therefore were "inconsistent with the character of God." They should be regarded "as only the odes of a Pious King, who yet had all the frailties of a man." As he wrote to his nephew Columbus Greene a few weeks later, he continued to believe that the "Books of the old and new Testament . . . [were] written by men inspired by God, for certain purposes," but he no longer thought these men had been "inspired at all times."[14]

Parker had adopted the liberal approach to the Bible. He was now "exercising his reason upon it perpetually." Convers Francis had opened a door in his mind through which, as his studies advanced, he would admit the radical German biblical criticism of De Wette and Strauss. But this was in the future. In 1834, he could still write to Greene, when asked about the nature of his faith, that "I believe in the Bible." Throughout his stay in Watertown, and long after, he remained deeply reverential toward "Sacred Scripture." In the "History," he had attacked those who thought the writings of the Greeks more beautiful than those of the Hebrews, while two years later he criticized Greene for "the unholy manner" in which Greene had "quoted sacred writ" in a letter.[15]

When he encountered actual "infidelity"—that is, outright disbelief in the accounts of the Bible and in the miracles—his reaction was very sharp indeed. One summer evening in 1833, he had a heated discussion about Christianity with George T. Bigelow, a young law student (in later life, a prominent jurist)[16] who made the case that "skepticism alone is rational." The next day, Parker, quick with a reply as ever, wrote Bigelow a satiric letter in which he thanked him for proving his point:

I had long been accustomed to believe the events recorded in Scripture, partly from internal evidence and partly from the concurrent Testimony of contemporaneous historians and such scholars as Leclerc, Grotius, Leibnitz [*sic*], Newton, Locke and an host of others foolishly considered learned, and foolishly regarded as wise. I must now set aside all their pretensions as useless, their arguments inconclusive, and even the very Religion they attempt to defend a mere farce!!! It cannot be defended without begging the question, which is ridiculous[,] or supposing impossibilities (E.G. miracles) which is absurd.[17]

He goes on to "prove," using Bigelow's skeptical methods, that the story of Columbus discovering America was a fabrication.

Bigelow's response, in a letter written the next day, is interesting because he sounds not unlike Parker himself a few years later. Bigelow criticized his friend for using "the frailest and least honorable of all weapons — viz — *Ridicule*," and pointedly asked him whether he ought not to "illustrate the truths and virtues of the Christian religion — if any it has —, so as to make them attractive to the unbeliever, — rather than to drive him from investigation by ridicule and reproach?"

I find that the Bible, — the *corner stone* of your belief — cannot be measured by the square and compass of reason, nor be weighed in the balance of truth and *love*. . . . I can worship my Creator with as sincere and heartfelt a devotion, as you can —, with all your faith — and your systems of theology — for I kneel at a shrine — not made with hands, nor fashioned by human iniquity, while you bow at an alter, "so crossly indented, and whimsically dove-tailed," that it appears, what in truth it is, the museum of absurdities of every nation, sect and age.[18]

ON A SUNDAY afternoon in late October 1833, Parker walked from Watertown to Lexington and announced to his father that he was engaged to Lydia Dodge Cabot. The old man, normally so reserved, was visibly moved. "A tear actually started to his aged eye," wrote Parker to Lydia, with evident surprise. The couple did not plan to wed until Parker had gone through theological school and was settled in a parish, a process that they expected would take four years. John Parker thought this was "a good while to wait," but he gave his consent. "I should be happy with anyone you select, Theodore," he told his youngest child, "but now you must be a good *man*, and a good *husband*, and that is no small undertaking." The words, Parker told his fiancée, "sank deep into my heart."[19]

They had met in spring 1832, shortly after he arrived in Watertown, at the house of Nathaniel Broad, where Parker was boarding. The Broads seem to have been friends of Lydia's family, and she came to stay with them for a season; while there, she taught Sunday school in Francis's church. Parker never failed to notice a pretty girl, and she was a tall eighteen-year old with fine features, large blue eyes, and long, straight brown hair. Even better, she had qualities befitting the wife of the minister Parker planned to be: gentility, a good education, and, above all, piety.[20]

Like many ambitious young men, Parker hoped to "marry up"; the farm girls of Lexington had not been for him. Lydia's family had money and position; they were a cadet branch of the famous Cabots. Her great-uncle George Cabot, the senator, had chaired the Hartford convention, and her first cousin Amelia Lee Jackson would wed the elder Oliver Wendell Holmes and become the mother of the Supreme Court justice. Her father, John Cabot, the only surviving son of a wealthy merchant, had married his own first cousin, Lydia Dodge. Not an apt merchant himself, partly because he suffered from ill health, Cabot had used his inheritance to retire at thirty and live as a country squire in Newton, where he and his wife reared three children. Lydia was the youngest and the only daughter. By the time of her engagement, she was living most of the time with her father's sister Lucy in Boston.[21]

Lucy Cabot, nearly fifty years old when Theodore and Lydia fell in love, owned a fortune in stocks but, like her brother, suffered from a variety of ailments. She had never married and needed a companion; Lydia seems to have filled this role from an early age. In return for her service, Lucy, who was also something of a bluestocking, oversaw her schooling. Aunt and niece had grown so close that some people mistakenly thought Lucy was Lydia's foster mother. They lived apart only occasionally, as when Lydia stayed at the Broad's place (why she was away from Lucy in the spring of 1832 is unclear). The two women seem to have had an understanding that when Lydia married, their arrangement would continue. Parker must have realized they were inseparable and so tried to like his future in-law, who struck him as a rather difficult person. In the spring of 1836, he took pains to write in his journal some "kind remarks about Aunt L."[22]

Lucy had given her niece a good education by the standards set for women of that day. She had found for her excellent teachers; one of them was the Transcendentalist and educational innovator Elizabeth Palmer Peabody. Peabody later would vouch for her former student's intelligence, but little evidence of Lydia's learning survives. Her few surviving letters show impeccable grammar, spelling, and penmanship, but no erudition. She could read enough French to help her fiancée translate some papers of Lafayette for the historian Jared Sparks in 1834, but seems to have had little training in the three principal scholarly tongues of early-nineteenth-century New England: Latin, Greek, or German. Parker's letters to her do assume, however, that she was familiar with contemporary literature and that she kept abreast of current events, both political and religious. He assumes, too, her thorough knowledge of Scripture and discusses with her his critical readings of certain passages.[23]

This knowledge indicates her piety, a quality they had in common. They shared a deep interest in Sunday schools, in which they both taught. He often expressed his support for them. His Commonplace Book, which he started in 1835, is full of Sunday school lessons, and has in it several passages refuting the claim that Sunday schools "do no good"; in 1837, he contributed a number of (anonymous) articles to the *Sunday School Teacher, and Children's Friend*, a Unitarian Sunday school periodical. Lydia's support for Sunday schools was so strong that she criticized Theodore for not supporting them enough. She also copied by hand tracts for the American Sunday School Union.[24]

Parker's own religious and moral qualities evidently drew her to him; no doubt she extolled them to her parents, in successfully persuading them to consent to the match. Years later, she would recall with approval the young schoolmaster's "habits . . . of strict industry, frugality, & temperance," and how "he bore himself above reproach." She noted with approval how he "anxiously inquired" after his students' "purpose in life," and how he carefully watched over the moral condition of the five or six of his scholars who boarded with the Broads: "Of these he took particular charge with reference to their deportment as members of the household. They all sat and ate at the family table, at which they were accustomed each day to listen to Mr. Parker's invocation of the blessing of Divine Providence." She was impressed that, although poor himself, he taught for free a bright girl who could not pay him.[25]

She may have been drawn to him, too, by a maternal interest in his health. She worried with reason that he overworked himself. She saw him out every day at dawn chopping wood for the school stove, yet she knew that he had been up to all hours reading, because his lamp was always empty in the morning (and the Broads, she knew, did not scrimp on oil). In his spare time, besides pursuing his biblical studies, which included walking to Charlestown every week to learn Hebrew from James Seixas—a convert to Christianity from a prominent Jewish family who had become a respected teacher of the language—Parker read all of Tacitus and most of Cicero, Herodotus, and Thucydides, translated most of Pindar, Theocritus, and Aeschylus and read in the works of Coleridge, Cousin, Goethe, Schiller, and Klopstock. He regularly attended Lyceum lectures and sometimes even wrote them. In the winter of 1831-32, he had written his first lecture, on Poland; part of another early lecture, on Cuba, still survives. The bad effects of his intemperate work habits were aggravated by alarming ascetic impulses: when he boarded himself he had a tendency to eat nothing but dry bread and crackers. After he and Lydia were engaged, she issued orders that he go to sleep by eleven and repeatedly urged him to read less and exercise more. "You are quite too fearful of my *over*-studying," Parker complained to her in 1836. "Now I tell you that I know best about these matters, and that my conscience would as little permit me *study* too much as to *drink* too much."[26]

Parker could laugh off Lydia's maternal worries, but that she had them probably helped him to idealize her. He seems to have projected on her all his hopes to recreate the childhood home that he had lost as his mother and sisters died one by one. These hopes, charged with a jolt of half-submerged sexual longing, conjured in his mind a powerful image of his fiancée as an angel—he regularly called her "sky born"—who would become his perfect wife. Such projection was made easier by a certain passivity in her personality. Once, in a letter to him, she referred to "poor weak women," among whom she seems to have numbered herself. Such a self-image might explain what Parker later called her "reluctance . . . in conversing at all." When he talked, she probably listened quietly, and he took her silence for sympathy. Moreover, during the years of Parker's schooling, and while he was searching for a pulpit, he and Lydia seem to have spent long periods apart, during which they knew each other mostly from letters. But Lydia was "not one of the writing caste more than of the talking." And so Parker never really got to know her until they were married.[27]

PARKER CLOSED his Watertown academy in March 1834. On the final day, his students presented him with an engraved silver cup as a token of their affection, and he wept—but the sadness was mixed with excitement, for he was about to achieve his longstanding ambition to study at Harvard. With Francis's encouragement, he was joining the junior (that is, first year) class of the divinity school at midyear. By not waiting until the fall to join the next junior class, he planned to shave a year off the three-year program, which would allow him to find a pulpit and marry Lydia that much sooner. On 1 April, he moved into a room on the fourth floor of Divinity Hall and began classes two weeks later.[28]

It was a long, four-story brick building that had been opened only nine years before and stood in a "rustic woodland" at the end of elm-shaded Divinity Avenue, about a quarter of a mile from Harvard Yard. It held student accommodations, recitation rooms, a small chapel, and a library. The latter was also small, but the students had access to the college library, with its more than 20,000 volumes. Most of the students boarded at the college commons for $1.90 a week, although Parker, in a burst of asceticism and frugality, for a time brought his expenses down to fifty cents a week by eating only dry bread (he evidently stopped this regimen before succumbing to scurvy). Although the divinity school had but thirty students and three professors, it was the principal place to train Unitarian ministers. Its faculty would have denied that they were conducting a mere sectarian seminary, for neither they nor their students were required to swear to a creed. One historian has aptly remarked, however, that the "distinction between a Unitarian Divinity School and a school conducted by Unitarians for 'impartial, and unbiassed investigation of Christian truth,' resulting in well-trained candidates for Unitarian pulpits, is too metaphysical . . . to grasp."[29]

The Unitarianism of the school was evidence that Harvard was changing its social role. Under the administration of its dour president, Josiah Quincy, it was turning into a private cultural training ground for the new merchant and manufacturing elite of Boston—most of whom were Unitarians.[30] The college was still little more than a boarding school and a rather rowdy one at that. In the spring of 1834, Harvard Yard was the scene of a major student riot that grew from a protest over Quincy's stern disciplinary measures. Parker apparently made no comment on this event, perhaps because the divinity school and the college seemed, despite their proximity and connections, to belong to different worlds.

The divinity students formed a close group, studying, eating, singing, and praying together, bursting into each other's rooms at odd hours and talking all night. Their sense of common purpose was so high that in the spring of Parker's senior year, when for a period of two months all three faculty members were either ill or absent, the students continued to hold their classes according to the regular schedule. Many of them would have notable careers, although not all in the ministry. George Ellis, after a distinguished career as a pastor, was to return to Harvard as a professor of theology. Henry Bellows was to take an important pulpit in New York and later organize the National Sanitary Commission and the National Conference of Unitarian Churches. Cyrus Bartol was to become the eminent minister of the West Church in Boston, sometimes associated with Transcendentalism. Other future Transcendentalists were Christopher Cranch, who soon abandoned the pulpit for the writing desk and the easel, and John Sullivan Dwight, who never found the ministry congenial and became a Brook Farmer and later an influential music critic. Cranch and Dwight became Parker's friends, but his closest friends—dozens of affectionate letters to them from Parker survive—were probably Sam Andrews and above all William Silsbee. Neither was later to rise to eminence. Andrews, who was never to be ordained, became a clerk in the police court at Salem. Parker probably came to know Andrews through his townsman Silsbee, Parker's "most intimate" friend of all. Silsbee came from a prominent Salem family (his uncle was a U.S. senator from Massachusetts), with a scholarly bent and Transcendentalist leanings. He had published doubts about the authority of Scripture as early as 1834.[31] Yet he was to have an unremarkable ministerial career.

Parker plunged enthusiastically into student life. He became active in the Philanthropic Society, an organization of theological students that provided religious instruction for inmates at the state prison in Charlestown (at one point, he was visiting the prisoners three times a week), and that usually met every other Wednesday evening to discuss the "moral and religious wants of our community, and the various benevolent projects of the day." He gained a reputation as the best public speaker at the school, not only in the society debates, but at the religious discussions that the whole school would have every Thursday evening. One of his fellow students remembers him in these "conversations," "sitting still in his seat, and tying noiseless knots in his hand-kerchief, every one of which . . . meant some argument for which he had a reply." [32]

In September 1835, he became an editor, with Silsbee and Ellis, of the *Scriptural Interpreter*; the little journal, founded by a fast-rising young Boston minister, Ezra Stiles Gannett, was intended to help its Unitarian subscribers with family Bible study by making available to them fruits of biblical criti-cism. That same year Parker was appointed an instructor at the college, where he assisted John Gorham Palfrey in teaching Hebrew. Parker earned money in his spare time by translating French and German writings and by privately tutoring college students in German, Latin, and Greek. He wrote dozens of poems and religious articles, many of which he published anonymously in the Unitarian weekly, the *Christian Register*. All this activity was in addition to his reading, which soon became legendary as among the most extensive of any student in the history of the school. [33]

Parker's friends later remembered him as a "prodigious athlete in his studies" with a "restless ambition to excell," yet "full of exuberant life," and possessed of a temperament that seemed "charged full of electricity, so that he was literally *snapping* at times with sparks of fun and satire."

> Two or three of us divinity students . . . [recalled Christopher Cranch,] were in full musical blast at something—fluting or singing, I forget which—in one of the rooms of Divinity Hall. Immediately opposite was Parker's room. He was evidently engaged in much more serious study, and more in line with his future profession, than we were. Still we were quite unaware of our disturbing him. . . . Presently, there was a peculiar "movement" in the entry, just outside our door, executed upon a pecu-liar and by no means musical instrument . . . thrown in as an accompani-ment to our strains. On opening the door . . . there was Theodore, who had left his folios of the Latin fathers, had rushed into the cellar, and brought up a wood-horse, saw, and log of wood, on which he was exer-cising his vigorous sinews—see-saw, see-saw—to our utter discomfiture and amusement. As for Theodore, he barely smiled. [34]

His friends also remembered darker aspects to Parker's character—his sharp tongue, volatile emotions, and quick temper. One friend recalled an argument he had had with Parker over Henry Taylor's drama *Philip Van Arte-velde*. At one point in the play, Artevelde, a fourteenth-century Flemish patriot fighting a war with France, executes two villains. The friend thought this act was a "great blemish," for Artevelde should have shown mercy. "No," cried Parker, "it is just; it is good; it is Christian." "It is downright murder," the friend replied—and Parker furiously ordered him out of the room. He later wept with regret that he had lost his temper.[35] On another occasion, he asked Dwight to point out to him his faults, a favor he had already done for Dwight. Dwight's reply offers a remarkably accurate insight into Parker's character:

> You distrust those who are unlike yourself. You fancy them restraints upon you and then your faith in your own energies and ideas speaks out in a tone of almost bitter contempt for the world and those who do not think and feel as you do. You feel that such sentiments as you cherish ought to triumph, but you find the world courting men who pursue inferior aims. Coupled with your high ideal is an impatient wish to see it immediately realized, two things which don't go well together; for the one prompts you to love, the other soured by necessary disappointments, prompts to hate, at least contempt.[36]

PARKER LEFT vivid impressions, but no one remembers him as having been a religious radical at Harvard. "Great things were prophesied of him," recalled the Transcendentalist Cranch, "but it was supposed he would be little more than a scholar. . . . None guessed that . . . later he was to do battle for pure, unadulterated Christianity."[37]

Just how unradical he was comes out in a letter he wrote to his nephew Columbus Greene the day after he moved into Divinity Hall. The first principle of his faith, he says, is belief in the Bible, although he thought the writers of the Bible were not inspired at all times. He believed in "one God" (not in the Triune God), who is "almighty—good and merciful—will reward the good and punish the wicked—both in this life and the next." This punishment "may be eternal." He believed that Christ was "the Son of God, conceived and born in a miraculous manner," that He "came to preach a better religion by which mankind may be saved," but not that "our sins will be forgiven because Christ died." Parker did not believe in total depravity, "or that Adam's Sin will be imputed to us"; rather, he thought that "if a man leads a good and pure life he will be accepted with God." The means of religion consisted of "reading the Holy Bible, attending prayers, professing Religion and pious conversation."[38]

This confession of faith would have provoked no objection from even quite conservative Unitarians. His position on the Trinity and original sin

An Immense Change

were standard among them. His description of the means of religion might have been lifted straight out of Henry Ware Jr.'s *On the Formation of the Christian Character*. His admission of the possibility of Hell placed him to the right of many Unitarians, who believed in universal salvation, and contradicts his later recollection that he had abandoned the idea of damnation by the age of seven. He also contradicts his later accounts with his unqualified affirmation of belief in the supernatural birth of Jesus, which he claims to have doubted well before he came to Harvard. In June 1834, he could write to Greene that he believed "Christ was miraculously conceived; John the Baptist was, so was Samuel, and Isaac."[39]

IN LATER YEARS, Parker the radical prophet would make disparaging remarks about the divinity school. He would recall how his professors milked the ram, and the students held the sieve. Yet at the time, he expressed nothing but high regard for the views of his professors, whose ideas were in many ways representative of Unitarian opinion.

The senior member of the faculty was old, bald Dr. Henry Ware, who taught Natural and Revealed Religion, Church History, and Dogmatic Theology. Ware bore his seventy years with a patriarchal air, which he had acquired while fathering and rearing nineteen children. It had been his election to the Hollis Professorship of Divinity thirty years before that had triggered the Unitarian controversy, and he had been a liberal stalwart in the debates that followed. His pamphlet exchange of the early 1820s with his Orthodox counterpart at Andover, Leonard Woods, had run to some eight hundred pages. Never a man of acute intellect (he admitted, for example, that he never really understood the ontological argument for God), he had grown uninterested in innovation. He now liked rereading old devotional books and listening to familiar hymns, and out of simple inertia would keep wearing his great winter cloak well into the spring and his thinnish summer garments into October. Still, Parker admired him and was one of the students who in 1836 signed a letter of appreciation to him, in which they thanked Ware for his "kindness, attention and urbanity towards us," and for the example he had set of "diligence in examining, of patience in reasoning, and of benevolent candour and impartial love of truth in deciding."[40]

Ware's lectures advance no original ideas, but they do provide a clear exposition of the system of apologetics that undergirded Unitarian opinion, and that modern scholars identify as "supernatural rationalism."[41] According to the supernatural rationalist system, people could with their unaided "natural" reason discover certain basic religious truths. Someone could reason from the observations that every effect has a cause, and that the universe is apparently well designed, to the idea that there was a God who was a First Cause and Designer. The observation that things are so constituted that virtue tends to lead to prosperity and vice to ruin, and the awareness of one's own conscience, might result in the discovery of the Goodness of God, God's Providence, and the Moral Law. The thought that, despite these, virtue does not always appear to triumph in this life, possibly could lead to the conclusion that there was a Future State of rewards and punishments that would provide compensation.

Although Ware believed unassisted human reason was able to discover these truths, he thought the history of the Heathen world indicated that it would not do so. How "full of absurdity and error has been the religion, not only of barbarians, but of the nations most enlightened and refined," notes Ware in one of his lectures; "and not only the popular opinions, on the subject of religion, but those of the great masters of human science." Their opinions were "vague and uncertain," their reasonings "feeble, defective, and false," on "the first principles of religious faith, which Christians regard as the very elements of the religion of nature!" To remove absurdity, error, and uncertainty, God had given us a supernatural revelation of religious truth in the Bible.[42]

The Bible, Ware argued, strengthens the truths about God and immortality taught by natural religion. The Old Testament teaches us there is but one God, the Creator and Sovereign of the universe, who is infinite, eternal, omnipresent, omniscient, omnipotent, and whose attributes are perfect Holiness, Goodness, Mercy, and Veracity. The New Testament casts "a far clearer light" on immortality, "the most important doctrine of the Christian religion," than any other ancient religious text. Jesus and the Apostles speak emphatically of a future state of rewards and punishments, in which the soul lives eternally.[43]

Moreover, many essential truths of religion, although not contrary to Reason, are beyond its powers to learn without the Bible, especially those concerning Christ and His mission. On these matters Ware thought as a Unitarian: Scripture did not teach the Trinity, original sin, or vicarious atonement. It did teach, Ware claimed, that Jesus was God's "messenger, agent and visible representative"; that we are fallen from a primitive condition of innocence and purity, to our present state of "weakness, but not of absolute helplessness, of temptation, but not without power of resistance, of danger, but not without the means of escape"; and that Jesus "is the medium by which are communicated to us the blessings and hopes, that relate to the forgiveness of sin, the favor of God, and another life." Jesus by his life reconciles us to God, said Ware; he does not by his death reconcile God to us, as the Orthodox maintain.[44]

Parker still accepted the basic distinction between natural and revealed religion while he was at Harvard. So in a sermon on "Retribution," which he wrote as a class exercise and preached to his fellow students shortly before he graduated, Parker argued that the certainty of a future state of retribution could be proven three ways, by reason, experience—but "most of all . . . by Sacred Scripture."[45]

The distinction between natural and revealed religion was an ancient element of Christian thought, hardly unique to the supernatural rationalist tradition. More distinctive was its method of confirming that the Bible really was a revelation. For if the Bible is to help us, we must be sure the truths in it truly come from God. Ware, like other Unitarians, argued emphatically that the only decisive proof of the divine origin of the biblical truths was the miracles that surrounded their transmission via inspired messengers. Miracles, roughly defined, were suspensions of the laws of nature. As these laws had been established by God, God would not suspend them without a good reason—such as to confirm a revelation. The New Testament miracles had been visibly performed before numerous reliable witnesses and so were reasonable evidence that the Christian revelation was of God.

Parker nowhere, in his surviving writings from divinity school, explicitly says a revelation can be confirmed only by miracles. But he often writes on the Bible, and his comments show clearly the influence on him of Unitarian biblical criticism, which was based on supernatural rationalist assumptions.

He had been exposed to criticism of the Old and New Testaments by Convers Francis; at Harvard these subjects were taught by John Gorham Palfrey, dean of the school. Palfrey, not yet forty, had a face that suggested his character, with blunt features and close-set eyes, indicating a forceful man of action (he would later be elected to Congress), and a high, broad forehead, indicating intellect and cultivation (he edited the *North American Review*). Parker and the dean liked and respected each other. Parker probably saw Palfrey as the model of a poor boy who had risen fast in the ministry—a charity student at Exeter who had become minister of the prestigious Brattle Street church at age twenty-two and a dean by thirty-five. Parker's commonplace book for 1835–36 contains several highly appreciative summaries of Palfrey's sermons. When the dean fell ill for a time that winter, he had Parker take over his Hebrew class; one of Parker's detailed letters to him, describing what he had been assigning the students, is signed "affectionately yours."[46]

When Palfrey was appointed dean in 1831, he was also appointed Dexter Professor. The chair in biblical criticism had recently been vacated by Andrews Norton, who had retired from teaching to devote his full energies to completing his monumental work on the New Testament. Palfrey had had no desire to compete with his good friend Norton and so had made the Old Testament his specialty. When he did write on the New Testament, he, like Norton, defended the authenticity of the Christian books and the reality of the Christian miracles. Unlike Norton, he tolerated the opinions of others and so created an atmosphere in which his students could reach their own conclusions about Scripture. This was especially so because when he wrote on the Old Testament, he was something of an iconoclast. He defended certain traditional ideas—for example, that Moses wrote the Pentateuch; but Parker believed, as he later wrote, that Palfrey was the only biblical critic in the English language to "look the Old Testament in the face." Palfrey unwittingly prepared students to accept radical ideas about Scripture he himself did not condone.[47]

Behind Palfrey's willingness to treat the Hebrew Scriptures more daringly than the Christian ones lay a commonly held Unitarian view, which Parker shared, that religion had developed progressively through history. Unitarians challenged the Orthodox belief in the unity of the Bible, on the grounds that the Old Testament often showed marks of being written in a primitive era and was therefore not of equal value with the New. "The dispensation of Moses, compared with that of Jesus," William Ellery Channing had said in his sermon *Unitarian Christianity*, "we consider adapted to the childhood of the human race, a preparation for a nobler system, and chiefly useful now as serving to confirm and illustrate the Christian scriptures." Parker echoed this view in an article in the *Scriptural Interpreter*, published in 1836: "How much must mankind have advanced between Moses and Paul! what a difference in the subjects and style of these two illustrious writers! The writings of Paul would have been unintelligible to the contemporaries of Moses. . . . The doctrines . . . which are taught in the Bible are such as the people 'were able to bear' at the time they were published."[48]

Palfrey, assuming that the Old Testament was historically conditioned, could be much freer in his treatment of it than he could with the Gospels. For example, he was quite willing to declare many of the miracles of the Old Testament to be mere natural phenomena or poetic stories.[49] He was firmly convinced, based on his supernatural rationalist principles, that the only valid miracles were those that confirmed a revelation.[50] That Parker accepted this line of reasoning is suggested by an article on Job that he wrote for the *Scriptural Interpreter* in December 1835. He argues here that the miracle of the whirlwind "is certainly inconsistent with the general tenor of the government of the world," because its purpose was merely to "convince five disputants of an error." A "miracle is never wrought unless the occasion be adequate, which no one will contend in this instance." Although he did not go on to say what would be an adequate occasion, it is reasonable to assume he believed that the confirmation of a revelation would be one.[51]

More dramatic evidence of the potential radicalism of this line of reasoning was an article Parker published in April 1836 on the passage in Isaiah about the "suffering servant" (52:13–53:12). Parker denied the view, widely held by Unitarians and others, that the passage predicts the coming of Christ. He carefully reviewed the possibilities as to who the suffering servant might be. It was not Jesus, because the figure had some worldly dominion (53:12), and should be buried with the wicked (53:8); the term "Servant of God" is never used in the Old Testament to refer to the messiah; the passage discusses past events, not future ones; the context of the passage is a description of Jewish sufferings in the exile and their present deliverance; the other prophecies of the Old Testament are general and vague, not specific, like this passage; the writers of the New Testament do refer to this passage, but only for illustration, not because they thought it was a prophecy. Although many other interpreters thought the suffering servant was Israel, Parker believed that this was stretching the metaphor. "To me," he concludes, "the writer laments the untimely fate of some virtuous and patriotic Jew who had been associated with him in attempting to relieve the distress of his countrymen."[52]

This article caused a small controversy. An "eminent Doctor of Divinity, settled in Boston"—almost certainly Dr. Nathaniel Frothingham of the First Church—"found fault" with the piece and told Parker he was "sorry to see it."[53] Far more distressed was a subscriber to the *Interpreter*, who sent the editors an anonymous letter:

> I read . . . the article on the 52nd chapter of Isaiah, and with unmingled surprise and horror. What could possess you? What is the object of the theologians at Cambridge? Are they determined to break down the prophecies, and make our blessed Saviour and his Apostles impostors and liars? Cannot our doctrines be sustained in any other way? Must the pious Christian be compelled to give up one passage after another, one book after another, one prophecy after another, until he has nothing left to stand upon but what is in common with the Deist? . . . Pause then, I beseech you, before it is too late. . . . I am one of the household of your faith. But another such a blow and I must quit all I value; my religious faith above all things else. I cannot part with it. To escape, therefore, shipwreck, I must jump overboard before the last plank is taken away.[54]

The editors responded with "their most hearty thanks for the kind caution, which the writer expressed with so Christian a spirit," and with assurances that "the writer's objections may be removed," if they could only learn "by what title to address him." They never learned.[55]

The scattered reproaches Parker's article received have earned it a daring reputation among his biographers.[56] But the issue of prophecy had been raised before the Unitarian public almost two years earlier. In July 1834, George Rapall Noyes, the Unitarian minister at Brooksfield and a distinguished scholar of Hebrew, published an article in the Unitarian quarterly, the *Christian Examiner*, in which he argued the Old Testament prophecies could be interpreted to predict the coming of Jesus only by making use of unreasonable methods of exegesis; true, the Apostle Paul had interpreted the prophecies this way, but Paul, said Noyes, was wrong.

Public reaction was swift and furious. Noyes was denounced in the newspapers, and there were even calls for his prosecution under the state blasphemy law. But leading Unitarians defended his right to think and speak freely. Norton wrote a stinging attack on Noyes's accusers; Palfrey, in his diary, noted the attack on Noyes, and commented: "Oh what a despotism does one live under, where all one's neighbors want to be tyrants over him."[57]

Both Palfrey and Norton actually agreed with Noyes. Norton, in a letter from 1836, said he did not believe the prophets "claimed a miraculous power of predicting future events, or were supposed by their contemporaries to possess it"; there was no reason to suppose they did possess it. Palfrey published his opinion on the prophecies some years later, when he delivered his *Academical Lectures on the Jewish Scriptures and Antiquities*. He then argued that the only miraculous dispensation in the Old Testament was that of Moses (that is, as found in the Pentateuch). The prophets were not miraculously inspired; the messiah they predicted was not like Jesus. Fittingly, when Palfrey retired from Harvard, in 1840, Noyes was appointed his successor as Dexter Professor.[58]

By 1836, when Parker published his article on Isaiah, the rejection of prophecies, although still the minority opinion, was becoming a respectable one in Unitarian circles. It grew logically from the claim that God used miracles only to justify a revelation. So Parker's article provoked only one alarmed letter, and when Nathaniel Frothingham, who himself privately doubted the prophecies, criticized Parker for publishing the piece, Parker understandably thought him inconsistent. Parker himself, like Palfrey and Norton, could reject the prophecies while accepting many other miracles. "I do not doubt that Jesus was a man 'sent from God,' and endowed with power from on high, that he taught the truth and worked miracles," Parker wrote in his journal a month after the publication of his article, "but that he was the subject of inspired prophecy I very much doubt."[59]

On one point, Noyes was more daring than Parker: he said Paul was wrong about the prophecies, while Parker claimed the New Testament writers, properly understood, were not wrong. This claim fitted the usual Unitarian approach to New Testament criticism, which again evolved from supernatural rationalist apologetics. Having shown that miracles could happen because God had a good reason to employ them, Unitarians now had to show that miracles in fact had happened—in other words, to prove that the biblical accounts of certain miracles, above all the Gospels, were accurate.

In attempting to prove their accuracy, most Unitarians rejected another unnecessary miracle—the plenary inspiration of the Gospels. In 1836, Norton stated their position in a letter: "I ascribe the authorship of neither the Gospels nor the Epistles to God, and cannot call them in any sense the Word of God." These Unitarians denied the Evangelists were miraculously inspired on the grounds that they were plainly not infallible; their stories were obviously inconsistent on some points. But Norton thought the accuracy of the Gospels could be proven by the standard rules of testimony. First, they could be proven "genuine": that is, they could be shown to have been written by the eyewitnesses or contemporaries to whom they are traditionally ascribed, and to have been passed down from ancient to modern times in substantially unaltered form. Norton tried to prove just these two points in *The Genuineness of the Gospels*, a book on which he labored seventeen years. Once the Gospels were proven genuine, one needed only to prove the Evangelists were credible witnesses—by showing, for example, that their testimony jibed with known facts.[60]

The case of the Apostle to the Gentiles was more complicated than that of the Evangelists, for almost all Unitarians held that Paul was miraculously inspired in some sense. Even Noyes held that although Paul was an all-too-human exegete, he was infallible when he spoke of religious truth. Parker took a more conservative position. In October 1835, he published in the *Interpreter* a commentary on the second epistle to the Thessalonians, in which he set out to prove that Paul had not believed the Second Coming was nigh. Had Paul preached such a doctrine to the Thessalonians, Parker argued, and the prediction failed to come true, then not only would they have "lost confidence in his teachings," but "we ourselves could scarcely place the same unbounded trust in his other doctrines."[61]

PARKER RESPECTED Dr. Ware and Dean Palfrey, but for Ware's son, Henry Ware Jr., the Professor of Pulpit Eloquence and the Pastoral Care, his feelings were deeper. In an 1834 letter to Columbus Greene, Parker not only recommended Ware's *On the Formation of the Christian Character* and *Life of the Savior*, he judged their author "one of the finest men I have known." Even a dozen years later, after much had happened to sour Parker's memory of his Harvard years, he recalled Ware's "presence at our religious meetings" as that of a "saint": it "was the fragrance of violets in the library; and we felt it."[62]

The younger Ware—or "Mr. Ware," as Parker referred to him—had a puny frame wracked by illness, but his large head gave him the impression of size. He dressed with severe plainness, and his public manner could be just as severely formal. Parker recalled that he "was not always equal—sometimes was absent, and *seemed* cold." Yet his fervent, understated piety and quietly heroic unselfishness gave many the impression of a volcano in ice, and in private company he could be "an exceedingly agreeable gentleman" whose conversation was "delightful and instructive." Emerson, who had succeeded him as minister to the Second Church in Boston, thought him a "soldier that flung himself into risks at all hours, not a solemn martyr kept to be burned once." Still, Emerson doubted if the spirit really moved in Ware; his theology was too traditional. Parker, however, saw the spirit of Transcendentalism in his professor, even without the theology. In 1839, after he heard Ware pray at an ordination, he told a friend the prayer was "savory enough without Transcendentalism."[63]

In Ware's years at the Second Church, he had fostered one of the most successful pietistic revivals and was regarded as a model pastor, until ill-health forced him to retire. The Professorship of Pulpit Eloquence and Pastoral Care then was created for him, but he would not let it become a sinecure. He worked more closely and extensively with the students than did either his father or Palfrey. Not only did they take classes with him, notably on the preparation of sermons, but he would often meet with them individually in their rooms; by such careful attentions, he hoped to prepare them "in principle and action, in mind and heart," for the duties of their profession.[64]

A demanding teacher, he held his students to the same exalted standards of duty, morality, and religiousness as he held himself. Parker recalled that he "never flattered. He told the truth . . . even though it was a painful truth." Ware spoke one such painful truth when Parker preached his first sermon, on "Idolatry," as a "theological school exercise" before his fellow students and Ware at the school chapel in the early spring of 1836. It reads as a somewhat dry, bookish effort, and Ware bluntly told Parker it was unworthy of him. Parker, ever sensitive to criticism, retired to his room and wept. But he resolved to do better and meet the standard that the Professor of Pulpit Eloquence had set.[65]

Ware condemned, in his lectures, the idea that pulpit eloquence was "a thing external," consisting of "appliances & methods & contrivances, which are capable of being learned in a course of methodological training." Such a concept was a "fatal error"—eloquence without spirit was death. Sermons did require "painstaking discipline of the pen," but they must not be intellectual and exclusive of feeling. For the minister's office "is far more to persuade than to instruct—to move to duty . . . than to teach it—to incite to virtue than to make it known." People cannot be moved to action by mere "calm & philosophical statements respecting truth & duty," nor by orderly demonstrations respecting God, Providence, or Eternity. Such an intellectual approach touches "[n]ature only in one spot, & that not the spot in which the government resides." If a preacher is not to speak in vain, he must address himself to the "moral sense, the great instinct of duty, the warm and deep affections." It is only by their operation that "character is formed."[66]

The pastor must help his people perfect their characters. Ware most fully expressed the theme of perfecting character in *The Formation of the Christian Character*. Religion Ware here described as an extensive thing: a principle of the mind; a sentiment of the heart; a rule of life. Religion implied "the absolute supremacy of the soul and its interests over all the objects and interests of the present state." The "primary characteristic" of religion is not "external conduct" but "a certain state of mind and affections." To attain and perfect such a state "is to be the object of your desire, and the business of your life." This lesson Parker took deeply to heart. It was to form a central element of his own preaching.[67]

ANOTHER ESSENTIAL lesson Parker absorbed from Ware was that "cowardice" in a minister was "inexcusable." In his lectures on preaching, Ware condemned the "fear of giving offense; a disposition to soften down the requisites of duty to the standard of opinion & character of the respectable men with whom we live—a cowardly silence condemning fashionable sins, a cowardly connivance at public follies . . . & an avoiding of such subjects as virtue, piety & judgement to come, lest some honorable Felix should have cause to tremble—hence some very smooth preaching—hence the cry of peace peace when there is no peace."[68]

Parker often would echo Ware's words in his later preaching; he became famous for attacking real public sins and naming names. Yet at the time that he was Ware's student, he seems disengaged from social issues and even from his times. The political and social issues that embroiled Jacksonian America are scarcely mentioned in Parker's surviving journals, letters, or published writings from his time at Cambridge. The hullabaloo of the age, it would seem, did not even rattle the window panes of his room at Divinity Hall.

This impression may be an illusion created by gaps in the sources, but perhaps it is not wholly mistaken. Parker himself later recalled that he was at this period "so lost in Hebrew, and Grecian, and German metaphysics," that he did not read the newspapers. Yet however much Parker was preoccupied with theology in these years, evidence indicates he had some social concern. It also indicates that he was far from being the radical reformer he would become. His political and social views appear to have been about as moderate as his theology.[69]

They are implied by his involvement in the debates of the Philanthropic Society. The standard procedure of the society was to appoint an ad hoc committee to examine a certain topic. The committee would issue a report and propose resolutions, which the society as a whole would debate and then vote on. Parker's name first appears in the society records in July 1834, when he was appointed to a committee on "wages and means of honest occupation for females" (a committee that issued no report nor offered any resolutions).

Over the next two years, he served on several other committees and is noted as having taken part in various debates, although his remarks and votes are not recorded.[70]

The society had been formed by the students in 1831, at Mr. Ware's suggestion. The immediate need was for an organization to supply teachers to the Sunday school in the Charlestown prison, but Ware saw the society as a means for training the students "to be active and benevolent, as well as learned, ministers of Christ." The constitution of the society, reflecting Ware's vision, gave it a mandate to determine how best to promote "the spread of Christian principles and practice" by "Missionary, Bible, Tract, Prison Discipline, Temperance, and Peace Societies, Sunday Schools, Education generally, the prevention of crime, poverty, &c."[71]

As this list suggests, the society aimed to promote a certain kind of conservative social leadership. Its character was "benevolent"; it assumed an unequal and stable social order, one in which there were those who dispensed benevolence and those who received it with deference and gratitude. These assumptions surface in the resolutions proposed in June 1835, by a committee on Almshouses and approved by the society as a whole. They state that it "was particularly incumbent upon the clergymen to have the poor always with them" and to improve their condition, but that care must be taken not to "arm the poor & ignorant with jealousy towards the rich & educated" and that any compulsory legal provisions for the poor, excepting only those sick and "impotent," were "injudicious & injust." Another resolution stated that a principal way to help the poor was to encourage temperance; the idea was that moral reform and education of individuals were the keys to social progress. Such opinions, shared generally by Unitarian moralists, were shared by Parker as well. He was one of the three members of the Almshouse committee.

The only brush Parker or the society had with radicalism during these years was in late 1835, when the students took up the explosive issue of slavery. On 14 October, the society had a discussion on mobs, in which Parker did not participate; at that meeting, a committee on slavery was appointed. The association of mobs and slavery was not accidental, because anti-abolitionist riots already had occurred in several cities. It was also prophetic. A week later, there was a major anti-abolitionist riot in Boston.

Calls for emancipation provoked violent reaction among whites because many whites perceived them as assaults on property rights, on the Constitution, on the prosperity of those New Englanders, such as cotton mill owners and workers, whose livelihood depended on slave products, and, above all, on white supremacy. The only somewhat acceptable expressions of antislavery sentiment were vaguely hopeful pronouncements about the eventual demise of human bondage, or joining the American Colonization Society, an organi-

An Immense Change

zation that encouraged private manumissions—provided that the freedmen emigrate to Africa. In 1833, the Philanthropic Society had itself endorsed colonization as the best means to "relieve our Country from the evils of a free black population."

Totally unacceptable was to endorse the abolitionist program of "immediate emancipation." This was the platform of the American Anti-Slavery Society, of such affiliated organizations as the New England Anti-Slavery Society, and of William Lloyd Garrison, who edited the most famous abolitionist newspaper, the *Liberator*. Garrison and the abolitionists repudiated colonization as a fraud and supported equal rights for blacks; abolitionist organizations were racially integrated. Abolitionists not only had a radical program, but used radical tactics. They were notorious for denouncing slaveholders as criminals and sinners. They flooded Congress with antislavery petitions; southern members protested so strongly that in 1836 they succeeded in passing a gag rule that tabled all such resolutions before they could be read. Meanwhile, agents of the abolitionist societies were traveling the North, spreading the word. The arrival of one of these abolitionist evangelists in a town was often the occasion for a riot. The rioters were often cheered on by the local press.

Such was the case on 21 October 1835, in Boston. The itinerant British abolitionist George Thompson had come to speak before the first anniversary meeting of the Boston Female Anti-Slavery Society, a Garrisonian group. After threats started to circulate that a mob would break up the celebration and maybe lynch Thompson, who was excoriated in the press as an outside agitator, his hosts canceled his appearance and instead invited Garrison, who was at least a Bostonian. The concession made little difference. A mob attacked the gathering anyway. Garrison was seized and very nearly lynched. The rope was already around his chest when he was rescued with the help of the mayor and sheriff. The next day, several Boston papers blamed the abolitionists for having provoked the violence by outraging community feeling.[72]

Slavery was the great burning issue for the abolitionists, but for most Unitarian moral reformers, it was but one problem among many. For Parker himself, abolition would not come to dominate his reform agenda until 1850, when he began to protest the Fugitive Slave Law. Nonetheless, as one historian has justly remarked, the problem of slavery "was surely the most vexatious and troubling of the social issues confronting the wisdom and virtue of the Unitarian moralists." The vexations were evident in the actions of two of the most prominent Unitarian moralists, who both had a deep influence on Parker: the younger Ware and William Ellery Channing, the minister of the Federal Street Church in Boston. Both men wished to oppose slavery, but both were repelled by the radicalism of the abolitionists. They struggled and failed to find a middle ground.[73]

Ware publicly endorsed antislavery in the spring and summer of 1834, just when Parker became one of his students. He founded the Cambridge Anti-Slavery Society (among the members were Dr. Ware, Karl Follen, and Frederic Henry Hedge). At the first meeting, in June 1834, he declared slavery wrong and said everyone must work to end it. He announced a meeting of his society from a pulpit in Boston, after a Sunday service. He also addressed the radical New England Society.

His aim had been as much to moderate the abolitionists as to encourage emancipation. His proposed platform for the Cambridge Society declared that emancipation measures "must be conducted with great wisdom and gentleness, in a tone of Christian kindness and meekness." Appeals for emancipation should be addressed above all to the slaveholders, "by bold yet kind representations, of the sin and dangers in which they and country are involved." And it was "desirable to countenance and advance the efforts which are making to provide abroad a refuge for those persons of color who desire it, and to build up a colony for the establishment of Christianity and civilization in Africa." Ware proposed similarly "temperate" resolutions to the New England Society. He also asked a friend to ask Garrison if he would submit all articles for the *Liberator* to a committee of "six or seven gentlemen, of calm and trustworthy judgment," who would screen out anything that showed an "unchristian spirit" and had an "objectionable tone."[74]

Ware's efforts to establish a middle ground came to nought. On the one hand, the abolitionists would not be moderated. Ware's resolutions to the New England Society were rejected, and Garrison must have found his proposal for a board of censors amusing. On the other, the larger community branded him an extremist. The newspapers attacked him, especially for mentioning antislavery in a pulpit; his friends remonstrated with him, saying he was compromising his effectiveness; one story has it that Harvard undergraduates pelted him with acorns. Ware continued to insist that he was in principle an abolitionist, but by 1835 he had ceased antislavery activities and let his society go moribund. "He had not that kind of nerve, which qualifies for a great work of reform in the external condition of things," wrote his brother and biographer, years later. Emerson might have been describing Ware's experience when he noted in his essay "Character" that "I knew an amiable and accomplished person who undertook a practical reform, yet I was never able to find in him the enterprise of love he took in hand. He adopted it by ear and by the understanding from the books he had been reading. All his action was tentative, a piece of the city carried out into the fields, and was the city still, and no new fact, and could not inspire enthusiasm." Yet at least one prominent Unitarian did express enthusiasm for Ware's efforts, announcing that he subscribed to the principles of his society. This was William Ellery Channing.[75]

An Immense Change

Parker probably first came under Channing's direct influence while at the theological school, going to hear him preach and calling on him at his home on Mount Vernon Street in Boston. Like all the other Transcendentalists, Parker would remember Channing as an inspiration and mentor. This small, slightly stooped man in his mid-fifties, frail and pallid, was not a prepossessing figure, and his manner was more formal and distant even than that of Ware, who could unbend in private. Channing never did. Everyone referred to him only as "Dr. Channing." The use of the title was also a sign of respect. Parker, for one, thought him almost as great a saint as Mr. Ware, and a deeper thinker. Certainly, he had broader interests, was a better scholar, and was less obviously committed to traditional theology.

Also, his influence was wider. Channing was the only Boston minister with an international reputation. His 1819 sermon *Unitarian Christianity* had been hailed on both sides of the Atlantic, and his later writings were admired, both in Europe and America, for their simple eloquence, liberal sympathies, and high moral tone. By the time Parker got to know him, he was regarded as the spokesman, even the embodiment, of American liberal Christianity. In the 1830s, however, Channing's interests underwent a controversial shift, from theological to social reform. At the center of this shift was his developing critique of slavery.

He had hated slavery since he was a young man, when he worked for two years as a tutor in Richmond; these feelings were revived in 1831 when he came face to face with the institution again, on a lengthy visit to Santa Cruz. When he returned to Boston, he preached a sermon condemning slavery. He started to write an essay that did the same, but set it aside. Perhaps he had no wish to be associated with Garrison, who was just then gaining notoriety. He did, however, befriend two Unitarian abolitionists, the writer Lydia Maria Child (who was also the sister of Convers Francis) and Samuel J. May, a minister close to Garrison, and through them he had followed, privately but closely, the development of the antislavery movement, including the founding of the New England Society in 1832 and the American Society in 1833—the year Great Britain emancipated the slaves in its West Indian colonies. What kept him from joining Ware's Cambridge Society, in 1834, was an aversion, both temperamental and ideological, toward association work.

That summer, Channing learned of an anti-abolitionist riot in New York City, which lasted several days and in which blacks were attacked. What shocked him was that the mobs were tolerated "by the *respectable* part of the community," revealing its "willingness that free discussion should be put down by force, and that slavery should be perpetuated indefinitely." Characteristically, he did not find the abolitionists blameless: they had "unnecessarily" outraged the feelings and prejudices of laboring whites and "done much to intoxicate the colored people" by calling for immediate emancipation and equal rights for blacks! Still, he noted in a letter that he was filled with "indignation and grief" at the event and did not believe the abolitionists should recant anything, lest they be seen as giving in to fear. But in public he said nothing.[76]

In the fall, he received a visit from Samuel J. May. As May recalled the conversation, many years later, Channing complained to him at length about the harshness and vehemence of abolitionist rhetoric. May, somewhat to his surprise (he was usually very deferential to the great man), found himself responding with some warmth:

> Dr. Channing, . . . I am tired of these complaints. The cause of suffering humanity, the cause of the oppressed, crushed colored countrymen, has called as loudly upon others as upon us, who are known as Abolitionists. . . . We are not to blame if wiser and better men did not espouse it long ago. . . . [We] are just what we are,—babes, sucklings, obscure men, silly women, publicans, sinners; and we shall manage the matter we have taken in hand just as might be expected of such persons as we are. It is unbecoming of abler men, who stood by, and would do nothing, to complain of us because we manage the matter no better. . . . We are not to blame, sir, that you, who more, perhaps than any other man might have been heard throughout the length and breadth of the land,—we are not to blame, sir, that you have not so spoken. . . . Why, sir, have you not moved, why have you not spoken before?[77]

This remarkable appeal, vehement and yet redolent with Unitarian assumptions about benevolent, paternalistic reform, struck home to Channing. "Brother May," he said, after a long pause, "I acknowledge the justice of your reproof; I have been silent for too long."

He was responding to this conversation when, in October, he delivered a sermon that denounced the riots of the previous summer; as he later said, "I was induced to preach on this subject, in part by a desire of freeing myself from the painful consciousness of unfaithfulness to the interests of liberty and humanity." Although in the sermon, as in his correspondence and private conversation, he criticized the abolitionists for "bitterness of language," "precipitancy," and "needlessly outraging public feelings or prejudices," he argued now that fanaticism usually accompanies a good cause and is no reason to abandon it. This sermon was hailed by the abolitionists, and he was urged to print it. He demurred. Were he to publish, he said, he would feel compelled to enlarge on abolitionist errors, especially that they needlessly outraged the feelings of the South.[78]

Channing did not resolve to make a published statement until the following summer; perhaps he was prompted by news of the anti-abolitionist meeting at Faneuil Hall that August, which he feared would disgrace Boston by approving proslavery resolutions. He stayed quietly through the fall at his summer home in Newport and wrote a small book, *Slavery*, which was ready for the press in early November.

Like Ware and his Cambridge Society, Channing aimed with his book to establish an antislavery position distinct from abolitionism. Slavery he condemns on principle. To hold and use a human being as property is a violation of that person's humanity: "He is a person, not a thing. He is an end, not a mere instrument or means. He was made for his own virtue and happiness. Is this end reconcilable with his being held and used as a chattel?" To be held as a slave obviously violates a person's inherent and inalienable right "to inquire into, consult, and seek his own happiness." Channing also, with professed reluctance, describes the evil effects of slavery. For the slave, it degrades the moral character, prevents intellectual development, destroys domestic relations. It gives license to cruelty. For the master, it nourishes his passion for power and thus counteracts the spirit of Christianity. In the most provocative section of the book, Channing argues that slavery inevitably tempts some masters with sexual licentiousness; even worse, the children of master-slave unions are often left in bondage, or sold—"one of the greatest enormities on earth." Slavery is also ultimately hostile to free institutions and is contrary to the spirit of the New Testament.

Channing refuses, however, to condemn individual slaveholders, many of whom he insists are good people trapped in an evil system; some are enlightened enough to recognize slavery as wrong and to abhor it. On the other hand, he does condemn those "who hold their fellow creatures in bondage from selfish, base motives." These masters must learn to set virtue above gold.

When Channing turns to the means for removing slavery, he (not unexpectedly) rejects immediate emancipation and chastises the abolitionists for their fanaticism and agitation, although he says there "is a worse evil than abolitionism, and that is the suppression of it by force." But he does not endorse colonization as a means for removing slavery, as "to rely on it for this object would be equivalent to a resolution to perpetuate the evil without end." Rather, the first step must be that slaveholders admit the principle that "man cannot be held rightfully as property." Further steps toward emancipation would include training the slaves to support themselves, by paying them wages, for example; making their domestic relations "inviolate"; stopping the domestic slave trade; giving slaves religious education (Sunday schools might be established for them). Channing closes the book with a plea for the free states to be "firm, but also patient, forbearing and calm."[79]

Just as Channing was finishing his book, George Thompson's visit prompted a proslavery riot in Boston. Only a week after these disturbances, the slavery committee of the Philanthropic Society presented its resolutions.[80] Despite the charged atmosphere of the moment, the students evidently wanted to hold the middle ground alongside Ware and Channing. The resolutions declared that "to hold fellow men in Slavery is an outrage against the dearest rights of man & a sin against God," that "the laws relating to slavery are such as to hinder the development of those intellectual and moral powers wh[ich] it is the highest duty . . . [and] the most honorable privilege of man to cultivate," and that "laws relating to the free people of color in some of the states are unjust & unconstitutional." Other resolutions defended free speech, affirming the "inalienable" right to discuss slavery and the Constitutional one to present antislavery petitions to Congress and denouncing the "conduct of some of our papers," which "tends to shackle free enquiry & countenance mobs."

Another resolution, however, sought to remove the blame for slavery from the South: Great Britain was held largely responsible for the introduction of slavery into the country. Still another expressed concern for the effect of slavery on the slaveholder. Also, the "abuse of Mr. Geo Thompson" was criticized for showing "as little dignity as his conduct does judgement"; in other words, he was partly to blame for the late riot. (This was Ware's position, too; as he declared in a letter written only two days after the riot, Thompson "had no business in the country.")[81] The "criminations & recriminations" of the Anti-Slavery Society and the Colonization Society were called "unkind & unjust," and colonization was pronounced the method "best adapted to promote the safety & happiness of both master & slave." Only the final resolution veered to radicalism: if "no plan for colonization can be adopted the slaves should be emancipated here *immediately*."

This last resolution, with its endorsement of the abolitionist motto, was necessarily the most controversial. The debate over it, in which Parker participated, grew so heated the vote was postponed. When the society next met, two weeks later (Parker gave the opening prayer), the debate remained divisive and the vote was postponed another week. At this third meeting, Ware himself was present. He gave the opening prayer and participated in the discussion. Perhaps at his suggestion, the words "here *immediately*" were struck out. With this amendment, all the resolutions were approved.[82]

The length of the debate over immediatism indicates that some students were more radical than others. Where, then, did Parker come down? He was probably one of the moderates. To this point, he had shown no abolitionist tendencies. When he was teaching school in Watertown, a black girl had tried to enroll in his academy; when white parents protested, he sent her away without much soul-searching. Again, he later recalled that the very day of the 1835 Boston riot, he had gone into the city to spend the evening with some of its "most respectable inhabitants"—probably his fiancée's relatives. Although his hosts "did not exactly commend the mob; or approve of the means," they commended the end that was accomplished "and thought, on the whole, [that] the mob was a very good thing, and that . . . [the abolitionists] had deserved it all." Years later, when Parker told this story, he was appalled by these opinions—but he did not remember voicing any objections to them at the time.[83]

The image of Parker's moderation is reenforced by his reaction to his first sight of slavery, during the snowy April of 1836, when he traveled by steamboat, rail, and stage to visit Philadelphia, Baltimore, and Washington. It was only his second trip outside of Massachusetts (the previous summer he had seen Niagara Falls with Lydia and Aunt Lucy), and his first below the Mason-Dixon line. Yet in his letters to his fiancée in which he described his travels, he never professed shock or outrage at what he saw. In fact, in his description of Baltimore, he failed to mention slavery at all. In Washington, he was excited by the chance to see Henry Clay and John C. Calhoun on the floor of Congress. He never noted that they were both slaveholders, nor that one of the largest slave markets in the country was operating only a few blocks away, in clear view from the Capitol. Parker did report reading an advertisement in the newspaper that offered " 'cash for seven hundred negroes of both sexes,' " but his only comment was that such language sounded "harsh to northern ears." Seeing "negroes" in large numbers was for him a new experience, and he seemed to have difficulty empathizing with them. They struck him as "a queer set, . . . some of them very merry, dancing and capering about on the sidewalk as if they had nought to do but dance." He was surprised when he came across "two negro *lovers* walking about *cooing* and *billing* as if they could not restrain their joy in one another's presence!" Then he questioned his reaction: "Why should their *colour* prevent them?"[84]

THE PHILANTHROPIC SOCIETY was not Parker's only extracurricular activity. He was pursuing his own, private studies with ardor, making far more extensive use of the college library than anyone else at the school. The library charging records show that between July 1834 and June 1836 he checked out some four hundred volumes, over a hundred of which were not in English. Other sources, such as his journal and references that he makes in his writings, reveal that these were by no means all the books he read. The library records indicate that between July 1835 and June 1836, Parker charged out 149 volumes, while his journal shows that between July 1835 and November 1836 he read 320.[85]

These private studies, at least until the fall of 1835, do not at first glance suggest a religious seeker. Rather, they bring to mind Emerson's remark about the German mystic Böhme. His aim was "to know not one thing, but all things. He is like those great swaggering country geniuses that come . . . to college and soon demand to learn, not [only] Horace and Homer, but also Euclid and Spinoza and Voltaire and Palladio and Columbus and Bonaparte and Linnaeus." Sure enough, on Parker's library charging list appears Paulus's edition of Spinoza, a volume of Voltaire, the four volumes of Irving's *Columbus*, and a volume of Scott's *Napoleon*. Parker had already read Euclid, but Newton's Conic Sections is on the list, and if Linnaeus and Palladio are not, there does appear Kirby and Spence's *Entomology* and Boccaccio—as well as Boswell's *Journey to the Hebrides*, Bullock's *Six Months in Mexico*, Gibbon's *Decline and Fall of the Roman Empire*, Cuvier's *Essay on the Theory of the Earth*, Buckland's *Reliquiae Deluvianae*, and even a *System of Anatomy*.[86]

Other library charges indicate that Parker had already conceived of the hubristic project that he was to announce, a few years later, to Convers Francis: to become acquainted with the literature of every known language. Before he arrived at Harvard he could read Latin, ancient Greek, Hebrew, French, Spanish, and German. The charges for the fall of 1834 show him working on Arabic (with Chappelon's grammar, Richardson's Arabic-English dictionary, and an Arabic version of the Gospels). In November 1835, he began to study Danish and Swedish (with Brunnmark's Swedish grammar and Rask's Danish grammar, among others) and within a few weeks was commenting on Swedish poetry in his journal. In the same month he worked on Persian (Jones's Persian grammar) and checked out a modern Greek New Testament; by early December he was studying Anglo-Saxon. According to recollections he wrote ten years after his graduation, he also studied Italian ("and read the great authors of Italy—from Dante downward"), Portuguese, Dutch, Chaldic, Coptic, "Icelandish," and "a smattering of the Aethiopic." He attempted Russian, too, "but could not master the sounds of that . . . alphabet without help." In 1837, he was to wonder in a letter to Lydia if there was "any money-getting virtue in the knowledge of *some twenty* tongues." Yet this knowledge, impressive as it was, had decided limitations. He knew the grammatical structure and some vocabulary in each language and probably could translate them all into English. But he rarely did so for most of them. His surviving translations almost all come from a shorter, but still impressive list: Latin, Greek, Hebrew, German, and French. Also, his was almost exclusively a reading knowledge. He did not dare write Germans in their own language, and when years later he tried speaking in French to native speakers, they could not understand him. Latin was the only foreign language he felt comfortable writing; Latin passages appear often in his journal and he occasionally wrote humorous letters in Latin to friends.[87]

Parker's studies seemed to range so madly that his friends worried about him. "I think your love of learning is a passion," Dwight told him, "that it injures your mind by converting insensibly what is originally pure thirst for truth into a greedy, avaricious, jealous striving not merely to know, but to get all there is to know." Henry Ware Jr., meanwhile, was concerned lest Parker's studies interfere with his work as a pastor.[88]

Faced with these criticisms, Parker grew somewhat defensive. In his first sermon, from the spring of 1836, he took care to condemn the "xclusive [*sic*] pursuit of knowledge for itself": "The desire for Knowledge when unconnected with any wish to xpand [*sic*] our own Souls, or to benefit others . . . is by no means praiseworthy. . . . It is only when placed under the control of conscience & pursued for the Glory of God, that it becomes a moral act." Similarly, he argued in "The Godly Student of Theology, and How He Deporteth Himself," a piece written in a mannered, antiquated style and published over the name "Agapa" in the *Christian Register* shortly after he left Harvard, that those who get knowledge without wisdom "be *pedants*, not *scholars*."[89]

Here he outlined what he considered his plan of study to be. The Godly Student, declared Parker, reads histories of nature, "for therein be set down no few of the marvellous things of the Lord," and "histories of man" to learn how "weak and little we be," to observe "the way whereby states (and men no less) do climb up from a low place to a brave eminency" and "how the finger of Providence doth help on a reward such as be virtuous, and contrariwise doth punish and cast down all men that go astray after inequity." He reads "the Poets also, for they be the interpreters of nature, or, or be rather like her High Priests." He reads the Orators, ancient and modern, "because his soul receiveth great delictation thereat, and no little profit, by beholding the manner of the speaker's address, and by what springs he moveth the heart." Of all "profane Books," the Godly Student delights most in Philosophy: "Here he doth not scorn a volume, though it be folium which escaped the Saracen, and written in crooked Greek, or the perverse character of the East. . . . He careth little for weariness in such a pursuit, and though he may sometimes outwatch the nightingale, yet he never outsleepeth the cock." But above all, the Godly Student loves the Bible. He compares it "with all good Books, and beholding its exceeding excellency he cleaveth fast unto it, striving to understand its dark sayings. . . . He maketh it the constant rule of all things."

Parker was arguing that everything was relevant to his studies. Perhaps he was right. Most of them in fact can be grouped around a religious theme. Learning Arabic, Persian, Coptic, Chaldic, and Aethiopic, for example, was a necessary part of serious biblical study; Dean Palfrey himself encouraged students to study the ancient "Oriental" languages for this purpose. Parker also may have learned languages in order to study comparative religions; he later claimed to have pursued such a study, and although no religious writings outside of the Jewish, Christian, Greek, and Roman traditions appear in his journal or in the library charging records, in one of his articles for the *Scriptural Interpreter* he cites the "Coran." The travel accounts he read were also part of his effort to learn about the religions of many lands.[90]

Until the fall of 1835, none of these studies seem to have pushed him outside the Unitarian mainstream, as represented by Palfrey and the Wares.

The library charging records indicate that his readings were weighted toward modern English and ancient Greek and Roman writers—all respectable in Unitarian circles. Suddenly, in his senior year, his work took a new direction and he began reading Germans.

THE UNITARIAN intellectuals who became Transcendentalists shared an enthusiasm for the new theology, philosophy, and biblical criticism coming from Europe. Their excitement had a religious source: the belief (as George Ripley described it) that "the prevailing philosophical theories in this country are not completely adequate, to say the least, to the scientific grounding of a spiritual religion." The prevailing philosophy came from British thinkers; it had its origins in John Locke's *Essay on Human Understanding*, published in 1689. Locke's concern was to build a rational epistemology. He rejected theories that ideas could be innate—that we are born with ideas in the soul. Instead, he argued that ideas are derived from sensations; they are how sensations are represented to the mind. Knowledge consists of the understanding determining the relationship between ideas. All knowledge, therefore, derived from experience.[91]

The Transcendentalists polemically labeled Locke's theory a form of "sensualism" and argued that its inevitable consequences were philosophical and religious skepticism. That all Lockeans were skeptics was certainly false: Locke was not, and Unitarians generally revered him as an early liberal Christian. But the rise of skepticism in Britain and France in the eighteenth century was linked to thinkers working out problems raised by Locke.

The most important of these was the relationship between ideas and reality. Locke assumed the real existence of things and that ideas represented this reality. He then asked how accurately they represented it. He argued that some "primary" qualities, like "figure," did exist in things themselves and were represented directly by ideas to the mind, while "secondary" qualities, like color, were purely subjective. But were his assumptions warranted?

Many believed they were not—most notably the great Scottish skeptic David Hume. If all we know are sense impressions, he argued, then the external world is a fiction; all we can say about the world is that certain relations between impressions, such as cause and effect, are customary. We can be sure of nothing, not even the continuous existence of our own mind; belief in reason, senses, and memory is merely instinctive. We can only make probable conjectures from common experiences. From this position, Hume was able to counter all theistic arguments. We cannot argue for God from the design of the world, because the origins of the world are beyond our experience. God in this instance is merely a hypothesis. The miracles of Scripture defy common experience. We should only believe them if the testimony for them outweighed common experience, which it does not.

Hume's skepticism met with two major philosophical responses. One came out of Scotland: the "Common Sense" philosophy first articulated by Thomas Reid. Reid modified Locke's system to eliminate its dangerous tendencies. First, he abolished Locke's theory of ideas. Sensible things could be direct objects of knowledge; what we perceive really exists. Second, he rejected Locke's idea that there was nothing innate in the mind. God has placed principles there that order our sense experience, such as cause and effect. God would not deceive us. Therefore, it was rational to make predictions about the real world based on these principles. As one historian has justly remarked about Reid's philosophy, "It was a brave front, and, for a time, it helped stave off intellectual chaos." It was accepted by the Unitarians, because it seemed to rescue supernatural rationalism.[92]

The other major response, which ultimately had the most influence on the Transcendentalists—it even gave Transcendentalism its name—was German. It received its first expression in the writings of Immanuel Kant, starting with his most important book, the *Kritik der reinen Vernunft* (Critique of Pure Reason), the first edition of which appeared in 1781. Kant's answer to Hume was far more radical than that of Reid; it has been called a "Copernican revolution" in philosophy. He drew a distinction between things-as-perceived (phenomena) and things-in-themselves (noumena). The former consist of the data from our senses. These data have been reshaped according to basic mental categories of space, time, and causality—categories Kant called "Transcendental." All knowledge is built from things-as-perceived; things-in-themselves were unknowable. From concentrating on the effects on the mind of the object perceived, Kant had shifted philosophical speculation toward exclusive attention on the mind perceiving.

His impact on traditional metaphysics was as devastating as that of Hume. Kant separated faith from knowledge. Faith consisted of the soul encountering God in the noumenal realm; knowledge, and therefore science, being of phenomena, could not affect faith. The traditional philosophical arguments for God, therefore, could not stand. The ontological argument (that is, that in order for the idea of God to exist, God must exist) failed because ontology was impossible. The cosmological argument (that the rule of cause and effect required the existence of a First Cause) did not hold up because it assumed the ontological argument and because it did not recognize that cause and effect were but mental categories. The extremely popular teleological argument (that the beautiful design of the world implied the existence of a Designer) mistakenly sought to use data from the phenomenal realm to prove the existence of something in the noumenal realm.

Unlike Hume, Kant offered an alternative for what he had destroyed. Religion, he believed, consisted of practical morality, and the only proof of God he thought valid was the moral proof. Our conscience impels us to do our duty, regardless of whether or not duty produces happiness. On the other hand, we believe that the performance of our duty (being virtuous) should produce happiness, which we know is impossible without God. By performing our duty, we thus show our faith in God and in an afterlife in which happiness will be proportionate to virtue.

Kant is regarded as the founder of German Idealism, but none of those philosophers and theologians who came after him—notably Jacobi, Herder, Fichte, Schleiermacher, Hegel, Schelling, De Wette—agreed with him entirely. Some disagreed profoundly; they also disagreed with each other. Friedrich Schleiermacher, often called the "father of modern theology," was widely understood to promote a religion of emotion in contrast to Kant's rational religion of morality; Schleiermacher separated religion not only from knowledge, but from morality. In his famous *Speeches on Religion to its Cultured Despisers*, published in 1799, he asserted that religion was a feeling—what he later identified as a "sense of dependence." Hegel, by contrast, held that religion was not a matter of feeling but of reason. Only reason is uniquely human: animals have feelings, although we attribute no religion to them; feelings, too, cannot be communicated, as can reason. Although as a young man Hegel was a Kantian, in his mature writings he rejected Kant. Hegel wanted everything to be knowable and so objected to Kant's unknowable noumena. He therefore forged connections between humanity and God (he preferred to call God the Absolute, so as not to confuse it with the Judeo-Christian God). The mature Hegel saw the Absolute as immanent in human history, which was the dialectical process of God attaining self-consciousness.

The ideas of various German thinkers gradually gained currency in Britain and France. Their attractiveness was largely that they placed the soul at the center of philosophy and so seemed to put philosophy at the service of religion. German philosophy was rarely, however, accepted completely, even by its leading British and French interpreters. Yet New Englanders were often introduced to these new ideas by these interpreters, most notably Samuel Taylor Coleridge, Thomas Carlyle, and Victor Cousin. Emerson excitedly read Coleridge's *Aids to Reflection* and wrote that his distinction between the Reason and the Understanding was "a philosophy in itself"; he later became Carlyle's friend and correspondent. James Freeman Clarke remembered that reading Carlyle's early essays had made him feel as if he had seen "the angels ascending and descending in Jacob's dream." George Ripley and Orestes Brownson both championed Cousin's "eclectic" philosophy.

For his part, Parker later remembered reading Coleridge and Cousin while living in Watertown. He refers to them occasionally in his surviving letters and later in sermons; when he came to write his *Discourse of Matters Pertaining to Religion*, the writings of both are cited, and quotations by Coleridge are used as mottos for a section. But at most they served to provoke and stimulate him. He never became a follower of either.[93]

Although he later praised Coleridge for emancipating young minds, he criticized his "lack of both historic and philosophic accuracy, . . . the utter absence of all proportion in his writings; . . . his haste, his vanity, prejudice, sophistry, confusion and opium." Parker never adopted Coleridge's sharp distinction between the Reason, which directly perceived divine truth, and the Understanding, which organized sense experience. He preferred to distinguish four elements of mind—the rational, moral, affectional, and religious—each of which could perceive a different aspect of the divine mind—Truth, Justice, Love, and Holiness. Cousin's eclectic philosophy, which he later called a "brilliant mosaic," and of "great service," was ultimately unsatisfying. Cousin proposed to build an absolute religion by taking the best elements from all earlier forms of religion. Parker eventually concluded that no combination of historical religions would result in the absolute religion, for all truth is not contained in the past. Also, the act of deciding what is best in other religions requires a standard to judge by; the answers are decided by the questions.[94]

Parker later confessed his indebtedness to Carlyle and especially to Carlyle's seriocomic novel of ideas, *Sartor Resartus*. It is supposedly a memoir of Diogenes Teufelsdröckh, professor of "Allerley-Wissenschaft" at the University of Weissnichtwo in Germany and the author of an epic Philosophy of Clothes. The story traces how Teufelsdröckh developed his philosophy from his struggle to reject the "Everlasting No" of skepticism and find beneath the surface (e.g., clothes, the central metaphor of the book) a spiritual "Everlasting Yes." Parker later recalled reading one of the first copies of the book to reach America—one of a handful that had been sent by the author to his friend Ralph Waldo Emerson for him to distribute to the cognoscenti. Emerson lent a copy to Convers Francis, who after he had read it sent it along to Parker. Parker remembered that the book "opened my eyes"; he brought the book in turn to William Silsbee. They read it together and agreed it should be published in America. With the help of Francis and others, they gathered a long enough list of subscribers to ensure the work would be printed and sold by prominent Boston publisher James Monroe.[95] Yet despite Parker's efforts for *Sartor Resartus*, he was never an uncritical admirer of its author. His most interesting, if indirect, comment on Carlyle is an anonymous, satiric short story, titled "Einlieben," published in the *American Monthly Magazine* for November 1836.

"Einlieben" is "a Romantic Tale" about a beautiful princess who falls in love with the King of Flowers; it is supposedly a translation "from the nightbook of Gottesgabe Von Thiergarten." The pseudonym is a play on the author's own name: "Gottesgabe," like "Theodore," means "gift of God"; "Thier" ("animal") sounds like "Theodore"; "garten" can mean "park"; "Thiergarten," of course, is the German word for "zoo." "God's gift from the zoo" is also an evident allusion to the equally absurd name of Diogenes Teufelsdröckh.

The editors of *American Monthly* played along with Parker's joke. "Herr Gottesgabe von Thiergarten must be a very illustrious author," they write, "though we are not prepared to state we have ever heard of him till now. The admirers of double-refined transcendentalism will be in ecstasies with his style." The style is certainly remarkable:

> The King of Flowers . . . twice clapped together his small palms, when their mysterious silver-ringing was replied to by six snow-lilies, and a rose, which rolled themselves into a fair, flame-colored chariot, beautiful as virtue; with purple linings, and rich, half-drawn snow-white curtains. The soft, yielding, voluptuous air-cushions receive[d] the night travellers of the untracked sky. As borne by invisible wing-steeds, upsprang the wonder car a thousand leagues above the earth. Clouds, vapors, and the pure heaven light curled musically around them as the swift car floated upwards and on. Now from the unseen centre of a rose-colored purple-edged cloud outswelled the soft, perfume-melody of love! Flower like, soul-moving, heart-stirring, wonderful was the flower-melody, as it arose in all the voluptuous swell of infinite harmony. It cheered, and welcomed, and encouraged them on as they passed, and again repassed, the irregular floating and full-animated life-cloud.[96]

The structure of the sentences is so painfully Germanic, and the imagery so (literally) florid, that Parker can only be satirizing the excesses of Carlyle's prose.

Parker did not need the mediating services of Carlyle, Coleridge, or Cousin. He could read German well enough to go straight to the source of the new thought. He later remembered that Kant's writings, which he read while at Harvard, had been especially important in setting him "on the right road." But this recollection appears not to be accurate. It was not Kant who most influenced him, but some of his successors, who were on some points highly critical of Kant.

Parker's interest in German writers and thinkers grew steadily during his stay in Divinity Hall. In 1834, he checked out only three German books from the college library, as well as a copy of Madame de Staël's *de l'Allemagne*.[97] In the first nine months of 1835, he checked out thirteen more—although several of these were not contemporary (one was a volume of Luther's *Schriften*).

His decisive confrontation with the Germans began in the fall of 1835, when he undertook a project for the Philanthropic Society. In the meeting of 2 September, he and Henry Bellows were appointed to the committee that chose topics for discussion. Two weeks later, he and Bellows proposed, along with slavery and nineteen other topics, "the state of Religion in Germany." Parker made this project his own and presented a "Report on German Theology" nine months later, on 31 May 1836. In the introduction he claims to have "laboriously *perfoliated* upwards of sixty 'close printed, close meditated volumes, such as appear no where but in Germany.'" The claim is plausible. Although he checked out only forty-nine German books from the college library during these months, many of which are referred to in the "Report," many others referred to there are not on the library charging list.[98]

Why did Parker undertake this project? He may have become interested in German thought through German romantic literature, for which he showed an appreciation long before he accepted any of the conclusions of the German theologians or biblical critics. In Watertown, he had read and admired Goethe, Schiller, and Klopstock; in January 1834, he had written to Lydia that he had found "some beautiful pieces of poetry in Schiller." In early 1835, now at Harvard, he had charged out a copy of Klopstock's *Werke* and four volumes of Schiller from the college library; his journal reveals that in December of that year, after he started to research the "Report," he read Carlyle's translation of Goethe's *Wilhelm Meister* (both the *Lehrjahre* and the *Wanderjahre*). He was later to read his way through Goethe's complete *Werke*, at least twice. Still, Parker's enthusiasm for German poetry and fiction was never deep. At bottom, he thought Goethe was a "selfish rogue," and later confessed that he had always disliked Schiller: "He is proud, inflated, stiff, diseasedly self-conscious."[99]

Parker was, however, a true enthusiast for German biblical criticism. The "Report on German Theology" is preoccupied with biblical criticism; at the time, Parker may even have thought it was the whole of German theology. No serious biblical critic could avoid exposure to German thought, because the Germans were producing the most thorough and exacting biblical scholarship, as even those who disagreed with their conclusions admitted. At the divinity school itself, German was a required language, and in Dean Palfrey's classes, Griesbach, Rosenmüller, and Jahn were required texts.[100] Parker read well beyond these. His articles in the *Scriptural Interpreter* for 1835–36 refer not only to the writers just named, but to De Wette, Ammon, Eichhorn, Michaelis, Paulus, and Herder.

Herder seems a clear example of a major philosopher whom Parker approached first through his biblical studies. In 1835, Parker translated a passage from Herder's *Spirit of Hebrew Poetry* for the *Interpreter*; in December of that same year, he bought Herder's complete *Werke* in forty-five volumes—surely the largest single purchase of any sort Parker had ever made.[101]

There is no record of Parker's buying a book by Kant, nor does he even mention Kant in any surviving passage of his journal from these years, nor in any article in the *Interpreter*, nor in any surviving letter until January 1837. He did check out a single, unspecified volume of "Kant's Works" from the college library in March 1835 (and did not renew it).[102] In his "Report on German Theology," Parker does refer to Kant a number of times, but most of these references show only that Parker knew Kant to have been important, without making quite clear why. For example, Parker notes that at the end of the eighteenth century, "Germany presented an host of Biblical scholars: There were the Michaelises, Herder with his heavenly piety, Ernesti and Morus, Dathe and Doederlein, Reinhard, Eichhorn, Noesselt, Bauer, Kant [n.b.], Staudtein, Ammon, Tychsen, Vater, the Rosenmuellers, Boehm, Gesenius, Paulus, Teller, Wolff, Storr, Hengstenberg, Hahn, Planck and young De Wette when morn gave omen of a golden day. Then too arose Fichte and Schelling, Jacobi and Schleiermacher!"[103]

What does it say of Parker's appreciation of Kant, that he buries the philosopher's name between Bauer and Staudtein? Parker does, however, twice cite books by Kant in the "Report." He refers once to Kant's *Anthropology*, and once calls attention to Kant's "remarkable" note on the Virgin Birth in *Die Religion innerhalb der Grenzen der blossen Vernunft* (Religion within the Limits of Mere Reason), which, however, Parker mistitles as *Religion du Reinen Vernunft* [*sic*] (Religion of Pure Reason). He obviously had confused the title of this book with that of Kant's *Kritik der reinen Vernunft* (Critique of Pure Reason). The first concrete evidence of Parker having read this, Kant's most important work, comes only years later.[104]

The references to Kant in the "Report" are meager and vague—but the most important evidence that Parker did not yet appreciate Kant is that he fails to portray him as the central figure in the development of modern German theology. That role Parker assigns to the deist H. S. Reimarus, whose *Wolfenbüttel Fragments*, published posthumously by G. E. Lessing in the 1770s, Parker portrays as having shaken Germany from its dogmatic slumber. There were seven fragments; today, the seventh, "The Aims of Jesus and His Disciples," is the most famous. In it, Reimarus argued that Jesus was merely a Jewish eschatological preacher, who thought he was the messiah and so expected God to make him the king of Israel. When he was crucified instead, the disciples were out of work. So they stole Jesus' body, claimed he was resurrected, and began preaching that Jesus would soon return to establish his kingdom. Reimarus was a cogent scholar and his writings demanded reply; in fact, they provoked an uproar that launched the "quest of the historical Jesus," which was to occupy German scholars until Albert Schweitzer.

Interestingly, Parker does not mention this most famous fragment in his report. He only seems to know of the first five fragments: one showing how reason was being frightened from the pulpit; one arguing against the idea of a revelation all could rationally believe; one attacking the credibility of the story of the Red Sea crossing; one arguing that the Old Testament was not intended to reveal a religion; and one attacking the credibility of the story of Jesus' Resurrection. Parker acknowledges the existence of the sixth fragment, concerning the toleration of deists, in a footnote—but does not seem to realize it was part of the series. Clearly, Parker has not yet read Reimarus; that came some years later.

Parker argues in the "Report" that German scholars, in trying to refute Reimarus, launched a theological revolution that produced four "classes" of theologians: a small group who follows "the Deists and Free-thinkers of England and France" and believes that revelation is nothing but superstition; another small group, among whom Reimarus should be numbered, that attempts "to advance natural religion at the expense of Christianity"; a large group of Supernaturalists, many of whom adhere "to similar doctrines with the Orthodox in our own country," but the more profound of whom are "moderate"; and a large group of Rationalists. It is the Rationalists who most interest Parker. He devotes more than twenty pages of the "Report" to them, more than ten times as to the other three classes combined.[105]

All Rationalists believe that Christianity was a "divine beneficent dispensation," that Jesus was "a messenger of divine Providence," and that the Holy Scriptures contain "a true and eternal word of God"—but "they deny any supernatural agency of God in producing Christianity." Rather, it is produced by God's general providence. A revelation is therefore impossible, being "at variance with the *omnipotence, wisdom* and *goodness* of God." The most important disagreement among Rationalists is over the origin of religion: Some believe religion originates in the "understanding," and others in the "feelings." Parker directly identifies no members of the latter group and dwells on the former one, the chief members of which are Paulus, Rohr, and Wegscheider. He describes in some detail their informed view of the "Sacred Scriptures." They regard them as full of "mythi," particularly in the Old Testament accounts of the appearances of the Deity and of the Creation. The miracles of both Old and New Testaments they explain away. Moses saw the setting sun through a thicket, which looked like a bush that burned without being consumed and which he interpreted as a good omen. Lazarus was only apparently dead; Paulus provides numerous examples of men who lay as if dead for several days before "they were restored or 'came to.' " Rohr, in his *Briefe über des Rationalismus* (Letters on Rationalism), argues that miracles are no proof of doctrine: at most they prove one a worker of wonders, not an announcer of truth. The Rationalists do not consider writers of the Bible to have been supernaturally inspired, nor do they accept the prophecies, which "labour under greater difficulties than even the doctrine of miracles." None of the

Rationalists believe in the supernatural birth of Jesus, although many believe in the Resurrection and all praise "his Spirit and his heavenly doctrine."

Although Parker clearly disagrees with the Rationalists on many points, he admires them. "A characteristic of the Germans is love of Truth *as Truth* . . . ," he writes. "They prove Christianity to be true by its character and revealed by its history. They do not write like the English divines of 'the advantages of a Revelation,' 'the benefits of Christianity,' 'the blessings of the immortality of the soul.'" Although he believes they have been "deservedly censured for their manner of explaining away all miracles," he thinks that the most severe censure comes from "the most ignorant." If "the Germans have wandered widely from the right path, . . . let their aberrations be compared with the gigantic dimensions of their own orbits, not by our narrow circles." They fearlessly follow their principles wherever they may lead, careless of consequence, because they "trust the power of Truth, for they know it is God's[,] and fear nothing but falsehood."[106]

Strangely, Parker does not discuss directly the class of Rationalists he agrees with the most: those who believe that religion originates in the feelings. "The fact that religion does originate in the feelings is one of the grandest discoveries of modern times," he enthuses, "and was discovered and made use of by"—and here there is a maddening blank in the text. Today, most scholars would fill the blank with "Schleiermacher," but it seems doubtful whether Parker would have. In the "Report," the references to Schleiermacher are even more meager and vague than those to Kant; he is mentioned as a mediating figure between the Rationalists and the moderate Supernaturalists (e.g., C. F. Ammon and K. G. Bretschneider).[107]

One "feeling" Rationalist who had an unquestioned influence on Parker's thought can, however, be identified: Wilhelm Martin Leberecht De Wette, whose works are cited nine times in the "Report." Parker came to know De Wette through his biblical criticism; the earliest reference to him in Parker's writings is a passage in his journal, from early 1836, on De Wette's interpretation of Isaiah, and his works are several times cited in Parker's *Scriptural Interpreter* articles. Moreover, Parker spent years, after leaving Harvard in 1836, translating and expanding De Wette's *Einleitungen die kanonischen und apokryphischen Bücher des Alten Testements* (Introduction to the Canonical and Apocryphal Books of the Old Testament).[108]

De Wette is remembered today principally as a biblical critic. One recent historian has said that his work "inaugurated a new era in critical Old Testament scholarship," because he was the first Old Testament biblical scholar to use "critical method in order to present a view of the Israelite religion that is radically at variance with the view implied in the Old Testament itself." His decisive technical contribution, still accepted by biblical critics, was to show that Chronicles was a late compilation from Samuel and Kings, and "an entirely tendentious account of Israelite religion that falsely presented David as the founder of the postexilic Levitical-Mosaic ceremonial tradition." More generally, De Wette was important in advancing the idea that much of the Old Testament was myth.[109]

He remained a pious Christian, however, and made imaginative efforts to reconcile his criticism with his faith. These efforts account for his considerable appeal as a theologian. His reputation was high in Germany, where his was the only portrait hanging in Schleiermacher's Berlin office. His standing abroad may have been even higher. "Of all German theologians of the new era," wrote a reviewer in the *Christian Examiner* in 1838, "De Wette is the most congenial with English readers." At Harvard, he had strong personal connections: his friend Karl Follen taught church history and his son-in-law, Karl Beck, was a professor of Germanic languages. Yet even over at the Orthodox seminary, Andover, Moses Stuart would often quote from his writings, and Edward Robinson praised his "taste and poetical susceptibility." As Parker himself wrote to De Wette in 1839, "Your works are more read & appreciated among us, than those of almost any of your theological contemporaries. They are valued not merely for their accurate erudition & the philosophical profoundness they display, but for the deep vein of piety which pervades them all." Parker's opinion was confirmed even by Andrews Norton, who, in an essay attacking the "modern German school of infidelity," singled out De Wette because "no theologian of the German school had more direct influence on opinion out of Germany."[110]

The most accessible presentation of De Wette's theological views is in his semi-autobiographical, didactic, two-volume *Bildungsroman*, first published in 1822, *Theodor oder des Zweiflers Weihe: Bildungsgeschichte eines evangelischen Geistlichen* (Theodor, or a Skeptic's Conversion: The History of the Culture of a Protestant Minister). Parker read it in the spring of 1836, just as he was completing his "Report on German Theology," in which he cites it twice. *Theodor* is not successful as a novel; De Wette, by his own admission, was uncomfortable writing fiction. His hero is a kind of intellectual Everyman given to making long speeches, his other characters are little more than representations of certain intellectual positions, and his plot, especially in the first volume, is a mechanical contrivance to shuffle these intellectual positions on and off his stage as they are needed for his argument. Although there are aspects of De Wette's argument that Parker never appreciated (notably De Wette's aesthetics), it seems that Parker saw in *Theodor* a kindred religious spirit.[111]

The Theodor of the novel, like Theodore Parker himself, is attracted to Rationalism, but finally rejects it and with it partially rejects the philosophy of Kant. The novel opens with Theodor, a young man from a pious country family who intends to become a minister, going to an unnamed university. He attends lectures on rationalist biblical criticism that shake "all his former opinions respecting the Origins of Christianity." He encounters the moral philosophy of Kant and is strongly attracted to the "thought of the self-dependence of the reason in its utterance of laws; of the freedom of the will, by which it is lifted above nature and fate; of the disinterestedness of virtue . . . ; of pure respect for a self-imposed moral law." Yet the effort to interpret Jesus' teaching along Kantian lines further shakes Theodor's beliefs, for "the suspicion crept in that Christ had either adapted himself to the superstition of the times, or had not been wholly free from enthusiasm." Kant's writings eventually produce in Theodor a crisis of faith; above all, Kant's "doctrine of the Deity . . . fell like a thunderbolt upon his soul, and extinguished the flame of its devotion, and left behind a sad and melancholy darkness." Virtue, according to Kant, "in herself has no need of God,—she has her law and her power of reason; but that she may more easily conquer in the battle with sense, an Almighty God must be near, as judge and rewarder." Theodor finds this thought "proud," but "sad" and "empty of consolation": "We cannot say then that God *is*, and we in him, through him, and by him; but Reason *is*, and he on her account, and through her. Is *that* the true and living God, and not much rather a shadow of our own thought?"[112]

Theodor tries to pursue his theological studies, but can find little consolation in either of the prevailing theological schools. The Rationalists, whose scholarship and independence of mind he admires, think "reason is the fountain of religious truth," and thus reduce God to a mere "intellectual process," which leaves him feeling cold and empty. He finds wholly unacceptable the alternative of the Supernaturalists, with their "arbitrary, extraordinary" revelation.[113] Finally in despair, he gives up the ministry, moves to the capital, joins a circle of worldly sophisticates, and becomes a government official.

The remainder of the novel is about how Theodor finds his way back to the ministry. His crucial first step in this direction is to attend the lectures of Professor A. (modeled on De Wette's own intellectual mentor, J. F. Fries), whose philosophy places a heavy emphasis on feeling. The professor argues that faith is a "primal consciousness," from which are derived the spiritual faculties of the Understanding and the Reason. Understanding is the "lower and mediate" faculty; through it we perceive the world as it exists in time and space. Reason perceives the facts of faith directly. Its knowledge is thus intuitive and immediate. It cannot err. From the Reason comes "inward revelation," that is, innate religious knowledge; but we can recognize the truth of an "external revelation," that is, the revelation of another, such as that of Christ, only through feeling, "which is strongly moved by the divinity which appears in the mediator of a revelation." Theodor reads Schleiermacher's *Speeches on Religion to Its Cultured Despisers*, a book that Professor A. highly recommends, and there learns that religion itself is neither knowledge nor morality, but feeling.[114]

Parker would have found a religion of pure reason wholly inadequate, just as the Theodor of De Wette's novel had. Insofar as Parker thought Kant was advocating such a religion, he would have rejected him. In fact it was the "grand discovery" that religion "originated in the feelings," and not the technical philosophy of Kant, that turned him into a Transcendentalist.

FINALLY, in July 1836, came Visitation Day, the equivalent at the theological school of a commencement ceremony. The morning exercises, when all the senior class gave brief orations before an assembly of distinguished guests, went off well. Parker's subject was "Gnosticism"; he described it as an ancient species of "eclectic philosophy" (Gnostics sincerely but mistakenly attempted to answer the skepticism of their age by blending materialism and idealism) and learnedly analyzed allusions to it in the New Testament. The talk was received with approval, and soon afterward he printed it in the *Interpreter*. The afternoon services dragged heavily, as the feeling sank in among the seniors that these happy few, this band of brothers in Christ, would soon be scattered. It was "a 'day of trembling,' of sad uneasiness to most of us, a day of perplexity to all," wrote Parker in his journal that night.[115]

He then reflected on his two years and three months at Harvard, time that had passed so speedily away. "What an immense change has taken place in my opinions and feelings upon all the main points of inquiry since I entered this place!" He had come there a conventional, even conservative, Unitarian, but his reading in German biblical criticism had propelled him across a threshold. While still barely aware of the implications of the change, he began to blur the distinction between natural and revealed religion. Blurring or obliterating this distinction was to become a basic characteristic of Transcendentalist theology.[116]

More specifically, Parker began to doubt the religious significance of the historical evidences of Christianity—and above all of the miracles. The distinction between "internal" and "historical" evidences for the truth of the Christian religion was traditional and held to be obvious. The argument from internal evidences was that Christian doctrines were so well suited to the needs and aspirations of the soul and so generally reasonable, and that their revealer, Jesus, had a character so excellent, that both doctrines and revealer had to be of God. All Unitarians admitted that these evidences of Christianity were exalted and spiritual; to contemplate them was widely extolled as an aid to piety. Most Unitarians also believed, however, that the internal evidences alone were insufficient, partly because they were merely "subjective," and partly because they left room for doubt that Christianity was uniquely divine. Hence miracles were the only decisive, "objective" proof of Christianity. Yet Parker, under the influence of the German biblical critics, began to move away from this external evidence. As he noted in the "Report on German Theology," the Rationalists he admired "do not rely upon the Prophecies or Miracles for proof of [Jesus'] divine doctrines, but they press the internal evidence." [117]

As it happened, in May 1836, the same month he presented the "Report," Parker listened to a Dudleian Lecture by Orville Dewey on revealed religion. Parker in his journal called it "the best, perhaps, I have ever heard"; Dewey had "removed the presumption" against miracles and "overturned" objections to them. Parker still thought miracles had happened. Yet, significantly, in the same passage he judged miracles "the least interesting part of the Evidences of Revealed Religion." [118]

This lack of interest seems innocuous enough, suggesting merely a shift in emphasis from one traditional form of evidence, the historical, to another, the internal. Surely, this is how Parker conceived the shift. But behind it lay his deepening conviction that religion was innate in human nature. He was learning from De Wette and others that "religion does originate in the feelings"—a claim that jibed with his own religious experience. If religion was a sentiment, then the truths of religion could be proven "subjectively," with internal evidence, and "objective" proofs like miracles became simply irrelevant. If miracles were no longer needed to confirm a revelation, then the whole fabric of supernatural rationalism would unravel. The distinction between natural and revealed religion begins to blur, because all religious truth could be discerned "naturally." Parker's thoughts began to take this direction in 1836. Such thinking, of course, was in keeping with the times, for this has been called the "Annus Mirabilis" of Transcendentalism.

An Immense Change

Chapter Three

Period of Disappointment

Parker preached to a "real *live* audience" on 3 July 1836 for the evening service at the First Parish meetinghouse in Cambridge. He was unhappy with his debut. He had not been able to "get into" the sermon, having had to "do the agreeable" for an hour before preaching. It was his first lesson on the realities of the ministry, but he blamed himself and prayed: "Oh, God, wilt thou help me to become more pure in heart, more holy and better able to restrain all the impetuous desires and unholy passions." Three Sundays later, he conducted his first full-day service at Convers Francis's church in Watertown. "I felt more alarmed and agitated than I had anticipated," he confessed to Samuel Andrews, "though I had been dreading it for a whole month." He had had "jactitations" Saturday night, and had delivered the two sermons with a "vile tremor" in his deep voice. But he lived through the day. His friends liked his style; many thought the tremor "affecting." Even though he preached the following Sabbath in Roxbury, he considered the next fortnight a vacation, spent "loitering about, idling away time, and living at ease; now strolling about with Lydia, and now picking cherries and flowers alone." But soon he was restless to get on with his life: "I have sterner deeds to *do*, greater dangers to *dare. I must be about my work.*"[1]

He had to find a permanent pulpit. Candidating involved travel back and forth to wherever a congregation of Unitarians sought to settle a likely young man: to Concord, where young Hersey Goodwin had unexpectedly died; to West Roxbury, where George Whitney was leaving for a pulpit in a neighboring parish; and so on across New England and beyond, from brick chapel to clapboard meetinghouse. A church would somehow get word that a certain candidate was worth a hearing. If he was lucky, his friends would "lay out" the parish for him, by meeting with members of the church committee and talking him up. The committee then would invite him to come for a trial engagement, which could last for months. The process was an ordeal for both parties. An unlucky church might go without a permanent minister for years; an unlucky candidate might never be settled. For Parker, the process lasted till the following summer, during which time he continued to grope his way toward Transcendentalism.

He hoped to settle in Concord, although he intimated this wish only to his closest friends. To them he said enough for one of them to begin calling the place "Parker's Jerusalem." The attraction could not have been the low salary. Could it have been the presence there of Ralph Waldo Emerson? Parker had met the tall, slender Emerson, whose sharp Yankee features were softened by a reserved and spiritual bearing, in January 1836, when the divinity student had gone to Concord to deliver a lecture at the Lyceum and had passed the evening at Emerson's house. He found his host to be "most delightful" and praised his wife, Lidian, as *"faith put into action."* About the same time, Parker had become acquainted with Emerson's younger brother Charles, of whom everyone expected great things. When Charles died suddenly in May 1836, Parker lamented his passing in a letter to Columbus Greene.[2]

Emerson's literary reputation was all in front of him then: seven years Parker's senior, he was about to publish his first book. His early career had been conventional. He followed his late father into the Unitarian ministry and in 1830 became pastor of the Second Church in Boston, succeeding Henry Ware Jr. when the latter retired to become a professor. Two years later, Emerson resigned the position. He told his congregation that he could no longer conscientiously administer the Lord's Supper. Behind this stated reason was his creeping dissatisfaction with the ministry itself. Although he continued to preach on a "supply" basis (temporarily filling pulpits for pay), he began to change professions. In the winter of 1834, he delivered a series of lectures in Boston on natural history and the following year another on the lives of great men. He drew an audience with his increasingly unconventional eloquence and emerging "spiritual" philosophy. Parker attended at least some of these lectures; in early 1837 he told his friends he was grieved that candidating kept him from hearing Emerson that season.[3]

Parker admired Emerson, but did not always agree with him or even understand him—as can be seen from his reaction to Emerson's first book, which came to be regarded as one of the preeminent Transcendentalist statements. Parker read *Nature* as soon as it came out, in September 1836, and wrote to Silsbee that the little book was "queer," for Emerson "absolutely" denied the existence of matter, "a violent assumption" in Parker's opinion. On the other hand, it was "full of Beauty" and "overflowing with Truth," and he wished that he and Silsbee "could sit down together and read over these glowing pages, and talk of the high matter it handles." In fact, Parker misread Emerson on the existence of matter, which was easy enough to do (Parker was not alone in doing so). Emerson had written a prose poem on natural theology, not a treatise of natural philosophy, and his point, made more with imagery than argument, does bring him to the borderlands of ontological idealism. Nature—all that is not human or produced by human art—does not dominate the soul, as the carnal person and materialist philosophy would have us believe, but serves it. Nature provides us not merely with physical benefits, but with spiritual ones: our sense of beauty; the roots of our language; means to discipline our understanding, reason, and conscience. Emerson admits the attraction of the idealist argument that "matter is a phenomenon, not a substance," but he accepts it as only a "useful introductory hypothesis, serving to apprise us of the eternal distinction between the soul and the world." He is more interested in engendering greater spirituality and originality of thought than in discussing metaphysics.[4]

Emerson may have been the reason Parker wanted to settle in Concord, but the young man preached there only once, in October 1836. In December, he learned the church had given the call, unenthusiastically, to Barzillai Frost, a pedestrian preacher who had graduated from the theological school the year before. Frost accepted the offer. "So go down my ancient hopes," wrote Parker when he got the news.[5]

It was not Concord, but Barnstable that gave Parker his first extended experience of what a minister's life was really like. He arrived there early in the morning of 4 August on the packet schooner from Boston after an overnight trip in which he found, to his embarrassed amusement, that the berth at his head, the one at his feet, and the one above him were all occupied by young women ("I had the *poet's* corner," he remarked in his journal). The appearance of the little Cape Cod village struck him as odd, with its single-story houses, mostly of unpainted shingle, scattered irregularly along a crooked road. The inhabitants seemed "spiritually dead": they were unwilling to "talk on religious subjects," preferring instead to "ask about the weather, the passengers on the Packet, the Love Stories, and gossip and scandal of every little Family in Town." This impression of religious coldness was understandable, coming from a young man who had just stepped from the hothouse of theological school into the temperate air of daily life. Exposure quickly modified his opinions. A number of parish visits, social calls, evening gatherings, and afternoon teas later, he admitted that "*some* of these people have *religious feelings*." After a few more weeks, he could tell Lydia that he was "exceedingly pleased" with the "good people" of the place, partly, no doubt, because they were "models of attentiveness" when he preached—"they seem to *grow into you*."[6]

Even on his first Sunday, despite an awkward unfamiliarity with the open pulpit in the small East Parish Church, he thought he had never been in better spirits for speaking and "not only delivered the written word, but added much that was better and more *reaching* extemporaneously." Soon he spoke with "more ease and freedom, of mind and body" than ever before. A fellow boarder called one of his sermons the best he had ever heard. More and more people came to hear him. By his third week, extra chairs had to be brought. Gratified by this response, he wrote nearly a dozen new sermons.[7]

There were harder things to do than preach. One day, early in his stay, the deacon arrived at Parker's rooms and asked him to perform a funeral service. As the young minister was being escorted to the widow's house, he confessed with "fear and trembling" that he had never done a funeral before. "There must be a first time," came the reply — "which wonderful truth," wrote Parker to Lydia a few days later, "inspired me with all the fortitude you can imagine to flow from such a fountain!" A sign painter had been ruined and killed by drink; his noble wife was left with no money and five young children. "I went and said all I could, but I *felt dumb* before such a picture of real grief." Still, Parker had himself known real grief, and he thought his prayer "struck and affected" his hearers.[8]

The following Sabbath was even more trying. First thing in the morning, he was asked to open the Sunday school with a prayer. Then came a full day of church services: Scripture, hymns, sermons, and more prayers. As he finished in the afternoon, he was handed a note requesting him to come at once to the funeral of an infant who had just died. Despite fatigue and a headache, he went, prayed publicly again, and followed the sad procession. He returned to the boardinghouse — only to be called to the sickbed of an old woman, where his prayers brought tears of pious joy to her and her family. By the end of that long day, Parker calculated he had prayed publicly seven times.[9]

"How disqualified we are for contact with the real world," he wrote shortly afterward to his classmate Silsbee. "I felt when first shown a real live man, and when brought to speak with him, utterly at a stand. I rarely knew what to say." But he thought he was making rapid progress. Near the end of his August sojourn at Barnstable, he wrote in his journal that his experience there was like a "wire touching the chaotic liquid"; "crystallization had begun." He had a large store of knowledge. Now, as he quietly turned twenty-six, he was learning how to use it.[10]

Not, of course, that he had stopped adding to his store. He explored the sandy roads, collecting and pressing unfamiliar flowers, including a scarlet pond lily. He learned how to handle a skiff and, with some friends, sailed thirty miles down the cape to investigate a camp meeting in Eastham, where he witnessed "a plenty of shouting, praying, singing, and of shouting 'Glory to God,'" but happily "none of the naughty doings that are said to take place on such occasions." Parker only noted in passing that various people there raised the issue of slavery; like Dr. Channing and Mr. Ware, he was still uncomfortable with abolitionism.[11]

His "favorite employment" remained reading. He brought an eclectic library of books with him to Cape Cod, including editions of Shakespeare and Byron; biographies of Captain John Smith and the ornithologist and poet Alexander Wilson; the "Revised Statutes"; and Schelling's lectures on academic study, which he found "an ideal within his own subjectivity, which is an impossible real, and contains elements of its destruction, since it involves a contradiction." He also commenced a long-contemplated labor, the translation of De Wette's *Critical and Historical Introduction to the Old Testament*. The project had been suggested to him by Moses Stuart, the noted biblical critic at the Orthodox seminary in Andover, but Parker, perhaps fearing he would fail in the undertaking, as yet revealed it only to a few friends. It "would take a giant many a day to finish," he wrote Lydia; "me a much longer time." Still, within weeks he could boast to a friend of having translated "hundreds" of pages. In fact, he completed a draft of the whole two-volume work by the following May.[12]

Parker expected an invitation to settle in Barnstable; he knew he had made a favorable impression on the Cape Cod men and women. "Do not think however I have any desire to take up my abode here," he reassured Lydia. That "would please me as little as it would them." He might have added that Lydia and her Aunt Lucy, who was planning to follow Lydia into her new home, would have been equally displeased. They did not want to live out among the sea captains.[13]

Parker told his fiancée that questions about settlement "rest with you, mainly"—by which he meant with her and with Lucy. But he was not really so amenable. Between the lines of Parker's surviving letters to Lydia can be discerned a debate over where they should live. Nowhere was disagreement sharper than over the Spring Street parish in Roxbury, near Boston.

West Roxbury, as it was also called, was a tiny parish; it had once been known as "Skunk's Misery," and at the theological school Parker's classmate George Ellis used to tease him about how he would have to settle there. Yet it appears to have been favored by Aunt Lucy. While Parker was still in Barnstable, she "laid out" the place for him. When Parker learned of Lucy's efforts to secure him an invitation, he tried to discourage her in a letter to her niece. "Why now admitting they would want me there, which is not at all likely, what is there to do?" he asked Lydia. "To preach to some 40 of 50 people at the most, and to go about and talk about all their *little* matters, from the sickness of their *cats* up to the age of their great grandmothers, is not much more agreeable to me than the old practice resorted to by an old Closet-Scholar, who made Speeches to an audience of Cabbages! . . . [I]t would be equally inspiring to preach to a congregation of that size and to a collection of Cabbages. (The latter certainly would never disturb you by a *yawn*)." Parker adds that some things are "absolutely necessary to make a parish bearable," among them an "income sufficient for the body and a little for a rainy day" and access to "intellectual and refined society." He evidently thought West Roxbury was too small to provide either. Why then did Lucy like it? Perhaps because she owned land in the area and members of the Cabot family lived nearby: Lydia's parents were in neighboring Newton, and Lucy's first cousin Frederick Cabot summered with his family in West Roxbury itself. The issue of income was unimportant to the wealthy spinster. Parker seems to have wanted to live independently of his future in-law's largesse.[14]

Despite his initial reaction, the question of West Roxbury was not closed. A few days later, he wrote Lydia that he would "settle in Spring Street or Concord or anywhere you please." They surely talked over the matter when they next saw each other, after he returned from Cape Cod at the end of August. He needed an acceptable alternative to Lucy's choice, but could find none. Over the next few months he did mostly supply preaching and often did not know from one Sunday to the next in what pulpit he would stand.

In September, he was in Portland, Boston, Watertown, Lowell, and Keene, New Hampshire. The following month he went to western Massachusetts, carrying with him his De Wette manuscript and, for pleasurable reading, some of Goethe's plays. The society in Northfield needed a minister for its new, gothic-style meetinghouse. Parker drank in the Connecticut River Valley scene, with its high and handsome hills. He was flattered when one Mrs. Rice told him she knew him already, from his pieces in the *Interpreter*. But Northfield was too isolated. He told his friends he would rust there. He could study, but with no one to talk to, the Everlasting No would be before him, above him, around him, and within him. When, in early November, the Northfield church invited him to settle there, he declined at once.[15]

By this time he was back in Barnstable, which looked "a little gloomy and dismal, with sandy hills and mean houses, instead of the everlasting mountains and the beautiful white houses of the valley of the Connecticut." Already weary of candidating, Parker began to think again about Spring Street. He informed to Convers Francis that "sundry of my friends wish me to settle" there and asked him if doing so would be a good idea. Parker conceded that "it is not regarded as a *desirable* parish by most men," but indicated "certain reasons" that made him "look towards it more favorably." The principal of these was that cultured society, including Francis, and the College Library, would be within hail. Francis's reaction to this rather tepid endorsement of West Roxbury is lost. Parker later recalled consulting one of his theological school professors—probably Mr. Ware—about the place and being told that it was too small for him; he would be tempted by "the seductions of an easy chair." So Parker's wayfaring life continued. In mid-November, the good Christians of East Barnstable formally invited him to settle with them. He declined.[16]

During these draining few months, Parker had had a few respites. One had been to attend the Harvard Bicentennial on 8 September. President Quincy's oration was, in his opinion, awkward, clumsy, and tasteless—he would have much preferred a speech by the eloquent governor of Massachusetts (and former Harvard professor), Edward Everett—but Parker enjoyed the colored lights illuminating the college buildings and, like Emerson, who was also there, was moved by the long, winding, torchlit parade of alumni through Harvard Yard. That night, at Willard's Hotel, Emerson met with three other ministers who were in town for the celebration: George Ripley of Boston, Frederic Henry Hedge of Bangor, Maine, and George Putnam of Roxbury. The group decided to gather again. Eleven days afterward, the new club, later remembered as a node of Transcendentalist activity, had its first meeting at Ripley's house. Parker, who was in the area at the time, might have been present. Long after Parker's death, Hedge remembered him there, but no contemporary evidence supports the claim.[17]

Parker probably did meet with Ripley some time that September. They talked about a potentially controversial review of *The Rationale of Religious Enquiry*, by the English Unitarian James Martineau, that Ripley was writing for the *Christian Examiner*. Ripley, a witty, energetic man of thirty-four, with short curly brown hair and the pale face and gold-rimmed spectacles of a scholar, pastored the new Purchase Street church in Boston and was regarded as a rising star of Unitarianism. Parker had been introduced to him by George Ellis, his theological school classmate and fellow editor of the *Scriptural Interpreter*, perhaps during the winter of 1835–36, when Parker was writing his report on German theology and Ripley was writing major reviews for the *Examiner* on Herder and Schleiermacher. Parker had probably wanted to borrow books and discuss their common interest in German thinkers. Ripley, for his part, liked Parker's work for the *Interpreter*, and, in December 1835, recommended the little magazine to the public in an effort to win it subscribers: "Such productions from the pens of our young men give an omen of happy promise."[18]

He and Parker struck up a friendship that in the coming years was to deepen. It already was close enough in 1836 for Ripley to discuss with the younger man plans for turning the review of Martineau's book into a major Transcendentalist statement. Martineau's little collection of sermons had been written by the Manchester minister to challenge a conservative British audience with the idea, already familiar in Boston, that the only sure guide to religious truth was human reason. Ripley thought the book would "do good work," as did Parker, who had written a favorable notice of it for the August *Interpreter*. But Ripley disagreed with Martineau on the inspiration of the Apostles and the miracles of Jesus. His arguments on these points carried him beyond supernatural rationalism into Transcendentalism and would surely provoke a protest. Parker warned Ripley that "the first one who lifted a hand in this work, would have to suffer," and urged that "some old veteran German," who would not mind a few blows, be pushed "into the fore front of the battle." Parker was suggesting, in other words, that Ripley should publish his ideas by summarizing the opinions of a German thinker with whom he agreed, as he had done in his earlier reviews of Schleiermacher and Herder. Ripley responded that he expected the controversy to cause him "no danger."[19]

On inspiration, Martineau took a straightforward position, shared by Andrews Norton and John Gorham Palfrey, that the Apostles made mistakes and so could not have been inspired. Ripley argued that they were inspired, despite their being as fallible as Martineau believed. This claim might seem conservative, yet Ripley evidently intended it to be radical. If the sacred writers could be regarded as divinely inspired simply because they knew religious truth, then any person who knew religious truth was also divinely inspired, and inspiration was not, as most Christians believed, supernatural and limited to a few historical characters who had special religious authority, but rather was, as the Transcendentalists held, natural and universal. In the published review, Ripley does admit the existence of "supernatural" inspiration— but then claims it is merely an extraordinary form of natural inspiration. "The revelations of . . . natural inspiration are the absolute claims of reason, which lay claim to necessary and universal validity," he writes. "The primary truths which are independent of experience and demonstration, the perception of the Just, the Holy, the Perfect, the Infinite, upon which all religious faith is founded, proceed from this source. . . . And just in the proportion in which the supremacy of these ideas transcends the ordinary, the natural effects of culture and reflection, we pronounce them supernatural." Ripley seems to want to eat his cake and have it. Despite the naturalness and universality of inspiration, he wants the Apostles, and especially Jesus, somehow to have been inspired in a unique way. Ripley is probably not trying to be obscure so as to avoid controversy, because he makes no effort to avoid it in the section of his review on miracles, where he is quite unambiguous.[20]

Martineau claimed that anyone who denied the miracles of Jesus could not be called a Christian; Ripley flatly disagrees. He admits the miracles happened, but argues that Jesus did not intend to use them to verify the truth of what he had to say—in fact, that they could not have verified it. Physical facts, he says (echoing Kant), cannot prove spiritual ones. Instead, Ripley argues that the beauty of Christian doctrines, and the evident greatness of Jesus' character, proved that both were of God. He is dismissing the historical evidences of Christianity as irrelevant and arguing that internal evidences were the only relevant ones.

The issue of inspiration was logically prior to that of miracles: if inspiration were universal, then anyone could recognize religious truth and miracles would be unnecessary. But it was Ripley's straightforward comments on miracles, not his unclear ones on inspiration, that provoked the first skirmish of the Transcendentalist controversy. On 5 November, shortly after the Martineau review appeared in the *Examiner*, Andrews Norton, who had once taught Ripley biblical criticism at the theological school, wrote a sharp letter to the *Boston Daily Advertiser*. Norton had been one of the founders of the *Examiner* and was still listed among its supporters, but he now dissociated himself from the journal in order to protest their tolerance of Ripley's ideas: "I consider them as vitally injurious to the cause of religion, because tending to destroy faith in the only evidence on which the truth of Christianity *as a revelation* must ultimately rest." Anyone who controverted doctrines perceived as vital to faith should form his opinions with great caution and should publish them "in such a form, as far as may be, that they will first go into the hands only of those who are capable of judging their correctness."

Several days later, Ripley replied with a long letter to the *Advertiser*. The largest part of the reply was a collection of citations and quotations, which Ripley presented partly to show that his position on miracles was not novel, but was supported by Scripture, the church fathers, the early Protestants, and modern theologians (especially the German ones), and partly to refute Norton's implied accusation that he was an inadequate scholar. Ripley called for free discussion. Only that and "scientific enquiry," "in which the love of truth shall be blended with a heartfelt trust in its power," would relieve the "scepticism and vague thought" on religion that characterized the modern age. He concluded by remarking that the differences of opinion between himself and Norton rested on a "radical difference in our philosophical views": "You are the disciple of the school which was founded by Locke—the successor of Hobbes and precursor of Condillac and Voltaire. For that philosophy I have no respect." In other words, Norton assumed that knowledge could come only through the senses, a view that, according to Ripley, could only lead to atheism and materialism.[21]

Parker was in Barnstable when he read this exchange. He thought that Norton's letter surpassed his "previous arrogance": "*Is he the people? Will all truth perish with him?*" Such accusations of dogmatism had followed Norton throughout his long career. He was remembered by an alumnus of the theological school for dropping students who disagreed with him; the students, in turn, secretly referred to him as "his Highness" and gave him the waggish title of "Unitarian Pope." He had always responded that what drove him was not dogmatism, but rational conviction. His definitions and arguments were so clear in his own mind that he was unable to understand how any reasonable person could honestly differ with him. His most common charge against his opponents in debate was that they were incoherent and misused terms. Parker, while researching his Visitation Day talk on Gnosticism in May 1836, had been introduced to Norton at his handsome house near the theological school, and his first impression of the former divinity school professor was never to change: "He certainly is a very urbane man, and very mild and gentlemanlike in all his deportment; but a bigot in his opinions."[22]

Parker thought Ripley had "floored" Norton with his reply, but the debate was not over. Norton's opinion was respected as that of the greatest Unitarian biblical critic. Even Parker, who rejected his conclusions, could write after a visit to him in early 1839 that he was "delighted to see so profound & accurate a scholar."[23] Norton's view on the importance of miracles, moreover, was widely shared. In November, Palfrey canceled his subscription to the *Examiner* to protest the Ripley piece, and in December, when the debate was joined in columns of the *Christian Register*, after the Norton-Ripley exchange was reprinted there, most of the correspondents sided with Norton. But Parker was sympathetic to Ripley's positions, not only on miracles but on inspiration. Just as Ripley's positions were not without their ambiguities, however, so Parker's were still unsettled.

Parker, in his writings from these months, showed himself increasingly sure that religious inspiration was universal. In the first part of a 102-page *Scriptural Interpreter* article, published in July, on the laws of Moses, Parker still drew a distinction between natural and miraculous inspiration. He tried to prove that the "Lawgiver" was miraculously inspired, because some of the laws he gave to the Jews in the desert were "prospective" in character, dealing not with their present nomadic life, but with their future life as settled farmers in the promised land, and "various little crimes and difficulties are provided for, which no human sagacity could foresee, much less remedy."[24]

Although the Transcendentalist controversy hinged on the inspiration issue, Parker's mind was far from settled on it, as revealed by his inconclusive struggle in the article with the problem of whether or not the seemingly wicked laws commanding Jews to extirpate the Canaanites actually came from God. Parker admits that some critics "think it no grave heresy" to deny that these laws were inspired; they "think too that such interpreters, as ascribe all these *sanguinary laws* to the inspiration of the Almighty 'take more upon their critical shoulders than Atlas would bear.' They admit the inspiration of Moses, but do not suppose *every word of the law*, of divine origin. . . . They think too, that the oriental custom of ascribing all remarkable events, wonderful appearances, and striking thoughts to the immediate action of God, explains the *alleged* command of the Almighty." Parker sounds open to such opinions, but does not endorse them. In fact, he seems to endorse the other side. He remarks that the exterminated nations were "exceedingly vicious and corrupt," and that had they been suffered to remain they would surely have led the Jews astray from the true faith. He concludes: "If nations are by divine permission, visited by earthquakes and pestilences, why may not the sword be employed for the same purpose?"[25]

In the sermons Parker wrote that summer and fall, however, he spoke with growing confidence of there being "naturally within us an aspiration after spiritual things," of how the dominion of God is "stamped by God's hand upon the human Soul, & stamped so deep that nothing can erase [it]," of how faith is "natural to man."[26] In his concluding remarks for the *Interpreter*, published in November (the same month that Ripley's Martineau review appeared), he declared:

> Our own investigations have assured us that [religion] is deeply laid in nature and in the human heart. Error as well as truth may be built upon it, for the superstructure is the work of man. Past generations have ever found enough to satisfy their religious wants, and to guide and support their hopes. Our wants are the same, our hopes cannot be brighter or holier than theirs. It is a soothing thought that the same book which nourished the flame of piety in the ages of darkness—gives the guiding light to all mental progress—and throws a bright radiance onward into the future where it mingles its returning rays with its own eternal source.[27]

If religion is natural to human nature, as Parker says, then religious inspiration, by implication, can also be natural; Parker implies here, too, that there are "rays" of inspiration beyond the Bible.

He still claimed that Jesus was somehow divinely inspired and performed miracles—but, like Ripley, he denied the miracles were religiously significant; he pressed the internal, not the historical, evidences for Christianity. In a sermon on the "Greatness of Christ's Character," which he wrote during his August visit to Barnstable and preached seven times during his candidacy, he argues that Christ's greatness did not come from "the miraculous *wisdom* conferred upon him, great indeed as was the revelation made him & miraculous as his powers were," because if this were so, he would not be great of his own will. Nor did his greatness "consist in his power of working miracles,—for others before him possessed this astonishing power, in whose character no such moral sublimity appears." Instead, his greatness "consisted in his acting according to the Laws of the spirit of life as shown & xemplified [*sic*] in *Love to Man, [&] all nature*."[28]

During Parker's November visit to Barnstable, while he sorted out his ideas and Ripley sparred with Norton in the newspapers, he received a letter from Lydia with the news that John Parker had died in Lexington. Theodore had anticipated the old man's death, but when it came, he felt "ten times" more grief than he had expected. Sitting lonely and silent by his boarding room fire, he forgot his father's austere reserve and remembered only being "cradled in his arms, fed by his hands, blessed by his prayers, and moulded by his tender care."[29]

Did Theodore then feel a psychological cord snap that bound him to his past? Certainly, after November, the development of his thought rapidly accelerated, and he sped beyond the Unitarianism of his father. In a sermon from December, he boldly asserted that Christianity "creates nothing new in man; it calls for the exercise of none but human faculties, but it awakens the deepest, the divinest powers in man, powers that slumber in too many a heart." In other words, Christianity was natural, not miraculous. In the next sermon he wrote, he asked an obvious question: If Jesus had created no truth, "but merely *presented* it to man, why could not man have discovered it for himself!" Why then did we need the mission of Jesus? No doubt, Parker answered, "in Time man would have discovered these truths," as children would discover on their own, by observation, many truths that they learn instead from their parents. But still "it is kind & wise . . . [of] the Parent to anticipate the child's xperience [*sic*], & lead him onwards the more pleasantly, & the more swift!"[30]

He soon began to ask a host of questions he had never dared ask before, not even in his journal. But they spill onto the page in a journal entry from early 1837: "What is the extent of known supernatural Revelation to man?" "What is the foundation of the authority of Jesus Christ?" "How is Christ more a Saviour than Socrates?" "Why did the world need a Saviour?" "What is the foundation of religion in Man—the Design of Miracles—the pretense of them in other Religions?" On the next page, under the heading "Questions in Scriptural Criticism & Exegesis," he ponders the "Authenticity of the beginning of the Gospels of Matthew and Luke—the Miraculous Conception," and even "The Resurrection—why was the body of Christ raised?—why 'carried up?' How is the resurrection of matter proof of the Immortality of Spirit? Is not the material Resurrection of the body of Jesus Christ unspiritualizing?"[31]

The practical question of where he was to settle remained unanswered. He spent most of December preaching on supply in Salem and much of the first month of 1837 in pulpits near Boston. In February, he went west again to George Ripley's hometown, Greenfield. At first, Parker reacted to the place unfavorably; he found five societies for two thousand people and detected a "mean and jealous Spirit between some little ones of the sects." But he was still looking for an alternative to West Roxbury, and soon his letters to Lydia reveal him tentatively trying to persuade her and Lucy of the merits of the place: "Were it not for *some* things"—Lucy's plans, perhaps?—"I should be glad to stop here for some few years. One of these—but no, let it all end here!" He felt inspired by the wintry scenery, which he called a "System of Divinity" that could teach him more than Emerson's lectures; so he learned a lesson in tenderness when, walking through the snowy woods one bright, cold day, he found a sturdy young hemlock, cradling in its branches the great, old fallen oak that had long given it shelter, while beneath them bubbled a pure, unfrozen spring. Such scenes made Parker "almost begin to hate the City again." He told Lydia that he had given up "all notions" of a settlement in Boston. He admitted that any place within ten miles of Cambridge (which included Spring Street) would do, "but to go further than that—to settle in some dull stupid place,—where there was not a single Soul to sympathize with me in literature[,] philosophy, and noble enterprise, this were worse than—Death I was about to say." Greenfield was far from the good books of Boston, which gave him pause, but he did find there a sympathetic spirit, George T. Davis, whose wife had been to school with Lydia. This friendship encouraged Parker enough that he wrote to his fiancée: "*I* should much rather be settled in Greenfield than anyplace I ever preached in . . . but I say nothing." Lydia and Lucy remained unpersuaded. So Parker left Greenfield behind and made a second visit to Salem, where he stayed until April. While there, he visited with Elizabeth Palmer Peabody, Lydia's former teacher, and Sophia Peabody, Elizabeth's sister, and noted that a Salem man, Sophia's future husband, Nathaniel Hawthorne, had published "quite a clever little volume" of short stories—his first book, *Twice Told Tales*.[32]

Meanwhile, he and Lydia had decided, finally, to marry. The wedding took place in Boston on 20 April 1837, a sunny spring Thursday, at four in the afternoon in the Church on Church Green, with the portly, stately Reverend Alexander Young presiding. The groom was twenty-six, the bride twenty-three. The couple then left for Lowell, to spend one or two days in "the sweet leisure of one another's Society."[33]

Less than two weeks later, Parker began his candidacy in West Roxbury. It lasted four successive Sabbaths; during these weeks he stayed with his new wife's family in neighboring Newton. Each Sunday morning, he would drive a carriage down to the little white, steepled church facing Center Street. Lydia and Lucy would come with him and listen to him preach both morning and afternoon sermons from the old-fashioned high-box pulpit, then return with him to Newton in the evening. On 22 May, the parish committee voted unanimously that Parker "settle with us in the Gospel ministry." The salary would be but $600, to be paid in semi-annual installments. Parker accepted the offer—with, as he later wrote, a "good deal of unwillingness" and "against my ⟨will⟩, judgement and ⟨common sense⟩."[34]

Now that he was living with Lydia and Lucy, he must have had difficulty withstanding their lobbying for Spring Street. Besides, there were new financial considerations. When he and Lydia became engaged, four years earlier, they sensibly had resolved to postpone marriage until he was settled. Whatever their reason for changing their minds, Parker could not now afford to be so picky about a parish. His income as a candidate was scarcely enough to support a wife, much less the family he and Lydia both expected. His money worries probably were intensified by the panic of 1837, which was raging that spring. Parker himself witnessed many of the "best men" of Boston become bankrupts overnight. He probably felt it wise to try to appease the wealthy Lucy, even if doing so made him financially beholden to her—as he soon became, when she bought a house on Spring Street, near the homes of some of the wealthiest families in the parish. She moved in with her carriage, pair of horses, servant, and footman; the Parkers moved in with them.[35]

Shortly afterward, on a Wednesday afternoon, 21 June 1837, the longest day of the year, Parker was ordained. The ordaining council included both Henry Wares, and, as delegate from the Unitarian church in Quincy, John Quincy Adams, congressman and former president. Convers Francis preached the sermon; Caleb Stetson, the minister at Medford, gave the Charge to the Congregation; the younger Ware made the prayer; and George Ripley, who presented the "Right Hand of Fellowship," the traditional fraternal welcome to a new clerical colleague, praised Parker's "studious energy." Theodore Parker was held to be a young man of great promise, and not only as a scholar, but as a member of the new school of Unitarians: Francis, Stetson, and Ripley were all regular members of the Transcendentalists' little club. Perhaps to balance both these expectations, Ware prayed that "no fondness for literature or science, and no favorite studies, may ever lead this young man from learning the true religion, and preaching it for the salvation of mankind!" Parker thought the remarks of his favorite professor were "beautiful."[36]

The ceremony having ended, the company retired to Taft's Hotel, about a mile away, for tea and refreshments. By some oversight no one provided the new pastor with a carriage or horse, and by the time Parker reached the reception on foot, he found only scraps of food on the table. Many years later, he wrote that he often thought of this incident as "an *omen* of much of what was to come."[37]

THEODORE HAD set aside the misgivings with which he came to Roxbury. But they did not go away. Some five months into his pastorate, he penned a poem in his journal:

> On all this Earth there lies not that for which
> I wish to live. There was a time—how swift
> It went—when all before my face shone bright.
> ⟨. . .⟩
>   Oh then I saw
> A Field wherein to labour long & see
> A net reward. But no, this is denied,
> Scanty my field. Ambition, Hope to the dead![38]

More than two years later, he wrote in his journal that preaching to a hundred persons, half of them "babies," did not answer the "purposes of life."[39]

The people and place may be quickly sketched. The parish had been created more than a century before, by members of the old First Parish of Roxbury who had tired of trekking several miles every Sunday along muddy roads to the opposite end of town. The Second Parish had had an unremarkable history. The Great Awakening seems to have caused no stir, and the Revolution had inspired the usual patriotic ardor and sacrifices. During the Revolutionary era, the most notable event in the life of the parish was the construction of a new meetinghouse in the early 1770s, which, with a steeple added in 1821, was the same building Parker used in the 1830s and 1840s; its interior had an old-fashioned feel, with a high-box pulpit and family-box-style pews.[40]

During the long pastorate of John Bradford, who became the minister in 1785 and served until his death forty years later, the church had quietly turned Unitarian, although a minority had retained Orthodox views. Bradford seems to have been like Jonas Clarke in Lexington: he was able to use his long-standing ties to the community to keep united a church whose members held diverse theological opinions. Clarke's successors could not hold his church together; those of Bradford similarly failed in West Roxbury. He was followed by John Flagg, whose ill-health prevented him from being too active in a parish that was starting to divide, and who died after only five years in the pulpit. Flagg's successor was the boyish George Whitney, an earnest, sunny, guileless man, who also suffered from ill-health, and who himself died not long after relinquishing his pulpit to Parker; in Parker's opinion, his predecessor had had no religious life, "and could not impart[,] poor man, what he did not possess."[41]

Whitney had been unable to prevent a schism in his church. A sign of it, if not the proximate cause, was the adoption of a new church covenant in August 1832. The original, from 1712, had been a somewhat lengthy, solidly Calvinist document, whose signers spoke of being "in humble dependence upon free grace for Divine assistance & acceptance," of having to depend "wholly on the free mercy of God, & upon the merits of Jesus Christ" for salvation. The Unitarian majority now found this language distasteful and so had scrapped it in favor of something much shorter and more liberal: "We . . . declare our belief in the divine authority of the Holy Scriptures; and cheerfully receive them as our rule of faith and practice; promising to conform to their demands, according to our ability in that sense in which they seem to us individually to be enforced. And this we consider to be a Church of Christ, pledging ourselves to walk together as brethren, in all the commandments and ordinances of the Lord blameless."[42]

This language must have upset the Orthodox minority. By March 1833, they had organized a separate meeting with a minister from Dedham, and in April, eight former members of the Second Church joined with others to form the West Roxbury Evangelical Society, proclaiming they felt "the necessity of hearing the gospel preached in its purity, as it was taught by Christ and the Apostles, and as it was formerly believed and taught in this place by our forefathers." Their new minister was one Christopher Marsh. Once, after Parker had been told that Marsh was "uncommonly prayerful & pious," he noted in his journal that he was "glad of it & hope it is true," but that it would not be easy to convince his own parishioners of the fact.[43]

Despite this evidence of hard feeling, the schism seems not to have been too bitter. At least one family had members in both churches, and members of Marsh's congregation could be found attending Unitarian temperance lectures in Parker's meetinghouse.[44] The schism helped Parker because it removed from his church those who would most likely have objected to his developing Transcendentalism.

He was also helped by the ongoing evolution of his parish from an isolated village into a suburb of Boston—an evolution symbolized by the commuter stagecoach that left the tavern across Center Street from Parker's house every morning at eight, rattled its way inbound to the Boylston market, and returned every evening at five. The old families of the church, such as the Arnolds, Farringtons, Welds, and Whittemores, were local farmers; yet most of the men in the parish whose profession is recorded in the local histories are remembered as "merchants." They were probably farmers who made extra money as small traders and craftsmen. Serious, silent Deacon Farrington, who still wore a cue and moved so slowly he was reputed to take seven years to wear out a pair of boots, was simply a farmer; he did not supply much business to Deacon Arnold, who was also a bootmaker.[45]

Yet West Roxbury also had become the rural refuge, either seasonal or permanent, of some wealthy Boston merchants and professionals. Several parishioners were remembered as "men of leisure," and at least one, Robert Billings, became a millionaire. Parker once remarked that of the 120 in his congregation, some 20, drawn from these more elite ranks, were "intelligent." They would number among Parker's strongest supporters in the parish.[46]

Among the summer residents was the family of his wife's cousin Frederick Cabot, a retired importer who now managed textile mills. His brother-in-law was the German radical Karl Follen, and he would name a son Follen Cabot. Several of these Cabots show up in the list of members of Parker's church, and he was to grow closer to them than to any other members of his wife's family. Years later, when he made out his will, he would turn to Frederick Cabot and his children to witness it.[47]

Parker's immediate neighbor (they shared a garden) was George Robert

Russell, a merchant, now retired, who had traveled widely in the Pacific while making his fortune; he was a longtime friend of the Transcendentalist Orestes Brownson. Parker found, to his delight, that Russell had "much aesthetic culture[.] Understands paintings, & is full of poetry. He loves nature & is full of life. He talks like a living book."[48] In 1835, Russell had married Sarah Parkman Shaw, who came from a prominent merchant family noted for its wealth, liberal sympathies, and good looks. She was one of Parker's former students and became a member of his church. He was to become very close friends with the Russells and to baptize two of the Russells' children.

Parker became attached, too, to the family of other neighbors, Sarah's brother, Francis George Shaw, and his wife, Sarah Sturgis, sister to Caroline, the writer and Transcendentalist. Francis was one of those rare rich men sympathetic with radical reform; he became a benefactor of abolitionism and Brook Farm and a regular contributor to the Fourierist *Harbinger*. Francis and Sarah would become parents of three children whose names are remembered: Robert Gould, who would die an antislavery martyr commanding the first Union regiment of northern black soldiers in the Civil War; Anna, who would marry the literary editor and political reformer George William Curtis; and Josephine, whom Parker was to baptize, and who would, as Josephine Shaw Lowell, become a prominent philanthropist. Parker was also to be drawn to Francis's and Sarah Russell's younger sister, also named Anna Shaw.[49]

THE DAY of Parker's wedding, he wrote out a list of resolutions in Latin in his journal. They were translated into English and printed by one of Parker's early biographers:

1. Never, except for the best of causes, to oppose my wife's will.
2. To discharge all services, for her sake, freely.
3. Never to scold.
4. Never to look cross at her.
5. Never to weary her with commands.
6. To promote her piety.
7. To bear her burdens.
8. To overlook her foibles.
9. To love, cherish, and ever to defend her.
10. To remember her always most affectionately in my prayers; thus, God willing, shall we be blessed.[50]

How these resolutions fared is indicated by another list, again in Latin, that he wrote in his journal a few months later, after he, Lydia, and Aunt Lucy had settled together in West Roxbury. These "rules to observe" with his wife have never before been translated into English or printed:

1. Never contradict.
2. important[:] Frequently praise her Virgin [i.e., Aunt Lucy].
3. Never touch on her prejudices.
4. Smother the ferocity of her "no's."
5. Exercise silence rather than conversation.
6. Ignore her scolding.[51]

On the same page appears a poem lamenting that

'Tis hard, 'tis very hard to find,
One's bosom partner prove unkind
I grasped at gold, it is but dross,
Oh grant me grace to bear the cross.[52]

What life was really like in the Parker-Cabot household is difficult to reconstruct, in part because most direct references to it in the Parker manuscripts are missing or edited out. In 1860, when Parker died, his papers passed to Lydia, and, after her death, in 1883, to the author and editor Franklin Benjamin Sanborn, who had been close to Parker in his last years. Some of Parker's letters to Lydia during their courtship were still extant in Sanborn's time (he made copies of them in the 1880s) but have since disappeared. Of Parker's letters to her during their marriage, not even copies can be found. Lydia apparently blotted out many passages in her husband's journal that related to their marriage—although, ironically, the notes she made in this process preserved some passages that otherwise would have been lost. Sanborn, when he got the journal, appears to have made deletions of his own. A researcher of the journal must therefore spend hours under a bright light, trying to decipher ink-smeared sentences. In addition, Lydia apparently destroyed her own papers systematically and perhaps the papers of her Aunt Lucy: just three sentences in Lucy's hand are known to survive, and nearly all of what little survives by Lydia herself dates from either the final year of her husband's life or after his death.[53]

The available evidence concerning the Parkers' marriage comes mostly from passages in Theodore's journal that escaped bowdlerization. These present only his view of events. Furthermore, Parker wrote as if Lydia might read what he had written and react badly. "I have not been in so good spirits as usual today," Parker wrote in an entry from the summer of 1838. "Indeed for a whole fortnight—& that in the most beautiful season of the year I have been as good as dead, for reasons not to be named in this book—lest W[ife] should tear out the leaf, as the wont is."[54] To evade such wonts, he recorded some of his most personal comments in Latin, or disguised his words by writing them in Greek or Hebrew characters. He sometimes wrote about his situation in

Period of Disappointment

the third person, or as a fable or in a poem, which he then carefully would label as a translation from some obscure ancient tongue. Sometimes he even seems to have scratched out passages himself.

The recurring theme of his surviving complaints is his loss of hope for a happy domestic life. Seven months into his marriage, he lamented in his journal that

> A Twelvemonth since, & who so blithe as I?
> My Hopes were rainbows, of most brilliant die.
> Without no fighting, as within no fear.
> Sure Peace & joy, I said, shall wait me here
> Here on the Earth I'll build an Heaven of bliss,
> For Heaven above's no more secure than this. . . .
> Deceitful dream—E['e]n now Thou comst to view,
> As in that Season when I deemed thee true. . . .
> Yet what are Hopes, Oh false & perjured Thou. . . .
> Oaths are but words, & words but very wind.
> The tie still binds—but where[']s the bliss of Love conjoined.[55]

Several months later, in his journal for early 1838, he wrote that he "had no hope," for he had been told that people shunned him and that no one loved him. "And indeed," he adds, "when *the* one who before God's altar swore to love me is found an enemy more cruel than death or the *grave*, . . . where can I hope for Love[?]"[56] In the fall of 1838, he preached a sermon on the "Uses of Sufferings." After providing poetic accounts of various kinds of afflictions, such as "undeserved" poverty and the loss of loved ones, he announced with sudden, startling vehemence that a "still worse case" was

> when that friend selected from the world, loved in the heart's heart: the very idol of affection: the centre whence hopes, beautiful as dreams extend outward to all the world: the one chosen as a companion for time & eternity to multiply joys & divide sorrows, to be heart of our heart, & soul of our soul, the ark of our refuge, a Pillow in the tempest, a friend when all friends forsake, when this one prove recreant & poisons the cup it should have blessed: curses that home it should have endowed, leaving the confiding one betrayed, & comfortless, then is the cruelest suffering produced. So the ivy clings to the tree & tieing [*sic*] round pole & branch affords beauty while it receives support. But when the faithless tree proves rotten & falls, disappointed [*sic*] its trust, the faithful vine falls a melancholy ruin to the ground, still to linger with ineffectual endowments & live a life of mildew & disappointment. Many evils are there in life. But *no evils* like this.[57]

In his journal from early 1839 there appears a poem titled "Omens," which Parker supposedly translated "from the Siriak." He scratched it out himself, but it is still legible:

> Two ravens on my marriage day
> Attended me to wife:
> Were with us, in their dark array
> To curse the new wed life.
> Oh sad & sinister their croak,
> Wicked the words the Ravens spoke,
> True harbingers of strife.
> The wedding Bell
> Was a funeral knell
> For buried hopes it tolled
> Yet glad I heard its summons fell
> Affection made me bold.[58]

The Parkers did not divorce, but this is unsurprising: in New England at that time, divorce was legally difficult and, especially for a minister, socially unacceptable. The Parkers did have the option to separate. That they did not is a sign that their marriage may not have been as disastrous as the quotations above indicate. Parker admitted to Lydia that "whatever [is] disagreeable haunts me," and he does appear to have been more likely to write at length about his bad times than his good ones. His writings may therefore give disproportionate weight to the bad moments of a generally workable marriage. Part of the problem, too, is that among the missing sources are some that might have balanced the picture. So in June 1841, when Lydia was away on a trip, Parker claimed he was writing her almost every day, and these letters may have contained expressions of affection—but none survive.[59]

In the sources that remain, Parker occasionally compliments his wife, or expresses affection for her. Yet even taking these remarks into account, the bad times in the Parkers' marriage seem to have come so often that his friends noticed them. After he had been married several months, his friend Samuel Andrews told him he seemed discontented. Parker responded to Andrews by confessing he was right, but would not tell him why. "I always knew I had trouble in store," Parker added, "but never thought it would come in the present shape." In 1839, Elizabeth Palmer Peabody, who was aware of some of the Parkers' problems, wrote them with friendly advice. Unfortunately, only Parker's acknowledgment of her "fine and comforting" letters survives.[60]

Few marriages are perfect, but the problems of the Parkers persisted long enough that they need to be explained. One difficulty may have been a commonplace one, which Parker identified in a sermon from 1841 as "the most fertile of all difficulties between man & wife," that is, "a cessation of *the kind*

& *tender offices* deemed necessary to secure affection." Those who think they love one another before marriage tend to make professions of kindness and show abundance of self-sacrifice. After marriage, however, they may take one another for granted, and the attentions cease: "It must be a sad thing for he who has been worshipped as a *Goddess* [*sic*] . . . to be tended with neglect—perhaps coldness. Sad to him whose coming had been looked on [as] a great blessing, & anticipated with a trembling heart to be met with indifference, or even aversion. To find his fancied angel—a very cold piece of clay."[61]

That Parker would be disappointed in his expectations for married life is understandable: they were impossibly high, probably because he longed so deeply for the domestic life he had lost when his Lexington family was destroyed by disease. In a sermon from 1838, he held up to his congregation, as a model of home life, a "nameless Christian family" that is obviously the Parker family in the 1810s: "It is a Sunday Evening in summer. . . . The father[,] strong in the grey hairs of 60 winters, hold[s] in his hands hardened by humble toil[,] hands wh[ich] were his children's bread, the well-worn bible of his father. From this & his own heart he teaches his youngest son, who sets upon his knee. The mother is teaching the daughter some sacred book, or telling some instructive tale, not to be forgotten. Ten older brothers, & sisters, are discoursing with pious cheerfulness of the events of the day." Parker must have had such an ideal scene before him when he told Lydia before their marriage that he hoped they would found a family "which shall bear up our names, honor our virtues, reflect the Sunshine of our hearts, and *finish our work*."[62]

This dream, as Parker slowly and sadly came to see, would never be fulfilled. He and Lydia had no children. In 1839, when he heard that his friend William Silsbee would become a father, wrote him a note of congratulation tinged with envy: "I used to hope the Lord would favor me equally, for a Parker or a Cabot that had no children is something unheard of in the history of our families." Privately, he lamented: "Alas is [it] not to be my lot to enjoy the raptures of Paternity? God grant me patience, even here." A few months later, he noted in a sermon on "sorrows," in a passage he later scratched out, that the man without children is "discontented & sad."[63]

That he and Lydia were childless may indicate that they were sexually incompatible, although they do not seem to have been abstinent, at least in the early years of their marriage. The day after their wedding, Parker elatedly wrote his friend Silsbee that Silsbee, too, should marry and end his "pilgrimage in the desert (of Celibacy, where I trust you will not continue 40 years. . .)." Parker never ceased to condemn celibacy as unnatural and pitied the fate of bachelors and old maids, "who grope their cheerless pilgrimage along the dry and dusty way of time never getting a mouthful of fresh air." He also expressed hope for years that he would become a father, implying that the union was not void of sexual relations. Yet he may have been referring to his own marriage when he wrote in his journal that he knew "a man whose wife has no *passion*—sentiment enough, but the passional part of marriage is hateful to her. In this point then, the Man is not married." Sexual incompatibility may also be implied by a passage in his journal from the summer of 1840. It has often been cited as evidence that Theodore and Lydia were happily married; he was indeed feeling lonely because his wife was out of town (in this case, for a trip to visit her brother in New Jersey): "I miss her absence [*sic*]—wicked woman most exceedingly. I can not sleep or eat, or work or live without her. It is not so much the affection she bestows as that she receives by which I am blessed. I want someone always in the arms of my heart, to caress & comfort[;] unless I have this I moan & weep." There seems to be a sexual subtext to this passage, indicated by his identifying her as a "wicked woman," whom he wants to "caress & comfort" in his "arms"—albeit, the arms of his heart. When he says he is blessed by the affection he bestows on her more than by that which she bestows on him, is he merely restating that "'tis better to give than to receive"? Or is he indicating who is more active in "bestowing" sexual affection?[64]

Parker's deepest frustrations with his marriage, however, were not sexual. What he missed the most from his childhood was the support and companionship his mother and sisters had given him—what he came to call "sympathy." In 1841, he wrote in his journal, in a passage obviously referring to himself, that the "man without brothers or sisters, with no father nor mother, with none about him of the companions of childhood[,] cut off from his mother[']s grave: with no past brought daily to his recollection—yet putting out his arms for an embrace. He it is that needs S[ympathy]."[65]

Parker perceived the greatest obstacle to his receiving sympathy at home to be Lydia's sickly, strong-willed Aunt Lucy. He felt that she dominated his household and resented her for it. He surely intended to belittle her when he referred to her as "the Virgin," which he did repeatedly in his journal, but certainly never to her face. The nicest surviving comment he wrote about her comes from his journal in 1841 and was hardly an unalloyed compliment: "While I honor the good of my Aunt, I still think she does little to make a house pleasant. Her kindness to L——a [Lydia] was pure, loving & true. Her own ill-health & natural temperament is the excuse for all she is & does." In Parker's darker moods, he was unwilling to excuse her. He noted rather too often in his sermons that a single, peevish, fault-finding person could destroy the peace of a whole family.[66]

Parker secretly vented his frustrations with Lucy in sharp-edged satiric sketches, which appear from time to time in his journal. In one, supposedly "from Zacateces" (in Mexico), he writes about a middle-age virgin, "Donna M Lucia Gabbatti" (the name is crossed out but can still be read), who dies

Period of Disappointment

and arrives at the gates of Heaven. She is disgusted to see the "vulgar rabble" crowding in. Not doubting her own welcome reception, she demands of St. Peter to see her "Uncle Jorgio" (Lucy's uncle was the prominent Federalist senator George Cabot). Peter tells the "defunct virgin" that he is not there— whereupon she flies into a rage and so is sent to purgatory.[67]

In another sketch, this one supposedly a translation from an obscure language, Parker describes one "Miss Dorothy," a "virgin" who was "a little turned of fifty" (Lucy was fifty-three at the time) who "fancied herself as young as ever." She had "never been selected as the most amiable, in any circle, it has been the writer's fortune to meet, & as to her personal Beauty, though no enemy to praise & adulation," she had never been "sought out by all the people . . . of a city, & compelled to exhibit herself to the public twice a week, as once happened to a Beauty."

> The most striking trait in Miss D., [he continues] & all her traits were striking, was this. She never did any thing wrong. Yet she was often a confessor of faults in general. She was "a frail creature," "Of short memory," "Full of faults," "Laden with follies." Here was a profession of Frailty, which would have satisfied a Moravian. But in the concrete[,] matters wore a different face. She did not commit an error. Here she bore uncontested superiority, to . . . the Great Mogul, & the Pope,— who cannot but *do* err. Was a misstep taken in Miss D's family, It [*sic*] was the cook or the footman, who was at fault. . . . Of course she was always surrounded by the imperfect. Her servants were the most inattentive; Her friends the most careless. Her own family—for though a virgin she was surrounded by a *circle*—the most negligent & [unchristian] assemblage to be found out of the domain of the great god of flies. She was never at Peace, except when at war: was only quiet when she stormed: & chiefly pleased with being out of humor.[68]

The following year, when Parker preached a sermon on "Pride," he paraphrased this sketch of Lucy when presenting a portrait of a "proud man": "Does the proud man speak of himself, he is the frailest of creatures. You would fancy a saint was confessing a sinner[']s faults, so long is the list. . . . He will confess to you all *general faults*, but charge him with error in any one instance . . . [&] He will show it *was impossible*. The church of Rome claims to be infallible, but confesses she has often committed errors. The proud man differs from that church, for he claims to be the most fallible of men, but denies that he ever commits a *fault*."[69]

How Lucy reacted to having this sermon preached at her is suggested by a note Parker made on the first page of the manuscript: "Not to be preached again, for though I like it I doubt that others do." In a later sermon, however, he noted that the fault-finder, who has no satisfaction except with displeasure and is at war with all, dies unmourned; still later, in a sermon on the uncanonical sin of "peevishness," he paraphrased his description of Lucy yet again: "the Peevish man confesses he is the most fallible of mortals. . . ."[70]

Parker disliked Lucy most for her influence on Lydia. In 1838, he noted that Lydia had made a comment that displayed her "usual good sense," but added, "when she is allowed to use it, which is *seldom*."[71] That the force he thinks restraining her was Lucy is suggested by another journal passage, in which Parker condemns "unparents," who train their children not in love, but fear. He names no names, and indicates he is talking about a mother and daughter, not an aunt and niece, but there is no doubt that he is really judging how Lucy reared his wife:

> A case familiar to me when a woman educates a daughter in this way. The d[aughter]. is of a nature & merit different from & far superior to the teacher & educator. Love visits her rarely. Fear is her constant companion. All independent action, is forbid, the beautiful soul marred in its action. Deception was taught. Shows made to seem better than realities. There was an outward calmness, even indifference, but an inward warfare. The delicate soul was maimed, became little, timid, peevish, revengeful, jealous. She had been trained never to disagree with the educator, but to take all her opinions, think her thoughts, obey her commands, because hers. . . . She was taught to think the Educator a prodigy of Intellect, though of a mind commonplace, & shallow,—a wonder of attainments though they were the most ordinary, & to count her a . . . miracle of goodness & benevolence, though her temper would have disgraced a shrew, & her benevolence was confined to a few shillings. The result need not be written.[72]

Worst of all, Parker believed Lucy was setting his wife against him. In his journal, on a page that has since been inked out, a sentence can still be read in which he complains that he must "share the house with one who *tells my wife she should think she would wish* [three words illegible] *to her father's to get away from her husband*!!!!"[73]

Lucy, for her part, doubtless disdained Parker, partly because he was socially beneath her—but more important because she disliked his Transcendentalist theology. In 1838, Parker noted in his journal that a "certain Lady" had just pronounced him an *infidel* "in good set speech." The name of the lady has been scratched out, but "Miss L" is still legible; it was almost certainly Miss Lucy. She disagreed with Parker's claim that the authority of Jesus rested only on the truths he taught. To her mind, people should obey what Jesus taught even if it did not seem true to them. "If sentences of his did not seem true to me," replied Parker, "I should reject them"—although he insisted to Lucy that he revered Christ as much as she did, if not more. Lucy later retracted the word "infidel," but, wrote Parker angrily, "this does not mend the matter."[74]

Lydia herself may not have thought her husband an infidel, but she appears to have had little interest in the intellectual matters that consumed him; Parker often noted that she was not a scholar, or a writer, or a conversationalist. Even worse, he now perceived her spirituality to be conventional and thought her incapable of sharing his exalted, Transcendentalist aspirations. In 1840, he wrote grimly in his journal of dark hours "when the remembrance of affection ill-met, of love placed on objects not deserving," rose up as specters: "These hours are dreadful, they come oftenest to the most acute of sensibility. He who is linked to a mass of obdurate clay—how often must he feel it."[75]

Parker came to feel more and more constrained around Lydia and Lucy. In 1841, shortly before he preached the "Transient and Permanent in Christianity," he wrote in his journal that there are those "who breathe freely in all places but their own fireside; who can trust all but their own household; who never hear a foot approach their room, but they send for their caution, & huddle their loose thought, & high fancies out of sight." He then reveals that he is referring to his own situation: "Oh were the Devil to come from Hell methink there are who would give him new lessons on the art of torture. . . . Well, so be it. God's ways are dark, but they end in Light. Each true man's path is a radius which leads back to the central sun, at last. What are these seventy years? Forty years hence no man will know the sorrows I have smothered in my heart. Then I shall have outgrown them all. This is a pleasant thought. If Hell is my ——, why let it be so."[76] The unwritten word, obviously, is "home."

Parker gave his most detailed picture of his home life in a thinly disguised comic fable from 1840. "The Swallow and the Tortoise" is about the "strange affair" of a young gentleman swallow who woos and weds a lady land tortoise. As the swallow matures he wants to fly, but his wife declares his "aspiration for the skies" "preposterous"—because no member of her distinguished tortoise family had ever flown. " 'Go to now,' " she tells him, " '& behave like the Tortoises as other people do. That alone is respectable. Don[']t break your wife's heart, kind & condescending as she has been to marry you[,] you thin-skinned, shelless son of an Egg.' "

The swallow tries to behave as his wife would like, "walking awkwardly enough in the dust, eating roots & the like & sleeping after dinner." He attends the Tortoise family meetings, tries to dance as they dance and even think as they think. "But it would not do. He was not born for a Tortoise." His instinct calls him to the clouds, where his "eye was keen & brilliant, his wing quick & dazzling glanced in the sun as his cheerful, sharp twitter broke merrily from his beak." At night he returns "faithfully to the shapeless rest of . . . the Tortoises" but rises early to go on his "celestial journey." "Still he is faithful, for Conscience in the Swallow overbounds Desire."

Nonetheless, the wife-tortoise and her family, including her "mother," "Miss Snap Turtle," who glimpse him "dallying" from afar, reproach him for not being as merry with her as with his friends of the air. "You never twitter with me," says Mrs. Tortoise Swallow, "nor fly round & round, & beneath & above me—nor catch summer flies from the surface of the lake, for my palate, as for Miss Swift-wing, Miss Fork-Tail, & Miss Fair-Shape." "Alas," the Swallow replies with a sigh, "I am aweary, & aweary, & aweary. . . ." "When she disturbs him as he stops on the ground, wh[en] she claws him in the night, bites him in the day, or breathes out a hateful venomous breath upon him,— He only twitters. But his heart will break, & the widow will wed a more fitting mate."[77]

About the wife-tortoise's reproaches concerning Misses Swift-wing, Fork-Tail, and Fair-Shape, more will be said later. Yet the question arises as to how the Parkers' marriage looked through Lydia's eyes. No direct testimony survives, but she must have found it excruciating to be subject to conflicting demands for loyalty from her husband and aunt. Theodore, moreover, seemed to make little effort to understand her problems—or for that matter, those of any woman.

He would later become justifiably famous as an advocate of women's rights, but in his preaching from the first years of his marriage, he hardly mentions women, although they made up most of the membership of his church. Beginning in 1839, he did preach occasionally on motherhood, and in 1840, he tentatively started to recognize the problem of the "condition of women." In his sermons on the home, however, he failed to explain how women were supposed to benefit from domestic life and spoke of the family only as a refuge for men from the harsh world. He seems to have been so concerned by how Lydia had failed to turn his home into a refuge for himself that he seldom considered her intellectual or emotional needs.[78]

He may not have appreciated her intellectual potential. In 1839, when he heard that Margaret Fuller was to launch the first of what became a famous series of intellectual conversations for women, Parker wrote to Elizabeth Peabody that although Fuller's plan was "excellent," Lydia declined to attend owing to "a reluctance she feels at conversing at all." In fact, although she was by all accounts shy, she only needed encouragement to be persuaded to participate; Elizabeth Peabody may have been the one who provided it, because in the end Lydia did go to some of the conversations (there is no record of what she said). Parker may not have encouraged her himself because he doubted the ability of most women to talk on deep subjects. Later in 1839, he wondered in his journal why women are *"so fond of little things about persons, which are of no consequence?"* He speculated on an answer: "1. Are they weak and frivolous by nature? 2. Is their education so scanty & defective as to disenable them to think of anything better? 3. Has the tyranny of man over powered her better spirit?"[79]

An incident in 1837, meanwhile, seems to illustrate Parker's insensitivity to Lydia's emotional needs. That November, her oldest brother, John, died in New York. Everyone knew he had led a dissipated life (Parker discovered some years later that John had fathered an illegitimate son). Parker reacted mildly to the death of his brother-in-law: "John had suffered so much, and so rudely, from this rude world . . . that for his own sake, I doubt not, the change was for the better." He noticed Lydia was "full of sorrow" but thought she sorrowed "*not* as one not to be comforted" and bore the loss well.[80] That Parker may not have appreciated the full extent of her grief is suggested by the only sentences in Aunt Lucy's hand that survive. They appear as a note on the cover of a manuscript sermon that Parker preached in late January 1838. She asks Parker to "gratify Lydia with the 424"—that is, to have this particular hymn sung at the service. "I would not ask you," Lucy continues, "if I did not know from experience how soothing it is. Please to gratify your wife in this & me."[81] The 424, in the book of psalms and hymns used by Parker's church at that time, is for "comfort in trouble":

> When floods of grief assault the mind,
>   And o'er the conscience roll,
> Where shall the mourner comfort find
>   To soothe his troubled soul?[82]

Lydia was likely still in need of comfort two months after her brother's death; yet Parker had to be told of it by Lucy. He may have been self-centered for a reason: he was himself mourning the death, in December 1837, of his last remaining sister, another Lydia. Yet the suspicion of insensitivity lingers, reinforced by an entry in his journal at just this time. The following prayer hardly gives the impression that Parker was "soothing" or "gratifying" his wife:

Increase my patience. Help me to submit quietly, when reviled may I not revile again, when persecuted let me not complain. If I am to be tried by a fiery trial let all the Sin be burned up. Bless my Soul Oh Lord. Let this visitation be for my good; And wilt Thou bless one still so near & dear to my heart. Let her yet turn from the evil path while it is yet day. Create in her a new heart. Pardon her offenses. Bless her in all things. Wilt Thou also forgive me for little Patience. If I am guilty of unkindness, or want of due tenderness, blot out my transgress[ions] & assist me to shew forth the spirit which stirs within. Give me more meekness, more charity, more heavenlymindedness.[83]

Here may be the preserved echo of Lydia's voice: Has she accused him of lacking patience, kindness, and tenderness? Here, too, is evidence that the intolerant streak John Sullivan Dwight identified in him a few years earlier was not confined to the classroom: "You distrust those who are unlike yourself. You fancy them restraints upon you and then your faith in your own energies and ideas speaks out in a tone of almost bitter contempt for . . . those who do not think and feel as you do."

PARKER WAS seeking those who thought and felt as he did when, in the late summer of 1837, shortly after his ordination, he attended a meeting of an informal conversation club at Emerson's house in Concord. The eleven men present, all Unitarian ministers except for one, Bronson Alcott, drank cold water while they discussed the topic of the evening—"Does the Species advance beyond the individual?" What Parker thought of the discussion is lost, but he must have found it more stimulating than the cold water because he kept attending the meetings, each in the house of a member, for the next three years. In 1840, he even hosted the group in West Roxbury.[84]

For Parker, the "club," as he called it, became a refuge from the "foolish & unmanly tattle" he felt he had to put up with every day. He frequently complained in his journal of "wasting" an afternoon in making social calls and chaffer with Lydia and Lucy. Even worse was slanderous village gossip. In a sermon in 1839, he made a point to condemn an example of particularly vicious innuendo, which he claimed came from a "popular modern writer," but which must have struck close to home: "It was remarked in a company that a certain young woman was remarkable for her faithful attendance upon her aunt, who they observed was very ugly, very sick, very peevish, & —very *rich*, Added the false witness, who made part of the company. It was utterly impossible to show this uncharitable insinuation was without foundation." In contrast to such talk as this, how rare was "*real talk*, i.e. the saying *something* of *something*"; how delightful it was "to converse with true friends, wise, moral, religious men." He found such talk and such friends at the little club.[85]

It had no name. Emerson sometimes called it the "Aesthetic Club," and sometimes, jokingly, "Hedge's Club," because it met when his friend Frederic Henry Hedge, the Unitarian minister in Bangor, Maine, was in town, and perhaps also because it was Hedge who had first proposed the idea for the club to him. Alcott referred to it grandly as the "Symposium." Long after it disbanded, it came to be remembered as the "Transcendentalist Club" because so many of the prominent Transcendentalists were at some point members. It was hardly the only club to which Transcendentalists belonged, but it is a useful window into their movement.[86]

The club was born in a May 1836 conversation between Ripley, Hedge, and George Putnam, the young Unitarian minister in Roxbury, at the annual

Unitarian conference at the Berry Street Vestry of Dr. Channing's church in Boston. A few weeks afterward, Hedge recalled that they "all remarked the lamentable want of courage shown by the members in their discussion of subjects, & the utter neglect of truth for expedients." Putnam then asked, "Why could not a parcel of us have a conference among ourselves where we could speak our minds boldly without fear of our elders or betters?" Hedge and Ripley concurred. This "symposium," they agreed, should have "no constitution, no officers, no formal debates," but concentrate solely on conversation. Its members should be "men who earnestly seek the truth & who, with perfect freedom in the avowal of their own opinions, . . . unite perfect toleration of other men's freedom & other men's opinions." The members should be, it was thought, all ministers.

When Hedge, Ripley, and Putnam drew up a preliminary list of possible members, they immediately thought of Emerson; Hedge soon proposed the idea to him in a letter. Emerson responded warmly: "I confess the experiment you propose has never been fairly tried by us. And I will hope from it a pure pleasure." He also suggested his friend Alcott as a member; although not a minister, Emerson thought him a "God-made priest."[87]

Emerson, Hedge, Ripley, and Putnam did not get a chance to meet until 8 September, when they attended the Harvard College Bicentennial Jubilee. After the festivities, the four gathered at Willard's Hotel. They decided that although the club should have no formal debates, each discussion should revolve around an agreed-upon question. Ripley volunteered his house in Boston for the next gathering, on Monday evening, 19 September 1836, usually counted as the first real meeting of the group. It continued to meet irregularly for the next four years; the intervals between the meetings varied from two weeks to five months.

The members of the club had diverse, even divergent, interests and temperaments; Emerson later recalled that they were surprised to find themselves called a "school or sect"—"and certainly at the name of Transcendentalism, given nobody knows by whom." This alien-sounding name (derived from German, but with Old French and Latin roots) had been coined decades earlier, as British commentators struggled for language to describe the idealism of Kant and Schelling. Before long, the neologism had picked up negative connotations in the Anglophone world, becoming a synonym for the extravagant, vague, and irrational in language or thought. In New England, the term had been circulating among the cognoscenti since at least the late 1820s. By 1836, when the little club was being gathered, Bostonians had become aware that "new views" were circulating among them, especially among the rising generation. In January 1837, Francis Bowen, a hard-headed young tutor of philosophy at Harvard, published a review of Emerson's *Nature* in which he denounced this "new school of philosophy" called "Transcendentalist," accusing it of mistakenly trying to revive the dead bones of Platonism and charging its proponents, in particular Emerson, with wooly-headedness and affectation. Bowen's attack may have been the first acknowledgment, in print, that such a "school" existed in New England.[88]

Broadly speaking, the "new school" shared the view that religious truths could be known intuitively and a sense that they were part of the Movement, not the Establishment. They also held in common (more or less) a closely linked cluster of notions, likes, dislikes, and interests—although the composition of this cluster, like the composition of the Transcendentalist circle itself, changed over time. In 1836 and 1837, however, Transcendentalism included as its key elements a perfectionist piety influenced by Platonism; a preference for the internal proofs of Christianity over the historical ones; an enthusiasm for modern continental, and especially German, thought and literature; a sense that neither American society generally nor Unitarianism in particular was spiritual enough; a strong commitment to individual freedom of expression and the free exchange of ideas; a certain sympathy with social reform; and an excited expectancy that great changes in American religious life were at hand. None of these elements was peculiarly Transcendentalist, but the cluster as a whole, held together by intuitionism and an anti-establishment tendency, comprised a distinguishable, although not yet distinct, position within Unitarianism. It would become distinct only in 1838, when some Transcendentalists began explicitly questioning the authority of historical Christianity.

Just as the ideological boundaries of Transcendentalism were not fixed, neither was membership in the little club. Many people dropped in for only one or two sessions; the usual attendance was between ten and fifteen, and about fifty people in total took part in one or another of the conversations. Emerson, Hedge, Ripley, Alcott, and Convers Francis attended regularly from beginning to end. Putnam, although one of the founders, dropped out after a year, possibly because the mood of the club was becoming too radical for him. Ripley's friend Orestes Brownson was present at the first few meetings and even hosted one, but soon left because he was felt by the others to be uncomfortably argumentative. Meanwhile, the club began to admit women; at later meetings, Margaret Fuller was often present, Elizabeth Palmer Peabody attended several times, and other women made occasional visits. The remaining regulars were all Unitarian ministers: Cyrus Bartol, Caleb Stetson, James Freeman Clarke, William Henry Channing (Dr. Channing's nephew), and Parker's theological school classmates John Sullivan Dwight and Christopher Cranch.[89]

Parker was close to some members of the club already and made new friends there. Convers Francis he had known since running the academy in Watertown, but there had always been a certain distance between them, as between a teacher and student; their letters to each other had been addressed "My dear Sir." In the club they met as equals; their letters began to be addressed "My good Friend." Their friendship was founded on mutual admiration and a common love of scholarship. "I think of your literary & theological labors with greatest delight," wrote Francis to Parker in early 1838. "There is no name among us, with which my hopes for theology & general learning are so connected, as with yours." Parker, for his part, praised Francis's acuteness of mind, depth of knowledge, and elegance of expression; he praised his letters for being "like what the Preacher says of the words of wise men[,] 'They are as *goads*' for they stimulate & make one ashamed of his ignorance & Sloth." Theirs became a wide-ranging intellectual exchange. In a letter from late 1839, Parker asked Francis if he knew anything about the hymns of the early Christian church, if he knew whether the story of Cupid and Psyche originated with Apuleius, and if he knew about the origin and nature of the Milesian fables; in Parker's journal, there is a list of "Questions for Dr. Francis" that includes queries on the "Metaphysics of Matter," the "Metaphysics of Property," Matthew 6:23 ("Get thee behind me Satan"), which Parker suspected was spurious because Jesus called Peter a devil, whether the "savage" has "ever been directly benefitted by the civilized," and what Francis thought about using prepositions at the end of a sentence.[90] Their friendship appears to have been especially close in 1839 and 1840, when Parker trusted Francis enough to voice to him some of his most skeptical statements about Christianity and Jesus.

If Parker's friendship with Francis was based on intellectual fellowship, his friendship with Elizabeth Palmer Peabody, although it had an intellectual aspect as well, was more emotional. He borrowed books from Francis, while from Peabody he borrowed not only books, but her private journal, parts of which he copied into his own. He met her as early as the winter of 1835–36, before the club began to meet, when he was still a theological student and she was assisting at Bronson Alcott's school in Boston. They were probably introduced by Lydia, her former student; Peabody also was friendly with William Silsbee's family. During Parker's candidacy, he visited Salem several times and called on her and her sisters, and when he and Lydia married in the spring of 1837, Peabody sent flowers. That summer, she visited the Parkers in West Roxbury. She and Parker seem to have become close sometime in late 1838 or early 1839, when his letters to her became frequent, and the salutation on them changed from "Dear Miss Peabody" to "My dear Elizabeth." Parker even called her "my dear Sister"—words that carried for him a strong emotional charge. At the same time she maintained her friendship with Lydia and apparently addressed letters to both Parkers.[91]

She was six years older than Theodore; they would joke that they looked a little like one another (although she had, unlike him, a "white fence of teeth").

The oldest child of a physician and a schoolmistress, she built on the excellent education she had received from her parents; eventually she learned to read ten languages. She had her greatest impact on American life much later, in the 1860s and 1870s, when she led the movement for kindergartens in America. But even by the 1830s, Peabody had accomplished much, starting schools, serving as secretary to Dr. Channing, and writing significant articles for the *Christian Examiner*, including one on Herder and the spirit of Hebrew poetry. In 1834, she became Alcott's assistant and "Recorder" at his experimental school in Boston. The following year, she published a *Record* of the school that received widespread attention. In 1836, she parted company with Alcott (owing largely to the controversy surrounding his *Conversations with Children on the Gospels*). In 1840, she opened a bookstore in Boston that specialized in a foreign inventory and so became a Transcendentalist center; Parker made a point of buying books from her and sending her books to sell.[92]

They talked about theological and spiritual questions, like the meaning of sorrows and afflictions. Parker received many hints for sermons from Peabody; she told her friends that Parker was a "son of Thunder," whose preaching could move her as she was seldom moved. Peabody was also one of the few people who seem to have been able to talk to both Parkers about their marital problems. In August 1839, she sent him a letter full of "unmerited praise" and "wise hints." The letter is lost, like almost all her letters to him, but his response indicates that it concerned his relations to Lydia: "Both L. and myself are highly edified by your letter. I am highly grateful for the advice you offer, and doubt not it will bear fruit." In another letter, probably from 1840, he tells her that "[y]ou have said many, very many good things in your letters to Lydia and myself." Peabody, in turn, unburdened herself to Parker about a private suffering of her own involving a loved one. Who this was, and what this person had done, Parker's letters do not specify, but he was sympathetic and encouraging. "I can't think the person you speak of will always remain in the dark on this point," he wrote. "Sometime the light must fall on his veiled lids—and he will see the deep of affection he has disturbed, and all the sorrows he has poured out on one whose celestial temper it is plain, he could not interpret or comprehend." In a later letter, Parker told her that learning of what she had borne only confirmed his high opinion of her religious character: "I regard you, my dear Sister—I will say it, as a colossus of Christian obedience and resignation, and a colossus on the top of Olympus too. If Christian tranquillity has not revealed *all* its depth of Beauty yet;— though I know no person who has so much of it, and you therefore have often sat for that excellent Grace in my sermons—yet it will come." Parker added, "Love is its own reward, but when changed to a different feeling,—to one almost opposite—there is nothing but Christian faith that can bear it." This "disappointment is truly greatest"; it was a disappointment he knew well.[93]

No such emotional confessions seem to surface in Parker's relationship with George Ripley, one of the founders of the club. Their friendship did become close, although scant record of it survives because their correspondence from this period has been lost. One event that marked it was a week-long vacation Ripley and his wife, Sophia Dana Ripley, spent in West Roxbury with the Parkers in July 1839. "We were full of joy & laughter all the time of their visit," wrote Parker in his journal. It was a week neither Ripley nor Parker ever forgot; twenty years later, they could look back wistfully to the languid hours they spent lying under the great oak near Parker's house or riding together down the wild little village lanes. Ripley remembered this episode as the "causal & immediate antecedent of Brook Farm." That October, he, Parker, and another friend, Henry Lee, went on a two-week hike together across Massachusetts and around the Berkshires. Over the following year, George and Sophia would often visit West Roxbury.[94]

Parker and Ripley were both scholars and so shared literary projects. They regularly borrowed books from one another, and in 1838, when Ripley launched the *Specimens of Foreign Standard Literature*, his series of translations of French and German writers that he billed as an effort to present "the best productions of foreign genius and study . . . in a form that shall be accessible to all," Parker promised to translate a major work, C. F. Ammon's *Progressive Development of Christianity*.[95] More important, when Parker began to think more deeply about social reform, he seems to have developed his ideas in dialogue with Ripley. Ripley, meanwhile, was also in a dialogue with Orestes Brownson—probably his closest intellectual companion of these years. Parker, Ripley, and Brownson would become radical reformers together.

Parker was never personally close to Brownson, who had stopped coming to club meetings before Parker began attending them. Although Parker expressed respect for Brownson's obvious bravery and ability, he admitted that he "doubt[ed] the man a little." Brownson was black haired, tall, and lean; his plebeian habits, like chewing tobacco, put his humble origins on display. He displayed, too, a powerful intellect and was an extraordinary autodidact: Parker, during his candidacy, heard Brownson converse and wrote a friend that "I was so much ashamed of my ignorance . . . that I have not held my head up since." His religious history was marked by a remarkable series of conversions: reared in poverty in Vermont as an Orthodox Congregationalist, he became by turns a Presbyterian, a Universalist minister, and a freethinker and journalist associated with the Workingman's Party in New York. In 1830, he found his faith again as a Unitarian. He also resumed his ministerial career, first in Walpole, New Hampshire, and then, in 1834, in Canton, Massachusetts, where Ripley had preached his installation sermon. In May 1836, Brownson founded his own Unitarian church in Boston, the Society for Christian Union and Progress; he wanted to find a middle way between those who proposed radical social reform without religion—like his old associates in the Workingman's Party—and the approach of most ministers, who ignored social reform and stressed only individual salvation. His society, too, was meant to provide a spiritual home for the unchurched laboring classes of the city, and so it did away with proprietary pew-holding and opened membership to all who were moral, open minded, and reformist.[96]

Brownson himself saw the driving force behind his spiritual pilgrimage as the desire to work out the logic of his positions and to act on whatever conclusions he reached. His story should have made him a chief exhibit for the virtues of liberal religion: Orthodoxy had driven him at last to infidelity, while the enlightened, rational faith of the Unitarians had saved him. But many Unitarians thought him too mercurial. Over the 1830s, he shifted away from supernatural rationalism and became a disciple of the French eclectic Victor Cousin—such a prominent disciple, in fact, that Cousin acknowledged and publicly praised him. Brownson evidently had not yet found his spiritual resting place.

Then, too, he had become a public supporter of the Democratic Party and prominently associated with its radical wing, the so-called "Loco-Focos." Most Unitarians were Whigs, while the Transcendentalists as a group had a strong distaste for electoral politics. One of Parker's reasons for distrusting Brownson was his fear that he "looks out for political life" and might become the Loco-Foco candidate for Congress. Once, Parker heard Brownson lecture before a group of Democrats, and although he found the talk "good tempered, sound, Judicious, truly [Christian] & eloquent," he complained that Brownson was false "in calling the democratic party the chief recipient of the great Ideas of humanity."[97]

Finally, Brownson was disliked for his arrogance. He had pushed himself quickly into prominence in Boston. Shortly after he moved to Walpole, his powerful essays found their way into the *Christian Examiner*. In 1838, he founded his own journal, the *Boston Quarterly Review*, because "the oracle within will not utter his responses, when it depends on the good will of another whether they shall [*sic*] to the public ear or not." On the other hand, he was eased out of the little club because he liked to destroy the logic of his opponent's position. Even Parker distrusted his overbearing manner. After dining with him in 1840, Parker thought he "was very wicked. I despair at his *morale* & *religieuse* [*sic*]. He has a great deal of the 'better reign in Hell than serve in Heaven' principle. Indeed he *commended* Satan for that saying."[98]

Parker was also ambivalent about Bronson Alcott. The tall, slender Alcott, with his sky-blue eyes and long, thinning reddish hair now turning grey, was Brownson's distant cousin, but a very different man—so different, that when the English journalist Harriet Martineau visited Boston in 1836, she concluded Brownson was a genius and Alcott a fool, while noticing no common, Transcendental ground between them. Brownson was a lucid writer, while Alcott's prose had an unfortunate tendency toward magniloquence and vapor. But many prized his high ideals, pure motives, and "majestic" talk.[99]

Born into humble circumstances in western Connecticut in 1799, Alcott, like Brownson, was entirely self-educated. Parker probably first met him in September 1835, at the theological school, when Alcott came there to talk about education. How his talk was received by the students is not known, but the day before, their Philanthropic Society had voted to commend Elizabeth Peabody's *Record* of Alcott's school to every Sunday school teacher, in the hopes that it would counteract the "unsettled, immatured [*sic*], mechanical & unphilosophical" character of most Sunday school education.[100]

Alcott had made his mark as an educational reformer. He founded a series of remarkable schools; although all failed financially (and he was almost always in debt), his innovative methods attracted influential interest and attention. By 1834, when he started the Temple School in Boston, he had the patronage of Dr. Channing and was able to attract as his assistants Elizabeth Peabody and later Margaret Fuller. Alcott believed that children were close to God and that the duty of a teacher was to unfold their innate divinity. Toward this end he made many practical pedagogical innovations: he tried to turn his classroom into a beautiful, inspirational setting; he had the children sit at individual desks, often arranged in a circle, instead of the usual long benches; he made physical exercise part of their education (because the body housed the soul); he persuaded the children to agree to how they would be disciplined; used the ferule sparingly; and for a time even punished misbehaving students by insisting they strike *him* (his students agreed this was the most effective discipline he ever devised). Most significant, perhaps, he dispensed with rote learning in favor of directed conversation.

At conversation he was an acknowledged master. Parker thought his talk worth more than that of anyone else at the club. Emerson once remarked that while he himself accommodated to his conversant by sinking to his level, Alcott remained serenely spiritual and pulled others up to his higher ground. The self-containment Emerson praised, however, was thought by some of Alcott's critics to be extraordinary self-conceit. Even Elizabeth Peabody, in her *Record*, conceded that "Mr. Alcott is very autocratic."[101]

Alcott respected Parker—he called him "one of the true men of the Age"; the two were able to work together, notably at the Groton and Chardon Street Conventions in 1840. But Parker disagreed with many of Alcott's ideas, in particular those about God. In early 1838, Parker in his journal noted a conversation with Alcott in which Alcott had spoken of "the *progress* of God: the Almighty going forward to His own infinity—progressively unfolding himself." This vaguely Hegelian idea Parker found "revolting." In November 1838, Parker recorded a meeting of the little club, in which the topic was "Pantheism." Although he thought Alcott had made some "good remarks," he could not make out whether Alcott believed in the existence of "an objective god, who was *intelligent* & *conscious*." Alcott affirmed that God was conscious, but in an odd way: he claimed that Justice, Love, and Truth were themselves conscious entities. Alcott again brought up his "revolting" idea of a progressively more perfect God. "Now if this means more than the old notion of a progress in affairs," responds Parker, "I must reject it." It was like a triangle becoming a circle while remaining a triangle! On the next page of the journal, Parker recorded a list of "Doubts" about Alcott, among them: "Does he believe in a *self-conscious God*?" "Is he to be put among the Philosophers?" "When examined to the Bottom is he anything more than a very spiritual & highly religious dogmatist?"[102]

Parker's doubts about Margaret Fuller were even stronger. He and Fuller were introduced at a party in Boston in April 1837, during Parker's candidacy, but they had little to do with each other for the next two years. The earliest surviving reference to her in his journal is from June 1839, and she rarely mentions him in her surviving letters. They had few common concerns: Parker wanted to reform theology and the church, while Fuller, at this stage of her career, wanted to foster American literary genius. The two developed an "intense subtle antagonism," according to Caroline Healey Dall, who knew them in the early 1840s.[103]

Fuller, only a few months older than Parker, already was regarded in Boston circles as perhaps the most brilliant woman in America.[104] Her father, Timothy, a prominent lawyer and congressman, had seen that she received the same education that would have prepared her for the college at Cambridge had she been a boy. As it was, she had to pursue advanced studies on her own. In the early 1830s, a tight circle of young intellectuals formed around her, among them Hedge and James Freeman Clarke. In 1835, she swept into Emerson's life and almost demanded his close friendship, which—somewhat to his surprise—he gave her. To support herself, she taught with Alcott and later at another experimental school in Providence. From 1839 to 1842, she held conversations for women (the ones Lydia was persuaded to attend); the tickets for a series cost $10, and the participants often met at her friend Elizabeth Peabody's bookstore. Fuller's ambition, however, was to be taken seriously as a woman of letters. In 1839, she published a translation of Eckermann's *Conversations with Goethe* for Ripley's *Specimens of Standard Foreign Literature*. By 1840, her reputation as writer and critic was so high among the Transcendentalists that she became the first editor of their journal, the *Dial*.

She was easier to caricature than to describe. Fair-haired and graceful, with plain features and constantly blinking eyes, she was considered by many to be both attractive and repulsive. Her brilliant conversation could be by

Period of Disappointment

turns profound and sarcastic. She could form intense, sympathetic friend-ships with others, as she did with the somewhat overwhelmed Emerson, yet she was possessed of what he called "Margaret's monstrous ME." Dall com-plained that while Parker treated her as an equal, Fuller never did. But at bottom, the problem most people had with her was that they did not know what to make of a woman who was so aggressively and assertively intellectual. Parker himself did not.

He did respect Fuller's ability as a conversationalist. When he first heard of her plan to hold conversations for women, he wrote to Elizabeth Peabody that Fuller "will *awaken* minds, to think, examine, doubt and at last conclude, and will set them an example of conversation, for she smites and kindles, with all the force, irregularity and matchless beauty of lightening." After he first heard her talk at the little club, he found her "full of thought" and announced in his journal a few days later that she "resembles *Mme de Stael* more than any woman I know" because she "has such knowledge, back looking & for-ward seeing, & that matchless power of putting into speech the elements of thought that people her mind."[105]

Parker was unable to see her, however, as his intellectual peer. He once noted in his journal that he had met with Fuller but "did not get much." "I sel-dom get much from her," he added. "Is it my fault? No doubt." After another meeting with her, he wrote: "I should like to hear her bright sayings, but have not now the time." Evidently, he did not think her "bright sayings" worth the effort. He would admit she was a "critic," but thought she was not a "creator," nor a "philosopher," nor even a "good analyst." But he sometimes disparaged her ability even as a critic. When she edited the *Dial* he often accused her of printing worthless pieces, and years later, when he founded the *Massachu-setts Quarterly Review*, he told friends it would be an improvement over the *Dial* because it would be "the *Dial* with a beard." Was this a belated swipe at Fuller?[106]

Parker several times expressed strong doubts about her religiousness. In his first entry on Fuller in his journal, he says she came to visit and that he was "pleasantly disappointed in her" because there had been no "scoffing."[107] A little later he noted that although she was a "prodigious" woman, she "puts herself upon her genius too much" and "has [nothing] to do with God out of her."[108] In other words, she was too conceited to hear the voice of God. But his most memorable comments about Fuller come from this outburst that appears in his journal in September 1840:

But what shall I say of Miss F.? I grieve to say what I *must* say. I have lat-terly seen in her deportment indications of the same *violence* & *unregen-erate passion* so strongly marked on her face. I did not think Religion had softened a spirit naturally so austere; nor that charity had tempered a . . . [character] so selfish & tyranaical [*sic*] by birth. I did not dream those silken cords had joined her so softly to the sky. But I did dream that considerations of Prudence, suggestions of the Understanding, not a little experience of the world, & a very subtle understanding with considerable insight into first principles—had done the work as well such agents could effect it. Now I see my mistake. Nor that alone but my old Rule—to which in her case I was making a conjectural exception—that Rel[igion]. alone can regenerate a spirit at first ill-born, holds good. I need not mention particulars to prove these statements. It is enough that I find the worst suggestions of Mr. All[cot]t [*sic*] confirmed, & I am filled with grief at the discovery. After wandering some 30 years in the Saharas & Siberias, the Englands & Egypts of life finding a sad mingling of Earth & Heaven,—to see one of vast gifts of intellect, great & diversified culture in elegant letters & the arts—of deep experience, in the detail of life, one tried by suffering mind & body,—to see a woman giving way to petty jealousies, contemptible lust of power, & falling into freaks of passion . . . it is . . . ludicrous first, & then it is melancholy. It is not for me to forgive anything. Thank God I have no occasion, but it is for me to pity & to mourn.[109]

What unmentioned "particulars" about Fuller had so provoked him? A hint is provided by the remark that Alcott's "worst suggestions" about her had been confirmed. At the time of this journal entry, she was serving as editor of the *Dial*; the first issue had come out in July 1840, and the second was about to be printed. The first issue had published a long list of aphorisms by Alcott, which he called "Orphic Sayings." A few of them met Friedrich Schlegel's standard for a good aphorism—that, like a hedgehog, it must be compact and have many points. But too many of them suffered from the usual faults of Alcott's prose style: They were not orphic but orotund. Fuller had only used them because, as Emerson said, those who knew Alcott "will have his voice in their ear as they read."[110] Once published, however, they had been widely ridiculed as Transcendentalist malarky, and Fuller chose not to print any more in the second issue, although she did print a few small pieces by herself. Her decision angered Alcott, who evidently had told Parker that she was "selfish" and "tyrannical." Many writers have harbored similar feelings about their editors. Why then did Parker take Alcott's complaints so seriously? His own writings were amply represented in the first two issues of the *Dial*.

Caroline Dall suggested an answer: "It seems to me that Theodore Parker hates Margaret, and I can never understand why, unless it be that in their *faults*, they resemble each other." In her experience, both "required a sort of personal submission before new comers could be admitted to a cordial understanding." Fuller was plainly unwilling to submit to Parker. When she became editor of the *Dial*, she insisted that Parker "cannot be the leader of my journal." And Parker certainly was unwilling to submit to her. Could he have disliked any woman having authority over him, whether it be Fuller or Aunt Lucy?[111]

PARKER'S RELATIONS with Fuller's good friend Emerson were never so complex. Emerson himself was later to call them "quite accidental." From his perspective the statement seems correct, for Parker seems to have had little influence on him. But he unavoidably influenced Parker. By 1838, as a contemporary noted, he had come to be recognized as the leader of the Transcendentalists, because "his published writings have made a stronger impression than any others of this class." Parker had to react to Emerson's pronouncements, and he did.[112]

The young minister not only bought *Nature* as soon as it came out and praised it, its phrases stuck with him. Echoes of them can be heard in unexpected places. For example, Emerson, in *Nature*, described exhilarating moments when "almost I fear to think how glad I am"; Parker, in an 1838 sermon, described "hours in a man's days which seem crammed with the life of years: when the man lives really: is full of thought: full of virtue: full of holiness: full of resolution. He is almost afraid to think how happy he is."[113] Every winter, meanwhile, Parker would attend as many of Emerson's regular lectures as he could. In 1837, he went to the Harvard commencement to hear Emerson deliver his famous Phi Beta Kappa address, *The American Scholar*, and in the refulgent summer of 1838, he was in the small audience at the little Divinity Hall chapel that heard the Divinity School Address. When this last was printed, Parker bought six copies.

Nothing by Emerson ever impressed Parker more than the Address. Emerson had been invited by the small senior class of the theological school (only seven students that year) to deliver "the customary discourse, on occasion of their entering the active Christian ministry." They had wanted something eloquent; at least two of them admired Emerson's oracular style and tried to imitate it in their own Visitation Day speeches that year. What they got from him was not merely an eloquent speech, but a Transcendentalist manifesto. "On this occasion," he told them, "any complaisance, would be criminal, which told you, whose hope and commission it is to preach the faith of Christ, that the faith of Christ is preached."[114]

He began by presenting his Transcendentalist view of inspiration. For Emerson, there was no special, supernatural inspiration; all inspiration was natural and universal. The Address opens with an evocation of the beautiful laws of nature, and of that most important and beautiful law of the soul, the "sentiment of virtue." This sentiment, "a reverence and delight in the presence of certain divine laws," is "the essence of all religion." Emerson conceived of inspiration as somehow partaking of the laws of the soul. He saw these laws as divine; they were God. He seemed to be saying that someone who partakes of these laws becomes an expression of God—in a sense becomes God: "The intuition of the moral sentiment is an insight of the perfection of the laws of the soul. These laws execute themselves. They are out of time, out of space, and not subject to circumstance. Thus; in the soul of man there is a justice whose retributions are instant and entire. . . . If a man is at heart just, then in so far is he God; the safety of God, the immortality of God, the majesty of God do enter into that man with justice."[115]

Having laid out his position on inspiration, Emerson attacks the traditional understanding of Jesus and the miracles. Alone in all history, says Emerson, Jesus estimated human greatness. He said he was divine, that through him God acted and spoke, as God would act and speak through you, if you thought as he did. But this "high chant from the poet's lips" was distorted by uninspired minds in the next age, who said, " 'This was Jehovah come down out of heaven. I will kill you, if you say he was a man.' " Jesus spoke of miracles, "for he felt that man's life was a miracle. . . . But the very word Miracle, as pronounced by Christian churches, gives a false impression; it is Monster. It is not one with the blowing clover and the falling rain."[116]

Emerson now moves from bold assertion of principles to scathing critique of traditional doctrine and the state of the church. The church, he says, makes two errors "which daily appear more gross from the point of view we have just now taken." First, it "dwells, with noxious exaggeration about the *person* of Jesus." Yet "the soul knows no persons"; thus the church "shows God out of me" and "makes me a wart and a wen." Second, "Men have come to speak of the revelation as somewhat long ago given and done, as if God were dead." But the need was never greater for a new revelation than now. There was an "ill-suppressed murmur of all thoughtful men against the famine of our churches."

In these two errors, Emerson finds "the causes of that calamity of a decaying church and a wasting unbelief, which are casting malignant influences around us, and making the hearts of good men sad. And what greater calamity can fall upon a nation, than the loss of worship? Then all things go into decay. Genius leaves the temple, to haunt the senate, or the market. Literature becomes frivolous. Science is cold. The eye of youth is not lighted by the hope of other worlds, and the age is without honor." What then is to be done by us in these despairing times? "It is the office of a true teacher to show us that God is, not was; that He speaketh, not spake."[117]

To do this a preacher must go on alone, and refuse even the good models. "The imitator dooms himself to hopeless mediocrity. . . . Yourself a newborn bard of the Holy Ghost,—cast behind you all conformity, and acquaint men at first hand with the Deity." Emerson rejects all attempts to "establish a

Cultus with new rites and forms." Faith makes its own forms; "let the breath of new life be breathed by you through the forms already existing." Yet he closes with an extraordinary call for a new revelation, greater even than the Bible: "The Hebrew and Greek Scriptures . . . have no epical integrity; are fragmentary; are not shown in their order to the intellect. I look for the new Teacher, that . . . shall show that the Ought, that Duty, is one thing with Science, with Beauty, and with Joy." [118]

Only a few hours after Emerson finished speaking, Parker sat at his desk back in West Roxbury and wrote in his journal this thrilled report:

> After as usual preaching, Sunday-schooling, teachers-meetering &c wife & I went over to Brookline & took Mary Anne [probably Lydia's cousin, Marianne Cabot Jackson] & proceeded to Cambridge to hear the Valedictory sermon by M. Emerson. In this he surpassed *him*self as much as he surpasses others in the general way. I shall give no abstract, so beautiful, so just, so true, & terribly sublime was his picture of the faults of the church in its present position. My soul is roused, & this week I shall write the long-meditated sermons, on the state of the church & the duties of these times. [119]

Shortly afterward he did write two sermons titled "The State of the Church" and "The Duties of these Irreligious Times," which he preached two Sundays later. [120] On the intervening Sunday, his topics had been "Christianity as Old as Creation," a sermon he had written months before but had delayed preaching, and "Peculiarities of the Christian Religion," which he had just written.

The titles alone of these four sermons indicate that Parker shared with Emerson an agenda of religious reform. Both men believed that the times were irreligious. Both believed that to revive religion, one must challenge the traditional distinction between natural and supernatural inspiration; for both, Christianity was not a historical revelation, but a continual one, built into the laws of the universe—it was, in Parker's words (echoing those of the eighteenth-century deist Matthew Tindal), "as old as creation." Both believed one must rely not on the religious authority of tradition or Scripture, but on the voice of God in the soul; one must have faith in human perfectibility. This, they agreed, was the message of Jesus—for Parker, it was what made Christianity distinct from all other religions.

They disagreed on certain theological points. Shortly after the Address was printed, Parker admitted that although he still thought it "the noblest, the most inspiring strain I ever listened to," it contained "some philosophical untruths." The most important of these, for him, concerned the nature of God. Parker read Emerson as saying that not only were people like God, they were God. In early August, when Parker sent a copy of the Address to his friend Silsbee, he wrote, "I do not believe it all. Emerson mistakes *similarity* for *Identity* and so confounds man and God. Alcott does the same, and the Mystics to a man. It is the *Capital fault* of all of them." In his journal, Parker sought to refute their error with a homely analogy: Being like God was no more being God than ten peas in a pod were a single pea.[121]

Behind this objection was the problem of how each man portrayed God. Emerson could describe obedience to spiritual laws as being God, because he portrayed God as impersonal, made up of these laws. By contrast, Parker was committed to describing God as a father. This language appears most strikingly in his "State of the Church" sermon. Why did the message of the early Christians succeed, Parker asks? Because "Mankind was told there was still a god, that god a father!" Again, later in the sermon, Parker notes that people say God "is good and kind, a Father. Do they feel all the Beauty of the Goodness, Kindness and fatherly regard?"[122]

Parker could not help but wonder if Emerson believed in any objective God at all, and he was not the only Transcendentalist to ask the question. It had been raised even before Emerson delivered the Address. In February 1838, Parker had met with Ripley, Hedge, Alcott, and Dr. Channing in a conversation club called the "Society of the Friends of Progress" (Emerson did not belong); the topic was Emerson's last lecture of the season, "Holiness," in which he had first presented some of his views about the nature of God. "It was thought Mr. E's doctrines were dangerous," noted Parker in his journal; "that he denied the personality, which is, practically speaking, to deny the existence of the Deity. Mr. Ripley accused him of maintaining that God was only an idea formed in the mind of the individual, and then projected into omnipresence. It is the idea of power, love, &c., without any substance to which these attributes belong." At the time, Parker demurred, saying that although some of Emerson's phrases could almost justify the construction Ripley put on them, he took it that Emerson had merely denied the materiality of God. After he read the Address, however, he was no longer so sure. "Is there not this fundamental doctrine at the foundation of all his philosophy," wrote Parker to Elizabeth Peabody in early 1839, "the moral and religious ideas we form are God? This is to project God—so to say, out of ourselves."[123]

Brownson had raised a similar objection in his review of the Address that appeared in the October 1838 issue of the *Boston Quarterly*. Brownson liked the "life and freshness," "freedom and independence," "richness and beauty" of the Address; he respected Emerson's attempt to get people to think for themselves and recognize that Truth is as available now as in former days. But he voiced stinging criticism of Emerson's philosophy, which he described as "undigested" and "inconclusive." He labeled Emerson a "Transcendental egotist" who exalted the capacities of the soul and called them God. Emerson's motto was "obey thyself" when according to Brownson it ought to have been "deny thyself." To be truly exalted, wrote Brownson, we still must submit to a higher power. Two years later, Parker was to echo Brownson's criticism in his journal: "Mr. RWE is a great Egotist. His *sage* is himself, his prophet— himself, his scholar—himself, his [Christ]—himself. His God is subjectively projected out of himself."[124]

Yet these theological differences between Parker and Emerson were perhaps less important than they at first appear. Parker was willing to concede that the distinction between a personal and an impersonal Deity may be logical, not actual, and that personality is in the mind of the thinker, not in God. Further, Parker came to recognize that Emerson's language about God was ambiguous, which is apparently what Emerson intended it to be. Some months after the Address was published, Elizabeth Palmer Peabody wrote to Parker that when Emerson said, "If a man is at heart just, then in so far is he God," what he meant was, "If a man is just he has God on his side." Parker replied: "Does he really mean this? I have no doubt he means something very good, if we can just tell what it is. But this is the question." Parker pointed out that Emerson had been unable to explain what he meant either to Henry Ware Jr. or to Parker's friend Silsbee, who had written Emerson a letter asking him to explain this passage and had received an unsatisfactory reply. "You need not suppose I am falling off from Mr. Emerson," Parker continues, "or ceasing to admire him, for I never can. I see more and more in his writings and lectures every day, but I find perhaps the most light from him, when I differ most from him."[125]

THERE WAS SOMETHING else in the Divinity School Address that caught Parker's attention. Emerson gives a vivid example of what disaster befalls the worshiper when the pulpit is "usurped by a formalist." In a famous passage, he describes the case of a "clamerous" young preacher he once heard who sorely tempted him to say that he would go to church no more: "A snowstorm was falling around us. The snowstorm was real; the preacher merely spectral; and the eye felt the sad contrast in looking at him, and then out of the window behind him, into the beautiful meteor of snow. He had lived in vain. He had no one word intimating that he had laughed or wept, was married or in love, had been commended, or cheated, or chagrined. The capital secret of his profession, namely, to convert life into truth, he had not learned."[126]

When Parker sent a copy of the Address to his theological school classmate George Ellis, who was then traveling in Europe, he called his attention to this passage. "Some say *Seiders* sat for this picture," Parker noted, referring to Reuben Seiders, their classmate whose short (apparently unsuccessful) ministry in Wayland was just then drawing to a close, "but I suspect *another man*, whose name I will *whisper* sometime, but not write, for 'scripta manet.'"[127]

Did Parker guess the truth—that Emerson was in fact referring to Barzillai Frost, the man chosen over Parker for the Concord pulpit in 1836, not two years before? Emerson, in the privacy of his journal, had made repeated complaints about Frost's preaching, and many of these passages had been transferred into the Address as complaints about preaching in general. The image of the spectral minister in the real snowstorm may even have been a play on Frost's name. Emerson's complaints about Frost were, perhaps, driven by a need to justify himself. He had only stopped supply preaching at East Lexington that spring—the effective end of his ministerial career. When he wrote in the Address that thoughtful men were fleeing the church in disgust, he was in part explaining his own decision. Yet his disgust at Frost, which echoes so sharply through the Address, seems to have been grounded in fact; even Frost's good friends admitted his preaching was flat and dry.[128] Had the Concord church made a different decision—had Parker settled there instead of West Roxbury—had Emerson been listening to his warm words every Sunday, instead of the cold ones of Frost—would his attack on the church have been less severe and his Address therefore less controversial? Might the Transcendentalist controversy then have taken a very different shape?

WHEN PARKER turned twenty-nine, he reflected on his life in his journal. The years from ages one to seven had been a "period of unconscious joy"; from seven to twenty-six (that is, until his graduation from the theological school) a "period of hard & successful struggle"; but the years since had been a "period of . . . disappointment." In his journal the following spring, he elaborated on this theme: "I am thoroughly disappointed in all the essentials of outward life, viz. a . . . ⟨home⟩; children; & a good professional sphere. All fail me, & all equally." But if disappointment marked Parker's private life, it also characterized the history of the Transcendentalist movement.[129]

The year 1836, when the Transcendentalists' little club was gathered, has been called the "Annus Mirabilis" of the movement. The little club was formed in September, and over the following months a spate of important Transcendentalist declarations saw print. Emerson's Nature was one of these. So was Ripley's review of Martineau, and his Discourses on the Philosophy of Religion. Orestes Brownson published a major review of Victor Cousin's works in the Examiner, and a book, New Views of Christianity, Society, and the Church. Bronson Alcott's Conversations with Children on the Gospels also appeared. Convers Francis caught the excitement of the moment when he wrote in his journal in early 1837 that "the spiritualists are taking the field in force," and added, "I have long seen the Unitarians must break into two schools—the old one, or English School, belonging to the sensual and empiric philosophy, and the new one, or the German School (perhaps it may be called), belonging to the spiritual philosophy."[130]

Francis turned out to be something of a prophet: Unitarianism did divide. But it did not divide in quite the way that he, or any other Transcendentalist, expected. The new school seemed to have broad support within Unitarianism—certainly broader than the confines of the little club itself. For one thing, prominent Transcendentalists belonged to other conversation clubs. In early 1838, only a few months after Parker joined the little club, he reported in his journal that he had attended three meetings of the "Society of the Friends of Progress" in Boston, along with Ripley, Hedge, and Alcott. The "Friends" included others not in the little club: the young Wendell Phillips, just starting his career as an abolitionist agitator; Karl Follen, the radical German exile who had recently lost his teaching position at Harvard for his antislavery views and was now starting a ministry in East Lexington; the philanthropist Jonathan Phillips, at whose house the "Friends" met; and Dr. Channing himself. The "Friends" had a somewhat more formal atmosphere than the little club, probably owing to the presence of Dr. Channing, who, as Parker once remarked, was obscured by thick wrappings of reserve, and "whom I venerate, perhaps, too much." Dr. Channing tended to dominate the talk; Parker called one meeting "Socratic" and added, "Dr. C. is the Socrates." By contrast, no member of the little club was yet so eminent.[131]

The omission may have been merely accidental. When the little club was first discussed by Hedge, Ripley, and Putnam, they considered inviting several leading Unitarians: Dr. Nathaniel Frothingham, the elegantly literate minister of the prestigious First Church, Boston; Orville Dewey, a New York minister who was one of the leading Unitarian preachers; and James Walker, the editor of the *Christian Examiner* and future president of Harvard. Again, when the club had its first meeting, that fall, there was talk of bringing in Walker, Jonathan Phillips, and Dr. Channing.[132] Channing actually attended one meeting of the club, in 1839.

The Transcendentalists had no sharp sense of being distinct from the Unitarians. They thought many Unitarian leaders shared their general outlook, and they had reason to think so. Nathaniel Frothingham was conversant in German ideas and was known to believe privately that the Gospels were inauthentic; in the fall of 1836, he wrote a sympathetic review of Carlyle's *Sartor Resartus* for the *Examiner*. Walker publicly advocated the "marriage of philosophy and religion," and in July 1838 he delivered a lecture on "Transcendentalism," in which he was highly appreciative of Kant. As for Dr. Channing, most of the "spiritualists" looked to him as their leader. Parker, for one, thought of Channing as the real head of the "Progress Party" and regularly paid him visits in Boston to consult about matters of religious reform.[133]

Besides, the leading Unitarian publications, both literary and religious, were all either controlled by Transcendentalists, or open to them (excepting the Olympian *North American Review*). The *Western Messenger*, published in the Ohio Valley, is usually remembered as a Transcendentalist periodical, partly because it was edited by club members James Freeman Clarke and Christopher Cranch. But at the time it was regarded as the leading Unitarian periodical outside of the Northeast. Brownson's *Boston Quarterly*, founded in 1838, was taken for a Unitarian publication, at least at first. The weekly *Christian Register*, which had been founded by Ripley, kept its columns open to the new school while under the editorships of Sidney Willard and Chandler Robbins; Robbins, a friend of Emerson, himself occasionally attended meetings of the little club. Meanwhile, Walker, at the *Examiner*, was publishing major articles by Hedge, Ripley, Brownson, and, later, Parker. In March 1837, Walker and his associate editor F. W. P. Greenwood made their policy clear: When there were questions on which leading figures of the denomination differed, or had not made up their minds, both sides must be allowed to speak. The next year, when Brownson put out his first issue of the *Quarterly*, he conceded in his introductory remarks that the *Examiner*, "a periodical for freedom and freshness unsurpassed in the world, has always been open to me." The principal difference between the *Examiner* and *Register*, as opposed to the *Review* and the *Messenger*, is that the *Examiner* and *Register* felt obliged to be balanced and to print not only the views of those sympathetic to Transcendentalism, but also those of their opponents.[134]

Andrews Norton had established himself as just such an opponent when he attacked Ripley's rejection of miracles in the Martineau review. Another was Francis Bowen, the young tutor of philosophy at Harvard who, in early 1837, had assaulted Transcendentalism when he panned Emerson's *Nature* for the *Examiner*. Parker, at that time wandering in the desert of his candidacy, read Bowen's article and, in a letter to a friend, snorted with contempt at Bowen's presumption: "Bowen! Tutor Bowen!! has written a piece in the Examiner on —what think you? Why upon Emerson's Nature! P-r-o-d-i-g-i-o-u-s.... He has given Transcendentalism 'sich a lick,' that it is almost dead. Kant, Fichte and Schelling appeared to me in a vision of the night and deplored their sad estate. Transcendentalism is 'clean gone' said Kant. 'verdammt'! said Fichte. 'What *shall* we do!' exclaimed Schelling."[135] Bowen would later become a prominent figure in American philosophy, but at the time he was considerably less eminent than Emerson.

With the exception of Norton, no important Unitarian minister or theologian was willing publicly to condemn the Transcendentalists in 1836 or 1837— a fact that Norton himself lamented. The Transcendentalists who were ministers continued to be seen as Unitarians in good standing. As late as June 1838, Ripley, the Transcendentalist then most active in denominational affairs, was elected a member of the executive committee of the American Unitarian Association and a trustee of the Unitarians' Massachusetts Evangelical Missionary Society.[136]

Again, with the exception of Bowen's review of *Nature*, Transcendentalist books received favorable, or at least respectful, notices in the two leading Unitarian periodicals, the *Examiner* and *Register*. The *Register* praised *Nature* as a "beautiful production," a "work of genius," and "throughout tributory to the purest devotion." Ripley's *Discourses on the Philosophy of Religion*, made up of sermons he had preached to his congregation in 1834, were published after Norton had tried to arouse public alarm against his opinion about the miracles. The book was in fact a response to Norton's strictures; Ripley aimed to prove the truth of Christianity without miracles, by arguing that it must be true because it corresponds so beautifully with our spiritual needs. The work was praised highly by the *Register*, which said it "cannot fail to do good to every reader who is conscious to himself of possessing a spiritual nature," and by the *Examiner*, which called it "one of the happiest among the many indications we have had of late, of a disposition to introduce a higher tone of spirituality into the preaching of Unitarians." The *Register* also published a column by "A Unitarian," which commended Ripley's book. Miracles "silence, astonish, more than they convince," says this anonymous correspondent, while the kind of evidence for Christianity Ripley discusses is "perfectly conclusive and satisfactory." [137]

The reviews of Alcott's *Conversations with Children on the Gospels* are even more interesting, because they were written in the teeth of a storm of popular criticism. Alcott had collected Elizabeth Peabody's transcriptions of group discussions about the early life of Jesus he had held with his young students, all under age twelve, at the Temple School; he had published them along with an essay on human culture. The work provoked an outcry, loudly amplified by the two most influential newspapers in Boston, the *Advertiser* and the *Courier*. Alcott was accused of promoting "indecency" because he at one point directed his class to talk about the "origins of the body," and a six-year-old boy announced that the body was made out of "the naughtiness of other people." [138] This was shocking enough to many, but it was not all. Alcott's overall philosophy emphasized the power of spiritual instinct. He thought people worshiped instinctively. He viewed children as closer to God than adults and so more capable of seeing religious truth. All this was attacked as nonsense at best, pantheism at worst. Norton is supposed to have remarked that Alcott's book was one-third absurd, one-third blasphemous, and one-third obscene.

The furor closed Alcott's school, as parents hurriedly withdrew their children; he and his family were not to know financial security again for twenty years. But he also had his defenders. Among the staunchest was Robbins at the *Christian Register*. In March 1837, he wrote an editorial in which he said of the *Conversations* that "no book has ever been treated more unjustly, and uncharitably in a Christian community." Alcott's views on the subjects of education, culture, and discipline were novel, open to criticism, and sometimes even to censure, but he had not yet been given a full and impartial hearing. In fact, his fundamental ideas were true and important: that the ideal of human culture is to perfect the soul, and remake it in the image of the Creator; that the model teacher was Jesus, who also relied on the Living Word. The following month, Robbins published a column by "A Frequent Spectator," who tried to "adjust the balance" of criticism on Alcott's behalf; although the writer disagreed with Alcott on points of doctrine, the thrust of the piece was that Alcott had indeed found a way to awaken the souls of his students, and they would not again sleep. In the same issue, Robbins published a letter by James Freeman Clarke, then living in Louisville, who had highly praised Alcott's book in the *Western Messenger*, and now was called on to defend himself. "A LYNCHING seems quite as fashionable with you in the East as with us," said Clarke; were not the newspapers trying to incite a mob against the Temple School? As for the charge that Alcott's book was indecent, there "is such a thing as prurient modesty, there is a morality of so straight laced a character as to excite strong suspicions of its not being the genuine article." Robbins himself commented that "we came very near to suffering martyrdom ourself, nay were verily threatened with the Inquisition, because we had the audacity to say a word in defence, of a man who appeared to us to have been generally misunderstood, and maltreated." Over at the *Examiner*, Walker also tried to present a balanced view of Alcott, writing a review, published in November 1837, that pronounced Alcott's methods worthy of attention (although Walker judged unsound the specific application Alcott made of them).[139]

The reaction of the *Register* and *Examiner* to the Alcott uproar was reminiscent of their defense of George Noyes, three years before. When Noyes published his article in the *Examiner*, denying that the prophets had predicted the coming of Jesus, there had been a popular hue and cry, and the Attorney General had wanted to prosecute Noyes for blasphemy. But the Unitarian clergy and the denominational publications had rallied to Noyes's defense, even though many Unitarians disagreed with him. The treatment of Alcott, as the treatment of Noyes, revealed that many Unitarians were committed to free speech. It seemed also to reveal some sympathy, especially among leading Unitarian ministers, for new ideas and Transcendentalism in particular. This sympathy, however, would prove to be shallow.

Much of it was the result of ambiguity. In 1838, Parker's friend Silsbee could write to Emerson that he, Silsbee, was often perceived to be a Transcendentalist, and called upon to defend their positions, but he was not sure what these were; he asked Emerson a series of questions that Emerson was unable to answer to his satisfaction.[140] In fact, the Transcendentalist positions on the key issues were at first cloudy. Once a few Transcendentalists worked out radical implications of their views, many who thought they were members of the new school—Silsbee among them—disassociated themselves from it.

One key issue was that of inspiration. All Unitarians, Transcendentalist and non-Transcendentalist alike, rejected the doctrine of the plenary (that is, absolute or perfect) inspiration of the Bible. All agreed that Jesus and at least some authors of sacred Scripture were inspired by God. But there was considerable confusion over the nature of that inspiration: Had God inspired Jesus and the biblical authors in a special, miraculous way? At first, the Transcendentalists seemed to fudge the issue. Ripley's Martineau review is a good example: he asserted that the writers of sacred Scripture were "supernaturally" inspired, but then seemed to suggest that supernatural inspiration is only an extreme form of natural inspiration. Similarly, Brownson insisted that to understand religious truth, we still needed "supernatural," but not "unnatural," inspiration; for once, his ability to make clear, nice distinctions failed him. Again, shortly after Silsbee wrote to Emerson, he wrote to Parker and asked him some of the same questions, such as, "Do you believe we can attain to all religious truth without Revelation?" "No. No. No," replied Parker. "To none at all—But how comes the Revelation? It is a revelation in consciousness, made on the single condition that the man lives by the 'Law of the Spirit of life,' and always made when that condition is fulfilled." All truth, said Parker, was an inspiration, although there are different "modes" of truth and "degrees" of inspiration.[141]

Between the idea that the truths of the Bible were the product of a special inspiration, and the idea that Jesus and the sacred writers were inspired in the same way as we are, but to a different degree, lies a great gulf. To take the latter position was to be open to new revelations and future Christs. The Bible and Jesus would then have no unique authority. And yet, the issue of authority, too, remained for some time nebulous. Did not all Unitarians agree that the words of the Bible had to be weighed by Reason? Yet for some, we only had power to determine what the inspired writers of the Bible really meant; to that meaning, we must then submit. For others, we could reject the authority of the Bible, if we found its meaning repugnant to our own Reason and Conscience.

Because the issues of inspiration and authority were not yet sharply defined, the miracles question was misunderstood. Ripley, in his Martineau review and *Discourses on the Philosophy of Religion*, raised the question of whether miracles were necessary to prove the truth of Christianity. Those who believed they were necessary held firmly to supernatural rationalist principles and argued that the special authority of Christianity could not be sustained without miracles. Yet the new school was not at first seen as denying this authority. Rather, it was thought simply to prefer the internal evidence of Christianity over the historical evidence.

This position was widely respected, even by many of the Transcendentalists' opponents. They admitted that the historical proofs of Christianity could be emphasized to the detriment of spirituality.

> Sadly, mournfully indeed has the doctrine of a miraculous revelation been perverted, [admitted one of these opponents,] when that which was but a circumstance has been transformed into the main cause and end, and the great interposition of inspiration and miracle, which was intended to bring men back to the perpetual inspiration of the soul and the miracle of the universe, has absorbed all our religious thoughts into itself; and, instead of drawing us to Father now, serves only to show what he did thousands of years ago, — the dim footprints of a Father who once was here, but now has left us orphans.[142]

The internal proofs of Christianity were admitted by all to be of vital use in preaching; they were conceded to be much more likely than the historical proofs to quicken the spirit. Norton argued nonetheless that without miracles there could be no religious authority; other opponents of Transcendentalism were less certain. One correspondent to the *Register* conceded that some "instructed and thoughtful" minds could find "ample" grounds for persuasion of the proof of Christianity without miracles, but that the "mass of men" needed miracles to convince them.[143]

Such a view assumed that miracles were not an essential part of faith, at least for the educated and spiritually minded. And they were not, so long as the authority of the Bible was assumed, and the distinction was maintained between natural and supernatural inspiration. Transcendentalism received much of its initial support because it was perceived as a more "spiritual" and "philosophical" form of Unitarian Christianity.

For many of these supporters, Emerson's Divinity School Address administered a terrific shock. Emerson's attack on miracles carried special force, in part, because he seemed to suggest, for the first time in the debate, that they had not happened at all. More important, he explicitly denied supernatural inspiration, claimed we could all be Gods like Jesus, and anticipated a modern and better revelation than the Bible. Suddenly, Transcendentalism began to appear to some of its sympathizers as an alternative to Christianity.

The rumble of protest against Emerson's Address began from the expected quarters. A few days after he delivered it, Parker was back in Cambridge to attend the Visitation Day exercises; there he heard Dean Palfrey announce that that part of the Address which was not folly was impiety. Commented Parker in his journal: "Why not add 'He hath a devil & is mad' a capital wholesale criticism once uttered."[144]

Not long afterward, when the Address was printed, a vituperative attack on it appeared in the *Daily Advertiser*; Parker pasted it into his journal under the heading "A Strange Article," and speculated that it was by Francis Bowen, because of its "Hatred of 1. Germans 2. Carlyle 3. Emerson," its "Ignorance of Germans, Carlyle, Emerson," and its "Bad Spirit." But Parker quickly corrected his error. The piece was by Andrews Norton.

It begins as polemic against the "New School in Literature and Religion": "The characteristics of this school are the most extraordinary assumption, united with great ignorance and incapacity for reasoning." It owes its origin "in part to ill understood notions, obtained by blundering through the crabbed and disgusting obscurity of some of the worst German speculatists," which notions have been received at second hand through Cousin, "that hasher up of German metaphysics," and Carlyle, "that hypergermanized Englishman." " 'Silly women,' it has been said, and silly young men, it is to be feared, have been drawn away from the Christian faith, if not divorced from all that can properly be called religion." The evil is becoming "disastrous and alarming," and the most "extraordinary and ill-boding evidence" of this was the publication of Emerson's Address. Emerson "rejects all belief in Christianity as a revelation." Norton strongly condemns the graduating class of the theological school for inviting him to speak there, thereby associating these opinions with the institution. "The words God, Religion, Christianity, have a definite meaning, well understood," he concluded. "We well know how shamefully they have been abused in modern times by infidels and pantheists; but their meaning remains the same; the truths which they express are unchanged and unchangeable. The community know what they require when they ask for a Christian Teacher; and should any one approving the doctrines of this discourse assume that character, he would deceive his hearers; . . . he would consent to live, a lie, for the sake of being maintained by those whom he had cheated."[145]

Norton's vituperations seem to have done his cause more harm than good. Even conservative Unitarians condemned his tone. Yet the newspaper exchange he had initiated would not be stilled. Parker continued for months to paste examples into his journal.

Then in September, Parker's favorite professor, the younger Henry Ware, preached a sermon on "The Personality of the Deity," which, although it did not name either Emerson or Transcendentalism, was correctly perceived as a significant reply to both. Like Parker, Ware disagreed with Emerson's portrayal of God as consisting of impersonal laws. For Parker, however, the issue was speculative. For Ware, it was vital. The difference between a personal and impersonal God produced a radically different experience of faith; Ware compared it to the difference between a child being cared for by a "judicious and devoted mother" and one "under the charge of a public institution, which knows nothing but a set of rules." The concept of an impersonal God amounted to a virtual denial of God; it destroyed worship; it removed the sense of personal responsibility; it stood "in direct contradiction to the whole language and teaching of the Old and New Testaments." Further still, it destroyed "the possibility of a revelation in any sense which makes it peculiar and valuable, by making all truth a revelation, and all men revealers. It takes away all special divinity and authority from the gospel, reduces it to a level with any other wisdom, and thus robs it of its power over the earth."[146] Jesus himself becomes a pretender and a fraud for professing to be sent from God.

Parker made no direct public comment on these events, but he made an indirect one in "Three Ways to the Name of Atheist," a short satiric piece written in a deliberately old-fashioned oratorical style and published in the *Register* over the colorful pseudonym "Senex Who Hath Crept Out of His Cave." In old times, says Senex, people were called atheists because they denied the existence of God in good set speech: "Such were Leucippus, and Democritus, and Protagoras, and Lucretius, with diverse others, well known; the which did glory in their shame, that they were atheists." Occasionally, people in old times were called atheists because, while saying there was a God with their tongues, they denied him with their hearts. "But now-a-days, it hath some how gotten to be the fashion to neglect such atheisers, and call them by sleek, smooth names, if so be they have a dainty seeming." A much surer method of getting the same atheist is "by being more spirituous, in thought, expression and in life, than other men." The image of Emerson hangs over Senex's remarks:

> Because [genius] doth outrun the dull fancies of other men, who being unable to pack all of the truth he brings in their panners—(not on account of the fulness, but the craziness thereof) straightway they call out, 'madman, fool,' and sometimes even worse. So if any man be so devout, that the most wonted forms of devotion, (albeit they be useful to others)—do not square with his desires, nor express the prodigious aspirings of his soul; nor serve to bear him upward in his loftiest soarings, but he fashioneth other wings for himself; and giveth vent to his piety in unwonted exclamations, even in words unusual, incoherent, and, peradventure, not always fitly spoken, he also is surest of coming under the ban of these men who call that water cursed which is not drawn in their pitchers; and all gourds deadly, unless seethed in their pots. . . . So went the old world in the Lord's time: and matters be not over-much mended in these days, we fancy.[147]

In private, Parker tried to laugh off the controversy. It is thought, he said in a letter to a friend, that chaos is coming back, the world is coming to an end, that Christianity will not be able to weather the gale: "For my own part, I see that the Sun still shines, the rain rains, and the dogs bark, and I have spread doubts, whether Emerson will overturn Christianity at this time."[148]

Would he overturn Unitarianism? In January 1839, Chandler Robbins took pains in the *Register* to refute the growing speculation that Unitarians would divide. To break up the Unitarians, he said, is no easy thing: "It is impossible to produce any lines of division that shall practically answer to such a purpose, or abide." But Parker believed he saw the line. Shortly before Robbins's editorial appeared, Parker attended a meeting of the Boston Association of Congregational Ministers, and the members, all Unitarians, debated the question of whether Emerson was a Christian. "The opinion was quite generally entertained that he was not," Parker later recalled; "for 'discipleship was necessary for Christianity' . . . [and] 'the essence of Christian discipleship' was thought to consist in 'sitting at the feet of our blessed Lord (pronounced Laawd!) and calling him Master, which Emerson certainly does not do.'" Several members even proposed writing a creed, "lest the New School among the unitarians should carry the whole body up to the height of Transcendentalism." Describing this meeting to a friend, Parker, like Convers Francis two years earlier, asserted that there were "two parties among the unitarians." As Parker defined them, "one is for Progress, the other says 'Our strength is to stand still.' Dr. Channing is the real head of the first party. The other has no head. The oyster, which never moves, has none, and needs none. Some day there will be a rent in the party, not soon I trust, however." Parker still believed, as had Francis, that if the split came, the leading Unitarians would fall toward the Transcendentalist side. He would be quickly disabused.[149]

Just a few months later, Parker in his journal recorded a conversation with Dr. Channing on the authority of historical Christianity. Channing's comments obviously surprised him: "Said [Christianity] could not be separated from [Christ]! J[esus] had a miraculous [character], different in *kind* from ours. To him was made a mirac[ulous] *revelation* different in kind from that made to other men, xcept [*sic*] the old Prophets & apostles. Believe[s] the Bible miracles, not those of other people &c." From this moment, Parker realized that the "head of the Progress party" was quite traditional in his core beliefs. Although Parker continued to respect the older man, a space had been opened between them that was to grow. A year after this conversation, Parker took tea with Margaret Fuller, and they "lamented at the condition of Dr. Ch-n-n-ng, & his fear of the new."[150]

Around this same time, the *Examiner* and the *Register* were changing editors. With new men came a new tone. The *Examiner*, under Walker, had sought to maintain balance between the new school and the old. Articles attacking Transcendentalists appeared alongside temperate or even warm reviews of their works. In his last issue, from September 1838, he published a glowing article on De Wette. His successor, William Ware (another son of old Dr. Ware), saw no need for balance; during his tenure he published nothing that explicitly expressed sympathy for the Transcendentalist position. Parker's articles continued to be published in the *Examiner* until 1841, but only because he became increasingly careful about expressing his real opinions in the pieces he submitted. He learned this lesson in early 1839, when he submitted a long article on mysticism to Ware, who hung onto it almost a year before rejecting it with the comment that he "wishes to show *some* among us how 'Infidelity gross as that of Hume, Rousseau or Mr. Emerson, can wear the [Christian] name.' "[151] Meanwhile, in the spring of 1839, Robbins had relinquished his desk at the *Register* to Rufus Johnson. Johnson kept his columns more open than Ware did his pages; the Transcendentalists could still express their views there. But Johnson, in his own editorials, did what Robbins refused to do: he emphatically endorsed Norton's sternest strictures on Transcendentalism. Norton's *Discourse on the Latest Form of Infidelity*, delivered in July 1839, received glowing attention.

In this new editorial climate, is it any wonder that the members of the little club felt a pressing need for a new journal? The discussions that led to the founding of the *Dial* began in earnest only in the fall of 1839, because only then was a separate Transcendentalist publication really needed. The original hopes of movement, that it could carry Unitarianism with it, had noticeably dimmed. The Transcendentalists came to see themselves as a persecuted minority; for Parker, this sense of persecution was a goad to radicalism.

Chapter Four

I Preach Abundant Heresies

Parker's life as a country parson is usually described as an idyll. Here he is, on a spring morning, sauntering along the dirt roads, broad-brimmed straw hat pushed back on his head, carrying a spray of flowers picked along the banks of a nearby stream, greeting every child he meets with the offer that they take some. Here he is, on a summer afternoon, riding a horse along a path through the green fields toward the nearby meander of the Charles River, with the object of taking a swim, or, on a crisp day in winter, crunching his way purposefully through the gleaming snow on the same path, skates slung across his neck. Here he is, in his black clerical suit at his high-box, white-painted pulpit, preaching a sermon to the quiet congregation, but pausing to take a longing glance out the tall church windows toward the nearby woods. For he was fond of trees—certain ones especially, such as the great pines just out his front door, or an ancient oak in a field about a half-mile north of his house, which was remembered as the "Parker Oak," because he so loved to lie under it.

Such sepia-tinted images obscure what it was really like to minister to a village: the banalities and challenges and duties involved in living religiously. An obvious locus of religious life was the meetinghouse. Sabbath morning services there opened about ten o'clock with a short prayer, followed by a Scripture reading, two or three hymns, a general prayer, the sermon, a third prayer, the doxology, and the benediction. Then came the midday break for dinner. Afterward, the congregation would reassemble (the audience was usually somewhat larger in the afternoon than the morning) to sing hymns, pray, read more Scripture, sing more hymns, hear the second sermon, pray again, sing yet more hymns, and be given a second benediction.[1]

These services presented special challenges for a minister. "The act of prayer is tender and sublime," wrote Parker's first biographer. "To pray tenderly at eleven o'clock precisely, every Sunday morning, is a preciseness which the spirit declines to accommodate."[2] But the two sermons were surely the greatest challenge. Parker often planned his discourses months in advance; at the beginning of every year, he would make a long list in his journal of possible topics to address. He usually wrote a sermon the week it was to be preached, but sometimes he would wait months to preach it—in a notable case, thirteen months.

A sermon would begin simply as a title, suggesting a subject. Then Parker would work up an outline, either on scraps of paper or in his journal; when he came to write a sermon out, he did it fast, usually in one sitting. He avoided the small octavo booklets favored by most ministers and used quartos instead—his scrawling hand, which grew increasingly hieroglyphic as the years passed, racing across the large blue leaves. On the title page of each sermon he would jot down in pen where he had preached it and the passages of Scripture to be read with it, and would note in pencil the numbers of the hymns to be sung. The hymns he chose, from a standard collection published by Carter, Hendee & Co., would reflect the subject of his sermon. In Puritan days, even in Jonas Clarke's time, ministers were known to deliver discourses that ran for hours; now, the people could only bear such length in a grand oration by Webster or Everett. Parker's sermons were usually eighteen to twenty manuscript pages long; they probably took him about fifty minutes to read—more if he added extemporaneous comments, as the manuscripts often indicate that he did.

He found the usual problems with the sermon form itself. He later complained that it "seems invented by the genius of dulness for the sake of putting to sleep." True, it was not as rigid as it once had been. In the late eighteenth and early nineteenth century, New England ministers, and especially liberals, had expanded its literary possibilities. A Unitarian preacher could now depart, if he chose, from the old three-part Puritan sermon structure of exposition, doctrine, and application, and Parker typically did so. But as a practical matter, he found something like this structure hard to avoid. His sermons frequently were about applications—applying "religion to life," for example, or "common sense to theology"; some even conclude with a section explicitly on "the application of this discourse." Then, too, if he did not pull his doctrine from a biblical text, people would say he was delivering a lecture and no sermon at all. So when Parker started preaching, he made exposition of a biblical text part of every sermon and sometimes devoted an entire sermon to exegesis. Over time, he began to use the Bible in a less authoritative way. He would take his texts from the Apocrypha, for example (he was fond of the Wisdom of Solomon and of Ecclesiasticus). Later, he would abandon exegesis altogether, and use biblical texts merely as mottos. Sometimes, he would announce that although the writer of the text meant one thing, he would use the words in another sense to make his point.[3]

I Preach Abundant Heresies

As for subject matter, he was expected to stick to certain traditional themes with which his congregation was already familiar—sometimes all too familiar. So he opened a sermon on "Contentment" with the observation that the topic was "proverbially dull": "When the subject is announced men usually display this virtue by resigning themselves to quiet positions & comfortable repose." Certain occasions mandated a special sermon. One for New Year's was needed, as was one for Thanksgiving and for Fast Day, which fell in April. Parker's first two sermons to his congregation after his ordination show the restrictions under which he labored. The occasion prescribed the theme: the duties of the minister and of his parishioners. Emerson had preached on the same theme the Sunday after his ordination, eight years before. Both even preached on texts from Romans and second Corinthians. Hundreds of other young men, at the inauguration of their ministries, surely had done the same.[4]

Besides preaching, Parker performed marriages, baptisms, and, most frequently of all in his aging parish, funerals. Baptisms took place in the church. At the beginning of the morning or evening Sabbath service, an infant would be brought forward to be sprinkled at the bowl. Funerals required a service outside the church, although it was expected that those who had died the previous year would be recognized in the regular New Year's sermon. Every six or seven weeks, Parker administered communion. As tenuous a place as the Lord's Supper held in Unitarian theology, it was still an important part of Unitarian spirituality. Despite Parker's own growing private distaste for administering this sacrament, he continued to do so because members of his congregation wanted it.

With his wife, he was expected to make parish calls and run the Sunday school. Then, too, all the ministers of the town routinely served some time on the Roxbury School Committee. Parker did his duty. As a committeeman, he conscientiously inspected every school and wrote letters of recommendation for young school masters or mistresses. Ministers commonly took on pupils for private lessons, and Parker was no exception. He routinely tutored children in Latin, Greek, history, and mathematics.[5]

Parker had a hundred other obligations to his parishioners. A church member, up for election as selectman, was falsely accused of intemperance; Parker wrote a letter vouching for his good character. In 1838, while the church was planning to renovate the meetinghouse and carpet the aisles, word got back to Parker that a member would desert the congregation unless the church bought a new organ. In private, Parker wondered at the "very slender ties" of Christian fellowship, but he supported the request. A new organ was installed, and the potential lost sheep became the organist and held the position for the next forty-three years.[6]

Besides such duties to Spring Street, Parker had obligations to the Unitarian denomination, with which he continued to identify himself for some years. He became a member of the regular Unitarian organizations, the Boston Association of Congregational Ministers, which he joined just after his ordination, and the American Unitarian Association (AUA). In 1837, he let Charles Briggs, his old minister from Lexington who was now secretary of the AUA, give a lecture to drum up support for creation of a local auxiliary. Parker also could be found every May at the Unitarians' Berry Street Conference.

The principal organization of denominational fellowship was the Boston Association, made up of all the area Unitarian ministers. They met every fortnight at the house of one member or another, to discuss issues of common concern and plan denominational activities. Parker always went, even if he had to walk several miles through an icy winter night into Boston and back. Once, he hosted a meeting, although he felt he lacked the knack for pulling such an event off. At these gatherings, Parker got to know his "Brethren," among them some of the most prominent names in American liberal Christianity: Ezra Stiles Gannett, Dr. Nathaniel Frothingham, Dr. Francis Parkman, John Pierpont. By tradition, each member of the Boston Association was expected to deliver the weekly "Great and Thursday Lecture" (actually a sermon) at the First Church of Boston, in a rotation that took about seven months, the order determined by the date of the preacher's graduation from college (for this purpose, Parker was reckoned Harvard '32); the other members would try to attend.[7] Parker naturally took advantage of these opportunities to be heard by a wider audience. He exchanged pulpits often with his Unitarian colleagues and gave his first of many Thursday Lectures in March 1838.

PARKER ALWAYS said that a minister must be a scholar. He harshly judged those clergy who shirked their duty to find out the facts of religion for themselves. He naturally was inclined toward such a view of ministerial duty—his own ambitions far transcended that of parish pastor. When he was still in theological school, he wrote Lydia that they must live in a house where he could have a study; it was, he said, a matter "somewhat important to one who is to *read*, more so to one who is to *write*, to *make others think* [and] so build up a reputation." He set up a study as soon as he moved into the house on Spring Street, lining it with floor-to-ceiling bookshelves that soon were filled to capacity. The room was on the ground floor, facing northeast; the window, framed on the outside by two tulip trees, overlooked the garden. Next to the window (beside a pot of corn in the winter) Parker moved a large table that served as his desk. He stacked the books he was using beneath it; on top he kept the manuscripts on which he labored—always several at once. He confessed to feeling heavily pressed, "consumed by self-reproach" when he was not at work, which was seldom. In 1840, he wrote to his brother that he could

I Preach Abundant Heresies

find ten hours a day, five days a week, "to devote to works not directly connected with the exercises of the Pulpit, and yet neglect no duty I owe to any one man, or to the whole Parish."[8]

Parker always seemed to be dashing off some short piece for the weekly *Christian Register*; by 1841, he estimated he had written more than a hundred articles for them. These are somewhat difficult to trace, because the correspondents to the *Register* almost always used pseudonyms. Parker used a host of them, including "Agapa," "Veritas," "GG" (for "Gottesgabe" — "Theodore" in German), "W." (for West Roxbury?), and "Senex Who Hath Crept Out of His Cave." Parker's pieces that have been identified include notices of books and sermons, homilies and homiletic fables, translations from French and German (including dozens of Herder's parables), and even satires, such as "A Law Case: *Duty vs. Appetite*: Report of an abridged case in the High Chancery of Justice, his Honor, Universal Reason, on the Bench," published in March 1839. Parker continued to publish poetry, too, although less often than when he was a student. The muse, he complained in his journal, visited him less often.

Despite this variety of output, Parker's principal literary aim in these years was to establish a scholarly reputation among the learned. His great project remained the translation of W. M. L. De Wette's introduction to the Old Testament. He completed a draft in the spring of 1837; by November, he felt so confident the work would soon be published that he began circulating a prospectus and, in December, put an advertisement in the *Register* asking for subscribers. Sometime that winter, however, he conceived a much more ambitious plan than a simple translation. As he announced it to William Silsbee in May 1838, he would enlarge De Wette's work with "all that is most valuable in *Eichhorn* and *Jahn* and some dozen more lying under my table," plus notes and a "huge appendix" of his own. "The original was designed as a sort of guidebook for teachers and learners," he later explained. "If it were simply translated, it would be intelligible to but a few." He would have to supply what the author took for granted. He expected the new project would take him the better part of a year to complete. In fact, "De Wette" was to remain on his lists of "work to do" for over five years.[9]

Meanwhile, in the summer of 1837, when he still anticipated the swift completion of the De Wette, he took on another large translation project: C. F. Ammon's four-volume *Fortbildung des Christianissmus* (Parker's title was the "Progressive Development of Christianity"). Ammon's book was probably suggested to him by George Ripley, who announced in 1838 that it would be published as part of the *Specimens of Foreign Standard Literature* series. Although Parker worked on the manuscript intermittently for five years and translated hundreds of pages, he never saw fit to publish it.[10]

His other long "extracurricular" writings before mid-1840 also show his scholarly bent. In 1838, he published a fifty-page review in Brownson's *Boston Quarterly* of John Gorham Palfrey's *Academical Lectures on Hebrew Scriptures and Antiquities*, and in 1839, a review of John Sullivan Dwight's translation of minor poems by Goethe and Schiller. That same year, in the *Christian Examiner*, he published a significant review of C. Ackermann's *Das Christliche im Plato*, two long articles on the life and works of the seventeenth-century English Platonist Henry More, and, in Moses Stuart's *Biblical Repository*, an article on the origin of writing in Greece and Egypt, on which he had labored over a year. That year, too, he wrote an article on Ralph Cudworth, another English Platonist, which was published in the *Examiner* in January 1840, and also submitted to the *Examiner* an article on mysticism, on which he had worked at least a year, but which was rejected by the editor, William Ware, because it had Transcendental overtones.

WHEN PARKER was not writing, he was reading. Books he could not buy, he borrowed from the college library (as a theological school alumnus, he retained charging privileges), from friends like Convers Francis, George Ripley, and Alvan Lamson, and from fellow biblical scholars like Andrews Norton and Moses Stuart. On his list of "books read" in the back of his journal for July 1838 to December 1840 are some 270 titles, many of them multi-volume works, including books in German, French, Latin, and Greek. And this list is not complete; a comparison to the list of more than 100 titles of books Parker charged out of the college library over the same period reveals only about thirty titles in common. Besides, Parker wrote reviews and notices of books on neither list, and there is anecdotal evidence that he read still others.

The voracious and omnivorous study habits manifest at theological school had not lost their force. Among the books Parker devoured from 1837 through 1840 were David Brewster's *Treatise on Magnetism*, Goethe's *Farbenlehre*, and (possibly as an antidote to Goethe) Brewster's *Treatise on Optics*, with notes by Alexander Bache; travel books, such as those by Carsten Niebuhr, Johann Burckhardt, and Marco Polo (as translated by William Marsden); volumes of ancient English and Spanish ballads; *An Historical Essay on Architecture*, by Thomas Hope; the first volume of Tocqueville's *Democracy in America* (as translated by Reeve), and Fourierist works; *Oliver Twist, Nicholas Nickleby*, and even a few volumes of English and American poetry.

Parker organized his studies roughly into courses. In 1838, one of these was on English Platonism; he read books by and about Cudworth, More, and John Smith. In the spring of 1840, he began to "restudy" all of Goethe, speeding through the complete *Werke* and Döring's *Leben*, while jotting copious notes in his journal. On 1 June of that year, he began a systematic survey of Greek literature, which ran well into 1841. Those Greek writers he knew already, he examined more carefully. He was already quite familiar with Homer's epics; in the summer of 1837, he had been reading a passage of the *Iliad* every day. Now he examined different Greek editions of the *Iliad*, the *Odyssey*, and the "Hymns," translations by Chapman, Hobbes, and Voss, and numerous commentaries, including those of Friedrich Schlegel. Then Parker worked his way in a similar fashion through Hesiod, Pindar, Solon, Phocylides, Aeschylus, Sophocles, Euripides, Anacreon, and Meleager (whose odes to what Parker called the "odious vice" of homosexuality disgusted him).

The major part of Parker's reading, like his principal writing projects, concerned philosophy, theology, and especially biblical criticism and ancient and church history. His reading lists are crowded with introductions, commentaries, *Lehrbücher*, and *Handbücher*—among them, *Wolfenüttel Fragments* (which he finally read), Richard Cumberland's *Essay on Jewish Weights and Measures*, Georg Adler on biblical voyages to Rome, Heinrich Hävernick's handbook of historical-critical introductions to the Old Testament, Heinrich Gesenius on Isaiah, Johann Michaelis on Jeremiah, Johann Eichhorn on the Hebrew prophets, Ernst Rosenmüller on Daniel, and several major works by the reactionary confessionalist E. W. Hengstenberg. In 1842, in Parker's essay on German literature, he was able to reel off scores of names of the German scholars with which he was familiar. Yet Parker seems to have had comparatively little direct contact with the writings of the major modern German philosophers and theologians—Kant, Fichte, Schleiermacher, Schelling, and Hegel. Just how little is indicated by a letter to him from Frederic Henry Hedge, written in August 1838.

Hedge was responding to a letter from Parker, now lost, in which Parker had asked him which German books he should read and purchase. Hedge was the obvious person to ask: he had studied in Germany when young and knew German philosophy and literature better than anyone else in the Transcendentalist circle. He urged Parker to read Kant, "whose every word is valuable"; to begin with his miscellaneous writings, or the *Anthropology*, then make enough of a study of the *Critique of Pure Reason* to "get a good idea of its leading positions," move on to the *Critique of Practical Reason* and *Critique of Judgement*, and then return to the first *Critique*. Other titles that Hedge recommended for purchase were Fichte's *Bestimmung des Menschen*, which he considered the philosopher's great work, as well as his *Wissenschaftslehre*, "the most thorough & systematic work of philosophy since Spinoza's *Ethics*," Schelling's *Von der Weltseele*, *System des transzendentalen Idealismus*, and *Naturphilosophie*, and, too, Hegel's *Encyclopädie*.[11]

Hedge wrote as if Parker had been a tyro in the field; Parker probably approached him in this guise, but it may have been something of a pose. Parker occasionally feigned ignorance when asking experts what books to read on a topic, hoping thereby to get a complete list. Yet Hedge's perception that

Parker knew little may have been accurate. Although there is evidence that Parker had read Kant's *Anthropology* and *Religion within the Limits of Mere Reason* while at Harvard, no book by Kant is on Parker's reading lists until December 1841, when the *Religion*, the *Critique of Pure Reason*, and the *Critique of Practical Reason*, suddenly appear. Was Parker merely seeking citations, while he rushed to prepare his *Discourse of Matters Pertaining to Religion*?

What was true of Parker's reading in Kant was also true of the other major German thinkers. Of all them, he seems to have been most directly familiar with Schelling: he read the German's lectures on academic study in the summer of 1836; charged his *Ideen zu einer Philosophie der Natur* out of the college library in January 1839 and again in May 1841; that same month charged out his *Einleitungen zu dem Entwurf eines Systems der Naturphilosophie*; and in January 1842, a volume of his "philosophical writings" appears on Parker's reading list. Parker evidently read some Fichte while studying ethics in the summer of 1837, but no other work by him appears on Parker's lists until 1841, when the *Critique of All Revelation* shows up. No work by Hegel appears until the *Philosophy of Religion* in late 1841. With Schelling, Fichte, and Hegel, as with Kant, Parker appears to have been adding footnotes to the *Discourse* in late 1841 and early 1842. At no time does Parker make a systematic study of any German writer other than Goethe.

If Parker's reading in the German idealists themselves was haphazard, he did read extensively in the German secondary literature. Observations on Kant, Hegel, and Schleiermacher, for example, all appear in his journal in the summer of 1838; they were copied out of F. C. Baur's *Christian Gnosticism*. Other observations in his journal on the German intellectual scene were culled from various German journals that came Parker's way, such as the Jena *Allgemeine Literatur Zeitung*, the Berlin *Jahrbuch*, or *Studien und Kritiken*.

Occasionally, the ideas and terminology of a German thinker did stick with him. Parker absorbed Herder's theory, for example, that each people was to develop an idea in history. Again, Parker adopted a famous definition from Friedrich Schleiermacher. Several works by the "Father of Modern Theology" appear in Parker's lists of the books he read or are referenced in Parker's writings. From these sources, he appears by 1842 to have looked through or perused Schleiermacher's lectures on the New Testament, his commentary on Plato, his *History of Christianity*, and his magnum opus on Christian belief. Parker came to use Schleiermacher's best-known idea, that religion is grounded in an innate "sense of dependence." Parker used the term "sense of dependence" for the first time in a sermon from October 1838; thereafter it became his standard way of describing the "religious element in man."[12]

Insofar as Parker did understand the great German thinkers, he often disagreed with them. In 1841, for instance, he translated into his journal F. C.

Baur's comments on Hegel's Trinitarian Christology. As Parker reads Baur, Hegel believes that the nature of God is to objectify God's self, but God must remain identical with God's self. So there is a separation in God that is immediately restored in the divine idea. The Son proceeds from God and stands beside God, but this division returns to unity in the Absolute Spirit. Parker rejected this entire line of reasoning out of hand: "It seems to me the whole question seems to rest on a false position viz that J[esus] of Naz[areth], was the *Supreme Being*. Admit that he was a man—the noblest man who ever lived, admit that if I do my duty as faithfully I shall be equally accepted by God— the mystery is all over. I am perpetually astonished that men should reason so—on such notice." A little later, he wrote to his friend Silsbee, quoting "a Hegelian" (Baur?) who thinks that God first comes to consciousness in Adam (that is, in a human being), and to self-consciousness in Christ who is the sum total of humanity. Thus God could never say "I" nor distinguish between the divine "me" and "not me" until the birth of Jesus. "With all Reverence for Philosophy," comments Parker, "I would ask, 'Who told him this?' "[13]

Parker's ideas remained closer to Platonism than to German idealism. Hence Parker found "revolting" the Hegelian concept of God developing self-consciousness through human history. This was antithetical to his Platonic idea of God as the ultimate perfection and to his fundamental belief that we must strive to become as perfect as God. Yet Parker was willing to adopt a piece of Hegelian terminology when it served his purposes; so in 1841 he began to call his conception of the religious ideal toward which humanity had been striving throughout history "Absolute Religion."

Parker's debt to the German biblical critics was not as superficial as to the philosophers. Biblical criticism had a clear effect on him: it undermined his early faith in the authority of the Bible and historical Christianity and forced him to consider rebuilding theology on a new basis. The critics who most influenced Parker in this period were the most radical, De Wette and David Strauss. Parker's early and enduring involvement with De Wette has been noted. As for Strauss, Parker later recalled reading the first copy of his explosive *Das Leben Jesu* to reach America, brought in 1836 by a student who had been studying in Germany.[14] In the winter of 1839–40, Parker made a careful study of Strauss in order to write a long review of his book for the *Christian Examiner*, and so read the second and third editions, as well as the *Streitschriften* the book had engendered.

Parker quickly absorbed De Wette's deconstruction of the Old Testament, no doubt because it was not so important to his religious belief. The New Testament was central. Strauss's work, which undermined the historical credibility of the Gospels, was therefore much harder for him to accept. If Parker first read Strauss in 1836, then it took him more than two years to begin to face his arguments.

Strauss was less than three years older than Parker and an even greater prodigy.[15] He was only twenty-seven when, in 1835, he published the first edition of his *Life of Jesus*. It had an unsettling effect not only on Parker, but on everyone who read it. Strauss advanced a comprehensive critique of the two prevailing interpretations of the Gospel stories. The Supernaturalists accepted the accounts as literally true; Strauss believed that their view was unreasonable and begged too many questions. The Rationalists, who included many prominent German biblical critics, thought the Gospels were based on fact, but argued that the truth had been obscured by legend and poetry; the miracle stories were exaggerated accounts of natural events. The Rationalists, Strauss argued, made unwarranted assumptions and their explanations were often convoluted and unconvincing. Strauss's view was simple and elegant: the Gospels emerged out of an unconscious myth-making process. The Jews had expected a messiah, these expectations had somehow latched onto the historical figure of Jesus, and almost all the Gospel stories, above all the stories of the miracles, had arisen from the effort to make the life of the historical Jesus match these messianic expectations. Strauss thought that we can know nothing of the historical Jesus, who has been lost in a haze of myth.

Parker felt the power of Strauss's argument years before he would accept any of the German's conclusions. The idea that such a plausible case could be made against the historicity of the Gospels raised at least a doubt in his mind. Theology, obviously, had to be constructed on a new foundation. But how was this to be done?

Parker's answer, which he came to quickly, was that theology ought to be a "science." It should be based on hypotheses that could be tested against facts. He first suggested this publicly in a short article he wrote for the *Christian Register* in the fall of 1837. In this satiric piece, Parker assumed the voice of an alarmed young conservative. Many sciences are advancing, he says here, "some perhaps have passed already through two of the three stages which all must permeate — to wit, *hypothesis, experiment* and *internal development*" — while theology, the science of sciences, remains stationary. But is this not, comes the ironic question, because theology is already perfect? The critical study of Scripture places theology on a level with the other sciences, casting off error and adding truth. If this is done, "what becomes of the infinite perfection of theology?"[16]

WEEK IN and week out, Parker in his preaching set out to foster among his congregants a perfectionist, Platonic piety. This piety, although not unique to Transcendentalism, was for Parker an essential part of it. This spirituality grew from his own experience and reflection; in the way he described and applied it, it was necessarily bound to the attitudes and biases of his time and place, even as Parker aimed to transcend them. Yet for him it was the fortress from which he would launch his attacks on traditional theology and social injustice; it was the rock on which he could build. It was for him the essence of Absolute Religion.

His sermons elaborated certain "truths of faith": the divine nature of man; the human capacity for endless spiritual growth; the immortality of the soul; the perpetual presence of God and so of God's perfect Wisdom, Goodness, and Love; and "a confidence that this world is the best world possible, or even conceivable, that it will work out an infinite Good to each Soul at last."[17]

The key proposition was the "nobleness of man's nature." The expansive force of our intellect, Parker believed, is seen in the development of the individual and of our institutions, laws, and sciences. Our moral qualities are even loftier, for although our intellectual achievements may be the result of selfishness, we are capable of disinterested love for Justice and Truth. Above all are our religious instincts, which make us aware of the perpetual presence of God. Hence arises our love of God, for we only love what we know.[18]

And what we resemble: "*We are the offspring of God*—therefore *God is our father, we are like him in nature, in attributes*." Thus we are spiritual beings and possessed of an immortal soul "which is without doubt nobler & more valuable than all the universe of matter." To say God is infinite and man finite is false, for the human spirit is immortal: "[Is] there not trace of Infinity in man? Is not each of his noblest affections infinite?" We must share with God our spiritual qualities. How could we speak of God's Goodness, Wisdom, Justice, and Love if we did not know from within ourselves what they were? True, God is infinitely superior to us in these qualities ("like the sun to a lighted cigar"), but our duty is to perfect them all, that is, to perfect our character. Perfection was the standard Parker actually set for daily life: listed among his New Year's resolutions for 1840 was the awesome injunction to "do nothing imperfectly."[19]

There is, Parker believed, "not only a natural tendency towards a perfection in all noble & divine attributes, but a *deep want* of it in the human heart." So the average of thought and religion always was progressing through history; "humanity has been going up for 6000 years." Parker admitted that history presents us with "a tissue of complicated wickedness that perplexes the subtlest understanding." In the summer of 1839, he read a history of Asia and wondered in his journal how its kingdoms could rise and fall, seeming to "leave not trace in the world," producing a "wall of tears & blood—fanned & blown upon & heaped up by prayers, curses & groans of soldier, widow, orphan, violated virgin, yet no good end produced thereby?" Why is there "all this prodigious waste of pain & blood & life?" Reason could offer him no answers. "But happily there is a better guide. Faith . . . assures that all these seeming evils are so contrived that no real sorrow can befall the soul, but for its own good." As he said in a sermon a year later, Religion enables one to see that "this abomination of sin[,] this administration of crime[,] are but the first awkward & mistaken steps, the boy man essays to make, in his early attempts to get forward."[20]

Man, then, according to his nature, is a being who "never stands still, completely satisfied with his attainments. The spot his young eyes looked upon as the very top of the mountain, he has left far beneath & behind him as he has traveled upward & on & still the way lengthens before him." Parker, like Wordsworth and Bronson Alcott, thought that children were closer to God than adults: "Heaven is about us in our infancy but the Shades of the Prison house soon begin to close in upon us . . . & soon this day-spring from on High fades away into the light of common day." Still, if we educate ourselves properly, we naturally will find within us as we mature "an Idea of Being every way perfect, just, powerful, lovely, holy." This idea is always before us as a model. Thus we can understand Jesus when he says, Be perfect as your Father in Heaven. "Am I told," Parker cried, "that . . . there is no resemblance between man & God? That we can never imitate even in the remotest degree the wisdom, love, Holyness [sic], perfection of God! If this be true then perish Truth, Perish [Christianity], Perish man's hope in life, his Hope in death. A worm is he, a worm he shall continue."[21]

God has given us means to perfect ourselves as boundless as the need; the "whole world is his seminary for training up the Sons of man."[22] Christianity is one such means. Although Parker came to question the miraculous authority of the Christian revelation, he held that we have been helped immeasurably in the pursuit of perfection by its influence and above all by the epochal example of Jesus. Jesus came closest of anyone in history to fulfilling the law of God in the soul; he was the model man who revealed to us our potential. Parker expressed this view in December 1836, during his candidacy, in a poem he wrote in his journal. Originally titled "Jesus," it was published in the *Register* a few months later; a later version of it was to become by the end of the century a popular Unitarian hymn:

> Jesus, there is no name dearer than thine,
> 　　Which Time has blazoned on his ample scroll:
> No wreaths, nor garlands ever did entwine
> 　　So fair a Temple or so vast a Soul.
> Ay, every Angel set his comely seal
> 　　Upon thy brow, and gave each human grace,
> In a sweet copy Heaven to reveal,
> 　　And stamp Perfection on a mortal face:
> Once on the earth, before dull mortal eyes,
> 　　—Which could not half thy sacred radiance see,
> (E'en as the emmet cannot read the skies,)

For our weak orbs reach not immensity—
Once on the Earth wast Thou a living shrine
Where shone the GOOD, the LOVELY, the DIVINE.[23]

The church, too, was at least potentially a means of perfection: "Every faculty has its own machinery in the world, so if there are schools for the head there are churches for the heart." But the voice of the church is but one in a thousand. God employs all of nature to educate us.[24]

Like Emerson, Parker thought every natural object had spiritual significance. What use is the beauty of flowers? To teach us some lesson. Why are morning and evening "dressed in holiday robes"? Not just to please the eye, but to awaken the soul to all that is grand and noble. The stars do not merely guide travelers: "He that looks on them after his day of toil & disturbance, feels unconsciously a cool tranquillity steal into his breast."[25]

Parker was here, in a sermon from the summer of 1839, referring to a personal experience. One night the previous winter, he was walking home from Boston after a meeting of the Boston Association. "The stars were unusually bright & large," he wrote in his journal. "The pale northern lights came out. . . . The air was clear, cool. The great bear looked like a constellation of suns, that kept watch over the Earth. I had become somewhat excited by silent meditation, when I stopped to look on the H[eavens] more attentively. A little brook—not bound by the frost ran beside th[e] road & emitted that clear tinkle so remarkable when white ice covers part of the water." Inspired, he composed a poem:

> The things that are around us
>   What wondrous truths they tell
> Though flesh to Earth hath bound us
>   It doeth its office well.
> The sunshine in its splendour
>   The meeker moon by night
> The stars that do attend her
>   and people the Vast night
> The holy ear address,
>   and tranquilly they whisper
> Their word of holiness.[26]

Tranquillity was one of nature's greatest lessons. "In God's universe there is nowhere any rest—but never any hurry. All the creative work is done in silence, without haste." Parker often returned to the subject of tranquillity because he thought the lack of it was a sign of the times—and perhaps because he perceived tranquillity as "one of my *attainable* but unattained virtues"; among his 1840 New Year's resolutions was "Become tranquil." In nature, every law is perfectly obeyed, because each thing is simply the expression of a law: "At the formation of each particular thing certain laws were impressed upon it which the thing obeys, e.g. a trout must swim in the *water* & a blackbird fly in the air." According to Parker's neoplatonic understanding of natural laws, the law is the "essence" of the object, as heat is the essence of fire, so that "the object could not exist without the L[aw]." The law of nature is the action of God in nature. Because God is perfectly obeyed, all creatures are perfectly fulfilled. "You shall search all the birds of all the flocks: do you find one melancholy or wretched?" [27]

We are meant to be industrious, temperate, intelligent, just, and holy, but unlike the things of nature, we are free to disobey the laws of our being. And we all do disobey them to some degree. In the grave and tranquil world of nature, "man is the only joke." [28] The perfect fulfillment of the law of God in nature reveals to us, by analogy, the life we should lead.

Parker conceded that there were things in nature he found "utterly incomprehensible." Animals appear to be cruel to each other, as the cat to the mouse. They often seem to behave immorally: the eagle robs the fishhawk; the alligator devours its young; red ants enslave black ones. Then there was the troubling sexual behavior of beasts. Parker himself had seen two older male squirrels castrate a young one. What to make of dogs who "wanting females commit sodomy" (a "crime against nature")? Or of the "onanism of apes"? Or of frogs sitting on the backs of trout and casting their seed? Considering all these things, "I should think there was a dark ground in the cause of the world," wrote Parker in his journal, "or that matter had some qualities which *the Deity* could not control, were it not inconsistent with common sense." At one point, Parker privately speculated, with Bronson Alcott, that "the world is the product of all man. So long as men do such things animals will do likewise." The "world we life [*sic*] on is a good type of man. It resembles him quite closely. The animals . . . prefigure all his vices." His basic response, however, was one of faith — "*Trust then the all-father.*" As Parker said in a sermon, "*If all things are [not] ordered for the good of* EACH, *if there is in the world any pain not compensated for, any evil not liquidated by a good at last, there is no certain hope for you or me, now or for eternity.*" [29]

An even more important means of perfection than nature was the home — or at least, the home as it ought to be. It was the "only institution on Earth formed by God — & unchangeable." The moral nature of children was educated mostly in the home, and it was the seat of religious education as well. Parents are to "tempt forth the little spirit" of their child, teach it duty and self-denial, afford it precepts and silent examples. "The Spirit of the Mother will interpenetrate the Spirit of the child. . . . The Father has a divine right over the mind of his child. It is given by God himself. Religious impressions made early on the mind rarely fade out even . . . in the deeps of old age." Be-

I Preach Abundant Heresies

yond this, the family relation cultivates our social feelings: "How wondrously is the lot of daily household life woven up, of small kind offices, wh[ich] seem insignificant; the kind greeting; the gentle reply; the delicate enquiry; the bland smile; the anticipation of a wish; the prevention of a want!" Only in the home do the "genial feelings of the soul have free play."[30]

The home "as it is" was not like this, as Parker himself knew all too well. Men and women "will not control passion or suppress anger." They "are too indolent to be kind & affectionate." The father is passionate; the mother is irritating. Small incidents set off quarrels that last for hours and are remembered for months.[31]

Nonetheless, Parker liked to contrast the ideal home with the larger world of toils, which "blunts the better feelings, makes men circumspect, watchful, jealous, selfish." The home, he said, "should be a green bower in the heat," an "ark in the storm, to bear us above the troubles of the world." The ideal family "is the nearest & most beautiful type of Heaven ever yet devised." Heaven itself "is only a larger home, where God is the parents, all men brothers & sisters, united by love."[32]

Despite Parker's claim that the world of toils "hardens a man & renders him selfish," and his recognition, after 1838, of the problems of labor exploitation, he held that every legitimate human occupation was potentially a means of educating the soul. Labor should not be seen as a curse, or a disgrace, but a blessing. It is the law of the body, producing not only food, raiment, and all desirable things, but strength and bodily health. Labor educates the intellect, for a man must exercise the mind to ply his trade. It strengthens a man morally, for in the world his morals are constantly tested; also, through toil for others, as a father for his child, we learn selflessness and how to brave difficulties. And a man's religious sentiments are excited by his calling, as when the farmer learns by experience how the laws of nature work for him.[33]

Nature, Christianity, the home, labor—Parker found it "melancholy" that with all these means of perfection available to us, most people failed to take advantage of them. Here we are, he would say, possessed of a soul, the crown of the Almighty's works, that can never end, that is designed for everlasting improvement until it "outshine the seraphs," that is surrounded by the spectacle of nature, "visited & sustained by the spirit of the living God"—and yet we live without an effort to improve. We sit complacent on our achievements. But what man has achieved in virtue and holiness is "only a whisper of his capacities & as no more to all he can compass in his path than a single leaf to the forest."[34]

Parker thus lamented "the degradation of men at this time, their low aims, and worthless pleasures." The young minister would return often to the case of men and women just starting out in life. What goals do they set for themselves? Young men seek Fame, Pleasure, and Wealth; or they wish to be

Heroes, "brave, bold, daring, sudden & quick in a quarrel, fearless in speech, & not restrained by any puritanical scruples." Young women, although in Parker's view more inherently religious than men, care mostly for bodily beauty, gaiety of garment, and "foolish things." Both men and women want to take the most from society and give back the least. They do not wish to be like God. They value Seeming over Being. Why do they not aim instead to perfect all their spiritual faculties, intellectual, moral, and religious—especially the last two?[35]

The moral faculty was Conscience, "God's Vice-Regent on Earth," the part of us that "most resembles the Supreme Being." At the level of theory, Parker argued that the conscience was infallible. In January 1839, he had a discussion with Dr. Channing on the subject. Parker held that the conscience could not be educated and could not err, but Channing hesitated to agree with him. Seeking common ground, the younger man wondered if the problem was only that "the understanding should be rendered capable of presenting the case distinctly to the conscience." Channing "seemed to favor" this idea, yet he doubted that people needed an infallible guide, for "the belief in such a beast had led to the theory that S[acred] S[cripture] was inspired word for word." Parker insisted that conscience "will always decide right if the case is fairly put, & old habits have not obscured its vision." Channing was more moderate: if a man began to use conscience only late in life, he would doubtless make great errors; yet, "[o]n the whole, if a man should begin early to ask for the Right, with sincere wish to find it, he would never get far out of the way."[36]

Channing's reservations apparently led Parker to modify his opinions somewhat. A few months later, when he returned to the subject in a sermon, he continued to hold that "C[onscience] in itself is doubtless infallible," but stressed, perhaps more strongly than he had earlier, that "in practice it commits missteps, or rather, the understanding does not state the case clearly for the conscience to decide." In a sermon a few months later still, he was willing to concede Channing's point, that a conscience "*imperfectly* trusted, or only now and then obeyed, often misleads." Yet sin, for Parker, remained the "voluntary violation of what we know to be right."[37]

As a practical matter, Parker always urged moral education and improvement. Here he faced a familiar problem for New England ministers: his congregation, with a few exceptions, was made up of "good, quiet, sober, church-going" people, who seemed pretty moral already. In familiar New England fashion, he held that this was not enough. The "rule of morality," he claimed, "is stiff without being very high." Public opinion mandates outward morality, so actions "cease to be the test of the motives of goodness." Good deeds lose their goodness if done from bad motives, and our motives are low. People are honest only because it is the best policy. People are charitable only because

I Preach Abundant Heresies

public opinion would condemn us if we were not. People wish only to be as moral as everyone else. People believe sin is sweet and are as sinful as they think they can get away with.[38]

Parker repeatedly urged "self-examination." We must measure ourselves every day by ultimate standards. We must always ask, "What is the law of my nature, or what is the will of God, that I ought to keep?" We should want to do the best things in the best way from the best motives. No foible or fault is too small to correct. He who "despised small things . . . falls by little & little, but just as certainly, as a stone falls from a high place, with increased swiftness to the ground."[39]

Being moral, however, was not enough; we must also be religious. Parker always distinguished between the two. In his most popular sermon (he preached it twenty-five times between 1838 and 1841 to congregations around Boston), he attacked the idea that "a man is *religious* just so far as he is *moral*, & no farther." People may be just, unselfish, and benevolent, and yet not be religious. "The principle of morality is obedience to the Law of con[science]: the sentiment of M[orality] is love to your fellow men." The principle of religion was that we "feel naturally, allegiance to a superior Being: dependence upon him & accountability to him"; the sentiment of religion, meanwhile, was love of God.[40]

Being religious required prayer. "No feeling is more deeply planted in human nature than the tendency to adore a superior being," he said, "to reverence him, to bow before him, to feel his presence, to pray to him for aid in times of need[;] to bless him when the heart is full of joy." He recognized the "indirect benefits" of prayer—that in order to pray a worshiper had to "compose his spirit" to do what must be done and bear what must be borne. But he denied that prayer only affected the one who prayed. Our relation to God "is the most tender & intimate: that of a child to its Father. [D]oth not the Father listen to his child; does he not grant his requests?" We do not know how prayer influences God, but we know that God rewards such as diligently seek him.[41]

Prayers could be vocal or silent, but they should be regular. Prayer fortifies us against the difficulties of life. By timely prayer we "renew & strengthen the soul" for the trials of the coming day. The length, vehemence, and frequency of prayers should not be prized of themselves. He noted that sincerely religious Unitarians are "abashed & discouraged" by the evangelicals who claim they can pray all night, without food or sleep. But a short prayer is better than a long one, for "our petitions can be addressed in very few words." A prayer should be a "mild, gentle breathing of the soul." And one well-done prayer is better than many ill-done ones. Prayer is an act of the intellect as well as the heart. The whole mind should be awake during prayer; prayer should not be performed in the drowsy time between sleeping and waking. Prayer is an act of faith: a strong and unhesitating confidence that God will order all things so as in the best possible way to produce our well-being in time and eternity. Prayer, then, was a means of achieving Godliness. And Godliness is "Godlikeness"—that is, resemblance to God.[42]

Our failure to perfect our character and become Godlike exacts on us a retribution, and not just in the future: "No[,] the Almighty reckons with us every day."[43] God has so ordered the universe that each of us is rewarded in this life for his character, and this recompense is generally just. Temperance usually leads to health, industry to competence, contentment brings happiness, while honesty brings respect, and so on. Yet compensation in this life is never complete.

As Parker's thought matured, and he reflected on his own experience, he became more alive to the apparent unjustness of suffering. In a sermon from October 1837, he could declare that "Job & others in very rare cases might say they did not deserve the treatment they received," but within a year (the year he was married and settled), he had decided that the picture Job presents is "very common." After his thirtieth birthday, he would say in a sermon that to "a thoughtful mind, most faces that have seen 30 winters & summers are scarred all over with the wounds they have got in the battle of life." Sorrows are not avoided by doing right. Did not Jesus and Paul suffer? Like them, we suffer from the sins of the others. And, as we grow more perfect, we suffer because we are all the more aware of our remaining imperfections. This world is, then, not the house of happiness. The end of life is not happiness but education, and sorrows have their lessons.[44]

Sorrows, afflictions, and failures, more than anything else, impart nobleness of soul. Here Parker felt he was teaching from experience. In a parable, "A fable of Calid," which Parker wrote in his journal in the summer of 1839 and used in a sermon some months later, the prophet Mohammed asks a friend to bring before him "the man who had done the noblest & most in life." After a long search, the friend brings Calid to Mohammed. Calid had been born poor and ignoble, but was now rich, honored, wise, and successful in all he had undertaken. Mohammed smiles and says that although Calid has used his success wisely, it now enfeebles him, because he rests satisfied with his attainments. Mohammed then turns to Calid's slave, who was born noble and rich, whose life has been one of outward failure, and says that "the world has been of more use to him than to thee or me, though called the great Prophet. He has wisdom, we cannot measure. . . . His disasters forced him to rely on himself, so there stands a man whom all the world teaches." Mohammed then allows his friend to see the angel of death take Calid and his slave from their mortal surroundings. Although Calid's soul is "glowing & majestic," that of his slave "towers above him like a colossus."[45]

I Preach Abundant Heresies

In this world, then, a man "should remember that every act of his, nay every word—nay every deliberate thought—every cherished feeling—is a seed corn cast into the ever-living & germinating Soil of his Spirit." Everywhere in the universe, "there is a perfect system of Profit & Loss. . . . The time a man steals from his proper devotions & hours consecrated to the improvement of his immortal self—& what he foolishly squanders—is just so much taken from . . . [his] happiness." Because our spirit is immortal, the consequences of our all acts, thoughts, and feelings are eternal.[46]

Parker denounced the "monstrous doctrine of eternal punishment" as "extravagant," contrary to reason, and to our understanding of a just God. But he found equally extravagant the opposite doctrine (promoted by Universalists like Hosea Ballou) that there is "no retribution at all for offenses." He thought the vice of Universalism "is that it overlooks too much the exceeding sinfulness of Sin; the horrors of an outraged conscience, nay the power of conscience itself, & the fact that Sin, is the greatest of evils, a man endure[s], & must continue so long as the Sin lasts, & this can only be removed by man's own act, though Providence offer never so many occasions for regeneration." Someone who loses willfully the years of this life in sin "can never stand just as he would have stood—had those years been wisely spent in holiness." Hell, like the Kingdom of God, is within us, and the "Prince of Darkness is every wicked man."[47]

Still, fear of retribution, or desire for happiness, in this or a future life, were low, "commercial" reasons to be religious. Was religion to be merely a "working for wages"? How foolish to think that humility will be rewarded with splendour, and self-denial with luxury! No—"Character itself is its own recompense." Parker speculated that there was a hierarchy of religiousness: "fear" of God was found among the savages; the Jews "venerated" an Almighty, but unlovely God; the religion of the Greeks and Romans was marked by "hope"—they had to hope, for they knew nothing certain of life after death; "faith" marked the religion of the early martyrs and the Puritans; but the highest religion was that of Christ, Paul, and John: a religion of "perfect, divine love."[48]

The essence of this Absolute Religion is not just right action; nor just raptures and prayers, which of themselves have no more influence on our lives than the reflection of a rainbow has on a lake; nor a negative "statute law," which says "hitherto shall thou come & no further," and so acts as a lion in our path; nor a sentiment, here today and tomorrow gone. No, the essence of Absolute Religion is "a union with God, a *binding together* of what has been long separated. It is a participation of the divine nature, & therefore *it is a divine life*: A life which is animated by those *feelings* & *prayers*[,] perhaps those raptures, which with some make up the whole of Rel[igion]. A life which shows itself in action, in honesty, prudence, charity. . . . Thus it is a rule of life, not a statute law, but a law of the spirit of life, & a sentiment wh[ich] steals freshly up to God."[49]

"I PREACH abundant heresies," announced Parker to William Silsbee in a letter from the fall of 1837, "and they all go down—for the listeners do not know how heretical they are. Nay I preach the worst of all things[,] Transcendentalism, the grand heresy itself—none calling me to account therefore, but men's faces looking like fires new stirred thereat." Parker here suggests boldness—and prudent duplicity. The latter impression is reinforced by another letter to Silsbee, written a year later: Parker says he feels bound to communicate his views "just so fast and so far as men understand them, and no farther." From 1837 to 1839, Parker grappled with the thorny problem of how fast and far he should communicate the increasingly radical ideas about religious authority that were coming to characterize his Transcendentalist theology.[50]

The first two sermons Parker preached as pastor of his congregation, on 25 June 1837, the Sunday after his ordination, can be read as examples of his couching new ideas in traditional language. Parker adopts a cautious and conservative tone. The ministry, he says, is based on an innate human need to develop our spiritual powers; he would seem to have no truck with radicals who would dissolve the institutions of the church and "priesthood." The means of a minister, he continues, are of "God's appointment." Among them are the public reading of Sacred Scripture: "Here is an authority, the irresistible authority of Truth. . . . Who would *dare* teach on such subject[s], with only his own wisdom to guide and suggest!" He urges his parishioners to attend services even if the preaching is dull, because eloquent preaching is rarely the most profitable, and hearing Sacred Scripture is worth a dull sermon. He concludes his second sermon with a traditional exhortation that sounds almost like that of a fusty old Federalist in President Jefferson's day: "I need not say that the support of religious institutions is the duty of every man who has a soul—for he knows that he has as great an interest in them as every other man . . . nor of every patriot—for who does not know that no state can stand a twelve-month unless rel[igion] be the deep foundation thereof: nor of every father, brother, sister . . . for they too must know that without Rel[igion] the altar of Home is desecrated[,] the Peace of families destroyed & misery made to take the place of domestic bliss."[51]

Yet these sermons, despite their old-fashioned sound, provide the first hint of how rapidly Parker's thinking on authority had evolved in the year since he left theological school. He bases the authority of the church and of Scripture not on miracles and tradition, but exclusively on nature and Truth. In the second sermon, he says that the only authority is that of Truth: "Even the apostles who had miraculous powers taught nothing by other authority:

I Preach Abundant Heresies

never asked men to believe from hearsay but to prove all things & hold firm to that wh[ich] was good. Jesus even appeals only to this. Nay, his highest claim was that he was the king of Truth & for that end was sent into the world."[52] Although Parker assumes that miracles happened as the Bible says they did, he holds that they were not needed to prove that Christianity was a divine revelation. He seems to believe, like Ripley in the Martineau review, that miracles cannot be used to prove a revelation, but he does not say so explicitly. Like Ripley, Parker calls for free inquiry.

Parker continued to attack the authority of tradition and to call for free inquiry in both public and private writings from the remaining months of 1837. "If I were a painter," wrote Parker to Silsbee in November, "I would represent AUTHORITY—the 'great GODDESS' of the conservatives—as a giant of prodigious strength, seizing her followers by the 'handle of the face' and dragging them onward—herself going *backward* all the while—*looking* backward also, and by standing before the eyes of her followers preventing them from seeing the ditch they are all—leaders and led—about to fall into."[53]

He pursued the assault (with less vivid imagery) in some of his sermons. In one, on the foundation of morality, he argued that it was based on the innate knowledge of right and wrong, and not on the command of God in the biblical revelation: "With all due deference for Revelation, it must be remembered that without some rule of Right [within,] we can never distinguish the revealed from the common. . . . What is not in man can not be got *out of him*." In a sermon on the meaning of truth, he attacked those who had preconceived opinions, judgments before the fact; they had inherited their ideas from their ancestors, "along with their landed estates." He urged that no one "ought ever to fear to stand alone in the defense of a Truth." In a sermon on the Lord's Supper, delivered on the first Sunday he administered it, he defended the rite as "one of the most important helpers and assistants" on a soul's spiritual course, yet insisted that if "after the faithful use of all one's faculties . . . [a man] thinks it is *not* his duty, then plainly it is not for another to say *it is*."[54]

Parker was risking controversy to suggest that the Lord's Supper was a matter of individual judgment. But no evidence of a controversy survives, although members of his congregation surely felt more strongly about the Lord's Supper than he did. Parker often remarked that the communion service was helpful to "old women." The speculation is irresistible that Aunt Lucy was one of the old women he had in mind. The doubts of the Aunt Lucys in his congregation probably were eased, because Parker was willing to continue to administer the bread and the wine.

Besides, the Lord's Supper was not at the heart of the problem of authority. The Bible was. The covenant of Parker's own church, approved only a few years earlier, recognized the "divine authority of the Holy Scriptures" and made them the "rule of faith and practice." Yet the whole course of Parker's thinking was to question the authority of the Bible. It might have "the authority of Truth," as Parker said it did in his "Christian Ministry" sermon, but that was all the authority it could have. What, then, if the Bible was not true?

Parker concluded it often was not. In 1837 and 1838, before he began seriously to confront the problems raised by Strauss, his concerns centered on the Old Testament and had two different sources, one critical, the other pastoral. His critical study of the Hebrew books, made while he labored on his edition of De Wette, had convinced him that they were largely inauthentic and mostly "mythological." In late 1837, after he read a German translation of Palaiphatos, an ancient Greek rationalist who tried to debunk Greek myths by arguing they were only highly embellished accounts of mundane events (e.g., the Hydra that Hercules fought was not really a many-headed serpent, but a town called Hydra defended by fifty bowmen), Parker commented that "such books do good," and added: "I wish some wise man would now write a book . . . and show up the absurdity of certain things commonly believed, on the authority of old Jews. To be plain, I mean the Old Testament miracles, prophecies, dreams, miraculous births, etc."[55]

He expressed these concerns in a short but important piece published in the *Christian Register*. When he submitted it to Chandler Robbins, the editor, he enclosed a note saying he hoped it would stir up zeal for a careful study of the Bible. Published in November 1837, it appeared over the pseudonym "W." Its title was "Reasons why a clergyman should not study the Scriptures carefully and critically."[56]

The ironic tone of the title is maintained throughout. The piece purports to be a letter from W., "a very young minister," who is full of doubts, to "a very old one," apparently his mentor, who holds conservative views. W. worries that there are "many *dangers*, real dangers," attending the critical study of the Bible. It leads to new opinions, "which are always dangerous, as you have often told me, and above all dangerous in matters of religion." It casts doubt upon many matters, "which, as you say, is bad upon any subject and sinful in religion." And it leads to the wrong notion of inspiration. "I confess, my dear sir," concludes W., "that I found so many difficulties and dangers attending the study of the Scriptures . . . I intend to abandon it altogether."

W.'s comments on inspiration are clear evidence that Parker had by this time concluded there was no distinction between natural and revealed religion. Careful examination of Scripture, says W., shows that a vicious man is never inspired to teach virtue, nor a foolish man to impart wisdom. Instead, "those men accounted the most highly inspired, were, *naturally*, men of a far reaching intellect, and a mighty grasp of thought." Great powers of mind and body are called inspiration, "if one looks critically."

I Preach Abundant Heresies

Parker then turns to the problems of miracles and of the authenticity of biblical accounts—especially the Old Testament miracles and accounts.[57] After searching the Scriptures, says W., he could not fail to doubt that Moses wrote the Pentateuch, that God commanded Abraham to murder his son, or that Noah, "so soon after the creation, could build an ark as big as the Capitol in Washington, and still less that he could get all the beasts to go into it." How could David give gold and silver valued at 3,936,525,000 dollars toward building the temple, when elsewhere the Scripture says he was poor? W. finds it difficult to believe that all the books of the Old Testament were written by the authors whose names they bear—for example, Daniel and the latter part of Isaiah. How could Jonah live for three days in a whale, and even more, compose a hymn there? "I find it difficult to believe that Balaam's ass spoke— you will say, that he may have been *inspired*—but without exciting your laughter by speaking of an *inspired ass*, for the subject is too grave for ridicule—I would ask if then he would not have spoken to the point?" God spoke to Jacob in a dream. Does this not mean that Jacob dreamed God appeared to him?

Parker's article prompted letters of protest to the editor. The writers ignored Parker's remarks about inspiration, but were outraged by his comments on authenticity and miracles. One said that W.'s article would have been better printed in the paper of Abner Kneeland, the convicted blasphemer, than in the *Register*. Another, from "A Lover of the Bible," complained that W. had not spoken of his difficulties with the miracle stories "in a way less offensive to pious ears": "I confess I never could endure to hear even the strangest stories that we find in the Bible, mentioned in a jesting way. . . . I may possibly be as liberal in my interpretation of the passages referred to in that communication as W. himself; but my feelings and my judgment would forbid me to speak of them in a way [which] would be likely to grieve any lowly disciple of Jesus, or that would give occasion to the enemies of the Bible, to blaspheme."[58]

In private, Parker was appalled by the rebukes. "That anyone could be *such* a dunce," he wrote to Silsbee, "as to take [the piece] in earnest and others such *bad* men as to attribute an evil motive to W!!" He continued: "I might have drained a Black Sea full of ink in scribbling about the importance of the Bible," and been ignored. But in public Parker apologized, in an unsigned letter published in the *Register* on 18 November.[59]

Reading the strictures on his article, he says, has been so agitating that "I can scarcely write, my heart beating *audibly*." If he did wrong, it was with the best intentions—to arouse people to study Scripture. Why, he asks, is the Bible "so little read by thinking, yet imperfectly educated men? This, I believe, to be the reason. *They cannot understand it 'unless someone guide them;'* and where are such guides? . . . I have seen men—strong minded men, struggling with these difficulties; they pressed them like an incubus, which they could not shake off, and which threatened to stifle the life of God in their souls,—what shall these men do?"

Parker does not here challenge the authority of the Bible. But he intimates why he might do so, and his principal reason has nothing to do with either theology or biblical criticism. Rather, his concern is pastoral. In these enlightened times, he is saying, the Bible, improperly understood, has become an obstacle to faith.

So it really seems to have been for many Unitarians of that period. The Old Testament in particular was widely perceived as presenting difficulties. The tendency seen in the writings of Channing, Norton, and Palfrey, to discount the religious significance of the Hebrew Scriptures, was reflected even in weekly preaching. Parker preached from New Testament texts almost three-fifths of the time and from Old Testament texts only a third of the time; the remainder came almost wholly from the two wisdom books of the Apocrypha, Ecclesiasticus, and the Wisdom of Solomon. In the more than 300 sermons he preached in his first seven years as a minister, Parker never chose a text from twenty-six of the thirty-nine Old Testament books. He avoided the Law and the Prophets, the most important parts of the Jewish revelation, concentrating instead on the Psalms and Proverbs; half of all his Old Testament texts came from these two books. By contrast, in the same period, he took texts at least once from twenty-one of the twenty-seven New Testament books. His favorite sources of texts were, in order of preference, Matthew (by far), John, Luke, and Romans. The New Testament books he avoided included the ones he considered the most Jewish in outlook. He never, for example, preached on a text from Mark.[60]

Bias against the Old Testament was not confined to Unitarian intellectuals, but had penetrated deep into the spirituality of the laity. Parker knew of a "wise and thoughtful layman," old but with young children, who would not let them read the Old Testament "lest it should injure their religious character." Parker also recalled talking to a man who had read the "first part" of the Old Testament again (the Pentateuch, presumably), "& *he was sorry he had read it, because he could not believe it, & before he thought he believed all.*" Parker was not the only one to perceive the problem. James Walker, writing in the September 1838 *Christian Examiner*, said that the question "'What shall we do with Old Testament?'" is "of such frequent recurrence among laymen as well as clergymen, that any well-considered attempt to answer it, or supply the means of answering it, is almost sure of hearty welcome."[61]

This question lay behind Parker's call, in his letter to the *Register*, for a new interpretation of the Bible. The people need an interpretation, he says, that "takes human reason as its starting point," clears up the difficulties the Bible contains, reconciles its contradictions "(easily done by the learned—impos-

I Preach Abundant Heresies

sible to the ignorant,)"—"and in one word, sets the whole Bible in the fair, impartial light of Reason." About the time Parker wrote this letter, he attempted just such an interpretation, by writing two sermons on "The Contradictions in Scripture"; Parker came to see these discourses as a turning point in his career. One of their striking features is criticism of the Old Testament.

Because they are animated by Parker's pastoral concern to maintain faith, he bypasses questions of criticism and nowhere discusses the authenticity of any biblical book. But in the first sermon, he does discuss apparent contradictions to reason and to morality in the Bible; all his examples come from the Hebrew Scriptures.[62] Among the contradictions to reason, he explicitly excludes miracles, which he says do not contradict reason; like the other Transcendentalists, Parker still believes that most of the wonder stories in the New Testament literally describe actual events. He believes that those of the Old Testament, however, when literally interpreted, contradict reason. The Creation story in Genesis, for example, contradicts the known facts of science: the Creation did not take six days, but millions of years. He explains that we must simply separate the essential part of this story, that God created the world, from the primitive, poetic dress in which it appears. Similarly, the miracle story of Joshua making the sun and moon stand still, which Parker had defended as literally true seven years before, in his "History of the Jews," he now explains as simply a highly colored, poetic rendering of the Jews pursuing their enemies after the sun set by the light of the moon. Then he notes the intellectually troubling passages in which God appears physically on Earth—for example, walking through the Garden of Eden in the cool of the day. Parker explains these by pointing to a progressive spiritualization of the portrayal of the divine in the Bible that corresponds with the level of civilization in which the particular book was written. In the "rudest" books, God appears physically; in more advanced books, only angels appear; as progress continues, God appears only in visions, and then only in dreams.

More disturbing to him than problems such as these are the apparent contradictions to morality, above all when immoral and evil acts are attributed to God; again, his examples all come from the Old Testament. For instance, Moses orders the Jews, on the authority of God, to massacre the inhabitants of Canaan, a peaceful people at least three million in number. Parker had struggled to defend this command as late as the fall of 1836, in his *Scriptural Interpreter* articles on the "Laws of Moses." Now, just a year later, he condemns the "shifty interpreters of the S[acred] S[cripture]" who "have been at infinite pains to reconcile this with God's justice." They will never succeed, he says, because the heart feels this action is unjust. He argues instead that, in such cases, human action was being attributed to God, something that was commonly done among ancient peoples. "Thus sayeth the Lord" meant merely "Be it enacted."[63]

In the second sermon, Parker takes up the problem of the Bible contradicting itself, as when it teaches different doctrines at different times. He points out that most of these contradictions appear between different parts of the Old Testament, or between the Old Testament and the New Testament. He solves this difficulty by radically separating the two revelations from each other. The doctrines of the New Testament, he declares, are "quite independent" of those of the Old: "They rest on different authority: They are of a [Character] vastly dissimilar. It is often argued . . . that [Christianity] & Judaism must stand or fall together. . . . But this is not the truth. [Christianity] has no connection with the religion of Moses, which is [by] comparison, cold, formal, outside though superior to all the old religions of the world."[64] He goes on to call the Old Testament a "yoke too great to bear," and asks that no one think him impious for saying so, because "it is *for the sake of piety*— for the sake of Truth—for the sake of man[']s comfort & progress in virtue & religion that it is uttered."

Having found the Old Testament religiously superfluous, Parker can discount much of it. If Ecclesiastes preaches sensual gratification, we can ignore it. If the Jewish books do not talk about the immortality of the soul, this is not a problem. He concludes, in words that echo those of Dr. Channing in *Unitarian Christianity*, that we should respect the "dispensation of Moses" as the highest thought that men could produce at the time, but it was meant for the infancy of the world, while the dispensation of Jesus was for its manhood. At the very end of his second sermon, Parker finally turns to the apparent contradictions in the New Testament—for example, that Peter and Paul disagree over whether or not the Jewish law has been superseded. All such contradictions mean, says Parker in conclusion, is that the Apostles were not infallible.

Parker may not seem to be saying anything very radical for the times. His sermons have a plainly apologetic purpose. He would show that, properly understood, the Bible does not contradict Reason or Morality or even itself. He says nothing against the miracles, and all his major critical points had been anticipated by Andrews Norton and John Gorham Palfrey, who had proven themselves quite willing to be critical of the Jewish books, even as they defended the Christian ones. Norton and Palfrey would also have agreed with him that Apostles were not infallibly inspired. Besides, some of Parker's points had been preached by other ministers to their congregations. Convers Francis had made similar arguments about the Creation story in a sermon Parker heard while living in Watertown.[65] Yet Parker's sermons were bold nonetheless, because these ideas do not seem to have been preached very often; even Francis kept some of his views confined to his study.

Besides, Parker's sermons do break new ground. He is seeking a more radical separation between the Old Testament and New than most Unitarians

I Preach Abundant Heresies

would accept; the enlightened James Walker could say that belief in Christianity is "wholly independent" of belief in Judaism, but he admitted that "the truth and divine origin of Judaism seemed to be involved in Christianity, considered historically."[66] Parker denies even this. And Parker's solution to the Old Testament "problem" is to argue that the ultimate standard of truth and morality lies in the soul, not in the Bible. He therefore challenges the authority of all Scripture. Understandably, then, Parker was worried about how these sermons would be received. In the first sermon, he admits that his "explanations may sound new to most of us: strange to many, & some may be *shocked* at such interpretations," but he urges his congregation not to reject them simply because they are new. Even the small protest against his W. article had made his heart "beat audibly," and these sermons risked distressing and offending his own congregation.

At one point he confided his fears to a "wise & distinguished layman." This unidentified man, "old, with large social experience, and much esteemed for sound sense," was the same one who would not allow his young children to read the Old Testament, fearing its effect on their religious character. He "knew the difficulties of the case," and admitted to Parker that there was no doubt Parker's view of the Bible was correct. Yet he thought "silence wiser than speech":

> If you preach what you believe on this matter, why the Great Vulgar who hear but little of the sermon & remember but little will say, "He doesn't believe in the Bible." The Little Vulgar who hear less & understand less, will say yet more. They have not *thought* upon the subject[;] they will not think. They will only be offended, so you will do more harm than good. But if you think that you can tell the truth so that men will understand it as you do & not shock their prejudices, why you will do an unspeakable service & a wide one, for at this day the popular notion about the Bible is a great impediment in the way of [Christianity]. But at any rate, if you undertake this never so carefully, YOU WILL HAVE ALL THE CLERGY ABOUT YOUR EARS.[67]

Besides this obvious worry was another: Would he disturb the faith of the people and put nothing in its place? Such concerns were not unique to Parker. When Parker asked various "wise & old ministers" whether he should preach the "Contradictions in Scripture," he was told that the people must be taught with traditional authority. He recalled one minister telling him that it was useless to disturb the popular religious belief: "If I were to go to a Mahometan I should never point out any faults in the Koran."[68]

Some Transcendentalists believed authority was at least a provisional necessity. In 1839, Parker wrote Convers Francis, exclaiming how different the Bible was as they studied it at home from how their parishioners heard it in church. "Is it necessary there should always be this *clerical-view*; and this *laical-view* so different from it?" he asked. "Now would not the people be *better, wiser, & holier* if they were emancipated from this stupid superstition which now hangs like a millstone around their necks?" Francis agreed it was a "strange idea" that the Bible, a volume of mostly uncertain authorship, its books written at intervals over three thousand years for the most diverse occasions, "at all periods of culture including largely the lowest and rudest"—that this volume should be held up to enlightened and cultivated nations as their last spiritual and moral guide, never to be questioned. And yet he cautioned that "the passive & undiscriminating faith in the Scriptures as an ultimate authority" has been and continued to be "a condition of soul-culture fitted to its place as a help to something better"; we must teach the "vast multitude" upon authority just as we do children, "to prepare them for independent & spontaneous developments in [the] future." That even Francis should think like this shows what Parker was up against.[69]

So 1837 closed and 1838 passed, and the "Contradictions in Scripture" lay on Parker's desk, unpreached. He continued to read and study, and his own critical views of Scripture continued to mature. He expressed them most fully in the spring of 1838, when he undertook to write his first major article: a fifty-page review, for Brownson's *Boston Quarterly*, of the first volume of the *Academical Lectures on the Jewish Scriptures and Antiquities*, by Parker's old professor John Gorham Palfrey. The review was anonymous, and Parker admonished Silsbee to tell no one who the author was: "My hair stands up when I think of what I have written." He had reason to be nervous. The article was quite critical. When it was published that July, Palfrey thought it was written by George Bancroft, with whom he was feuding at the time; moreover, Parker's strictures were weighty enough that James Walker, in his review of the book for the September *Examiner*, felt obliged to try to answer them. But more important, Parker for the first time in print breaks explicitly with supernatural rationalism.[70]

Parker had some praise for the dean's book. It was better, he wrote to a friend, than "all the contemptible trash in the English language." In the review itself, he explains that Palfrey abjured the false principles of his predecessors, who had assumed the Hebrew books were inspired in their entirety, so there could be no error in them. These scholars had begged the question at the outset. Palfrey did not. He held truth to be more important than tradition. He admitted that some of the laws of Moses may have been decreed not by God, but by Moses himself in God's name. This latter claim Parker believes to be the most important of the book, because it allows us to evaluate Moses' laws for ourselves. Parker also praises Palfrey's conclusion that the Old Testament canon was not settled until three or four centuries after Jesus, and although Parker appears to disagree with Palfrey's decision in favor of the

Mosaic authorship of the Pentateuch, he does not say explicitly that Palfrey was wrong.[71]

Parker does attack Palfrey's supernatural rationalist assumptions—that God spoke audibly in Hebrew; that the religious principle, although the most important in human nature, is too weak to discover truth; that there can be no objection to a miracle when there is an occasion for one, as to confirm a religious truth; and that we need a revelation to know religious truth and can recognize this revelation only if it is accompanied by miracles. Parker argues that Palfrey on miracles goes either too far, or (as Parker evidently believes) not far enough. "While he admits the abstract credibility of miracles," writes Parker, "he seems desirous of restricting the miraculous agency to the smallest sphere possible." Palfrey believes miracles must be rare, unique events that God uses to confirm a revelation. He tries to apply this criterion rigorously and so accepts some miracles while rejecting others. He does not allow us to receive the miracles as we have been taught to receive them since childhood, but he will not allow us to regard them all as natural events, "which, through the long lapse of ages, men's ignorance, superstition, and natural love of the marvelous have greatly exaggerated."[72]

More fundamentally, Parker rejects the distinction between natural and revealed religion: "Is there not a sentiment in human nature, which impels us to worship the Infinite God? If not, religion has no foundation in man's soul, and divine communications would find no ear to listen."[73] History shows that religious knowledge came naturally. The miracles did not successfully persuade the Jews of the truth of Moses' teaching. They remained idolaters. Meanwhile, Abraham found God without miracles.

Parker concludes by criticizing Palfrey for ignoring the contemporary German biblical critics, including De Wette. They are never cited; it "is clear the author has never seen them." His book was not what the public expected, nor did it satisfy the deepest wants of the public, nor was it a work a liberal Christian professor at Harvard should have produced. But it did show an "earnest desire to do something."[74]

Parker had a similar desire. What he accused Palfrey of failing to do, he tried to do in West Roxbury. Although he held off preaching his sermons on the "Contradictions in Scripture," he quietly readied the good folk of the place to receive them. He attacked biblical authority indirectly, by attacking its theological underpinnings.

Here Parker faced the various problems surrounding the miracles. He no longer believed the miracle accounts of the Old Testament and thought such disbelief affected no important doctrine.[75] But he did not yet consider them to be "myths" in the sense of De Wette and Strauss—that is, to have no basis in fact, but to be "expressions" of the religious desires of the Hebrews. Parker never declared such views in 1837 or 1838. Rather, as he wrote in the Palfrey review, he still thought of the miracle stories as "greatly exaggerated" accounts of actual events.

In a sermon in April 1837, he suggested that the miracles of the Old Testament were less believable than those of the New, especially than those of Jesus. In January 1838 he began a long series of sermons (he was to preach them on communion days over the next two years) on the life of Jesus, in which he showed little sign of questioning the authenticity or accuracy of the accounts in the Gospels. That November, he wrote to Silsbee that he believed "most heartily" in miracles described in the Gospels and the Acts.[76]

Parker's preference for the miracles of the New Testament over those of the Old was at bottom evidence of his Unitarian biases. But he did have reasons for his preference. His critical work on the Hebrew Scriptures had convinced him that their historical credibility was weak; but he still believed in early 1838 that the historical evidence for the New Testament miracles was strong. As he said in a sermon about the miracles of Jesus: "Here are 4 independent writers attesting to the facts, writers whose works bear every mark of honesty. . . . 2 of these writers [Matthew and John] were eye witnesses to the events. They could not be deceived as to the facts. The M[iracles] were wrought publicly: before great multitudes." Jesus' miracles had to be regarded as historical facts, resting on sufficient evidence, and therefore to be "reasoned upon & examined" like other facts. "These miracles *were real*," he insisted. "The [character] of J[esus] shows that he could not attempt to work a M[iracle] when he only did a common act in a mysterious manner."[77]

There were certain New Testament miracles, however, that Parker preferred to explain in natural terms. For example: What happened to Saul on the road to Damascus? When a man asked Parker this question in August 1838, Parker told him that the future Apostle had been overtaken by a thundercloud. The man responded that Parker's explanation "made it all plain." Parker would give out similar, naturalistic explanations for the liberation of Peter, the death of Ananius, and Paul's visits from the angels. When he turned to the Gospels themselves, he challenged various accounts, including those of the Nativity, the Temptation, the Transfiguration, and the Ascension. But not those of the Resurrection itself—although he may have had doubts as early as 1838, when he preached a sermon describing the death of Jesus, but making no mention of His being risen.[78]

Why was Parker willing to defend some miraculous accounts of the New Testament and not others? The answer lies in his understanding of what a miracle was, which he first made explicit in his sermon on miracles from spring 1838. By the conventional definition, a miracle was an interruption of the laws of nature. Parker says this definition is "unwise," "since as yet we know so little of these laws." Parker preferred to think of miracles and miraculous ability in the same way as he thought of revelation and inspiration—as the product of a natural power that we all possess, but that Jesus possessed to an extraordinary degree. "We have all power over matter," Parker asserted in a sermon, "power over living men. This power is a miracle to ourselves. We cannot comprehend it. . . . Now of this power all men have a little, J[esus] had much. Ours is therefore *common*: his a miraculous power. We are all conscious of something divine *in* us. . . . To the same source J[esus] refers his acts."[79] Such an understanding of miracles would predispose Parker to see as plausible any miracle directly effected by the personal power of Jesus, but to doubt all others; Parker would dismiss out of hand stories involving angels, demons, or the Devil.

This naturalistic understanding of Jesus' wonder-working was gaining acceptance among Unitarians in the late 1830s. It was attractive for a variety of reasons. In 1836, William Henry Furness, a minister from Philadelphia and a close friend of Emerson, had published the first edition of his *Remarks on the Four Gospels*, in which he argued against a supernatural view of miracles on the grounds that it denied the immanence of God in the world: If God must interrupt the natural order to perform a miracle, then God must not be in the natural order. Furness's point was well taken, and the book had some influence. Views similar to his started to be voiced even by some conservative Unitarians, but found readier acceptance among Transcendentalists. Such views fitted well with the Transcendentalist faith in human potential, and their belief in the power of spirit over matter. In the summer of 1839, after Parker had noted in his journal that Jesus' miracle working was an "element of the soul" that appears throughout history, he added that we "all feel this power *ideally* (Alcott says *actually* likewise & perhaps he is true. I feel something of it. Supposing it is what Emerson calls demoniacal influence). J[esus] a greater man than ever lived before, or since, lived it actually[;] his miracles therefore were natural acts, not contrary to outward nature, but above it."[80]

The nature of the miracles was independent of the problem of their significance. Did they give special authority to historical Christianity or not? Furness himself believed that they did—that no one could truly be a Christian who did not believe in the miracles of Jesus and understand their importance.[81] George Ripley and other Transcendentalists disagreed.

By the time Parker settled in West Roxbury he had already sided with Ripley, but for the first ten months of his ministry he did not explicitly deny the religious significance of the miracles in a sermon. Only in April 1838, in his sermon on miracles, did he make his position clear. Great stress, Parker says, has often been laid on the miracles as proof of the divine authority of Jesus. It is said that he wrought miracles and therefore is a teacher of true doctrine. But, counters Parker, "his doctrine is true if he wrought no miracles.

No one of his precepts . . . derives the smallest force from the fact that it was uttered by a worker of M[iracles]. . . . We have a standard in the heart, whereby to try all questions of this nature."[82]

This sermon on miracles was one of several in which Parker set out to re-define the authority of Christianity. All these sermons risked controversy, and he held off preaching some of them for months after they were written. In a sermon on the "Three Primal Duties of Man," which Parker wrote in February 1838 but did not preach until December, he argued that there is nothing in Christianity that "revolts a man's calm, pure reasonings." Christ and the Apostles never teach "on any other authority than that of *Reason & Truth*. This Reason in man they make the standard measure of all things. What a man deems reasonable he is to *receive*: what irrational he must reject. . . . *Man's Reason therefore* is made the measure of revelation."[83] Jesus, Parker goes on to say, brought the principles of human nature to light, as Newton had dis-covered the laws of the material world: "All that was revealed by J[esus]. or published by the famous astronomer—*was the disclosure of these Laws*, wh[ich] had been in operation since creation."

A few weeks later, in March, Parker returned to this theme, and wrote "Christianity as Old as Creation," which he did not preach until after he heard Emerson's Divinity School Address several months later. Here Parker argued again that the laws of human nature were eternal, and that "Jesus re-presented to all men what is in each man if he have but the skill to find it." It is, in fact, "a well-known truth that there is not an important doctrine or beautiful pre-cepts [*sic*] in the N[ew] T[estament], which is not to be found in some writer before the time of Christ." The agreement between Jesus and "the greatest & best of men antiquity & of every land" was one of the strongest arguments for Christianity.[84]

The most important of these "great & best men" to Parker was Plato, as he made clear in a review of C. Ackermann's *Das Christliche im Plato* ("The Christian in Plato"), which he wrote sometime in 1838, and which was pub-lished in the *Christian Examiner* in January 1839. Parker presents Ackermann's views with enthusiastic approval and fleshes them out with quotations from other writers, including the English Platonist Henry More. This article is perhaps the most overt expression in print of Parker's Christian Platonism.[85]

Ackermann argues, like many Christian scholars since the early days of the church, that Plato and Jesus, despite specific differences, were deeply alike in doctrine, tone, and spirit. Plato spoke of the "existence, attributes, names, and works of the Supreme Being in a Christian sense." He was a monotheist; he calls God "Father; Father of all, — Creator; the only existing King or Gov-ernor of the world." He enjoins prayer " 'in Spirit and in Truth' " and holds that pious sentiments and a virtuous life are the sacrifices most acceptable to God. Plato is no "cold rationalist" who derives these truths from the human understanding. Rather, he derives them from "tradition" and "the life of God in the human soul"; Plato "refers to the writings of the old Poets, as Jesus and his disciples quote the works of the Prophets and Psalmists." Both Jesus and Plato recognize that "all tradition is only the well-trod path that leads to the fountains of living water in the souls of old men eloquent." Plato believes that truth is nothing mortal, or subjective; it flows like a pure stream into every soul, and all receive some portion of it. "The soul of man is entirely different from all material things; it belongs to the higher sphere of spiritual and immortal essences." Our present degradation is a result of our voluntary fall from a state of purity. The Bible treats extensively of sin, while Plato was one of the rare ancient writers to do so; he dwells "long and earnestly" on the subject. His ethics are pure. He regards piety to God the highest virtue.

Yet the "Christian element in Plato is not to be discovered mainly in his opinions, though he thinks like an angel, but in his spirit and his life." Like Jesus, he understands our need for salvation, and is moved at the "sickness of suffering humanity." "A melancholy earnestness pervades all the writings of Plato. In this they differ essentially from the other productions of laughing Greece." Evil he attributes to sin, and sin "is the disobedience to God's law written in human nature"—that is, alienation from God. Plato attempts to convince us of the need for salvation, and then to excite within us "a love for God, a love of the true, the holy, and the good." He believes men must be born again, and does not limit salvation to this life.

Was there anything then distinctive about Christianity? Parker insisted there was. When he preached "Christianity as Old as Creation," the Sunday after he heard Emerson's Divinity School Address, he joined it to another sermon, "Peculiarities of the Christian Religion," which he had just written. Here he insisted that the idea of Christianity (as opposed to its actual state, which falls far short of that ideal) is the best of all religions, and free from their faults. Christianity alone values "man as man." Even Plato wrote for the great, the rich and wise, while the Jews restricted their affections "to the narrow limits of Judea." Christians, however, saw the likeness of God in all persons and so were the only ones to try to go abroad to teach truth. Similarly, Christianity had a higher idea of God than any other faith—not partial, unjust, or capricious, as in the Old Testament, but a father. Above all, Christianity alone teaches "perfect compensation": "*every man receives or will receive [reward or punishment] by the unchanging laws of God, as the just recompense for his [character]."* [86]

Parker elaborates this argument in his article on Ackermann, for Ackermann also asks what is peculiar to Christianity. He answers that it is not the doctrines of divine Unity or of the soul's immortality, as had often been claimed. "He says nothing of the miracles," reports Parker, "and seems to think that Christianity is not dependent upon them for its establishment or support." Rather, he believes Christianity is uniquely suited to promote the " 'progressive development of the soul' " toward its ideal.

Nature aids us in this work; it satisfies all natural instincts. "Christianity is no appendix to creation. Whatever its design, it can never fill up a chasm originally left in the creation." Naturally, we are to live a good and improving life. But nature has a "melancholy reverse." Without "an higher influence, it is not the Human, but the Animal, which is developed, and the Animal speedily becomes Bestial." We perceive our fate and complain of our lot—"It is the voice of a noble prisoner who sighs for freedom." The more society is developed, the more acutely does humanity feel how far below the ideal is its actual. Hence arises human restlessness and discontent. We seek salvation in art, philosophy, civilization, and morality, but in vain. The soul seeks God; nothing else will restore it, and only Christianity will provide it. Parker made a similar point in his journal in July 1838, when he fantasized of writing an epic poem, set in first-century Greece, in which the hero seeks answers in nature, art, philosophy, and finally Christianity, where he eventually "finds all, and at last." In his article on the "Christian in Plato," Parker says even Plato is ultimately an insufficient guide. In him is little of the true, universal philanthropy that "breathes in every word of Jesus." And at bottom, Platonism aims at salvation through thought—an abstraction—while Christianity alone has the power of salvation, because it is unique "in the power of idea and emotion, in the life and love of the Holy on the earth, in the incarnation of the divine Word"—that is, in the example provided by the life of Jesus.[87]

What, then, was the role of Jesus? Karl Barth once remarked that Jesus was a "problem child" for all theologians who try to ground religion on psychology and anthropology. Parker was no exception. In a sermon he wrote and preached in June 1838, he made the inevitable concession to the logic of his position. Let it be proved, he said, "that J[esus]. never taught, *died* or even *lived*, still the real vital word of God as it speaks in the N[ew] T[estament] is just as true as ever."[88] But this answer was unsatisfactory, and to no one more so than Parker himself. Why so is suggested by his first sermon on the life of Jesus, which he preached in January 1838. In the most intriguing passage, Parker stops to consider Jesus as he was in his teens and twenties:

I delight to dwell upon this portion of the life of the Savior. I see him struggling with poverty—learning thereby a giant strength: his spiritual yearning answered only by the cold, withering sneer of the Pharisee, yet his soul suppressing its righteous indignation & turning away from the broken cisterns of tradition & conventionalism, to refresh itself from the deep fountain of the spiritual life, wh[ich] springing directly from God, well[s] forth in every pure & noble heart. I contemplate him not as a miracle worker feeding a multitude with a few loaves, but struggling for daily bread, for himself, his mother & brother: not as a teacher but as an humble hand, aspiring by study—in hours wrested from sleep, wh[ich] the toil-worn body craved—to liberate his soul from the shackle of ignorance & solve the great problem of the world.[89]

The Gospels provide no information on this portion of Jesus' life. Why then does Parker "delight to dwell" on it? Was it because this was when Jesus was the same age as Parker, who was twenty-seven at the time? Parker identified emotionally with the historical Jesus; and in fact, this portrait of the young Jesus looks strikingly like its painter—a poor boy, studying far into the night.

Jesus had to have some special role. In "Christianity as Old as Creation," Parker suggests that Jesus had not only put the truths of Christianity in a "clearer & stronger light": his chief distinction lay "in the beautiful spirit with which he embodied all these truths in his own [Character]," for "all improvement in the world is effected by great examples."[90]

This was also Ackermann's answer, as Parker presents it in his review: "Before man could pass from the earthly to the heavenly life, some one was needed to fill up the immense chasm between the Actual and the Ideal." Such was the mission of Jesus: "In him is the love of God perfect; communion with God never interrupted. His freedom is his union with God; for freedom and oneness with God are identical. He is the perfect Actual and loftiest Ideal. The son of God is one with the son of man; humanity and divinity are equally incarnated in him. . . . His whole life within and without is the life of the Divine; he is the kingdom of Heaven."[91] Despite Parker's eloquence here, he had not found his final answers about Jesus; here, he unites the ideal Christ with the historical Christ. Later, they would begin to separate in his mind.

While Parker was developing these positions on revelation, miracles, Christianity, and Jesus, he held off preaching the "Contradictions in Scripture." Yet the overall effect of his preaching must have been to undermine the traditional authority of the Bible. His efforts bore fruit in mid-1838, when his church quietly revised its covenant.[92] The language of the new covenant is that of Parker himself. Gone is any reference to the "divine authority of the Holy Scriptures." In its place is a simple statement: "We whose names are written underneath this do constitute ourselves members of the Christian Church, and unite for the purpose of promoting Goodness and Piety amongst ourselves and others." A long list of names follows—far longer than had signed the 1834 covenant—starting with Deacons Farrington and Arnold, and including all the old families of the parish.

Having achieved this political triumph and after preparing the congregation for thirteen months, Parker finally hazarded to preach the "Contradictions in Scripture" on 13 January 1839. "I did not dare look you in the face while I spoke," he later recalled to his parishioners. "I clutched at the cushions of the pulpit and read with a trembling heart."[93] The day finished without incident, and he waited anxiously for a reaction.

It came back gradually. The kind of specific responses he received are indicated by comments he later attributed to his two deacons, on the tendencies of his preaching. They disagreed with him but remained magnanimously open-minded. Slow-moving, deliberate Farrington told him that although he thought very differently about the Old Testament, and the New Testament, too, he should be very sorry to have Parker not preach what he thought, for it would be almost as bad as to preach what he did not think, and would soon lead to that. Arnold, meanwhile, told him that the problem lay in "rightly dividing the word of truth": there were things in the Bible he was sorry to see there, but he did not think it possible to set the Truth all on one side, and the rest on the other, without doing violence to the "good parts." As the new wine is found in the cluster, destroy it not, for a blessing is in it—but if Parker could get the blessing out of the grape skin, "that is all we want!"[94] In general, Parker found that his sermons were "most acceptable" to the "most intelligent & religious" people in his parish, who were glad to find religion was one thing and the Bible another.

"My eyes were at once opened," wrote Parker later. "I saw that intelligent men & religious men had not built their faith on mere authority as I had all along been taught." He called the preaching of the "Contradictions in Scripture" a "crucial experiment" and a "guide-board instance," in which he learned "that the mass of men need not be led blindly by clerical authority, but had competent power of self-direction, and while they needed the scholar as their help, had no need of a self-appointed master." After this "joyful discovery," "I did not wait thirteen months again before I . . . exposed a theological absurdity, or ventured to preach a truth not preached before."[95]

In his excitement and relief, was he willing to voice long-harbored doubts about the New Testament? A new radicalism abruptly appears in his private writings. In a letter to Convers Francis, written only a few weeks after preaching the "Contradictions in Scripture," Parker speculated that in the future, the New Testament would be dropped from the churches.[96] Several weeks later, in another letter to Francis, Parker shows that now, nearly two years after he first had read David Strauss's *Life of Jesus*, he was willing to confront directly some of its arguments:

> Is not this plain that the N[ew]. T[estament]. contains numerous mythi? . . . Now the Gospels are not without their mythi. The miraculous conception, the temptation, &c. Now the question is where are they to end? Who will tell us where the mythi begin, & the history ends? Do not all the miracles belong to the mythical part? The resurrection, is that not also a myth? I know you will not be horror-struck at any doubts an honest lover of truth may suggest. & certainly I see not where to put up the Bar, between the true & the false. [Christianity] itself was before [Abraham] & is *older* than the creation, & will stand forever.

I Preach Abundant Heresies

But I have sometimes thought it would stand better without the N[ew]. T[estament]. than with it. Certainly I would not send a sceptic to the Bible to convert him. . . . Is not Strauss right, in the main, when he says the N[ew]. T[estament]. is a collection of mythi? No doubt he goes too far, but pray tell me where *is* far enough?[97]

PREACHING THE "Contradictions in Scripture" was a major turning point in his Parker's early ministry; only one other event was as important. In the night of 15 July 1838, in a flushed high only hours after hearing Emerson's Divinity School Address, he announced in his journal that he would write two "long-meditated" sermons on the state of the church and the duties of the times. He did write them and preached them two Sundays later.[98] These sermons mark a watershed in Parker's preaching, not about theology, but about the sins of society.

In his early sermons he says little about what he later called political and civil sins, such as slavery or the problems of labor. In part, he was responding to a tradition that such matters should rarely be made the subject of preaching. By convention, a distinction was made between two types of sermons, regular and occasional.[99] A regular sermon was preached on an ordinary Sunday and was expected to address problems of individual salvation. The other kind of sermon was preached for a special occasion; its subject matter was more flexible. It was considered acceptable, in an occasional sermon, to preach on the state of society.

Two occasional sermons were built into the preaching calendar: Fast Day, which fell on a Thursday in April, and Thanksgiving. As Parker once pointed out, "etiquette" demanded that in Thanksgiving sermons, as in Fourth of July orations, "the present state of things be presented flawless." For Fast Day, however, as Parker noted in his first such sermon, "more latitude is usually given to the Pulpit than on other days." Only on Fast Day might a minister be expected to call his nation to task for its sins. These sermons were naturally the most poorly attended of the year. In 1840, Parker could note in his journal with justifiable pride that the attendance at his Fast Day sermons had risen from thirty-five in 1838 to over ninety two years later. Still, even in a Fast Day sermon, it was considered inappropriate to raise an "exciting" (i.e., controversial) topic, like slavery, and the tone of the sermon, at least in Unitarian pulpits, was expected to be genteel. As Parker said in his first sermon to his congregation after his ordination, preaching must be "calm & tranquil": "He is a madman who paints vice, sin, unbelief in its most appalling features." Most Fast Day sermons revolved around general themes.[100]

Parker's first Fast Day sermon is a fair specimen of the genre. In "The Signs of the Times," which he preached in 1837, during his candidacy,[101] he praised his age for an "earnestness of spirit which characterizes men in all their undertakings," a skill in controlling the material world, and desire to advance our weaker brethren, evidenced by the movements for prison reform, schools for the indigent, and temperance. On the other hand, our earnestness becomes impetuosity; we lack tranquillity. Our desire to control Matter results in our forgetting Spirit; our love of things leads us to forsake thoughts and feelings; our love of utility leads us to lose sight of Duty and Truth; we gain the world but lose our souls. Our zeal to improve others can lead us to neglect ourselves. We become mere instruments in the work of society—"not men but only halves & quarters of men," narrow and intolerant. Parker closes with an injunction against the "tyranny of popular opinion": "All men are tried by the same conventional standard instead of being measured by their own selves & the rule of truth."

This sermon, with its balanced, careful tone, is no jeremiad. Parker seems generally content with the state of New England society, and this impression is reinforced by his other sermons. In one of the earliest, he said we must be grateful to God that "equal laws distribute justice unto all—that the rich oppress not the poor, nor the poor hate the rich, but that all are so curiously . . . knit together, that each worketh for the other's good, & all are blessed by the labours of each."[102]

Complacency is suggested, too, in Parker's next Fast Day sermon, an ambitious effort titled "Peace," in which he argues against war (easy enough to do, when the country was not fighting one). All men are brothers, he says, both because we descend from a "common stock," and because we share a "common nature." Christendom seems, however, to have forgotten the brotherhood of man. All Christian nations prepare for war, yet the spirit of war itself is a product of a low stage of human development, when the physical force predominates over moral and intellectual. As human nations advance, Parker hopefully argues, wars become less cruel and frequent. Kindness eventually will triumph because human affairs wear a "simpler aspect" than ever before, so the sentiment of peace may be more easily diffused. The business of the world is effectively managed by only three Christian nations, the English/American, the French, and the German. As Christianity takes hold in these nations, they will first attempt to raise the low and degraded in their own lands. Ministries to the poor, prison discipline societies, temperance societies, education reform—all will seek to put the soul above the senses. Then violence will be limited by courts of law. Capital punishment will be abolished, then piracy, and finally armies. Parker is advancing an almost millennial vision, but his tone is hardly urgent or radical. Progress is inevitable, he says, and we are at the forefront of it.[103]

Parker's cautiously liberal tone was that of the Boston elite, which he still aspired to join. He did, however, consistently press one "exciting" topic—temperance. Parker had a personal interest in the issue; both his brother

Hiram and his brother-in-law John Cabot were drunkards. Besides, he saw "the Old Destroyer" at work in West Roxbury. In his church records for 1838, he records burying a woman who died of "fever & many hardships"; her husband was a drunkard. Three years later, Parker buried this man and listed the cause of death as "intemperance." And he attributed at least two other deaths (one man and one woman) partly to this cause. Moreover, the problem was larger than a few poor topers. One of the wealthiest and most respectable members of his church, Reed Taft, the owner of Taft's Hotel, sold strong drink at his establishment. Besides, temperance was emerging as a hot political issue; in 1837 Massachusetts voters elected a pro-temperance legislature, which passed a controversial law severely restricting liquor sales. In the fall of 1837, at the height of the election season, Parker delivered a temperance lecture; he later recalled that in doing so he offended not a few of his parishioners. Yet Parker's position on the issue was not extreme. He did not advocate total abstinence and exempted beer and wine from his list of spirits to be abjured.[104]

Later in 1837, in a sermon on "Christianity—Past, Present, Future," Parker broached a topic even more "exciting" than temperance—slavery. In a carefully worded passage, he listed the attempt to abolish it among the good works Christianity was "attempting at this moment" and defended his right to mention such a divisive subject in the pulpit; he would be false to "my convictions & my trust," he declared, if he did not condemn an institution that, like slavery, warred with the Golden Rule. Parker's position, however, was "moderate"; like the younger Ware and Dr. Channing, he condemned both slavery and the "intolerance & violence" of the abolitionists—this at a time when abolitionists were being mobbed and even lynched. Despite Parker's attempt at moderation, and his statement about having to speak out, he may have decided in the end to keep quiet on slavery. On the manuscript, a pencil line is drawn through this passage, possibly indicating that he did not preach it.[105]

In general, Parker's early position on social reform seems similar to that of Channing, Ware, and the Philanthropic Society at the theological school. He was cautious and moderate in both tone and aims. He said little in public that indicated budding radicalism. But in private, a storm was brewing, as suggested by a letter Parker wrote to his friend Silsbee in September 1837. "Touching things *carnal*," said Parker,

I assure you I am more disturbed than I had ever anticipated—this is between you and me—Men of the ACTUAL and their name is "legion" have a very cheap sort of logic amounting to this. "My way is perfectly right," this is the first axiom—an undisputed truth self-evident. Then cometh the second, viz. "All important things are comprised in the actual, which alone should engross one's attention." This is the theory of these worthies. Now for the practice. They see other men doing different from themselves, so they condemn them under the first axiom. They find them thinking of other matters than Potatoes and Turnips—and Railroads—Specie currency and the manners of their next neighbors—to wit thinking of God, of *Duty, Nature, Destiny, Cause, Consequence*, the *Right*, the *Beautiful*, the *Good*—and so they condemn these under the second. Then yearn their bowels of tender mercy—(the tender mercies of the Actualists!) and they attempt to *reform* the thinkers, i.e., to make their talk of Turnips etc. and failing herein they beset one, till flesh and blood cry out like that of Abel for vengeance.

Parker adds that "I feel much of this harassing." The next section of the letter has been deleted from the surviving copy.[106]

Parker seems to be describing his unhappiness with Lucy and Lydia; his stifled discontent with his domestic situation must be kept in mind to understand Parker's electric reaction to the Divinity School Address. What excited him about Emerson's "true," "just," and "terribly sublime" pronouncement was its tone. Transcendentalist statements to that time had been scholarly, like Ripley's Martineau review, or contemplative, like Emerson's own *Nature*. Here, Emerson issues a cry of protest against the spiritual famine of the ministry; his sense of urgent aspiration for something beyond the actual inspired Parker to write his two "long-meditated" sermons, one on the "State of the Church" and the other on the "Duties of these Irreligious Times." The first of these is the more important.

It shares themes with Emerson's Address and echoes its language. Parker, like Emerson, attacks the spiritual deadness of the church. But there is an obvious difference: Emerson condemns the clergy, Parker the congregation. Emerson says that the soul is not preached, so the people, hungering for real religion, are either leaving the church in disgust or drifting away from it in apathy. The ministry bears the brunt of his scorn, which climaxes in his scathing portrait of the dull, "spectral" preacher who almost leads him to say he would go to church no more. By contrast, Parker makes only one comment on the ministry, near the end of his sermon: "Let it not be supposed that the blame [for spiritual deadness] falls on the Laity alone for there are faithless shepherds, as well as wandering sheep." [107] Parker identifies the people of New England, not the ministers, as the principal problem.

Partly, this difference was due to his addressing, and trying to challenge, a different audience than Emerson—not a group of prospective pastors, but regular lay listeners. The more important reason for the difference, however, is that the two men had different life experiences. Emerson was in the process of abandoning the ministry; his private frustration with his profession is expressed in the Address as part of a general indictment of the church. In Parker's case, his private frustration with his household was voiced as part of

I Preach Abundant Heresies

a general indictment of society. The "State of the Church" is Parker's "cry of vengeance." It sounds quite unlike anything he had preached before.

Its tone is suggested by his texts, two verses from the Book of Revelation (this is almost the only time he used it as a source of texts): "Thou livest and art dead," and "I know thy works that Thou art neither Hot nor cold. I would thou wert cold or hot." The sermon falls into two unequal parts. The first concerns the age of Jesus and the Apostles, at which time, Parker argues, Christianity was a real, vital religion. In the second, contrasting section, about twice as long, Parker denounces the religious indifference of New England in his own day.

Religion in New England, he says in this second section, is no longer what it was and should be, "*a thousand voiced Psalm—from the heart of man to his invisible Father.*" Rather, it is a prudential calculation, "whereby some smaller quantity of earthly enjoyment may be exchanged for a larger quantity of Heavenly enjoyment. Thus religion too is Profit, a working for wages."[108]

How many youths, Parker asks, when forming their life plan, say that "I must be an whole man"? I must reverence conscience, be wise and above all religious; I must reverence God in my prayers and my life. For every one such youth, you will find 999 who care for nothing but gold, pleasure, and reputation, good enough in their places, but contemptible as goals for life. Moreover, how many adults, who have lived long enough to tell wisdom from folly, try to make religion the concern of their daily lives and nightly prayer, and seek to train up their children for the Kingdom of Heaven? For every one such, you will find 999 who care only to raise a fine crop of corn, and gain new wealth and splendor. Cries Parker: "Can these things be so in a religious community!"[109]

Most people go to church, Parker says, but only because it is respectable and an established custom. People praise one discourse as profound, interesting, beautiful, and curse another as stupid and worthless, yet never think to lay to heart the truths they contain. Others support religion because it is useful in comforting the sick and keeping social order. "In their eyes, religion is as indispensable to the State as the Poll-tax, or the militia system. . . . [The] Hope of Heaven might rank with money at 3 per cent."[110]

Parker's language in the closing pages of the "State of the Church" echoes both Emerson's Address and the Book of Isaiah:

> Few men seem to understand the nobleness of their souls. . . . They distrust reason, they fear to follow *conscience*, & so make a half-service to expediency. They say there have been Revelations. It is true, most noble revelations. Moses & Jesus will never die. Their revelation is eternal. But are they all? Have they exhausted the deeps of man's nature, & drained the fountain of eternal wisdom? Why are there not revelations now? Men distrust their own spirits. They seem . . . |impiously| to

dream that God is superannuated, that he now makes no revelations of himself. But if a man be faithful to his own soul . . . [he] may have and *be* a revelation as glorious as that of Moses, or Paul, of old. Is infinite wisdom exhausted! Has the allmighty withdrawn from the works of creation! Has man no further intercourse with his maker! Does not God's spirit still speak in creation, in the soul of man! The sky is no less deep & blue, than of old time; the grass is equally green, the sun as bright, the storm as loud. Why is not every man a revelation from God? . . .

Is the picture presented in this discourse a false one? Would it were. They who sit quiet in parlors & studies will say it is false. The newspapers tell them of new churches built, new bibles printed, donations made & Priests installed. But they who go to & fro in the land with eyes open, to read men's lives [*sic*] as well as their speeches, they who feel the pulse of the people, know that the religion of the community is waxed cold, that Justice is turned away backward & justice standeth far off. . . . Truth is fallen in the street & Equity cannot enter. . . .

But . . . there is no room for . . . despair. . . . Man is still made for religion |& [Heaven]|, though he spurns his birthright. There is indeed cause to mourn for the state of Religion, but no one need mourn as those without hope. Perhaps there are some who standing high on the mount can see the Light, before it is risen to others. |To them we say watchman, [what of the night?]| . . . Well if they ever say "the morning cometh." God grant it may come speedily. That the fire may be kindled on cold alters, & a new spirit awakened in the dry leaves of old tradition.[111]

Here Parker for the first time speaks in the voice of a prophet. Society, he says, requires a revival of real religion. How was this revival to be effected? Parker answers this question in "Duties of these Irreligious Times," the companion sermon to the "State of the Church." If the case is as I have represented it, says Parker, "it behooves each man to be on his guard . . . that he may escape the evil which oppresses many." He must examine himself, and ask, "How do I stand affected towards religion?" In the "vast majority" of cases, the answer would be, "I have cultivated my hand, & can work, my feet, & can walk, my ear, my eye, my palate, all my senses, & each of these has received more of my attention than my soul. In a word, I have cared less for Religion, than for all other concerns."[112]

If the man should resolve to be truly religious, his course of action is clear. He must be true to his convictions: "A man's conscience is never to be sacrificed to any thing or to any man." It is not enough to attend church; he must keep the devotional feelings active. "It is not enough to listen to the words of holy writ, to the stirring, or stupefying discourses which may be eloquently, or churned feebly forth—but to catch every true word, and to apply [it] to . . . your self." A man desiring to be religious "will bestow as much thought on his chief concerns, as on his humblest duties." He will not pretend to seem good, but will try to be good. "He will look in his heart—& will find counsel, for God has put his inspiration there. He will watch—watch. . . . He will work. *He will pray.*" As sure as man is man and God, God, his watching, working, and praying will not be in vain.[113]

Parker's parishioners may have been perplexed by the vehemence of his exhortations in these two sermons. A few days before he preached them, he went fishing with a member of his congregation, the farmer Cornelius Cowing. Between casts, Parker apparently started complaining about the state of the church and so gave Cowing a preview of the upcoming discourse. Cowing heard him out, but remained unconvinced; you are "mistaken," he told his pastor.[114] But Cowing failed to douse Parker's fire; he still burned with the idea that American society lacked real religion. As his thinking on this problem developed through the autumn of 1838 and the winter following, he moved swiftly from making a general indictment of American irreligion to attacking specific manifestations of it. With this shift, he moved from calling for individuals to reform their character to endorsing specific social reforms.

The transition can be seen in "What our People Need," a sermon written and preached in September 1838. Here he identified the evils of the age as a "great preponderance of the animal powers & wants over the intellectual & spiritual," seen above all in an "excessive love of wealth," and "extravagance in expectations & [e]xpenditures." Reform societies aim to remove specific evils—"temperance societies, anti-slavery societies, . . . health societies"— but they too are extravagant. They believe that remedying their particular evil will destroy the poison tree, when in fact they only attack a branch. Here again, as in the "Duties of these Irreligious Times," he calls for an infusion of "deep, vital practical religion." But now he also talks about "education": We must teach our children that they are not animals but souls. This education must be universal, must come to the houses of the poorest, must begin early and continue late. It must involve not only parents but (Parker evidently had in mind the efforts of Horace Mann) the common school system. Parker challenged parents not to remove their children from school in order to work: often this is done when the exigency of the parent does not require such a "monstrous sacrifice" from the child.[115]

The problem he identified here led him inevitably to the abuse of labor and social inequality. He first raised these issues in a sermon written in November 1838 and preached the following March. Is there not, he here asks, "too much of L[abour] now required of men, for their bodily, & mental, & spiritual welfare? Is that system of things right wh[ich] demands 12, 14, 16 & even 18 hours of toil f[ro]m men day after day, year out year in? . . . Will not this process destroy body, M[ind] & S[oul]?" If doing all the "work of the world" required seven-tenths of the people to be cursed with "ignorance & rudeness," and if doing the work of the world less perfectly would allow "all men" to "cultivate all their faculties," true Christianity would not hesitate to have the work of the world less perfectly done.[116] Parker thinks, however, that the problem can be solved if labor be "more equally distributed" and machines be invented that will "free a large portion of men's time."

In another sermon, Parker linked exhausting labor with intemperance: men forced to toil sixteen hours out of the twenty-four end their day "*depressed, dejected*, without Spirit," and the "maddening cup" offers "momentary life." Parker had brought up the "exciting topic" of temperance repeatedly in sermons from the fall of 1838 before he wrote and preached this one in November, but it was his first entire discourse on the subject. He began by saying that he had "long desired" to speak about temperance, but had waited until after the November elections, in which it had been a hot issue. He did not want even the "over scrupulous" to think that "this sacred place (where no public answers can be given to arguments & assertions) was perverted to improper uses & from a desire to influence votes." Nonetheless, this was Parker's most political sermon to date: he all but endorsed the new state law restricting unlimited liquor sales.

His principal complaint against intemperance is not that it produces poverty, wretchedness, and bloated hideousness for the drunkard, and misery for the drunkard's family. These evils are obvious enough, he says. But such "outward" wretchedness is nothing, when voluntarily borne. The Saviour did not know where to lay his head. The men of the Revolution were often half-fed and half-clothed; in winter, their naked feet "bedewed the Ice with blood"; yet because they fought battles for freedom, and a divine flame burned in their hearts, these evils were light things. No, the worst wretchedness of the intemperate man is inward: He has lost self-command; he loses self-respect; he loses his reason; he deadens his conscience. Similarly, the principal cause of intemperance is not the liquor itself. Rather it is the "want of spirituality among us." We lack spiritual aims, so our pleasures are animal. Temperance societies and laws do good, but more is done by education—intellectual, moral, and religious.[117]

A few weeks later—in, of all places, his 1838 *Thanksgiving* sermon!—Parker launched his first full-throated attack on the way America treated its Indians; he also condemned slavery. Parker's remarks on Indians were prompted by the United States forcing a blatantly fraudulent treaty on the Cherokees in 1835, then using it brutally to expel a peaceful people from their ancestral lands in Georgia. Almost nine-tenths of the tribe signed a remonstrance, which the government ignored. Many in New England were appalled. In April 1838, Emerson had written a public letter of protest to President Martin

I Preach Abundant Heresies

Van Buren: "In the name of God, sir, we ask you if this is so? . . . Such a dereliction of all faith and virtue, such a denial of justice, and such deafness to screams for mercy, were never heard of in times of peace, and in the dealing of a nation with its own allies and wards, since the earth was made." Parker, in his sermon, spoke of the Cherokees' "wail of desperate distress," and their "shriek of despair & indignation": "Is there not a sin of the deepest die committed against these poor sons of the Forest? . . . I cast no blame & no insinuations upon any part[y], for they are all implicated. . . . The blood of the red man cries out to Heaven." Slavery was a sin of equally dark dye: "I do not speak as a Partisan. . . . But all men will acknowledge that slavery is a curse, a sin."[118]

That Parker was now willing to raise such "exciting topics" in a Thanksgiving sermon shows how far he had come in only a few months. By the following spring, he was even permitting himself to entertain thoughts of utopia. In March 1839, he submitted to the *Register* "Boston in the Year of Grace 3839." Chandler Robbins published it at the end of the month.

It is the account of "A Dream by a Very Old Man." The narrator, "Senex," says that in his dream he passed several days in the Boston of the future. Two millennia hence, says Senex, the present century is remembered as the "age of Worcester, of Channing and of Garrison"; but in the bookstores he found "not one of the familiar faces, so dear to scholars of those days," not even "the venerated names of sages whose voice has been heard these five thousand years, were known to the booksellers of the 39th century." He visits the courthouse and discovers that the judges "referred to no Law Book, but decided on the eternal principles of Justice and Equity." Violence is never used to enforce judicial decisions, yet they were always obeyed. Senex learns that there are no criminals in 3839; there have been no prisons for over a thousand years. The government had dwindled away: "[Someone] showed me the 'Revised Statutes' of the commonwealth, a small pamphlet not as large as a printed sermon of our times. The Legislature came together every year, rather to reciprocate good feeling than to enact laws. There were no executive officers, excepting a governor and council, whose chief business was to do the honors of the state, to strangers who visited the place." The people are prosperous and happy. Some are rich and some poor, but none are crushed by opulence or disturbed by poverty; the distinction of master and servant is gone; people of all conditions freely and gaily socialize together. Children sing beautiful songs in the streets, and the two million residents of the city were like a prodigious tide, "that flowed gracefully, and happily over the smooth pavements."

The world, Senex learns, has been Christianized—although it is a Christianity of an uninstitutional, untheological sort. Not only has a "Christian school" arisen in art, but "no man now thought of proving the truth of Christianity, still less the existence of a God, or the religious sentiment in man."

Senex finds that the Lord's Supper now takes place in private parlors: "A few gathered together in the houses of the wise and gifted, a prayer was put up, an hour was spent in religious conversation, and bread and wine were handed by the host to his guests." More important, people finally understood the meaning of the sayings, "He that is greatest among you let him be your *servant*," "All ye are *brethren*," and "I and my father are *one*."[119]

Finally, Senex attends a historical lecture on the nineteenth century. The lecturer regards it as a dark age, but marked by great achievements nonetheless—notably the application of steam to locomotion, and the abolition of capital punishment, slavery, and war. Still, nineteenth-century philosophers were fettered. Their theologians thought "man made for the Bible not the Bible for man. So they defiled the Bible and degraded man." The folly of that time can be seen in the clothes people wore. The lecturer shows the audience full-length drawings of a nineteenth-century lady and gentleman in full dress; the audience falls into a roar of laughter, and Senex feels so ashamed of his own "barbarous costume" that he rushes out of the hall to find a tailor—and awakes.[120]

Parker's piece is lighthearted, even humorous. He may not have taken his "dream" too seriously when he wrote it. But it raised themes that would soon be important to him. Soon, he would become a reformer in earnest.

Chapter Five

All the Force of Transcendentalism That Is in Me

Parker was nearing thirty now, and his brown hair was thinning alarmingly; a few years more and he would be quite bald. But he was sturdy and energetic, and capable of prodigious amounts of literary work. Convers Francis persuaded Harvard that someone of Parker's learning ought to have a degree of some sort (the theological school had only given its students certificates in 1836); in September 1840, therefore, he was awarded a master's degree—something Harvard apparently had never before done for a man without an AB. He seemed well on his way to fulfilling his early ambition of becoming the Reverend Doctor Parker. Moreover, he had become a forceful writer. The mannered quality of his early prose had vanished in the crucible of weekly preaching. His mature style—"loose, copious, expansive, eloquent," as one of his biographers has aptly described it—had taken shape in his sermons.[1]

He was gaining, too, a reputation as an effective preacher. Elizabeth Peabody said that when she went to hear him preach it was "always good—better than others: & sometimes—frequently—*very great.*" People commented on the power of his voice—Peabody called it "deep" and "organ-like," while others heard in it a resonant, nasal tone.[2] And he projected a sense, unusual for a Unitarian, of terrible earnestness. His genteel audiences were startled and stirred to see him so moved by what he was saying that he clutched the pulpit for support and sweat broke out on his brow.

He had avoided public involvement in the Transcendentalist controversy. His best-known published writings until 1840 were probably his articles for the *Examiner* on C. Ackermann's *Christian in Plato* and on the English neoplatonists Henry More and Ralph Cudworth. Almost all his published writings, whether poetic, homiletic, or scholarly, whether serious or even satiric, had been nonpartisan. The few exceptions had been published anonymously or pseudonymously; for one of these, his "W." article for the *Register*, he had publicly apologized. His most "heretical" sermons he had preached only to his tiny home congregation, whom he had carefully prepared to receive them. When he preached on exchange or went to Boston to deliver a Thursday Lecture, he made no pronouncements on disputed subjects such as inspiration, the Bible, or miracles. The topics of his most popular sermons through the middle of 1839 (he preached each at least ten times) were "The Law of the Spirit of Life," "Self-Denial," "The Character of Paul," "Tranquillity," "Morality and Religion," and "The Fall of Man."[3]

Parker was pushed to find a more radical public voice in part by his need to break the confines of West Roxbury. He was glad his church tolerated his Transcendentalism, but his ambition had not stilled and he craved a wider audience. "I came here *against* my own consent," he reminded his brother Isaac in January 1840, and "could wish with all my heart for a larger Sphere,— a greater number of hearers—and those more intelligent and cultivated than the majority at Spring Street." In April, he noted that he was "ill at ease with the world" and not "answering the purposes of life" by preaching to one hundred persons, half of them "babies." He reminded himself repeatedly in his journal that he was not settled permanently.

Nonetheless, in early 1840, he turned down two attractive offers to move. One, communicated by, among others, his brother Isaac, was to return to his boyhood church in Lexington; the second was to settle at the fine, large society at Waltham. His stated reason for staying put was his obligation to his parishioners; they were so few and had so little money, they would have a hard time finding a good minister to replace him. Besides, West Roxbury was so small he had time to pursue his literary projects, and another church might not accept his radical opinions. But he also admitted to Isaac that he had "private reasons" for staying. If he moved, "Miss Cabot" (Aunt Lucy) would be out of reach of her relations, and. . . . The rest of the letter has been deleted.[4]

A move was blocked, it would seem, by Lucy's commitment to West Roxbury, and his wife's commitment to her. This spousal obligation must have been doubly galling for him, because his marriage was entering one of its most difficult periods, and some of his most pointed comments about Lydia and Lucy appear in his journal.

As he there confessed, when he came to West Roxbury he saw that the people and place "must be idealized to be made bearable." He idealized both and dreamed "with the most inveterate obstinacy." But "I shall soon awake— & then—& then—I will not say what then." "I hate to preach to my own people," he continues. "It is a duty I now perform with reluctance." He trusts that he will soon leave Spring Street, but "the evil will not be removed by removal. It is not the *where* but the *what*." For the first time, Parker seems to have serious doubts about the ministry itself: "I often say to myself that

All the Force of Transcendentalism

I have mistaken my calling, but if so it is too late to turn back." His resolution is to write books, "& if I cannot address a large circle of hearers, I may address a large circle of readers."[5]

MEANWHILE, the difficulties in Parker's marriage were being exacerbated because he sought refuge from his wretched home life in outside female companionship. Not that he ever had an affair. As he wrote in his fable about the Swallow and the Tortoise, "Conscience in the Swallow overbounds Desire." Besides, the sexual infidelity of a village minister would have been impossible to conceal, and when discovered, would have ruined his career. Nonetheless, he did seek out the company of certain young women from whom he tried to find the "sympathy" he felt he could not get from Lydia. The most significant of these "sympathetic" associations was with Anna Blake Shaw, the younger sister of his neighbors Francis Shaw and Sarah Russell.

Anna Shaw was "like a Saxon princess," in the opinion of Sarah Freeman Clarke, who met her about the same time Parker did: "Gentle and wise, beautiful and modest, with ringlets like the daughters of Odin, and a slightly Transcendental cast of intellect. This is something in a belle and an heiress, is it not?" Unfortunately, only a few letters by Shaw survive, all from her later life, after she had married William Batchelder Greene. The letters reveal little, but her choice of Greene as a husband is interesting: He was a dashing soldier who became a Unitarian minister, a contributor to the *Dial*, and a radical Democrat who claimed to be one of the earliest American followers of the French anarchist Proudhon. Also interesting is another fact known about her—that she took part in a number of Margaret Fuller's conversations between 1839 and 1841. Like other members of the Shaw family, Anna appears to have been open to reformers and Transcendentalists.[6]

Parker met her in the summer of 1839, just before his twenty-ninth birthday, and just after she had turned twenty-two, when he preached on exchange in Boston at the church of her uncle, Dr. Francis Parkman. His first impression was of a "nice girl, not so handsome as her sister" (probably he was referring to her younger sister Elizabeth, who was also widely admired), "but deep, full of aspiration, charged with soul." She apparently was religiously troubled and beginning seriously to question the supernatural rationalism in which she had been reared and which her conservative uncle taught his people so confidently. She confessed to Parker her doubts and fears, which he thought "deep" and "wide." He suspected she had not told him everything.[7]

There is no record of them talking again until the following May, when she apparently visited her siblings in West Roxbury. In the previous few months, her doubts had grown. She had become phrenologically inclined and now agreed with Robert Owen that "everything is forecast in the mental & physical structure of the man" (at one of Fuller's conversations that took place about this same time, she maintained there was no such thing as "will"). Parker stuck up for the power of spirit over matter. Privately, he thought she was going through a stage.[8]

Over the course of the month, Shaw and Parker met other times, either at her brother's house, or more likely next door at the Russell place, which Parker visited almost every day. Parker found in her an attractive young woman with whom he could actually talk about his ideas; she was, too, like his wife, a woman of high social status—higher, in fact. Her father, the eminent merchant Robert Gould Shaw, was much richer than old father Cabot. Parker's feelings for her developed quickly. On 20 May, he wrote a poem, "To A. S.," in his journal:

> I've been told
> By poets of old
> That Jove came down in showers of gold,
> To bless the grecian girls;
> But never I knew
> The story was true
> Till your fair form ⟨enchanted⟩ |first met| my view
> *Maid of the golden curls.*[9]

On the same page, he noted that the "luminous cloud on my horizon" had not yet floated off: "It still reflects the sun as sweetly as before, & continues near me." Again on the same page, he wrote out a translation from Homer:

> Ah happy is the man, who says of thee 'My Daughter'!
> Thrice happy is he who calls thee 'Sister dear'!
> But happier than the Gods who calls thee 'wife'!
> And holds thee fast, with warm embrace, forever.

The following day, he wrote another poem "To A. S.," which reads in part:

> I would I were the Sun,
> Then wherever I shone
> I would see thee all the day . . .
> I would I were the Grass,
> When thy tiny footsteps pass
> I would greet thee all the day . . .
> But I'd rather be the Skies
> For then with thousand eyes,
> I . . . would ⟨gaze⟩ bless thee all the day.[10]

Not long afterward, she evidently decided to live with her brother or sister for a time, because Parker begins to refer to her as his "neighbor." Over the following year, they seem to have met often and taken long walks through the woods together. Parker apparently gathered flowers for her, and when they were alone they would have deep talks. He records one of their conversations in his journal, in which he described woman as a vine, adorning the tough oaken branches of the man, "giving round out gracefullness" to the male tree trunk, and "hanging his boughs with purple clusters of love." Men and women, responded Shaw, were like two trees that grew up side by side and intertwined their branches. Parker conceded she was right: "If woman were not deemed a VINE, & so inferior to man, the present abominable abuses could not take place."[11]

Entries in his journal indicate that his infatuation with her did not fade quickly, as when he wrote this "original conundrum" in early 1841: "Why is Anna Shaw like a city of Salem? Because famed for her witchery." The most tantalizing entry comes from the fall of 1840. At first glance, all that seems to be on this page are a few mundane lines describing what Parker did on 26 September—but above them, in very faint pencil, is written "Anna Anna Anna," and below them are several erased lines, which still can be partly deciphered: ". . . Anna . . . if it were not for my wife . . . keep me from . . . tempter . . . sometimes. . . ." The rest of the page has been cut away.[12]

If this journal entry means what it implies, Parker must have realized he was treading close to the edge of the abyss. The following month, when he returned to the Homeric theme to describe Shaw, he made careful modifications, which indicate that he had checked himself:

> Who calls thee FRIEND—is richly blesst
> SISTER or CHILD—hath heavenly rest
> Who calls thee WIFE—becomes divine.[13]

This time, he has added the category of "friend" to the possible relationships, and has replaced the suggestive "holds thee fast, with warm embrace, forever," with the infinitely more chaste "becomes divine."

He thought the poem now safe enough to publish. In 1841, he combined it with a new version of one of his other poems to Shaw ("I would I were the Sun") and submitted it to the *Dial* with a note to the editor, Margaret Fuller. He here confessed, "*sub rosâ rosissimâ*," that the "bits of verse" were his: "I don't think of myself made for a poet, least of all an *amitory poet*. So if you throw the 'lines' under the grate of your critical wisdom, I shall not be grieved, vexed or ruffled." Fuller happened to like "Protean Wishes," as the poem was now called. It appeared in the July 1841 issue.[14]

Parker's intimacy with Shaw inevitably created troubles at home. Things seem to have come to a head in April 1841, when he noted in his journal that Aunt Lucy, "in her wisdom," had reproached him for visiting his "*neighbor*" too much. Parker's response, self-righteous as it is, throws perhaps the clearest light on the problems of his marriage:

She [Lucy] does not conceive of *friendship*—the friendship of two souls. My love for —— is ideal. It were the same if she were a man. [I]t is a brother's love, nothing less. I crave sympathy, a sympathy L[ydia] does not yield me,—for my *thoughts*, my imagination, my prayers. I ask a place where I may feel safe—where no rude tongue may assault me—when I find it, *there I will go*. But I would not for the world harm a thought of L[ydia]'s heart, nor give her a twinge of the lip. If she is less a *wife* than a *niece*—& such is the fact, it is more her misfortune than her fault.[15]

In the journal a few pages later, with this conversation obviously still on his mind, he wrote that without sympathy, "marriage is but a copulation of bodies—adultery made easy."[16]

OUTSIDE THE Parker household, accusations of another kind of infidelity—the theological sort—had been causing much stir. On 19 July 1839, Andrews Norton delivered his *Discourse on the Latest Form of Infidelity* to the association of the Harvard Theological School alumni, meeting at the First Parish Church in Cambridge. Parker was there and knew what was coming. "I flutter on the wings of expectation, for his ejaculations," he had written sarcastically to William Silsbee a few days earlier. "Andrews the Only" did not disappoint. Which is to say, he did. Parker thought the speech had "great merits of style," but was otherwise a "complete failure." It was published in August. George Ripley quickly decided to respond. A pamphlet war was underway. This most famous exchange of the Transcendentalist controversy would continue for ten months. Parker gradually would be drawn into it, as he edged closer to becoming a public figure.[17]

Unlike the old, avowed, and zealous form of infidelity, says Norton in his *Discourse*, the new one assumes the Christian name "while it strikes directly at the root of faith in Christianity, and indirectly of all religion, by denying the miracles attesting the divine mission of Christ."[18] The entire history of Christ is miraculous. To remove from it what directly or indirectly relates to his miraculous authority and works would leave nothing that was consistent or coherent. If no miracles in fact occurred, then the Gospels are fabulous—the products of utter folly or gross deception. We either believe that Jesus Christ was commissioned by God to speak to us in God's name, or we know nothing about him. We would have no grounds to venerate him or to consider his teachings of importance.

Norton also claims that reliance on the historical evidence for Christianity is the only way to maintain social authority. In a note to the published version of the *Discourse*, he addressed the argument that since Christianity is a universal want, God would meet it with a universal principle intrinsic to our nature. Advocates of this view think historical Christianity cannot be the basis for belief, because it is based on testimony, which is extrinsic to our nature; even worse, the vast majority of people lack the scholarly skills properly to investigate the Christian books. Norton responds that although the want of religion is universal, religious belief can only be established "by the exercise of reason, by investigation, by forming a probable judgement upon facts." All higher knowledge, including the religious, requires labor, thought, and learning to effect its development, clear exposition, and general reception. In all knowledge, the benefits of the many are derived from the efforts of the few. We must accept religious truths as we do all other truths—on the authority of others more learned than ourselves. There can be "no intuition, or direct perception, of the truth of Christianity, no metaphysical certainty."

Norton's *Discourse* demanded a reply, and Ripley, his disputant of 1836, was the obvious man to write it. He had *The Latest Form of Infidelity Examined; A Letter to Mr. Andrews Norton*, ready for the printer by the beginning of September 1839, when he read the manuscript to Parker. The younger man found it "strong, clear and very good," "excellent in design and execution, equally fine in manner, matter and spirit." Yet he thought there was "a higher word to be said on this subject than Ripley is disposed to say just now." [19]

The problem with Ripley's *Letter* is that despite its length—almost 160 pages—it does not directly address Norton's underlying point: that Christianity must be received as a uniquely divine, supernatural revelation. He devotes the bulk of his pamphlet to an attack on Norton's adherence to the "exclusive principle." Norton wants the Unitarians to choose sides. Ripley replies, in effect, that they should not have to. He accuses Norton of making the criterion of Christian belief his own conviction that "*the miracles recorded in the New Testament are the ONLY PROOF of the divine origin of Christianity.*" A denial of the miracles is not a denial of the "divine origin" of Christianity; the two points are logically distinct. He then presents forty-five pages of quotations to prove that other kinds of evidence have been accepted by the Christian fathers, Protestant reformers, and modern liberal divines, including Norton himself (Ripley cites his opponent's earlier writings to prove his point), and recommended in Scripture. [20] Ripley's argument is much weakened, however, because he never says whether or not by "divine origin" he means, as Norton does, "exclusively supernatural origin."

Ripley is on stronger ground when he turns from scholarly arguments to pastoral ones. Undue emphasis on the historical evidence, he says, makes for deadly preaching; Norton's fondness for such evidence stems from his lack of practical ministerial experience. He unfairly questions the sincerity of a great many ordinary believers, whose faith rests on other evidence. Ripley strongly objects to the implication of Norton's doctrine, which Norton himself seems to admit, that ordinary people must depend for the fundamentals of their faith on a class of "scholars and antiquaries." Norton thus denies the Protestant principle that people should judge the truth for themselves, denies the religion of the heart, and repudiates the example of the Savior, who found his disciples among unlettered fishermen, not learned rabbis.

Parker agreed with Ripley, as far as he went. In a sermon on the "Evidences of Christianity," preached just as Ripley's *Letter* went to press, Parker also held that the unlearned cannot find out the facts of the miracles for themselves. The best proof of Christianity, he argued, and the only one that need not be learned from the pulpit or by rote, is that Christianity answers the wants of the soul.[21]

Parker here, like Ripley in his pamphlet, did not address the fundamental question of whether or not Christianity is uniquely supernaturally revealed. But he did address it elsewhere—most publicly in two Thursday Lectures, delivered (as were all Thursday Lectures) at the First Church in Boston. In the audience would be members of the Boston Association of Congregational Ministers, the organization of Unitarian clergy who had charge of the Lecture. Making a Transcendentalist statement about revelation before his "brethren" was a bold thing to do, as most of them agreed with Norton about the importance of miracles.

In "The Relation of the Bible to the Soul," Parker attacked the idea of a special historical revelation. He had written this sermon early in 1839, in the excited weeks after he successfully preached "The Contradictions in Scripture"—and therefore months before Norton delivered his *Discourse*. Parker surely meant to reply to Norton, however, when he chose to deliver the discourse as a Thursday Lecture on 1 August, only two weeks after Norton had spoken. Elizabeth Peabody, who probably heard the Lecture, must have sensed his new willingness to risk public controversy because a few weeks later, she wrote him urging caution. "I have precious little of the spirit of a martyr," he responded confidently, "but inasmuch as I fear no persecution, I fancy I can 'say my say,' and go on *smoothly*: but if not, why well, I can go roughly."[22]

The Lecture is bold and daring; it anticipates in many of its points Parker's enormously controversial sermon on the "Transient and Permanent in Christianity," preached almost two years later. Parker informs the Brethren that the Bible is neither the master of the soul nor the foundation of religion, nor is the New Testament the foundation of Christianity. "If it could be shown," he declares, "in opposite [*sic*] to the &c that all the facts of the N[ew]. T[estament]. were no facts (though there is the strongest historical proof of this truth) [Christianity] were just as true. Just as lasting as now. Its truths were laid in human nature." The Bible is a teacher, but with no supernatural authority.

What it teaches us, "we could all find out by ourselves at some period of our lives": the nobility of our nature, our duty to be perfect.[23]

Inspired teachers, says Parker, in art or science as in religion, are those who see what others do not dream of. They "have a greater portion of the Soul, that is in all other men." But pupils outgrow their teachers. They *can* outgrow them because they start from higher ground; they *must* outgrow them to be true to themselves; they *do* outgrow them every day in science, art, and even in religion. Moses was a great and prophetic man, but the peculiar institutions of his system have long since fallen ino decay, the ruin (evidently he means Judaism) "only tenanted by ignorance & superstition which linger about the tent of that great man, as Owls & Bats, wh[ich] cannot bear the light, seek shelter in rotten trees & old forsaken buildings." Moses' system has served its purpose, having fitted us for higher instruction.[24] Parker again, as he had in the "Contradictions in Scripture," radically separates the Old Testament from the New.

This line of argument leads Parker to a disturbing question: How do we know that Christianity in turn shall not be passed by and forgotten, having "prepared the way for a more beautiful manifestation of man than [Christ] himself?" There are those even today, Parker provocatively insists, who understand Christianity better than James and John, Peter and Paul. Yet Parker seeks to reassure his audience: "[Christianity] itself, in its essence, can never pass away." This "essence" Parker defines as the Christian ideas "of God, of man, of the connection between them: Its account of man's duty & destination: of God's love that broods like the day over beast & plant & man; the prophetic prayers for the [Kingdom] of [Heaven] on earth; all these are immortal as Thought, Religion & God."[25] Parker seeks to defend Christianity, in other words, by extracting its "permanent" element and separating that from Scripture; according to this apologetic, Norton's concerns about the subversion of Christianity are misplaced.

Parker risked controversy again when he returned to the First Church on 2 January 1840, and delivered a Thursday Lecture on "Inspiration." He had written this sermon in November 1839 to complement another one, on "Omnipresence," but soon realized that the topic lay at the heart of the Transcendentalist controversy. He therefore decided to present the discourse before the Boston Association and even wrote an "enlarged & Improved" edition for the occasion.

Inspiration, Parker here told his assembled Brethren, is the *"direct & immediate action of God upon the soul."*[26] To understand it, observe God's influence on matter; the action in both is the same, only the manner is different. God is everywhere in nature. No part is devoid of the divine influence. Because God is everywhere the same, the law on which nature rests is fixed and immortal. The obedience to this law in the inanimate world, and the animate world outside of humans, is perfect. This is why we find the influence of God in the hills and meadows "more congenial to the growth of Morality & Religion than the close contact of conscious men in crowded towns."

The divine "substance & energy" not only constitute the life and law of outward nature, they also "possess" the human soul. This possession we call inspiration. The fact of inspiration has been generally believed. The doctrine of the church is that God has spoken to some men, such as the prophets, Paul, the Apostles, and Jesus. We therefore think of their words as having authority. This is wise, for they were doubtless inspired. But has God seen fit to inspire only "some score of men"? To speak directly "only in the early ages of the world" and "only to a single race," and "in the Hebrew tongue"? Parker says not: "[I]n all ages from the dawn of time to this moment—in all the families of men[,] the spirit of God has flowed into the Soul." The list of inspired men should include Socrates, Confucius, Zoroaster, among many others.

There can be, says Parker, only one *kind* of inspiration: "It is the direct & immediate perception of Truth in some important mode—e.g., religious or moral." There can be only one *mode* of inspiration: "It is the constant presence of the Most High in the Soul, imparting this truth; the felt & acknowledged presence of Him as Truth, Charity, Holiness, Justice or Loveliness, infusing himself into the soul & giving it new life." There can be only one *criterion* of inspiration: "The truth of the thought, feeling or doctrine." There are many *signs* of inspiration, ranging from deep conviction to miracles; but none of these are *proof* of inspiration. Jesus had the highest *degree* of inspiration ever possessed; but he and other sages had the same *kind* of inspiration. He will continue to hold his exalted place until God creates a soul yet larger and nobler. Not until then can a more perfect religion be proclaimed.

When the lecture ended, and as the audience dispersed, Parker stopped to chat with Convers Francis and another minister. Suddenly, Dr. Francis Parkman, the senior Unitarian clergyman in Boston and Anna Shaw's uncle, came up and addressed him sternly. Parker later set down in his journal a phonetic transcription of what Parkman said: "When you write about Ralph Cudworth" (Parker's article on the neoplatonist had just appeared in the *Examiner*), "I read ye & like ye—but when you talk about 'future christs,' I can't beâr ye." Parkman accused him of impiety and more. Parker felt so "grieved" by this surprise attack that he abruptly left the building and "went weeping through the street."[27] Parker had assured Elizabeth Peabody that he was ready to "go on roughly" if required, but in fact he was not ready at all.

Meanwhile, the Norton-Ripley debate had veered into secondary matters. About a month after Ripley's *Letter* to Norton came out, Norton's *Remarks* on it was in the press. In January and February 1840, Ripley published two more *Letters* in reply. Just the opening few pages of Norton's pamphlet, and

All the Force of Transcendentalism

the closing few of Ripley's second pamphlet, concern the basic questions of inspiration and authority.[28]

Norton insists that a miraculous revelation can only be confirmed by tangible miracles: We "have no grounds for believing anything miraculous, where nothing miraculous appears." He denies Ripley's accusation that he believes only in the historical evidence for Christianity. There is an obvious difference, he says, "between the evidence necessary to authenticate the fact of a divine revelation, and necessarily implied in the existence of the fact," and the evidence we may now have that a revelation was once made. This latter evidence is vast, various, and persuasive. But it all bears on one point: that a revelation was made by God and authenticated by the miracles of Jesus Christ. Norton, as he had done in his *Discourse*, wholly rejects the idea that we can perceive truths of religion directly in the mind. This view is "utterly inconsistent with any belief in Christianity as a revelation from God."

Ripley's reply, when it finally came at the end of his *Third Letter* in February, was to call "revolting" Norton's claim that the soul could not perceive religious truth. This idea, says Ripley, is contradicted by "the universal consciousness of man." We never have been shut out from intercourse with our Maker. To rely on "external" testimony alone is to make certainty impossible, as Norton admits; yet the "soul of a Christian . . . seeks a higher boon than this." Mere probability, decided by intellectual researches, leaves the heart "dry and impoverished." The tone of faith "is that of confidence; in its best moments of triumph; habitually, of serene and joyful trust." It beholds the presence of God.

This exchange touches on vital matters and even indicates a fundamentally different religious temper. Ripley, in this sense like the Quakers and Anne Hutchison before him, sought religious certainty, while Norton, in this sense like the old New England Puritans, made lack of assurance an element of true faith. But the bulk of Norton's *Remarks* and of the two pieces by Ripley concern literary questions.

Norton, in his original *Discourse*, had in passing attacked Spinoza, whose system "may appear like a text-book of much that has been written in modern times." The seventeenth-century philosopher affected religious language, but his system is founded on atheism, because it holds that the laws of nature bind God. Spinoza's "God" is thus mere nature and not God "in the proper sense of the word." Norton had gone on to attack the modern Germans. In a note to the published version, he accuses De Wette, Schleiermacher, and Strauss of hiding infidel opinions behind prose that was incoherent—at least according to the sample translations he provides. Ripley, in his first *Letter*, had taken time to defend Spinoza from the charge of atheism. He had also accused Norton (with justice) of egregiously misinterpreting and mistranslating De Wette and Schleiermacher. Ripley may have felt compelled to broach these scholarly matters because he had long championed the writings of the two Germans: he was publishing several volumes of De Wette translations in the *Specimens of Foreign Standard Literature* and had written a long essay in the *Examiner* extolling Schleiermacher. As Norton himself pointed out, Schleiermacher had himself extolled Spinoza. Ripley may have thought that defending the German theologian required defending the Jewish philosopher.

Norton used his *Remarks* to make an extended rebuttal of Ripley's attack on his scholarship. He defended his translations of Schleiermacher and De Wette and his assessment of them and of Spinoza. Ripley, in his *Second Letter*, protested that Norton had given the debate a new direction: "You have taken it from the people, and given it to the scholars. You have confined it to points, in which few take an interest." Unfortunately, he took up the challenge. His second and third *Letters*, which have a cumulative length of over two hundred pages, are almost wholly devoted to defending these three thinkers from Norton's aspersions. This exchange at least served one purpose: it raised public awareness of Schleiermacher, De Wette, and especially Spinoza. As Parker acidly remarked, he doubted that even Norton had read Spinoza's chief works before the controversy began. Now long summaries of the philosopher's views were being published in the *Register*.[29]

Still, Parker complained in his journal that the debate had turned "personal & literary," and "the question between [the two men] is lost." "I wish some one would move the previous question," he writes, "viz. *How does man attain to Religion? Whence get the fundamental truths of Religion?*"[30] He resolved to write a pamphlet on this theme under the pseudonym "Isaac Smith." The name was in part a stratagem. Parker had a reputation as an expert on German theology and would be expected to defend it if he published a controversial pamphlet. A plain-spoken, square-toed Yankee like "Isaac" would not.

Yet Parker did want to defend the Germans. Back in September 1839, he had contemplated in his journal writing an article on German literature.[31] And he now delayed writing his "previous question" pamphlet until he had completed a long review of David Strauss's *Das Leben Jesu*. Parker finished the review on 1 April; some two weeks later he brought it over to the *Examiner*, where it was published in July.

To say a temperate word about Strauss in Boston in early 1840 took some courage. Strauss, as has been noted, held that popular expectations about the messiah gradually and naturally attached themselves to the figure of Jesus and that the miracle stories in the Gospels were all "myths"—that is, fictions that sprang up from a desire to make the history of Jesus conform to these expectations. Norton, in the notes to the published version of his *Discourse*, had attacked Strauss along with De Wette and Schleiermacher, but Ripley had not even attempted to defend him. How could he defend a writer who taught, in Norton's words, that "the account of Jesus in the Gospels is destitute of historical truth"? If some in New England saw Schleiermacher and De Wette as infidels thinly disguised, most thought that Strauss had torn off the mask. In April 1839, Parker had spoken with Dr. Channing about translating Strauss's book into English; Channing had advised him against it, adding "very archly" that he should not be sorry if some of the followers of the convicted blasphemer Abner Kneeland should undertake the work. (In the end, the English Unitarian Mary Ann Evans, who later became a famous writer under the pseudonym George Eliot, did the translation, which was published in 1846.)[32]

Parker was requested to write his review of *Das Leben Jesu* by the editor of the *Examiner*, William Ware. Four years after the book appeared in Germany, this was to be among the first serious notices it received in America — or even in English; Ware may have decided a review was needed now, since German theology had become a topic of heated public debate. That he asked Parker to write it indicates Parker's standing as a scholar. Still, Ware worried about the young man's Transcendental leanings. In February, he rejected an article Parker had written on mysticism, saying that it was too tolerant of infidelity. Ware was sending a clear signal that the *Examiner* would publish nothing too controversial. Parker wrote his review accordingly. "I could not say all that I would say, from the stand-point of the Examiner, for this is not allowable," he noted in his journal when he finished the manuscript, "but the most the readers of that paper can bear."[33]

What Parker might have said, had he spoken freely, is indicated by his unpublished writings. He himself had begun to take Strauss's argument seriously only in early 1839, after he had preached "The Contradictions in Scripture." Until this point, his doubts about the Bible had been almost exclusively over the Old Testament. Now, he suddenly became concerned with the problem Strauss posed: "What are the historical facts at the basis of the Christian movement?"[34]

In February 1839, Parker wrote to Convers Francis that "*no learned & free [Christian] thinker believes all that is contained in any writer of the N[ew]. T[estament].*" Parker was concerned above all with the historical accuracy of the Gospels. Even before 1839, he had said he did not literally believe the account of the Temptation. In 1839, he said privately that he did not believe in the miraculous conception, the stories of demonic possession and exorcism, the accounts of the dove descending on Jesus at his baptism and of the articulate voice proclaiming him "my only begotten son," or the stories of the Ascension (which Parker called "old wives fables"). He began to doubt the miracles happened, wondering why Paul never mentioned them; if Paul knew of Lazarus, why did he say Jesus was the first raised from the dead? Parker also professed to doubt Jesus' predictions of his death and even the Resurrection itself. He compared, in his journal, the stories surrounding Jesus with the myths surrounding Hercules, suggesting that they were equivalent: both were sons of the supreme being by an earthly mother; both encountered temptation; both worked wonders; both were put to death by their enemies; both descended to Hell for the "benefit of the race" and ascended to Heaven and were exalted. Due in part to such skepticism, he speculated in his journal that the "ideal Christ is what we are to preach, & perhaps we shall not need the Gospels very much, in delineating him."[35]

Parker left such speculations out of his Strauss review. Still, when he read part of the article to Ware, he noted that the editor of the *Examiner* "looked very suspiciously upon me." Ware printed it, but had reason for suspicion. The article was a comment, albeit indirect, on the Norton-Ripley debate. Norton had condemned modern German thought wholesale and had cited as evidence of its low state that writers like Strauss had not been greeted with "universal wonder and derision." Parker therefore opens his piece with a comparison of German and English theology.[36]

Eighty years ago, he says, the English stood far in advance of the Germans. The most notable German theologian of the day was the Lutheran dogmatist Sigismund Baumgarten; philosophy was ignored and critical inquiry suppressed. By contrast, England was full of great thinkers and new ideas. The Deists had spoken; great men—the Broad Churchmen and Liberals—had risen up and given unprecedented progress to the Protestant Reformation. The works of Montaigne, Malebranche, Bayle, "even" (a quick glance toward Norton) "of Spinoza," had English readers. Yet Germany has since made a great advance. "Men study theology as the English once studied it,—as if they were in earnest." The English, meanwhile, have not been merely stationary, they have gone backward. Their theology now bears little fruit.[37]

Strauss's book, then, cannot be dismissed out of hand because it is a product of German theology—nor because its conclusions are unsettling. Parker understood that his readers had a deep aversion to Strauss's effort to reduce the New Testament to mythology. Although he himself strongly disagrees with Strauss on key points and even thinks his book savors of Pantheism ("using Pantheism in its best sense"), he is careful to portray the German as a reasonable and serious man.[38]

He calls *Das Leben Jesu* of "profound theological significance" (which was true), and claims (plausibly) that it was "the most remarkable work that has appeared in theology, for the last hundred and fifty years." He favorably contrasts it with other "attacks on Christianity." It surpasses its predecessors in "learning, acuteness and thorough investigation," and although it is not written in a religious spirit, it is marked by a "serious and earnest" tone. "There is none of the persiflage of the English deists," Parker points out, and "none of the haughty scorn and bitter mockery of the far-famed Wolfenbüttel Fragmentist." Parker emphasizes that although Strauss does not think the Gospels factual, he insists they were not intended to deceive. Parker portrays Strauss as more Christian in expressing his unbelief than certain conservative theologians, like E. W. Hengstenberg, are in professing their faith.[39]

Parker may also be trying to portray Strauss as reasonable by the way he summarizes his principles, methods, and conclusions. This summary takes up the bulk of the review and is fair and accurate. Still, Parker seems to take what opportunities he can to present Strauss's conclusions in a way that fitted with widely accepted Unitarian ideas. He twice cites Andrews Norton's *Genuineness of the Gospels*, for example, to show that Strauss and Norton agree about the spuriousness of Matthew's genealogy and the legendary character of Luke's nativity narrative. He emphasizes, too, Strauss's attacks on narratives that he knew many Unitarians, besides himself, had trouble accepting literally, such as the Temptation and the driving of the demons into the swine. He also is careful to point out times when Strauss seems to admit that an event or text was not wholly mythical (e.g., Strauss thinks that John really did baptize Jesus and that some of Jesus' controversial narratives are genuine).[40]

Parker makes clear that he disagrees with Strauss. He was not feigning his criticisms for the sake of William Ware; they are too cogent (they are partly derived from some of Strauss's more formidable German critics, notably De Wette), and they match what Parker says elsewhere.[41]

He holds that Strauss's methods have led him to exaggerate the mythic content of the Gospels. Parker engages in a little persiflage of his own, applying Strauss's principles to American history to "prove" that the Declaration of Independence was a myth; Parker here sounds much like the young schoolmaster ridiculing George Bigelow's infidelity back in Watertown years earlier. More to the point, Parker notes that although other critics have maintained the New Testament contains myths, only Strauss thinks that there is no fact behind these myths and that they arose purely out of popular beliefs. Parker rejects this interpretation of myths; they are not, he argues, made out of air, but historical materials. Parker thinks Strauss reverses the order of things — makes the effect appear in the cause and the idea appear in the mass before it appears in the individual. "If there was not an historical Christ to idealize, there could be no ideal Christ to seek in history."[42]

The view of Scripture Parker recommends as most compatible with both a "cultivated understanding" and a "pious heart" is neither that the Bible is entirely historical nor that it is entirely mythical, but that it "always rests on historical ground, though it is not common historical ground, *nor is it so rigidly historical that no legendary or mythical elements have entered into it.*"[43] Parker seems to have needed the Gospels to delineate the ideal Christ, more than he was sometimes willing to admit.

Despite his criticisms, he insists that Strauss has done valuable work. Strauss represents the crisis of the age. He has "done what many wished to have done, but none dared to do," and his work will help mankind over the "great chasm" between, on the one side, "the frozen realm of stiff super-naturalism, and lifeless rationalism," and, on the other, "*free religious thought, where the only essential creed is the Christian motto, 'Be perfect, as your Father in Heaven is perfect,' and the only essential form of Religion is Love to your neighbor as to yourself, and to God with the whole heart, mind, and soul.*"[44]

Within days of sending off this manuscript, Parker began writing a "New Opus," his pamphlet on the "previous question" between Norton and Ripley. Here he would engage for the first time directly in their debate and address some of the points he had avoided for tactical reasons when reviewing Strauss. Even though he planned to publish under a pseudonym—the name evolved, as he wrote, from "Isaac Smith" to "Levi Blodgett"—he felt he was taking a terrific risk by expressing such views in print. In early April 1840, when he worked up a "rough sketch" of the "Opus," he wrote in his journal that "I have raised a spectre that will not down charm I never so wisely, & therefore I shall shut him up in my secret dark, where somebody will find the heretical [manuscript] when I am dead, & wonder what it meant." He planned to "warm my own fingers at the flame of this fire, though I may not exhibit the cinders to the gaze of the public."[45]

A few days later he went into Boston, read the manuscript to Ripley, then visited Margaret Fuller, who read him a "discouraging Epistle" from Frederic Henry Hedge. Fuller was at this time in the thick of putting together the first issue of the *Dial*. She had assumed, like everyone else, that Hedge would be a major contributor. At the end of March, however, Hedge had written from Bangor that if he identified himself publicly with the Transcendentalists, he would be seen as an "atheist in disguise." He "advises us the Transcendentalists 'to drink beer & dance with the Girls,'" commented Parker in his journal. "He fears he will lose his influence & his bread & cheese. I fear neither." Having rallied his courage, Parker quickly finished the "Opus" and sent it to the printer. It had scarcely left his desk when he got word of a new pamphlet issued by Norton, "containing a furious & false expose of *Transcendentalism.*"[46]

Norton had refused to respond directly to Ripley's last two *Letters*, pre-occupied as they were with scholarly matters. He thought that if he did re-ply, the public would believe he was acting from personal motives and ignore his arguments. He knew, too, as he wrote with sarcasm to William Ware, that many now regarded him "as a bigot, a holder of obsolete doctrines, a man of obsolete learning, and narrow-minded and over-zealous about trifles." Searching for ways to turn the issue away from himself, he urged his friend Palfrey to reply to Ripley and even sent the former dean materials to write a pamphlet, but Palfrey was too busy with his own projects.[47]

Norton turned to unlikely allies. In February, he began to call the attention of his friends to an anonymous article that had appeared the previous month in the *Princeton Review*, the journal of Presbyterian Orthodoxy. Written, as it turned out, by that formidable Calvinist stalwart Charles Hodge, it begins as a review of Norton's own exchange with Ripley. Hodge criticizes Norton for believing that miracles alone could confirm a revelation; the Holy Spirit, says Hodge, can also do that. He also indicates that he believes Norton's biblical criticism goes much too far. But he thinks Norton right to say that those who denied the miracles denied Christianity. The review then turns into an extended attack on Hegelianism as the leading philosophy of Germany and the logical outgrowth of Transcendentalist thought. Hodge draws his strictures mostly from the polemics of E. W. Hengstenberg, the Berlin professor and great champion of biblical literalism and strict Lutheran confessionalism. Hegelianism is divided into warring right and left wings, says Hodge: the difference between them is that the former are "outwardly decent" while the latter are "openly indecent." But they all are more or less openly pantheistic. Their philosophy undermines Christianity and morality.

Norton must have seen in Hodge, who in normal times would have been his theological foe, a disinterested and therefore credible ally. In February, he wrote to Ware asking that Hodge's review be noticed in the *Examiner*, and the following month, one of Norton's supporters got long excerpts from it printed in the *Register*.[48] Meanwhile, Norton had written to New Jersey and received permission to reprint the article as a pamphlet; with brahmin discretion, he removed the part that reviewed his debate with Ripley. Norton also received permission to reprint another *Review* article, written by two other Princeton professors, James Alexander and Albert Dod, which had been published in January 1839. This piece was an anti-Transcendentalist broadside, attacking Kant, Fichte, Schelling, Hegel (who believes "God himself is nothing"), Cousin, and Emerson. When *Two Articles from the Princeton Review, Concerning the Transcendental Philosophy of the Germans and of Cousin, and Its Influence on Opinion in This Country* appeared in early April, with a commendatory preface by "A. N.," it was, at a hundred pages, the most comprehensive polemic against the new thought yet published in New England.

Parker hoped that Ripley or even Hedge (whose knowledge of the Germans was extensive) would write a reply. "I am now too busy for anything of the kind," wrote Parker his journal, "though I fear I shall be drawn into some folly of this sort."[49] Folly or not, a little more than a week later he wrote "Transcendentalism," a satirical notice of the pamphlet for the *Register*. Parker may have decided to act because he sensed no one else would do it. Hedge stuck to his resolution not to get involved in public controversy. As for Ripley, his interests had already started to shift toward reform of church and society; in only five more weeks, his thinking on these subjects would prompt him to offer his resignation as pastor of the Purchase Street Church. He would write theological polemics no more.

Parker's satire took the form of a letter from an old man—yet another "Senex." He tells of reading A. N.'s pamphlet, learning with alarm about this "very naughty thing" called "Trans-*cend*-ent-al-ism," and falling suddenly into a profound slumber, where he is visited by a "very remarkable dream." In the dream, he stands on a Cape Cod beach and watches the approach over the sea of a cloud miles across and deep beyond measure. It is made up of flying men, divided into smaller parties of Left, Right, Centre, and Extreme, all furiously arguing with each other in incomprehensible languages. They alight on the shore and, maintaining their Left, Right, Centre, and Extreme positions, sit down—some on the great books they carried with them, some on nothing Senex can see, some on kegs, wine-skins, and fifteen gallon jugs—and begin smoking large tobacco pipes. But they keep talking fiercely as before in their strange tongues, each party making insulting gestures toward the other.[50]

While still absorbing this remarkable scene, Senex is approached by a man who announces himself to be a deacon from Munich and a spy for Hengstenberg. The spy informs him that this frightening and fantastic assortment of people—drawn from tombs, pulpits, professorial chairs, parlors, beer shops, and "places still worse" than beer shops, all "thrown together in the greatest confusion, without any regard to age, opinion or character"—were the Transcendentalists, who had fled across the sea because Hengstenberg had harried them out of Germany. At this news, Senex cries out in alarm: "We be all dead men, for the Transcendentalists have come! They say there is no Christ; no God; no soul; only 'an absolute nothing,' and Hegel is the Holy Ghost!" The spy reassures him that Hengstenberg himself will soon come to set things right.

Senex again looks over the ocean and sees a giant figure approaching in the sky. "It was Mr. Hengstenberg himself, mounted on a monstrous broom, alike his weapon, and his chariot. . . . Wonderful to tell, he grew smaller, and smaller as he came near us, till at last he was an homunculus, 'no bigger than a tobacco seed'; still he made a great cry. But soon he recovered his original size, and seemed a mere mortal, like ourselves."

To combat Transcendentalism, Hengstenberg announces to Senex, we must go back to the thirteenth century and believe the Old Testament letter for letter. We "must never consult Reason, but bow to the letter, and reckon a doubt as a sin not to be pardoned." Least of all "should we make the slightest attempt to reconcile Faith and Reason, Religion and Philosophy." Senex is awestruck: "We will do it all, . . . illustrious sage, or angel if thou art!" Whereupon he awakes—to find the pamphlet of one hundred pages lying before him, and his pipe broken at his feet.

All the Force of Transcendentalism

The *Register* published "Transcendentalism" on 25 April, but did so under protest. According to a note printed along with the piece, it was allowed to appear only because the editor, Rufus Johnson, was away for a few weeks, and his assistant did not feel he had the authority to reject an old and frequent contributor. Still, the assistant continues, he does not like the spirit or tone of the satire. Norton's pamphlet deserves a "grave reply." "It is not to be met with ridicule, a weapon commonly regarded as the last resort of weakness."[51]

Stung by these strictures, Parker produced a second piece, this time over his own initials, which he called a "Desultory Notice" of Norton's pamphlet. The *Register* published it on 16 May. It took up the entire first page of the paper and two columns of the second.[52]

Parker dismisses out of hand the reprinted article by Hodge, on the grounds that he draws "his facts, arguments and conclusions" from Hengstenberg, "one of the most violent polemics in Europe—a man whose theology belongs to the dark ages." Instead, the "Notice" concentrates on the other article, by Alexander and Dod.[53]

Parker's principal objection to their attack on German philosophy is that they are ignorant of it. None of their criticisms of Kant have to do with substance of his system; rather, they simply abuse his philosophy as obscure, abstract, and "extravagant." They attack Fichte, Schelling, and Hegel as pantheists and atheists. Yet they quote no work by the first two, and evidently have read nothing by them; their attack on Hegel, meanwhile, quotes him out of context and blames him unfairly for the occasional excesses of his followers.[54] When the Princetonians turn to Cousin, they also quote his writings out of context, while inaccurately making him out to be a disciple of Schelling and Hegel, when in fact he disagrees deeply with some of the ideas of these philosophers. Finally, they use Emerson's Divinity School Address as evidence that Transcendentalism—and thus Pantheism—was spreading among New England Unitarians. The Princetonians associate Pantheism with heartlessness, godlessness, and libertinism. Parker demands to know who these heartless, godless, and libertine Unitarians are.

Parker, like Ripley in his pamphlets, demands the debate be kept open. Let the errors of Transcendentalism exposed, but only in a fair and Christian spirit. Parker compares Americans to Jews wandering in the Wilderness, "parched with thirst, and pinched by hunger," looking longingly "not back to the flesh-pots, and leeks and garlics of Locke, and the Egyptian bondage of sensualism, but forward to the promised land of Truth, Liberty and Religion." Coleridge and Cousin, "the Caleb and Joshua of the new philosophy," give a favorable report that the promised land is near and bring "huge clusters of grapes, 'pomegranates, and figs.'" Yet we trust the others who say that "'the land eateth up the inhabitants thereof . . .'" and cry out "to stone them with stones."[55]

Meanwhile, only two days after his satire "Transcendentalism" appeared, *The Previous Question between Mr. Norton and His Alumni*, by "Levi Blodgett," went on sale. It was the first of more than a hundred pamphlets Parker would publish over the next twenty years. Historians have praised it, with justice, as perhaps the clearest short statement of the Transcendentalist theological case.

Parker had taken on the homely guise of Blodgett in part to avoid issues like those he raised in the Strauss review or the "Desultory Notice." He opens by apologizing to Norton and Ripley for the "humble style and uncouth phraseology of my letter, [which] I trust you will candidly excuse, when I assure you that 'ower much o' my life has been spent at the plough, and ower little at the college or the schule.' " [56] He does not take this disguise too seriously; bits of erudition are embedded everywhere in the text. Still, the Blodgett byline serves another purpose: it allows him to write a very lively essay. Costumed in Blodgett's comfortable clothes, he can be light-footed and even a little humorous ("uncouth"), as he could not had he come forward in his sombre minister's suit. Similarly, he could only have written a piece like "Transcendentalism" when disguised as "Senex."

The only question of real moment in your debate, says Blodgett to Norton and Ripley, is whether people believe in Christianity solely on the grounds of miracles. Yet the problem of the evidences of Christianity has difficulties not easily removed. Before we can touch it, the "previous question" must be answered: "HOW DO MEN COME TO HAVE ANY RELIGION, or, in other words, *on what evidence do they receive the plainest religious truths?*" The evidence for religious truths in general cannot be different from the evidence for the special religious truths of Christianity. "I do not see how there could be two *kinds* of evidence, any more than two *kinds* of right; but you Gentlemen, are learned, and can settle difficulties that puzzle simple folk." [57]

Blodgett identifies two truths of religion, without which "I cannot conceive any religion possible": "A BELIEF IN THE EXISTENCE OF GOD" and (proof that Blodgett, despite his lack of "schuling," had read Schleiermacher) "A SENSE OF DEPENDENCE ON HIM." How do men come to believe these truths? Blodgett's answer: "I reckon man is by nature a religious being; i.e., that he was made to be religious, as much as an ox was made to eat grass." The existence of God "is a fact given in our nature . . . given outright by God; a truth which comes to light as soon as self-consciousness begins." A sense of dependence on God is "a natural and essential sentiment of the soul, as much as feeling, seeing, and hearing, are natural sensations of the body." [58]

Blodgett tries to prove the existence of a religious nature; Parker would turn to these proofs often in the coming years. Blodgett says it would be absurd to think (like Norton) that God created man dependent on God and religion and did not give him "power in himself to become perfectly assured in his own heart, of the existence of God, and his sustaining power on which

All the Force of Transcendentalism

we may depend." There is an analogy in the natural world: "All animals are perfectly suited by their natures, to the sphere they move in, and it is absurd, even impious, to suppose that man is an exception to this law."

Also, an analysis of the powers of the human soul proves that belief in God is an indestructible element of the soul—"You come back to this fact as you examine and analyze any faculty of our nature." Moreover, looking back through history, you find no nation that does not admit of the existence of God and the sense of dependence on him. Blodgett says he is aware that "some of you" will say that the Creator made a miraculous revelation of religious truths "from without, and through the senses." But an outward revelation could be only the occasion of manifesting the innate "germs" of religion in us.[59]

The religious instincts, says Blodgett, must express themselves in action. They are wakened by the influence of "various objects of nature, and events of life, and intercourse of man with man." The form of religion therefore changes to suit the culture of the age. As the "tribe" or "race" improves, its religion becomes more perfect. Blodgett now presents a theory of religious history that Parker would develop in his *Discourse of Matters Pertaining to Religion*.

Religion is advanced as other human interests are, says Blodgett, by "distinguished individuals": "At the head of all departments of human thought, or interest, stand individuals, who are in some measure the concrete type of that interest." The higher the department of thought, the rarer and nobler the "guides or types." Religious teachers are the rarest and noblest.[60]

Blodgett asks how these teachers know what they know, and so he addresses the great issue of inspiration. All people have two "*direct* channels of communication with God, viz., Conscience and the religious Sentiment." "One reveals the moral law; the other the Beauty of Holiness." Original religious teachers "are enlightened directly from God, for the religious sentiment and conscience, 'his greater and lesser light,' shine straight into them. It is no figure of speech to say these men are inspired. . . . But though inspired, their inspiration was no more strange and out of the way, than that of the Poet or Painter, the Philosopher, or the Artist; it is only higher, and greater in degree, and more intense in its action."[61]

Blodgett denies that inspired teachers need to work miracles to confirm the revelations they make. People appreciate the powers of a great religious teacher, he says, as they appreciate the superior talents of a great general or artist. No miracle was needed to convince them that Caesar possessed more martial skill than they, or that Homer sang sweeter. They required no "foreign proof"; the works of these men was sufficient. So "in the case of a religious teacher men listened to Zoroaster, or Budha [*sic*], or Fo" (he evidently means Confucius), and felt their superiority.[62]

Blodgett does not deny that these men worked miracles, although (as Parker and the other Transcendentalists had done for years) he conceives of "miracles" as natural, if extraordinary, phenomena: "If a man is obedient to the law of his mind, conscience and heart, since his intellect, character and affection are in harmony with the laws of God, I take it, he can do works, that are impossible to others who have not been so faithful." But Blodgett confesses that he cannot determine the kind or number of miraculous acts performed by any of these teachers. Their powers have surely been exaggerated: "Legends, (or *mythi*—I think the learned call them) increase in number, and marvellousness [*sic*], in proportion to the sensuality of the people where they originate, or in proportion to their ignorance of the facts of the case." Even when the possession of miraculous power can be proved, it is only a *sign* of the genius of a religious teacher, never a *proof*.[63]

Blodgett now turns from religion in general to the particular case of Christianity: true Christianity he "reckons" to be the highest form of religion. He expands on this idea in a passage that touches on themes Parker had voiced in his "State of the Church" sermon and that he would soon develop in "The Christianity of Christ, of the Church, and of Society": "The Christianity of the church is, gentlemen—you know better than I what the Christianity of the church is,—what the average morality and religion of the community, and therefore of the church, which only subsists by representing and slightly idealizing that average morality and religion. But the Christianity of Christ is the purest, the most intense, and perfect religion ever realized on earth. I say *realized* for it was realized in its arche-type and founder, though perhaps never since then." Blodgett admits, however, that Christ may not be the ultimate incarnation of God, "for I cannot measure the counsels of the Infinite."[64]

Blodgett suggests what a future and greater Christ would look like. Jesus represented only the moral and religious side of our nature, says Blodgett. Perhaps someone will be created who is "the full measure of perfect humanity," uniting "the poetic, philosophic, artistic, political and religious archetypes in himself." Such a person would be a more perfect incarnation of God than Jesus was—but not a more perfect incarnation of moral and religious excellence. "Of course, he could not reveal more perfect religion, as I take it." Therefore, Blodgett takes it for granted that Christianity is "absolute religion."[65]

Blodgett finally returns to the problem of the Christian miracles. Christianity must start, he says, from the same primary, general truths as other religions: belief in God and sense of dependence. Christ, like his predecessors, always assumed these truths as self-evident. No miracle was needed to confirm them. Therefore, no miracle was needed to confirm any of the other truths Christ taught. These are derived from the primary truths, and "I am

All the Force of Transcendentalism

told by my minister, who is an argumentative man, it is a maxim of logic, that what is true of the genus is true of the species."[66]

Still further, Christianity is either the perfection of a religion whose truths are innate in the soul, or it is the perfection of religion whose truths are not innate in the soul. If it is not in the soul, then miracles would be necessary to establish the divine authority of a teacher. Yet devout people, if they found a religion unnatural and repugnant, must reject it even if the teacher of that religion had satisfactory "credentials of his divine office." Suppose, for example, that a miracle worker "should assure a large audience in Boston, that it was a moral duty to lie, steal, and kill; and, at their request, as proof of his divinity, and the truth of his doctrines, should feed that large audience to satiety, with a single loaf of bread; would they believe the new doctrine in opposition to conscience, reason, and religion? If they did thus believe, the fact would only prove that their senses were more active than their souls."[67]

Blodgett says he believes that Jesus, like other religious teachers, wrought miracles. But the character of Jesus gives value to his miracles; they do not prove his divinity. Many others wrought miracles (and even if they were not real, they were as good as true to such as believed them), yet the effect of these miracles was trifling, because no great soul worked them.[68]

Also, there are historical difficulties establishing *all* the miracles Jesus wrought: "I reckon it would be difficult to prove in a court of justice the reality of any one of the miracles ascribed to Jesus in the Gospels, with the exception of his resurrection," which is not Christ's miracle, but God's act. The Epistles, "though older than the Gospels, as you tell us," mention no particular miracles; if Paul had known Lazarus and two others were raised from the dead, would he have called Christ "the first fruits of them that slept"? The authority of the Evangelists is not quite satisfactory. "I have read in some of the religious papers" (Parker's own article in the *Examiner*, no doubt) "that a German critic — Dr. Strauss I think — has explained a great deal of the New Testament into *Mythi*, as the papers called them, which had no foundation in fact." Blodgett says he does not like "Mythi" ("that Hebrew word") but has long thought there was "something legendary" in the stories of Christ's birth, early life, and ascension.[69]

Now since these things are so, "it seems to me much easier, more natural, and above all more true, to ground Christianity on the truth of its doctrines, and its sufficiency to satisfy all the moral and religious wants of man in the highest conceivable state, than to rest it on miracles." The spiritual elevation of Jesus is a more convincing proof of his divinity than his miracles. "I take him to be the most perfect religious incarnation of God, without putting his birth on the same level with that of Hercules."[70]

Happily, Blodgett concludes, the miracles question is one of theology, not of religion. But do you wish for us to rest our theology and even our religion on a ground so insecure? If the groundwork of Christianity is to be left at the mercy of scoffers, or scholars and critics, what are we, the unlearned, to do? Blodgett beseeches Norton and Ripley, "in behalf of numbers of my fellows, pious and unlearned as myself, to do one of two things, either to prove that the miraculous stories of the Bible are perfectly true . . . or leave us ground our belief in Christianity on its truth,—which is obvious to every spiritual eye that is open. . . . Until you do one of these things, we shall mourn in our hearts, and repeat the old petition 'God save Christianity from its friends, its enemies we care not for.' "[71]

The purpose of the Levi Blodgett pamphlet had been to push the Norton-Ripley debate back to basic issues. But neither Norton nor Ripley was interested in continuing their exchange. Perhaps as a result, the pamphlet received comparatively little notice, and its author remained anonymous. Even two years later, in the review for the *Examiner* of Parker's *Discourse of Matters Pertaining to Religion*, the reviewer could comment that the author had used an astonishing variety of sources, "from Homer and the early fathers down to an obscure pamphlet by one Levi Blodget [sic]." But Convers Francis was in the know and wrote Parker asking him to thank Levi, when he saw him, for writing "one of the best pamphlets ever published."[72]

Others read more critically. One of the only notices of the pamphlet appeared in the July *Examiner*; the reviewer was William Ware. He accused "Mr. Blodgett" of reducing Christianity to natural religion. We had natural religion before Christ came, says Ware, and can have it now in Africa or the Pacific islands; we value Christianity because it is something more. The views of this pamphlet are injurious to Christianity, for insofar as the miracles are made out to be other than what the Evangelists claim them to be, just so far is the New Testament shown to be worthless. Although Ware admits that Blodgett does not deny the reality of the miracles, he notes presciently that it is "hardly conceivable" that anyone who did not see the miracles as proofs of Christ's authority would long admit them as facts, except "through mere force of habit."[73]

A few months earlier, in late May, Parker probably had heard David Damon, the Unitarian minister in West Cambridge, attack the Blodgett pamphlet in his address to the annual Berry Street Conference. Damon set out to answer various arguments that had been advanced against the traditional understanding of the significance of miracles—including those of Ripley and William Henry Furness. The miracles have no other obvious purpose except to confirm a revelation, Damon insists; and without them, Jesus would be today half-forgotten. To the objection (voiced by Blodgett) that we would not believe a wonder worker who urged us to do evil, Damon responds that "I wait, and expect to wait, for the presentation of this difficulty in the shape of facts." He asserts that the "unbelief that is most rife and most to be dreaded is unbelief of the miraculous facts," and points with alarm to Blodgett's suggestions that the "authority of the Evangelists is not quite satisfactory" and that the miracles could not be proven in a court of law. Yet he concludes his address mildly, urging only free discussion of the subject.[74]

Some of the brethren felt less tolerant. After Damon's speech, the conference debated whether or not "differences of opinion on the value & authority of miracles, [ought] to exclude men from [Christian] fellowship & sympathy with one another?" Parker, who was present, recorded in his journal that Ripley, Hedge, and Caleb Stetson had defended the New School (although he thought they had not touched the "fundamental questions"), and that the conference had resolved to respect differences of opinion. Parker was nonetheless "horrified" that the question had been raised at all: "This in the 19th century! This in Boston!! This among Unitarians!!!"[75]

The debate at Berry Street was an omen. By raising the specter of infidelity, Norton had forced the question of exclusion, previously unthinkable, onto the table. He may have complained that few leading Unitarians would support him in publicly denouncing the Transcendentalists, but he had successfully changed the terms of the controversy. When the difference between the New School and Old was seen as whether or not to "spiritualize" Christianity, the New School had had the advantage. Despite the efforts of Ripley and Parker, Norton had made the issue to be one of Christianity or No Christianity. This fight the Old School would surely win. Hedge had sensed the new climate of opinion when he had declined to write for the *Dial*.

Parker sat silent at Berry Street. He was still hesitating on the brink of becoming a Transcendentalist spokesman. Yet Dr. Parkman already had denounced him as "impious," and in April, Parker had written in his journal that many of the brethren, including William Ware, no longer regarded him as a "safe man." Now the debate at Berry Street seemed to fire him with new resolve. When he got home that night, he wrote in his journal: "I intend in the coming year to let out all the force of Transcendentalism that is in me, come what will come."[76]

PARKER NOT ONLY resolved, he acted, and over the coming months his friends noticed the change. "I want you to hear Parker preach *now*," wrote Elizabeth Peabody to John Sullivan Dwight in September. "He has got on fire with velocity of his spirits speed—and the elements melt . . . in the fervant [*sic*] heat of his word."[77]

His new willingness to speak out boldly is seen by his decision to publish many more potentially controversial articles. Some of them were a direct extension of his involvement in the Norton-Ripley debate. For example, he published his two daring Thursday Lectures. He produced a third draft of

"Inspiration," changing it from a sermon to an essay, retitled it "The Divine Presence in Nature and in the Soul," and submitted it to Margaret Fuller. It appeared in the first issue of the *Dial*, which came out in July 1840. Parker would go on to publish a number of major articles in the Transcendentalist magazine, including one in each of the first five issues. He also revised "The Relation of the Bible to the Soul," making numerous stylistic changes and adding a paragraph that reflected his current thinking about the Bible: in the original version of the sermon, he had criticized only the "imperfections" of the Old Testament; in the new paragraph, he says the New Testament also contains errors. He submitted the revised sermon to the *Western Messenger*, where it was published in two parts during the winter of 1840-41.[78]

In January 1841, he published in the *Dial* his long-contemplated defense of German literature. Parker had conceived of the project in September 1839, when he noted that he should write a review of "Felton's book" when it came out. He was referring to a survey of German literature by the Stuttgart literary critic and journalist Wolfgang Menzel, which was being translated into English by Cornelius Felton for Ripley's *Specimens of Foreign Standard Literature* series. The translation finally appeared in the summer of 1840, and Parker had his review completed by early November. Only the final third of the article, however, concerns Menzel's survey. (Parker did not like it; he found Menzel too superficial and opinionated, with an exaggerated dislike of Goethe.) Rather, Parker uses the review to carry forward the apology for German literature that he had begun in early 1840 with his article on Strauss and in his "Desultory Notice" of Norton's *Princeton Review* pamphlet.[79]

Parker opens "German Literature" with laughter at the polemics of Norton and the Princetonians. If we are to believe what is currently reported, Parker writes, there exists in New England a "faction of discontented men and maidens" who love everything Teutonic, "above all the immoral and irreligious writings, which it is supposed the Germans are chiefly engaged in writing, with the generous intention of corrupting the youth of the world . . . and thus gradually preparing the way for the Kingdom of Misrule, and the dominion of Chaos and 'most ancient night.'" Yet, Parker reports, he has never met any of these dangerous lovers of all things German. Those he knows who read German literature "are mostly,—yes, without a single exception, as we remember—unoffending persons." They go their own way and leave others the same freedom; they have scholarly habits and some have no contemptible erudition; they study German literature as they would that of any other nation, for the good in it.[80]

On the other hand, "we are told—and partly believe it,—that there is a party of cool-headed, discreet, moderate, sound, and very respectable persons, who hate German literature. Of these we speak from knowledge." They are numerous as acorns in autumn. Their hate is mostly based on prejudice, and "on the most utter ignorance respecting the whole matter." Their judgments are like those of those medieval monks who condemned the revival of classical learning, or like the Turkish justice, who saw no reason to try a criminal before passing sentence. Let us embargo German works, suggests Parker ironically, as we do India crackers. Let us then pronounce on German works, as the medieval monks did on the classics: *Anathema sit!*[81]

Turning serious, Parker departs from this "high court of Turkish justice," and proclaims German literature to be "the fairest, the richest, the most original, fresh, and religious literature of all modern times."[82] He picks up where he left off in the beginning of the Strauss review and extends his comparison between the literatures of Germany and England. Parker has given himself the chance to wear his erudition, won with such toil, as a dazzling coat—and he seizes it.

He starts with classical scholarship. From whom do we get the editions of the classics worth reading, "in which modern science and art are brought to bear on the ancient text"? Why, the Germans. "We do not hesitate to say, that in the present century not a Greek or Roman classic has been tolerably edited in England, except through the aid of some German scholar." The English provide the white paper and the luminous type; the Germans alone provide the diligence, profound knowledge, and philosophy.

> Whence come even the grammars and lexicons, of almost universal use in studying the ancient authors? The name of Reimer, and Damm, and Schneider, and Büttman, and Passow, give the answer. Where are the English classical scholars in this century, who take rank with Wolf, Heyne, Schweighauser, Wyttenbach, Boeckh, Herrmann, Jacobs, Siebelis, Hoffman, Siebenkees, Müller, Creutzer, Wellauer, and Ast? Nay, where shall we find the rivals of Dindorf, Schäfer, Stallbaum, Spitzer, Bothe, and Bekker, and a host more? for we have only written down those that rushed into our mind. What English name of the present century can be mentioned with the least of these? Not one.[83]

Parker here bludgeons his opponents with intimidatingly long lists of German names; he writes as if none of them need introduction, although he knows few of his readers will have heard of them. Convers Francis, when he read the piece, understood Parker's intended effect: it "must strike our foolish babblers dumb."[84]

Parker keeps up the barrage through the article, arguing that no English scholar can match any of the formidable number of Germans he names in the fields of ancient history, physical geography, general civil and political history, the history of science, art and literature, biblical criticism, ecclesiastical history, or (notably) theology: "Wegscheider's Theology is doubtless a poor work; but its equal is nowhere to be found in the English tongue. Its equal, did we say? There is nothing that can pretend to approach it. Where, then, shall we find rivals for such theologians as Ammon, Hase, Daub, Baumgarten[,] Crusius, Schleiermacher, Bretschneider, and De Wette? even for Zachariæ, Vatke, and Kaiser?"[85]

Yet the strength of the Germans in these fields is not, says Parker, the chief merit of their literature. It has lately produced four philosophers who hereafter will be named among the great thinkers of the world: Kant, Fichte, Schelling, and Hegel. "Take Kant alone, and in the whole compass of thought, we scarce know his superior." Philosophy is "epidemic almost" in Germany, and "a score of first-rate American, or half a dozen English reputations, might be made out of any of their writers of fourth or fifth magnitude." Moreover, they are also eminent in other departments of elegant letters. Here Parker voices some criticism of German writers, many of whom he accuses of weakly imitating foreign models. But "the staple of their literature," he insists, "is eminently original. In point of freshness, it has no equal since the days of Sophocles. Who shall match with Wieland, and Lessing, the Schlegels, Herder, so sweet and beautiful, Jean-Paul, Tieck, and Schiller, and Goethe?"[86]

The greatest charm of German literature, he continues, is its religious spirit. It is the most religious literature the world has seen "since the palmy days of Greek writing." "We had almost said it was the only Christian literature the world has seen," but no one has yet even dreamed of realizing the idea of a Christian literature. Parker's article, which opens satirically, now turns prophetic. Using evocative imagery from the Gospels of Matthew and Luke, he suggests we have as yet only the "cradle song of Christianity":

Christianity is still in the manger, wrapped in swaddling bands, and unable to move its limbs. Its Jewish parent watches fearful, with a pondering heart. The shepherds, that honor the new-born, are Jewish still, dripping as yet with the dews of ancient night. The heathen magicians [who] have come up to worship, guided by the star of truth . . . are heathen even now. They can only offer "gold, and frankincense, and myrrh." They do not give their mind, and still less their heart. . . . The Herod of superstition is troubled, and his city with him. . . . [H]e would gladly slay the young child, that is born King of the world. But Christianity will yet grow up to manhood, and escape the guardianship of traditions, to do the work God has chosen. Then, and not till then, will the gospel of beautiful souls, fair as the light, and "terrible as an army with banners," be written in the literature, arts, society, and life of the world.[87]

All the Force of Transcendentalism

Parker in this article presents a formidable scholarly front. But the long lists of names he provides are grouped indiscriminately. His familiarity with German thought seems broader than it is deep—an impression perhaps unfairly reinforced by his rhetorical strategy of providing no analysis of what the Germans were saying. Moreover, he unwittingly indicates the limits of his German reading. The names he can rattle off most readily are those of professors in classics, biblical criticism, ecclesiastical history, and systematic and practical theology. Here, evidently, he is on very familiar ground. But when he turns to German philosophy he only lists the most obvious figures.

This article was not his last word on the Norton-Ripley debate. That appeared two months later, in March 1841, and seemed to be about something else entirely. "The Life of Saint Bernard of Clairvaux: a Chapter Out of the Middle Ages," presents itself as an assessment of the great twelfth-century abbot. That William Ware missed its implications is undoubtedly the reason he allowed it to be published in the March 1841 issue of the *Examiner*—despite his deepening suspicion that the young man was "unsafe."

Why did Parker feel the need to write about Bernard, who, in Parker's own judgment, "belongs to that long list of middle-age scholars, on whom the world has passed the bitter doom of forgetfulness and night"? His books are now dusty and worm-eaten, and when opened seem to the modern reader strange, barbaric, uncouth, and repellent. He is among the authors "before whom Industry folds her hands, and gives up the task; from whom Diligence, with his frame of iron and his eye of fire, turns away, dispirited and worn down." The Middle Ages were not a popular subject of study in New England at that time, and Parker may have conceived of the article as filling a scholarly gap. At least, his original journal entry concerning the article, from September 1840, implies nothing more: he proposes to write two pieces, one on Bernard's life and another on his works (similar to Parker's earlier articles on the neoplatonist Henry More), and appends a long list of sources to consult.[88] But Parker often sketched studies in this journal that he was never to pursue. What sustained his interest in this project? Could it have been his realization that hidden behind this medieval rood screen, he safely could handle the charged issues of the day—miracles and the division among Unitarians over religious authority?

Parker, as he unfolds Bernard's life story, dwells on the many miracles the saint is supposed to have performed. Such stories, he comments, mark a credulous age, "when a sharp distinction was not made between the miraculous and the natural; when the effects of imagination, of a strong will, or sensitive nerves, were less understood than now, and when 'wonders' were expected of each very holy man. Where they are expected, or looked for, they always come." In 1842, Parker would make explicit the radical implications of his argument. "There is far more testimony to prove the fact of miracles . . .

in times comparatively modern," he would write in his *Discourse of Religion*, "than to prove the Christian miracles." St. Bernard of Clairvaux, for example, "cures the deaf, the dumb, the lame, the blind, men possessed with devils, in many cases, before multitudes of people. . . . His wonders are set down by the eye-witnesses themselves, men known to us by the testimony of others. I do not hesitate in saying that there is far more evidence to support the miracles of St. Bernard than those mentioned in the New Testament." If modern, rational Unitarians do not feel compelled to admit Bernard's miracles, why should they feel compelled to admit those of Jesus?[89]

Parker also discusses Bernard's suppression of heretics, notably Abelard. In the "German Literature" article, Parker had compared the hostility of certain medieval monks against classical learning to the hostility of contemporary conservatives against German thought. Now he extends the analogy. When light began to dawn on the world once more, says Parker, and the ancient sages or poets were rediscovered, men wiser and holier than the church rose up. Two parties appeared. One "stood on authority, and adhered strictly to the old theological formulas, and if they could not find expressed therein the sum of wisdom which they sought, they found it by implication." These "conservativists . . . dealt out, with a lavish hand, the thunders of the Church, and its fire and fagots too, against all who dared to look forward." The "other party, few in numbers, but often mighty in talents, relied on no authority, however great and good. They referred all to the human soul, or rather to the Spirit of God in the soul of man."[90] When Parker goes on to detail the suppression of the Abelard, giant of the New School, by Bernard, champion of the Old, he implies that the judgment of history will be against Norton and Hodge: Abelard could be suppressed, but the truth he uttered could not.

Parker's article on Saint Bernard appears in part to have been a sly satire—the slyest he ever wrote. Despite growing disapproval of his increasingly radical views, he had slipped an attack on Norton past William Ware and into print. Soon after, Parker would be wholly shut out of Unitarian publications. His piece on Bernard was his last article to appear in the *Examiner* for seventeen years.

IN THE FALL of 1837, Parker had said that he was preaching "Transcendentalism" to his congregation. His sermons indicate that by "Transcendentalism" he meant a certain set of positions on the theological issues of inspiration, miracles, and authority. By the spring of 1840, when he resolved to let out all the force of "Transcendentalism" in him, his understanding of the term evidently was evolving: radical social reform was emerging as a significant element of it. In June, he wrote two sermons that were major statements of his new position, "A Lesson for the Day, or the Christianity of Christ, of the Church, and of Society," published in October, and "A Sermon of Work," which he turned into an essay and published the following April as "Thoughts on Labor."

The idea that society needed to be changed had appeared back in the summer of 1838, when he heard Emerson's Divinity School Address and preached on the "State of the Church." He had started to argue that the spiritual state of society was low and that certain social ills were the result of this low state. In his sermons over the next year and a half, he had supported some specific reforms—stricter temperance laws and universal education—and had denounced slavery, the Cherokee expulsions, and the exploitation of labor. He continued to preach on these topics, but they became part of a deeper indictment against the social order, one grounded in the idea, central to his weekly preaching, that our duty was to perfect the soul. Now he saw the social order as an obstacle to that perfection.

As he said in a sermon in the fall of 1840, the efforts of the temperance societies, abolition societies, and peace societies were good, noble, and even divine. At a time when Christianity "nods over her Bible, & sleeps in her pew of a Sunday, while she makes slaves & keeps them, & strives to render the rich richer & the poor poorer all the week, the world cannot afford to be nice & criticize the only men who are awake." Yet the aim of these reformers is superficial and partial. They do not ask why the inmates of our jails are there; why seventeen men out of every score live in fear of poverty their whole life; why three-fourths of men and women must toil so much that they have nothing left for intellectual improvement. He wrote in his journal that he felt deeply the wrong of society: "A Reformation will scarcely suit me. It must be a Revolution that sets the world right."[91]

The scope of his indictment against "things in general" is indicated by various journal entries from the spring and summer of 1840. The state he calls *"a bundle of shams"* because it is based on force, not (like real Christianity) on love. A Christian state is "like a square circle, that will not be found even in dreams, for as [Christianity] goes up the state goes down."[92]

Parker in particular condemns how the laws "degrade half the human race" —women—and "sacrifice" them to men. An example is prostitution, in which "embraces, like beef, are bought and sold": "Oh the damnableness of this taint on social life." But even marriage, as it now exists, is a disgrace: "Man at marriage promises to endow his wife 'with all his earthly goods,' while at that moment she is one of them, & can't inherit in her own right a farthing of her own estate, or what was hers a moment before."[93]

He accuses society of causing the crimes and hanging the criminals. Our prisons make more criminals than they mend. And those called criminals are often less sinful and guilty "than such as wear the red livery of municipal justice." Such thoughts were on Parker's mind in August, when he watched a black man on trial for beating his wife. He was on a trip to New York (his first out of Massachusetts since 1836) and had stopped by the imposing new courthouse and jail, built of marble in the fashionable "Egyptian" style, and popularly called the "Egyptian Tombs":

> It seemed to me [he comments in his journal] the place was well called "Egyptian" from the darkness that covered over justice in that place; and "tombs" for it appears, as all our court-houses are, the Sepulchre of Equity. How can it be "Justice" to punish a crime the institutions of society render unavoidable? . . . This poor Negro at trial for a crime showed me in . . . miniature, the whole of our social institutions. 1. He was the victim of [Christian] cupidity, & had been a slave, 2. From this he had probably escaped by what was counted a crime by his master, or else was set free — by charity, perhaps trying to cover up its own sins. 3. He was cast loose in a society, where his colour debarred him from . . . the rights of man, & forced him to count himself a beast, with [nothing] to excite self-respect, either in his condition, his history, or his prospects. Poor wretched man, what is life to him! He is more degraded than the savage, has lost much in leaving Sahara, & gained — infamy, cold, hunger, & — the white man's mercy — a prison of marble.[94]

Parker's discontents with his marriage and his position, which were becoming acute at this time, surely contributed to his sense that all was not right with the world. The journal entry in which he announces a revolution is needed to set the world right, for example, is headed "Misfortune," opens with the comment that "My life is very sad & dull," and closes with his familiar complaint that he is preaching to an audience of only seventy adults.[95] Yet the sources of Parker's social radicalism cannot be entirely personal; Emerson, Alcott, Ripley, and Brownson were moving in the same direction in 1840.

In a sense, the Transcendentalists were merely keeping up with the times. By 1840, reform of every kind was in the air. Garrison was agitating for immediate abolition of slavery; the Grimké sisters had given their famous abolitionist lecture tour, which had provoked the opening controversy of the women's rights movement; Horace Mann, secretary of the newly formed Massachusetts Board of Education, was starting to professionalize the public school system; Sylvester Graham was promoting his new diet and system of hygiene; labor reformers were demanding a ten-hour workday; socialists were trying to establish ideal communities; and Edward Palmer was pursuing his solitary experiment of living without money. Behind this ferment were secular social changes — the beginnings of industrialization and all the rearrangements of life that went with it, especially the emergence of a new, self-conscious, urban middle class.[96] Yet the reasons for Parker's especially intense interest in reform in 1840 cannot be attributed directly to such general causes.

All the Force of Transcendentalism

Was his interest a response to the lingering effects of the panic of 1837? The panic had hit during Parker's candidacy, when a sudden international contraction of credit had precipitated bank and business failures across the country. Parker had been shocked to see "the best of Men . . . daily suspending Payments, and going to pieces in the Storm of the currency." While staying in Boston that May, he had written to a friend that people "gather by twos and threes in the Streets . . . all talking of the hard times, telling who has failed, who will fail, who not." The flood of failures eventually slowed (although there was another surge in 1839), but money remained tight, and the depression lasted for four years.[97]

Ripley and Brownson seem to have been goaded to radicalism in part by the panic. With their urban ministries, they could not ignore the resulting distress among the "laboring classes." Ripley's Purchase Street Church was an oasis of gentility in a deteriorating and increasingly Irish neighborhood down near the wharves; when he walked to work from his home at Rowe Place, he did not close his eyes. He later said that he could not "behold the degradation, the ignorance, the poverty, the vice, the ruin of the soul, which is everywhere displayed in the very bosom of the Christian society in our own city, while men look idly on, without a shudder." For Brownson the problem was even more acute. He had established his free church, the Society of Union and Progress, in order to reach the unchurched laborers of the city, and he quickly sensed "more hatred of the rich" in his congregation than he had expected. The panic appears to have prompted him to preach about the "contest" between the "privileged and underprivileged" and to call for giving everyone "equal chances to wealth."[98]

Yet the panic seemed only to perplex Parker. As he said in a sermon in November 1840, "We have continually for the last 3 years been complaining of *hard times, hard times*, when the country was full of wealth." Living in the midst of comfortable farms, he seemed to have difficulty believing the depression was real. He mentions the economy rarely in his preaching and then only to insist that the commercial distress had been "slight." He seemed to blame the hard times on a failure of will. "The buyer complained that he could not purchase," he said in a sermon, "the seller that he could not buy. The lazy man that he could find no work, & the profligate because he became poor . . . and the fault was all laid on the door of *the hard times*. Were it not so melancholy it might make a man smile." Parker certainly did not see the recession as a reason for reform. Young nations, he said, like young men, "are prone to excess in all they undertake" and "will suffer one year because they purchased more than they could pay the year before, & will be happy in laying the blame on the National Bank, or the N[ational] Government."[99]

Many Americans did lay the blame on the banks or the government. The economy became a major political issue. Democrats, now led by President

Martin Van Buren, held the hard times to be the result of currency manipulation by greedy speculators who controlled the banking system, which needed reform. The most radical Democrats, the "Loco-Focos," demanded the abolition of banks and paper money. The newly organized Whig Party, meanwhile, which favored a strong banking system, blamed the hard times on the political high-handedness and financial recklessness of the Democrats in power. Partisan strife reached a new high in 1840, the first two-party presidential election in the modern sense. The Democrats accused the Whigs of being the party of the money power. The Whigs accused Van Buren of indulging in aristocratic extravagance at the people's expense and claimed that their candidate, the war hero William Henry Harrison, was a sturdy republican who would be content with "a log cabin and a jug of hard cider." The Whigs' exciting, ballyhoo-filled "hard cider" campaign brought droves of new voters to the polls while the depression sapped Democratic morale. Harrison and his party won in a landslide.[100]

The interest of the Transcendentalists in political matters could not help but rise with that of the country. Several Transcendentalists deliberately broke with the Whiggery of most Boston Unitarians and voiced sympathy with the principles, at least, of the Democratic campaign against privilege. Emerson's introductory lecture for the 1839 season, on "The Present Age," was "*democratic*" and "loco-foco throughout," according to Parker. But only Brownson, of the early Transcendentalist circle, actually endorsed the Democratic Party. Emerson liked the Democratic cause, but thought the Whigs had the "best men"; he styled himself an "indifferent Whig" and was happy to see Van Buren lose (if for no other reason, Emerson excoriated the president's Indian policy). Parker also liked Democratic doctrines more than their leaders, and, like Emerson, appears to have voted Whig in the 1830s. He came to dislike Whig policy, however, and to distrust the two most prominent Whig politicians, Daniel Webster and Henry Clay. Months before the 1840 election he privately decided he would not vote: "Then I shall have a vantage ground I can't possess now."[101]

Parker was not a disinterested observer of party politics. Politics came to disgust him. In a sermon preached a week before the 1840 election, he noted that "[m]any men are sanguine in their hopes if this party succeeds, or that." But he asked his congregation if they thought the leaders of either party would heal the evils of society? "Oh no," he answered, "they do not even dream of it. Believe them not."[102]

His contempt surfaced again in April 1841, when President Harrison, only a month in office, suddenly died. Parker's comments in his journal were not sad but sardonic: "All this tempest of words, those cataracts of hard cider to make [*sic*] the old General out of the world." He added that the president's death "could not be more opportune for the clergy of Massachusetts."

The news arrived just before Fast Day and so would "furnish such a fund of Homiletical capital for fast-day sermons."[103] Parker himself preached a short, rather noncommittal eulogy for Harrison as one of his two Fast Day sermons that year. His other sermon included an attack on Jacksonian political culture.

In "The Mechanical Tendency of the Times," Parker complains that Americans are partisans more than patriots, and "care more for their party, than they do for the *measures* of their party, though everybody knows the Party is of no value except to achieve the measures of the Party." We have many politicians, he says, who know how to service certain trades and interests, but have no "Great *Statesmen*" who "look forward & see what is good not only for a single state but for the whole land for centuries to come." Education, most notably, is neglected, even though everybody knows that "the defense of the Republic is in the minds & hearts of its sons and daughters." But politicians do little "except just on the eve of an election, when they know how to go to their districts . . . & talk [to] the farmers of learning, colleges & common schools, till the poor electors fancy the gods have come down to us in the shape of men & would offer slain beasts & sacrifices, calling one Jupiter, the other Mercury." Because education is neglected, we have an ignorant population, ignorant electors, corrupt newspapers, and wicked rulers. For these plagues the people can only blame themselves. Whenever "they are deceived, blindfolded, cheated as they have been—oftener than once in the last 13 years" (that is, since Andrew Jackson won his first term as president), "& that too by more than one political party, let them lay their hand on the afflicted spot & say my own sin has come back on my head."[104]

Parker said in another sermon that if America had a truly Christian government, there would be no need for "an army of office holders greedy to kepe [*sic*] their station, & a larger army of office hunters greedy to get station." The government would be a simple affair, consisting "of a few clerks at the capitol, with a moderate salary, whose office was to keep the books of the nation, & do the honour of the place to strangers, & reciprocate the good feeling of the similar clerks in other nations, & so keep at good understanding the world over."[105] This ideal, which Parker had first set out the year before in his "dream" about Boston in the year 3839, was hardly unique to him. The desire to minimize or do away with the state was pervasive among nineteenth-century reformers and radicals, from Dr. Channing to Karl Marx.

Neither the rise of political partisanship nor the economic downturn seems to have turned Parker toward reform. The source of the change seems to have been the Transcendentalist controversy. The conservative reaction against the Transcendentalists left Parker feeling alienated from conventional society and above all from the conventional church. He always linked political and social reform to religious reform, and when he attacked the evils of society, he also attacked those of the church.

The church was based on a "sham"—the infallible authority of Scripture. The practice of the church separated it from life, so that it could not meet the vital spiritual needs of the people. As he wrote in his journal in June 1840, many who were confined by the unchristian necessity to hard work all the week can find

> no amusement & recreation on Sunday but must sit hours in the church & hear two sermons on abstract subjects, written in a language peculiar to sermons, filled with sentences taken from an old Hebrew or Greek book—which though produced in the rudest age is appealed to as the infallible canon, the standard of all truth. . . . A sermon delivered in a tone never heard out of the pulpit, by a pale man who knows nothing of real life, except for stolen glances at lying romances, who is never seen in places of amusement, but is restricted to the company of . . . old women of both sexes, or none at all, a man who as the symbol of all this humbugging, is clothed in an antique dress [the black robe and white collar] never seen out of the church, & defunct colleges. This is the entertainment provided for real living men & women, & served up twice a . . . Sabbath from week to week, year out & year in, & the unfortunate man is lucky if he is not forced to . . . |take| [in] three of these feasts in a day. This is not all—if any could be fed by this food it is babes only, yet are forced also to come in, & eat & be filled. . . . Worse & worse the church, once catching a man never lets him go. . . . He may have sucked dry the paps of the church, she still hold out her dry breast & says, Come to unto me all ye that hunger.[106]

"Yet," Parker adds, with an apparent jolt of self-recognition, "I am in the pale of the church, am a clergyman!"[107]

Similar thoughts helped drive Ripley from the pulpit. Parker's solution was to try to redeem his position. As a symbol of his effort, he refused to wear the "humbug" ministerial costume of black robe and white tie. More important, he sought to preach down the shams, both religious and social, that he saw around him. With this goal in mind, late in June 1840, he wrote "A Lesson for the Day, or the Christianity of Christ, of the Church, and of Society." He preached it six times in the next few months (at Ripley's church, among others) before publishing a somewhat expanded and revised version in the October *Dial*.

A few days before Parker began writing the "Lesson," he had been talking to George and Sophia Ripley about the state of the church. They all agreed it was very bad. Yet when Parker noted the conversation in his journal, he maintained that "there has never been a time since the first settlement of the country when morals or Religion, were really at a higher flood." He would complain as loud as any about the lowness of the "common actual" and of

All the Force of Transcendentalism

the "common Ideal," "but I would not look back on any one age & say we are worse than our fathers—but forward to an *ideal* and say we are worse than that."[108]

Such is the strategy Parker adopts in the "Lesson." He opens with the claim that every nation, like every individual, has an ideal floating before it. The Christian ideal, "the stature of the perfect man in Jesus Christ," is what we are striving to realize in life. There is a great gap between the ideal and the actual; even worse, there is a gap between our *ideal* and the ideal of Christ. The Christianity of Christ is the highest ideal possible; the Christianity of the Church the very different thing held before our eyes; the Christianity of Society is that of the church, but imperfectly realized, and "has but the slightest affinity with Christ's sublime archetype in man."[109]

Parker's inspiration for the "Lesson," it quickly becomes clear, is Emerson's Divinity School Address. Emerson's cry against the spiritual famine of the churches, two years before, had prompted Parker to write his own sermon on the "State of the Church," which had echoed Emerson's language and tone and had marked the beginning of his prophetic preaching on social reform. Now, Parker draws off his old sermon to write the new one. He takes the same text from Revelation as he did before: "Thou livest and art dead." Most of the first section of the "Lesson," on the Christianity of Christ, is lifted almost word for word from the "State of the Church."

His picture of the times of Jesus once again bears strong resemblance to his image of modern New England: the religious form was "outgrown and worn out, though the State yet watched this tattered garment with the most jealous care, calling each man a blasphemer, who complained of its scantiness or pointed out its rents"; no wise man anywhere had faith in the popular religion, "except so far as he found it a convenient instrument to keep the mob in subjection to their lords." Once again, Parker echoes Emerson's Address, as when he calls Jesus "a true man; such as had never been seen before," and adds that Christ "found men forgetful of God. They seemed to fancy He was dead. They lived as if there had once been a God, who had grown old and deceased. . . . Accordingly they believed there had been Revelations, in the days of their fathers, when God was alive and active. They knew not there were Revelations every day to faithful Souls."[110]

Parker draws off his "State of the Church" sermon when he describes how multitudes of the poor in spirit heard Jesus, but that he was put to death by such "as thought old things were new enough, and false things sufficiently true, and like owls and bats shriek fearfully when morning comes, because their day is the night." Parker's explanation for how Christianity triumphed over the world, despite "fearful odds," is almost identical to what it had been two years earlier: "We are sometimes told it was because that divine youth had an unusual entrance into life; because he cured a few sick men, or fed many hungry men, by unwonted means. Believe it you who may; it matters not. Was it not rather because his doctrine was felt to be true, real, divine, satisfying to the soul; proclaimed by real men, true men, who felt what they said, and lived as they felt?"[111]

Parker's section on the Christianity of the church has no parallel in his earlier sermon, but does have one in Emerson's Address. In 1838, Parker had not responded to Emerson's condemnation of the church and the ministry. But he himself condemns them now—revealing how far the controversy of the previous two years had alienated him from his profession.

What is taught as Christianity, says Parker, is almost the opposite of what Jesus taught. The Christianity of Christ is about leading a divine life; that of the church is about belief in certain doctrines. To enter the Kingdom of Heaven, the church demands that you assent to its arbitrary creeds, and "bow the knee" to its forms. It therefore "insults the soul, and must belittle a man before it can bless him."[112]

Little is heard in our pulpits of the great doctrines of Jesus; still less are they applied to life. "The church is quick to discover and denounce the smallest deviation from the belief of dark ages, and to condemn vices no longer popular; it is conveniently blind to the great fictions which lie at the foundation of Church and State; sees not the rents, daily yawning more wide, in the bowing walls of old institutions." If Paul should come back to earth, he probably would not be admitted to the church, for he ventured no opinion on the nature of God and the history of Christ, while our churches utter dogmatic and arbitrary decisions and condemn as infidels all who disagree with these. And certainly, adds Parker, with the Transcendentalist controversy obviously in mind, if Jesus brought to New England the same boldness of inquiry and love of truth he showed in Judea, he would also be called an infidel by our churches and be abused by our newspapers.[113]

The Christianity of our churches "enslaves men to the Bible; makes it the soul's master, not its servant; forgetting that the Bible, like the Sabbath, is made for man, not man for the Bible." The church worships not God, but Jesus, "a man born of woman." He has been made to speak with authority greater than Reason, Conscience, or Faith. But since he was a "hero of the soul"—the noblest and largest the world has ever seen—"perhaps the idolatry that is paid him is the nearest approach to true worship, which the mass of men can readily make in these days."[114]

The influence of real Christianity is to restore the man to his nature, until he obeys Reason, Conscience, and Religion and is made free by that obedience. But those who accept the Christianity of the church "are, in the main, crushed and degraded by their faith." Theirs is not true faith, but merely fear. "They resemble the dwarfed creed they accept. Their mind is encrusted with unintelligible dogmas. They fear to love man, lest they offend God. Artificial in their anxiety, and morbid in their self-examination, their life is sickly and wretched."[115]

Below the deep of the Christianity of the church is a lower deep—the Christianity of society. For this section of the "Lesson," Parker takes arguments and language from his "State of the Church" sermon, although he improves the material by rewriting and rearranging it. He once again complains that Religion is not a " 'thousand voiced psalm,' from the heart of man to man's God," but a "compliance with custom," a "prudential calculation," whereby people hope to give a little time and money and gain the treasures of Heaven; that it has become "a working for wages"; that people think Religion useful only for the old and sick and poor, or as a valuable tool to keep social order; that they "deem it needful as the poll-tax, or the militia system"; that "the Hope of Heaven, or faith in Christ, might be summed up in the same column as money at one per cent." Parker once again asks how many young men—and, he now adds, women—ever set their hearts on a divine life? He again answers that "the mass of men care little for Christianity."[116]

Yet there are differences between his old discussion of the Christianity of society and his new one. He now says more about social sin than he did before: "Where shall we find a savage nation on wide world that has, on the whole, been blessed by its intercourse with Christians? Where one that has not, most manifestly, been polluted and cursed by the Christian foot?" He remarks too that if the people truly cared about Christianity, "the sins of the forum or the market-place, committed in a single month, would make the land rock to its centre." Yet Parker is not aiming in this piece to outline specific social evils he wants to eliminate.[117]

The most important difference between the old sermon and the new is in his discussion of how the people respond to the low state of the church. Here he takes images from the Divinity School Address. Like Emerson, he complains that Religion is so disregarded, "talent and genius . . . float off to the market, the workshop, the senate, the farmer's field, or the court-house, and bring home with honor the fleece of gold." Parker then provides his own gloss on the famous passage of the Address in which Emerson complains of a "clamorous" young minister (actually, Barzillai Frost): "Meanwhile, anointed dulness, arrayed in canonicals, his lesson duly conned, presses, semi-somnous, the consecrated cushions of the pulpit, and pours forth weekly his impotent drone, to be blest with bland praises, so long as he disturbs not respectable iniquity slumbering in his pew, nor touches an actual sin of the times, nor treads an inch beyond the beaten path of the church." Emerson had not mentioned that the dull preacher ignored iniquity, nor that he was praised for doing so.[118]

Emerson had said the soul was not preached, and so the people were falling away from the church. Parker says the people complacently *accept* the Christianity of the church and that this is a sign of the low state of religion among them. The times, he insists, are skeptical—people doubt "man's moral and religious nature." Even if they embrace Christianity, they do not make Jesus a brother, the archetype of divine life, but accept the doctrine that he is "an unnatural character; . . . amphibious; not man and not God, whose holiness was poured on him from some celestial urn, and so was in no sense his own work, and who, therefore, can be no example for us." Christianity is not for most people love to God and love to man, but instead "some perplexing dogma, or some oriental dream."[119]

At the end of the "Lesson," Parker turns to the problem of what is to be done. In 1838, he had proposed individual self-examination. Now, he seems to suggest that promoting the Christianity of Christ requires doing away with the institution of the church: "Use good words when we can find them, in the church, or out of it. Learn to . . . make Religion daily work, and Christianity our common life. All days shall then be the Lord's day; our homes, the house of God, and our labor, the ritual of Religion."[120]

As the structure of Parker's sermon suggests, he still believed that the church, even as it was, stood in advance of society. If the church were transformed, he believed, society would surely follow. Such ideas would become the heart of his social reform program.

IN 1840, the Transcendentalists grew deeply concerned with the reform of property and labor. At their club meetings, the Transcendentalists never seem to have discussed the problem of labor, but in May 1839 they did tentatively raise the issue of property. According to Parker's report of the meeting in his journal, "very little was elicited on this subject," beyond Alcott's statement that property "was not based on an instinct of the soul"; Hedge's comments were "guarded." Parker thought that there would doubtless always be property, but that "it may be distributed more wisely." He hoped rather vaguely that property may someday educate the moral powers as it now does the intellectual powers.[121]

Ripley, who was at this meeting, evidently said nothing that Parker found memorable. Over the next year, however, Ripley's growing estrangement from the church brought on by his controversy with Norton and his running dialogue with Brownson led him to question all social arrangements. In June 1840, he announced to Parker that he opposed the transmission of property from parent to child.[122] The following month, Brownson proposed the same idea in a famous article on "The Laboring Classes," which he published in his *Quarterly*. Abolish inherited property, he says:

> We see no means of elevating the laboring classes which can be effectual without this. And is this a measure to be easily carried? Not at all.

All the Force of Transcendentalism

It will cost infinitely more than it cost to abolish either hereditary monarchy or hereditary nobility. . . . The rich, the business community, will never voluntarily consent to it, and we think we know too much of human nature to believe that it will ever be effected peaceably. It will be effected only by the strong arm of physical force. It will come, if it ever come at all, only at the conclusion of war, the like of which the world as yet has never witnessed, and from which, however inevitable it may seem to the eye of philosophy, the heart of Humanity recoils with horror.[123]

Brownson's article sparked uproar, in no small part because he was a prominent Democrat and this was an election year. As Parker explained in his journal, the Whigs, "finding their sacramental idea—Money—in danger," attacked Brownson "with fire-brands & like weapons." The irony was that they thereby spread his doctrines, which if left alone "would come only to scholars." Parker professed to "like much" of the article, but disagreed with Brownson's ideas on property. He could not take lightly "the slight evil of killing millions of men," which like Brownson he assumed the abolition of inherited property would entail. This was not, however, Parker's only grounds for disagreement.[124]

He said many times that the "present system of property" brought "great evils" to society. He noted in his journal that "17/20ths" of crimes are committed against property, which showed him that "there is something wrong in the state of property." But unlike Brownson, he did not conceive the problem in class terms: he thought the current system hurt both the rich and the poor. Rather, the basic problem was spiritual. As he told Ripley, the "sin lies deeper than the *transmission* of property. . . . It lies in the *love of low things*."[125]

In his sermons, Parker emphasized the spiritual dimension of property—an idea he may have derived in part from Emerson. In *Nature*, Emerson had said that although certain farmers may own the fields and woods, "none owns the landscape": "There is a property in the horizon which no man has but he whose eye can integrate all the parts, that is, the poet. This is the best part of these men's farms, yet to this their warranty deeds give no title." In 1838, two years after Parker had read *Nature*, he had said in a sermon that we may possess the whole world, in a spiritual sense, but only if we are unselfish, good, and wise. We would then see that a legal title was the smallest part of property. Far more people can enjoy looking at "gay & costly raiment," for example, than can wear it.[126]

In August 1840, Parker elaborated on this argument in a sermon on "Property." We should not envy the holdings of the rich, Parker says, "for we can enjoy so much of what they possess." If someone has a fine house and beautiful lands, the "meanest passenger [*sic*] in the street may call them his so long as he rejoices in their beauty." We delight in the beauty of the butterfly with-out envying it. Can we not delight as wisely in the "fine raiments, worn by our human fellows, though it outshine our own plain apparel"? A woman who wears costly jewels is a public benefactor, for she sees less of her own splendor than the "unconcerned looker-on."[127]

If Parker was attempting to answer Brownson with this sermon, he fails. Privately, Parker himself admitted as much. He professed to be appalled by social inequality. "The houses of the rich are 'confection shops, where you get champagne & strawberries,' " he wrote in his journal, while those of the poor are "sheds": "Benumbed with ignorance & bowed down by labour, they render their homes too often like stalls for cattle, where they eat & where they sleep, where they are born & perhaps die, less lovely than at birth."[128] Parker, who himself had grown up in very modest circumstances, did not romanti-cize poverty. He insisted that the first condition of spiritual development was an "outward competence."

He obviously did not intend, in "Property," to justify social iniquity. Rather, his message here is part of his larger effort to turn both poor and rich away from low things. "Property" is addressed to those of slender means, yet Parker was painfully aware that he was not speaking to the truly wretched. "I cannot attend a Splendid Ball or soirée of the lettered few," he wrote in his journal, "but I think of those who sit in the outer darkness, & I cannot reach them. I sit down with a few gifted men & talk . . . [while] those who in the desperate vice of the Grog-shop & the Brothel find their satisfaction & I can do nothing for them."[129]

Instead of addressing such "weak" members of society, Parker typically tried to reach the "strong" ones—the wealthy, educated, and powerful. The injustices of society, he believed, were due far more to the selfishness of the strong than to the foibles of the weak. His message to the strong was there-fore consistent: Help the weak. He had in mind not charity, but social justice. This became clear when he addressed the problem of the "laboring classes."

Surely the starkest statement of it was made by Brownson. "All over the world," he writes in the "Laboring Classes," "this fact stares us in the face, the workingman is poor and depressed, while a large proportion of the non-workingmen . . . are wealthy." Brownson dismisses out of hand the idea that "any considerable proportion of the present generation of laborers" will ever work their way out of the laboring class. Some laborers have become rich, but "no man born poor has ever, by his wages, as a simple operative, risen to the class of the wealthy." His analysis of the workers' situation, published eight years before the *Communist Manifesto*, sounds presciently Marxist. The old struggle between the King and Barons is over, he says, as is the struggle between the Baron and the Merchants and Manufacturers. The coming war will be between Wealth and Labor—that is, between the middle class, or employers, and their natural enemy, "actual laborers, who are laborers and not proprietors, owners of none of the funds of production, neither houses, shops, nor lands, nor the implements of labor." [130]

Parker differed with Brownson on labor as he differed with him on property. He admitted the exploitation of laborers, but did not conceive of the problem as one of class struggle. In his journal, commenting on Brownson's article, he asks himself if one man may serve another for wages without being degraded? He answers yes, except that "I have no moral right to use the service of another, provided it degrades him in my sight, in that of his fellows, or himself." "It is surely unmanly," he writes elsewhere, "to receive a favor you would not give." [131]

As these remarks suggest, Parker's focus was less on the "laboring classes" than on "labor"—that is, work. He presented his ideas on the subject in his June 1840 sermon on "Work," which he later revised and published as "Thoughts on Labor." Here he conceives the problem of laborers to be at bottom the false idea *"that work degrades."* [132] He therefore asserts that work is not a curse, but a blessing, desirable in itself, and enjoyable.

By "work," he has in mind especially manual work. He deplores the widespread aversion to it. Young men, he says, children of hard-toiling parents, are ashamed of their fathers' occupation and seek to flee it. Parker relates an anecdote about how a shopkeeper and a blacksmith had lately advertised for an apprentice, and how fifty "beardless youths" had applied to the haberdasher and not one to the craftsman. The "terrible moral" to the story, comments Parker, is that "forty-and-nine out of the fifty were disappointed at the outset" (that forty-and-eight would have been disappointed regardless does not seem to occur to him). Moreover, this aversion for manual labor, "this selfish desire to escape from the general and natural lot of man, is the sacramental sin of 'the better class' in our great cities." Manual labor is in fact a blessing, a dignity; but even assuming it were a curse and a disgrace, "would a true man desire to escape it for himself, and leave the curse to fall on other men? Certainly not." Christianity goes even further and makes human greatness consist in the amount of service a person renders to the world. When Jesus washed the disciples' feet, he "meant something not very generally understood perhaps in the nineteenth century." [133]

More generally, Parker counts work to be any productive activity. Thus he says that someone who "invents a machine, does no less a service than he, who toils all day with his hands." Above all, and quite consistently with his overall worldview (and necessarily, considering his own career), he counts those who teach moral and religious truth the greatest benefactors of the race: "That is a poor economy, common as it is, which overlooks these men. It is a very vulgar mind, that would rather Paul continue a tent-maker, and Jesus a carpenter." [134]

Yet Parker sympathized with an idea suggested by the analogy of Paul and Jesus, and well articulated by George Ripley, that there should be "a more natural union between intellectual and manual labor than now exists." Ripley, in a letter to Emerson, presented as the goals of Brook Farm "to combine the thinker and the worker, as far as possible, in the same individual" and "to guarantee the highest mental freedom, by providing all with labor, adapted to their tastes and talents, and securing to them the fruits of their industry."[135]

In a "rational state of things," Parker agreed, labor would be enjoyable. Duty and delight would go in hand. "The duty of labor is written on a man's body; in the stout muscle of the arm and the delicate machinery of the hand. That it is congenial to our nature appears from the alacrity with which children apply themselves to it, and find pleasure in the work itself, without regard to its use. The young duck does not more naturally betake itself to the water, than the boy to the work which goes on around him. There is some work, which even the village sluggard and city fop love to do, and that only can they do well."[136]

Parker had long held that work was the "Great law of the body, mind and soul," as he had said in a sermon written in 1838, but the idea that particular kinds of labor were especially delightful to particular people, and that society could be rationally ordered to match the person with the work, was new to him. His thinking was probably influenced by Ripley, and through Ripley by the French socialist Charles Fourier. It was probably Ripley who called Parker's attention to *Social Destiny of Man, or Association and Reorganization of Industry*, a book by Fourier's leading American disciple, Albert Brisbane. Ripley, Brownson, and Emerson, as well as Parker, read Brisbane's book in 1840. When Parker did so (after he wrote his sermon on "Work"), he commented in his journal that "I have never seen so excellent a portrait of society as it is."[137]

The book is full of Fourier's peculiar ideas and technical jargon, but driving it was a powerful idea, very congenial to the Transcendentalists: that social iniquity would vanish if society were reshaped to conform to human nature. Human "passions" were good, thought Fourier, and if the social system were properly organized, people would be able to fulfill all the work of society by following their impulses. This way, in Brisbane's words, "*Labor*, which is now *monotonous, repugnant and degrading*, can be *ennobled, elevated* and made *honorable*;—or in other words, . . . INDUSTRY CAN BE MADE ATTRACTIVE." Parker, in his "Thoughts on Labor," sounds something like a Fourierist when he envisions a society in which "labor would never interfere with the culture of what is best in each man" because each would be doing "what nature fitted him to do." Even before Parker read Fourier, he had held that labor should be a "school to aid in developing the whole man, body and soul"; Fourier helped him to see that making labor an agent of human development would result in

All the Force of Transcendentalism

a sweeping transformation of society: "Then a small body of men would not be pampered in indolence, to grow up into gouty worthlessness, and die of inertia; nor would the large part of men be worn down as now by excessive toil before half their life is spent. They would not be so severely tasked as to have no time to read, think, and converse."[138]

Fourier was very specific as to how social reorganization should be accomplished. He planned for people to live in "Phalanxes"—communal dwellings of three to four hundred families—the design and organization of which he worked out in minute detail. In a Phalanx, not only would everyone be assigned work according their inclinations, but they would enjoy the benefits of concerted action; Fourier and Brisbane savaged the "incoherence and waste" of individual households. Parker was skeptical about the Phalanx idea, although he admitted it did not "appear less natural to me than a city would to Patriarch Abraham."[139]

Parker thought of the Phalanx as at best a long-term solution to the problems of society. But he thought there were other remedies at hand. The first, which he had proposed as early as 1838, was to distribute the work of society more equitably. The problems of society, Parker believed, were due to the "treachery" of one part of it—the wealthy who force others to work for them but do not themselves work. If it is true, he says, that we must choose either living as we now do, which requires that "seven-tenths of men and women should, as the unavoidable result of their toil, be cursed with extremity of labor, and ignorance, and rudeness, and unmanly life," or lessening the work of the world, which would require that we "sleep less softly, dine on humbler food, dwell in mean houses, and wear leather like George Fox" for the sake of a "wide-spread and generous culture"—if such were the choice, there would be no doubt how "Common Sense, Reason and Christianity" would choose: "Wisdom, virtue and manhood, are as much better than sumptuous dinners, fine apparel, and splendid houses, as the Soul is better than the Senses."[140]

In 1838, Parker had declared for wisdom, virtue, and manhood and stopped there; now, in "Thoughts on Labor," his thinking has grown more sophisticated and he denies that the choice is a real one. He embraces something analogous to the Marxist conception of "surplus value"; Marx argued surplus value produced economic crises, while Parker saw it as causing moral problems. Parker illustrates his thinking in a fable about a village named Humdrum. At the beginning of the story, the people of Humdrum work fourteen hours a day that they "may all be housed, fed, and clothed, warmed, instructed and made happy." Then some ingenious hands invent watermills, which allow all the old work to be done in only five hours. Nine hours a day have thus been freed for "study, social improvement, the pursuit of a favorite art, and . . . for amusement also." But the "longest heads of Humdrum," having selfish and not Christian hearts, "persuade" the laborers to keep working fourteen hours.

The state of society in Humdrum becomes unnatural, because so much more is produced than consumed. The "wise men" send off the superfluities and bring back luxuries for themselves. They live in palaces, their children do not work, they fare sumptuously, they are clothed in purple and fine linen. As for the common people, working as long and a little harder than before, they are spiritually debased. Parker believes that what today is called the "standard of living" has been gradually rising; the common people have some things their parents did not: French gloves, English cloth coats, red drapes for their windows. But for these "blessings," the laborer has agreed to part with the nine hours a day that the machinery has saved. He "will make his body a slave, and leave his mind all uncultivated": "He is content to grow up a body— nothing but a body. So that if you look therein for his Understanding, Imagination, Reason, you will find them like three grains of wheat in three bushels of chaff. You shall seek them all day before you find them, and at last they are not worth your search."[141] Parker wants laborers to set their sights higher, but the thrust of his argument is to blame their condition less on them than on the "wise" but selfish men who have exploited them.

The "artificial" state of society in Humdrum prompts nature to revolt. It is "scarce right for bread to come fastest into hands that add nothing to the general stock," so the people grow restless and begin to steal. Crimes become numerous, "the result of want, indolence, or neglected education"; they are mostly committed against property. To remedy this unnatural evil, judges, lawyers, courthouses, and jails are needed. Those jailed are sacrifices "to the spirit of modern cupidity; unfortunate wretches, who were the victims not the foes of society; men so weak in head or heart, that their bad character was formed FOR them, through circumstances far more than it was formed BY them, through their own freewill." Artificial diseases spread, caused by indolence on one hand and overwork on the other. Unnatural remedies are needed to treat them, so Humdrum must create a medical faculty.[142]

Parker believes the condition of Humdrum is the condition of our society because "the beastly maxim is even now prevalent, that the Strong should take care of themselves, and use the weak as their tools, though to the manifest injury of the weak." This maxim must be supplanted, he says, by the Christian idea of wealth and the Christian idea of work.[143]

He asserts that "if all men and women capable of work would toil diligently but two hours out of the twenty-four, the work of the world would be done" and we could be as comfortably fed, housed, and educated as at present. In fact, our condition would improve, because one class would no longer be crushed by toil and the other oppressed by indolence. We should then hear no more about "the sickness of sedentary rich men"; exercise for the sake of health would be given up; yet everyone would have more opportunity for study, social intercourse, and recreation.[144]

Caprice, ostentation, vanity, and luxury are what oppress the world, he says. If these are renounced, "and each performs what is due from him, and strives to diminish the general burden and not add to it, then no man is oppressed." We are meant to return to society, with the work of our head and hand, what we have received; those who do not are sluggards and robbers. If one cannot work, due to "weakness," infancy, age, or sickness, the rule of love is that such a one should be fed. But if "one will not work, though he can—the law of nature should have its effect. He should starve." Those who prevent themselves from starving by getting the earnings of others (i.e., the idle rich) "should properly meet with the contempt and stout resistance of society." [145]

We must, says Parker, reduce the number of "unproductive classes" (he includes traders, who he asserts create no wealth) and increase the classes of workers and thinkers. We must, too, let the mind do the body's work and allow the new machines we invent to set free the labor of many hands. [146]

In "Thoughts on Labor" itself, Parker is vague about how these changes are to be brought about, and at one point even suggests that it may be "best that man should toil on some centuries more before the race becomes of age, and capable of receiving its birthright." But he suggests a less passive approach in "The Beavers," a "new fable" that he wrote out in his journal in December 1839. [147]

One day, Parker begins, as the chief beavers were planning a new dam and village, there rose to speak Castor, a young beaver "of great acuteness & parts." It seems the "internal arrangements" of the beavers in those days were that the few who were wise stayed at home and "by dint of thinking" made others their "slaves." Castor announces that this system is wrong: "Hitherto the strongest of us have forced the weak & foolish to build the dams & cabins, & prepare the food for the whole race. Let it be so no more. Let the strongest do the work—the wisest the thinking, & let the most prudent be the Heads & the . . . bravest the soldiers of the whole race." Then, predicts Castor, there "will be no Sluggards to die of the Gout, & no workers laid up with Rheumatism from excessive labour & continual exposure."

The greybeards receive this speech with "great disgust." One (a rodent Dr. Parkman) tells Castor that "*he could not bear him.*" Another, a young beaver named Pollux, rises to answer Castor and the two debate. Pollux argues that the exploitation of the weak by the strong is the general law of nature and cites as examples the lion, queen and drone bees, and man. Castor replies that strong lions bring home food for the old and weak; that among bees the queen works more than any other—planning for the good of the race and being mother to the other bees of the swarm—and that drones do not dominate the hive; and as for humans, they were a "most frightful anomaly in nature, and their case does not apply." [148]

Castor then announces that he will debate no more. He wants his scheme to be tried, "& since I am the strongest Beaver in the race, & of the most ancient family—& already have such a name for wisdom that the degree of *Great Dam Projector*—has been conferred on me this early, I shall go to work & take the lead of the rest in the most difficult labour of planning & building." The greybeards, afraid to sit still, joined him; the rest fell "merrily" in. They built better than before, and there has never since been a quarrel about mine and thine, for all have enough to spare.

There is an authoritarian element in this fantasy of which Parker may not have been wholly conscious. The idea of a single, heroic genius reorganizing a society resembles Jean-Jacques Rousseau's equally authoritarian concept of a national "Legislator."[149] Parker's intended moral, however, seems to have been simply that society could be reformed if the true ideal were set before it—work he believed the "strong" members of society were both suited and morally obligated to undertake. Parker approved when George Ripley founded Brook Farm in 1841 on a democratic plan of mutual education: laborers and scholars would work side by side and teach each other. Yet Parker himself never joined Brook Farm, although he lived only two miles away. He believed his principal contribution to social reform would be made by transforming the church.

"It makes me groan to look into the evils of society," wrote Parker in his journal in July 1840. "I thank God I am not born to set the matter right. I scarce dare attempt a reform of theology, lest I be in for the whole, & must . . . condemn the state & society no less than the church."[150] Yet if Parker chose to focus his energies on reforming theology and the church, he did not believe he was thereby neglecting social reform. Rather, he placed religious reform at the center of his social reform plans.

So did the other Transcendentalists. At four of the five meetings of the little club in 1840, the discussion revolved around reform and the creation of a new church.[151] Brownson, Ripley, Alcott, and Parker, who differed with one another on many issues, all agreed that without religious reform, social change was impossible.

Once the Transcendentalists' ideas about religious reform are understood, some apparent disagreements between them diminish. For example, Parker says many times that although Christianity must be applied to the state and society, the "chiefest" and "best" way to apply it—the way that will ultimately do the most social good—is to the individual. Trust not to society, he says, to do the work of a divine life. Brownson, by contrast, in his articles on the "Laboring Classes," dismisses the idea society can be transformed by converting individuals to Christianity. This is "doubtless a capital theory," he says sarcastically, "and has the advantage that kings, hierarchies, nobilities,—in a word, all who fatten on the toil and blood of their fellows, will feel no diffi-culty supporting it." It also is "exposed to one slight objection, that of being condemned by something like six thousand years' experience." The evils of society are not individual in character, says Brownson, nor can individuals, by directing their efforts to their own character, remove it. "Could we con-vert all men to Christianity in both theory and practice, as held by the most enlightened sect of Christians among us," he asserts, "the evils of the social state would remain untouched. . . . The only way to get rid of its evils is to change the system, not its managers."[152]

If read more carefully, however, Brownson is saying that it is useless to con-vert people to the Christianity of the *church*, even in its Unitarian form. He believes the world would indeed be changed if people were converted to the Christianity of *Christ*. The church "makes its deluded disciples believe that they have done their duty to God when they have joined the church, offered a prayer, sung a psalm, and contributed of their means to send out a mis-sionary to preach unintelligible doctrines to the poor heathen." By contrast, Christ demands that we "labor to reform society, to mould it according to the will of God and the nature of man." Parker's own distinction between the Christianities of the church and of Christ was similar.[153]

Parker and Brownson, as has been seen, did disagree about inherited prop-erty. But in view of their ideas about religious reform, this disagreement does not appear so important. Brownson himself admits that any change in prop-erty relations would be a long time coming and then only after a mighty struggle. Our first task, he says, is the abolition of the "priesthood"—that class of persons which pretends to mediate between humanity and God. Fun-damental change in the church, he and Parker agreed, was a priority.

Brownson locates the historical origin of social injustice in the priest-hood.[154] Early in human history, he says, certain people arose who took ad-vantage of the natural human religious sentiment and the popular deference given to the wise to enslave their fellows and ensure honors and emolument for themselves. In this process, they brought to an end the wild freedom of the savage state and moved the race onto the first stage of civilization. The priesthood, therefore, is found everywhere as humanity rises out of savagery, ruling with an iron hand. The priests set up systems of social inequality that persist to this day, Brownson believes, and are the ultimate cause of the con-dition of the working classes.

The removal of social inequality, then, requires the destruction of the priest, that universal enslaver of his brethren. Brownson condemns all clergy, both Catholic and Protestant, as "priests": "Both are based on the principle of authority; both deny in fact, however it may be in manner, the authority of reason, and war against freedom of the mind; both substitute dead works for true righteousness, a vain show for the reality of piety, and are sustained as the means of reconciling us to God without requiring us to become godlike." Let us, says Brownson, have no professional class of religious teachers: "Let every man speak out of his own full heart, as he is moved by the Holy Ghost, but let us have none to prophecy for hire, to make preaching a profession." Parker was thinking along the same lines. He wished to deconstruct all ecclesiastical institutions, not only the ministry, but the Sabbath and church.[155]

He wanted to remove from each any vestige of divine authority. People must recognize that each was merely a human institution, which did not stand between them and God, and which they could freely alter to meet their religious needs. And how might they alter them? Parker was not too concerned with changing the rites of the church. They did not disturb him much, perhaps because he did not think them too important. Besides, baptism, one of the two rites Unitarians retained, still "meant something" to people. Nonetheless, in the summer of 1840 his complaints in his journal about the other rite, the Lord's Supper, became more vocal. In June, he called it "heathenish," and said it now meant "very little" to anyone. In August, he said it troubled him more and more, and he would gladly abandon it. He would rather meet in a private house in the evening for religious conversation, and prayer if needed, "& bread & wine might form part of the entertainment." "Cast away the elements," he wrote elsewhere in his journal, "but let all who come into a parlor have a social religious meeting . . . a conversation, free & cheerful on moral questions, or simply personal good feelings & prayers, only let all be natural & real."[156]

DISCONTENT WITH the state of the church circulated far beyond the Transcendentalist circle in 1840. It helped fuel a series of major religious conventions at Groton and at the Chardon Street Chapel in Boston. Parker became involved with all of them; in the process, he grew increasingly excited by the possibilities of church reform. He also began winning a reputation, in certain Unitarian circles, as a dangerous radical.

His decision to go to Groton seems almost light-hearted.[157] He appears to have been motivated in no small part by simple curiosity: the convention promised to draw together a host of religious reformers with whom he had never before had contact, including many from the lower classes. Then, too, Lydia appears to have been out of town, and the late summer was a good time for an amble across the New England countryside.

He set out on foot for Groton on 10 August 1840. In his journal, he describes the trek as a jaunt. He was accompanied by Ripley and Ripley's friend E. P. Clarke, and the company soon was joined by Christopher Cranch. They sauntered along, enjoying the weather and scenery, stopped frequently for refreshment, and made talk of all sorts to beguile the time. By late afternoon, they had reached Concord—about midway between West Roxbury and Groton. They called on Emerson, took tea, strolled with him and talked (Parker complained that nothing good was said), and tarried in the town overnight. The next morning, joined by Bronson Alcott, who now lived in Concord with his growing family, they were off again along the dirt roads and made it to Groton by evening.

What Parker found there astonished and impressed him; he devoted six pages of his journal to the convention. Its effect on him was similar to that of preaching "The Contradictions in Scripture," a year and a half earlier. Then, he had learned that plain folk could be taught religious truth without reliance on authority. Now, he found plain folk who had gone further and "emancipated themselves" from the "shams" of the church—who could "now worship God at first hand & pray largely & like men."

The Groton convention had been organized principally by Second Adventists, also called Millerites. They followed William Miller, a Baptist minister and chiliast from Vermont, who interpreted the Book of Daniel as predicting that "all the affairs of our present state would be wound up" on 23 October 1843.[158] He had found a wide and fervent following for this bold and bald prophecy. Among his sympathizers was a young Groton man, Silas Hawley, who edited the *Christian Reformer*, a religious newspaper. Hawley won the support of his local minister, a Dr. Farnsworth, and issued the call for a convention of all "Friends of Christian Union," regardless of affiliation, to meet in his hometown and help bring an end to sectarianism.

His hope, apparently, was to unite all Christians in preparation for the last days. But his call was answered not just by millenarians and a few curious Transcendentalists. As Ripley noted, the delegates came from "far and near" (some walked a hundred miles) and from "every sect, every Christian connexion, with every variety of faith, opinion and character." Groton became a magnet for anyone in New England who felt "a deep and heartfelt dissatisfaction with the religion of the age."[159]

Sectarianism—the conflict between sects—was widely perceived as a failing of the church. Parker himself saw it as such. Unlike some antisectarians, he did not believe all Christians should be united in one visible church. As he said in a sermon, sects "arise naturally & unavoidably from the nature of man." As Christianity enters the soul, it affects all the "active powers." When it touches our minds we devise creeds; our consciences, we institute rites; our hearts, we produce "symbols," like baptism and the Lord's Supper. "All this is natural & beneficial, so long as no man forces another to accept his creed, rite or symbol." But forcing happened all the time. Here was the real evil of sectarianism. Behind it lay a fundamental mistake, made by almost every sect: religion is made to consist "in belief of a certain creed, & not a dispensation of the heart, which affects the whole [character] & becomes the man's life."[160]

Opposing sectarianism on such grounds, Parker could not help but be quickly disillusioned with the conference organizers. He concluded that they only wished to tear down all the other sects to make room for their own, "which will probably be worse than its predecessors." Almost as soon as the Transcendentalist contingent arrived in Groton, they met "Brother" Hawley, who struck Parker as "cunning," "designing," and "ambitious." Hawley told them that two questions were not to be discussed: What constitutes a Christian? What constitutes a Christian church? "Here we saw for the first time the mark of the beast," commented Parker, "& the print of his foot." Parker and the others were then invited to attend a discourse that night by "Brother" Jones (probably the Millerite Henry Jones), who would hold forth on the return of Christ in three years' time. Commented Parker: *We could not wait so long.*

Fortunately, there was more to the convention than Millerism; more, too, than the "simple, scriptural and Christlike" meals provided for attendees in the local church vestry—a menu consisting of "good cold water, bread and boiled flesh in cold slices; with occasionally, crackers, butter and cheese and no apologies" (understandably, the Transcendentalists ate at the local tavern). On 12 August began the sprawling, chaotic debates, as the assembly considered an unwieldy list of resolutions. Here questions were raised that Parker and his friends found much more interesting than the date of the apocalypse. The two questions that Hawley said could not be discussed inevitably came up.[161]

Parker himself spoke to the convention at least three times. For the most part he developed themes he had stated elsewhere, particularly in "The Christianity of Christ, of the Church, and of Society," which had not yet been published. He defined sectarianism as any departure from the "simple method of Christ." By this standard, modern Christianity was almost entirely sectarian. Christ had insisted only on a life of outward goodness and inward holiness. If the Christianity of Christ is tried by reason, nothing in it is found to conflict with human nature; if tried by conscience, nothing is found wrong, harsh, or arbitrary. Today all churches trust in their creeds and not in divine life. Parker called for Americans, known for their good sense, to apply it to religion, for then we would only have to fear flesh and the devil; but "so long as we have the flesh in the world, and the devil in the church, there is much to fear."[162]

Parker also took part in a lengthy debate over whether "the outward organization of the Church [was] a human or a divine institution." Most of the discussion assumed the authority of the New Testament and revolved around the intentions of the Apostles—did they command outward organizations or not? Parker predictably took a different tack: He denied the Apostles were infallibly inspired. They had a better idea of Christianity than modern churches; the Apostles all insisted on divine life; nonetheless, they all departed from the Christianity of Christ. Parker here advanced a new idea for him, that there was sectarianism even in the New Testament.[163]

According to Parker, Paul said that to be saved you must "believe in the Lord Jesus Christ," by which he meant, "believe in Christianity." But he also seems to have regarded baptism as essential. The "inconsistent" and unreliable Peter (whom Parker portrays almost as the villain of early church history) departed even more from the simplicity of Christ. With "right Jewish narrowness," Peter did not think there was salvation outside of the church. At times, too, he insisted that the old law, "wrathful, foolish and absurd as it was in its form, should be bound like a millstone, on the disciples' necks." The "most revolting rite of the law" (circumcision) "was selected as the point not to be given up." Paul "withstood Peter to the face" on this; the conflict between them, who "seem to represent the two Poles of the new religion," was sent to a council in Jerusalem, which said Christians must abstain from eating blood, things strangled, and all food offered to idols, "of which Christ had said not a word."[164]

Parker disagreed with many at Groton about the authority of Scripture. But among the 275 "brothers" and "sisters" who officially had enrolled their names and the hundreds more who had come to wonder and perhaps to pray were others with whom he was in closer accord. One was Joseph Palmer of Leominster, with his flowing white beard that he would not trim, because he thought God had given it to him for "some good purpose" (he had been imprisoned two years for assaulting some men who had tried to shave him). Parker thought Palmer had seen through "most of the shams of the present day, — & it requires a long life to see through them all." Palmer believed that people could be inspired as in old time; he took the Bible "for what it is" and Christ as a brother, not a master; he was "an abolitionist; a no property man; a non-resistant, & a no government man, all this with very little culture by means of books." Then there was the young D. W. Dwyer, a preacher with the exterior of a rough working man and no book learning, who believed that Christ was Truth, and Truth Christ, and that salvation came from becoming Christ—a view Parker thought startlingly like that of the seventeenth-century English neoplatonist Ralph Cudworth. But the strongest impression was left by a contingent of twenty or thirty "Come-Outers" from Cape Cod. The Transcendentalists were so taken with these plain saints, all laborers and fisherman, that they invited them back to their room in the local tavern. There, as Parker later told Silsbee, "we had a little convention of our own."[165]

They had all "come out" of other churches. One woman, "Sister" Olive Bearse, the wife of a skipper, told her apparently typical story to the convention, her husband beside her "cheering her on." She said she had been "converted into the spirit of Christ" at age twelve. At first she was "free indeed" and loved the spirit wherever she found it, "in black or white—rich or poor—high or low." Then she joined a church (probably Calvinist). Soon she learned that she "must love the members *there* a little *better* than those that were as truly members of Christ's family, though not of that denomination." She "struggled along"; was persecuted ("I was put down by a preacher in my own father's house"), and finally asked for her dismissal. When her church would not dismiss her to any other denomination, she left anyway and joined the Free-will Baptists. They claimed to have no creed and told her she could come and go with them as she wished. For some time she again felt free, but as the church grew she sensed "a little less willingness that they should come and go according to their own views of the teachings of the spirit." So she left them, too. Ever since, she said, she had "felt it to be my duty to come out wholly from every visible Church"; she would join no "visible company" that would assume to judge her or to stand between her and Christ. Parker thought her remarks "showed plainly she spoke from the divine life."[166]

The Come-Outers and the Transcendentalists both disliked the ambition of the Millerites: Sister Bearse feared that a new sectarianism would rise out of this "anti-sectarianism," while her husband told Brother Hawley, "I see you wish to pull down these little Babels, to take the combustible materials of which they are made & erect one Great Babel into which you may enter." But what particularly interested Parker was the way the Come-Outers organized their religious life.

Anyone could associate with them, or leave them. No one was asked to sign a creed, nor was anyone's name recorded in a membership book. When the Come-Outers were asked if they would accept someone as member who did not believe in Christ, or the Bible, or God, and even allow such a person to speak freely at their meetings, they replied, Most certainly. "Do you think we fear that error is stronger than truth?"

They worshiped in each other's houses. They thought all days were the Lord's Day, although they kept the Sunday for convenience, because custom left them free from toil. Christian ordinances they viewed as their daily work; they did not count a rite better than any other act. They rarely baptized anyone, but if someone wished to be baptized, and the spirit moved someone else to baptize them, it was done. Anyone could do it. The Lord's Supper was rarely administered; if someone was moved to eat it, bread and wine would be brought out. "All our meals," they told Parker, ". . . are the *Lord's supper* if we eat with the right heart." They prescribed no particular kind of prayer, although they thought prayer in words was "not the highest kind." Anyone could preach when the spirit moved them, for the Come-Outers believed that "*it took the whole church to preach the whole Gospel.*"

They did have ministers. One of these had been to a seminary, although he had triumphed over this handicap and become a useful man. But a minister

All the Force of Transcendentalism

among the Come-Outers was no "priest." "If he wants any thing, they give it to him. If they want he gives them, which is oftener the case—*for the fathers ought to lay up for the children*." Parker commented particularly on one of their ministers, Joshua Davis of Brewster, a rough-hewn "common laborer" with a "countenance full of the divine," who "worked out" for his daily bread, yet managed the year before to expend a hundred dollars in charity. He never slept more than four hours a night and rose at four every morning to pray. When the Transcendentalists asked him if he thought his calling sacred, he said yes, but no more than that of anyone among us, be she a sister six years old. All work is sacred.

Parker was "surprised & enchanted by these Cape Cod men," who "have made actual my own highest idea of a church." He, Alcott, and Ripley were so pleased with them, they planned to visit them on the Cape that fall. Although the trip does not seem to have come off, in early 1841 Parker did write an appreciative account of the Come-Outers for the *Monthly Miscellany*, a leading Unitarian periodical.[167] Such enthusiasm is telling. A modern religious historian might classify the Come-Outers as good specimens of a certain kind of radical Christian primitivism that surfaces from time to time in Western history and often in America. The Transcendentalists, as church reformers, were like European settlers moving into Indian lands. They imagined they were discovering a new world, but in fact they were following ancient paths, worn by the tracks of generations. Like the settlers, they transformed the land they occupied.

Groton gave Parker no new ideas, but did deepen his confidence in his old ones, "for I see they may be made actual." Even before he went to the convention, he had been planning a sermon on how the new wine of new teachings could not be put in the old wineskins of old institutions. In one of his speeches to the convention, Parker had called attention to the wineskins parable and claimed that Jesus had "nothing to do with . . . [the] organizations" of the Jews; he did not come to tear down the temple, but he knew it would fall at the voice of teachings like his. Immediately after Parker returned home, he wrote and preached his sermon on "Old Bottles." Here he says that if a system cannot receive a new truth, it must be destroyed. Familiar examples are the government of France before the 1789 revolution and "the old Jewish Church, which had not changed its [character] since [Christ's] times, wh[ich] scorns all truth, not previously admitted, & is therefore at this day really dead & become like the ruins of ancient cities,—the habitation of Infidels, Atheists, extortioners & nameless wicked men." Parker's zeal for "de-judaizing" Christianity was rising.[168]

He was not the only one fired up. Other delegates to the Union Convention wanted to call another convention for the fall, this time to discuss more directly "the fundamentals of the ecclesiastical state." The proposal floated about until 23 September, when there was a two-day meeting in Boston at the Chardon Street Chapel of "nonresistants"—Christian pacifists and anarchists, closely associated with William Lloyd Garrison. Many from the Union Convention were also there, including Joshua Himes, the minister at Chardon Street, some of the Come-Outers, and among the Transcendentalists, Ripley, Alcott, and Parker. Parker attended because he liked the "spirit & upward tendency" of the nonresistants, not because he considered himself either a pacifist or an anarchist. Ripley and Alcott both spoke at the meeting, but Parker did not; he may have been reluctant to do so, and besides, business called him away early on the first day.[169]

Certainly he was not there during dinner break on the second day, when "a small party of advocates of the movement," Alcott among them, while eating together at the house of "a hospitable friend," raised again the proposal to hold a new convention. Enthusiasm for the idea was found to be high. The group quickly constituted itself as the "Friends of Universal Reform" and by the next day had drafted a call. The convention would meet at Chardon Street in November. Invited were "all persons, who feel an interest in the momentous questions which it is the object of the convention to discuss"—the Sabbath, ministry, and church:

> They exist in our midst. Their influence, for good or for evil, is mighty. It is of the highest importance to the progress of truth to ascertain whether their claims to a Divine ordination be indeed valid, or whether they be but inventions and traditions of men. . . . If the institutions in question have indeed the Divine authority which they claim, they will be but more firmly established in the hearts of the people by a full examination of the foundation upon which they rest. If, on the contrary, they should be found, on careful inquiry, to be but human inventions, and that, consequently, the corruptions, abuses, and spiritual tyranny which have ever attended them, are but their legitimate results, the Glory of God and the good of man demand that their actual character should be exposed, and their power forever destroyed.[170]

The coming of the Kingdom of God on Earth, the call adds, "must, of necessity, be mightily hastened or retarded by the reception of true or of false ideas with respect to these important instrumentalities."

Whether Parker had any role in drafting this document is unclear. But he did sign it. Soon it was being reprinted in newspapers across New England, endorsed by twenty-four names, among them those of Alcott and Parker.

The call was quickly attacked and the convention denounced before it even met. As Parker noted only half-jokingly, its supporters were accused of having "the benevolent design to overturn the useful & restore the dominion of most ancient night." Even some of Parker's "friends after the spirit" blamed him

All the Force of Transcendentalism

for endorsing the call, and their criticism made him at least pause to question himself and "examine the whole matter." Dr. Alvan Lamson, the minister in Dedham, whom Parker thought a fine scholar and a "beautiful soul," feared "bad use would be made of truth." Dr. Channing, who planned to attend the convention as an observer, thought the call "looks like seeking agitation"; he feared the influence of some of the radicals who would participate.[171] "*Nous verrons*," wrote Parker in his journal. "I have my own *doctrines*, & shall support them think the *convention* as it may."[172]

When the Church, Ministry, and Sabbath Convention, popularly called the "Chardon Street Convention," finally gathered for its three-day session, starting Tuesday, 17 November 1840, the several hundred in attendance ended up discussing only the Sabbath. The issue of the ministry was deferred to a second convention to meet in March 1841, and that of the church to a third, to meet November 1841. Parker was to attend all three. He later said that they "vastly disappointed my expectations," although he still thought they did a "world of good."[173]

The most famous and colorful description of the conventions comes from Emerson and was published in the *Dial* in 1842:

> The singularity and latitude of the summons drew together, from all parts of New England, and also from the Middle States, men of every shade of opinion, from the straightest orthodoxy to the wildest heresy, and many persons whose church was a church of one member only. A great variety of dialect and of costume was noticed; a great deal of confusion, eccentricity, and freak appeared, as well as of zeal and enthusiasm. If the assembly was disorderly, it was picturesque. Madmen, madwomen, men with beards, Dunkers, Muggletonians, Come-outers, Groaners, Agrarians, Seventh-day-Baptists, Quakers, Abolitionists, Calvinists, Unitarians, and Philosophers, — all came successively to the top, and seized their moment, if not their *hour*, wherein to chide, or pray, or preach, or protest.[174]

Emerson leaves the impression of near chaos, and the group certainly had an anarchistic or at least libertarian spirit. Although the delegates were willing to elect officers (as chair they chose the abolitionist Edmund Quincy), they defeated a routine motion to appoint a committee of business. Nor did any of the conventions succeed in passing a substantive resolution, much to the chagrin of some present. But some substantive resolutions were voted down.[175]

First defeated was a resolution offered by Joshua Himes, the pastor at Chardon Street, that "the Convention adopt the scriptures of the Old and New Testament as the only authentic record of our faith and duty." This vote was later cited as evidence that the delegates were infidels, although their motive seems to have been to guarantee freedom of discussion. They then took up a resolution offered by a Unitarian, the combative John Pier-pont, pastor of the Hollis Street Church in Boston, "that the first day of the week is ordained by divine authority as the Christian Sabbath." Debate on this resolution occupied the rest of the convention. No vote in the end was taken, although at one point the delegates did defeat an amendment, evidently offered to appease those who thought Saturday worship was commanded, "that there is ordained by divine authority a weekly Sabbath [in other words, not necessarily Sunday], perpetually binding on man."[176]

Alcott, Ripley, and Cranch, as well as Parker, were in attendance. The Transcendentalist who left the strongest impression on the convention itself and the public at large was Alcott; Chardon Street proved to be an ideal forum for his idiosyncratic idealism and extemporaneous eloquence. Still, Parker did give a speech, on the morning of the first day, that delighted some of his friends. Convers Francis, who did not attend the convention (meetings of that sort, he told Parker, "are not to my taste"), heard glowing reports of Parker's address from the "good and wise": It "was spoken of as almost without par-allel," and Dr. Channing himself "could not enough express his admiration." "I believe your defense of the true idea of the Sabbath," Francis told Parker, "did more good than all the rest said or done at the Convention."[177]

Exactly what Parker said is not known, although two summaries by hos-tile observers appeared in print. The New York *Observer* reported that he had "avowed his belief that Moses was inspired just as all great legislators are, and that 'Thus saith the Lord,' in the Pentateuch, is exactly equivalent to 'Be it enacted' in our Statute books." Still, the report continues, Parker had "spo-ken eloquently in favor of the Sabbath as a very beautiful and useful institu-tion, though not of divine appointment, except as all good laws are so." An Orthodox participant in the conference, meanwhile, in a pamphlet published in 1841, says that Parker had argued no Sabbath existed before Moses, who instituted it not because God ordered him, but because "the Jews of his day were disposed to overwork themselves and their slaves"; the pamphlet also reports Parker affirming that he "would still cling to the Christian Sabbath, if it were only for the oxen and the horses," but that he wanted Sunday observed according to "liberal and enlightened views."[178]

That these are more or less fair summaries of Parker's position can be seen from a sermon he preached shortly before the convention opened.[179] Here he attacks the popular idea that the Sabbath originated with the creation of the world and that it was shifted to Sunday due to the Resurrection. He ar-gues that there was no Sabbath before Moses, and that the Mosaic Sabbath was enacted with no divine sanction. Moses evidently intended it as a way of restricting greed; it was simply a cessation from labor, with no religious sig-nificance. It gradually came to be used for social and then religious purposes, but at the same time Sabbath restrictions became oppressive. Such was the

All the Force of Transcendentalism

situation at the time of Jesus. He gave no command to honor the Sabbath, and the disciples wanted to meet every day; when this became inconvenient, they chose the first day of the week to distinguish their worship from that of the Jews. They continued to work on that day, because they thought labor sacred. The wisdom of a day of rest was gradually recognized; in A.D. 200, a church council resolved that to transact business on the Sabbath would be wicked. Roman law made cessation from work mandatory; a general church council later required attendance in church; English law followed this established pattern. Thus the Sabbath has no divine sanction. It is wholly a human creation.

Yet even if the Sabbath were merely a "break in the linked chain of worldliness & work" that binds us, it would be "the best institution that has come down to us from old times." "He must have toiled 16 hours out of the 24, & eaten hard bread, earned with the sweat of his forehead, before he knows the value of the Sunday." It is made even better when used as a day of religious and moral improvement. Even the Sunday as it now is, when people gather to hear poor sermons and prayers that sometimes smite and offend the true soul, is the only help available "to keep up religious decency, self-respect, morality, & in some sense Rel[igion] to the mass of men." The day could be spent better than it now is. Not in amusements—this would be "very bad"—but perhaps in "cheerful & pleasant conversation," or in taking a walk through the fields, or in intellectual improvement. Moral and religious betterment should remain the chief activity of the day. Parker strongly denies the popular "superstition" that holiness and prayer are more acceptable on Sunday than other days, or that one day a week is sufficient for religious improvement.

Such a position would probably have met with Channing's approval, if for no other reason than it was comparatively moderate. Garrison, for example, proposed to do away with Sabbath observance altogether. Parker sought instead to free people to use the Sabbath in the way they felt was best suited to meet their spiritual needs.

His views on the church and ministry, which he was to advocate at the later Chardon Street Conventions, were similar. He first presented them in a sermon written at the same time as his sermon on the Sabbath.[180]

Here again, as with the Sabbath, he challenges ecclesiastical authority with historical criticism. The primitive church, he says, was a very simple affair and claimed no authority from anyone. Only later, when it grew in wealth and power, did it claim rights; at this point religion left the church. Ministers, meanwhile, were originally merely "helpers." Now, all too often, they are the "helped." Parker finds it "surprising" that "grave men can be found in the 19th C[entury], who have not lifted their eyelids, and seen the absurdity" of any doctrine that grants authority to a minister just because of his office. Parker spoke from experience: "He has spent a few years at college, a few at theological seminary, & then a beardless stripling, utters with authority from the Pulpit what must not be called into question by his grand sire, though a hundred times more religious than he. Men pay peculiar deference to him, & the children run away when he approaches. He must not do all that others do, & must wear a peculiar dress, to distinguish him from the mass of the people." But in the early church, ministers were chosen by the people. Their authority came from the degree of their inspiration and talents.

The church and ministry, like the Sunday, were nonetheless valuable— although they needed reform. We all know, he says, that "there are those among us, who think the time has come when the present . . . institutions should be abandoned, & men should assemble of a Sunday with no minister to worship & pray, & instead of a discourse from one person who was paid for that service, that anyone who pleased should speak what . . . he had to say, that was profitable to the audience."

Parker's proposals for church and ministry sound radical, but he does not directly advocate them. Was it because he was preaching to his own congregation? He was not going to tell them to deconstruct their church. In fact, he never tried to implement at Spring Street the reforms he proposed.

Perhaps he thought they were not necessary in his own case. With his sermons on ecclesiastical institutions, he in effect had issued an emancipation proclamation to the good people of West Roxbury. He had told them no Christian institution had divine authority, so they were free to organize their worship however they wanted. But if they still found the old ways useful, as they evidently did, he would not try to force them to change. To do so would only harm their faith, not help it.

Was Parker being inconsistent? Certainly, he was not so bold as his friend Ripley. About a month before Parker wrote his sermons on Sabbath, ministry, and church, Ripley had written a remarkable letter to his congregation at Purchase Street, soon published, in which he laid down the conditions under which he would remain their pastor. The ideal of the church that he presents here, which he calls "social worship," is very similar to the one that Parker would soon present.

Ripley calls for the freedom of the minister to speak what is in his heart and on his mind and for the freedom of members of the congregation to come and go. He specifically criticizes the system of pew ownership, which he says keeps people attached to a church even after they have lost interest in the services. Sabbath services would be much more attractive and fruitful, he says, "were all such restrictions removed, even if we came together as the disciples did, in a large upper room, in a fisher's boat, or by the shore of sea."[181] Such worship should be founded only on perfect sympathy between minister and congregation.

Ripley eschews all ministerial authority. He has always, he reminds his church, "lived with you as a man with men, as a friend, a brother, an equal." It has always been his desire "to lead you to think for yourselves." But some in the congregation have disliked this course. They desired a "more authoritative and zealous mode of preaching"; they wanted "the days of the old priesthood restored, when the clergyman trusted more to his office than to his words, and advanced his opinions as oracles to be submitted to rather than as suggestions to be weighed and considered." Ripley thinks, by contrast, that if "it be an objection that a man speaks in the pulpit, as men speak anywhere else, on subjects that deeply interest them, the true man will soon find that he can speak more to the purpose in some other place." This is in fact what Ripley found. On 1 January 1841 he tendered his resignation, and on 28 March preached his farewell discourse. Immediately thereafter, he moved with his wife, Sophia, to West Roxbury. There, about two miles across the fields from Parker's house, they started Brook Farm. His old church began to consider Parker as his successor.[182]

PARKER'S INVOLVEMENT with the Chardon Street Convention, as well as his major publications that fall, began to win him notoriety as a Transcendentalist and reformer. The increasingly conservative Dr. Nathaniel Frothingham dated his alienation from Parker to the convention. By contrast, the aristocratic abolitionist Edmund Quincy, who had chaired the Sabbath Convention and recently befriended Parker, considered participation in the convention to be the "turning point" of Parker's life, because "it helped him get rid of a large proportion of that usefulness which is the first thing a man has to free himself from when he wants to be good for any thing—& moreover it conferred upon him a very wholesome share of odium—the true baptism by fire." Quincy believed Parker had "pretty nearly preached himself out of all respectable pulpits" and would soon "preach himself out of his profession."[183]

An incident a few weeks before the convention opened made clear to Parker his new reputation. He had written to James Thompson, a Unitarian minister in Salem, requesting a pulpit exchange some Sunday in December. He was still awaiting an answer when he happened to run into Thompson, "clad in a cloak as usual," at a Boston book store. Thompson, looking agitated, said he had just mailed Parker a reply and that "my health is *so delicate I think I could not go so far* as West-Roxbury in *the month of December*." But, he added, he might get better, "& if so I will let you know." Parker noted that Thompson's "colour came & went, his voice faltered & his hand trembled while he said all this stuff, & his eye did not meet me like a man's." Parker politely tried to act "as if I did not see the traverse he was working on me." Thompson's letter arrived the next day and revealed what Parker suspected: Thompson, obviously acutely embarrassed, admitted he had just been writing "a letter to you on some of your heresie[s]"—a letter he had intended to publish.

"Nemesis never sleeps," commented Parker in his journal. He had never exchanged with Thompson before and claimed to have expected one with him "as little . . . as with Mohamet." Still, the refusal "decides my course for the future." He had solicited exchanges repeatedly, and without success, from Alexander Young (the minister who had officiated at his wedding), Samuel Barrett, and even from Dr. Parkman. To ask these men again, he felt, would be "a dereliction from [Christian] self-respect." Such feelings probably prompted his resolve (an ironically prophetic one), which he recorded in his sermon record book in December 1840, to "preach at home more next year." He would continue, however, to request exchanges from conservatives, if only for the sake of experiment: "Let us see! I should laugh out-right to catch myself weeping because the Boston clergy would not exchange with me!!!"[184] The ties of Christian fellowship, which at Divinity Hall had seemed too tightly twined ever to break, were starting painfully to unravel.

Later that winter came an even more ominous development: for the first time, Parker was called an infidel in cold print. The charge was made in an article from the *New England Christian Advocate*, by one Amos Phelps. A volubly Orthodox minister, Phelps had attended the Chardon Street Convention and given an almost unendurable, four-hour speech defending the divine origin of the Sabbath. He was upset that the other delegates had failed to approve this position. By February, he had decided publicly to break with them. In his article, later expanded into a pamphlet, he attacked the opinions of several of the speakers as hostile to revealed religion. Prominent among those condemned was the Reverend Mr. Parker of Roxbury. Parker himself seems to have been unaware of the charges; Phelps traveled too far outside his orbit. But the Orthodox ministers around Boston quietly took note.[185]

MEANWHILE, the Transcendentalist movement was taking a new shape. One sign of this was the demise of the little club, which had its last meeting on 9 September 1840, at Elizabeth Peabody's bookstore. In part, it died because the Transcendentalists now had wider forums, like the *Dial* and the Chardon Street Convention; an intimate haven for free expression was no longer needed. Then, too, there were personal conflicts—notably between Alcott and the others. He was miffed by the lukewarm reception his "Orphic Sayings" had received from Emerson and especially from Fuller, who had printed some in the first issue of the *Dial* but refused to print any more. By the fall of 1840, he had decided that if the other Transcendentalists really wanted to hear him, they could come out to him in Concord. He would no longer go to them. Without him, the club was a less interesting place to be. "The talk was very good," commented Parker on the final meeting. "But we had little of inspired talk. We miss Alcott exceedingly. His talk would have been worth all the rest."[186]

More important, pronounced differences were emerging over the direction the movement should take. Emerson and Fuller were pulling it toward literature. Under their care, the *Dial*, which had been conceived as a vehicle for the bold expression of the new religious thinking, turned into a literary magazine. Of the few articles on religion they did publish, most were by Parker.[187]

The new journal met with mostly hostile reviews; Parker himself was disappointed in it. When the first issue came out, in July 1840, he greeted it coolly. The prose he thought by and large "Young-mannish," excepting only Emerson's "graceful & exquisitely well done" introduction, and two other articles—almost certainly his own "Divine Presence in Nature and in the Soul" and a review of Brownson's writings by Ripley. As for the rest, which included pieces by Fuller and the young Henry Thoreau, he thought it had "awkward lurching air." Thoreau's mannered early essay, "Aulus Persius Flaccus," an assessment of the Roman satirist filtered through Emersonian ideas about history, Parker thought "foolish." Such life as it had was "Emerson[']s, not Thoreau's, & so it had been lived before." As for the poetry—there were poems by Cranch, Dwight, and Emerson, among others—it was better than the prose, but hardly original.[188]

Parker was not uninterested in literary criticism, but his own passion in 1840 was for religious reform. He was therefore much less attracted to the *Dial* than to Brownson's *Boston Quarterly*. As he wrote to Francis in December 1840, if he were "to do the thing in paint" (although what he had in mind was less a painting than a cartoon) he would represent

a body of minute Philosophers—men & maidens elegantly dressed— bearing a banner inscribed with "The Dial." A Baby & a Pap spoon & a cradle should be the accompaniment thereof. The whole body should have "rings on their fingers & bells on their toes," & go "mincing as they walk" proceeded by a body of fiddlers—with Scot's [*sic*] Claud Halero "playin [*sic*] the first violin" & repeating "New Poetry." This body of the excellent should come out of a canvass city of Jerusalem, set upon a hill. On the other hand should come up a . . . small body of warriors looking like the seven Chiefs before Thebes & swearing as they did, with just about as modest devices on their shields; they should be men who looked battles, with organs of combativeness big as your fist. They should be covered with sweat & blood & dust, with an earnest look, & confident tread. "Sonorous metal blowing martial sounds" should encourage them. At their head should stand "Orestes Augustus Brownson" dressed like David; with Goliath's sword in one hand, & that Giant[']s head in the other. Would not this make a picture?[189]

Besides the question of literature versus reform, the Transcendentalists began to disagree over the nature of reform. This problem was thrown into sharp relief in October 1840, when Ripley, flush from baring his soul in his letter to the people of Purchase Street, began seeking support for Brook Farm. He asked Emerson to join. Emerson declined. As he told Ripley, a community was "a circuitous & operose way" of effecting his personal emancipation, "which I ought to take on myself."[190]

The difference between Ripley's emerging socialism and Emerson's individualism was not the only one dividing the Transcendentalists. Alcott was moving toward a position that some scholars have called "anarchist" and that he described as "Come-Outer." That spring, he had moved his family from Boston to Concord and taken up an austere life of subsistence farming in an effort to separate from the evils of existing social arrangements. By September, he could complain to Parker that both Emerson and Brownson were "partial" and did not "lay the axe manfully at the root of all sin." Alcott was entering a period of his life in which, as one historian has remarked, he "lived as if on the verge of the millennium," a period that would climax, three years later, in his disastrous attempt to bring Heaven to Earth at Fruitlands.[191]

Meanwhile, others in the Transcendentalist group were starting to retrench. After the penultimate meeting of the little club, which occurred on 2 September at Parker's house, Parker remarked that Hedge, Francis, and Stetson were "wedded to the past": "Now I love the past but would as soon wed my Grandmother whom I love equally well."[192] Hedge's letter in March 1840, in which he refused to help with the *Dial* for fear he would be labeled an "atheist in disguise," had been a bellwether. Although Hedge did patch things up with Fuller and Emerson, made some small contributions to the *Dial*, and even attended the three last club meetings, he refused any more to play a leading role in the movement he had helped to found. His own later development would be toward a strong sense of the importance of the church as an institution, liberally and broadly conceived.

As for Parker, he considered himself to be taking the middle ground in most of the Transcendentalist disputes about reform. He was neither an individualist like Emerson nor a communitarian like Ripley; he avoided both the anarchism of Alcott and the institutionalism of Hedge. It was in searching for a middle ground that he wrote *A Discourse on the Transient and Permanent in Christianity*, the sermon that would make him famous as a heretic prophet.

ON 19 MAY 1841, a cold, raw Wednesday, Deacon Arnold drove Parker over to the Hawes Place Church in South Boston, where he was to preach an ordination sermon, his first, for Charles C. Shackford. Parker arrived and met with the ordination committee while the church filled with enough people to make the air hot and close; in the audience could be seen the unmistakable bonnet of Elizabeth Peabody. At 2:15, the strains of a "voluntary" on the organ called the committee to their seats, and the service began. It unfolded in the usual manner: an anthem; an introductory prayer and a reading of selections from Scripture (both offered by Chandler Robbins, former editor of the *Christian Register* and pastor of the Second Church, Boston); and a new hymn (composed for the occasion by Andrews Norton). Then it was Parker's turn. He rose, climbed the pulpit, and opened his manuscript; several members of the audience, following the old New England custom, readied themselves to take notes. He announced a text from Luke: "Heaven and earth shall pass away: But my word shall not pass away." His topic would be "what is *Transient* and what is *Permanent* in Christianity." [193]

SHACKFORD WAS a Unitarian who had been trained at the Orthodox seminary in Andover. He evidently saw his ordination as a chance to promote harmony between people of differing theological opinions. He had invited the three Orthodox ministers of the neighborhood—a Congregationalist, a Methodist, and a Baptist—to attend. For his ordaining council, he had selected Unitarians from across the range of denominational opinion: conservatives and moderates would dominate, but a Transcendentalist would deliver the sermon.

Shackford was only casually acquainted with Parker, but knew his preaching had been well received in South Boston. Parker had been invited there on exchange five times before, most recently in January of that year. Also well received had been his performance at an earlier ordination—that of his friend William Silsbee to a church in Walpole, New Hampshire, the previous June. Parker had offered the Right Hand of Fellowship, and the *Christian Register* had praised his remarks as "an affectionate and beautiful welcome to the field of the Christian ministry." [194]

Shackford was not looking for Parker to write a Transcendentalist manifesto. Nor did Parker think he had written one. He later recalled thinking the sermon "poor," and that when he read it to a friend before preaching it, the friend—Ripley, almost certainly—had told him it was the weakest thing he had done in some time. [195] Parker claimed the sermon was hastily prepared when he was sick and "burthened with other work."

He does seem to have been suffering from various ailments that spring (he needed two fillings in his teeth in June), and he was also busy. In March, he had been preoccupied with the second Chardon Street Convention, on the ministry, which he attended and at which he spoke. Then in April, President Harrison died, and a National Fast Day had been called for 15 May. Parker appears not to have started writing his South Boston sermon (#238 in his sermon record book) until early May; he may have rushed to finish it to give himself more time to compose his discourse for the National Fast, "A Sermon on Post-Mortem Prophecies" (#239), which he had to preach five days before the ordination. He also had been pursuing a rigorous course of studies, reading heavily in biblical criticism and Greek literature, planning numerous articles and studies, and working almost daily on the De Wette; in April, he told Silsbee he expected soon to send the book, on which he had labored five years, to the printer.[196]

Yet the subject of the transient and permanent elements of Christianity had been on Parker's mind for some time. Although the topic is not on a long list of possible sermons that appears in his journal early in 1841, he had hinted at it in "The Relation of the Bible to the Soul," his Blodgett letter, and his speeches to the Groton convention. In November 1840, he had written in his journal that Christianity is "the Residuary Legatee of Jews & Pagans." Why, he wonders, does Christianity vary from age to age? Because of foreign accretions. As old religions die out, their estate is divided between antiquaries, poets, and oblivion, with Christianity getting the "Contingent remainders." He proceeds to list, haphazardly, the things accrued to Christianity from the old "Jewish worship," from "Greek & Roman worship," and from the worship of northern Europe. Among them are, from the Jews, the "Pharisaic observance of Sunday," the mediatorial character of Priests, an angry God, the Old Testament and the idea of its infallibility, and the miracles; from the Greeks and Romans comes worship both of saints and of the Trinity, each a relic of polytheism; from the northerners, Hell, the Devil, and the festivals of Christmas and Easter. One "formal" notion has been found in every age, that Christ is the "*highest manifestation of the Godhead.*" But what, Parker wonders, if one higher than Jesus appears? Then "this formal part [is] destroyed, & the essence still remains."[197]

Parker sharpened and expanded his argument in a sermon he wrote in January 1841, on the old topic of "Idols." He preached it at Purchase Street on 4 April, the week after Ripley's resignation. Present were Margaret Fuller and the young Caroline Healey, who would soon become Parker's good friend. Healey, hearing Parker for the first time, wrote in her journal that his sermon "startled" her and waked her "into admiration and dread." This is as Parker intended. Purchase Street was thinking of offering him Ripley's pulpit, explained Fuller to a friend, and Parker "wished to let them know all his thoughts as explicitly as they lay before himself." "Idols" may be read, then, as a programmatic statement.[198]

Parker here accuses modern Christians of idolatry. Real Christianity, he says, is the "true worship of God; the worship in spirit & in truth." The only belief it demands is that the Lord thy God is one God. The only form it demands is that one love your neighbor as yourself and love God with your whole mind and heart and soul. The only profession it asks us to adopt is to be perfect as your Father in Heaven is perfect. This, says Parker, is the religion of Jesus — "very simple, very beautiful: [nothing] can be thought of higher, more simple, more beautiful." But this is too high for most Christians, "as we call them," who have "taken into their houses a great deal of Heathen-ism, a great deal of Judaism, & very little of [Christianity]. Thus the pure waters of Rel[igion], have been . . . corrupted — filled with the mud & slime, & abominable things of Heathen countries, the sweepings of idol temples, the offscourings of Jewish cities. What we call [Christianity] has become but the residuary legatee of other Rel[igions], ceased long ago." [199]

Parker then points out two "modes" of modern idolatry, that of the wicked and that of the pious. In the section on the idolatry of the wicked, Parker re-states his criticism of New England society: the people love money, public opinion, and "show" over virtue, truth, and inner value. In the section on the idolatry of the Pious, he attacks the worship of the Bible and of Christ.

Parker prefaces this section with the remark that pious idolatry must "be touched with something of gentleness, for it is always dangerous to criticize the best of men." [200] As he had said in "The Christianity of the Christ, of the Church and of Society," he thought that the idolatry paid Jesus was perhaps the "nearest approach to true worship, which the mass of men can readily make these days." He therefore takes pains to praise the worth of the Bible and above all the nobility of Jesus, whose words judge the world and whose life is a rebuke to all that has come since.

Nonetheless, Parker must object when persons enslave their mind to the letter of Scripture and are willing to believe even "the greatest absurdity" that defies Reason, Conscience, and Religion — the story of Abraham and Isaac. That God would "excite weak men to sacrifice a human victim, [is a] thought at which nature revolts & the flesh creep[s]." Then, too, when people worship Jesus and turn him into God, his example can mean nothing to us.

When Parker finished preaching, Fuller later told a friend, he came down from the pulpit "in a fine glow." She added: "I quite loved him." [201]

About the time Parker preached this sermon, he noted in his journal that the Christianity most people embrace is a "poor thing" — just the stories of the New Testament, which "corrupt the truth. None of them rest on evi-dence." It is known that Jesus lived, died, and was crucified. "His life was higher I presume than anyone has described it. A great soul lay at the bot-tom of the [Christian] movement. Men do not tell such stories save of great men." But "the miracles — that contradict common Law — such as the tran-substantiation of Bread, water &c, the sending [of] the Devil into the swine, the resurrection of dead men — the resurrection of J[esus] C[hrist] itself — all these have [nothing] to do with [Christianity]. I do not know what to make of them." Our duties for the present, he says, are to "rationalize Christianity" and to "Christianize reason." In the margin, he adds a note: "[Christianity] is a field, in which the strangest crops, wood, hay & stubble, wheat & leaves may be raised. The soil remains, the crop varies."[202]

As in his sermon on "Idols," Parker here seems engaged in a dialogue with theological conservatives—those who base their faith on Christian traditions. To them he is saying that their Christianity is made up of Transient corruptions. But he also had a message for radicals—those who wished to do away with the traditions and "move beyond" Christianity. Among the latter he counted Alcott. In the summer of 1839, Parker had noted in his journal that he thought Alcott "desires to make a new advance: that he will eventually give up [Christianity] altogether as [Christ] did Mosaism & take some new measures." But he and those like him will not succeed, added Parker, for Christianity "has not yet lived its life, as Mosaism had then done."[203] In fact, Parker wished to argue that some part of Christianity—its "essence," the "soil" of Christian "field"—would never be transcended.

He was thinking of radicals, not conservatives, when he chose the title of his South Boston sermon. "Transient and Permanent in Christianity" is borrowed from, of all people, David Strauss. Three years after Strauss published the first edition of his *Leben Jesu*, he put out an article entitled "Über Vergängliches und Bleibendes im Christenthum" (On Transiency and Permanency in Christianity). Parker's theological school classmate George Ellis was traveling in Germany about the time Strauss's piece appeared; when he returned to Boston in early 1839, he brought with him at least a report of it and probably a copy. Although the German "Transient and Permanent" does not appear on Parker's journal list of "books read," he does mention it in a notice, which appeared in the *Christian Examiner* for May 1839, of "New Works Recently Published in Germany."[204]

A year later, when Parker wrote his review of Strauss's book, he made clear that he disagreed with its radically negative conclusions. As Parker said in his journal, a great soul must lie at the bottom of the Christian movement. Why then would Parker take his title from Strauss? Because for a brief period, Strauss had doubted that the Jesus of Scripture was almost entirely mythical.

His book had cost him his university position, and not a single theologian in Germany had stood up to defend either the book or him. Faced with universal condemnation, he began to make concessions to his critics (concessions Parker noted in his 1840 article on Strauss for the *Examiner*). In the third edition of *Das Leben Jesu*, published in 1838, Strauss admitted that perhaps positive statements could be made about the historical Jesus. Shortly afterward, he published "Über Vergängliches und Bleibendes im Christenthum"; the following year, he reprinted it in a volume entitled *Zwei friedliche Blätter* (Two Peaceable Papers). As the title suggests, Strauss conceived of his article as a peace offering to his opponents. It turns out to be the most positive statement about Jesus in the Strauss canon.[205]

The article takes the form of two dramatic personal addresses, or "soliloquies." The portrayal of Jesus here is of particular interest. Strauss denies the vicarious atonement, the miraculous conception, and even the incarnation — but he does say that the worship of genius was the order of the day and that Jesus was a genius. He was, moreover, a greater genius than any other in history. Most genius is directed outward, says Strauss, toward the creation of objective works, but the greatest genius is directed inward, toward the creation of a perfect soul, and Jesus was the fullest and highest of the inward geniuses. Strauss even argues that no one will ever be able to equal Jesus, because the historical conditions from which he emerged can never be reproduced.

Strauss, in his article, finds a permanent place in his faith for the historical Jesus. Parker may have taken his title from Strauss because he sought the same. But he rejects Strauss's idea that Jesus is an unsurpassable genius and should be worshiped as such. The worship of Jesus was idolatry, and Parker thought future and greater Christs were possible. Yet he believed that even if one higher than Jesus were to appear, the essence of Christianity would remain.

Parker places his faith not in the person of Jesus, but his words. Strauss himself seems to have given Parker permission to do so. In Parker's review of *Das Leben Jesu*, he had quoted Strauss's statement that the "granulary discourses of Jesus have not been dissolved or lost in the stream of oral tradition," but simply "loosened from their natural connexion, washed away from their original position, and like boulders rolled to places where they do not properly belong."[206] Even Strauss admitted that the words of Jesus had a historical basis. Parker builds on this idea in his sermon: My words, says the text, will not pass away.

Parker opens by identifying two groups that doubt Jesus' assertion. One (the conservatives) thinks that "the least doubt respecting the popular theology, or the existing machinery of the church; the faintest distrust of the Religion of the Pulpit, or the Religion of the Street, is supposed . . . to be . . . capable of shaking even Christianity itself." The other group (made up of those like Alcott and the Strauss of the first edition of *Das Leben Jesu*) tells us "the day of Christianity is past," that "Piety must take a new form; the teachings of Jesus are to be passed by; that Religion is to wing her way sublime, above the flight of Christianity, far away, toward heaven, as the fledged eaglet leaves forever the nest which sheltered her callow youth."[207] Parker proposes to prove both groups wrong.

He starts with an evocation of the words of Jesus, one that is eloquent even in the unpolished preaching text:

Nothing seems more fleeting than a word. It is an evanescent impulse of the most fickle element. It leaves no track where it went through the air. Yet to this, and this only, did Jesus entrust the truth with which he came laden, to the earth, truth for the salvation of the world. He took no pains to perpetuate his thoughts; they were poured forth where occasion found audience,—by the side of the sea, or a well, in a cottage, or the temple; in a fisher's boat, or the synagogue. He founds no institution as a monument of his words. He appoints no order of men to preserve his bright and glad revealings. He only bids his friends proclaim the truths they had received. He did not even write his words in a book. With a noble confidence, the result of his abiding faith, he scattered them, broad-cast, on the world, leaving the seed to its own vitality. Knowing that what is true and of God cannot fail, for God keeps his own. He sowed his seed in the heart, and left it there, to be watered and warmed by the dew and the sun which heaven sends. He felt that the good never perishes without doing its work, he knew his words were for eternity. So he trusted them to the uncertain air; and for eighteen hundred years the faithful element has held them good,—distinct as when first warm from his lips. Now it translates them into every human speech, and murmurs them in all earth's thousand tongues, from the pine forest of the North to the palm groves of eastern Ind. . . . In the mean time, the words of great men and mighty, whose name shook whole continents, though graven in metal and stone, though stamped in institutions and defended by whole tribes of priests and troops of followers—their words have gone to the ground, and the world gives back no echo of their voice.[208]

Here Parker, using images of transience to emphasize permanence and of permanence to emphasize transience, makes the key point of his sermon: the words of Jesus are eternally true; they are the permanent element in Christianity.

Having identified the permanent, he goes on to identify the transient. He makes the obvious point that the doctrines and forms of the church, which make up the bulk of what is usually taught as Christianity, have varied widely over the centuries, indicating their transient nature. But they are not Christianity, as he explains in a passage that echoes both his own earlier sermon on idolatry and Strauss on the words of Jesus: "As old religions become [*sic*] superannuated and died out, they left to the rising faith, as to a residuary legatee, their forms, their doctrines, their life. . . . Many of the doctrines that pass current in our philosophy, seem to be the refuse of idol temples; the offscourings of Jewish and Heathen cities, rather than the sands of virgin gold, which the stream of Christianity has worn off from the rock of ages, and brought in its bosom for us." Two "striking instances" of the "transitoriness of theological doctrines" are the "doctrine respecting the origin, authority and nature of the Old and New Testament," and that relating to the "person, nature and authority of Christ."[209]

This section of the sermon draws heavily from the section of "Idolatry," on the idols of the pious.[210] In his earlier sermon, Parker said such idols should be touched with "something of gentleness." Did Parker believe he was touching them with gentleness here? This section is addressed to the fears of the conservatives. Parker wishes to reassure them that no matter how bad things look for these two doctrines, the words of Jesus will stand firm.

He therefore makes things look as bad as possible. He asserts that every word of the Old Testament has been held as miraculously inspired and infallibly true; Christianity has been said to rise or fall on an immaculate Hebrew text. "On the authority of the written Word, men have been taught impossible legends, conflicting assertions; to take fiction for fact; a dream for a miraculous revelation of God; an oriental poem for a grave history of miraculous events." Such is the current opinion of the religious sects of our day. "Matters have come to such a pass that even now, he is deemed an infidel, if not by implication an atheist, who will not believe that God commanded Abraham to sacrifice his Son, a thought at which the flesh creeps with horror." But modern criticism is "fast breaking to pieces the idol men have made of the Scriptures."[211]

The same could be said of the New Testament: "It has been assumed at the outset, with no shadow of a sufficient reason, that all of its authors were infallibly inspired, so that they could commit no error of doctrine or fact." Yet there are obvious contradictions in it, as well as degrading legends. Which evangelist, apostle, prophet, or psalmist ever claimed miraculous inspiration? Did Christ ever demand assent to any part of the Old Testament, or to the writings of "those men, who, even after his resurrection, expected that he would be a great general or Jewish King; of men who were often at variance with one another and obviously misunderstood his divine teachings?"[212]

Then, too, every sect makes Christianity rest on the personal authority of Jesus. Yet the great truths of Christianity can no more rest on the authority of Jesus than the truths of geometry can rest on the authority of Euclid. If Christianity is true, "it would be useless to look for someone to uphold it, as for someone to support Almighty God." Parker reiterates an argument he first had made in "The Relation of the Bible to the Soul": "So if it could be proved, in opposition to the greatest amount of historical evidence ever collected on a similar point, that the gospels were a sheer fabrication, that Jesus had never lived, still Christianity would stand firm, and fear no evil. None of the doctrines of this religion would fall to the ground."[213]

Having (presumably) calmed the fears of the conservatives, Parker turns to the claims of the radicals. To them, he describes the religion of Jesus as

> absolute, pure morality; absolute, pure religion; the love of man; the love of God acting without let or hindrance. The only creed it lays down, is the eternal truth recognised by all religions, if that indeed be truly a creed—there is one God. Its watchword is, be perfect as your Father in Heaven. The only form it demands is a divine life: Love to God; Love to man; doing the best thing, in the purest way, from the highest motives. . . . Its sanction is the voice of God in your heart; the perpetual presence of Him, who made you and the stars over your head; a promise, that if you are faithful, both the Christ and the Father shall make their abode within you.[214]

Parker tells the radicals, in words that recall those of his opening, that no matter how high men soar on the wings of wisdom, religion, and love, "they can never outgo the flight of truth and Christianity."[215]

Parker exhorts his listeners to let the Transient pass away and urges Shackford to rely on the Permanent Christianity of Jesus. He closes by admonishing the new pastor not to think one thing in his closet while preaching another thing from his pulpit: "God shall judge him, not we. But over his study and over his pulpit we might write—EMPTINESS; and on his canonical robes, on his right hand and forehead—DECEIT, DECEIT."[216]

When Parker looked back on this sermon, he could say, with justice, that he had said everything in it before. He "had even printed matter much more hostile to the current opinions." His purpose at South Boston was to establish a permanent historical basis for Christianity. He may have been trying to fulfill Shackford's ecumenical hopes and show the words of Jesus to be the common ground on which all Christians could safely stand. Yet if Parker's intentions in the "Transient and Permanent" were irenic, his words had the opposite effect. Elizabeth Peabody, out in the audience, thought the sermon was "consuming fire."[217]

DURING THE hour and ten minutes Parker spoke, a member of the audience walked out. Was it just for fresh air? Some of the note takers grew pained and uncomfortable. Did their faces show it? Parker finished speaking and took his seat. Was there an awkward pause? Old Dr. John Pierce of Brookline rose, climbed the pulpit, and delivered the ordaining prayer. His language emphatically emphasized the authority of Christ. Was the prayer a response to the sermon?

If so, it was the only one. The ordination proceeded without incident: Samuel Lothrop, of the Brattle Square Church, issued the Charge; John Sargent, of the Suffolk Street Chapel for the Poor, offered the Right Hand of

Fellowship; George Putnam, of the First Church, Roxbury, delivered the Address to the Society; and after a hymn, Nathaniel Folsom of Haverill gave the Benediction. All these men would figure in the events that followed.

After the service, everyone stayed for dinner. When time came at last to leave, Parker congratulated the new Reverend Mr. Shackford and rode home in Deacon Arnold's chaise, unaware of the storm gathering over his head.

Chapter Six

Absolute Religion

Within hours of the service, rumor spread that Parker had preached a strange, possibly infidel, perhaps even blasphemous sermon. Yet the news cycle of the religious press was slow. Two weeks passed before any report of the discourse appeared in print. Then, in the opening days of June, three evangelical papers, the *Puritan*, the *Christian Watchman*, and the *Recorder*, simultaneously published a short communication that unleashed a deluge of controversy.

Three Trinitarian clergymen signed the article. They all had attended Shackford's ordination: Joy Hamlet Fairchild, the senior minister of the trio and an Orthodox Congregationalist; a Baptist named Thomas Driver; and Z. B. C. Dunham, a Methodist. They presented their own abstract of the "Transient and Permanent," in which the sermon appears both vehemently deistic and shockingly impious. In an open letter, they asked to be "informed" whether "the Unitarian clergymen of Boston and vicinity sympathize with the preacher in his opinions expressed on that occasion." The writers pointed out that at Shackford's ordination itself, after Parker finished speaking, no member of the ordaining council stopped the service to protest what he had said; the writers specifically mentioned their disappointment in the venerable Dr. John Pierce, who delivered the ordaining prayer, and Samuel K. Lothrop, who delivered the Charge to the Congregation. The Trinitarians requested the participants in the service, as well as the Unitarian clergy of Boston, to declare whether they acknowledged Parker to be a Christian teacher.[1]

This article was reprinted widely in both religious and secular papers. It provoked both Unitarians and evangelicals to write replies and responses. These prompted further replies and responses. What was published in one paper quickly would be republished in others, with commentary, which in turn brought on yet more replies and responses. Reading these crisscrossing polemics was like listening to a gun fight in an echo chamber. The noise would not die down for months, and ears would still be ringing years later.[2]

248

Parker's own response to the uproar was to "print" his sermon (he could find no one brave enough to publish it) as a forty-eight-page pamphlet on 19 June. Within a week, the run was sold. By September, it was in its third edition. That winter, in Boston and surrounding towns, Parker delivered a course of lectures, his first, on the subject of religion. He found packed halls wherever he went. People were curious to hear him, suddenly the most notorious Transcendentalist in New England. Meanwhile, the controversy pushed Parker to present his religious ideas in a systematic way, a process that revealed to him conclusions even he himself at first hesitated to accept.[3]

PARKER HAD BEEN launched into fame by that original, shocking report of his South Boston sermon, made by Fairchild, Driver, and Dunham. They claimed to have based their abstract on Driver's "copious" notes and Fairchild's recollections, which were recorded "soon after the service closed." Much of their report, they insisted, was verbatim, and "*all* the sentiments here expressed were avowed by the preacher."[4]

The preacher himself thought the report a gross distortion and beneath contempt. He made no direct reply. Instead, he printed his sermon so that readers could judge it for themselves. They certainly found marked differences between the two versions of what he had said, but the critics were hardly satisfied. Parker had made the tactical error of not printing exactly what he had preached. Here he was following his standard practice. He had published four other sermons over the previous year and had revised each of them extensively before putting them in print. In the case of *A Discourse on the Transient and Permanent in Christianity*, the alterations from the preaching text number (depending on how they are counted) from the hundreds up to three thousand. Almost all these, as Parker points out in his preface to the first edition, were stylistic: he smoothed the rough edges of the preaching text. He also, however, made two lengthy additions: several paragraphs praising the character of Jesus, taken from his earlier sermon on "Idolatry," and a long quotation from Francis Bacon.[5]

Parker no doubt had improved the literary merits of his production, but he also had opened himself to accusations of duplicity. The newspapers soon rang with the charge that the polemical deism of his original discourse was being toned down in the face of public outrage. The hue and cry was such that when Parker put out the second edition, he added a lengthy appendix in which he tried to list every deviation from the preaching text. A few of his more diligent critics did try to use the appendix to reconstruct at least parts of his original discourse, but in the end abandoned the effort, because they thought the appendix itself untrustworthy. Besides, no matter what his exact words had been, what he admitted to having said was enough to convince them he was an infidel. Parker gave up trying to mollify them and dropped the appendix from later editions.[6]

For his critics, the fundamental problem with his sermon was its underlying doctrine: the denial of the special, miraculous authority of the Bible and of Jesus. What language he used to reject them was a secondary issue. But for Parker himself, as for his friends, it made a great deal of difference that he was a Transcendentalist and not a deist like Tom Paine. As one acute Orthodox observer noted, Parker would "scorn to own an affinity with the sensual and low-lived railings of the pot-house"; in 1843, when a group of freethinkers invited Parker to join them in celebrating Paine's birthday, he declined, admitting disapproval "of Mr. Paine's character in his later years," and professing no sympathy whatsoever with "the spirit of his writings on theology and religion." Yet Fairchild, Driver, and Dunham wrote their report as if they had heard Paine, not Parker, in the pulpit.[7]

They portrayed Parker as having dismissed and ridiculed the Scriptures and Christ. The authors conveyed this impression by leaving out of their abstract Parker's praise for both; his thesis, that the words of Jesus are the absolute religion, was not even mentioned. Not that Fairchild and his colleagues ever claimed their abstract was complete. Rather, they merely were paraphrasing those statements and passages they found particularly objectionable. These all came from the middle sections of the discourse, in which Parker tried to address the fears of the conservatives and the claims of the radicals.[8]

A comparison of the paraphrases to Parker's preaching text does reveal inaccuracies and distortions. For example, he is reported to have claimed that "Real Christian life was *out* of the Church, and *in* the world for the first four centuries." This is a bizarre idea, to say the least, not just an offensive one— that real Christian life flourished not among the saints and martyrs but among the pagans and heretics. According to the preaching text, however, Parker's actual statement (in fact, only an aside) was more conventionally Protestant: that the "stream of Christianity has come to us through two channels—one through the Church, the other without the Church—and it is not hazarding too much to say, that since the fourth century the real life has been out of the Church, and not in it, in the ranks of dissenters."[9]

At another point, according to the report, Parker had advanced the deistical (and again somewhat bizarre) claim that "Christianity was the same nineteen centuries before Christ, as nineteen centuries after Christ." According to Parker's preaching text, however, his words were these:

What doctrine of Jesus is not eternal? The Truth is always the same . . . (whether) in Nazareth or New England; in the nineteenth century before Christ, and the nineteenth century after Christ. . . . The truth he brought to light must have been always the same before the eyes of all-seeing God, nineteen centuries before Christ, as nineteen centuries after him. A life supported by the principle and quickened by the sentiment of religion, if true to both, is always the same in Nazareth or New England.[10]

Fairchild himself, when he read this passage in the published version of the sermon, admitted that this sentiment, so expressed, was true — but denied that Parker had so expressed it at South Boston.[11]

No wonder Parker thought Fairchild's report merely a slick hatchet job. He insisted that he never uttered the impieties Fairchild, Dunham, and Driver attributed to him. Yet the three Trinitarians were hardly alone in believing he had said bad things. Some of his statements worried even a few of Parker's sympathizers.

Elizabeth Peabody and her young friend Caroline Healey are examples. Peabody was Parker's most reliable defender in the summer and fall of 1841, writing a number of replies to Parker's critics. She also became his publisher, putting out the second and third editions of the *Transient and Permanent* and selling it at her bookstore. Healey, the intellectually precocious daughter of a prominent Boston merchant, had Transcendentalist leanings; she had been impressed when she first heard him preach (in January 1841, on "Idols," at the Purchase Street Church) and she would soon start a lifelong friendship with him. But her comment in her journal, just as the controversy was starting, seems to reflect concerns the two women shared: Parker "is so afraid that he shall not be independent enough, that he foolishly says, more than he means, and abstract truths as other people state them, are taking the likeness of rankest infidelity in his pages."[12]

An example of the kind of passage that bothered the two women was one in which Parker urges that the "killing letter" of the New Testament be separated from its "living spirit." This was the sort of "abstract truth" to which no one could reasonably object. The way Parker does the urging is another matter. According to his preaching text, he said:

Men have been told to close their eyes at the obvious difference between Luke and John, the serious contradiction between Paul and Peter; to believe, on the smallest evidence, accounts which shock the moral sense and revolt the reason, which tends [*sic*] to place Jesus in the same line with Hercules, and Apollonius of Tyana, and to degrade the Infinite God to the same level as Neptune or Jupiter; stories which Paul in the epistles never mentions, though he also had a vein of the miraculous running quite through him.[13]

Here Parker presents, in epitome, more than two years of hard thinking about myth and "sectarianism" in the Christian Scriptures; he writes as if what he was talking about were self-evident. But Peabody heard him with furrowed brow. If Parker "must say that the New Testament has parts that *revolt* the moral sense," she later complained in a letter to John Sullivan Dwight, "I want him to *point them out* because these are so few places that most people do not notice them."[14]

Peabody nonetheless assumed that Parker here had pious intentions. Others in the audience at South Boston heard only impiety. They seem to confirm Healey's observation on the discourse when she finally read it in early July. From Parker's mode of expression, she writes in her journal, "a great many things may be inferred, which all who know Theodore Parker must know that he never intended to say."[15]

Thus Fairchild, Driver, and Dunham report Parker as proclaiming that the New Testament had "obvious contradictions and absurdities . . . which are everywhere apparent" and that it "contains stories the most incredible, and sometimes shocking to decency." What many found especially indecent were his comparison of the stories surrounding the Saviour to those of Hercules, Jupiter, and Neptune. Driver, in a letter published separately from his report with Fairchild and Dunham, detailed for "the injured public" the infamous sex lives of these figures from Greek myth so that "*all* may understand the allusions." One who understood them all too well was old Dr. John Pierce. Pierce, the conservative Unitarian who had given the ordaining prayer at South Boston and who had a legendary memory for facts, distinctly recalled Parker asserting that the "story of the miraculous conception of Christ is worthy only to be placed by the side of the amours of Neptune." Pierce turned Parker's perhaps tactless classical allusion (which Parker in fact left out of the published version of the sermon) into an outright vulgarity.[16]

Yet the problem for many of Parker's listeners and readers was not, as Peabody and Healey believed, simply his mode of expression. Rather, many were incapable of making sense of his Transcendentalist position on its own terms. Pierce is a case in point. In his journal entry on the South Boston ordination, he complains that Parker's "sweeping condemnation" of the Bible as well as the "license" he had taken with the sacred character of Christ left "no ground, on which to stand." Pierce found it "difficult" to "vindicate, or even to understand what the preacher meant" because he "did not make it plain . . . by which rule we are to distinguish what is true and valid, in scripture from the unauthorized additions and positions of fallible men."[17]

For Parker, the question was not what was "true and valid in scripture" versus what was "unauthorized." He believed that nothing in the Bible was authorized in any miraculous sense and that what was true and valid was intuitively obvious to all people. He assumed that what was mistakenly called miraculous inspiration was in fact natural, and that natural inspiration could be "divine" if it perceived Truth; many in his audience, like Pierce, Fairchild, and Driver, assumed that inspiration could only be "divine" if it was miraculous. What Parker saw as the heart of his sermon, his positive claims for the words of Jesus, therefore made no sense to them. And so they heard only what they did understand, his "sweeping condemnations" of historical Christianity. No wonder they lumped him together with the devils they knew— Paine and his deistical kind, whose scoffing impieties were at least familiar.

Driver, in his published letter, provides a good example of such misinterpretation. He cannot even accept Parker's defense of the words of Christ as sincere. He dismisses it as a verbal trick. When Parker speaks of the "words of Christ," writes Driver, he does not mean "the written words of Christ, but something out of sight, like water under ground, springing up in all hearts to some degree, aside from revelation." For Driver, Parker's main argument made no sense except as a thin disguise for old-time Deism. So he quotes Parker's remarks on the Old Testament and asks rhetorically, "Has . . . Paine done more to stigmatize it?"[18]

FOR WEEKS after the South Boston ordination, no Unitarian published anything against the sermon or spoke against it—not at the annual Berry Street conference in late May, nor even on 10 June, after the Fairchild report was in circulation, when Parker, following the usual ministerial rotation, preached the Thursday Lecture in Boston before members of the Boston Association (that only two members came to hear him, however, he took as a deliberate slight).[19] The first notice of the sermon in a denominational publication did not appear until mid-June, when Ezra Stiles Gannett published a short, dispassionate summary in his magazine, the *Monthly Miscellany*.

Why were the Unitarians initially so quiet? Once the newspaper war started, Orthodox polemicists supplied an answer: that in Parker's sermon, Unitarianism had borne its ultimate fruit. The whole tendency of liberalism since its inception, they claimed, was toward deism; Unitarian ministers, although professedly Christian, did not repudiate Parker because in their hearts they agreed with him.[20] No accusation galled the Unitarians more than this one, for it was maddeningly difficult to disprove.

Most Orthodox commentators, however, attributed the initial Unitarian silence to the liberal principles of fellowship, which they correctly and almost immediately perceived would now face a severe test. Only days after the Fairchild report came out and before any public response to it had been made, an unknown correspondent—he signed his name "J. T."—forwarded a copy down to the *New York Observer* with a commentary that nearly crowed over the Unitarians' dilemma.[21] Many Unitarians, "J. T." admits, "are unwilling to remain in their present connexion with those [like Parker] who propagate such rank deism." Yet if Unitarians denounced Parker and excluded him from fellowship, they would be guilty of what they have so often condemned as "theological despotism" and "would be eating the most efficient words they ever uttered against the 'Orthodox.'" Moreover, if they were to censure Parker for his opinions, they would have to start classifying opinions into those censurable and those not. "In short, notwithstanding all they have said against such things, they must begin to form a 'creed.'" This would lead to debates and dissensions they are no doubt anxious to avoid. Hence the Unitarians are trying to duck the issue altogether, he concludes, by maintaining an awkward silence.

The problem J. T. identifies was real enough, and the Unitarians themselves soon would be forced recognize it. But he was wrong to suggest that they had recognized it in the weeks immediately following the South Boston ordination. Rather, the position of most Unitarians appears to have been much more straightforward and unreflective. They did not believe they needed to say anything.

This at least was the claim of Nathaniel Folsom, the Haverill minister who had delivered the Benediction at South Boston. As a former Orthodox Congregationalist himself, he evidently had kept up his subscription to the *Puritan*. He read the Fairchild report as soon as it appeared and on 4 June wrote the editor a letter, published the following week, which was the first public response from a Unitarian the report had received.

Folsom makes clear that he disapproves of Parker's opinions. He tacitly accepts the accuracy of the Fairchild report and even says that he heard in Parker's sermon "another gospel from what Paul preached." Nonetheless, he is firm on the point that there had been no need to denounce Parker at the service. Fairchild, Dunham, and Driver will doubtless recollect, he writes, "that in the other performances, the recognition of Christ as Master and Lord, and of his gospel as words which he spake with authority, was full and explicit." As a result, if "there were those who might imbibe the erroneous sentiments of Mr. Parker, the antidote was administered . . . [a]nd, as the result proved, the people were of age, and could speak for themselves"—that is, most of the congregation had made clear to him that they were not poisoned. He concludes his letter with a display of his liberal bona fides: praise for Parker's character and love of truth, despite his errors.[22]

Behind Folsom's letter, and with it the slow Unitarian response to Parker's sermon, may have crouched painful memories of the previous few years. In 1838, Andrews Norton had denounced Ralph Waldo Emerson's Divinity School Address almost as soon as it was delivered. His subsequent steady drumbeat of polemics against the New Views did succeed in isolating Transcendentalists within the denomination, but at the cost of making many Unitarians very uncomfortable. Few had Norton's zeal for controversy, and many wished to put all this unpleasantness behind them. Norton himself, sensing the growing disapproval of his tactics, had withdrawn to his study in early 1840, and since the Berry Street conference of that year the theological controversy had been dormant. Folsom's position seemed to many the natural one: if each minister spoke from himself, all would be well.

The editor of the *Puritan*, however, rejected this position. Suppose, he replied to Folsom, the other ministers at South Boston had expressed different views from Parker. Was this all that was required of them, under the circumstances? "They stood before the people uniting with one whom one of the council now says preached 'another gospel,' in ordaining a minister. And their union with him in that act, unless the whole proceedings were a miserable farce, was a constructive acknowledgment of his character as a minister of the gospel of Christ. And while they refrained from disowning him, as the preacher of another gospel, their hearers were left to infer that what sentiments they uttered somehow consisted, in the main at least, with his."[23]

The editor here indicates why the "Transient and Permanent" posed a huge problem for Unitarians, while Parker's earlier pronouncements (many of which he himself considered "much more hostile to the current opinions") did not. The important thing was not so much what he had said, nor what he was accused of saying, but where he had said it. Before, his radicalism had been confined to statements he had issued on his own behalf—articles in the *Dial*, for example, or speeches at religious conventions. Although a few Unitarian ministers had ceased pulpit exchanges with him because of these statements, most had seen no need to do so. As long as he did not force his views on them, these ministers held his views to be his own affair.[24]

Now, however, Parker had spoken when joined with others in a common service. Technically (as Folsom quickly pointed out) ministers on an ordination council were united in fellowship not with each other, but only with the church that invited them; in other words, the ministers gathered at South Boston had been united only with the Hawes Place Church, not with Parker. Technically, too, the member of a council could be held accountable only for having approved the candidate being ordained—in this case, Charles Shackford. The sentiments of the preacher were, strictly speaking, not a councilor's responsibility. Yet such subtleties easily were lost on the public. Suddenly under pressure, many Unitarians leapt to the conclusion their original position was untenable.[25]

One of the first to make the jump, even before the report was published, was old Dr. Pierce. His initial response to the "Transient and Permanent" appears to have been not unlike that of Folsom. As has been seen, in Pierce's journal entry on the South Boston ordination, probably written only hours after the event, he disapproves of Parker's sentiments so far as he understood them. But he displays no outrage (only later did he remark on Parker's supposed comment about the "amours of Neptune"), nor does he say Parker should be censured. When the journal entry is read in its entirety, Pierce seems less interested in the sermon than in a break with established custom, on which he comments twice: that a senior minister like himself should offer the ordaining prayer while a much younger one, Samuel K. Lothrop, delivered the Charge to the Congregation. Here, says Pierce, is a "new thing under the sun"! Also, he is much more impressed by George Putnam's Address to the Society, which he calls "by far the most popular exercise of the occasion," than by Parker's "strange" discourse.[26]

Such was Pierce's view on 19 May. A week later, however, Fairchild called on him and told him of the report that he, Driver, and Dunham were preparing. Fairchild must have mentioned that Pierce himself would be criticized by name for not denouncing Parker's sermon immediately after it was delivered. Pierce, understandably upset by the news, assured Fairchild that the only reason he had not interrupted the service was that he had been taken by surprise.[27] Pierce obviously was trying to mollify the Orthodox minister. Just as obviously, he did not succeed: the report went out two days later and was published the following week. Still, Pierce had conceded Fairchild's key argument, that Unitarians were responsible for each other's opinions, and that he therefore was obliged to denounce Parker.

Another Unitarian who accepted the logic of the Orthodox argument was Joseph Buckingham, the splenetic editor of the *Boston Courier*, one of the most influential Whig papers in the city. At the request of a few "respectable" liberals, he reprinted the Fairchild report on 11 June, adding a commentary in which he reiterated the Orthodox ministers' question—whether Parker was a Christian minister—and demanded the Unitarian clergy make a distinct yes-or-no reply: "Their *affirmative* answer would save a world of controversy, and render entirely superfluous the study and labor of many a sincere, honest, and pious young man, who devotes himself to the profession of what he believes to be the *Christian* ministry." Over the coming weeks, Buckingham probably would do more than any other person to promote the controversy, opening the columns of his paper wide to polemical correspondence, both Unitarian and Orthodox, while demanding editorially that the denomination must "excommunicate" the minister from West Roxbury.[28]

In making this demand, Buckingham had crossed an ecclesiastical Rubicon. Individual Unitarians disavowing Parker's opinions was one thing; "excommunicating" him was something else altogether. So Nathaniel Folsom sternly reminded Buckingham in a letter to the editor. Any effort to "'excommunicate'" or "in a formal manner, 'disown'" Parker, he pointed out, would be "wholly inconsistent" with the fundamental Unitarian principles of "religious liberty and responsibility." Unitarians were "independent ministers of independent churches." Among such independent congregationalists,

Absolute Religion

"ministers, as ministers, have no authority to depose, or excommunicate one of their number. To his own particular church, and to his divine master, each pastor stands or falls."

Folsom held that Unitarians who thought, as he did, that Parker preached "another gospel," had only two courses of action open to them. The first was to meet in convention and "disclaim all sympathy with the views charged on them as a body." The Episcopalians in Virginia recently had done just this, repudiating the Oxford Tracts as "Popery in disguise." Folsom hoped, however, that the Unitarians would not follow the Episcopal example, for "it will not any more conciliate their adversaries, and there is a more excellent way shown to them by their master above." This was for each liberal minister, on his own behalf and only as he saw fit, to disclaim responsibility for Parker's sermon and if necessary, "withold [sic] all acts of direct ministerial fellowship."[29]

Folsom's position was strictly correct. The Unitarians had no mechanism to "depose" Parker. He would remain in the ministry so long as the West Roxbury church would have him as their pastor. Moreover, the withholding of the most obvious form of ministerial fellowship, pulpit exchanges, was in fact the principal sanction Unitarians would employ against Parker (although the ideas of a group disclaimer and even of expulsion would resurface). Yet Folsom left many practical questions unanswered.

How far, after all, did the denial of fellowship extend? "*Your acts of fellowship* continue," the Orthodox editor of the *Puritan* reminded the Unitarians, "in spite of the most offensive declarations of infidelity." You still come and "sit under his preaching" at the Thursday Lecture; you still "admit him into your clerical circles as a brother beloved"—for example, at meetings of the Boston Association, of which Parker was a member in good standing. How therefore can you claim to have disowned him in any practical sense?[30]

With such questions left hanging, Unitarians remained on the defensive in their debates with the Orthodox. Especially discomfited were Unitarian conservatives, who found themselves in the awkward position of having to defend their principles of fellowship on behalf of Parker, whose views they thought pernicious. None was more visibly uncomfortable in the summer of 1841 than Samuel K. Lothrop.

Lothrop had little truck with Transcendentalism.[31] As principal editor of the *Christian Register* since mid-1840, he had gone further than any of his predecessors in closing the Unitarian newspaper to the New Views. The South Boston ordination, however, put him on the spot. He had delivered the Charge to the Congregation, and Fairchild, Driver, and Dunham criticized him by name (along with Dr. Pierce) for not seizing the moment to disavow Parker's views.

Aggrieved by what he perceived as an unwarranted personal attack, Lothrop took it upon himself to respond for the denomination, first in an anonymous *Register* editorial, then in a public correspondence with Fairchild himself, which was printed in the *Courier* over several weeks in June and July and is remembered as the most prominent feature of the newspaper controversy. Lothrop charges Fairchild and his colleagues with trying to "increase sectarian 'capital.'"[32] Lothrop challenges the veracity and plausibility of Fairchild's stated reason for issuing his report—that is, his desire to be "informed" as to whether Unitarians approved of Parker's sentiments. Surely, writes Lothrop to Fairchild, you must have known that almost all Unitarians disapproved of Parker's sentiments. What, then, was your object and motive in making, "with some parade," such public inquiry? And if this inquiry were sincere, why did you publish it only in Orthodox newspapers, "which are seen by but a few Unitarians"?

Another main line of Lothrop's offensive is to force Fairchild to admit that Unitarians are in fact Christian ministers—an "acknowledgement which the Orthodox clergy have not been very ready to make." Such an acknowledgment was implicit, he insists, in Fairchild's query as to whether the members of the council thought Parker a Christian minister, for if Unitarian ministers are not Christian, then the query has no force. Do you then, Lothrop asks Fairchild, acknowledge *me* as a Christian minister?

Fairchild replied vigorously. Your questions to me, he says, are no more than a labored effort "to raise smoke and dust in order to conceal from the public eye the very point which ought to be distinctly seen."[33] He brushes off Lothrop's accusation of bad motives: If he really were someone interested in increasing sectarian capital, he would not have attended a Unitarian ordination in the first place. He also dismisses Lothrop's demand to be recognized as a Christian minister. Whether I do so, says Fairchild, is a personal matter between us. We are on higher ground. You Unitarians call *yourselves* Christian ministers. The question is, do you call Parker one?

Fairchild hammers home his questions: *Does a council assume no responsibility in uniting with a known deist, in the services of an ordination? and is an ordained deist regarded by the members of that council as a Christian minister? Is a man who denies the divine authority of the Bible as a standard of truth, recognized by the Unitarian clergy as a Christian minister? Does or does not the known fact that he is a deist, so disqualify him for your fellowship, that you cease to recognize him as a Christian minister?*

Lothrop struggled to provide answers. He goes as far as Folsom said a Unitarian could go, by declaring that "if I entertained some of the opinions which I understood Mr. Parker to present, . . . I should think I ought to leave the Christian pulpit; . . . but if Mr. Parker thinks otherwise, if he can find a people willing to hear him, and ministers willing to exchange with him, that is his affair and their affair, not mine." To have explicitly disavowed Parker's sermon at the ordination itself would have been absurd, says Lothrop; when he participated in an ordination, he need not stand up and express disapprobation and nonconcurrence every time he heard something with which he disagreed.

Fairchild had a ready response: Parker's sermon demanded a remonstrance because the question it presented "was not one concerning creeds, or slight differences of opinion among believers in Christ—but . . . *Christianity* or *Infidelity*; *Bible* or *no Bible*." That Lothrop eventually had made a remonstrance, and with it intimated that he would exclude Parker from his own pulpit, Fairchild acknowledges. But, Fairchild adds, "you do not say you would not aid in introducing him into other pulpits" by joining with him on an ordination council. For that matter, can you exclude him from your pulpit and stay consistent with your principles? Is he not of your number and in regular standing? Have you Unitarians not given him the Right Hand of Fellowship? Mr. Parker "claims the fellowship you promised him," you do not say he has forfeited it, yet in effect "you tell him he is not fit to stand up in your pulpit." This, however, writes Fairchild, "is his affair and your affair, not mine."[34]

Most observers thought Fairchild had the best of the exchange;[35] Lothrop, like most Unitarians, seemed flummoxed by the Orthodox attack. Yet Unitarians did have one response to the crisis that was apparent to Parker by the end of the summer: the large majority of the settled Unitarian clergy no longer would consider exchanging pulpits with him. Their decision to withhold this form of ministerial fellowship was made with comparatively little reflection, but it eventually would produce a crisis in the denomination.

HAD PARKER fallen victim to an Orthodox plot to embarrass the Unitarians? The question of Fairchild's motives, although he successfully dismissed it in his debate with Lothrop, lingers. Most likely, as Lothrop no doubt surmised, Fairchild was the principal force behind the report. At fifty-one, he was considerably older than Driver or Dunham and had the highest public standing. A Yale graduate and successful evangelist, he had come to Boston in 1828 to build up the tiny Phillips Church, which then had a congregation of fewer than forty, and had succeeded over the next dozen years in increasing its membership tenfold.

This achievement would mark the apex of Fairchild's career. In August 1841, the deacons of his church privately would accuse him of having an affair with a married woman in his congregation; he would resign his pulpit under pressure the following year and move to New Hampshire. Shortly afterward, the deacons would make a new accusation, this time publicly, that he had fathered an illegitimate child by a servant girl before he left South Boston. The charge would result in a sensational ministerial inquest at which a panel of his Orthodox colleagues determined him guilty, and then a lurid trial in state court, at which a jury acquitted him. In the course of Fairchild's ordeal he would reveal himself to be a ferocious polemicist, issuing vehement tracts (and then a book) accusing the Phillips Church deacons of conspiring against him.

Fairchild's later experiences show that, at the very least, he had a talent for polemics and that many people, including his deacons and a large number of fellow clergyman, did not trust him. Was he, then, the sort of man who would have tried to use Parker to manufacture "sectarian capital"? His evangelism does suggest that he was an Orthodox revanchist, anxious to regain the sectarian ground lost to the liberals of Dr. Channing's generation. Moreover, he had issued strong statements against Unitarianism (in a published sermon he had argued it was "another religion" from Christianity), and, like other evangelicals, had avoided all ministerial fellowship with liberals. He confessed to having heard no more than three or four Unitarian sermons in his life. One of them just chanced to be the "Transient and Permanent."

Or was it merely chance? By Fairchild's own account, he had accepted the invitation to hear Parker because he had friends and neighbors in the Hawes Place church, and because he expected "nothing exceptionable" would be said there. Yet in a letter to Lothrop, he argues that Shackford ought not to have invited Parker to preach, because the West Roxbury minister had already disseminated deistic views in his widely reported address to the first Chardon Street Convention and in "The Christianity of Christ, of the Church, and of Society," published in the October 1840 *Dial*.[36] By charging that Parker's opinions were well known before 19 May, Fairchild appears to be admitting that he himself knew them; this would be unsurprising, as the accusation that Parker was an infidel had been made in Orthodox papers before the South Boston ordination. In that case, might Fairchild have come to the service anticipating that Parker would give him an opportunity to challenge the New Views?[37]

AFTER THE first fury of the polemics had subsided, Parker announced that his ideas had emerged unscathed, for no one had adduced a real argument against them. The Orthodox had contented themselves merely with denouncing his infidelity while harping on his Unitarian affiliation. The title of an anonymous New York pamphlet sums up their approach: *Unitarianism Identified with Deism, Exhibited in a Review of a Discourse Lately Delivered by the Rev. Mr. Parker, in Boston.* Conservative Unitarians, meanwhile, scrambled to renounce the controversial opinions of their brother. Andrew Peabody, a minister from Salem who reviewed the sermon for the September *Examiner*, credited Parker only with "the ingenuity to touch in his forty-eight pages upon almost every objection to authoritative or historical Christianity and its evidences, that can be found in the works of earlier or later *unbelievers*, as they used to be called."[38]

Neither conservative Unitarians nor the Orthodox had any incentive in the heat of a sectarian brawl to provide thoughtful commentary on Parker's arguments. Meanwhile, the Transcendentalists, who might have elevated the tone of the debate, remained mostly silent. Ripley, for years their champion in theological controversy, had retired from the lists, beaten his pen into a ploughshare, and with his wife and friends was busy modeling the future at Brook Farm. As for the *Dial*, it reflected the attitudes of Fuller and Emerson; neither, in their letters, even refers to the storm surrounding Parker's sermon, nor does Emerson do so in his journal (except for the passing comment that Parker "has beautiful fangs, & the whole amphitheatre delights to see him worry & tear his victim").[39]

Emerson had no inclination to inject himself into a theological controversy—he hated controversy and had grown uninterested in theology. He was also busy with other work. Over the summer of 1841, while the newspapers were full of the South Boston ordination, he was struggling to prepare his oration on "The Method of Nature."[40] Fuller, for her part, was publishing articles and reviews in the *Dial* treating of religious and social reform, but most of these had been written by Parker himself, who served in effect as the special correspondent on these subjects. Because he chose not to write a notice of his own sermon, none ever appeared in the Transcendentalist magazine.

One Transcendentalist, however, did speak out on Parker's behalf. Orestes Brownson, who had given up regular preaching nearly two years earlier, unexpectedly announced in July he would deliver a new sermon on the twenty-eighth. A large, curious audience gathered at the Masonic Hall, on Tremont Street across from Boston Common, to hear him deliver what turned out to be an extended vindication of the "Transient and Permanent." Brownson later reworked his sermon, expanded it, and published it as a review essay in the October issue of his *Quarterly*.[41]

Brownson argues that Parker's views of the nature and authority of Scripture and of Christ, if correctly understood, are in keeping with orthodox Christian tradition. Parker was certainly no Deist, for a Deist denies the possibility of supernatural revelations from God to man, which Brownson understands Parker to admit. Moreover, even if Parker did deny that the Scriptures were inspired, this did not mean he denied Christianity, for as God and man are always the same, so Christianity is always the same. It is eternal and exists independently of how it was revealed to us, as the Scripture itself admits (e.g., "Before Abraham was, I am"). Those who think Scripture must be accepted as an infallible authority are wrong. No one accepts the Bible literally; its words must be interpreted by Reason—but, Brownson insists, *"only when Reason is taken absolutely, as God's Reason, and not as man's."*

As for Parker's view of Jesus, Brownson argues that it is not heretical so much as incomplete. The church has always insisted that Christ was fully human and fully God; insofar as Jesus was human, he "may be thought of and spoken of, as we would speak of any other man of equal piety, worth and goodness, providing such other man can be found." Parker speaks of Jesus this way. But Jesus in this sense is not the Saviour and Redeemer of the world; Jesus is such only as "the one living and true God in his connection with Humanity." Brownson therefore "cannot approve of the manner in which Mr. Parker has spoken of Jesus," for it is "not the whole truth." Brownson concludes his review with an uncharacteristic plea for moderation. Let the young prophets of humanity remember, he writes, "that a departure from old beaten tracks is not necessarily to be on the road to truth" and that "the world has existed for many years, and not altogether in vain."

The tentative tone of Brownson's review suggests some soul-searching on his part. His long religious pilgrimage was entering a dark valley of crisis, as he began to question the radical ideas, both theological and political, that he had championed over much of the previous decade. In order to see if he could justify Transcendentalism to himself, he had chosen to restate Parker's argument in his own terms. Yet his restatement seems strained. What if he concluded that, after all, he had misread Parker—that Parker's views really were outside any interpretation of orthodox tradition? This is in fact what Brownson soon did conclude. The turning point came within mere weeks of Brownson's publishing his defense of the "Transient and Permanent," when he heard Parker deliver his celebrated lectures on "Religion."

PARKER HARDLY participated in the controversy he had caused. By his own reckoning, one short letter to the *Christian Register* in late June was the only reply he ever made to his opponents. He wrote it in response to two Lothrop editorials on the "Transient and Permanent"—one in which Lothrop criticized Fairchild, Dunham, and Driver for holding up as representative the opinions of "an eccentric individual," and another in which Lothrop announced that although he was not responsible for Parker's opinions, he himself was sorry to have been associated with Parker at South Boston, for the preacher had "grossly outraged our feelings" with "sneer and ridicule." Although Lothrop gave no details, he declared that Parker deserved censure for recklessly encouraging the skeptical and for wounding the feelings of the faithful without doing anything to enlighten them. Parker's views on the Bible and Christ Lothrop called "absolutely subversive of Christianity."[42]

Upon reading these remarks, Parker fired off a letter to the editor. He icily dismissed being stigmatized as an "eccentric individual," pronouncing it " 'a very small thing that I should be judged of you.' " He then asked seven questions. The first five demanded Lothrop give specifics: for example, which passages contain sneer and ridicule? The last two epitomized Parker's basic response to his Unitarian critics: "6. Since you imply—to say the least—that *I have no claim to be called a Christian*, will you tell me whether you mean, a *Christian in belief*, or a *Christian in life*, and if you mean the former, to tell me, the *minimum* or *maximum* amount of belief necessary to constitute a man a Christian in belief. 7. Since you say that *you* are not responsible for *my* sentiments, . . . tell me *for whose sentiments you are responsible*—always excepting your own?"[43]

Lothrop answered at length. He declared it "easy to show" that the remarks he had made upon Parker's sermon were justified, and answered the first five questions by quoting the now-notorious red-flag passages. To answer the critical sixth question, Lothrop quoted a passage from James Martineau's *Rationale of Religious Inquiry*, in which Martineau insisted that only someone who admits the supernatural origin of Christianity can be called a Christian. As for the last question, Lothrop attempted to dismiss it: of course he is responsible for no one's views but his own.

Some years later, Parker noted that when he wrote "the seven-headed letter," he "intended to send another with ten horns to rejoin to the reply" but concluded that "on the whole it was useless to do so." His decision caught Elizabeth Peabody by surprise. She had even drafted for him a point-by-point rebuttal to Lothrop's editorial that she intended for him to rework and submit to the *Register* over his own name; he pasted the manuscript into his journal, but did nothing more with it. In September, she tried again, writing for Parker a preface to the third edition of the *Transient and Permanent*, in which she took on each of his critics in turn. Parker suspected, however, that any reply merely would invite further attacks and so give the wicked "an occasion to sin." He had her abandon the project.[44]

By avoiding head-on confrontation with his critics, Parker was being wiser than he knew. His letter to the *Register* shows the self-righteous streak always visible when he attempted to answer personal attacks, but best not put on display. Still, Parker's boast that he never engaged his enemies in controversy did not mean he turned the other cheek. He made an extended attack on the theology of his opponents in a course of lectures he delivered during the winter of 1841–42 and published the following spring, in expanded form, as *A Discourse of Matters Pertaining to Religion*. Parker's first book was a bold attempt to delineate, in a systematic way, the seemingly limitless, indefinable thing he had come to call "Absolute Religion." The *Discourse* remains the most comprehensive and revealing statement of his theological position.

SOME YOUNG WRITERS have careers like skyrockets. They shoot to fame on the strength of one dazzling early work—then disappear from sight. Parker would be different. When he followed the sensational *Transient and Permanent in Christianity* with the even more sensational *Discourse of Religion*, he gave notice that he would not fade away any time soon.

The idea for the *Discourse* was not Parker's own, nor can it be traced to any single person. It may have originated among Parker's supporters at the Church of the Disciples, the new, reform-minded Unitarian church in Boston where Elizabeth Peabody sometimes worshiped. The minister there, James Freeman Clarke, had exchanged with Parker a few days after the South Boston ordination. Sometime before 10 June, Peabody heard from a member of "James Clarke's society" that Parker would be asked to give a course of lectures in Boston "on Christ—Duty—&c," and was expected to draw "an overflowing audience."[45]

The actual invitation was dated eleven days later, shortly after the *Transient and Permanent* went on sale. The four signers aver, in the face of everything being shouted and whispered about Parker's infidelity, that they had "regard & respect" for his "character as a true & fearless minister of Christ," and request him to return to Boston that fall to deliver five lectures on Christianity. They express confidence that large numbers would pay to hear him.[46]

That this offer was made at all shows Parker's popular support to have been much greater than a perusal of the religious newspapers might indicate. As Elizabeth Peabody observed, he made "a prodigious impression on people in spite of clerical opposition."[47] The sponsors of the lectures, in their invitation, indicate why. They mention that Parker's "stirring words," which they had heard from time to time when he had preached on exchange in Boston, had quickened their faith in "the unseen & eternal" and kindled anew their "love to God & man." In fact, few preachers could match Parker's passion and eloquence, and none had so exciting a message—an exhilarating mixture of perfectionist spirituality and outspoken support for religious and social reform.

Parker appears, however, to have turned down the invitation. According to an account of these events he gave a year and a half later, he pleaded "youth" and "inability." But, he says, the sponsors prevailed upon him, pointing out that he was "excluded from the Pulpits of the Unitarians, for no sufficient reason." They wanted to hear what he had to say, and as they could not do so the old way, they wanted to try a new one.[48] Parker reports consulting with two ministers—most likely Convers Francis and another older colleague whose opinion Parker respected, Dr. Alvan Lamson. Both told him to accept. Only then did he do so.

There is no reason to doubt the facts of this account, yet it seems strange that he would consider passing up such a golden opportunity. As the invitation itself points out, the course would allow him to present his views "at great length & in a more connected manner than is practicable in a single discourse." In fact, a recurring criticism voiced against the "Transient and Permanent" was that it was "a hasty and offhand production," written in a "popular and diffuse" form instead of a "strict logical" one.[49] Parker admitted as much. He never had intended his South Boston ordination sermon to be a manifesto. Now, however, he was being offered the chance deliberately to write one.

Doing so promised to establish his reputation as a major religious thinker. For years, he had longed to win such recognition, but felt hampered by his "youth" and unprestigious parish. The fire of his ambition had sputtered on meager fuel: his translation and expansion of De Wette, still years from completion; his (often anonymous) articles in the *Examiner* and the *Dial*; his speeches at motley religious conventions. Now at last he might break out of the galling confines of Spring Street and reach a broad, sympathetic, influential audience.

Parker may have declined the invitation because he feared the course might fail, despite the assurances of the sponsors to the contrary. When their offer first arrived, the controversy over the "Transient and Permanent" was only a few weeks old, and its outcome unpredictable. Another possibility is that Parker wanted to test the sponsors to see if they wanted him enough to ask again. Too, he may have felt it unseemly to accept too readily and so felt obliged to engage the sponsors in a ritual dance of courtship.

He could not, however, despite his later claim, really have doubted his ability to write and deliver five lectures on religion. In Parker's journal for June 1841—either just after he received the formal invitation or possibly just before, when rumors were circulating that it was coming, but at any rate, before he possibly could have accepted it—he wrote an outline for a series of "10 sermons" on religion. It was not the proposal of a man lacking in self-confidence.[50]

He planned to start with a discussion of the religious sentiment itself, its permanence and universality, its relation to fanaticism and sainthood. Then he would move to the problem of inspiration—how the religious sentiment was linked to God—and attack common theories of natural and supernatural inspiration while setting forth the Transcendental theory. He next proposed to examine the various manifestations of the religious sentiment through history, from what he considered the lowest, "Fetichism," up through Christianity, which he would show was the "fulfillment" of the other religions, because it was the only one to insist on the "perfect development of man." After this, he would examine how the religious sentiment related to the Bible (he would include a history of "Christian mythology"), and to the church (he would show that it was based on the Bible, in contrast to Christianity, which is built on divine truth). Finally, he would examine the "Progressive Development" of Christianity, from Catholicism up through the Protestant sects, and conclude with speculation on its "Future prospects," including the possibility of future revelations.

The scope of the course Parker imagined seems hubristically broad. The topics he listed each would seem to require volumes to treat adequately. Yet this outline, audacious as it was, was more or less the one he followed after he finally decided to accept the invitation, possibly sometime in July.

By mid-August, the practical arrangements for the course had been worked out. Tickets would cost one dollar (a bargain for five lectures, but a higher price was thought too restrictive) and would be sold at selected Boston bookstores. An advertisement, written by Parker himself, would be placed in all the major daily papers. The first four lectures were to be given successive Wednesday evenings at seven o'clock at the Masonic Hall, starting 6 October; the last lecture would be given Thursday, 4 November (Parker was already pledged to give a temperance lecture that Wednesday). With this deadline now fixed before him, Parker sketched out in his journal an incomplete "Plan of the V Lectures." Parker then took a short vacation by himself to Maine to gather his strength and think; he passed his thirty-first birthday hiking alone in the woods near Augusta. On his return he began the most intense period of literary work in his life, in which he organized his ideas, developed piecemeal and in bursts over six years, into a powerful, programmatic statement.[51]

PARKER MUST have thought the June outline for the course plausible because most of the proposed topics were familiar to him. He at least had touched on many of them in his publications and sermons.[52] One subject, however, he had never before examined at length — the manifestations of the religious sentiment in history — and he was unsure how to approach it. In the June outline, he treats the subject in a separate lecture. In the August "Plan," however, he decides to group together discussion of "The R[eligious] Sentiment" and its historical "Manifestations" in the opening discourse. But he remained vague about which manifestations he would discuss. In June, his list of them is oddly catchall and repetitive: Fetichism, Polytheism, Monotheism, "Judaic," "Hebrew," "Heathen," Christian, "Mohometan." In August, Parker does not even mention the developmental history of religion.

While contemplating how the course should be organized, he apparently wrote little. At least, all that survives from his summer work on the lectures are the June outline and the August "Plan," as well as jottings on odd scraps of paper. Yet by Wednesday, 1 September, when he sat down at his study table with a stack of cheap blank booklets before him and a newly sharpened pen, the "Discourse" must have been largely worked out in his mind. After writing for about a week, he did have to pause to scrawl out an outline of the first lecture on the back of an envelope; it evidently was not the first one he wrote. Still, he worked with amazing speed. Despite the interruption of parish duties, he completed a draft of all five lectures—202 quarto pages of theology—in fifteen days.[53]

The opening lecture, still on "The Religious Sentiment & its Manifestations," now identified this sentiment as a "sense of dependence," and included a long section on comparative religion. The second lecture, on "Inspiration," followed his initial plan of criticizing "Rationalist" and "Supernatural" conceptions of inspiration while advancing his own; but he now added a section on the "Mystic" idea of inspiration as well. The lectures on Christianity ("the Greatest Rel[igious] Form"), and on the Bible (the "greatest of books"), included his argument that Jesus preached and lived the Absolute Religion, as well as Parker's latest thinking on biblical criticism. The last and longest lecture was on the church (the "greatest of human Institutions") and its future. Here Parker included a lengthy critique of Boston Unitarianism, accusing it of having contradictory ideas about religious authority and of abandoning its original principle of free inquiry.

Over the coming weeks, Parker copied the draft lectures into new booklets, this time made from larger, heavier sheets, revising as he went along. He made few deletions—one was of his attack on the "mystic" idea of inspiration—and many additions, as he amplified his arguments and illustrated his points. The manuscript as a whole nearly doubled in size, running to 375 pages. This new version of the course was the one he actually presented in Boston. Parker no doubt fussed over each lecture right up to the day he delivered it.

THE BOSTON lecture season that winter is remembered by literary historians for Emerson's series on "The Times," delivered December and January in the Masonic Temple. But to contemporaries, Parker's course on "Religion," delivered October and November in the same place, was the hot ticket. Certainly, it was by far the more controversial. The conservative Unitarian clergy were alarmed by the specter of this young infidel spreading his opinions. In July, the Boston Association considered condemning the lectures in advance. In the end, the Brethren decided that to do so would be injudicious, but the mood of the meeting is suggested by the exasperated query of Ezra Stiles Gannett, who wondered aloud why members of the Boston churches, people to whom he and his colleagues ministered, ever should have "asked the instructions of Mr. Parker." At another meeting, in August, some Association members complained that a way must be found to prevent the lectures from taking place. None, however, could be found.[54]

Parker's course turned out to be a smashing success. The lecture room of the temple was packed all five weeks. The audiences, described in reports as "intelligent" and "highly cultivated," included those who disagreed strongly with Parker, Gannett among them; but even Gannett had to commend the "remarkable vigour and beauty" of Parker's writing style, as well as his "warm full flow of sincerity." When Parker finished in Boston on 4 November, he started over in West Roxbury. At the request of his congregation, he delivered the "Religion" lectures as part of his regular Sunday preaching over five weeks. People walked out from the city to hear him, some for the second time. Then he took his course out on the lyceum circuit, lecturing in Providence, Plymouth, Duxbury, and New Bedford. He later estimated that altogether, between the beginning of October and the end of February, thousands of people had heard him.[55]

Among those who did, all at the Masonic Temple, were Caroline Healey, Elizabeth Peabody, and Orestes Brownson. They reacted in different ways because they came to the lectures with different concerns. Healey heard the lectures when her dissatisfaction with traditional theology was mounting; Peabody, when she was growing worried about certain tendencies in her friend Parker's theology; Brownson, when his doubts about the New Views were becoming profound. For these three, Parker's course served as a flash of light in the dark sky, illuminating the different paths on which each walked unaware.

Healey's enthusiasm for the lectures, as she expressed it in her journal, was of an intensity that perhaps only an adolescent could feel; one scholar has described the nineteen-year-old as undergoing a "Transcendentalist conversion experience." As the course progressed, she gushed to a friend that "these thoughts had been in me from my infancy and had never found the expression they wanted." She more than once declared that Parker's lectures had made her "stronger." She was in awe of Parker's bravery in speaking his mind and thought that if she lived in "the atmosphere of such a life as his," she "should be always right." His appeal to live a divine life made her ashamed of what she saw as her own "false and degrading" position; after the last lecture, she felt regret that she had "consented, but a few hours before to waste a day at least in preparing for a ball."[56]

It was Parker's commentary on Jesus and the Bible, however, that most forcibly affected her. Like most Unitarians, she did not mind when he attacked the plenary inspiration of Scripture (in fact, she thought he here was beating a dead horse). Nor was she troubled by Parker's criticisms of the Old Testament. On that subject, she "perfectly sympathized in every word he said." But when he discussed Jesus, and she found that she "must reject the miracles in toto," she "rather shrank hot—while he spoke." Still, she believed him, even as the young man accompanying her whispered repeatedly in her ear a paraphrase of Acts 28:23: "Their beginning at Moses and the prophets he expounded unto them. . . ."[57]

Later that evening, she and her friends gathered at her house to talk.

Everyone seemed "shocked" by Parker's view of Jesus, but Healey thought it "did not detract from the beauty of Christ's character—that on the contrary it involved more in him—than the wisest Divines had ever drawn out of him." Yet she was seized by the idea that if she declared her "new faith," it must separate her "forever" from her closest friends: "I had seen Mr. Parker making a great effort to speak what he believed to be the truth[,] the perspiration starting to his forehead—and his hands trembling as he said that he spoke—'well knowing what it meant—"what would close the door of every pulpit in the land against him—rob him of his brother's heart—put his hand against every man's and every man's hand against him—I had loved him for his independence—and I wondered if I too—could do this—[.]" Before retiring, she prayed earnestly for "truth[,] faith and power."[58]

Over the following weeks she often was restless and unable to sleep. She found herself defending Parker to her friends. In late November, she screwed up the nerve to write him a long letter, which Elizabeth Peabody hand-delivered for her, detailing to him her "spiritual history" and asking for clarification of his views on the Bible and miracles. His reply she found gracious and modest, endearing him to her further. In December, he called on her in Boston, but she was distracted by a tragedy. Her baby brother had taken acutely ill and later that month died. Parker offered her his sympathy, for which she was grateful, and when she was able again to think of metaphysics, recommended books for her to read.

Finally, on the evening of 17 April 1842, she made a public confession of faith. She announced to her women's Bible class that she was a "humanitarian" and "in part" a "disciple of Theodore Parker." This declaration sparked, as might be expected, a warm discussion, in which Healey nearly burst into tears. "I struck my own death blow," she wrote melodramatically in her journal that night, "God forgive me the suicide." She expected (perhaps even hoped) she would be made an outcast, like Parker himself. As it turned out, however, her heresy was tolerated by her friends and her minister, Cyrus Bartol, who must have thought she would grow out of it.

In this, they were mistaken. Her devotion to Parker continued and bore fruit for both of them. Parker's mentorship helped her, in later life, break from social and intellectual conventions and become, as Caroline Healey Dall, a significant figure in the women's rights movement. Parker's benefits from his friendship with Healey were more immediate and concrete. In 1845, a group of Boston merchants, styling themselves the "Friends of Theodore Parker," would organize for him a new church. Prominent among them, as chair of the provisional Standing Committee, was Mark Healey, Caroline's father. Mr. Healey was known to be considerably more conservative than the Rev. Mr. Parker in both politics and theology and claimed that he acted purely out of devotion to the principle of free speech: Parker had a "right to be heard in Boston." He undoubtedly had been influenced, however, by his daughter's recommendation of the man.

Peabody, like Healey, was moved by Parker's lectures, but in a different way. She had supported Parker staunchly through the "Transient and Permanent" controversy, but now found herself troubled by this fuller exposition of his views. "I felt more & more," she later recalled, "as Parker proceeded in his lectures, & as my own views matured,—that a refutation would come of all his errors—which were thrown out with such self abandonment of sincerity." Peabody in fact decided to make the refutation herself; as Parker's close friend, she apparently felt a special duty to criticize him when he erred. She wrote her refutation in the early spring of 1842; Orestes Brownson published it in the April issue of the *Boston Quarterly Review*.[59]

Peabody seems to have been most bothered by Parker's wholly naturalistic interpretation of Jesus. She revealed her concern about the tendencies of Parker's Christology just before he delivered his lecture on Jesus in Boston, when she urged him to "rebuke with *great eloquence* this miserable Cant . . . which has got talked to the name transcendentalism & which so many take it for granted you are going to endorse," the attitude of " 'damn Jesus' " and " 'I do not see much in Jesus.' " In her *Boston Quarterly* article, she argued that Parker courageously had shown the "logical tendencies" of Unitarian Christology and in doing so unintentionally had revealed Unitarianism to be an unsatisfactory faith. Parker had made her realize what Unitarianism really was: a protest of the "moral nature" against the "corruptions of the Orthodox church," which holds that only faith in Christ, not personal goodness, is a necessary part of religion. Unitarians had placed their whole reliance on the moral nature for salvation, while inconsistently insisting that Christ was somehow the Saviour. Parker had done away with the inconsistency, and conservative Unitarians recoiled—thereby acknowledging "that their first principles involved a vital error." Peabody interprets Parker as believing the Moral Law is the "Absolute"; she hopefully anticipates he will soon discover it to be merely *"relative"*—that God is not "an Inexorable necessity, whether called Law, or *called* Love," but is "the Living God, revealed in the face of Jesus Christ." Peabody herself, meanwhile, dramatically renounced Unitarianism ("I . . . decidedly pronounce dead the foster mother of my religious life"), although she refused to endorse Trinitarianism. Her position appeared hazy, because she could not reconcile the tension between her Transcendentalist sympathies and Christocentric sentiments.[60]

If the "Religion" lectures prompted Peabody to question some of her theological commitments, it led Brownson to throw his over entirely. Years later, he remembered Parker's course as a turning point in his long religious pilgrimage—the moment he realized he was not at heart a Transcendentalist.

As soon as I listened to his Lectures, [writes Brownson in his memoirs,] I perceived that, though we apparently held the same doctrines, there was and had been a radical difference between us. We had both, it is true, placed the origin and ground of religion in a religious sentiment natural to man; but while I had made that sentiment the point of departure for proving that religion is in accordance with nature and reason, and therefore of removing what had been my chief difficulty in the way of accepting supernatural revelation, he made it his starting-point for reducing all religion to mere naturalism.[61]

Seeing the doctrine thus "in its nakedness," Brownson reeled. The shock would propel him with breathtaking swiftness toward conservatism and Rome.

In November 1841, Parker delivered the "Religion" lectures in West Roxbury as part of his regular preaching; he therefore needed to write only one new sermon, the Thanksgiving discourse. He took advantage of this "break" to catch up on other work. The week of the fourteenth was marked by a flurry of literary activity. On Monday, Parker submitted to the *Dial* the manuscript of "Primitive Christianity," worked up from two sermons he had delivered in July. Wednesday, the revised manuscript of a lecture he had given in August on "The Education of the Laboring Classes" went out to the American Institute of Instruction. Thursday, the opening eighteen sections of the De Wette were sent out for stereotyping. Friday, Parker submitted to the *Examiner* a review of J. A. Dorner's *Entwicklungsgeschichte der Lehre von der Person Christi* (Historical development of the doctrine of the person of Christ), a book he first had read the previous March.[62] He was clearing his desk in preparation for the big project ahead: turning his lectures into a book.

What he hoped to achieve, the goals he set for himself as he began work, he laid out in his review of Dorner. Parker submitted it to the *Examiner* as a kind of test. He had tried to remain personally friendly with the editor, William Ware, even as the controversy over the "Transient and Permanent" raged; but he nonetheless suspected that his contributions were welcome no longer in the Unitarian journal. As anticipated, the piece was rejected. Parker then submitted it to the *Dial*, where it appeared in April 1842.[63]

The latter part of the article is taken up with his summary and criticism of Dorner's famous and formidable attempt to complete the "speculative construction of the Christ," while evaluating every historical form of Christology. Although Parker respects Dorner's effort, he at bottom thinks it misdirected. The Trinity, Parker thinks, is a merely heathen corruption of Christianity, not, as Dorner asserts, a philosophical necessity.[64] More interesting than the review itself, however, are the "Thoughts on Theology" that precede it. Here Parker sketches his vision of what he believes will be a new kind of theology, pursued with "the method of a science."

This vision rests on Parker's concept of the "scientific," which in turn was influenced by two contemporaries, each a historian and a philosopher of science. He makes reference to both of them in the Dorner article: William Whewell and Auguste Comte.[65] Whewell, master of Trinity College, Cambridge, wrote prolifically on scientific and religious subjects (he coined the terms "scientist" and "physicist"), but is best known for his *History of the Inductive Sciences* (three volumes, 1837), and his *Philosophy of the Inductive Sciences* (two volumes, 1840). Parker owned both these books, often referred to them, and would write a favorable notice of the *Philosophy* for the April 1842 *Dial*.

That he was aware of Comte at all is noteworthy, for the work of this brilliant, if mentally unstable, Frenchman, too eccentric and impolitic ever to secure a permanent academic position, was not yet well known even in Europe. Copies of the opening two volumes of his densely written *Cours de Philosophie Positive*, published in 1830 and 1835, respectively, did not reach England until 1837. That same year, remarkably, Parker seems to have found and purchased both in Boston.[66] Parker went on to purchase each of the subsequent four volumes of the *Cours* as soon as it crossed the Atlantic.

Whewell and Comte both believe that although science is fundamentally inductive — that it consisted (in Whewell's words) of "collecting general truths from particular observed facts" — pure induction is inadequate. Each man rejects pure induction for very different reasons. Whewell believes scientific knowledge is grounded not only on observed facts, but also on necessary ideas, which by their nature cannot be known from experience. For example, arithmetic, geometry, astronomy, and mechanics would be inconceivable without the ideas of space, time, and number. Whewell, who had strong affinities for German idealism, identifies necessary ideas with innate ideas. Comte would have no truck with idealism. He restricts scientific knowledge to phenomena and the relations we observe between them. He insists, however, that observation of facts was by itself meaningless, unless we were observing for the purpose of testing hypotheses.

Behind this disagreement over epistemology lies one more fundamental: the Englishman warmly supports Christianity, while the Frenchman is a self-professed Atheist. Comte describes history as passing through three stages: the "theological," in which people believed all phenomena were the product of intentional spiritual forces — an era which is almost past; the "metaphysical," the present confused period of transition; and finally the "positive," in which scientific explanations will dominate. All human departments of human knowledge, he argues, have passed through these three stages, with the more complex departments advancing more slowly. He organizes the sciences he discusses in his *Course*, therefore, from least complex to most—that is, from mathematics and astronomy, discussed in the opening volume, up to "sociology," the "science of society" that he named and helped to found, discussed in the last three. By contrast, Whewell carefully restricts his discussion to the physical sciences, and his theory of scientific progress is more straightforward and less schematic. According to Whewell, science advanced when facts were observed correctly, when correct principles were derived inductively from those facts, after which deduction from those principles could occur.[67]

Parker was much more sympathetic to Whewell's religious outlook, epistemology, and methodology than to those of Comte. But Comte, by his willingness to apply the "positive" philosophy to new realms, matched Parker's own ambitions. Moreover, Parker was attracted strongly to Comte's three-part, progressive historical scheme, and even to his criticism of "theology." In "Thoughts on Theology," Parker, like Comte, contrasts theology (at least as it had been practiced) sharply and unfavorably to science.

In all science, says Parker, the freer and more searching the investigation, the better. As a result, sciences "go smoothly on in regular advance." Theology takes the opposite rule, and so advances only by "leaps and violence." The events of the previous five months are clearly on Parker's mind: "It was no difficult thing in philosophy to separate astronomy from the magicians and their works of astrology and divination. It required only years and the gradual advance of mankind. But to separate religion from the existing forms, churches, or records, is work almost desperate, which causes strife and perhaps bloodshed."[68]

He believes that the modern theologian, like the astronomer of Galileo's time (and following the advice of Sir Francis Bacon), must "cast aside his idols of the Tribe, the Den, the Market-place, and the School, to the moles and the bats." He must search for all facts related to divine things that can be gathered from the soul or the history of nations; he must examine these "spiritual facts" with diligence and candor; "combine them" with philosophical skill; generalize from them to get the "universal expression of each fact"; and discover the "one principle which lies under the numerous and conflicting phenomena."[69]

Yet theological writers do not use the scientific method. Instead, they "set up some standard of their fathers or their own; so they explore but a small part of the field, and that with a certain end in view." The domain of theology thus remains under the czar of prejudice. "There common sense rarely shows his honest face; Reason seldom comes. It is a land shadowy with the wings of Ignorance, Superstition, Bigotry, Fanaticism, the brood of clawed, and beaked, and hungry Chaos and most ancient Night."[70]

Each department of thought, suggests Parker, in a passage that reflects the influence of both Comte and Whewell, advances through three stages. The first is that of *hypothesis*, "when observation is not accurate, and the solution of the problem, when stated, is a matter of conjecture, mere guesswork." Then comes the period of *observation and induction*, "when men ask for the facts, and their law." Finally, "there is the period when science is developed still further *by its own laws*, without the need of new observations"—in other words (although Parker does not use the term), a period of deduction. Theology, he says, is all too obviously stuck in the period of hypothesis.

Parker describes two "legitimate" methods with which to improve and advance theology: the philosophical and the historical. By the first, the theologian "begins anew," trusts "entirely to meditation, contemplation, and thought," and asks "WHAT can be known of divine things, and HOW can it be known and legitimated? This work of course demands, that he should criticize the faculty of knowing, and determine its laws, and see, *à priori*, what are our instruments of knowing, and what the law and method of their use, and thus discover the NOVUM ORGANUM of theology." The theologian next must look inward, "studying the stars of that inner firmament, as the astronomer reads the phenomena of the heavens," and outward, to read the "primitive Gospel" God has writ in nature and the events of human life. Thus using both "*reflective*" and "*intuitive*" faculties, "he is to frame the theory of God, of man, of the relation between God and man, and of the duties that grow out of this relation." In contrast to the philosophical method, the historical method attempts to construct a system of theology out of the sum of past theological thinking, without observation of new facts. Parker believes it "useful to show what has been done," but that it cannot lead to a perfect theology.[71]

Turning again to the philosophical method, Parker argues that there are two general "methods of philosophizing," that of the "Materialists" and that of "Spiritualists." He associates the Materialist approach with the *Novum Organum* of Bacon, and the Spiritualist one with Descartes's "Book of Method and of Principles." The latter method, which lays great stress on "the *inward* and the *idea*,—in the Platonic sense,—and at least in its onesidedness and misapplication, led sometimes to the visionary and absurd," has been abandoned in England and America. The Baconian method, which involves the denial of intuition and the reliance entirely on facts observable to the senses, is favored instead. Yet this philosophy "recognizes scarcely the possibility of a theology." It sweeps love, God, and the soul "clean out of doors," and as a result, can never argue down skepticism.

Despite the low state of theology, says Parker, certain great questions have come up in our own day to be settled. He lists them: "What relation does Christianity bear to the Absolute? What relation does Jesus of Nazareth bear to the human race? What relation do the Scriptures of the Old and New Testament bear to Christianity?"[72] These very problems are the ones Parker is hoping to address in his book, using scientific methods as he has defined them. Parker closes the Dorner article with a quotation, which he seems to have read as an endorsement of this project. The words are those of Leibniz; the translation, from the Latin, is Parker's own:

> We must demonstrate rigorously the truth of natural religion, that is, the existence of a Being supremely powerful and wise, and the immortality of the soul. These two points solidly fixed, there is but one step more to take, — to show, on the one hand, that God could never have left man without a true religion, and on the other, that no known religion can compare with the Christian. The necessity of embracing it is a consequence of these two plain truths. However, that the victory may be still more complete, and the mouth of impiety be shut forever, I cannot forbear hoping, that some man, skilled in history, the tongues, and philosophy, in a word, filled with all sorts of erudition, will exhibit all the harmony and beauty of the Christian religion, and scatter forever the countless objections which may be brought against its dogmas, its books, and its history.[73]

PARKER MUST have assumed, even as he wrote his lectures in September and October, that he was going to publish them. The lecture manuscripts are far longer than needed for the purposes of a course; when delivering them, he had to omit large sections to keep each lecture down to a tolerable length. The enthusiastic response the course received only strengthened his resolve to put them out as a book. He decided to do so, even if he had to print it himself. This proved unnecessary. James Brown, of Little and Brown, volunteered to take charge of the work (although, as he later told Parker, two wealthy gentlemen had urged him not to do so) and thereby earned the young man's lasting gratitude. The *Discourse of Matters Pertaining to Religion* thus appeared "with the advantage of issuing from one of the most respectable publishing houses in the United States."[74]

Parker began work by marking up the lecture manuscripts with orange crayon, to show where the chapter breaks would be, and with pencil and pen jotting notes in the margins and between the lines — points to expand on, references, and citations. Exactly when he started writing out his third draft, this time on white loose leaves, is unclear. But he probably began before 1 January 1842, when he confidently predicted to William Silsbee that the manuscript would be ready for the printer in March. Things went slower than the author expected. He probably did send off the first pages to be stereotyped in March, but April found him far from finished; he was laboring over manuscript and proof sheets fifty to eighty hours each week. He rearranged some sections, made thousands of verbal revisions, added almost three hundred footnotes, and even laid out each page of the book himself. The effort was so intense, he had no time to make an entry in his journal between February and May. On 6 May, the last proof sheets, of the preface (dated 7 May), were returned to him. The book was over 500 printed octavo pages long. First he felt sad to end a project that had been "so dear" to him. Then he sank into exhaustion. For two months afterward, he complained repeatedly in his journal of feeling "stupid" and unable to work, "never in such a state before etc."[75]

The structure of the completed *Discourse* closely follows that of the lectures, with each lecture becoming a "Book" in the new version; Parker adds to these a preface, introduction, and conclusion. He opens each book with a motto or mottoes; most of these quotations he takes from sources Unitarians would have found unimpeachable. Parker evidently wants to indicate to his readers that he sees himself as standing squarely within the mainstream liberal Christian tradition. The first two books, for example, on religion and inspiration, respectively, take their mottoes from Locke. The introduction and conclusion, meanwhile, are prefaced by apparently sympathetic quotations from none other than Andrews Norton! Parker wryly pairs the concluding Norton quotation, about how society can be improved only by knowledge of religious Truth, with a passage from the Divinity School Address, in which Emerson asks, "What greater calamity can fall upon a nation than the loss of Worship?"[76]

The most striking addition to the lectures was not the mottoes, however, but those 300 footnotes. In them, Parker cites an astonishing variety of sources: writers famous and obscure, ancient, medieval, and modern; works in Greek, Latin, Hebrew, French, and German. Parker had assimilated a great mass of reading, and the ideas of various thinkers left traces and even great marks on his book. No one thinker, however, decisively shaped his thought. For example, three modern philosophers—Kant, Benjamin Constant, and Auguste Comte—are featured prominently in the footnotes, and each has been advanced by critics and historians as having had an epochal influence on him. That they had some influence cannot be contested, but he was never the disciple of any of them.

Kant, as all Transcendentalists acknowledged, if only rhetorically, was the seminal modern philosopher of their movement. Parker himself had called Kant "one of the great thinkers of the world"[77] and later claimed that the Prussian philosopher had set him "on the right road"; several of Kant's major writings are cited in the *Discourse*. Yet Parker never claimed to be a Kantian, and, as has been seen, his knowledge of Kant's ideas came largely from German secondary sources. In the Dorner review, for example, Parker summarizes Dorner's account of Kant's Christology. There is no evidence that Parker actually had looked at a book by Kant since 1836, when he skimmed *Religion within the Limits of Mere Reason* and the *Anthropology* while preparing his report on German theology for the Philanthropic Society at theological school. Suddenly, in December 1841, Kant's *Die Religion*, as well as his *Critique of Pure Reason* and *Critique of Practical Reason*, appear on Parker's list of "Books Read." Here is the first record of Parker looking at either of the great Critiques.

That Parker could have got anything out of these books through such last-minute cramming is doubtful, notoriously dense and difficult as they are even when not in German and printed in *Frakturschrift*. Besides, by December 1841, Parker already had written his lectures and delivered them in Boston. His basic arguments were in place and before the public.

If Parker gleaned one point from Kant, it was the "insufficiency of all *philosophical arguments* for the existence of God." Yet Parker did not obey Kant's proscription of these arguments and in fact uses them in the *Discourse* itself. He claims that despite Kant, "the fact of the Idea [of God] given in man's nature cannot be got rid of."[78] Once this idea is recognized, Parker writes, it

> is afterwards fundamentally and logically established by the *à priori* argument [one based on "the eternal nature of things, and observations made in the spiritual world"], and beautifully confirmed by the *à posteriori* argument [one based on "considerations drawn from the order, fitness and beauty discovered by observations made in the material world"]; but we are not left without the Idea of God till we become metaphysicians and naturalists and so can discover it by much thinking. It comes spontaneously, by a law of whose action we are, at first, not conscious. The belief always precedes the proof; intuition gives the thing to be reasoned about. Unless this intuitive function be performed, it is not possible to attain a knowledge of God.[79]

Parker believes that by basing his system on a "fact" and not on any "argument," he has answered Kant's objections to the philosophical arguments for God and now can use them safely as important, if secondary, spiritual helps. Behind his reliance on "spiritual facts," however, are some obviously un-Kantian assumptions—most important, that the "truth of the human faculties must be assumed in all arguments, and if this be admitted we then have the same evidence for spiritual facts as for the maxims or demonstrations of Geometry." Kant thought that the evidence was not the same at all. Parker's epistemology actually was much closer to that of the Scottish Common Sense theorists than to any German idealist. Parker believes, for example, with the Scots, that there are "four sources of knowledge": "*perception* for sensible things; *intuition* for spiritual things; *reflection* for logical things; and *testimony* for historical things."[80]

A more obvious influence on Parker than Kant appears to be that of Benjamin Constant. The French writer and politician, remembered today principally for his tragic romantic novel *Adolphe* and as a champion of liberal political ideals (also for his long, tumultuous affair with Madame de Staël), was recognized in Parker's time as an important historian and philosopher of religion. At least one reader of the *Discourse* believed Constant's philosophy of religion lay at the foundation of Parker's book, "running through every part, and without which it could not have been written."[81]

Constant set out his religious ideas in his five-volume *De la religion, considérée dans sa source, ses formes et ses développements* (1824–31), on which he had labored the last years of his life, and his posthumously published, two-volume *Du polythéisme romain* (1833); Parker had purchased and read both works in 1836. In December 1841, as Parker prepared to write the final draft of the *Discourse*, he read them again and commented in his journal that he once more was "struck by the value of both." In the *Discourse* itself, *De la religion* is cited nine times—more frequently than all but one other modern work.[82]

The most obvious parallel between Parker and Constant is that they both describe religion as progressing through the three historical forms of Fetichism, Polytheism, and Monotheism. In particular, the concept that there was such a thing as a "Fetichistic" form of religion is associated closely with Constant, who popularized it in France and England. Parker himself, in his journal, credits Constant with some of the ideas he uses in *Discourse*: that the human race rose gradually from Fetichism to Theism; that Polytheism has much good in it; that there must be a hard struggle to pass from one religious form to the next. Constant portrayed the period of transition between forms as one characterized by skepticism and superstition—an idea Parker found especially attractive, for it allowed him to draw direct parallels between the age of Christ and his own.[83]

Constant was not, however, a profoundly original religious thinker, and many of his specific observations Parker could have found elsewhere. Even the idea of Fetichism appears in a number of other writers Parker cites, including some who preceded Constant, such as the German theologian Christoph Meiners. Moreover, Parker could be quite critical of Constant, attacking his "extravagant love of system," his "superficiality," and his excessive "hatred of the priesthood," which gave him a "one-sided view" that "pervades his entire work on Religion."[84]

Comte's impact on the *Discourse*, meanwhile, seems considerable. Not only had Comte helped shape Parker's general conception of his theological project, Parker cites his *Cours de Philosophie Positive* sixteen times, more than any other contemporary work. The *Discourse* has the distinction of being the first English-language book to take ideas from Comte.[85]

Not surprisingly, the only volume of the *Cours* that Parker specifically cites (he does so ten times) is the fifth. In the first three volumes, Comte had dealt with the development of mathematics and the natural sciences, while in volume four, published in 1840, he had described his vision for "sociology."

Although he already had made clear that he thought "theology" would be replaced by positive philosophy, he did not discuss religion itself at any length until volume five, in which he set out his sociological interpretation of history. Published at Paris in May 1841, copies had reached Boston by the fall. "Compte [*sic*] Cours Phil positif (V)" appears in hasty scrawl on Parker's list of "books read" in November, when he was delivering his lectures in Boston, and again in January 1842 (this time with the author's name and the title spelled correctly). Probably in January, he made careful and extensive notes on it in a small booklet, which survives.[86]

The dates are significant. Parker read Comte's fifth volume after his lectures were written, so it could not have shaped the basic structure of his arguments. A recent historian has argued that Parker took from Comte the idea that religion passed through the stages of Fetichism, Polytheism, and Monotheism. In fact, both Parker and Comte took the idea from Constant. Moreover, Parker's version of the concept is much closer to that of Constant than to anything Comte proposed. Comte saw the three stages of religion as parts of the "theological" stage of history, which already was behind us, as we advanced toward positivism. In Comte's view, Fetichism was pure theology, Polytheism the highest social development of the theological idea, while Monotheism represented a decline. By contrast, Parker, like Constant, saw the three stages as a straightforward progression toward religious truth.[87]

Parker recognized the profound differences in outlook between himself and Comte and frequently used the Frenchman as a foil. To the philosopher's belief that polytheism was "the period of greatest religious activity," Parker snaps that the "*facts* look the other way." Again, he dismisses Comte's claim that "the doctrine of pure Monotheism is perfectly sterile and incapable of becoming the basis of a true religious system": "Judging from experience, his conclusion is utterly false."[88]

Despite such disagreements, Parker refused to dismiss Comte's work. He praised it as "valuable and sometimes profound," and when revising his lectures into the *Discourse*, he modified and amplified his comments on Fetichism, Polytheism, and even on Catholicism to reflect Comte's insights. Parker accepted these, in part, because he was sharp enough to see what many contemporaries did not—that despite Comte's professions of Atheism, "he in many places gives evidence of the religious element existing in him, in no small power." When Comte in his later career tried to establish a "Religion of Humanity," to the dismay of some of his early followers, Parker was one of the few observers in a position to say "I told you so."[89]

Still, Parker was no more a Comtean than a Kantian, or a disciple of Constant. As Parker built his intellectual edifice, he took from each thinker many ornaments, even the occasional pillar. But the foundation was laid in his perfectionist, Platonic piety—a style of spirituality that his Unitarian audiences found warmly familiar—while the cornerstone was his radical attack on the authority of historical Christianity—which these same audiences found shockingly, excitingly strange. This striking mixture of old and new, comforting and disturbing, gave the *Discourse* much of its peculiar power.

THAT SOME readers found Parker's book disturbing is no surprise. Primed by the South Boston controversy to look for "gross impieties" in anything he wrote on religion, they found what they sought. An example of preconception shaping perception occurs in the first major review the *Discourse* received, which appeared in the July 1842 *Examiner*, written by J. H. Morison, a Unitarian minister from Salem. Morison was no hidebound theological reactionary; he was aware of German biblical criticism and Benjamin Constant, and his position on the nature and significance of miracles appears to have been similar to that of William Henry Furness. But he approached the *Discourse* so expecting to find it distasteful that he did not even bother to read it completely, and he certainly did not do so carefully. At one point, aghast, he quotes Parker as referring to "*the obsolete Religion of the sermon on the mount.*" In the passage cited, Parker actually writes about "the absolute Religion of the sermon on the mount."[90]

This kind of distorted reading was central to the controversy over the "Transient and Permanent," yet it was not so in debates over the *Discourse*. In this case, unlike in the former, Parker's text was never in dispute. Yet even when he was quoted correctly, his own strong, emphatic language at times got him into trouble. There are many examples. One is found in Book 3, at the end of a chapter on the "Main Features of Christianity," in a section on the Lord's Supper. Parker describes the ritual as "useful," "beautiful," and "comforting to a million souls," but he also calls it "milk for babes" and quotes Pope:

> Behold the child by nature's kindly law
> Pleased with a rattle, tickled with a straw
> Some livelier plaything gives his youth delight
> A little louder, but as empty quite.[91]

These lines Parker added to his text merely as a rhetorical flourish while writing the final draft of the *Discourse* (they appear in neither of the earlier drafts). Yet so many people, even among Parker's friends, heard a sneer at a hallowed rite, that Parker himself came to think the quotation out of place. In later editions of the book he relegated the verse to a footnote, with an explanation that he had merely meant that the ordinance, "in comparison with a Christian life and character," was "no more than rattles and straws of a child, compared with the attainments of an accomplished man," and that God's Providence was "beautiful" in allowing things which in themselves were "of no value" to "serve so important a purpose as the intellectual, moral and religious development of a man."[92]

The disturbing aspects of Parker's book lay not, however, in any specific passage. Rather, people were unsettled by general rejection of traditional sources of religious authority. He repudiated the authority of the Old Testament in an especially thoroughgoing way. How thoroughgoing is apparent from the evolution of his thinking, while writing the *Discourse*, on what he calls a "doctrine connected with religion," that of the "primitive state of mankind," a topic he addresses in Book 1.

Parker here wrestles with a particular problem, which he had never before given serious consideration: At what point did the human race start out, Civilization and Monotheism or Barbarism and Fetichism? This question he approached with a genuinely open mind. He thought when he began work on the book that each side in the argument had a strong case, and if anything he was inclined to believe that humanity had started high and fallen.[93] By the time he published the *Discourse*, however, he concluded emphatically that humanity had started low and risen.

Parker had been thinking about the problem even before he started writing the *Discourse*, when he was hiking through the Maine woods in late August 1841. In a letter from Augusta, Parker asked Convers Francis whether he thought "part of mankind" had been "Monotheist from the beginning"; Parker found much historical evidence massed against the hypothesis, but thought "all the metaphysical arguments" supported it. Over the coming several months, when writing the rough and final drafts of the "Religion" lectures, he continued to favor the metaphysical side. In both drafts, he asserted that philosophers since early times had divided over the primitive state. One school, of a "material tendency," asserted that the human race was born into cannibalism and Fetichism, and only gradually "have the spiritual triumphed over the animal tendencies." Other thinkers of a "spiritual tendency" had maintained that " 'God created man upright' " with "full maturity of his organization—with a direct, & intuitive [knowledge] of the one living & true God"; that the race fell, or at least some of the race, and gradually sank into Fetichism, out of which it has since attempted to rise, assisted by the others "who kept their first estate."[94]

The way Parker framed the debate in these two drafts, the "spiritual" position appears more attractive, which is why he gave it the nicer name. He seemed to like its underlying assumption that "spiritual truth must be earlier than error." More important, he felt, as he explained to Convers Francis in December 1841, "a strong repugnance to believe man was created in the grossest Fetichism." But he added, "there history would place me, & Philosophy does not land at a very great distance from it."[95]

In fact, over the winter of 1841–42, while he was turning the "Religion" lectures into the *Discourse*, his thinking on the primitive state underwent a revolution. He indicated his new view in a sermon he preached in February 1842, in which he described two theories of the progress of Sin. The first was the one Parker had called "spiritual": that there was a Golden Age from which man fell into a savage state. Parker now labeled this view of human history *"theological"*: "It may be |said of this notion that there are no facts in history to support it| & but a few principles in Philosophy . . . which look that way." The second theory, which held that humanity began savage but that the "majority of men have been gradually rising in the scale," he no longer calls "material" but "philosophical" because it has "a few facts & a little philosophy to support it."[96]

What had happened to change Parker's mind? He may have been influenced by his reading of Comte in December 1841. The Frenchman was a strong proponent of the theory that humanity rose gradually from savagery; Parker notes in the *Discourse* that Comte "pushes this doctrine to the farthest extreme." Also, as Parker considered the various arguments for the two versions of the primal state, those in favor of savagery came to seem stronger. Parker was more and more struck, as time passed, that human religion seemed "ruder" the further back in human history he went, and that it was "utterly impossible" to find a primitive nation in a high state of religion. Again, the case for a Golden Age seemed weaker the more he looked at it. Its proponents used as a key piece of evidence, for example, that there was a tradition of such an age in all primitive peoples. Parker came to realize, however, that this belief may have resulted from the "tendency of men, in a low state of civilization, to aggrandize the past." Proponents also asserted that in all history no nation ever rose out of a savage state without the aid of one already civilized, but Parker concluded on examination that this historical thesis was unproven: the Chinese, Mexicans, and Peruvians had no known assistance, and no one could show that the civilizations of Rome, Athens, or Egypt "came from the traditionary knowledge of some primitive people."[97]

More than any particular argument, however, Parker's decisive turn toward the origin-in-savagery view came when he began to associate the Golden Age theory not with philosophy and science, but with "theology" and the myths of the Old Testament. In the *Discourse*, Parker makes this association clear. In the earlier drafts, Parker had described the Golden Age position as one held by "philosophers," and delineated it in terms not specifically biblical. Now he says only "poets and dogmatists" believe it, and he delineates it using the imagery of Genesis: that a single human pair was created "in the full maturity of their powers, with a perfect morality and Religion"; that they fell from this state; that only a few kept the light of Truth. In favor of this view, Parker now declares there are no arguments, but only the "legendary and mythological writings of the Hebrews, which have no more authority in the premises than the similar narratives of the Phoenicians, the Persians, and Chinese. If we *assume* the miraculous authority of these legends, the matter ends—in an assumption."[98] So long as Parker thought a variety of witnesses supported the Golden Age view of human origins, he gave it serious consideration. Once he identified it exclusively with the Old Testament, he rejected it.

Parker is reacting against what he sees as the particularly Jewish parts of the Christian tradition. For years, he had been attacking the historicity of the Old Testament and insisting that Judaism and Christianity were founded on completely different principles. In the *Discourse*, he asserts that the Bible sets forth two widely different forms of religion, Judaism and Christianity, "the one ritual and formal, the other actual and spiritual; the one the Religion of Fear, the other of Love; one finite, and resting entirely on the special revelation made to Moses, the other absolute and based on the universal revelation of God, who enlightens all that come into the world; one offers only earthly recompense, the other makes immortality a motive to divine life; one compels men, the other invites them."[99] Judaism, as here characterized (or caricatured), was an unwanted "outside" influence on Christianity.

His attempts to de-Judaize Christianity appear throughout the *Discourse*. Parker attacks "the claims of the Old Testament to be a divine, miraculous, or infallible inspiration"; and in his chapter devoted specifically to refuting the miraculous authority of Hebrew books (Book 4, Chapter 2), he emphasizes their Jewish character by discussing them not as they appear in Christian Bibles, the supposedly chronological sequence with which his mostly Protestant readers would have been familiar, but rather in a sequence they would have found alien, the three-part division of the Jewish canon: Law, Prophets, and Writings. Throughout the *Discourse*, Parker stresses his belief that the Jewish books, especially the early ones, contain an inadequate idea of God. When discussing the New Testament, he stresses the separation of Jesus from the ancient Jews, whom he portrays in a harsh light:

> [I]n a nation of Monotheists, haughty yet cunning, morose, jealous, vindictive, loving the little corner of space, called Judea, above all the rest of the world; fancying themselves the "chosen people" and special favorites of God; in the midst of a nation wedded to their forms, sunk in ignorance, precipitated into sin, and, still more, expecting a Deliverer, who would repel their political foes, reunite the scattered children of Jacob, and restore them to power; conquer all nations; reëstablish the formal service of the Temple in all its magnificent pomp, and exalt Jerusalem above all the cities of the earth forever,—amid all this, and the opposition it raised to a spiritual man, Jesus fell back on the moral and religious sentiment in man.[100]

Again, Parker is often hostile in his references to Saint Peter, whom he repeatedly calls both a "liar" (presumably because he thrice repudiated Jesus on the night of Jesus' arrest) and "selfish." Echoing ideas put forward in contemporary German theology, Parker holds the chief Disciple in especially low regard for trying, after Jesus' death, to keep Christianity "Jewish"—that is, for resisting the entry of Gentiles into the church, then for insisting that those who did enter keep the Mosaic Law and be circumcised. Parker clearly sympathizes with the Apostle Paul, who on these issues "withstood Peter to his face."[101]

Parker's attacks on the traditional grounds of religious authority, although particularly pointed against what he perceived to be the specifically Jewish aspects of Christianity, extended well beyond them, and thereby furthered the skeptical trends that been developing in his thought for the previous few years. He had begun to question New Testament miracles in 1839. Now he does so in a more thoroughgoing manner. He flatly denies that miracles, in the sense of a "transgression of all Law which God has made," are possible, because God's law must be perfect and "in the nature of things unchangeable"; moreover, he finds that "the evidence for the Christian miracles is very scanty in extent, and very uncertain in character." "I cannot," he declares, "believe *such facts on such evidence*." Again, since 1840, Parker had seen the New Testament to be full of "sectarian" conflict, notably that between Paul and Peter. In the *Discourse* (as already has been indicated) he expands on that belief. But Parker also broke what was for him new skeptical ground when here, for the first time, he hints at doubts about the central character of the Christian story. The rising tide of Parker's historical criticism, which had overtaken first the Old Testament, and then the writers of the New, now lapped at the feet of Jesus himself.[102]

Parker long had denied any claim of miraculous authority for Jesus, but staunchly had maintained for him the authority of Truth. Parker in the "Transient and Permanent" had been unequivocal that the words of Jesus, because true, would never pass away. In the *Discourse*, Parker emphatically and repeatedly asserts that Jesus "taught absolute Religion, absolute Morality, nothing less, nothing more." He portrays Jesus as the greatest genius of history, who through unparalleled purity and divinity of soul rose above the limitations of his youth, his "rude" origins, his "superstitious" and "proud" nation, and his "corrupt" age to go "at one step" "whole thousands of years" before the world. Parker sounds confident in these passages—more so than he actually was. While writing the *Discourse*, he started to suspect that Jesus had made significant religious errors.[103]

Parker always had thought some statements attributed to Jesus in the Gospels—especially in Matthew, Mark, and Luke, the "Synoptic" Gospels—were wrong, but he had a ready explanation for them: Jesus had been misunderstood by his own companions, and their incomprehension and prejudices had shaped the Christian records. "I would state it as my own conviction," declared Parker in the "Religion" lectures, "that judging from the leading doctrines of J . . . |&| his life as inspired with doctrines then taught, . . . still more judging from the revolution he wrought in human affairs, & is still working—that the writers of the N. T. have much underrated J; that his was a soul so vast, a life so divine they could not comprehend half its lustre & so have set down the few imperfect observations they made on a star so brilliant & so high." This perspective allowed Parker to dismiss as "imperfect observations" those passages he disliked, and to admit as "most likely to be genuine" only Jesus' "loftiest sayings"—or, rather, those Parker considered his loftiest sayings. What, however, if the sayings Parker considered less "lofty," or even dangerous, turned out to be genuine? This was the problem Parker first confronted in 1841–42. His struggles with it can be tracked over the three drafts of his book.[104]

They are readily seen in his examination of Jesus' attitudes toward baptism. Parker, as pastor of Spring Street, bowed to convention and performed baptisms, although not often, because few children were born in his tiny parish; the West Roxbury church records reveal him sprinkling one child in 1841, two in 1842, and four in 1843. But while Parker performed the ritual, he thought it could not be an integral part of the Absolute Religion. As he writes, with reference to baptism, in the "Religion" lectures, "No outward acts can change the heart, & God is not to be served with"—and here in the manuscript he crosses out "tricks" and interlines "rites," a word less provocative but also less revealing of his growing dislike of ecclesiastical sacrament.[105]

For Parker, if Jesus preached the Absolute Religion, he would not have mandated that such "tricks" be a part of Christian life. In the first draft of the "Religion" lectures, Parker emphasizes that there are no limits whatsoever on the universality of Jesus' message, and as proof declares that Christianity "asked for [nothing] ritual [or] formal; laid no stress . . . |on| special days—or forms, or creeds. . . . It proclaims the [nothingness] of forms, the all importance of a divine life."[106] Yet Parker seems to have had a nagging doubt about whether Jesus really cared nothing for baptism. Not only had Jesus himself been baptized, but the Gospels report him bidding his disciples to teach all nations and to baptize them in the name of the Father, the Son, and the Holy Ghost (Math. 28:19 and parallels).

Parker questioned the authenticity of this passage. He pointed out that the command is not recorded in the Apostolic epistles, which his biblical studies had taught him were older and therefore more reliable historical documents than the Gospels. More important, he believed the command plainly "opposite to the general spirit of [Jesus'] precepts." Yet Parker still felt the need to come up with some sort of excuse. In the first draft of the "Religion" lectures, he claims that Jesus never preferred baptism himself, "but seems only to have enjoined [it] on his followers as a necessary accommodation" to a "common rite of the times." [107]

Parker felt unsatisfied with this explanation. As he reflected further on the problem he evidently realized, with some anxiety, that he had no hard proof to support his reading of Jesus' intentions in this matter. When he came to write the second draft of the "Religion" lectures, therefore, he reluctantly conceded that Jesus "fitted truth to the occasion," "gave somewhat of ritual," and "*enjoined Baptism.*" This "accommodation to the age & nation," insists Parker, did not mean Jesus "laid any stress" on baptism or intended its use to be permanent. Parker is forced, however, by the logic of his reasoning to admit that if Jesus in fact did either, then "it must be *A WEAKNESS*, |we must charge him with an ERROR|." [108]

This passage, with its hand-wringing double and triple underscores, Parker did not transfer to the *Discourse*. By the third time he turned to the baptism topic, he appears to have passed from desiring to deny that Jesus could have made a mistake to resigned acceptance that Jesus probably had made one. If the command to baptize the nations really did come from Jesus, Parker writes in Book 3, "we can only say, There is no perfect Guide but the Father." [109]

To admit that Jesus "erred" on baptism may have caused Parker some consternation, but doing so nonetheless fitted with his larger Transcendentalist program. He wanted to challenge all claims of miraculous religious authority; showing that Jesus made mistakes helped Parker's brief. Yet he also wanted to prove the exalted natural religious potential of humanity, and the example of Jesus was for him a critical piece of evidence. He therefore could reconcile himself to a fallible Jesus, but not to a flawed one. When he began work on his "Religion" lectures, he was sure Jesus had no flaws. By the time he finished writing the *Discourse*, his confidence appears to have been shaken.

Parker's growing unease can be seen in his various drafts of a section in Lecture (later Book) III on Jesus' "limitations" and "defects." Parker apparently intended to respond to certain deistic attacks on Jesus by showing that the indictments, even if true, were trivial. In the first draft of the "Religion" lectures, he seems sure that the task would be easy. He confidently dismisses the significance of three charges: that Jesus had a superstitious belief in demonic possession; that he either misunderstood or deliberately distorted the Old Testament passages he quoted; that he used a fierce, uncharitable tone when speaking of his opponents. Parker asserts the first two charges have no bearing on Jesus' religious character: he "never set up for a teacher of physiology—or Nat[ural] Phil[osophy]," nor did he pretend to infallible skill in the criticism of ancient documents. As for the third charge, Parker argues that even if we concede his denunciations of his enemies are not as spiritually elevated as his plea that God forgive them, and even if we (unfairly) choose to judge Jesus not by his "highest" moments, we nonetheless cannot blame him for calling sin by its right name. Besides, says Parker, Jesus was as gentle in his treatment of the individual sinner as he was harsh on the sin.[110]

Parker elaborated these arguments over the next two drafts, not always strengthening them. In the published version, he comments on Jesus' use of invective that when "the youth of the man" is considered, "it was very venial error, to make the worst of it"—a remark that offended many readers, who professed shock that anyone should try to excuse the Savior of a mistake on the grounds of immaturity. Still, none of Parker's additions indicate he ever felt much anxiety about this charge against Jesus, or the other two. A fourth charge, however, which first appears in the second draft of the "Religion" lectures, proved much more troublesome.[111]

What if Jesus were an "enthusiast"? What if he "fancied himself the Son of God" in some peculiar sense? What if he believed he was the messiah foretold by the Old Testament prophets? What if he thought that he would return in the clouds after his death to become a king on earth, and that his disciples should sit on the twelve thrones of the twelve tribes?[112]

Parker had been exposed to such questions by David Strauss, who raised them in passing in his *Leben Jesu*, and by the eighteenth-century German deist Herman Reimarus, whose final "Wolfenbüttel Fragment," which Parker read in 1839, bluntly charges Jesus with believing himself a political messiah. The questions were cast in new and, for Parker, more plausible form by the Englishman Charles Hennell, whose *Inquiry Concerning the Origins of Christianity* (1838) Parker read sometime between June and November 1841. He later reviewed the book for the *Dial*, and there pronounced that Hennell, a ribbon manufacturer and amateur biblical critic, had written a "manly," "tranquil" book that was "marked by candor, faithful research, good sense and love of truth to a degree almost unequalled in theological works." Hennell's intensive reading in the Scriptures, Josephus, and Philo had convinced him that the Gospel narratives were neither inspired nor historically accurate, that the authors in fact were fighting theological battles with each other, and that only a naturalistic reading of early Christian history made sense. With all these conclusions Parker agreed; they were for him independently confirmed by German scholars whose works Hennell apparently did not know, as he had attained his results through independent primary research. Parker in his review dissents strongly, however, from Hennell's analysis of the "character, views and doctrines of Christ." Hennell held that Jesus believed he would be King of the Jews and would restore the Kingdom of Israel by popular insurrection. This portrait of Jesus as an "Enthusiast" and a "Revolutionist" Parker finds "repulsive." He evidently was trying to respond to Hennell in the second draft of the "Religion" lectures, when he added a paragraph to the "Limitations of Jesus" section on the accusation of "Enthusiasm"—that Jesus "fancied" himself the "Son of God" and expected to return in the clouds.[113]

The idea that Jesus could have thought he had some unique relationship with God ran directly counter to Parker's Transcendentalist interpretation of Christianity. In a journal entry written early in 1841, prior to preaching the "Transient and Permanent," Parker declares that he could not put the terms "Son of Man" and "Son of God" in Jesus' mouth, because only a mortal of "unbounded arrogance" could utter them. Because an unboundedly arrogant Jesus was for him unthinkable, Parker in the "Religion" lectures insists that Jesus "never speaks of his own connection with God as *peculiar*; never calls himself the Son of God, in any sense wherein we are not all the Sons of God, never speaks of his doctrine, his works, as any things |miraculous, peculiar| which others could not do & teach." That he was the Son of God in this general sense was merely a fact, and declaring it was entirely "justified" by the "simplicity" of his character and that of the Jewish nation. Parker argues that even if Jesus thought he would return in the clouds, as the Evangelists "make it appear," this does not harm his authority as a religious teacher.[114]

Parker's arguments seem unconvincing even to him, and during the winter of 1841–42, he chewed on the "enthusiasm" problem. He reflected that the enthusiasm charge was supported by numerous German biblical critics, notably Reimarus. Meanwhile, Parker's own Gospel studies confirmed, as he concedes in the "Limitations of Jesus" section of the *Discourse*, that "a strong case, very strong, may be made out from the Synoptics to favor this charge." Parker admits elsewhere in the book that Jesus "speaks of himself—if we may trust the words of the record so minutely—as the *life*, the *light*, the *only way* to salvation, that is, the teacher who shows the only way." In another place, Parker argues against the idea that Jesus, if he were a revealer of eternal truth, must "never be mistaken in the smallest particular," by pointing that "this is contrary to fact; for he taught that he should appear again after his ascension, and the world would end in that age." In a footnote, meanwhile, he admits that the phrase "Kingdom of Heaven" is one "of no little ambiguity," and that in some biblical passages "it certainly *cannot mean a state of rewards and punishments in another life*, even if it ever have this meaning." This reflection leads Parker to leave open a possibility he in his "Hennell" review calls "repulsive": "Can it be that Jesus expected a visible kingdom on the earth; or were his followers perpetually mistaking his meaning? There can be no doubt the writers of the New Testament sometimes understood, by the *Kingdom of Heaven*, a local kingdom on earth."[115]

Parker continues, in the final, published version of the *Discourse*, to praise Jesus' "honesty, zeal, self-sacrifice, [and] heavenly purity," to question whether the "dull evangelists" had put words in his mouth, and to assert that even if the errors were genuinely those of Jesus, they would not militate against his exalted morality and religion. Yet deep doubts lingered. They are plumbed in a footnote to Book 3 that touches on the difficulty in "estimating the doctrines" of Jesus. Starting on familiar ground, Parker again reminds his readers that any careful interpreter must take into account how "the Synoptics had all strong Jewish prejudices, and . . . give a *Jewish coloring to the doctrine of Jesus*, which does not appear so strongly in the fourth Gospel, or the writings of Paul." With Parker's next remark, however, he takes a startling leap into the unknown: "But after all, the question, Whether this or that historical person taught Absolute Religion, is of small consequence to the race." Parker's claim to be a Christian rested on his belief that the historical Jesus actually taught the Absolute Religion. Parker seems to brace himself for the eventuality that this belief would be overturned.[116]

IN PLACE of a theology based on miraculous authority, whether of the Bible or of Jesus, Parker proposed to construct one founded on "facts," which were to be uncovered by "science." Parker had described his scientific methodology in "Thoughts on Theology": first, he would examine religious phenomena and from them induce general principles; second, he would look within himself for intuitive truths and from these deduce other truths. He uses both approaches in the opening chapters of the *Discourse*, when he tries to prove the existence of an innate "religious sentiment" and work out its implications.

The inductive approach comes first, perhaps because Parker thought his readers would find it more familiar. He points to the "common and notorious fact" that the "institution of Religion" is vast and takes a larger part in human affairs than any other; that it is, too, "coeval and coextensive with the human race." The only "wise" explanation for this phenomenon, he argues, is that Religion "comes out of a principle, deep and permanent in the heart." Turning from induction to intuition, Parker asserts that we "feel an irresistible tendency to refer all outward things and ourselves with them, to a power beyond us, sublime and mysterious, which we cannot measure, nor even comprehend," and we are "filled with reverence at the thought of this power." He analyzes this feeling and finds it to be an element distinct from the body, the understanding, the affections, and the moral sense. It is the "RELIGIOUS SENTIMENT OF MAN," which he identifies, again borrowing Schleiermacher's term, as "A SENSE OF DEPENDENCE."[117]

Parker had established to his own satisfaction that a religious sentiment existed and had described its nature; he then began to deduce "truths" from these "facts." "A natural want in man's constitution," he argues, "implies satisfaction in some quarter, just as the faculty of seeing implies something to correspond to this faculty, namely, objects to be seen and a medium of light to see by." So "a sense of absolute dependence . . . implies the Absolute on which this dependence rests, independent of ourselves"—in other words, God. Parker distinguishes between the "vague and mysterious" but universal "Sentiment of God"; the "Idea of God," which is "in theory" perfect and limitless; and our actual "Conception of God," which of necessity is shaped by our limitations. Later in Book 1, Parker uses induction and traces these limitations through history, showing the steady progress from Fetichism to Absolute Religion.[118]

Parker switches back and forth in this way between data and induction on the one hand, and intuition and deduction on the other, throughout the book. In fact, he would do so in arguments on many different topics made throughout his career. The inductive and intuitive modes, he believed, complemented each other and corrected each other's limitations: induction alone led only to probabilities and skepticism, whereas intuition alone led to wild speculation.[119] He came to apply the double method to a wide variety of subjects as his interests moved beyond theology, such as to the economics of slavery in the mid-1840s and to ethnology a little later.

Hints of the applications to come appear in the *Discourse* itself. In one particularly interesting footnote, which appears in the "Primitive State of Mankind" section, Parker asks whether "all the human race descended from a single pair, or started up in the various parts of the earth where we find them?" He here touches on the issue of racial polygenesis (whether the different human races are actually separately created species), a problem which, with its profound political and moral implications, would preoccupy him some years later. This footnote reveals him already gathering information on the subject. He cites a wide variety of authorities, from the ethnologists James Prichard and Samuel Smith to Kant and Schleiermacher. Yet his conclusion is reached not with data but by deduction from an intuitive truth: the "unity of the race is not to be made out *genealogically*; it is *essential to the nature of mankind.*"[120]

THOSE WHO loved the *Discourse* tended to respond most favorably to Parker's concept of inspiration and to his ideal of the heroic religious martyr. The former he later called "the cardinal point of *my* system";[121] the latter he forged from his own experiences, and his example gave it for many a special resonance.

Parker turns to the subject of inspiration in the second book of the *Discourse*. He champions what he calls the "Natural-Religious" view of inspiration, which he calls "Spiritualism" (a name that had not yet been claimed by spirit rappers and mediums). According to Parker, just as God is omnipresent in matter, so does God permeate the soul; access to God, and therefore to Truth, Virtue, Holiness, is possible for all; special, miraculous inspiration is impossible because all inspiration—intellectual, moral, and religious—is natural and divine. These ideas Parker had preached and written about for years, but although his West Roxbury congregation and his readers in the *Dial* were familiar with them, for many others they were a revelation, as diverse testimony shows.

That of a Boston printer and religious seeker named Charles K. Whipple is an example. Having grown up strictly Orthodox, Whipple abandoned his childhood faith in his twenties when he concluded that many beliefs in which he had been reared, in particular about the strict observance of the Sabbath, were unscriptural. He faced a second crisis when he discovered that Scripture itself contained contradictions. Now in his early thirties, still looking for answers to his many questions, he attended Parker's "Religion" lectures. He later recalled dissenting from much of what he heard, but "felt indebted to Mr. Parker for his clear statement and able defense of the great doctrine of Inspiration." Whipple found of "most material and timely service" Parker's demonstration that God "has lost neither the capacity nor the disposition to inspire men *now*," and that God "is always ready to give those who seek to do what they already know to be God's will . . . further illumination respecting it from His Spirit." Whipple felt that for the first time he had "heard the true preaching of the Gospel." [122]

Frances Power Cobbe, meanwhile, who lived a world away from Whipple both geographically and socially, found that Parker's theory of inspiration gave her safe passage through a difficult strait. An Anglo-Irishwoman in her early twenties, residing on her family's large estate near Dublin, she had been reared an Evangelical in the English church, but her wide reading led her to doubt the infallibility of Scripture, then to abandon the "Evangelical creed" altogether. Isolated from intellectual companionship, she privately started constructing a theology that made sense to her. In 1846, she discovered the *Discourse of Religion*, recently published in a London edition. She called it an "epoch-making" book that "threw a flood of light on my difficult way." The *Discourse* affected her in part because she found in it ideas that she had "hammered out painfully and often imperfectly" on her own, now "welded together, set forth in lucid order, supported by apparently adequate erudition and heart-warmed by fervent piety." But most important, Parker showed her that divine inspiration was not miraculous "and therefore incredible," but "normal, and in accordance with the natural relations of the infinite and finite spirit." [123]

What Parker had given Whipple and Cobbe in the *Discourse* was permission to believe in divine inspiration without having to believe in a miraculously infallible Bible. What he gave to many others, starting in the *Discourse*, was a paradigm for how to live a religious life—how, in other words, a modern saint was supposed to relate to the world.

Parker presents this paradigm in no one section or chapter of the book.

Rather, he assumes it and refers to it throughout. It is a model of incessant and inevitable conflict in religion. On the one side is the lonely man of Religious Truth. He has seen through the hypocrisy of the venerated traditions and institutions of his age and is driven by his conscience to declare their failings, at first with trembling lip, tearful eye, and throbbing heart, then with thunder and fire. Of course he is as a result unpopular. Although he wins a few usually brave, humble, and modest supporters, he is opposed by the powerful, complacent, condescending priests, "whom interest chains to the old form, though false," and by ignorant popular opinion, "not yet elevated enough to see the truth." The prophet is persecuted, but is elevated by his struggle and comes to face sacrifice with tranquillity: "What is it to such a man to be scourged, forsaken, his name a proverb, counted as the offscouring of the world? There is that in him which looks down millions." The saint is inevitably martyred, but his pyre lights the way for mankind; his blood softens the Alpine rock, smoothing the path for others to follow. The Truth he proclaimed inevitably triumphs.[124]

Such a model of sainthood described Parker's sense of his own situation. At least one critic was amused by the apparent, if implied, parallel. Noah Porter, an Orthodox minister with liberal leanings, reviewing the *Discourse* for the *New Englander*, remarked that Parker provides a "graphic portraiture" of the sufferings and trials of Jesus, "and then proceeds to show how the same thing is fulfilled in all the Jesuses before and since his time, and particularly in the case of Theodore Parker, hero and apostle of Absolute Religion. The picture is pleasant and not unaffecting, though it becomes somewhat seriocomic when we remember that he alludes to the scribes and chief priests of Boston and Harvard College."[125] In fact, there was little comic about Parker's situation in 1842. The persecution he faced was serious enough, and the threatened martyrdom, although social instead of physical, was excruciatingly real.

WHEN PARKER received the last proof sheets of the *Discourse* on 6 May 1842, he predicted in his journal "a great *noise*" might be made about it, but that it would "do a great work in the world." It in fact did make a lasting impression, both in the United States and abroad. In 1846, an official British edition appeared (an unofficial one already was in circulation), and in 1848, much to the author's delight, a German translation was published in Kiel. The book would stay in print, on both sides of the water, for forty years, and came to be regarded as the ultimate statement of New England Transcendentalist theology.

Yet Parker's circle, the New England Transcendentalists themselves, failed to embrace it. One or another of them might have been expected to publish a sympathetic notice, yet none did so.

Parker was especially disappointed in George Ripley. With other Brook

Farmers, Ripley would ride a wagon every Sunday to hear Parker preach at the Spring Street Church, where the farmers rented a pew, and when Parker was turning the "Religion" lectures into the book, he brought each section over to Ripley to discuss it. Yet Ripley refused to write a review; Parker privately thought he ought "to be *blamed*" for his silence. Ripley's reasons for not writing were probably personal. He had sacrificed a life he loved for Brook Farm and needed to make the break with his past complete. He probably told Parker that he could not get involved again in a theological controversy without "self-inconsistency" and "self-reproach." Parker may have appreciated his friend's feelings, yet could not help thinking him a "[t]imid fellow."[126]

In the end, the only member of Transcendentalist circle to write on the *Discourse* was Brownson—and his review marked the public close of his involvement with the movement. Since Brownson's epiphany at Parker's lecture course a year earlier, he had repudiated his earlier defense of the "Transient and Permanent," saying that he had attempted to open a door through which Parker could retreat, but that Parker had "not chosen to avail himself of it."[127] Meanwhile, Brownson issued a series of blazing pronouncements that chronicled his theological volte-face: a public letter to Dr. Channing, declaring that the mediation of Christ necessary for salvation; an essay in the *Quarterly* on the writings of the French theologian Hughes de Lamennais, calling for "Catholicism without the Pope"; and finally, a massive review of Parker's book assaulting Transcendentalism head on.

The review filled the entire October 1842 issue of the *Boston Quarterly*— 126 octavo pages—and even that was not enough: to fit everything in, the exasperated compositor had to set the last 21 pages in smaller type. Brownson refuted or denied Parker's arguments in detail, often chapter by chapter. At the heart of his critique was that Parker held all real religious inspiration to be natural, while he himself thought a supernaturalist view of inspiration, similar to that "taken by the catholic church in all epochs of its history," was the only one that could be sustained logically. At the end of the piece he pronounced it the "most important and most complete" of his theological publications; although Brownson insisted he had not changed his position, only clarified it, the review in fact marks his public break with Transcendentalism. Fittingly, the *Quarterly*, conceived in 1838 as a Transcendentalist journal, ended with this article. Brownson thereafter suspended publication.[128]

He evidently hoped the younger man would attempt to answer his criticisms. But Parker did not oblige him. You "have not shaken my position," he told Brownson in a letter, ". . . but on this point, of course, we shall not agree." Both our statements, he continued, are before the public, and if we have made mistakes our errors will by and by fall to the ground. "I think you mistaken— and you think I am mistaken—in certain points where we differ. Let the *wise* part of the public judge between us. If we should open a regular theological controversy . . . — why, what then? I think we should lose our time, and waste our oil, doing little good in the world."[129] Brownson was never satisfied with this lack of response and came to accuse Parker of intellectual dishonesty — that Parker never replied to his critics because he knew in his heart that they had exploded his arguments. Parker in fact knew nothing of the sort.

The breach that here opened between him and Brownson, which was to widen into a chasm over the coming years, turned out to have many parallels for Parker in the controversy-filled years of 1841, 1842, and 1843. He found former allies distancing themselves and old friends falling away. The pain of these experiences fundamentally changed him.

Engraving of Theodore Parker made from an 1846 "photograph" (daguerro-type?), now lost. Note that Parker wears a black tie instead of a traditional ministerial white one. Parker rejected any symbol, like the white tie, that set clerics apart as a distinct class.

Theodore Parker in 1850. This image captures some of Parker's intensity and spirituality.

The Spring Street Church in West Roxbury, where Theodore Parker was minister from 1837 to 1846.

Engraving of Lydia Cabot Parker made from an 1854 portrait by Seth Cheney. Julia Ward Howe thought the contrast between Theodore and Lydia was greater even "than the usual . . . between husband and wife."

Marital strife. Page 143 of Parker's Journal I, dated December 1841 or January 1842, at first glance appears to contain a copy of a passage in Greek. On closer inspection, the Greek passage turns out to be in English but written in Greek characters as a kind of code. Decoded, with the crossed-out passages indicated by angle brackets, it reads: "⟨There are times when the sadness of life oppresses a man; when⟩ Religion alone can sustain him; times when the wickedness ⟨of a friend⟩, her faithlessness, and hostility convince one that life is no place of enjoyment. God knows I expect nothing from this life, *But a place to do duty.* Go where I may, this fact stares me⟨m⟩ in the face ⟨My wife is a⟩ *DEVIL.* I. HAVE. NO. HOPE. in. LIFE." (Theodore Parker Papers, bMS 101, Andover-Harvard Theological Library of Harvard Divinity School, Cambridge, Massachusetts)

William Ellery Channing (Federal
Street Church, Boston). Parker worried
that he "venerated" Dr. Channing too
much. Portrait by Spiridone Gambar-
della, 1838. (Harvard University Portrait
Collection, Gift of Frederick A. Eustis,
Class of 1835, in accordance with the will
of Mary Channing Eustis, © President
and Fellows of Harvard College,
Harvard University)

Convers Francis (First Church,
Watertown; Harvard Divinity School).
Parker believed Francis, his teacher and
intellectual companion, abandoned him
in order to win a Harvard appointment.
(Watertown Free Public Library)

Henry Ware Jr. (Harvard Divinity
School). Parker thought Ware, his favorite
professor, had a "genius" for religion,
although too conservative in theology.

George Ripley. Parker was Ripley's ally in theological battle but disliked his turn to socialism at Brook Farm. (Massachusetts Historical Society)

Ralph Waldo Emerson. Emerson's Divinity School Address helped Parker find his own prophetic voice. (Boston Athenaeum)

Elizabeth Palmer Peabody. Peabody and Parker were intimates until Peabody angered Parker by intervening dramatically in his troubled domestic affairs. (Peabody Essex Museum)

Bronson Alcott. Parker liked Alcott's talk but doubted his theology. (Concord Free Public Library)

Margaret Fuller. Parker and Fuller never understood or appreciated each other.

Orestes Brownson. Parker admired Brownson for hard-headed radicalism but ceased to take him seriously when he became a Catholic. (Notre Dame Archives)

James Freeman Clarke (Church of the Disciples, Boston). Clarke, like Parker, was a clerical reformer (note the black tie), but the issue of fellowship with Parker produced a schism in Clarke's congregation.

John Pierpont (Hollis Street Church, Boston). Parker saw Pierpont, the embattled temperance advocate, as a hero. Portrait by Rembrandt Peale, ca. 1836. (Unitarian Universalist Association Portrait Collection)

John Sargent (Suffolk Street Chapel, Boston). Parker's "friend in deed," Sargent resigned his pulpit rather than exclude Parker from it. Artist unknown, ca. 1845. (William Sargent)

Ezra Stiles Gannett (Federal Street Church, Boston). Tireless, humorless, and possessed of a "very tender and very crotchety conscience," Gannett became Parker's most influential Unitarian critic. Portrait attributed to E. Billings, ca. 1840–60. (Unitarian Universalist Association Portrait Collection)

Samuel K. Lothrop (Brattle Square Church, Boston). Lothrop wanted to take radical action against Parker, such as expelling him from the Boston Association.

Nathaniel Frothingham (First Church, Boston). Parker considered the elegant Frothingham a hypocrite who condemned him as an infidel while privately sharing his skepticism about historical Christianity. (Massachusetts Historical Society)

Francis Parkman (New North Church, Boston). "Dr. Parkman will become a fool," wrote Parker privately of the senior Unitarian minister in Boston, "& the change will be so slight no-body will notice when it takes place." Portrait by Chester Harding, ca. 1830. (Harvard University Portrait Collection, Bequest of Eliza W. S. Parkman, 1906, © President and Fellows of Harvard College, Harvard University)

Theodore Parker's supposed delight on visiting a book store or library in Germany.

This cartoon by Christopher Cranch, inspired by Parker's visit to Germany in 1844, pokes fun at his insatiable appetite for German theology. It shows him in his parson's hat, dashing in from the street, filled with joy and longing, toward a case of formidable, multivolume tomes, while the shopkeeper or librarian, and two *Spitze*, react with alarm at the madman. (fMS Am 1506, Houghton Library, Harvard University)

Chapter Seven

I Can Stand Alone

"I can stand alone," wrote Parker in his journal as the polemics over the "Transient and Permanent" started to fly. "I know the stake I laid down, & am not unwilling to pay the forfeit."[1] In fact, he did not yet know how high the forfeit would be, nor was he prepared for what turned out to be the emotional trial of his life. Allergic to criticism, he too often responded to rebuff or rebuke with self-righteous declamations, accusations of hypocrisy and bad motives, and withdrawal. These behaviors appear during the opening weeks of the controversy, in disputes he had with the Church of the Disciples and with Ezra Stiles Gannett.

After the South Boston ordination, which took place on a Wednesday, Parker next was scheduled to preach "abroad" only four days later, for a Sunday evening pulpit exchange with James Freeman Clarke, minister of the Church of the Disciples, a Unitarian congregation in Boston that had been in formal existence barely a month. On Friday, however, two gentlemen from the church visited Clarke at his home in Newton and told him that they had heard bad things of the West Roxbury minister.[2]

They seem to have been responding to early rumors about the "Transient and Permanent."[3] They told Clarke that Parker was said to set too low a value on Revelation and the character of Christ and even to deny that Jesus was in any peculiar sense a savior or redeemer. Worse still, Parker was supposed to have spoken of Jesus publicly "in a way to hurt the feelings of pious people." They could not vouch for the truth of these reports. Still, they worried that the ties binding the Disciples one to the other were still new and feeble. Having Parker in the pulpit might cast a Transcendentalist pall over their church in the eyes of the community, and some "weak" brethren, who wanted more reverence paid to Jesus, might be offended. Under the circumstances, one of the gentlemen suggested, could not the exchange be postponed? If, of course, this could be done without any impropriety?

The young Clarke, himself sympathetic to some versions of Transcendentalism (he was a close friend of Margaret Fuller), did not hesitate to answer: a postponement would not be proper. Two days later, on Sunday following the morning service, he requested that members of the church stay behind, then spoke to their concerns in a friendly, informal way. He explained that to refuse an exchange with a minister because of his alleged opinions was to excommunicate him without trial. Besides, for the Disciples merely to allow Parker in their pulpit did not mean they were endorsing his views. When Clarke finished his brief remarks, the distinguished physician Walter Channing, brother of William Ellery Channing, stood and said that he himself, and he supposed everyone else in the room, was "perfectly satisfied." Channing then moved that the meeting be dismissed, because they should not discuss Parker in his absence. The motion passed without dissent. Parker arrived after the dinner break and preached on "Sympathy and Antipathy." Elizabeth Peabody, who was present, thought his sermon "charmed" the people, and he went home unaware anything unusual had occurred.[4]

Clarke might have congratulated himself for having skillfully navigated the dangerous headland of congregational unrest. But he had not counted on the whirlpool of Parker's feelings. Sometime the following week, Parker learned (perhaps from Peabody) of what had happened there. Either it was an exaggerated report, or perhaps he magnified it in his own mind. He understood that there had been a "widely felt" sentiment against his coming; that a major "protest" against him had been made; that the subject had been "agitated" at a "public meeting" Sunday morning. He responded by writing the church a letter, which he sent to Clarke with a note requesting him to lay it before them. Clarke somewhat reluctantly agreed to do so. He presented it to the Disciples at their next weekly "social" meeting.[5]

From Parker, they learned that their actions the Sunday of his visit were "contrary to the general rule of conduct in the congregational churches of our country & other lands." Parker says that he defers to them as his "superiors in years as well as wisdom": "It is not for me to . . . find fault though I think you have done a grievous wrong. Certainly it would well be reckoned a delicate matter to exclude a [Christian] minister from a [Christian] pulpit . . . without alleging any reasons for the deed. To do so . . . when the subject of debate was a man that was a stranger to you, whose preaching & principles you could only know of through popular rumor,—this is an unusual thing to say the least." Nonetheless, Parker continued, he would not complain, for it "is not for me to judge my betters." But he wanted it to be distinctly understood, that had he known that he was unwelcome, or even that a single person had harbored such sentiments, he would never have imposed himself upon them. Avoiding doing so would have saved them "the pain of hearing |words which| . . . must have . . . seemed . . . *idle* (if no worse)," and would have spared himself the "grief" of writing to them. He closed with best wishes and prayers for the success of their attempts "to found a new & more liberal church of our common Rel[igion]."[6]

Parker's strange missive provoked some "warm talk," as Peabody described it. The Disciples may have taken more than one meeting to discuss the matter. Some apparently thought Parker should be offered an apology and another exchange, but Clarke refused to offer either. He admitted there was now a rumor abroad that the church was "acting in a very illiberal manner." Yet he insisted, "We *have* done nothing against Mr. P." In fact, Clarke himself, and not a few members of his church, thought "Mr. P." had done something against them. They heard sarcasm in his reference to them as older as well as *wiser* than himself and in his wishing them success in their attempts to build up a more *liberal* church. Parker could protest that he never underscored the words "wiser" and "liberal," but to no avail. The hostile reaction to his letter was such that Clarke grew sorry he had presented it. He even persuaded himself that he had asked Parker to withdraw it, until Peabody rather sharply reminded him otherwise.[7]

A few weeks after the contretemps with the Disciples, Parker exploded again, this time at Ezra Stiles Gannett, who over the next couple of years would emerge as his most important Unitarian opponent. Gannett served as the assistant to Dr. Channing and soon would succeed him as pastor of the Federal Street Church. Forty, with a chin-strap beard, Gannett was humorless, tireless, excruciatingly conscientious, and physically disabled: a recent stroke had cost him the use of his right leg and forced him to gimp around the city on twin canes. He and Parker had been acquainted for more than a decade; Gannett had given him his first chance to publish biblical criticism by turning over charge of the *Scriptural Interpreter*, a magazine Gannett had founded, to Parker, George Ellis, and William Silsbee. After Parker's ordination, he and Gannett had met regularly at Boston Association meetings and become friendly. In April 1841, Gannett recorded in his diary that "Brother Parker" had called on him, that they had spoken for an hour on the "[religious] state of the community & [differences] of theological opinion among us." Although Parker already was winning a radical reputation, and Gannett was generally conservative, they probably agreed that the times were too "materialistic," and Gannett notes that he liked the young man "very much." The following month Gannett published in the *Monthly Miscellany*, a Unitarian periodical he edited, a short article by Parker on the Cape Cod "Come Outers." It came out just days before its author preached the "Transient and Permanent in Christianity."[8]

Gannett sat in the audience at South Boston, taking pencil notes in a little book, and reported what he had heard in the June issue of the *Miscellany*. By the time this notice appeared, Fairchild, Dunham, and Driver already were bludgeoning Unitarians with their inflammatory precis of what Parker had said. Gannett wanted to blunt this attack. Although he himself had listened to Parker's sermon "with pain," he tried to present the discourse in a more favorable light than had the Trinitarians. He made no attempt to hide the chief cause of complaint against Parker, that he had repudiated the authority of Jesus and the Bible, but he did take care to note what the three evangelicals had neglected to mention—that Parker also had stressed both "the permanence of the 'words' of Jesus" and the great value of the Scriptures. Again, Gannett attempted to soften the impact of one of Parker's most provocative statements. In the notes Gannett took on the spot, he recorded Parker proclaiming that we will be Christians as Jesus was Christ only "when we have no mediator, nothing between us & God." In the published abstract, however, Gannett left out the remark about needing "no mediator." As he later explained, use of "*that* particular form of expression" (which was associated with Deism) might have excited "needless prejudice" against Parker. In the whole report, Gannett added only one editorial gloss: he calls "singular" Parker's doctrine that Christianity would be "just as true" if the Gospels had been fabrications and Jesus never lived. Gannett later said the adjective was the mildest he could have used "without allowing the declaration itself to pass without any comment, which I did not feel myself able in justice, . . . |nor disposed| to do."[9]

Despite Gannett's good intentions, his article not only failed to still the storm around the South Boston ordination, it upset Parker, who sent the editor a stinging letter. His report, Parker complained, produced "a very mistaken impression" of "*my poor sermon.*" Parker had two specific grievances. First, the report has him say that "Christ added nothing to true religion." According to Parker's preaching text, what he actually had said was this: "The Word that was before Abraham, in the very beginning, will not change, for that is Truth, to which Jesus could add nothing, from which he diminished nothing; but to which he came to bear triumphant witness." Parker is not here suggesting, as Gannett implies, that Jesus added nothing to religion *in the historical sense*, but rather that he had not *invented* Absolute Religion (although he did bring it to light and live it out). Again, Gannett misheard Parker's peroration denouncing clerical hypocrisy as a statement that we "must not accept the Christianity of the pulpit or the people, on which is written 'emptiness and deceit.'"[10]

Gannett, like so many others, had not fully understood the "Transient and Permanent." Considering the mildness of Gannett's offense, however, Parker's reaction seems surprisingly strong. His letter is full of charged language: "an unnecessary *wrong* has been done"; "I take this treatment to be [unchristian] and unkind"; "I can claim *Justice*"; and even, "You may be offended because I write you this letter: you may *answer me sharply*, or accuse me of *arrogance*." Parker recognizes that Gannett did not intend to misrepresent him ("I would not believe it if an angel told me") but thinks Gannett should have shown him the abstract in advance to check its accuracy.[11]

Gannett seems to have been somewhat alarmed by this outburst—the first letter he ever had received from Parker. He not only wrote back at length to explain himself, he went to West Roxbury to call on Parker and clear the air. Gannett in his letter, and probably in person, noted that if the truth had been violated, "it has not only been, as you are ready to admit, without any . . . |design| on my part, but in the face of both an honest intention, & as I thought, sufficient care." Still, he promised to rectify any innocent misrepresentations he had made, and in the July *Miscellany*, as part of his notice of the published *Transient and Permanent*, he devoted half a paragraph to correcting "the erroneous exhibition which we gave in our last number of some parts of the discourse." Moreover, he took special pains thereafter to report Parker accurately. That winter, before publishing in the *Miscellany* his notice of Parker's "Religion" lectures, he let Parker vet the manuscript.[12]

Parker's strong reaction to the perceived slights of the Church of the Disciples and small errors of Gannett indicate his naive unreadiness for the coming ordeal. He seemed to require, as Clarke testily remarked to a parishioner, that "every body . . . say they like him."[13] Parker quickly would learn how unreasonable this demand was.

HE REMEMBERED the controversy as a time when he was persecuted for his beliefs. Yet he was never mobbed or assaulted, as were some of his dissenting contemporaries, such as the abolitionists and the Mormons. Nor was he ever prosecuted by the state for blasphemy, as the infamous freethinker Abner Kneeland had been only a few years earlier. Legal prosecution of Parker actually was suggested by an Orthodox writer in the *Puritan* at the start of the "Transient and Permanent" controversy, but was never seriously considered by the Massachusetts attorney general. Most Unitarians were unwilling to press the matter, regarding the Kneeland episode as a "farce of humbug and intolerance."[14] Nor was Parker ever subjected to a formal heresy trial, if, for no other reason, because Unitarians lacked the ecclesiastical machinery to conduct one. He was not even ignored. When he lectured, he found large and attentive audiences; when he published, his writings received wide sale or at least wide notice.

Nonetheless, he did face a social, professional, and emotional gauntlet— one that profoundly changed his understanding of himself. It forced him to abandon any hopes of conventional "success" or "respectability," discard long-held ambitions, and, most painful of all, reconsider cherished friendships. Under duress, he started to recast himself as a young prophet, hero-ically battling the Scribes and Pharisees, and in return enduring a kind of martyrdom of insults, snubs, and slights.

The insults, snubs, and slights were real enough. A dramatic example oc-curred in the spring of 1843. Parker was putting the finishing touches on his De Wette book when he called on Andrews Norton to ask for his help in find-ing a source—the kind of scholarly courtesy that he once took for granted. The resulting, very short interview, Parker recorded in his journal:

SCENE I

Mr. Parker solus. Room with books on the tables, stands & floor. A neat wood fire in the chimney, table before it with writing apparatus, &c &c.

SCENE II

Enter Mr. Norton.

M.P.   Good Morning, Mr. Norton. How do you?

M.N.   Good Morn—ing. -. -. Mr. . . -. Par—ker.

M.P.   Have you been well?

M.N.   Y - e - s. -! (Pause of 12 seconds, in which both looked at one another—& neither spoke.)

M.P.   My object, sir, in this visit is to see if you will have the goodness to lend me a book—Mr. *Movers* work on the Chronicles—which Dr. Noyes informs me you have.

M.N.   I - sent it—to—the—college—Lib - ra - ry.—! You—will—find —— it - there.

M.P.   Good morning, Mr. Norton!

M.N.   Good - morning ——!

Exit Mr. P.[15]

Not quite as awkward as a visit to Professor Norton, but still sometimes painful, were his trips to the West Roxbury post office, where he frequently found hate mail waiting for him. "A True disciple of the D——l & Tom Paine takes the liberty of sending you a line," begins an example from August 1841. "I am rejoiced to see you so vigilant & useful in the service of our Common Master." The writer continues in this ironic vein, using Germanized English to suggest a low opinion of German theology: "And now I say ahead-go and let going to be born generations know that Theodore Parker the magnificent once lived and was so zealous for the cause of truth as to remain in the service of a master who was such an imposture as to deceive and cheat the world for Eighteen Centuries and more." Epistolary abuse such as this usually became fuel for Parker's study fire; he probably saved this anonymous scrap of spleen (it is signed "Your friend in Satan, a Layman") because its author at least had displayed a certain degree of wit.[16]

More irksome for Parker than any letter he received were the invitations he was all too aware no longer came. Parker was blackballed by elite, Unitarian-controlled institutions, such as Harvard. In 1840 and 1841, he had helped to administer the Greek examinations there; in 1842, the faculty nominated him to the examining committee once again, but this time the college overseers struck off his name. He was never asked back.[17] A breach was opened between him and his alma mater. Later, he would become one of the severest critics of the college at Cambridge.

Parker also was frozen out of the denominational periodicals. The *Register* once had been his favorite publishing venue; now it would accept no article by him or his defenders. As for the *Examiner*, Parker gave up trying to publish there after the editor, William Ware, rejected "Thoughts on Theology." By 1842, the *Dial* had become his only periodical forum.

Parker's controversial status forced him to set aside his dream of eventually settling in a larger parish. The Purchase Street Church in Boston, which had been considering him as George Ripley's successor, dropped him as soon as he became hot. "There are some too timid to dare so bold a Spirit," commented Elizabeth Peabody.[18] Certainly, no other Unitarian society would dare. Parker now had to reconcile himself to staying permanently in tiny West Roxbury. Even worse, he had to face staying there without the relief of pulpit exchanges.

Swapping churches for a Sunday was a longstanding, popular practice among the congregational clergy around Boston. It had arisen as a matter of convenience. It saved ministers from having to write new sermons every week and allowed congregations to hear a greater variety of preaching. For Parker, settled as he was in a tiny parish, exchanges offered another key benefit: they were a routine, reliable way to reach a wider audience.

Before the controversy, he had tried to exchange as often as possible. In 1840, he had preached in other pulpits nearly every other Sunday. Yet even in 1840 some Unitarian conservatives had begun to avoid him; after the South Boston ordination, those ceasing ministerial intercourse came to include most of the Unitarian clergy, including almost all those settled in Boston. As early as August 1841, Parker in his journal could name only twelve ministers he thought might invite him to preach—and in the end, just five of these actually asked him.[19] The number of Parker's exchanges steadily fell: nine in the latter half of 1841; seven in the first half of 1842; four between July and December 1842; and over the next eight months, just three.[20]

This decline had for Parker potentially dire practical consequences. He feared being forced to write a hundred sermons a year that only the sixty adults of his tiny congregation would ever hear. As Parker saw the matter, he would then be like "a bull whose roaring can't be stopped, but who is tied up in the corner of the Barn-cellar, so that *no body hears him*." He then would be "in substance *put down*," and his opponents, whom he saw as the "enemies of the *freedom of mankind*," would have triumphed.[21]

Contemplating this black prospect, Parker more than once, in 1841 and 1842, considered resigning the Spring Street pulpit. He had no concrete plan as to what he would do next, but his general idea was to stay in West Roxbury, perhaps going to live at Brook Farm. He thought to spend the warm months studying and maybe laboring with his hands ("I knew [they] . . . could win my bread," he later wrote, "for they could toil at numerous crafts & were perhaps better educated than my head"). During the cold months he would lecture. He evidently found somewhat romantic the idea of going "Eastward & Southward & Northward & Westward" to "make the land ring": "If I could not find a place in church, then I meant to take it in a Hall, in a School-house, or a Barn—under the open sky [—] wherever a word could be spoken and heard." Besides, the success of his "Religion" course in the winter of 1841–42 had persuaded him that he might at least be able to earn in lyceum fees the meager $600 a year he would lose in ministerial salary.[22]

Yet Parker loved the ministry and hated to give it up. Besides, before he could live with the Ripleys he would have had to persuade Lydia to come along—a difficult task—and probably would have had to sever financial ties with Aunt Lucy. However much he begrudged the old lady's monetary support, he would have been hard pressed to live without it. Parker had spent much of his youth escaping the farm, and although he still extolled the benefits of manual work (and enjoyed working with his hands as a hobby, chopping down trees, for example, or building simple furniture), he in his heart had no desire to move back to the workbench and the furrow—even when, as would have been the case at Brook Farm, the shop operated under Transcendentalist auspices and the banner of universal reform flew over the field.

As things turned out, his preaching load never became unbearable. Ministers who could not or would not exchange with him nonetheless eased his burden by giving him a "labor of love" (preaching for him without asking for a sermon in return). Altogether, ten ministers gave Parker at least one "labor of love" between 1841 and 1843. Parker also halved his own sermon-writing requirement by the simple expedient, which he adopted in July 1842, of preaching one old sermon every week.[23]

The great variable in his decision to stay in the Spring Street pulpit was the support of his congregation. It could have fired him or (more likely) forced him to resign by making demands that he would never accept, such as that he not preach on certain topics. Parker expected his people would resent the opprobrium he was attracting, which reflected on them. The Second Church, Roxbury, was fast becoming a pariah. In August 1841, Parker reported in his journal that a member of the local Orthodox congregation had frightened

I Can Stand Alone

an aged Unitarian lady, confined at home, with the news Parker was "like Tom Paine," and that her fellow parishioners liked his infidel message. By October 1842, the feeling against Parker's society had grown so strong that when the South Congregational Church in Boston invited a delegation from West Roxbury to sit on the Ordaining Council of its new minister, Frederic Huntington, several other churches protested by declining to serve.[24]

To Parker's surprise, however, as the controversy waxed, so did the attachment of his church to his "doctrines, teaching & person." His years spent carefully cultivating his parish now bore him a welcome harvest. No member resigned from the congregation, all maintained friendly relations with him, and one family paid him the ultimate compliment, in August 1843, of having him baptize one of their sons "Theodore Parker Whittemore."[25]

With Spring Street so supportive, Parker in the end felt no need to resign. Yet lack of exchanges remained for him a critical problem. His supporters outside West Roxbury, especially those in Boston, still had difficulty finding a way to hear him.[26]

MANY OF Parker's colleagues worried that their treatment of him violated liberal principles—in particular, that it ran counter to Unitarian traditions regarding pulpit exchanges. These had arisen a generation earlier, during the Unitarian controversy, when evangelical ministers refused to switch places with their liberal colleagues on the grounds that doing so would facilitate the spread of deadly theological errors. The liberals had resented this treatment so strongly that some began to regard exchanges as a fundamental right of Christian fellowship, one confirmed at every Unitarian ordination by the ceremony of the "Right Hand of Fellowship," during which a clerical member of the ordaining council gave a short address of fraternal welcome to the new pastor. In light of this history, many Unitarian ministers believed that Parker indeed had a right to fellowship despite his skepticism about the authority of the Bible.

Yet most Unitarian clergy who thought this way were deterred from offering him an exchange by the political facts of ecclesiastical life. Although Parker seems to have had at least a few supporters or sympathizers in almost every congregation—the breadth of his following is indicated by the numbers that flocked to hear him lecture—in almost every congregation his detractors held the power. In many churches, notably the large, rich ones in Boston, Parker's opponents seem to have made up a majority of worshipers. But even where they were a minority, they usually could prevent their minister from inviting him to preach. Pastors liked to operate by consensus whenever possible; none wished to alienate a section of his congregation, especially not when it included, as the anti-Parker group almost always did, a disproportionate share of the oldest, wealthiest, and most active members.

Many ministers felt pulled in different directions by principle and prudence. Prudence usually proved more powerful. In the summer of 1842, Caleb Stetson, minister of the Medford Unitarian church, made some inquiries on Parker's behalf and found a number of the ministerial brethren who professed a personal willingness to exchange with him, but only if doing so would not "kindle up unpleasant feelings" among their people.[27] The condition always proved impossible to meet.

This clash between liberal professions and congregational pressure produced both inconsistency and embarrassment. Parker's theological school classmate George Ellis, now settled in Charlestown, insisted in late 1841 at a meeting of the Boston Association of Congregational Ministers that all members had a right to an exchange with all other members. He seemed to imply that this right ought to be extended to Parker. A few days after making this bold declaration, however, Ellis quietly sent his brother (also a clergyman) to meet with Parker and tell him not to ask for an exchange. George would have to turn down such a request, Parker was informed, lest some members of the Charlestown church be offended.[28]

Acute embarrassment, meanwhile, is evident in the case of Thomas Robinson, Unitarian pastor in Medfield. In July 1841, he wrote to Parker asking to "postpone" (in effect, cancel) an exchange that they already had arranged.[29] He claimed that had the matter been entirely up to him, they would swap pulpits as planned. He praises the "Transient and Permanent" as "one of the freshest, ablest, and most beautiful discourses ever preached" and dismisses the reports of it then circulating as "false and exaggerated." Although he calls Parker's rejection of "the miraculous character and origin of the gospel" a "wide departure" from "the true theory of our faith," he concedes that Parker's theological speculations are no grounds to withdraw "the hand of fellowship." Robinson insists that so long as Parker calls himself a Christian and appears to show a "Christian spirit," fellowship ought to be maintained.

Nonetheless, and while confessing feelings of "humiliation," he asks that Parker stay away. By allowing him to come, Robinson fears he will offend some of the "best members" of his society, who were all "old-fashioned Christians." Would it be right for me, he asks, "to carry out any abstract notions of freedom or consistency I may entertain to endanger the peace and well-fare [sic] of my society, or cart a stumbling block in the way of the weak, the ignorant and prejudiced?" For Robinson, the question was rhetorical.

Even more embarrassed than Robinson was Nathaniel Hall, the young pastor of the First Church, Dorchester. Hall had been on the ordaining council at South Boston and had listened to the "Transient and Permanent" with enthusiasm. He told Parker at the time, and many others over the following weeks, that he had "seldom, if ever . . . been so moved—so filled with a spirit of Faith & Love, as by the hearing of that Sermon." When the discourse was

I Can Stand Alone

published, he bought it, read it, and reread it. While admitting to Parker in a letter that they did not agree about everything, Hall declared that he was "sure" Parker held a higher spiritual vantage point than his own. In conversation with his Unitarian "brethren," Hall boldly announced himself willing to exchange with Parker. Not only did Hall say he sympathized with many of the accused heretic's "peculiar beliefs," but he pronounced him "eminently a Christian man," and believed his preaching "found a response" in the souls of First Dorchester. In fact, Hall's congregation did contain some ardent Parker admirers; one of them, a spinster named Patience Ford, conducted a long, warm, emotional correspondence with her hero. Sure of the support of Ford and others, Hall arranged an exchange with Parker for 31 October 1841, during the weeks when Parker was presenting his course on "Religion" in Boston.[30]

Then came trouble. In mid-October, Hall had a talk with Rev. Dr. Thaddeus Mason Harris, his recently retired predecessor in the Dorchester pulpit, who had been pastor there for four decades and who still enjoyed giving lessons from time to time to his "beloved Church and People." Harris, alarmed by the success of Parker's lectures, wanted to inveigh against "the Transcendentalist views," and so requested the pulpit from Hall on the last Sunday of the month. Hall informed him that the heresiarch himself was scheduled to preach there that day. What happened next Hall related to Parker in a letter: "The poor man seemed much shocked & disquieted when I told him that I had agreed to exchange with *you*. He would not believe me, until I had repeated it, in answer to his anxious question. He wondered how I could regard you as a Christian minister—& how I could take a step which would hurt the feelings of so many of my people & brethren. In reply to which, I expressed my strong confidence in & regard for you, & my comparative indifference to the consequences that might attend upon a step which I felt to be right in itself." Yet despite this professed confidence and indifference, and despite Hall's private conviction that for forty years Harris had fed the congregation on the mere "husks" of religion, he canceled the exchange.[31]

Hall explained to Parker that he felt "duty bound" to grant this wish of his former senior colleague and promised another date would soon be arranged. But somehow the exchange never happened. The reason is indicated in one of his letters to Parker: "I was brought continually, almost, in contact with . . . my elders, & superiors in learning &c—who are directly & warmly opposed to the views which I incline to." For someone like Hall—a modest man, predisposed to deference, disinclined to conflict—such contact proved stifling.

Of the ten ministers who offered Parker a labor of love, most were free to act on their sympathy for him because they did not need to answer to any congregation. Among these were Parker's divinity school chums Sam Andrews and Christopher Cranch, neither of whom had been (or ever would be) ordained, and John Dwight, who recently had resigned from a short, unhappy ministry in Northampton and joined Brook Farm. George Ripley, meanwhile, overcame his reluctance to perform ministerial offices and twice came over from Brook Farm to preach at Spring Street.

Labors of love usually were given by churchless clergy like these. Parker himself had given a large number of them as a ministerial candidate in 1836 and 1837, but only a handful after his ordination, and until 1841, he never received one from a settled minister. After the controversy began, however, several settled ministers gave Parker a labor of love in lieu of an exchange. Among these was Charles Shackford himself, whose ordination sermon had started all the trouble. Shackford must have felt obliged to show Parker some kind of support and so preached for him, but was unwilling further to blacken the reputation of his church by inviting Parker back into his pulpit.

THE WIDESPREAD concern among Unitarians, both lay and clerical, that by excluding Parker from fellowship they compromised their liberal ideals, rarely found public expression. Some of his potential defenders stayed silent due to their perceived obligation to present a united Unitarian front in the face of Orthodox attack. Others who were willing to write polemics on Parker's behalf, such as Elizabeth Peabody in 1841, were shut out of the denominational press.

Parker's opponents dominated the public discussion, and they had no qualms about treating him as a pariah. Samuel Lothrop, editor of the *Christian Register*, who had not exchanged with Parker for years but who nonetheless had announced in the first weeks of the controversy that he would no longer do so, bluntly presented the conservative position in two sermons he preached to his Brattle Square congregation in October 1842. He wrote them in response to an anonymous note he had received from a member of his church, possibly a Parker sympathizer, who had asked what "measure of faith" gave someone "claim to the Christian name and privileges," and what were the "principles of Christian liberty" and "how were they to be applied"?

Lothrop answered without hesitation that he would deny the Christian name to anyone who doubted the historical accuracy of the Gospels and rejected the miraculous authority of Christ. Although Lothrop did not name Parker, he made his target obvious by quoting from the *Discourse of Religion*:

> If a man merely bow to Christ as an extraordinary religious genius, whose character, though distinguished for its moral elevation and purity, was yet marked, he thinks, by some inconsistencies and imperfections, which, however, he is willing to overlook as, "considering the youth of the man, very venial errors," if he does not regard him as invested with any direct divine authority, as no more inspired than we all

may be, "if we will pay the price," . . . if this is the extent of his faith and acknowledgments, I am not prepared to give such latitude to the appellation of Christian, so to destroy all meaning and force in it, as to apply it to him.[32]

Abjuring such latitude, Lothrop insisted, did not violate Christian liberty. Christianity presumes some distinction between believers and nonbelievers, but the line must be drawn in the right place. Differences between Catholics and Protestants, the Orthodox and the Unitarians, were "*in*, not *of* Christianity." But refusing to recognize the authority of the New Testament was another matter: "He who does not stand upon this ground is not a Christian believer, and his complaint of bigotry and exclusiveness, because the Christian name is denied him, is . . . unfounded." A great many Unitarians privately questioned this conclusion, but more than two years would pass before arguments like those of Lothrop met with public reply.[33]

THE MOST severe emotional wounds Parker suffered in 1842 and 1843 were inflicted not publicly, by avowed enemies like Lothrop, but privately by those he had supposed to be trustworthy friends. One of these, William Silsbee, had been Parker's closest companion at theological school. After Parker settled in West Roxbury, he had wanted his classmate, who was still candidating, to find a church nearby; toward that end, Parker in 1838 "laid out" his childhood parish in Lexington for him. Silsbee finally settled further away than Parker would have liked—in Walpole, New Hampshire—but Parker reaffirmed their bond at the ordination, in the summer of 1840, by serving on the ordination council and delivering the Right Hand of Fellowship.[34]

Parker considered his friend a "noble soul" to "recruit" for the Transcendentalist movement and once even persuaded him to come to a meeting of the little club.[35] Yet in the late 1830s, as Parker sped on to increasingly radical views, Silsbee seems to have moved more cautiously. Parker's letters to him from this period are full of reassurances, indicating that Silsbee worried his friend was going too far, too fast.

Whatever concerns Silsbee had about Parker's tendencies, the controversies over the "Transient and Permanent" and the *Discourse of Religion* only magnified them. In February 1842, Parker was having to explain to him in a letter how someone so skeptical about the Scriptures as himself could know what Christianity was, and how the Absolute Religion could be "got at." When the *Discourse* was published that spring, Silsbee tried to be kind, writing a brief, neutral notice of it for the *Salem Gazette*, but when Parker met him shortly afterward, he immediately sensed a new coldness, and noted regretfully in his journal that "William Silsbee has been changed." Silsbee soon called on Parker to air his disapproval of Parker's course; what exactly he said is not known, but Parker later referred to this visit as "the most painful I ever received from any man." Silsbee continued to pay his respects to their old connection by offering Parker labors of love over the next few years, but despite having received the Right Hand of Fellowship from him, Silsbee never offered Parker an exchange. The former boon companions drifted inexorably apart.[36]

Parker was saddened by this development, but not altogether shocked. The defection of two other clergymen was another matter. "Their learning, their ability, their general manliness & liberality," he wrote in a sermon from 1843, "the opinions they had often expressed to me in private led me to look to them for support. The long & intimate friendship I have enjoyed with them led me to intensify my expectations. They have both failed me,—signally, utterly & with aggravations."[37]

Parker privately identified one of them as Dr. Alvan Lamson, pastor of a Unitarian church near West Roxbury, in Dedham. The learned Lamson, eighteen years Parker's senior, had made especially diligent study of the history of the early church, a subject for which Parker also had enthusiasm. They also shared, at least to a degree, a dislike of the dominant theological ideas; Lamson once admitted to Parker that miracles never proved anything to him and he never preached on them. The relationship between the two colleagues, full of visits and book swaps, grew so cordial that they exchanged pulpits twelve times between the fall of 1837 and the spring of 1841—more exchanges than Parker conducted with any other minister. Yet when the "Transient and Permanent" controversy broke, Lamson at first delayed offering Parker another exchange, then deferred it indefinitely.[38]

Lamson apparently thought Parker incautious in his theological speculations, or at least in airing them publicly, and may have worried about bringing someone now known as a preacher of such ideas before the Dedham congregation, who disliked controversy in the pulpit. That Lamson should have put weight on such considerations, however, Parker must have found especially galling, in light of the prominent role Lamson and Dedham had played in the Unitarian controversy a generation earlier. Lamson's predecessor at Dedham had been Orthodox and had refused to exchange pulpits with Unitarians. Liberals in the congregation, who made up a majority of the parish, had grown to resent this "exclusive" policy; in 1818, when their old pastor stepped down, they had sought to change things by calling Lamson, a liberal, as his successor. Dedham evangelicals, who favored exclusion, had objected bitterly. They had constituted a majority of the covenanted church (those who took communion), and they held that according to New England tradition only the church, not the parish, could call a minister. The dispute resulted in a celebrated court case (the "Dedham case"), which the evangelicals lost.[39]

Lamson had received his pulpit, in short, as a part of a famous protest against exclusive fellowship, yet now he was excluding Parker. He and Parker maintained a social relationship, but Parker's disillusionment with his "near neighbor" keens from this assessment, written in 1844: "I love [Lamson] much—but his timidity, his despair of man—I find no sympathy for. . . . He is liberal—but fearful; just—but rather over nice. He has a quiet murmur tho' a little sound. . . . He has too little hope—too much respect for precedents—too little intuition—nor half spontaneous enough. When he dies—men will say 'Here lies a Unitarian minister who had folios in his library & read the Fathers.' "[40]

The failure of Lamson to support Parker, however, shook him far less profoundly than did the defection of the other clergyman whom he says disappointed him. In June 1842, Convers Francis wrote to Parker requesting that they "set aside" an exchange they had arranged the month earlier.[41]

For a decade, since Parker was a raw youth running an academy in Watertown, he had regarded Francis as his mentor—the teacher who started him on the study of the Bible, the sponsor who gave him entrée into the Transcendentalists' little club, the older colleague who preached his ordination sermon—and a valued friend. Francis, meanwhile, obviously reciprocated the warm feelings, his affection for a protégé having grown over the years to a near awe-struck admiration for a prodigy. By 1838, Francis could effuse about Parker in his journal: "Glorious man! . . . His intellectual affluence exceeds that of any man I know, not only among his coevals, but among all others. The rapid expansion and powerful development of his mind, since he first came to me as a schoolmaster, have been [a] matter of amazement to me." He and Parker exchanged pulpits only about once a year, because Francis apparently preferred to preach at home, but they visited frequently, borrowed each others' books, and wrote often, their correspondence lively with humor and learning.[42]

Parker respected Francis's judgment, and whenever the younger man said or did something particularly bold, he would turn for encouragement to the older one, trusting him never to throw up his hands in disgust or flee in fear. Parker's earliest surviving declaration that the New Testament "contains numerous mythi," for example, appeared in a letter to Francis from March 1839, in which Parker also expressed confidence that Francis would "not be horror-struck at any doubts an honest lover of truth will suggest." Nor was he. Francis in his reply reassured Parker that the New Testament stories were appreciated best as poetic expressions of deeper truths, which is how their authors likely understood them. Again, a year and a half later, when Parker faced severe criticism for signing the call to the Chardon Street Convention and had started to doubt whether he had done the right thing, he wrote to Francis to explain himself. Francis's response was heartening: "My dear friend, I am sorry you could for a moment suppose that any thing *you* can do should need a justification to *me*: for when I can think you have done wrong, it will seem time to inquire whether the planets have not taken to devious courses in the firmament."[43]

When the "Transient and Permanent" controversy broke in 1841, Parker assumed Francis would stand by him, and in fact, on 13 June, just after Parker started to be denounced in the press, Francis conducted an exchange with him. That same day, Francis in his journal expressed outrage that his friend, "a man of sound Christian piety, of unequalled theological attainments, of the most Christ-like spirit," should be cried down as an infidel and blasphemer simply because "he has said we may be Christians without believing all that is written in the Old and New Testaments!" Two weeks later, Francis wrote to Parker dismissing as "clatter" the criticism of his South Boston sermon, which he called "a great, and good, and pious, and deeply Christian discourse." In December 1841, Francis wrote in his journal that Parker seemed, "notwithstanding his reputation of infidelity, more and more pious every time I see him," and that a "mind so affluent in learning and high thought I have never known."[44]

Yet behind Francis's reiterated expressions of admiration for Parker seems to have been a gnawing concern that his friend's pronouncements were becoming rash and unnecessarily confrontational. Parker, perhaps sensing these barely articulated reservations, began to feel he had outgrown his cautious, retiring teacher. As early as 1840, Parker had criticized Francis for being "wedded to the past," and in February 1842 Parker noted somewhat wistfully in his journal that although Francis was "urbane & genial & good as ever," his words failed to "stir me as once they did. Then I walked long days in the strength of the meat I ate. He solved problems for me. Now I look else-whither."[45]

The two men had started to drift apart, but neither apparently minded the gap until early 1842, when Parker, "out of a sense of personal gratitude," offered to dedicate the *Discourse of Religion* to his friend. The recipient of this honor apparently was surprised to receive it, and to Parker's own surprise emphatically turned it down. Francis, who shied away from notoriety, probably wanted no public association with a work that promised to be so controversial. He also must have realized, based on either hearing Parker's "Religion" lectures or reading reports of them, that he could not endorse all that his friend would say, and he did not want to appear to do so. Parker, stung by the rebuff, sent the *Discourse* to the printer with no dedication at all, and predicted to Francis (only half-jokingly?) that once the book came out the older man would never speak to him again, except to say, *Get thee behind me Satan*! Perhaps to allay Parker's fears, Francis in mid-May offered him an exchange for the following month.[46]

At this delicate moment came news that changed Francis's life: he had been invited to succeed the ailing Henry Ware Jr. as Professor of Pulpit Eloquence and the Pastoral Care at the Harvard Divinity School. The offer presented Francis with an opportunity to introduce the rising generation of Unitarian ministers to new ideas of theology and biblical criticism that hitherto had been neglected in Cambridge classrooms. Moreover, on a personal level, the Harvard offer salved a long-festering wound to Francis's pride.

To all appearances, Francis seemed content to live out his life a bookish pastor in Watertown. Deep down, however, he resented that his considerable scholarly attainments never had received what he considered proper recognition. In a letter to Parker from 1839, Francis lamented that he was "unqualified to find favor with the public," and so "must content myself with such pleasure as I can find, or such culture as I can make, in my 'inner kingdom,' & retire from all claims to notice." He added, in a self-confessed "burst of egotism," that this lesson had been "also taught me pretty effectually by the studious exclusion from all tokens of confidence or esteem, which I have met at the hands of those among us who dispense the honors of theology & literature." Francis's injured pride explains his uncharacteristically bitter tone in another letter to Parker, this one from 1838, when Francis learned that Charles Brooks, a Unitarian minister from a nearby town whom he had known since boyhood, had been appointed professor of natural history at the City University of New York. Francis dismissed Brooks as "ignorant . . . on every subject" and huffed that Brooks had only won his distinguished post by brazenly courting influential patrons: "It is humbling & discouraging to see what can be effected by cringing & artifice . . . [while] men of scholarship & talents . . . would fail from want of impudence. I am sick of such things, & begin to think with Hamlet the . . . times are out of joint."[47]

For Francis, the offer in 1842 of a Harvard appointment must have seemed like sweet vindication, and he immediately accepted the job. He knew it would lead to major alterations in his life: he would have to resign his pastorate and move from Watertown, where he had lived for twenty years, to neighboring Cambridge. He failed to consider, however, the possible consequences for his friendship with the notorious young heretic from West Roxbury.

These quickly became apparent. On 10 June, just two days before his scheduled exchange with Parker, Francis mentioned the upcoming event to his old friend James Walker, who taught natural religion and moral philosophy at Harvard (and who himself soon would be chosen university president). Walker, plainly worried by Francis's disclosure, suggested that, "*under existing circumstances*," the exchange ought to be suspended. Although Walker professed personally not to mind if the pulpit-swap took place, he feared that Orthodox critics would seize on it and raise the cry that the school had appointed a professor who maintained fellowship with an infidel. Francis relented without a fight. He immediately wrote to Parker canceling their arrangement—not, he insisted, because of his own feelings, but in deference to the feelings of others.[48]

The letter left its recipient thunderstruck. Parker jotted in his sermon book that "*Francis* fell back on [account] of the professorship at [Cambridge]" and scrambled to make alternative arrangements; he ended up giving a labor of love for an ill minister in Boston, while persuading a friend to fill the West Roxbury pulpit with a labor of love. A few days later, he called on Francis to talk about what had happened, but the meeting did not go well. Parker thought his old friend evaded his questions. Francis's wife, meanwhile, apparently told one of Parker's friends (possibly Lydia) that the exchange had been canceled because her husband had mistakenly scheduled another exchange on the same day. The fib, when it reached Parker, only worsened his mood.[49]

His journal from mid-June records his mounting anger:

June 12: "Francis is a good man & I love him, but this expediency doctrine I don't like."
June 15: "The more I think of this affair of Dr F, the worse it appears, & the more cowardly. That *he* should sneak off in this way."
June 18: "Poor Francis—How he is fallen. I can't bear to think of him. False to his idea. *He has no Root in himself.*"[50]

Parker could barely conceal his emotions in a letter to Francis on 24 June. "No one that *helped* in my ordination will now exchange ministerial courtesies with me," Parker complained to the man who had preached his ordination sermon. Parker attacked the Unitarian clergy for their cowardice, framing the indictment in a way that implicated Francis himself. Parker confessed he was disappointed with the Unitarian ministers; he once had thought they would be "true to an ideal principle of Right," but now found "no body of men was ever more completely sold to the sense of Expediency. Stuff them with good dinners & Freedom, Theology—Religion may go to the Devil for all time." Freedom of speech, Parker wrote, was either worth preserving or not worth preserving. "If the ministers think the *first* (as their life shows they do) let them say it plainly & manfully, that the public may no longer look to their clouds with out rain. If they think the *second*, then something must be done."[51]

Francis chose to infer no criticism of his own conduct from this letter. He convinced himself that Parker saw the canceled exchange "in just the same light" he himself did. He continued, too, to condemn as "abominable" the "unkind" treatment Parker received from other Unitarians. Yet a new, critical edge appeared in his remarks about his friend. Francis discovered he disliked the *Discourse of Religion* even more than he expected he would; what seems to have bothered him most was Parker's tone, especially when treating the Bible and Jesus. "The spirit of [the book] *seems* to be bad, derisive, sarcastic, arrogant," he commented sadly in his journal on 25 June, "—contemptuous of what the wise and good hold sacred." Although he reminded himself Parker meant "nothing of this," Francis wished his friend had held off publication "till years had brought more consideration." Shortly after penning this judgment, Francis called on Parker, who found him "[m]ore severe upon me than ever before." In Parker's eyes, Francis looked "pretty sober & a little sad, perhaps at leaving his old *friends* & going into new friends."[52]

Francis desired no personal break with Parker, but knew he had to establish some distance from him. Toward that end, when Francis's turn came at the end of July to preach the regular Thursday Lecture in Boston, he took the occasion to affirm his faith in the importance of Jesus to salvation. By his own account, the sermon "gave some satisfaction to those who have been disposed to accuse me of the horrible crime of transcendentalism!" This discourse may have been the subject of a conversation that Parker recalled many years later, in which Francis criticized his friend for denying the "supernatural in Christianity." Parker responded by asking which specific New Testament miracle Francis believed actually had occurred. Francis could name none, but still insisted that he "accepted the supernatural element." He probably meant that he still wanted Christianity somehow to be recognized as an authoritative revelation, but for Parker, Francis's position appeared illogical and even hypocritical.[53]

Still, Parker struggled to contain his sense of personal betrayal and see the larger context. Your becoming a professor at Harvard, he wrote to Francis in July, "is as great a gain for the College & for the whole community as [was] the accession of Dr Ware" almost forty years earlier. Just as the elder Henry Ware had brought Unitarianism to the University, so Francis would bring the ideas of the New School; therefore Francis bore "about the same relation to *the times* that Ware bore to that period." Parker also tried to "rejoice" in Francis's "prospect of long usefulness" and his having at last found "a society of men" that would appreciate him. But in his heart, Parker was not rejoicing at all.[54]

In early August 1842, worn down by the toil and distress of the previous months, he fled, alone, to far-off St. John's, capital of Newfoundland, for a short vacation. But he found the city and its inhabitants "ragged, straggling, dirty," and dull. He had little to do but brood over his slights, and they hatched at last in a short, despairing letter to Francis, which he could not even bring himself to sign. If the feelings of "the Brethren" are offended by your simply exchanging pulpits with me, writes Parker, an act that implies no more than "general Christian sympathy," "how much more would it shock their feelings & 'hurt your usefulness' to exchange any *social* intercourse." I do not, Parker insisted, "wish to stand in your way," so once you go to Cambridge, "I don't see how I can visit you as heretofore."[55]

Francis received this ultimatum with mixed emotions. In his reply, he insisted that Parker's notion of hurting him with social intercourse was but a "bugbear" and a "chimera," and even if it were not, "I am sorry you should pay me so poor a compliment as to suppose I should care a straw for the alleged danger." Francis evidently did not want the "discontinuance of an intercourse" that had been one of his "chief pleasures." Yet, as his new world opened up to him, he seems to have been unwilling to take action to see his relationship with Parker continued; he did not, for instance, offer to visit Parker in West Roxbury. Instead, Francis left the future of the friendship entirely in Parker's hands: "If you will allow me the pleasure of seeing you at Cambridge as much and as often as possible, I shall be greatly obliged to you; if you will not, the loss will be my own, and I shall bear it with deep regret."[56]

Parker exercised the second option. He did not go to see Francis in Cambridge. But he resented that Francis did not come to see him. In a sermon Parker wrote in the early fall on "Expediency and Morality," he seemed to have Francis in mind when he denounced the "expedient" friend who turns away "when the popular tide sets against you": "Can you lean on him? You turn to look for him—& he is hid in the dust far off on the horizon. |It would 'hurt his usefulness' to be found in your company. But he loves you very much &c|." Parker still felt he could share scholarship with Francis and even wrote in his journal a new list of "Questions Francisanea," all concerning biblical criticism. But he adds to them an angry memo: "Never ask him any questions relating to *Phil[osophy]* or *Morals* or above all *Religion* since his shabbiness." Perhaps to test whether their relationship could be recast along less intimate lines, Parker in September wrote Francis an encouraging, if soberly worded letter, telling him that he had heard the Divinity School already wore "a new aspect" since his arrival, urging him to reverse the trend toward "awful neglect of study" among young ministers, and sending him "a great pile of Reviews." He waited hopefully for a reply, but none came. After enduring several months of silence, Parker penned this pained comment in his journal: "I wrote Dr. Fr. a letter last Sept. . . . But thought then I should not soon get an answer from the *careless* P[ost]. O[ffice]. Never yet (Dec 22). He is very busy."[57]

Francis was in fact very busy, having assumed a heavy load of teaching with no classes prepared, but there seems to have been another reason for his neglect: he resented Parker for not visiting *him*. Francis felt as if *he* were the one being abandoned. Since coming to Harvard, he had encountered criticism from many old friends for having done so. Frederic Henry Hedge, for one, had written him a letter announcing, in terms very similar to the ones Parker had used, that he could not visit Francis as before, because "there are new considerations and responsibilities incident to your new position, which must necessarily affect, in some degree, the tone of your intercourse with old associates & especially with those who have incurred the stigma of transcendental and heretical tendencies." Francis felt rejected and exasperated. "If I have committed a sin not to be forgiven in coming to Cambridge," he wrote of Hedge's statement, "it would have been quite as kind to warn me of it beforehand, rather than cast it in my teeth now."[58]

Francis and Parker, harboring such mutual resentments, had no contact for six months. Then, in February 1843, they unexpectedly met in a bookstore, and to the surprise of both, had a cordial conversation. Parker, realizing how much he missed his old mentor, took the initiative in offering the olive branch. In a brief, somewhat nervously jocose letter, he teased Francis for his long silence ("Semper ego *scriptitor* tantura! nunquamne ressonas!! & that means as plain as Latin can speak it—are you going to answer my letter of last September, nor never to write again"), offered to come see him ("I . . . intend one of these days to invade your *Adyta* & steal away some of that herb which 'once plucked groweth not again'—to wit your *time*"), made a recondite query about the Dominican scholar Leonardus de Unterio, and reported the doings of some common friends, including jokes about Francis they had told. To this letter, Parker finally received a response. Francis dwelt mostly on Leonardus, griped about "sneers and sarcasms" in the jokes, and only turned to the heart of the matter in a slightly petulant postscript: "Why have I not written before this? I suppose I am lazy. I would only put in the plea that I have not had time to take a long breath more than once or twice since last September. If you deem me worthy to bestow your time upon, I can only repeat that I am always most happy to see you."[59]

Parker took this rather stiff answer as an opening and sent Francis back two brief but boisterous letters, in which he deflected the complaint of "sneers and sarcasms" by arguing, tongue in cheek, that Francis could only have seen them where they did not exist because he had experienced "a *visitatio diaboli*, to which Hieronymous, & Lutherus & many great Doctors & Professors of theology have been subjected before." Parker even enclosed a cartoon he had made of the Devil who had made the visitation. Francis, starting to warm, replied with a humorously "diabolical" letter of his own, speculating what it meant that Parker knew " 'old Hornie' " well enough to get such a good likeness. Parker answered in similarly silly vein, describing the satanic visitation at length, with the Devil taking the form of Andrews Norton and other prominent Unitarians.[60]

The reconciliation sailed forward in March and April 1843—but then it ran into a squall and nearly sank. Parker had by this time decided to escape the controversy by taking a sabbatical in Europe. He needed to find supply preachers to fill the Spring Street pulpit in his absence, and Francis, as they were now getting along, seemed an obvious choice. So in mid-May, when they ran into one another at the Little and Brown bookshop in Boston, Parker asked him if he ever supplied pulpits. Francis replied that he did, whenever he "got the chance." "Well," Parker asked, "will you supply mine, for I am going to Europe, in Sept[ember], to begin a year [there]?" To Parker's dismay, Francis suddenly hedged and hesitated, mentioned "difficulties," and said he would have to discuss the matter with the Spring Street parish committee.

> I took up a new [Edition] of Neal's Puritans . . . [writes Parker in his journal] & looked along in it, while he continued to talk in the same strain. I confess—I felt as if my heart would dissolve in tears, at this new instance of rottenness in Francis—& so I said . . .
> "Well I think I had better leave it to the Parish committee—if I go."
> (& we presently separated.)
> If Dr Convers Francis be not a rotten stick—then there is none in this world.⁶¹

Parker's bitterness at this moment would seem to make impossible any future relationship with Francis, yet somehow, in June and July 1843, the two men reached a new, stable understanding. How they accomplished this cannot be determined; no letters between them survive from those months, and their journals are silent on the subject. The key seems to have been that Francis decided, after consideration, that he would preach for Parker after all. In early August, he gave him a labor of love and after Parker left the country, filled his pulpit for some months. The record of their correspondence resumes in the fall of 1843, and by then their letters have a friendly, although not intimate, tone.

Writing in 1846, Parker denied that he ever had felt personal "ill-will" or "sourness of temper" toward any member of the "Unitarian clergy now living"—except one. He does not name the minister, but he certainly is referring to Francis when he confesses that of this man "I did, for . . . [some months], feel emotions that I did not justify, or approve, or even attempt to apologize for." He here writes about these feelings as if they had passed away altogether—but in fact traces of them lingered. In 1859, when he came to write his autobiographical *Experience as a Minister*, he made no reference in it to Francis. The omission was deliberate, explained Parker in a letter to George Ripley: "I don't mention Francis, to whom *I* owe much. But (1) He has been so false to the Idea & also to me that I thought he deserved no mention; & (2) he is so timid that he would shake all over for a month if I should name him in public as one of my acquaintances!"⁶²

THE WORST emotional gauntlet that Parker endured in 1842 did not involve Lamson, Silsbee, or even Francis. In fact, the intensity of his reaction to their respective "betrayals" may have been merely a byproduct of his discomposure due to deeper troubles at home.

How deep are suggested by an astonishing outburst from January of that year. Parker was delivering his lectures on "Religion" and working furiously to revise them into the *Discourse*, when he wrote in his journal what at first glance appears to be a transcription of a passage in Greek, but on closer inspection turns out to be in English, written in Greek characters to disguise it. Transcribed into Roman letters, with the crossed-out passages indicated by angle brackets, it reads: "⟨There are times when the sadness of life oppresses a man; when⟩ Religion alone can sustain him; times when the wickedness ⟨of a friend⟩, her faithlessness, and hostility convince one that life is no place of enjoyment. God knows I expect nothing from this life, *But a place to do duty*. Go where I may, this fact stares me . . . in the face ⟨My wife is a⟩ DEVIL. I. HAVE. NO. HOPE. in. LIFE."[63]

Some awful fight lay behind this entry. An entry twenty pages later indicates that things had been patched up, but only verbally. Parker here records that his predecessor in West Roxbury, the Rev. George Whitney, had died, leaving a wife, two children, a widowed mother, and two unwed sisters. Parker comments, with the scratched out (but still legible) passages indicated by angle brackets: "How surprising it seems that such as W. are taken away, & I am left. ⟨No one depends on me⟩—few would mourn at my departure. ⟨My wife, I doubt not would rejoice. Her actions not her words say this.⟩"[64]

The statement "No one depends on me" suggests two of the chronic reasons for household tension: Parker's frustration at having no children and his resentment at being financially beholden to Aunt Lucy. Between him and Lucy there was no peace. In another coded journal entry from July 1842, this one written in Hebrew characters (and therefore from right to left), Parker makes two "Resolutions," probably prompted by an argument that itself grew out of his criticizing his in-law, perhaps to Lydia: "1. To treat Lucy as a baby. 2. Never to speak of Lucy Cabot."[65] Overall, during these years of public controversy, Parker's emotional distance from his wife's family increased; most of them were conservative, establishment Unitarians repelled by his theological and political heterodoxy. Years later, he complained that after the South Boston ordination, the Cabots and their kin treated him as if he had committed a great crime.

The most acute source of tension in the household, however, appears to have been his feelings for Anna Shaw. Although Theodore insisted that this attachment was merely "ideal," his attentions to her led Lucy to accuse him in April 1841 of "visiting his neighbor" too much. Parker replied defiantly (if not to her face, then at least in his journal) that he would go wherever he found "sympathy," but he also had insisted that he would "not for the world harm a thought of L[ydia]'s heart, nor give her a twinge of the lip." In other words, he refused to end his friendship with Anna, but he seems to be saying he would try to see less of her in order to mollify Lydia.[66]

Whatever relationship he still had with Anna, however, soon became for Lydia and Lucy intolerable, because people started to talk about it. It was said that Theodore had "made a mistake in his wife," that he "neglected" her, sought the "society of other ladies," and was "pitied" by his female friends for not being free to marry Anna. The rumors had bite, for they match closely the image of the Parkers' marriage that emerges from Theodore's own journal. Whether or not Lydia's discovery of the gossip prompted the terrible argument of January 1842 cannot be known. What is known is that the rumors were still circulating the following summer, when Elizabeth Peabody recorded them in a letter to Orestes Brownson.[67]

This letter hints at a complex, intimate drama that apparently had been unfolding for many months. The personae of the play included not only Theodore, Lydia, and Anna, but Peabody, Brownson, and a young radical named William Batchelder Greene. The action reached its climax around June 1842 (coincidentally, just when Convers Francis shocked Parker by canceling his exchange) and the denouement found Parker's connection with Shaw severed and his close friendship with Peabody at an end. Shaw, meanwhile, found herself free to be wooed by Greene, the man she would eventually marry.

Greene, the principal beneficiary of the events, seems also to have been their protagonist. Tall, strikingly handsome, with a "royal, aristocratic" manner, he made a splash on the Transcendentalist scene in the fall of 1841, when he was just twenty-two years old. He lacked the usual Transcendentalist associations with Harvard, Unitarianism, and Whiggery; Greene was reared among Democrats and Calvinists (his mother's father had been a prominent baptist revivalist) and had attended West Point. But he had grown up among books and ideas. His father, Nathaniel, who skillfully edited pro-Jackson newspapers and held plum federal appointments whenever a Democrat lived in the White House, also taught himself French, Italian, and German and produced a stream of literary translations. Nathaniel befriended Orestes Brownson, himself among the most prominent intellectual Democrats, and William grew up a Brownson admirer. Although he did not subscribe to Brownson's theology—as a young man, he was attracted to the skeptical ideas of Shelley—he did, like his hero, become "mercilessly opinionated" and a skilled syllogist.[68]

In 1839, Greene left Boston for Florida, where he served as an officer in the Seminole War. While there he had a physical breakdown and a religious awakening, which together led him to return home, join a Baptist church, and, in November 1841, resign his commission. While his health recovered, he made plans to go to Europe, possibly to study, and so began to educate himself in continental philosophy, probably with Brownson's guidance. As part of this project, Greene visited Elizabeth Peabody's bookstore in July 1841 in search of a translation of Kant.[69]

He and Peabody fell into conversation, and she found herself "fascinated" by this much younger man. He apparently found her, or at least her store, interesting; he kept coming back, and they kept talking. Eventually she learned his name and where he lived. She started calling on him to check on his health and to have long discussions about religion. She introduced him to her friends, on whom he also made a strong impression. Margaret Fuller called him the "military-spiritual-herioco-vivacious phoenix of the day," while Emerson persuaded him to publish some of his theological musings in the January 1842 *Dial*. Greene, in turn, came to admire Emerson. But he refused to call himself a Transcendentalist. In fact, he respected Emerson because he considered him free from the evil tendencies of "Transcendentalism," under which heading Greene lumped, according to Peabody, "the errors of pure minds — with the bad passions of *modern french novels* & the moral indifferency of *Goetheism*." All these errors Greene thought embodied in Theodore Parker. He accused Parker of believing that people should approach one another for "purely intellectual purposes . . . as if every one was all sufficient to himself — & nobody had any duties to others."[70]

Greene was so voluble in his antipathy to Parker that Peabody puzzled for an explanation. At first, she guessed that Greene thought Parker, in his 1841 "Religion" lectures, had attacked "the sacred things of God" and so must lack "reverence or conscience towards God — *or* man." Peabody did not believe anyone who knew Parker personally could doubt his piety or upright character, but she did understand Greene's negative reaction to the lectures. She herself had criticized Parker's naturalistic Christology in her April 1842 article for the *Boston Quarterly Review*. She may have hoped this piece, which distinguished between the theology Parker espoused and the religion he lived, would "satisfy . . . [Greene's] prejudices, & . . . turn the scale to a more favorable judgment" by him of her friend. But Greene's judgment remained strongly unfavorable.[71]

She then began to wonder if Greene's antipathy to Parker might not be about theology at all. She remembered that Greene began to curse Parker only after enduring some "personally painful" experience and dramatically changing his plans: he would not go to Europe, but to divinity school near Boston. This shift had occurred in the winter of 1841. By the summer of 1842 he was preaching on supply at a Baptist church in Methuen, and in the fall he started attending the Baptist seminary at Newton. What Greene's painful experience had been, she did not know and thought it indiscreet to ask, especially in Greene's "nervous and excitable" state. Nonetheless, she started to suspect that his anti-Parker diatribes were "mystification in a degree—whereby he poured out the effervescence of his mind *on something*—not choosing to talk about that which really was touching himself." She worried that this *"something"* was somehow attributable to her, because Greene occasionally made strange remarks regarding her, such as that she was *"of a character* that he would not vote for . . . [her] to belong to his church."[72]

Finally, in the late spring of 1842, she received information from friends that shed new light on the whole matter. She learned that Orestes Brownson apparently had heard (from whom is unclear) some *"specific charges"* against Parker, believed them, and in late 1841 had told them to Greene. The charges concerned Parker loving Anna Shaw more than his wife.[73]

Peabody was a confidante of both Theodore and Lydia and knew their marriage had problems. She even was aware of Theodore's fondness of Anna, although she seems to have accepted his interpretation of the attachment as wholly innocent. In his correspondence with Peabody, he sometimes referred to Anna, evidently without fear that Peabody would disapprove. The most striking example dates from early 1842, when he remarked that in popular schemes of salvation, sin "can be brushed off like the moss that falls in Anna Shaw's hair, as she walks through the woods." Yet even this rather romantic analogy seems to have set off, for Peabody, no alarms. If she heard any rumors about Theodore and Anna, she ignored them, believing such "ludicrous" gossip would be discredited as soon as Parker's moral excellence became better known.[74]

Now she discovered that the "evil reports," so unfavorable to Parker's "reputation for manliness, proper reserve, &c," were circulating "with an extensiveness" she had never expected. She also believed she now understood Greene's negative comments concerning herself. He must think she was one of the "female friends" who "pitied" Parker for not being free to marry Shaw. Peabody, who saw herself as a "sturdy Puritan," was alarmed that Greene should consider her so "morally indifferent."[75] She wrote at once to Brownson, hoping to convince him of Parker's innocence, so he could in turn convince Greene.

In this long letter, Peabody denies that the Parkers were ill-matched, in the process indiscreetly revealing much about them. She admits that many people find the couple "less easy at home than when they are away from home," but argues that the awkwardness was only due to the residence in the household of a "third person" (Aunt Lucy), "the care of whose health and happiness preys on the spirits of . . . [the] anxious & conscientious wife—& therefore worries her husband." Peabody admits that many acquaintances think little of Lydia's mind, but that was due only to "her shyness, her low spirits, her humility of temper [which] prevents her from doing justice to [herself] *in company.*" Moreover, her shyness, combined with her duties to her sick aunt, keep her at home—and therefore her husband as well, as he does not like to

I Can Stand Alone

go out without her—while preventing them from having company. This lack of socializing, Peabody speculates, may vex Parker's friends and lead them to say harsh things about Lydia, "but they do not know how much she needs this tenderness of attention & the cheering effect of his presence,—& that |it| is because she *claims* so little—that he loves to do much." Peabody guesses, too, that people sometimes "do injustice" to Parker's "noble frankness & warmth of heart" because "he is not *au fait* in the etiquettes of life & apt to feel awkward & embarrassed," and besides, "he is so *earnest* he sometimes wants gracefulness & elasticity & misses the average tone of the conversation." In this awkward earnestness, Peabody rather tactlessly reminds Brownson, Parker is "like yourself."

To her own testimony, Peabody adds that of Anna's older sister, and Parker's neighbor, Sarah Shaw Russell, the wife of Brownson's friend George Russell. According to Peabody, Mrs. Russell thought the charges against Parker ridiculous: "She never heard from [him] any thing but the utmost tenderness & respectfulness of his wife—or saw any thing but the most devoted attention." Parker had been as intimate as a "brother" in the Russell household since he came to West Roxbury, yet he never even stayed for a meal without Lydia, who in turn spent part of every day with Mrs. Russell. As for Anna—when she visited, Mrs. Russell assured Peabody, the family always sent for both Parkers, and although Theodore "admired Anna as every body else does," he "did not see her oftener than once every six weeks." This statement no doubt accurately reflects the situation by mid-1842, after Parker's many arguments with Lydia and Lucy, but not the situation of 1840 and 1841, when he had seen Anna much more frequently and had taken walks alone with her.

Peabody's letter apparently convinced Brownson that the rumors about Parker lacked foundation. At least, no later evidence exists of gossip concerning Parker and Anna Shaw. Whether Peabody convinced Greene is less likely. He and Shaw became a couple in the summer of 1842, around the time Peabody wrote Brownson, and he could have learned from her directly what had happened between her and Parker.[76] Perhaps the "personally painful" event that Peabody associated with the start of his anti-Parker diatribes was his discovery that the woman to whom he was attracted had an awkward intimate friendship with this married man. In the end, she did not marry Greene until after he converted to Unitarianism, her family faith, in 1844. He transferred from the Newton Seminary to Harvard Divinity School; their wedding took place shortly after he finished his studies there in 1845. The handsome couple soon moved to the central Massachusetts town of West Brookfield, where Greene was ordained pastor of a Unitarian church.

Peabody's intervention had helped make this consummation possible, because it ended whatever relationship Parker still had with Shaw. No one in Parker's circle, including Parker himself, could now ignore the serious danger of public embarrassment for himself and Shaw if they continued to see one another. But Peabody seems not, by her actions, to have bettered Greene's opinion of her—if, in fact, his opinion of her was as critical as she assumed it was. She may have been reading too much into his offhand comments. In a letter to Brownson from August 1842, Greene complained that she applied every "general remark" he made to herself. He found her a "strange character—entirely too hard for me," and seemed exasperated by her ceaseless attentions and queries: "If I had known that this would have been the consequence, I should have been very careful of letting |her| become so well acquainted with me."[77]

How did Parker react to Peabody's intervention in his life? The answer may be supplied by a journal entry from late June 1842. Parker records receiving an "impudent" letter from Peabody, "which I burnt up, & shall answer politely." He does not say what she wrote that so upset him, nor does his "polite" reply survive, but the date of the entry correlates with hers to Brownson, while the next few sentences of the entry indicate his household troubles were very much on his mind: Parker complains that he "Can't do much," is unwell, and that the cause of his problem is "very obvious, external but not distant."[78] Had Peabody written him about Brownson, Greene, and Anna Shaw?

Parker had been increasingly exasperated with Peabody's course over the previous few months, as she tried to persuade him that his theology was mistaken. At first, he had been respectful. In early 1842, when she had shown him the manuscript of her *Boston Quarterly* article before publishing it, he had called the piece "eloquent" and suggested her disagreements with him were in fact minor. As the stressful months passed, however, and she continued to criticize him, he lost patience. In June, he bluntly refused to dispute with her further. Her "*method* of settling the question" was so "different" from his own, he told her, that he despaired of making any argument that she would find "tolerable": "[O]ur two positions are fundamentally hostile, and our Theologies can never be reconciled."[79]

As if this dispute were not bad enough, did Parker also feel that she had violated his trust by speaking to Brownson and Sarah Russell about his most private affairs without consulting him? Certainly, by December 1842 he associated her with other intimates who had abandoned him. "I need not tell how my old '*friends*' treat me," he wrote disgustedly in his journal, referring to "Dr. Fr.," "Silsbee," and "E. P. P."[80] Although Peabody was to maintain a friendship with Lydia for some years, she and Theodore were never again close.

Peabody felt Parker's new coolness toward her, but misunderstood it. She thought their "*difference of opinion*" on theological matters had "wounded" Parker's "*sensibility*"—a charge he denied. The principal cause of his alienation seems to have been her handling of the gossip about him and Shaw. He implies as much in a letter to Peabody from April 1845, in which he pointedly tells her not to come out from Boston to visit him, because Lydia is not home, "and the good *Puritans* of Spring Street, would think it very bad if a *single* woman should stop with the minister when his wife is gone!"[81]

PARKER PROBABLY saw Anna Shaw a few more times after the summer of 1842, no doubt in controlled settings such as those Sarah Russell described, with her family present and in the company of his wife. Perhaps one such occasion occurred early that December, when he penned in his journal a stanza addressed to a

> Fair maid, whose fairness is thy smallest part,
>   more wise than fair, & better still than wise!
> Thou hast a heaven in thy gentle heart,
>   not less than Beauty living in thine eyes.[82]

Here the verse breaks off.

In 1843–44 Parker was in Europe; not long after he returned Shaw married Greene and moved halfway across the state. News of her marriage led him to write another, somewhat clumsily worded poem in his journal that was probably meant as a mental farewell:

> Long may the angels meet thee
>   Maid of the golden hair;
> And long may Beauty greet thee,
>   And bless thee maiden dear —
>
> And oh when sober days shall come
>   In times fast speeding tide,
> My Fate assigns his fairest doom —
>   Be thy [*sic*] a blessed bride![83]

Parker himself moved to Boston in 1847 and so did not even see her family much anymore. In 1850, when Greene decided to quit the ministry and pursue a literary career in France, she followed him abroad. They lived in Paris for the rest of Parker's life. Their only child, a son, was born there in 1851.

Anna Shaw was gone, but she lingered in Parker's imagination. He expressed his persistent feelings in a peculiar kind of poem he would write from time to time in his journal or notebooks. Each of these verses is addressed to a (discreetly) unnamed, undescribed "thou" — a former cherished intimate (the sex is never identified, but obviously female) now absent in body, but not in spirit. One of these poems, from January 1847, describes the former closeness and regrets its passing:

Life of my Heart
Why wander I from thee?
The wedded stars even never part—
Through all Eternity!
Had I a pang 'twas ever known to thee
You thou didst feel my sufferings as thy own
And all my glee
& every groan
[were] in thy bosom—felt & known!
Now distance hides thy face—
But in every star I trace
Thy welcome look
In every book
I meet thy cheery mind—
Ah me, thyself I cannot find![84]

The theme of finding the absent "thou" everywhere recurs in another poem, this from March 1847. Here the speaker, wondering if "I can be absent Love from thee," answers to the contrary that "When I to the woodlands go / Thou walkest with me there / . . . I see thy face in every star / Thy radiance stealing from afar."[85]

Parker thinks of the missing beloved particularly when, as he says in a poem from 1852 or 1853, "I wander o'er each cherished spot / where you & I have been":

Alas my memory faileth not
    To sadden every scene;
For lacking thee I lack the sun,
    The moon & starlight fair
And without thee, most dearest one,
    Both Night & Day are bare.
Why is it that of all [mankind]
    I'm straightly joined to thee;
And yet continually find
    that we must severed be?[86]

Parker associates the absent "thou" with "woodlands"—and especially with walks in the woods and the gathering of flowers—both things he had done with Shaw. In 1856, after Parker had gone out from Boston to pay a late summer visit to West Roxbury, he wrote a verse lamenting that "Unheeded grow the precious flowers / No eye woos now their Beauty" and that "Nature without thy holy face / Will paralyze my feeling." The speaker notices in the woods "a pale but precious flower / In a consecrated spot" that he had "oft" gathered for "thee," but now he passes it by: "Why should I take it from the earth / It will not meet thine eye."[87]

Other poems describe ethereal visitations by the absent "thou." In 1847, one comes in a dream:

> I dreamed I was with thee
>   'Twas but a dream
>   A sweet auralean dream
> That fell on me
>
> I woke & was alone!
>   that was no dream
>   nor came a single gleam
> Upon my bosom cold as stone.[88]

In 1852, the visitation is more enduring:

> I know not what it signifies
>   Continual thought of thee
> But ever since the morning's rise
>   Thy soul has been with me. . . .
>
> I count it not a little Joy
>   Thine image comes in sleep,
> For time & space cannot destroy
>   The treasure that I keep.[89]

Perhaps the most poignant and revealing of all these poems, titled "Names written in the Sand," dates from the summer of 1847. Parker subtitles the verse, "Lines of a Lover":

> I wrote thy name with mine upon the sand
> And called thee all the tender terms I knew
> Unto the wave & wind. But the next wave
> Disjoined our joined names & mine was gone.
> But yet me thought the waters held delay
> Where I had writ thy dear & lovely name,
> As loath to desecrate so fair a word
> But soon there came a wave so tall & strong
> The giant broke the charm & tore away
> The name, thy name which I too faintly wrote
> 'Twas gone, all gone, no trace nor figure left.
> And so I threw away the little stick
> Wherewith I |fondly| wrote such tenderness
> And the continuous wave threw back the style

with which I wrote thy name. Lo here it is
The sole memento of the sweet fond things
My tenderness had writ. Even so are we
Joined & disjoined, & the uniting love
Lives on, amid the wind & wave & storm,
Even tho tis cast away a hopeless thing
Still wind & wave & storm will bring it back
For Love which joins so tenderly our names
Will not be lamented & cannot be lost.[90]

Parker may here be describing an actual incident (he sometimes did visit the seashore in summer), but if so the event seems transformed into a symbol, even an allegory, of what had happened between him and Shaw over the previous five years: their separation; her marriage to the "tall & strong" Greene (who "erased" her name in making her a "Mrs."); Parker's own persistent feelings, which now can be expressed only by his little "stylus."[91]

Parker suggests why he clung to Shaw's memory in a journal entry from 7 June 1851. During the day, he had visited West Roxbury and had unexpectedly met Anna's sister Sarah Russell. Back home in Boston that evening, he did not feel well and speculated in his journal that his health had been damaged by the "hardships of my early life"; the toilsome years from ages 17 to 26 "made a mark on me, not to be effaced." He then adds, in a sentence later scratched out but still legible: "The next period—the first 7 years at West Roxbury—made it *far worse*—that was a terrible time—relieved by one mortal angel!"[92]

PARKER FACED yet another family crisis in 1842. Late in the year, news reached him that he thought so shocking and delicate, he made no note of it in his journal, not even in code. What he learned at that time (years later, he would hear a very different story) was that his wife's brother, the late, dissipated John L. Cabot, had "seduced" a young Boston woman, Sarah Jane Goodhue, a pupil at a Baptist School in Charlestown, and that she had borne him a bastard in February 1836. John apparently had acknowledged paternity by paying the woman money. Later, after John's death, Sarah Jane married a man named Colburn, who a few years later either himself died or abandoned her. In the late summer of 1842, she herself died, leaving the boy, now six years old and called George Colburn, an orphan.[93]

All this information likely came from one of Sarah Jane's sisters, Mrs. Mary Ann Moses, who was taking care of the child. Neither Mary Ann nor her husband wanted to keep him. Perhaps they could not afford to do so. Recognizing this, Sarah Jane in her will had appointed a doctor she knew, John Hayden, to be little Georgie's guardian, but Hayden evidently found the re-

I Can Stand Alone

sponsibility "inconvenient."[94] Someone, therefore, probably Mary Ann, approached Georgie's now famous uncle to ask if he would take the responsibility. Court documents indicate his response: on 12 December 1842, the probate judge of Suffolk County appointed Parker the boy's guardian. Parker quietly arranged for Georgie to board and be educated at Brook Farm.

Parker evidently accepted the claim that John had fathered a bastard. So, apparently, did Lydia. Aunt Lucy, however, did not. Neither did Lydia's surviving brother, George Cabot, nor her parents. This split may be inferred from Georgie being sent away to Brook Farm. He was to reside there for the next four years, never living with Theodore and Lydia so long as they stayed in Lucy's house. As soon as the Parkers bought a home of their own, however, in early 1847, they moved Georgie in with them, and he shared their life thereafter. Could Lucy not tolerate the presence of what she saw as an infant impostor? The later testimony of Lydia's brother George lends weight to this speculation. Writing in the mid-1850s, he declared emphatically that Georgie was never "acknowledged as or believed to be, the son of Mr. John L. Cabot by any member of *his* family, other than Mrs. Parker."[95]

If Lydia's relatives rejected the imposition of a bar sinister on the proud shield of their family reputation, why did she accept it? Perhaps she projected onto the child her strong love for her late brother, whose death had sent her into a protracted period of mourning. She may have thought that although she had been unable to save him, she could at least save his son. Then, too, she wanted a baby of her own. Just as her husband was deeply disappointed that he was not a father, as his journals and letters abundantly document, so Lydia felt "great grief" that their "union was childless"; at least, such is the report of the writer and reformer Julia Ward Howe, who met her in 1844 and came to know her well. But Lydia's feelings are indicated more by her deeds than by any surviving testimony. She had a pattern of taking in abandoned children. Georgie was only the first. Many years later, after Parker had died, and Georgie had grown up and moved away, Lydia informally adopted a little girl whose stepmother did not like her, reared her to adulthood, and lived to see her married.[96]

Lydia's maternal feelings toward Georgie may explain Parker's decision, in 1848, to change Georgie's name. He successfully petitioned the state legislature to have it expanded from George Colburn to George Colburn Cabot. Parker took this action over the strong objection of his in-laws,[97] and the question must be raised as to why he bothered. Could Lydia have wanted Georgie's relationship to her formally acknowledged?

One aspect of Georgie's arrival in the Parkers' lives, however, is both sure and significant: it redrew the lines of battle in their household. For the first time, Theodore did not stand alone against Lydia, Lucy, and their family. Instead, he and Lydia stood together against the others. Although Theodore may not have recognized it during the awful emotional weather of 1842, the climate of his marriage was about to improve.

IN THIS long, dark season, Parker found some respite from his troubles at the place where he sent Georgie to live, Brook Farm. The little utopia George and Sophia Ripley had established two and half miles from Parker's front door had been flourishing, in spirit if not financially. Brook Farm at first was home to but an apostolic dozen, including the Ripleys and, for a few months only, Nathaniel Hawthorne. But as time passed the population swelled with immigrant idealists—often whole families of them—as well as with students attending the innovative school Sophia ran, and some long-term visitors. The number of residents occasionally swelled to over a hundred. Tourists were also a common sight, poking around the buildings and grounds, usually curious to see how these visionaries, only a minority of whom had any experience with simple living or manual labor, got on with tilling and manuring, cooking and scrubbing, abjuring middle-class amenities and dining together on plain fare at a common refectory.

The consensus report, one confirmed by the many memoirs of participants, was that they got on quite merrily indeed. They had dancing, singing, and theatricals, stimulating lectures and high-minded group "conversations." They gleefully adopted a flamboyant style of grooming and dress, the men with beards, unshorn locks, Byronic open-collared shirts, and belted linen tunics, the women with linen skirts and knickerbockers during the day, flowing dresses and wide hats in the evening, and wreaths twined in their long hair for festive occasions. They all punned constantly, gave every building and person comic nicknames, and amused themselves by using exalted, Transcendental language in mundane settings ("Is the butter within the sphere of your influence?" was a customary formula at dinner).[98]

Parker enjoyed the wholesome Bohemianism of Brook Farm as much as anyone, and he liked to take part in the fun. To him is attributed George Ripley's Brook Farm nickname—"Archon"—and one memoirist recalls him at social gatherings, "his nasal voice in subtle and exquisite mimicry reproducing what was truly laughable." Parker himself recalled the less serious aspects of life at Brook Farm when he later wrote that Georgie, while there, had learned "to spell—& collect hens eggs—& steal apples."[99]

Besides the pervasive good cheer, Parker was drawn to Brook Farm by Ripley. Parker was closer to Ripley in 1841 and 1842 than at any other time; not only did the two men see one another at least once a week when Ripley worshiped at the Spring Street Church, Parker seems to have had his friend read and comment on nearly everything he wrote. Their intense one-on-one conferences are remembered by Ora Gannett Sedgwick. After two or three hours of intellectual exchange in Ripley's study, she recalls in her memoir, when Parker would leave for home, Ripley would go with him so that their dialogue could continue. Halfway to Spring Street, when Ripley turned around, Parker would now become his escort. When they reached Brook Farm again, Parker would resume his original direction—and Ripley would again be his companion. "In this way," writes Sedgwick, "the two men, always absorbed in conversation, walked back and forth, until sometimes another couple of hours were added to the solid talk."[100]

Parker found Brook Farm attractive, but aside from low moments in 1841 and 1842, when he feared being forced from the ministry, he never seriously considered living there. Besides, he may have been aware early—and he certainly came to see over time—that commitment to Brook Farm was a risk, because the community faced constant threat of bankruptcy. He knew some of those who had advanced to Brook Farm its working capital. His neighbors George Russell and Francis Shaw were among them; Aunt Lucy, possibly with his encouragement, also had loaned a small sum.[101] He himself took out a mortgage on a piece of Brook Farm property (in effect giving the community another loan) when he sent Georgie there. Parker must have realized before too long that Brook Farm was hard pressed to pay its debts. As the son of a farmer and artisan, Parker could have guessed the key reasons why: the soil on which the community struggled to grow its crops was sandy (the previous owner of the fields had been sensible enough to use them only for grazing milk cows), while the community craft shops were not well enough organized to turn a profit. In short, the "Brook Farm Institute for Agriculture and Industry," as it officially was known, succeeded neither agriculturally nor industrially. The only profitable enterprise associated with it was the school.

More important, Parker came to realize that he dissented from the Brook Farm approach to solving social ills. For one thing, Ripley and his friends were more skeptical than he about the justness of private property. Brook Farm members shared living quarters and eating space, and turned over the money made by their individual labors to the community. Ripley himself (who had told Parker in 1840 he favored the abolition of inherited private property) wanted to make these cooperative arrangements more thorough-going. He admired the proposal of the French socialist Fourier that everyone should live in tightly planned "Phalanxes," with little private ownership; eventually, he would try to turn Brook Farm into a Phalanx. By contrast, Parker believed strongly in private property, as he makes clear in an 1843 sermon, which he may have preached with the "Associationist" contingent of his congregation in mind. Some of them undoubtedly heard it.[102]

Parker here specifically criticizes the idea, which he is careful to say has been advanced by "pious & philanthropic persons," that property should be held in common. Parker sees this proposal as a natural reaction of the heart against the excessive desire for gain in modern society. But he argues that private property is "an *ontological fact*, belonging to the Nature of man": man is a "hoarding animal"; mankind has a right to appropriate and hoard; the earth belongs to mankind; as mankind is made up of individuals, so property seems to belong to each individual. Parker's logic seems somewhat slippery, but for him, earning what you receive from life and paying as you go were strict moral imperatives.

How strict is evident in several other sermons, in which he denounces state debt repudiation as a grave political sin. The issue was an important one of the day. Many states, mostly in the South and West, had borrowed heavily during the speculative boom years of the early 1830s, usually from English banks to pay for internal improvements. After the panic of 1837, these states found themselves strapped to meet their repayment obligations. By the early 1840s, a few states, in desperation, tried to repudiate at least part of what they owed. Some pro-repudiation politicians, all Democrats, argued that the debts were "held by rich and selfish foreign capitalists, who care for nothing so much as to wring money from the hard earnings of our people."[103]

Financiers and Whigs thundered indignation at the repudiators, and so did Parker. In his Fast Day sermon for 1842, he seems scarcely able to contain his outrage that whole states would talk of "*refusing to pay . . . [their] just debts.*" The "plain English of the matter," he declares, is that the "*Strong & the many rob the few & the weak, ROB them.*"[104] Whether those being robbed were rich or poor did not affect the case. The popularity of repudiation was a sign of the low morality of the people, who would get wealth without working for it. A few months later, in another sermon, Parker decries the religious state of the American people, who not only justify slavery and crush "poor savages to the dust" but allow "a *state* not to pay its debts"; this last crime Parker evidently finds comparable in gravity to the other two. Parker raised the subject of repudiation again in the first of his "Six Plain Sermons for the Times," the lecture series he delivered in the winter of 1842. "What are we to think of the morality of Trade," he there wondered, "in a land where whole states, gravely, deliberately refuse to pay, what they have pledged themselves to pay, thus defrauding the deceived capitalist, the orphan & the widow! If a man steal the handle of an axe, or pass a forged note for 12 shillings—he is a felon, but let a man steal thousands: by that madness which sacrifices the property of others, to the passion of a . . . grovelling for wealth—his name is good as ever! let an institution *forge* bills for 100s/1000s, it is no crime! let a state rob men of 1000,000s,—whole parties will tell you it is 'patriotic,' 'for the *peoples* interest'; 'serving a turn.' "[105]

Most Brook Farmers probably did not disagree with Parker about debt repudiation; on a personal level, at least, Ripley himself was a firm believer in meeting personal financial obligations no matter how onerous. Even the disagreements between Parker and the Brook Farmers over private property were more latent than not, because altering property relations as such was not the main focus of Brook Farm. No one was asked to give up their private assets on joining the community, which in legal terms was set up as a joint stock company. Members bought shares and were promised (with excessive optimism) a handsome return on their investment.

Instead, Brook Farm had been founded principally to fill the social gulf between those who thought and those who labored. And on this issue, the most obvious practical difference between Parker and the Brook Farmers emerged. Both agreed that the gulf must be filled, but the latter tried to fill it by teaching scholars how to plow and plane. Parker sought to fill it by enlightening the workers. This is the theme of one of his most important reform pronouncements, "The Education of the Laboring Classes," delivered as a lecture in August 1841 and published as a pamphlet early the following year.[106] It builds on his 1840 "Thoughts on Labor." In that piece, Parker had held that manual labor was admirable and that certain work was suited for certain people. Now he links these points to a broad ideology of reform, which he here begins to articulate.

Parker opens with a critique of New England education, framed in the form of a fable about a mythical nation "in the heart of the African continent." He imagines this strange society as a mirror image of New England: the laborers are well educated, but the professionals are profoundly ignorant. The lawyers are legal drudges, scarcely able to read and write; the doctors take a few traditional rules of medical practice and apply them mechanically; the clergy, the most ignorant of all, know their prayers and rituals only by rote and tremble and curse when the least innovation is made in either.[107]

Parker contrasts the state of the professions in his fictional country with that of the laboring class, which he defines broadly enough to include "the farmers, the butchers, the mechanics, the traders, the haberdashers of all sorts." The laborers had free schools for all ages, supported at the public expense, and special schools for each art and science. They were "intelligent and instructed men; had minds well accomplished; good manners; refined amusements, and met together for the interchange of thoughts no less than words, and yearly grew up to be a nobler population."[108]

After Parker points out the obvious—that this "most foolish and monstrous" land is but a satirical, reverse portrait of New England—he sets out his thesis: that it is time New England began to act in earnest on the principle that "a man is to be educated because he is a MAN, and has faculties and capabilities which God sent him into the world to develope [sic] and mature." The world, he insists, is a school, and we are in it not "merely to eat and drink, and vote, and get gain or honors," but to grow up to our full measure and train up the next generation.[109]

He takes issue with those who hold that there must be a large ignorant class to perform the work of the world. Parker admits that precedents can be quoted in great numbers that the majority always have been ignorant. But he points out that the future need not be like the past: "God does not repeat himself, so to say, nor make two ages or two men just alike." Besides, the most striking fact of history, for him, is not the persistence of ignorance from age to age, but the "progress in man's condition, almost perpetual, from the first beginnings of history down to the present day." In our "free, wealthy, Christian land," Parker wonders, is it too much to hope that the "masterly accomplishment of mind," now attainable to only four or five men in a thousand, "shall become so common that he will be laughed at or pitied who has it not?" The expectation of that result is not, he believes, so visionary as our present state would have appeared even a hundred years ago.[110]

Infinite universal education is not only possible, but a social obligation. There are things "we all know" that a society owes to each member of it: "a defense from violence; justice in matters between man and man; a supply of comforts for the body, when the man is unable to acquire them for himself; remuneration for what society takes away."[111] But above all society must provide education. Were people not allowed to improve their minds, hearts, and souls, Parker believes, all other functions of society have no meaning.

In Massachusetts, he says, "it seems generally admitted, the State owes each man the opportunity to begin an education of himself." This idea has produced "the fair and beautiful fabric of our free schools," but this is only a beginning. "Our system of popular education, even where it is most perfect, is not yet in harmony with the great American Idea." Instead, our system is derived from the notion that the only ones who deserve a "liberal, generous education" are a few "children of wealth." To "enable laboring men and women to obtain a good education," says Parker, "we must have some institution to go further than our common schools." He specifically proposes a "higher series of free schools"; Parker is thinking of public high schools, which were as yet so uncommon that he would consider the founding of one such school in each county a major advance.[112]

The problem, however, runs deeper than institutions. Due to the "mechanical and material tendencies" of the age, laborers who strive to read and educate themselves are criticized for wasting their time. Instead, "[m]any laboring men now feel compelled to toil all of the week-days with such severity, that no time is left for thought and meditation,—the processes of mental growth, and their discipline of mind is not perfect enough to enable them to pursue this process, while about their manual work." Parker does not conceive of laborers primarily as working for others, but as independent farmers and self-employed mechanics. Their excessive toil, therefore, is not a consequence of direct coercion but the false social stigma attached to being materially worse off than one's peers. Meanwhile, the educated and wealthy falsely

I Can Stand Alone

hold work to be a disgrace, and so do not do their share of necessary social labor, which must be done by others. Yet blaming the rich and educated alone for the situation Parker finds "wicked." The "sin," he believes, "belongs to the whole community."[113]

Parker stresses that ordinary working people do have time for education. Hours can be set aside for reading, for example, on the Sabbath, or on the farm during the long nights of winter or the many days of bad weather. Then, too, when doing mindless toil, thoughts can freely roam. Parker notes that trade itself can be "a study": "To the instructed man . . . the tools of his craft are books; his farm is a gospel, eloquent, in its sublime silence; his cattle and corn his teachers; the stars his guides to virtue and to God." Making a "church and college" of daily work is not now possible for everyone, but one day work will be a "blessing to all."[114]

"The American mind will one day be turned to its greatest object," concludes Parker optimistically, "the rearing up of a manly people." He points to the many factors encouraging the work in America: freedom from war; the abundance of physical comfort; "the restless activity of the American mind"; the ease with which books are printed and circulated; the free schools; the "free spirit of our institutions"; and, above all, the religion of Jesus. "With such encouragement, who will venture to despair?"[115]

The lecture is perhaps most interesting because in it, Parker, for the first time in his writings, mentions the "American Idea," a concept central to his later political thought. He does not here define it explicitly, but he does imply a definition when he accuses the education system of being not truly American, because derived from times and governments that "knew little of the value of the human soul, the equality of all before God, the equal rights of strong and weak, their equal claims for a manly education."[116] This was the germ of much to come.

WHILE PARKER kept a friendly distance from the Fourierists, he edged nervously closer to making public alliance with the small, largely despised band of reformers agitating to overthrow slavery. After he denounced slavery in his 1838 Thanksgiving discourse, more than two years passed before he spoke publicly on the topic again.[117] Parker may have thought one antislavery pronouncement was enough for his small congregation; he may have been too preoccupied with church reform to say more on the slavery issue; he may have believed that he should not preach on such an explosive subject during the excitement of the 1840 presidential election. Whatever his reasons, he did not address slavery again in the pulpit until January 1841, several months before the "Transient and Permanent" controversy began, when he delivered an important sermon that led many abolitionists to expect he would soon join their movement. These expectations would not be met.

What Parker said in "Slavery" so delighted an abolitionist member of his congregation, the merchant Cornelius Cowing, that he promptly reported to his friends in the movement that his pastor had come out "thorough & no mistake" for the Cause. This news much pleased Edmund Quincy, who had kept an eye on Parker as a potential convert for a long time. Within a few weeks, Quincy had heard "Slavery" for himself, when Parker came to his house and read it to him. Quincy praised the discourse for eloquently "taking all the ultra ground," without any of what Quincy called "Emersonian or Channingite qualifications." [118]

Abolitionists like Quincy had never been wholly happy with Dr. Channing's antislavery stance. Channing had always sought to distinguish himself from the abolitionists. He believed they were wrong to tar all slaveholders as sinners and most northerners as enablers of sin; he thought that the characterization was inaccurate and that it roused needless opposition. Channing had an aversion to agitation and wanted the abolitionists to proceed without it. As important, he distrusted associated action, whether of denominations or reform societies, which he thought compromised individual integrity. [119]

Emerson, for his part, had delivered a single antislavery address (never published and only fragments of which survive) in 1837, before a meeting called in Concord to protest the lynching of the abolitionist editor Elijah Lovejoy. Most abolitionists had found Emerson's speech disappointing, because his position had been so like that of Channing. While condemning slavery, Emerson had urged abolitionists to moderate their attacks on slaveholders and insisted that "when we have distinctly settled for ourselves the right and wrong of this question, and have covenanted with ourselves to keep the channels of opinion open, each man for himself, I think we have done all that is incumbent on most of us to do." [120] In other words, Emerson also discountenanced collective agitation.

What made Parker's sermon distinctive was not that he dismissed as "premeditated wickedness" all proslavery arguments; Channing and Emerson had done the same. What Quincy liked was that Parker also strongly defended "the course & measures of the Abolitionists." Parker specifically addresses the charge that opponents of slavery used "extravagant" speech and called slaveholders "hard names," arguing these shortcomings are easily excusable: "What wonder is it that these men sometimes grow warm in their arguments! What wonder that their heart burns when they think of so many women exposed to contamination and nameless abuse; of so many children reared like beasts, and sold as oxen; of so many men owning property in their hands, or their feet, their hearts, or their lives!" The wonder is that abolitionists do not go to further, sinful extremes, "and like St. John in his youth, pray for fire to come down from heaven and burn up the sinners, or like Paul, when he had not the excuse of youthful blood, ask God to curse them." Yet abolitionists were pacifists; they "never think of an appeal to the strong arm, but the Christian heart."[121]

Parker also pleased Quincy by seeming to adopt the abolitionist opinion, which neither Channing nor Emerson shared, that northerners, not southerners, were the "chief criminals" in the slavery matter. The abolitionists understandably had such an outlook, battling as they were the indifference and often violent hostility of their neighbors, and believing as they did that if the North stopped aiding and abetting southern slavery, it inevitably would fall. Parker, in exhorting his congregation to action, naturally takes pains to attack the common and enervating New England notion about slavery, that " 'we have nothing to do with it.' " He calls attention to the "sugar and rice we eat, the cotton we wear" being "the work of the slave," and argues that the slave's "wrongs are imported to us in these things." More important than this economic connection, or the obvious constitutional ties between the sections, is that "socially, individually, we are brought into contact with [slavery] every day," for if "there is a crime in the land known to us, and we do not protest against it to the extent of our ability, we are partners of that crime."[122]

Besides, Parker finds the root cause of slavery, and of the willingness of some to defend it, in the "desire to get gain, comfort, or luxury; to have power over matter, without working or paying the honest price of that gain, comfort, luxury, and power; it is the spirit which would knowingly and of set purpose injure another for the sake of gaining some benefit to yourself." This spirit, Parker believes, may be found not only in the South, but quite pervasively in New England. That we have no slaves here, Parker believes, is not due to any "superior goodness" on our part, but only to the "fortunate accident" that slaves "are not profitable."[123]

Sentiments such as these warmed Quincy's heart and led him to hope Parker would take a much larger and more prominent abolitionist role. Parker did, in fact, start saying more against slavery than he had before, denouncing it frequently in his sermons and lectures. He also began putting his antislavery opinions in print. He published the "Slavery" sermon itself as a pamphlet after preaching it for a second time in the summer of 1843. That same year, Parker published an article in the *Dial* about the recently deceased German emigré radical and Boston Unitarian minister Karl Follen, in which Parker praised Follen's support for abolitionism and even sounded sympathetic toward the controversial William Lloyd Garrison, whose efforts on behalf of the slave Parker called "justly celebrated."[124]

Parker's most entertaining antislavery publication appeared in the 1843 *Liberty Bell*, the most distinguished abolitionist literary periodical. "Socrates in Boston" imagines the philosopher transported to the American Athens and in dialogue with a solemn-faced, narrow-minded Yankee deacon named Jonathan (an appellation that writers of Parker's day commonly applied to a symbolic American). Jonathan, as self-righteous as Euthyphro, believes slavery for blacks is consistent with American freedom and with Christianity. Also like Euthyphro, when he tries to defend his beliefs, he finds himself tied in logical knots by his interlocutor. In the end, Socrates forces him to confess that slavery is mere exploitation upheld by unjust law. Jonathan refuses to renounce slavery, however, and in the end leaves at the sound of a church bell, which calls him to hear a sermon by a Dr. Smothertext on "the danger of being righteous overmuch." Parker in this piece nicely captures the feel of a Platonic dialogue—and provides, in Jonathan, an acid-etched caricature of a pharisaical Calvinist bigot.[125]

Parker's publications show his new willingness to be known as an abolitionist sympathizer, yet he still refrained from committing himself to the antislavery movement. Even in the "Slavery" sermon itself, which had in it so much that Quincy liked, Parker seemed to hang back. He was careful not to devote the whole sermon to chattel slavery; much of the discourse he spends discussing another type of bondage altogether—"slavery to sin." Perhaps by adding this explicitly homiletic dimension to the discourse, Parker hoped to deflect criticism from those in his audience who would object to an entire sermon devoted to a divisive political issue.[126] His caution indicated an unwillingness to take a wholly exposed abolitionist position.

It was seen as well in his reluctance to speak at antislavery gatherings. In August 1842, Parker attended the annual Dedham picnic of the New England abolitionists, but deliberately stayed in the background; when Quincy, who was also present, asked him to speak, he refused. "Alas!" lamented Quincy later to a friend, "how long & difficult is the process by which a *Unitarian Minister* is transformed into a *man*!" Quincy noted that Parker had pleaded illness (he often felt sick in 1842, owing to the stress he was under), but found this an inadequate excuse: "I do not think a fair minutes talking would have hurt him, had his heart been in the matter."[127]

A few months later came a more dramatic test of Parker's heart, when Massachusetts was rocked by a fugitive slave case. George Latimer, a young man who had fled from Virginia with his wife and family, had reached Boston in early October 1842. He evidently thought he would be safe there, for although a federal law requiring the return of fugitives had been on the books since 1793, no fugitive had ever been taken back to the South from Massachusetts. But Latimer's master pursued him and, in late October, persuaded local officials to have him arrested.

Abolitionists mounted a campaign to free him that won unexpectedly widespread support. Many outside the antislavery movement, people with no interest in emancipating slaves in the South, thought it an affront to local sovereignty to have a slave imprisoned on the free soil of their home state. After a month of legal challenges and public meetings, a group of wealthy, conservative Bostonians, alarmed at how much political capital abolitionists were making from this issue, offered to settle the matter by buying Latimer and emancipating him. His master, wearied by popular and legal harassment, took the money and went home. By late November, Latimer was a free man.[128]

Latimer's arrest may have inspired Parker to write "Socrates in Boston," published a year later; the dialogue begins when Socrates asks Jonathan about a crowd in front of the city jail, protesting the capture of a fugitive slave. There is no direct evidence Parker was part of such a crowd himself, or that he attended the large protest meeting abolitionists held at Faneuil Hall shortly after Latimer's arrest. Parker did, however, object strongly to the arrest. Months before Latimer set foot in Boston, Parker had made clear he considered the rendition of escaped slaves (which had taken place in a number of free states, if not Massachusetts) to be immoral. In a sermon from January 1842, he had insisted that the only reliable standard of moral behavior was that set by the individual conscience, and that no other standard could be trusted, including the "law of the land." To prove the law a false guide, Parker had imagined an Algerian pirate kidnapping a Boston man, who somehow escapes and returns to his native city. If the Algerian pursued the man here, Yankees would defend him with their lives. But suppose a treaty made the Algerian's act legal? A man who took the law of the land as his moral standard would turn over his brother and even shoulder a musket to help the Algerian. Added Parker significantly: "If instead of Algerian Pirate, we read, some other names, the case is one of which often happens."[129]

Parker elaborated a similar analogy during the Latimer crisis itself, when he wrote a short, anonymous piece for the *Latimer Journal and North Star*, an ad hoc newspaper put out by protesters in November 1842 to keep the public informed about the case. In "A Dream," Parker once again envisions a Boston man enslaved by an Arab—in this case not an Algerian pirate but a merchant from Tripoli; again, Parker imagines that the slave has escaped home and that his owner has come to reclaim his human property. Parker has the owner be met with a "very obsequious" reception: "The lawyers, and the jailors, and the constables, and the bailiffs, and the tide-waiters, and the deacons, and the tithing-men . . . said, 'Let him have his own. This is a country of law, property must be respected. The laws of Tripoli are as much *laws* as our own, we will help the master to his slave.' So the deacon encouraged the bailiff, and the slave 'was had in ward,' and the law, before whose eyes justice is sacred, stood waiting till the shackles were made intending to deliver a man to his owner." Yet "the people" dissent. They gather at Faneuil Hall and swear "by him that liveth forever and ever, 'It shall not be so, a slave is our brother, God is *his* God.'"

Parker's narrator next dreams that yet another slaveholder has come to Boston to claim a "brother man"; this time the owner is not a foreigner but an American from "our own sunny South." A voice says to the people, "Shall it be?" and they assemble at Faneuil Hall. Gathering with them are ghosts — all the "grave and valiant" spirits of New England history, including the dead veterans of Lexington and Bunker Hill and other departed patriots. Finally, from across the sea, still "dripping with the frogs of the three thousand miles of water he had crossed," comes John Robinson of Leyden, who as the original pastor of the Pilgrims was seen to be the religious father of New England. After Robinson has been given the chief place at the meeting, he asks why he has been summoned. "We would give back a man to the master that brought him, as a strayed lamb to the butcher," answers one of the living members of the audience. "Will not God approve us for keeping man's law?" In reply, a huge, knotty hand appears over Robinson's head, and writes on the wall behind him: "IS IT RIGHT TO DO WRONG. WHETHER IT BE RIGHT TO HEARKEN UNTO MAN'S COMMAND AND VIOLATE GOD'S LAW, JUDGE YE." Here the narrator suddenly awakes.

The second part of Parker's "Dream" may have been inspired by actual images that came to him in sleep — at least, the reference to Robinson "dripping with frogs" is just enough grotesque and absurd (frogs in the Atlantic?) to hint at actual hallucination rather than mere awkward conceit. Whatever its origins, the article foreshadows the future. Later, when Parker would lead Boston resistance to the Fugitive Slave Law of 1850, he would position himself as a tribune of the "people" against the officeholders and churchmen, and in thunderous speeches at Faneuil Hall would justify his actions by citing the hallowed example of Puritan and Revolutionary War heroes. Yet in 1842, he showed no willingness to be an antislavery leader or spokesman.

His aversion is indicted by his actions during the "Great Massachusetts Petition" drive of 1842–43. Latimer's release had been an antislavery triumph, but abolitionists were not completely satisfied; they wanted to prevent an emergency like the Latimer case from arising again. They therefore launched a campaign for a state "personal liberty" law. Specifically, they petitioned the legislature to forbid state and local officials from aiding in the arrest or detention of alleged fugitives, to forbid jails and public property from being used to hold alleged fugitives once arrested, and to "propose such amendments to the Constitution of the United States as shall forever separate the people of Massachusetts from slavery." More than 60,000 people eventually endorsed this petition. But despite its popularity, in late November 1842 Parker decided not to read it after a public lecture — although he had earlier agreed to do so.

Why he changed his mind he tried to explain in a letter to a disappointed abolitionist. In October and November, Parker had been delivering his new lecture series, "Six Plain Sermons for the Times," to large audiences at the

Marlboro Chapel in Boston. Some days before he was due to deliver the last "Sermon," Frederick Cabot (his wife's cousin, a member of his Spring Street congregation, and Karl Follen's brother-in-law) approached him and asked if, at the close of the lecture, he would read the Latimer petition to the audience. Parker without hesitation said he would. After Cabot left, however, he had second thoughts. The final "Sermon" concerned the "Application of Religion to Life" in various modes, political, "social," and individual; it concluded with an emotional plea to lead a more moral and spiritual life. Parker began to worry that if he read the petition after such an exhortation, he would not serve its "special purpose . . . so well as by omitting to read it, and by leaving the sermon to produce what effect it might in that special direction." Parker agonized over what to do. He consulted with a "thorough-going" abolitionist friend—Edmund Quincy, no doubt—who, probably sensing his anxiety, reassured him that "it would do more harm than good to read the petition then." Parker decided not to read it. The day of the lecture, 28 November, he stopped twice by the Marlboro Chapel, looking for an abolitionist to inform of his decision, but found none. When he returned in the evening to speak, many still expected him to read the petition. What happened next was understandably awkward.[130]

Frederic Cabot approached him with the petition only minutes before he was about to speak. "I don't know what I told him," recalled Parker some weeks later in a letter to a disappointed abolitionist. "I was in a state of great anxiety, as I always am for half an hour before I begin to preach on such an occasion." Cabot looked surprised, and Parker said something like, "Do not think my zeal for the slave is cooling off." Parker then delivered his lecture, after which, he writes, "I could not, in the state of feeling it left me, have read the petition at that moment, even if I had promised to do so." Parker tried to justify himself to his abolitionist correspondent: "Now, my dear sir, you may condemn me if you please; but my own conscience acquits me of anything but the best motives. I may have erred in judgment, certainly not in motives. I thought I should offend some of the Abolitionists by refusing; but fear of man never stopped me yet when conscience said 'Go.' . . . Do you think I was afraid to read the petition, and thought I should hurt my popularity? Then either you know me very little, or I know myself very little. . . . If I had read the petition with the feelings I then entertained, I should have been false to myself, though all the men in the Hall had said 'Amen,' and signed it at once."[131]

Parker's defensiveness suggests he may have been more worried about his own motives than he admits. In fact, despite all his sympathy for the abolitionists, their fierce rhetoric and all-consuming dedication to their cause made him uncomfortable. So, in October 1842, he expressed the hope to his young friend Caroline Healey, who had left Boston temporarily to work for a planter family in Virginia, that she would have the "*fire* of antislavery without its fury."[132]

His ambiguous attitudes toward the antislavery movement can be seen as well in the first of the "Six Plain Sermons," on "Expediency and Morality." Parker strongly endorses abolitionism; he expresses outrage that slavery could find defenders in the United States, a free and Christian land; he professes disgust that those who "attempt to look this evil in the face" are treated with contempt and loathing. Yet Parker continues to follow Dr. Channing's lead and keep a condescending distance from the abolitionists. He expresses regret that "great men" do nothing for the slave, leaving the work to "humble capacities & minds unused to such mighty themes."[133]

Perhaps Parker's principal reason for staying out of the antislavery movement was that, like Channing and Emerson, he preferred working independently for reform rather than in concert with others. He expressed this preference in the last of the "Six Plain Sermons"—the one he presented on the evening he did not read the Latimer petition.[134] Parker here praises the work of "Associations"—societies such as those for temperance, peace, and abolition—in "applying religion to life." He takes pains to defend associations from the charge that they too often have only harsh words for those who were not "up to their level." Although conceding that they might be blamed for this failing in a higher state of society, Parker argues that in the present era of selfishness, those who make sacrifices to fight against sin should be spared criticism. He is emphatic, however, that the best way to apply religion to life is not "socially"—or, for that matter, politically—but individually. An individual, he points out, can go to work without waiting for others and can set the highest moral goals and standards without waiting for others to recognize that these are right.

Parker never explicitly committed himself to the antislavery movement, but many abolitionists admired him nonetheless. One of them predicted, after hearing Parker deliver his "Religion" lectures in Duxbury in early 1842, that "he will do more for the Abolitionist cause than direct agents. . . . His lectures are so calculated to . . . make . . . [one] feel dissatisfied with a low, selfish life, to feel interested in all reforms, and to carry out the law of love into every act."[135]

FOR PARKER, the ideal reformer was the solitary, heroic prophet. He was starting to see himself in this role. Others began to see him in it as well; in fact, they were thrilled to recognize a prophet in their midst. The extent of the excitement can be seen from the reception of Parker's "Six Plain Sermons for the Times." In October and November 1842, more than 3000 people packed the Marlboro Chapel each week to find out what Parker would say—

a turnout that Emerson, who had lectured often at the chapel himself, called "unexampled." Parker delivered the series five times more at lyceums in surrounding towns and preached them at the Spring Street Church. Everywhere, interest in them was high.[136]

The "Six Sermons" had originated during the summer of 1842, when some "young men" from Boston, anxious to hear Parker preach in the city, approached him with a proposal to rent a hall on Sunday evenings, where he could come every week after preaching in West Roxbury and deliver old discourses. He declined the offer (perhaps because the proposal seemed somewhat vague and open-ended), but suggested instead that he could deliver a series of discourses "as we needed for the times." The Bostonians accepted his proposal. By late June, Parker had written an outline for the course in his journal; the six sermons themselves he wrote out over the next several months. The manuscripts are as long as those of the "Religion" lectures, but Parker seems to have agonized less over writing them; he prepared each in only a single draft (although two of them he based on earlier discourses).[137]

The "Sermons" and the "Religion" lectures were linked in that Parker apparently intended the former to complement the latter.[138] In the "Religion" course, he had tried to lead people to a more religious life by correcting what he saw as popular mistakes in theology; now, although he would treat theological topics, he would aim more directly at popular misunderstandings of morality and piety. He would address not only individual religiousness but social injustice.

Parker gives the course a practical, pastoral focus throughout. In the opening "Sermon," on "Expediency and Morality," he contrasts the eternal, universal Moral Law with the rule of expediency that governs trade and politics, while condemning the sins of both (e.g., among political sins, debt repudiation, the destruction of the Indians, and slavery). In the next three sermons, when he treats "Morality and Religion," "Theology and Religion," and "The Application of Good Sense to Theology," his principal aim is to show, in practical terms, what morality and religion ought to be. For example, he illustrates what real religion is by showing what it is not: not morality, although it cannot exist without morality; not theology, which ought to be the science of which religion is the practice (Parker reiterates that the "popular theology" has nothing scientific about it); not "Formalism," which substitutes rituals and creeds for righteousness and piety, "Asceticism," which confuses religiousness with gloominess and penury, nor "Mysticism" (or "Antinomianism" — Parker uses both terms), which would rest religion in sentiment alone and make no attempt to apply it to life. A man may be *formal*, says Parker, and accept the creeds and forms of his church — may be *ascetic*, and forbear from the innocent amusements and pleasures, the grace and elegance of the world — may be *mystic*, and feel, now and then, the *spirit* of faith and love —

yet still violate every day the *laws* of justice, charity, and love. Real religion shows itself in real faith, which is not the "belief in whatever an orthodox priest bids you believe," but the "never failing" confidence that a "religious man . . . reposes in God."[139]

Parker is most obviously practical and pastoral in the final two sermons. In "Religion as a Subjective Matter, or the development of Religion in the Soul," Parker argues that there are three stages of religious growth. In the first, religion springs from fear of Hell, in the second, from hope for Heaven; although the latter stage is an improvement, says Parker, in both, religion is mixed with selfishness, and the religious person is good and pious only so far as required to avoid punishment or win reward. In the highest stage, religion springs from love of God, without regard to punishment or reward, so the religious person strives to be as religious as possible. Religion at this level, Parker believes, brings the great benefit of tranquillity.[140] Parker concludes the course with a sermon on "The Application of Religion to Life," in which he calls for religion to be applied politically (that is, by governments), socially (by churches and associations), and, above all, individually.

The "Six Sermons" contain, especially in the first and final discourses, some of the most specific public calls Parker had yet made for political and social reform. The sixth sermon, especially when he discusses the "political" application of religion, has an almost visionary quality.[141] He here imagines how dramatic would be the shift were religion to govern the relation between nations: "savage" tribes visited by the ships of civilized nations would be taught and blessed rather than plundered, corrupted, then butchered; forts and barricades would become relics like the Pyramids; soldiers would go back to useful work; and thus the massive toil wasted in the negative business of defense would be turned to improve the comforts of life. Internally, a religious nation would resolve to build up a population more comfortable, happier, wiser, and more holy. In such a country, Parker believes, men of talent and wealth would no longer use their gifts selfishly, but for others; pains would be taken to prevent poverty and crime and promote education of all aspects of the human spirit, intellectual, moral, and religious.

More striking, perhaps, than any reform Parker proposes is his implicit portrayal of himself as a young prophet, scorned by the Pharisees for teaching Truth. He more than once calls attention to his own unvarnished honesty—as in the title of the course, which self-consciously describes the "Six Sermons" as "*Plain*." Again, he repeatedly denies what his contemporaries thought obvious—that he was an eloquent speaker. "I have no eloquence to regale you with," he insists to his audience at the beginning of the first sermon, while at the end of the last he reminds them, "I told you I have no eloquence to charm you with—but could only speak plain right on—as my heart bid."[142]

One of the most self-referential moments occurs in the fourth sermon, when Parker describes how reforms in theology "are brought about."[143] What he provides as a general model is transparently an account of his own case, as he understood it, and a judgment on his Unitarian critics.

Reform begins, he relates, when there arise "liberal men" who call for "brave & fearless inquiry" in theology and "demand *toleration* for all." They themselves "do not often, (in public,)" question a "|popular| doctrine they know to be false," yet they "stimulate young men to think freely." By and by some "timid" man rises up and "is helped to think by his fathers":

> He sees the false doctrine bearing bad fruit; must speak. The cry of toleration is kept up. He goes further than his party—a noise is made. They begin to quibble, bid him be cautious, or he will "hurt his useful-ness," |& "get into trouble,"| meaning hurt *their* usefulness & get *them* into trouble. C[onscience]. bids him on. The more he *thinks*, & prays the larger truth becomes, the less to be held in. He speaks more. The liberal party fall back, construe their principles more rigidly, say "We are not responsible for that, & we . . . |cant| bear you." One after another his old friends drive off; . . . the man stands alone. His . . . |former party| would wipe off the injury of his doctrines from themselves—& cast him off, as not meant to sit in their synagogue, & all fellowship is at an end. . . . Abuse takes the place of argument. . . . "Heretic, Infidel" is the cry.[144]

The treatment the young man receives, says Parker scathingly, shows what manner of Christian is tolerated under the old theology. Yet this treatment also wins the young man a hearing (here Parker pulls his audience into the story he is telling) from those who had been taught toleration. As for the young man himself, the crisis leads him to look deeper, discover new truths, and find "courage & a voice." So it was in the time of Luther, Parker says, and so it will always be. He then leaves the matter and lets his auditors draw their own conclusions about whether he himself was a young man Luther.

One of the auditors who seems to have seen him this way was the twenty-five-year-old Elizabeth Cady Stanton. The future giant of the movement for women's rights (a cause with which she already identified herself) had just moved from New York to Chelsea, nearby Boston, with her abolitionist hus-band and baby son. An antislavery friend, Oliver Johnson, knowing that she was in "a transition state of thought" on religious subjects (she had been reared a Presbyterian), offered to escort her to the Marlboro Chapel to hear Parker, "the hero of the hour." She happily agreed to go.

Stanton found the speaker the most impressive she had ever heard. "The repose and simplicity of his manner and language," she would recall years later, "while hurling such thunderbolts of denunciation and defiance at the old theologies, carried his audience along with him, quite unmindful of the havoc he was making of time-honored creeds and opinions." For the whole duration of each discourse (and the first took more than two hours to deliver), the listeners feared "to breathe lest some brave word should be lost or mistaken." Although New England audiences in that era were "very undemonstrative," when Parker "unveiled some of the hypocrisies of the day, and pricked some of the popular bubbles, a gentle ripple of satisfaction ran over the audience, more impressive than loud applause." Stanton liked the "Sermons" so much she went to hear them again when Parker delivered them in Charlestown. She also read his *Discourse of Religion* and his collection of *Critical and Miscellaneous Writings*, published in January 1843. In February, she informed a friend that she had taken "deep draughts" of Parker's "wisdom," and it "refreshed" her. Parker had helped water the seed of her religious unorthodoxy, which many decades later would bear famous fruit in *The Women's Bible*.[145]

PARKER MADE his boldest move as a social reformer in the fall of 1842, when he allied himself with the other extremely controversial figure of Boston Unitarianism, the pastor of the Hollis Street Church, John Pierpont, who was engaged in a bitter public dispute with his church proprietors. The Hollis Street conflict had nothing specifically to do with Transcendentalism, but as Parker and many others understood the matter, it had everything to do with the treatment of prophets in the pulpit.

Pierpont, a prolific writer who belonged to Dr. Channing's generation of Unitarians (he turned fifty-six in 1841), shared with the Transcendentalists neither their theology nor their literary sensibilities. He firmly believed that Christianity was a miraculous revelation, and, judging from the reams of verse he wrote and published, he preferred poetry that was pietistic, didactic, and written in heroic couplets. Yet he showed an unconventional streak in his willingness, unusual among the Boston Unitarian clergy, to take sides publicly on contentious political issues. Over the course of his long career he spoke out against imprisonment for debt and in favor of emancipating the slaves (although, like Channing, Emerson, and Parker, he kept his distance from the abolitionists). But the issue with which he had identified himself most strongly was temperance. In 1838, he led the public crusade that resulted in the "fifteen gallon law," the first serious attempt to restrict retail liquor sales in the state, by forbidding the sale of liquor in quantities less than fifteen gallons. Meanwhile, in speeches, sermons, poems, songs, and even plays, he condemned the sinful traffic in ardent spirits.

His activism deeply offended prominent members of his congregation—many of them, not coincidentally, distillers or grocers, who had made their money in a heretofore respectable trade. In 1839, they demanded Pierpont resign, charging him with having "hurt his usefulness" by introducing "exciting" topics (temperance and slavery) into his preaching. He refused to step down, claiming that the temperance cause and freedom of the pulpit were at stake. His opponents denied both claims, charging instead that he was unfit for his position. In 1840, they formulated a long list of complaints against him, drawn from the whole course of his ministry (he had been ordained in 1819). They charged, among other things, that he had been abusive in the pulpit, neglectful of his parish duties, and dishonest in both his public statements and private business dealings. Pierpont rejoined with accusations of slander and base motives.

During this protracted and increasingly acrimonious exchange, much of it carried on in pamphlets and in the press, Pierpont held the support of the majority of his congregation. His enemies, however, were richer than his friends, and they exploited their advantage to buy up a majority of the meetinghouse pews. Hollis Street, like most other New England churches of that era, resembled in legal terms a joint stock company, with the pew owners, or "proprietors," functioning as shareholders; the proprietors owned the property of the church and contracted to pay the minister's salary. Once Pierpont's enemies had a controlling share (something they accomplished with the help of wealthy allies who had never worshiped at Hollis Street), they began withholding his salary until they could void his contract.

By state law, there were only two ways to void it—either with his consent, which he would not give, or with the approval of an ecclesiastical council, which would act like a special court and judge whether Pierpont's behavior warranted such an extraordinary action. Pierpont, for his part, also wanted a council, because it would give him a chance to refute the proprietors' charges and vindicate his name. After protracted, difficult negotiations, a council was called. Twelve Boston churches were represented by distinguished laymen and by such prominent clergymen as Dr. Nathaniel Frothingham, Ezra Stiles Gannett, Samuel K. Lothrop, and Dr. Francis Parkman. The panel held its hearings in the summer of 1841—by coincidence, just when uproar raged over the "Transient and Permanent in Christianity."

That August, councilors issued their "Result," in which they apparently tried to split the difference between the two sides. They cleared Pierpont of the charges of professional negligence and personal malfeasance and pronounced insufficient the grounds presented to terminate his contract. Yet they hardly gave him an unqualified endorsement. They denied his claim that freedom of the pulpit was at stake, suggested he lacked sufficient "calmness" and "moderation" in advocating temperance, and criticized the harsh language he used in addressing his opponents. These the council did not rebuke, saying nothing against their motives or their tactics. The council concluded its "Result" urging the two sides to reconcile.

This recommendation pleased no one. The proprietors rejected it immediately, and their dispute with Pierpont dragged on, now in the regular courts. Pierpont's supporters and sympathizers, meanwhile, were disgusted. With this latter group stood Parker.

He viewed Pierpont as an ally. They agreed on the temperance issue: Parker had been preaching or lecturing for the cause since 1837 and himself had endorsed the 1838 law. They also shared a commitment to the Unitarian tradition of an open pulpit. After the South Boston ordination, Pierpont refused to denounce Parker, declaring only that he disagreed with "some things" the young man had said,[146] and thereafter was the only minister of a large, old Boston church to maintain ministerial fellowship with him. They exchanged in March 1842 and June 1843.

Above all, Parker admired Pierpont's willingness to preach down a sin actually found in his parish — a sin, moreover, cherished by parishioners with means and influence. Most Boston pastors, Parker believed, behaved very differently; he inevitably contrasted their treatment of himself with their treatment of the well-connected, elegantly dressed malefactors sitting in their own pews. In a sermon he preached the day after he published the *Transient and Permanent*, and just before the Hollis Street Council convened, on the pertinent topic of "Infidelity,"[147] Parker declared that "the rule in theological matters" is "that if a sin xists [*sic*] which is practiced by wealthy, respectable & powerful men, it must not be meddled with: but if a thought is put forth, — not perfectly in harmony with what passes for Orthodox, — that no quarter shall be shown to that thought — or its author." A few months later, in an article published in the *Dial* on modern "Pharisees," Parker reiterated the charge with greater eloquence:

> If there be a sin in the land, or a score of sins tall as the Anakim, which go to and fro in the earth, and shake the churches with their tread; let these sins be popular, be loved by the powerful, protected by the affluent; will the Pharisee sound the alarm, lift up the banner, sharpen the sword, and descend to do battle? There shall not a man of them move his tongue. . . . But let there be four or five men in obscure places, not mighty through power, renown, or understanding, or eloquence; let them utter in modesty a thought that is new, which breathes of freedom, or tends directly towards God, and every Pharisee of the Pulpit shall cry out from Cape Sable to the Lake of the Woods, till the land ring again. Doubtless it is heroic thus to fight a single new thought, rather than a score of old sins.[148]

Because the Hollis Street Council failed to commend Pierpont for his bravery, Parker judged it a craven document. In his journal, he copied from the published "Result" a passage in which the councilors, referring to Pierpont's temperance activities, remarked that "the circumstances of his parish, and the condition of things in that quarter of the city where his ministry was chiefly exercised and its influence exerted, were peculiar, and such as called for a large measure and constant exhibition of that wisdom which is from above." What the council meant in plain English, Parker scoffed, was that the parish required a minister "cunning enough to soften the doctrines of [Christianity] down to suit the Rum-sellers case."[149]

Even worse than being cowardly, Parker thought the "Result" fundamentally duplicitous. He believed the council feared reformers and wanted to censure Pierpont outright, as most of them had censured Parker himself, yet they had been afraid to do so, because Pierpont was popular and his proprietors were not (they were widely perceived as pettifoggers opposed to religious freedom). Therefore, the council had sought to undercut Pierpont without seeming to do so, by suggesting that his temper and judgment were questionable and shifting public attention away from the important issues of temperance and ministerial free speech toward the minor one of Pierpont's sometimes harsh rhetoric. When Parker learned that after the council issued its "Result," only three of the eleven clerical members continued to offer Pierpont pulpit exchanges, he considered this positive proof of the council's sympathy with the proprietors.[150]

Many shared Parker's negative assessment of the council and its work. His favorite professor, Henry Ware Jr., admitted to him just as the Hollis Street hearings were getting underway that although he "loved and honored" the ministers involved, he expected no justice from them. If they "let [Pierpont] off with no censure," Ware explained, "they condemn themselves, for God knows they have not undertaken his work." Edmund Quincy, meanwhile, denounced the council to Parker as an outright "farce": "The Boston ministers, instead of trying Mr. Pierpont, ought themselves to be brought before a council for *not* having done in a good spirit, what he is accused of *doing* in a bad one."[151]

These opinions were privately expressed; no one, at least no minister, was willing to speak out publicly against the large weight of respectable opinion that the council represented. By 1842, Parker realized that he alone, who had no reputation to lose, would be the only cleric willing to raise his voice. He awaited only an opportunity. In April, just as he was finishing the *Discourse of Religion*, Ralph Waldo Emerson unintentionally provided him with one.

Emerson had taken over as editor of the *Dial* a month earlier, after Margaret Fuller, who had been in charge of the little magazine for its first eight numbers, decided she no longer could sacrifice so much labor for no financial reward. He felt no little trepidation at shouldering the responsibility — perhaps, he wrote Fuller, "I shall rue this day of accepting such an intruder on my peace such a consumer of my time as a Dial" — but, unwilling to see the publication cease or pass out of friendly hands, he dutifully began soliciting manuscripts. On 6 April he wrote to Parker, begging him to supply a paper for the next issue. Parker promptly suggested a review of the *Proceedings* of the Hollis Street Council, the official record of its work, which had been published as a pamphlet of nearly 400 pages the previous fall. Parker told Emerson that the council, which he referred to as the attempt to "silence & tame" Pierpont, was worthy of notice as a "sign of the times."[152]

Emerson reacted coolly to the suggestion. Although he did not reject the topic outright, he requested that if Parker must write a notice, it ought to be short. Emerson not only thought the topic inappropriate for the *Dial*, which he wanted to be a strictly intellectual and literary publication, but he also had much less sympathy for Pierpont than Parker did. Emerson conceded that the "injury done to Mr. Pierpont . . . may be indefensible *in the forms*," but felt that "there probably existed in this case the *general objection* to the pastor which could not get stated, yet which is felt in the mind of each parishioner as the highest reason for displacing a pastor." He reiterated this opinion in another letter to Parker written a few months later: "I think the people almost always right in their quarrels with their ministers, although they seldom know how to give the true reason for their discontent." While Parker embraced Pierpont as a fellow combatant in the cause of righteousness, Emerson dismissed him as "that most unpoetic unspiritual & un Dialled John Pierpont," no bard of the Holy Ghost, whose long-suffering parishioners had rebelled against his barren religiousness the only way they knew how.[153]

These divergent views of Pierpont grew out of basic differences between Emerson and Parker, apparent as early as the Divinity School Address. Emerson, in that speech, had charged the clergy with failing to meet the spiritual aspirations of the people; Parker, in his sermons written in response to what Emerson had said, had charged the people with low, materialistic aims. Despite Parker's disdain for ecclesiastical authority, he remained sure that ordinary people needed clerical leadership. Emerson lacked this conviction, which may be one reason why he left the ministry while Parker did not, and why he was less prone than Parker to see ministers as heroic. Even more fundamentally, the two men separated on what constituted real religiousness. Emerson had a strong tendency toward mysticism. For him, inner light seemed to be everything, and it manifested itself most importantly in independence and originality, qualities he believed had a strong moral component, but which might not be associated, at least in any overt, practical way, with what society called "good works" or "just causes." But for Parker, as Emerson himself later observed, "the essence of Christianity is its practical morals; it is there for use, or it is nothing."[154]

Emerson did not succeed, however, in discouraging Parker from writing about Pierpont. Parker intended to dash off his Hollis Street article right after the *Discourse* went to press in May 1842, but discovered that his toils on that manifesto had "left him in a very bad state of brain"—unable to read and scarcely able to think. Before he had a chance to recover came the emotional trials of that miserable summer. Parker found that to write was "now almost as painful . . . as to walk on burning coals." What energy he had, he needed for other work, including writing the "Six Plain Sermons." The "Hollis Street" manuscript took months to complete and did not arrive on Emerson's desk until early September.[155]

When Emerson saw the contents of the packet, he confessed that his "heart sank." Parker had written him that he should feel free to reject the article ("I am not a *baby* to be vexed with you"), but Emerson felt he could not spurn a submission from so faithful a friend of the magazine, especially not one who felt so strongly about his article and had worked so hard on it. Emerson decided at once that the Pierpont piece "should be received & printed purely out of honor to the contributor, and it should be his affair, & no other man should claim it as a precedent for our admission of strange gods into our Dial or Temple of the Spiritual Sun." He sent the paper off to the printer without reading it.[156]

Had Emerson done so, he would have found that Parker had tried to meet his objections about the subject. In order to better suit the "philosophical" character of the *Dial*, Parker avoids discussing the sensational details of the Pierpont case (they are, he asserts, "unfortunately too well known, and require no reiteration"), but does remark on the long history of ecclesiastical councils, which he sums up as a sad record of "human folly and bigotry." He also provides a lengthy exposition of the "position of a minister in general." This last section reveals as much about Parker's understanding of his own situation as of the problems Pierpont faced.[157]

A minister, Parker asserts, has a speculative duty—to teach Truth—and a practical duty—to promote Goodness. This twofold work has in turn a twofold aspect, one positive, "sowing the seeds of Truth and Goodness," and one negative, "confuting Falsehood and exposing Crime." These tasks are, however, generally "thankless," for "the tellers of Truth and promoters of Goodness have rarely been popular till after death."

Yet a minister is "sometimes heard of" who is not serious in his calling. He "takes the general average of theological opinion in his district as the standard of truth, and the general average of popular virtue as the standard of goodness, and never goes beyond either." He preaches "profound, speculative sermons (sound in more than one sense,)" on biblical antiquities, or "smart practical sermons" against "obsolete vices, . . . doubts that nobody shares, and extinct or unpopular classes of unbelievers." In his spare time he dabbles in literature, or "plays on the surface of some easy science." Such a one, Parker writes contemptuously, never gets into trouble. "He is born for his tucker and his bib, and never sells his birthright."

If a minister decides to promote Truth, Parker continues, he will certainly get into trouble. If he asks what Truth is, he will find himself differing from the theological opinions of the public, "just in proportion to his ability, activity and honesty." Then comes the question, Shall he disclose his convictions? "If he is a serious man, he will do as Luther and Paul, and not 'shun to declare the whole counsel of God,' asking no question, whether public opinion will tolerate or condemn him." Then the church, the "great guardian of established opinion," will come to him and say, " 'Sir, you hurt our feelings.' " In the speech of the church that follows, Parker satirizes what so many had said to him over the past two years: "It is better for you to give up thinking altogether, till you can think and feel as we do. We are good Christians, and would not disturb freedom of thought and speech for the world! Nay, we prize that above all things. But if you preach such opinions as we dislike, we will burn you alive, if we can, and at all events will give you a bad name in this life, and the expectancy of damnation in the next."

If a minister turns from theology to practical work, he gets into trouble nonetheless. "He comes to conclusions respecting the public virtue, which differ from the opinions commonly entertained, just in proportion to his ability, activity, and honesty." Again, the question comes whether he should be silent, and again, the examples of Luther and Paul favor speaking. But if he publishes his opinions about the selfishness, sensuality, and sin of society, the world, "the great guardian of established usages," comes and says to him, " 'Sir, you have hurt our feelings.' " In the speech that follows, the world speaks in the imagined voice of Pierpont's proprietors: "You have spilled our rum, and put out the fires of our distilleries. . . . We are good Christians, but we get our living by what you call *sin*; we must get our living, and our way must be right, for it has always been followed 'from the beginning.' . . . We are patient men; but when you talk about our wrong doings, and sins we commit, we can't bear you, and we won't. . . . If you will continue . . . we will give you a bad name, and starve your wife and babies."

The minister who takes both horns of the dilemma, says Parker, and exposes the falsehood of popular doctrines *and* the sin of popular doings—his case is very hard. The church and the world are upon him. He is branded an infidel, atheist, madman, reformer. Both the church and the world want to crucify him.

Having drawn such distinctions between the "frivolous" and the "serious" minister, Parker can respond to Emerson's criticisms of Pierpont. If a minister is of the frivolous sort, Parker argues, and takes the average standard of opinion for truth and of duty for morality, then there is so little difference between the pulpit and the pews that "quarrels between a minister and his people in general come from a want of prudence, rather than from a superabundance of wisdom or zeal on his part; and in *such* quarrels we think the minister is almost always the party to be blamed." Parker does not consider the "quarrel" at Hollis Street to belong in this category, because Pierpont's moral standards were clearly superior to those of his opponents.[158]

Parker addresses the conclusion of the council that Pierpont had used inappropriately scornful language addressing these opponents by conceding that Pierpont did not, in this regard, come up the "ideal measure" of a minister or a man. Yet Parker goes on to quote Jeremiah, St. Paul, and St. James to show these canonical figures had not spared their enemies either. Besides, "there is no little palliation for the pastor": "Mr. Pierpont came forward as a Reformer, a rare character in the Pulpit, at a time when there were no honors to be won, no victory to be rejoiced in. The 'peculiar circumstances' of his parish were Rum-selling, Rum-making, Rum-drinking. The head and front of his offending, we honestly believe, is this, the crime of preaching against the actual sins of his own parish."[159]

According to Parker, Pierpont's course offended not only the sinners in his congregation, but his clerical colleagues. Parker cites examples from the *Proceedings* to show council members were hostile to Pierpont and concludes that "no plain man, who reads the volume before us, will doubt which way the prejudice of the council tended, or what would have been the decision of at least some of its members, if public opinion, the despot of the vulgar, had not so plainly favored" the accused. Parker quotes (identifying the sources only as "grave" and "pious" men) the harsh judgments of the council expressed to him by Henry Ware and Edmund Quincy. Parker brands the council "Result" a "piece of diplomacy,—designed to serve many ends," and hence "worthy of a college of Jesuits." He concludes his review with a fable about ancient Israel, in which a prophet named Zadock is tried before the hostile Sanhedrin, which, fearing his popularity, resolves to "speak him fairly with our tongues, but with our actions cut him to the soul," and thereby "insinuate evil with good words."[160]

When Parker sent the completed article to Emerson, he apologized that if "my health had been better so would the paper have been."[161] In fact, the piece could have stood some of the editing Emerson declined to give it. In places, it is repetitious, and there is an apparent contradiction in Parker's analysis. He makes unpopularity the sign of ministerial seriousness, and holds up Pierpont as an example of a serious minister, yet argues that Pierpont was not condemned outright by the council because he was too popular. Parker offers no explanation for Pierpont's popularity—or his own. Implicitly, however, he does provide one: the "unpopularity" he speaks of is not necessarily with ordinary people, but with the rich and powerful. For Parker, to be "unpopular" was to be opposed not by anyone, but by the "respectable" elite.

The "Hollis Street Council" article, despite its drawbacks, caused a sensation when it appeared. The *Dial* sold out its October run in a matter of days, and the demand for Parker's piece was such that an offprint was issued separately as a pamphlet. Pierpont's supporters reacted to the review with predictable enthusiasm and ever after regarded Parker warmly. Margaret Fuller, meanwhile, who had not before shown much interest in Parker's pronouncements, told Emerson that she liked the Hollis Street piece "much": "It is excellent in its way[;] the sneer is mild, almost courtly." Other readers, however, reacted only with outrage. No doubt the controversy roused by the article helped turn the "Six Plain Sermons," which Parker started to deliver in Boston on 24 October, into a popular triumph. Yet the article only intensified the hostility between him and his clerical Brethren in the Boston Association of Congregational Ministers.[162]

BY THE WINTER of 1842, this hostility was darkening the emotional sky like the onset of a nor'easter. Finally, in January 1843, the tension was released in a great, icy blast. Its howl was slightly muffled by the glass panes and lace curtains of liberal ideology, ministerial decorum, and Victorian sentimentality, but the sharp wind penetrated these thin defenses, and Parker felt a deep chill.

With no Unitarian organization was he more intimately involved than with the Boston Association. Since joining the Brethren just after his ordination, he faithfully had attended their fortnightly meetings and dutifully had preached the traditional Thursday Lecture when his turn came up in the rotation. But as his heterodoxy grew, so had his alienation from his associates. A turning point had been in January 1840, when Parker preached his Thursday Lecture on "Inspiration" and Dr. Francis Parkman told him that "I can't bear ye," prompting the young man to flee in tears. Over the next few years, Parker went less and less often to the Association meetings, and when he did attend, he professed sorrow that he had. "Stupid as usual" was his private assessment of a meeting in February 1842.[163]

The failings of the Association Parker personified in two of its most prominent members, Dr. Parkman and Dr. Nathaniel Frothingham. Frothingham represented for Parker sleek clerical hypocrisy, while Parkman stood for ministerial "narrowness, frivolity, selfishness & bigotry."[164]

Clerical hypocrisy Parker denounced repeatedly. In the peroration of the *Transient and Permanent*, he condemned the "man who consents to think one thing in his closet, and preach another in his pulpit": "Over his study and over his pulpit might be writ—EMPTINESS; on his canonical robes, on his forehead and right hand—DECEIT, DECEIT." Again, in his mordant *Dial* article on various types of modern "Pharisee," Parker came down most severely on the "Pharisee of the Pulpit," who zealously defends in public ideas in which he no longer believes. In the study, Parker says, this man freely admits that "the Testament is a collection of legendary tales," but in the pulpit he proclaims it the Everlasting Gospel: "If any man shall add to it, the seven plagues shall be added to him; if any one takes from it, his name shall be taken from the Book of Life." [165]

More than one observer wondered why Parker should be so concerned with this problem. Was he insinuating that some of his colleagues secretly agreed with his assessment of the Bible? He always replied that in neither the *Transient and Permanent* nor the "Pharisees" had he intended to criticize any specific person. Yet privately he did think a number of his colleagues spoke differently in the study and in the pulpit, and that Dr. Frothingham, the elegant, urbane pastor of the First Church in Boston, was in this regard one of the most egregious offenders. [166]

When Parker came to know Frothingham in the mid-1830s, he appreciated the older man's sophisticated literary taste, recondite learning, and apparently open mind about the ideas of the New School. In 1836, Frothingham had written a friendly review of *Sartor Resartus* for the *Examiner* — one of the most prominent notices Carlyle's book received in America — and was nearly invited to join the Transcendentalists' little club. When Transcendentalism became controversial, however, Frothingham sided emphatically with the conservatives.

Frothingham's disapproval of Parker's own course grew stronger over time. He stopped offering Parker exchanges after 1839 and later joined in the chorus disapproving Parker's involvement with the Chardon Street Convention. In 1841, he let it be known that he could think of no "logical definition" of Christianity that would include either Parker or his South Boston sermon. Later, he wrote to Parker that the *Discourse of Religion* was "utterly subversive of Christianity . . . both as a faith & an institution," and in spirit both "arrogant" and "scoffing." [167]

Parker found these rebukes ironic, because, in his opinion, "good Dr. Frothingham" was not himself "the stricter sort in matters of belief." [168] To document this assertion, Parker carefully recorded in his journal a number of statements made by his older colleague, underscoring those he thought especially significant.

He recalled Frothingham's assertion, in a conversation from 1836 or 1837 about Strauss's *Leben Jesu*, that "if Strauss had made a small book, in a single volume, & had made it popular instead of designing it for the learned alone, *it would have about done the thing for historical Christianity*." Parker remembered, too, a meeting of the Boston Association around 1837, at which Frothingham had mused aloud that although Christianity had been thought to rest on the twin pillars of prophecy and miracles, just as the Temple at Jerusalem had rested on the pillars called Jachin and Boaz, George Noyes had now "knocked down" prophecy and George Ripley toppled miracles, yet Christianity stood. At the same meeting, when a few of the Brethren had asked Frothingham if he believed the prophets had foretold the coming of Christ, he had answered that they had, but only "as every imperfect thing is a prophecy of the perfect." Again, at another Association meeting in the winter of 1840-41, Parker had asked Frothingham how he reconciled the conflicting accounts in the Gospels of Jesus' appearance after the Resurrection, and Frothingham had replied that he did not try: "*I look upon them as mythologico-poetical, fact & fiction are jumbled together in the strangest way. You can't tell when fact begins & fiction ends, nor whether there is any fact at the bottom or not.*"[169]

From such statements, Parker inferred a certain skepticism about the Scriptures on Frothingham's part—and did so correctly. Like many Unitarians, Frothingham did not regard the Hebrew Scriptures as historical or authentic; like a respectable minority, he did not believe the prophets really had foretold the future; more unusually, he questioned the genuineness of the Gospels. In 1837, he had a private debate with Andrews Norton in which he provoked the former professor with the argument (which he had absorbed from certain German scholars) that the Gospels gradually had taken shape over hundreds of years and that "nobody" had written them.[170]

Parker evidently assumed that anyone who doubted the genuineness of the Bible could not really accept its authority—but here he erred. Frothingham (like Convers Francis) maintained a faith that something miraculous really did lie behind the sacred stories, despite all the legendary material mixed in with them. Moreover, Frothingham had made his most daring remarks in the mid-1830s. As the Transcendentalist controversy unfolded, he recoiled from his more radical opinions, writing to Parker in 1843, "Ever since I saw,—or thought I saw, that the new liberality was employing itself in defacing the monuments & breaking the images of ancient reverence,—in flouting the holy guides of the past, & making inroads into the 'vast obscure' of mystic or philosophic speculation, I ceased to be a liberal."[171]

Frothingham's unwillingness to voice his doubts from the pulpit, moreover, does not necessarily mean he was dishonest and hollow. He seems to have feared feeding strong meat to babes. He thought a pastor should strengthen the faith of his people, not risk undermining it by voicing what Frothingham thought mere scholarly speculations. On similar grounds, he carefully avoided preaching on doctrinal questions; he even refused to declare himself a Unitarian until 1836, the twentieth anniversary of his ordination.[172] Frothingham's approach to the ministry was hardly heroic, but from a conservative point of view it was not despicable, either.

Parker despised it. He would delight when, in 1845, Emerson referred to Frothingham as "*the Artful Dodger of the Boston Clergy.*" What Frothingham came to represent for Parker can best be seen by his use of another Frothingham statement. At a Thursday Lecture, not long after Emerson delivered the Divinity School Address, Frothingham, in a conversation with Convers Francis, referred to Emerson as an "infidel." Francis, surprised, had clapped

I Can Stand Alone

Frothingham on the shoulder. "Come, come, Brother Frothingham," Francis had said, "that will do well enough for men that don't know any better. But you know that Emerson is no more an infidel than you and I are!" "I know that," Frothingham had answered. "But what is the use of talking of it?"[173]

This rhetorical question nagged at Parker, and when he wrote the *Discourse of Religion*, he placed a variation of it into the mouth of a great Pharisee. In a passage on the clerical opponents of Jesus, he imagines an illustrious rabbi privately reporting the Sermon on the Mount to his disciples in Jerusalem. "This new doctrine will not injure us, prudent and educated men," the shrewd man says, ". . . but what is the use of telling it? The people wish to be deceived; let them."[174]

If Dr. Frothingham was Parker's prototypical Pharisee, Dr. Parkman—whom Parker called, by way of rebuke, "a favorable specimen of the Boston clergy" in point of "[character] & heart & morâle"—was what we today might call his prototypical Colonel Blimp: the narrow-minded, reactionary blowhard. Most people treated Parkman with respect. He was the senior Unitarian minister in the city; he pastored the rich, distinguished New North Church; he came from a rich, distinguished family and lived splendidly in an inherited mansion on Bowdoin Square; he was considered amiable, charitable, and witty. Parker, however, dismissed him as comically contemptible. "Dr. *Parkman* will become a fool," wrote Parker in his journal, after listening to him pontificate on a trivial issue at an Association meeting, "& the change will be so slight no-body will know when it takes place."[175]

Parker recorded in his journal various instances of Parkman's buffoonery, as when, in a much-publicized sermon, he had attributed to Jesus the saying, "All that a man hath he will give for his life"—a sentiment the Bible in fact credits to Satan (Job 2:4). Again, Parker noted the time a newspaper mistakenly listed the name of "Francis Parkman" (instead of "Francis Jackson," the prominent abolitionist) at the head of two petitions to the state legislature calling, respectively, for the legalization of interracial marriage and the desegregation of public conveyances. The misprint so alarmed Parkman that he sent letters to both the Massachusetts House and Senate, denying he had headed the petitions—which no informed person seriously suspected, because Parkman was well known to despise the antislavery movement. Such an incident, wrote Parker, "could have happened to none but Dr. P."[176]

Even Parkman's physiognomy Parker found clownish. He laughed at a "wicked" witticism that the reverend doctor's nose resembled the latest novel of Dickens, because both were "all-of-a-twist." The laugh turned into a snort of disgust when Parkman announced at an Association meeting in 1841 that he would deny ministerial fellowship on frivolous grounds, such as that a brother had "an unfortunate *twist* in the face . . . or any peculiarity that would make the audience smile." Parkman may have been trying to make his Brethren smile with this example (he apparently twisted up his face as he spoke), but Parker failed to see the humor. "Nemesis never sleeps" was his comment later to a friend.[177]

Dr. Parkman most disgusted Parker by playing a key role in determining the outcome of the Hollis Street Council. Parkman was its president. The single strongest piece of evidence confirming Parker's view that the council had a hidden agenda was a statement by Parkman, which was reported to Parker in confidence (probably by either Francis Shaw, Mrs. Russell, or Anna Shaw, who were his nephew and nieces). Parker thought the remark so damning that he recorded it in his journal, along with his gloss, disguised in Greek characters, as a kind of code. Transcribed into Latin letters, the passage reads: " 'The Council would not condemn Mr. P[ierpont]. for that would only produce a reaction in his favor, so strong was the public opinion of his merit.' Dr. P[arkman]. counted this a fine piece of diplomacy. Is it not Christian?"[178]

Parker wrote his Hollis Street article so convinced of Parkman's malevolence that he put words in the man's mouth. Parker quotes from the council *Proceedings* a statement by Parkman: "I have not a doubt that temperance is three quarters of all our trouble." Parker here seems to admit that he agreed with the analysis of the Hollis Street crisis propounded by Pierpont and denied by the proprietors; Parker, recognizing the significance of the concession, places it in small capitals. Yet Parkman never uttered it. It is in fact a statement addressed *to* Parkman, by a Pierpont supporter. (Parker had to apologize to Parkman for misquoting him.)[179]

The publication of Parker's attack on the Hollis Street Council seems to have provoked the Boston Association finally to take some sort of collective action against him. As his disdain for the Brethren had grown, so had their discomfort at being connected to him. Most of them either agreed with Brother Lothrop that Parker was not a Christian, or feared, like Brothers Hall and Shackford, that he was too controversial to invite to preach in their church. By the fall of 1842, only two of the twenty-nine Association affiliates still were willing to offer Parker a pulpit exchange: one was Pierpont; the other was John Sargent, minister of one of the Unitarian Chapels for the Poor, who would soon play a significant role in Parker's career.

Yet Parker retained his membership and therefore his place in the rotation to preach the Thursday Lecture at the First Church—Dr. Frothingham's pulpit. Whenever Parker delivered a Thursday Lecture (as, for instance, in June 1841), Frothingham was not the only one made uneasy. The Brethren were accused by at least one critic of doing as a group what most of them refused to do as individuals: recognize him as a Christian teacher.[180]

For a long time, however, the Association saw no obvious action to take. To expel the troublemaker looked too much like an excommunication. The Brethren saw themselves as good liberals and were anxious to keep their lib-

I Can Stand Alone

eral bona fides on display. Even as they denounced Parker's theology, therefore, and barred him from their pulpits, they took pains to say they still considered him a "Christian in life," and insisted that they were his warmest friends. Lothrop himself professed that he "ever entertained a high regard" for Parker on a personal level and declared himself willing to bear "public testimony, though it is not needed, to the singular purity of his life and character." Dr. Frothingham, meanwhile, told friends he thought Parker "eminently religious," and he assured Parker himself that he would be "really grieved" if the differences between them "should interfere with any feelings of personal good-will." With even Lothrop and Frothingham able to make such declarations, expulsion of Parker seemed impossible, and the Brethren did not, for the time being at least, seriously consider it.[181]

Some hoped that Parker would resign his membership. In early December 1841, at an Association meeting Parker happened to attend, Dr. Parkman announced that if a member (Parkman named no names) held and preached opinions that the majority of his fellows found distasteful, and that brought scandal upon them, it was his duty to withdraw. Parker, taken aback by this broad hint, asked Parkman to repeat himself, which he did. Parker said nothing, but his back must have stiffened. A few weeks later, when describing the incident to a friend, he declared that "I would be *last to abandon a right*, especially when assailed."[182]

So the matter rested for some months, as tensions rose. Parker seems to have passed on the chance to preach a Thursday Lecture in 1842 (he had much else to do) and so avoided aggravating his colleagues in that way, but he made their mutual ties chafe nonetheless. Most of the Brethren felt "startled" and "shocked" by the opinions he had expressed in the *Discourse of Religion*. Even worse, they accused him of making remarks "derogatory to the professional honesty of the Brethren," most flagrantly and explicitly in his attack on the Hollis Street Council. Dr. Parkman and ten other members of the Association had sat on the council and had reason to resent being likened to a scheming "college of Jesuits."[183]

After the "Hollis Street" article appeared, in early October, Parker became the principal topic of conversation at a series of Association meetings, from all of which he was conspicuously absent. On 10 October, William Lunt of Quincy complained that some of the "blame and odium which the religious community in general attached to the sentiments of Mr. Parker" had fallen on the Association. He urged that the Brethren issue a disclaimer of Parker's views. This proposal, discussed that day and on 14 November, in the end was not approved, perhaps due to doubts about whether a collective disavowal would be a better vaccine against embarrassment than the many individual disavowals members had issued.

At the 14 November meeting, Samuel K. Lothrop, fresh from preaching his sermons declaring Parker an infidel, made a more radical suggestion: disband the Association. Its meetings, after all, were often mere social occasions, and few people other than Association members usually attended the Thursday Lecture. The cost of maintaining such an organization, Lothrop argued, was not worth staying in fellowship with Parker. A majority of the Brethren, however, seemed to have agreed with Ezra Stiles Gannett that "it would be better to attempt to revive the interest of the Members in the Association, & to increase its value, than to destroy it."[184]

Gannett emerged from these debates as the Association point man on the Parker issue—an informal and thankless office he would perform for the next few years. He was qualified for the position in a special way: unlike most liberal leaders, who shied away from any suspicion of "sectarianism," he envisioned Unitarianism as an organized denomination. He was better able than anyone else to consider the Parker problem in the context of strengthening Unitarian institutions.

Gannett did not doubt that Parker "uttered the . . . earnest convictions of his soul," and in his reviews of Parker's pronouncements, he praised not merely the "remarkable vigor and beauty" of Parker's literary style but his "*heartiness*—something more than sincerity." Yet Gannett firmly believed Parker was wrong, even dangerously wrong, to insist that intuition was the only adequate foundation for faith. As Gannett once told him, "I could not be a Christian on your grounds." In Gannett's experience, the only solid basis of religious belief was "the authority of a Divine messenger, established by sensible proof, and made clear to us by historical evidence." Parker might reply (and in fact did reply) that he could not be a Christian on Gannett's grounds, and Gannett did not doubt him. But Gannett maintained that "the ground of individual faith . . . sufficient for him who so esteems it . . . [may] yet be far from sufficient for men generally," and may even "create general unbelief." Gannett was convinced that although Parker's intuitionism might work for him, it would not work any more for the "vast majority of mankind" than it did for Gannett himself. As for Parker's disparagement of religious authority, Gannett considered it "a hurtful error, the tendency of which must be to unsettle people's minds and leave them unsettled, uneasy, skeptical and irreligious."[185]

As important for Gannett as resisting Parker's theology was disassociating Unitarianism from it. In Gannett's notice of Parker's "Religion" lectures for the *Miscellany*, he pointed out that Parker had expressed "but partial sympathy with any denomination, and his remarks upon the Unitarians, if those of a friend, were not less harsh than if they had come from an enemy." He concluded that "Mr. Parker certainly is not the representative of Unitarian opinions, and should not be so considered,—he probably would say, in justice to himself,—. . . [I] as decidedly say, in justice to them." In another *Miscel-*

lany article, Gannett insisted that Parker had no grounds to complain that the Unitarians were violating their liberal principles because they attacked his views: "Here there is no persecution, nor injustice, but the fair conflict of opinions and arguments."[186]

By mid-1842, Gannett had defined the threat of Absolute Religion and worked out a coherent Unitarian response to it. He probably expected no new provocations from Parker. Parker's denunciation of the Hollis Street Council blindsided him.

Gannett had been one the principal figures on the council — in fact, he had authored the "Result" that Parker excoriated. Most of those who signed that document, like Dr. Parkman, saw it as a devastating rebuke of Pierpont and thereafter treated him as they did Parker, refusing him ministerial fellowship. Gannett himself, however, seems to have taken what he wrote at face value: as an even-handed critique of a good pastor whose excessive zeal on a particular issue had led him to treat his parishioners uncharitably. Gannett therefore did maintain fellowship with Pierpont, one of only three ministers on the council to do so. He found nearly libelous Parker's accusation that the "Result" aimed to undercut Pierpont because Pierpont opposed rum selling.

Yet when the Boston Association debated what to do about Parker in November 1842, Gannett looked beyond his personal complaint. The only major charge he laid against Parker at the meetings was that he had caused an "uneasiness" among the membership that stood in the way "of the future harmonious and efficient action of this Association."[187] Gannett not only wanted to prevent such discomfort from destroying the Association, but to use the crisis to make the organization stronger.

On 14 November, after he persuaded the Brethren not to disband, he talked them into letting him "report upon the future action of the Association."[188] At the next meeting, a fortnight later, he made an elaborate presentation. He suggested a number of changes to the Association bylaws that he hoped would encourage attendance at the meetings, make them more substantive, and raise interest in the Thursday Lecture. He also proposed that Parker meet with the other members so that "a frank & friendly exchange of views & feelings [could] take place between" them.

Gannett's bylaw reforms received respectful attention; they were discussed over the next few meetings and most of them seem to have been enacted. But the talk about Parker was passionate. The opinion "appeared to be very nearly unanimous that the Members of the Association had sufficient reasons for feeling aggrieved by Mr. Parker's remarks [against them], & that certain of his opinions were at variance with Christianity considered as a particular system of religion." There was also, however, a general feeling that this train of talk should not continue in their errant brother's absence. The members professed regret that Parker could not hear "what they felt it their duty to say . . . in a spirit of Christian forbearance & love." Gannett's suggestion for a conference, therefore, had wide support. There was apparently, however, some concern that a meeting with Parker would descend into a fruitless debate over points of theology, so the Brethren decided not to talk with Parker about doctrines.[189]

Another difficulty presented itself. Because Parker had a right to attend Association meetings, some felt it inappropriate to invite him to one. Gannett therefore proposed a resolution, which after much debate was accepted, expressing the "wish" that Parker would attend the next meeting so that he could "participate" in the discussion about his "writings & remarks." To deliver this suggestion, the Brethren, again at Gannett's suggestion, chose the "Moderator (pro tem.)" of the meeting that evening—who was none other than John Pierpont! Gannett probably calculated that Parker would be more likely to respond if the request were delivered by the man he had defended.

When Pierpont delivered the message a week later, Parker found it somewhat ominous. "The Brethren wish me to come before them," he wrote in his journal, as if he were being asked to face a tribunal. But he told Pierpont that he was "gratified with the course the Association had taken" in regard to him and would meet with them as soon as his schedule permitted. He happened to be preaching the "Six Sermons" in Charlestown on Monday evenings, when the Association assembled, but he promised that he would come to the first meeting after the Charlestown course was completed. The conference therefore was postponed from mid-December until 23 January.[190]

Parker and the Brethren had more than a month to think over what they would say to one another. Dr. Frothingham wrote Parker a letter in early January, presenting a sample of what he planned to say. "I have no sympathy with your views," Frothingham wrote, "with the tone & temper which you have seen |fit| to present them, nor with the public course you have taken." The *Discourse of Religion*, Frothingham denounced as "vehemently deistical" in the "old-fashioned [i.e., Tom Paine–like] sense of that word." Frothingham complained that Parker "would merge the Gospel in the great ocean of the Absolute; while I hold it to be too precious to be thus drowned."[191] Parker did not answer these accusations right away, but over the next few weeks worked out in his mind an elaborate reply.

He was given another preview of what lay ahead in a dramatic December confrontation with George Putnam, an Association member and pastor of the large, rich, First Church of Roxbury. Parker, as pastor of the Second Church, had worked closely with the slightly older Putnam for years on local affairs (they had served together on the town school committee). In 1836, Putnam had been one of the founders of the Transcendentalists' little club, and although he soon had withdrawn from it, probably because it was becoming too radical, he did support Parker after the "Transient and Perma-

I Can Stand Alone

nent" controversy broke in June 1841. In July 1841, Putnam gave Parker a pulpit exchange.

Then Putnam distanced himself. He soon informed Parker that it would be "inexpedient" to exchange again, because some in his congregation would be offended. In 1842, after Parker published the *Discourse of Religion*, Putnam reportedly told Parker that "it augurs ill for a man, *within* the Church, to break its windows; we should more naturally expect, that they should be broken from *without*." Parker in his journal reports that Putnam had voiced the view that "the pulpit is not the place to stand in to reform the church," and that because Parker was an "enemy of the church" he ought to stand outside it. Putnam professed still to think well of Parker intellectually, morally, and religiously, but Parker warned himself to "put no confidence in George Putnam."[192]

Parker nonetheless was quite unprepared for what happened next. On 19 December, he walked over to Roxbury to deliver the first of his "Six Sermons" at a lyceum there; on the way, he made what he thought would be a friendly call on Putnam. But as Parker describes the encounter in his journal, he received an icy reception. Putnam announced that he had been thinking "hard things" about Parker and asked, in a way Parker found "wicked & coarse . . . both in tone & expression," what he was doing. Putnam told Parker what people were saying about him—that is, what Putnam had heard at the last several Association meetings:[193] Parker was trying to "do away with" Christianity; he "did nothing but pull down"; he "reviled the church, the Bible & the clergy." Putnam did not make these accusations "hypothetically" but "as if they were notorious facts."

Shocked, Parker began to defend himself. Then he began to cry. Putnam was abashed. Parker rose and, still teary, put on his wrap. Putnam awkwardly asked him to stay. They shook hands at the door. They were never friendly again.[194]

Parker managed to pull himself together and deliver his lecture. But he believed he now knew what to expect at the conference with the Association the following month. "What I have to hope from the '*brethren*' is plain enough," he wrote in his journal that night.[195]

PARKER'S MEETING with the Boston Association was the only time a Transcendentalist debated clerical opponents at length and face to face. Parker himself thought the event "significant" and "not unworthy to be remembered," and he took care to make an elaborate record of it.[196]

For some time he had been interested in documenting what had been happening to him. As early as 1841, he had clipped newspaper stories and set aside letters related to the controversy, mostly sent to him by fellow Unitarian clergy. By late 1844, he had bound both collections in notebooks, which he kept on hand for the rest of his life; he supplemented notes to the correspondence volume as late as 1855.[197]

He preserved his account of the "Conference with the Boston Association" in his journal. Usually, his journal was a spontaneous and intimate document; entries were composed quickly and meant for his eyes only. There was nothing spontaneous, however, about the "Conference" narrative. Parker set aside fully twenty pages at the outset, then worked for weeks writing, revising, and adding documentation. His intended audience was posterity, as he makes explicit in the first line, a suggestion that what follows be published in 1899, "*as a memorial of the 19th century.*"[198]

No one else involved in the event cared to remember it so minutely. Ezra Gannett, in his diary for 23 January, wrote only, "Convers[ation]. with Parker 3 hours." The minutes of the Boston Association, meanwhile, provide a mere *aperçu* of the discussion. They indicate that the Brethren told Parker, "without a dissenting voice," that his *Discourse of Religion* and other publications had "Deistical & Infidel character & tendencies," and that Parker had responded by "plainly . . . [avowing] himself a Disbeliever in the 'supernatural' claims of the New Testament." The Brethren also objected that Parker's "Hollis Street Council" article and other writings were "unjust & ungenerous to his professional associates"; Parker replied he was "not responsible for the inferences that might be drawn from his words, and that he was not prepared to soften or take back anything he had said." Finally, Parker is recorded to have "avowed his intention to remain a member [of the Association] unless the Brethren themselves should exclude him."[199]

For the Brethren, in sum, the conference ended in frustration and impasse, which may explain why Gannett, who in his diary had described the 14 November meeting regarding Parker "very animated" and "very satisfactory," in this case tersely avoided all adjectives. Parker gave the conference different treatment because he saw it differently—not only as an informal heresy trial, and so the baldest example of Unitarian illiberalism, but also as the emotional climax of his ordeal, the moment when feelings long suppressed burst to the surface.

As Parker portrayed the event, he was the humble, faithful young cleric, facing down an array of older, more esteemed, more powerful, but blind or hypocritical teachers. Parker was indeed outnumbered, and his opponents all pastored churches larger, and in most cases far wealthier, than he did. Yet there is another way of viewing the scene. He was now more famous than any of his interlocutors. And in this situation he was more powerful than they, for the outcome of the meeting rested largely with him.

Here is the scene. The Association gathers, in a dim winter afternoon, at the townhouse of Robert Cassie Waterston, who pastored one of the two

Unitarian Chapels for the Poor in Boston. Attendance is high—fully twenty, besides Parker, crowd into Waterston's second-floor parlor to take tea. Parker finds Dr. Frothingham, Dr. Parkman, and Ezra Gannett present and primed to talk. Samuel Lothrop is at the meeting, as is George Putnam. Also there, and treating him coolly, are George Ellis, his old divinity school classmate and former fellow editor of the *Scriptural Interpreter*, and Alexander Young, the minister who had officiated at Parker's wedding. Meanwhile, Parker's most conspicuous ally, John Pierpont, is absent—perhaps so that the "Hollis Street" article could be freely discussed. The only comparatively friendly faces in the room are those of John Sargent, who had given Parker an exchange in December 1841 and refused to rule out exchanging with him again, Nathaniel Hall, who continued to call Parker a Christian, and Charles Shackford, who had yet to condemn the preacher of his ordination sermon. Yet these three men think Parker at least partly mistaken, especially in his naturalistic interpretation of Jesus, and here, in the presence of their colleagues and ministerial elders, they seem reluctant to raise their voices on Parker's behalf.

With tea completed, a little after six o'clock, Dr. Parkman calls the conference to order and states with "a considerable degree of embarrassment" the business of the evening. Dr. Frothingham tells how the Association had felt a "delicacy" about discussing Parker in his absence. Chandler Robbins, pastor of the Second Church and scribe of the Association, reads the carefully worded resolution requesting Parker's attendance. Frothingham lays down a rule for the ensuing talk: Brother Parker "is not to catechize us, nor are we to catechize him."[200]

Preliminaries completed, Frothingham plunges *in medias res*, reiterating what he had written to Parker a few weeks earlier: they can remain personally friendly, but could have no more ministerial intercourse, because the *Discourse of Religion* is a "*vehemently deistical*" book that "*aims to dissolve Christianity in the great Ocean of absolute truth.*" Next, Dr. Parkman objects to Brother Parker's article on the Hollis Street Council because it "reflects on members of the Ass[ociation]." Parkman confirms Frothingham's judgment of the *Discourse*, but reminds everyone that the "*Doctrines of the Book are not a matter of discussion.*"[201]

Parker, now given the floor, responds with a long speech—one he seems to have been thinking about for weeks. He takes the spirit of their resolution, but sees "no good" can result from their meeting. He turns to a topic that Frothingham and Parkman evidently had not expected to discuss: ministerial fellowship. Parker claims he had "never complained on that account . . . felt an illnatured emotion, nor uttered an illnatured word respecting them, or any of them on that ground." (A scholar familiar with Parker's journal and correspondence must question these assertions, but he is quite correct in regard to his *public* pronouncements.) In passing, Parker mentions he had collected "very curious *letters*" regarding the South Boston ordination, a few from clergymen declining to exchange with him when they had agreed to do so before; these "might be printed after my death, or before it" (a possibility that Nathaniel Hall, who had written two of the letters, must have found discomforting to hear). The principal effects of your treatment of me, Parker continues, is that I was asked to deliver the "Religion" lectures and then the "Six Plain Sermons," and that thousands of people have come to hear me. Such, says Parker, has been the effect of your actions on the public. On me, he adds blandly (and inaccurately), your treatment has "had no effect." [202]

Turning to the *Discourse*, Parker pronounces "curious" their decision to discuss a theological book while forbidding discussion of the "subjects of the book," or "the doctrines on which we differed, or were alleged to differ." Parker apparently is well prepared to talk on just these topics, but he agrees to avoid "touching doctrines so far as it was possible." As he is "not to be catechized," he would "avoid catechizing others." [203]

Parker now launches on a rather technical (and to his audience, probably exasperating) defense of his theology. He challenges their definition of "deism." Although the term, broadly construed, referred to anyone who rejected the supernatural claims of Christianity, all deists Parker knows of "*deny the possibility of direct inspiration from God.*" By contrast, the "cardinal point" of his own system is that "all men" are "inspired just in proportion to their *quantity of Being* & their *quality of obedience.*" Therefore, he does "not come under the caption," or if he were a deist, he must be put in a class by himself, and then it would be "arbitrary to . . . call me by a name that did not describe my belief."

Parker denies his writings are "subversive of Christianity." In his own opinion, they are "*most Christian.*" Christianity, he elaborates, is either less than the Absolute Religion, the same as the Absolute Religion, or the Absolute Religion and something more. No one, he assumes "for argument's sake," would admit the first proposition; he affirms the second; they, as he understands them, the third. Therefore, "if they would first point out the precise *quiddity* that made Abs[olute]. Rel[igion]. Christianity they would do a great service. That other sects, defined the *shibboleth* of Christianity to their mind, but the Unitarians had no *symbolical books* & therefore a young man like myself & not learned finds a difficulty."

Parker must know that the answer to his question is "miracles" and the "authority of Christ," and that his colleagues do not regard these as "quiddities"; his reference to himself as "not learned," meanwhile, sounds almost cute. This attempt to score a debater's point is not appreciated, and when he turns to ask Dr. Frothingham "*to tell just what it was in which Christianity dif-*

fered from Abs[olute]. Rel[igion].," Frothingham cuts him short: *"I will remind Mr. Parker that he is not to* CATECHIZE *me."* [204]

Having been stopped on the subject of the *Discourse,* Parker turns to his article on the Hollis Street Council. It is "no wonder," he somewhat circumspectly begins, that men take "different views of that affair. I could not expect *them* to take the same view as myself." Gannett interrupts him—and finally unburdens what had been on his mind since the October *Dial* appeared. To Parker, he seems "very angry," but takes "great pains to keep cool." [205]

Gannett confronts his accuser: in your article, he says, you "held up the Council to the scorn & derision of mankind, representing them as a set of hypocrites, & double dealing knaves," and called the "Result in Council" a *"Jesuitical document."* As I was one of the council, and the one that drew up the "Result," you have traduced me; represented me as a "double-dealing & base man"; undertaken to weaken my influence, ruin my character with the world and my own congregation, and, so far as your influence went, you have done so. Gannett continues in this vein "at length, in language & manner which are peculiar to him." [206]

Parker cannot honestly respond that he did not mean Gannett when he wrote (although he seems to have had Dr. Parkman in mind more than Gannett), so he tries to sidestep the charge. One man, he points out, says I slandered the Brethren in my sermon of "Pharisees," another that I slandered them in the conclusion of the South Boston sermon, Mr. Gannett that I held him up to scorn in the article on the Hollis Street Council. In each case, "I am not accountable for their inference." [207]

George Ellis says he does believe Parker meant the Association when he denounced clerical hypocrisy in the "Pharisees" and the South Boston sermon. Ellis quotes an unnamed "orthodox gentleman in the country" who had told him that " 'You [Unitarians] have *maddened* Parker & in this way he shows his *spite*. He is in your confidence, & knew what you talk about in the Ass[ociation]. & tells your secrets.' " To this charge, Parker has a defense: the "madd[en]ing" did not begin until May 1841, but the "Pharisees" was written in December 1840. The sermon, he adds (with unintended humor?), refers to various classes of Pharisee, and "nobody complained but the Ministers"! Parker insists he "meant no personalities" in either that sermon or the "Transient and Permanent." [208]

Gannett jerks the conversation back to the Hollis Street Council. Since Mr. Parker refuses to say plainly that "he did not mean us," declares Gannett flatly, "I will take it for granted that he does." He presses Parker once more to clarify his "Hollis Street" article. Parker again says he "meant *no particular & definite persons, or body of men*" in either the South Boston Sermon or the "Pharisees." He aimed to expose sin and Phariseeism wherever they were—if in the Association, then there—but he had no "definite individuals" in mind when he wrote. The "Hollis Street" article, he finally concedes, "stands on a different ground," for in that case "it is plain who was meant." To that article he has "nothing to alter, or add."

A chorus of rebukes rises from around the room: "You called the Result in Council a *Jesuitical document*!" "You brought together a great deal of matter about Ecclesiastical Councils and about cowards and knaves and hypocrites. It meant somebody. I suppose it meant *us*!" "I did not read it very carefully for I disliked it so much!" "You quoted the words of somebody, 'Expect no justice from the Council,' as if you endorse them!"[209]

Parker breaks in. The offending prediction in fact came from the universally respected Henry Ware Jr., but Parker cannot say so, as Ware had spoken to him in confidence. So Parker says he did not "endorse" the words, because as they came from "a grave & wise man they require no endorsement of mine."[210]

"But you applied them" as if you expected no justice.

"I did so then, and I do so now." I expected no justice from the council at the time. When I wrote I considered the "Result" a most Jesuitical document and "*think so still*."[211]

As he says this, Parker notices portly Alexander Young—himself a signer of the "Result." The expression of the minister who had married him to Lydia, Parker thinks, was "such as I never saw surpassed for malignity in any human face"—and (recalling his life with Lydia and Lucy), "I have seen strange things in that way, too."[212]

Parker tries to defend himself from the charge of spitefulness. He says that he had not wished to write the article; that he had asked others to do so (probably George Ripley, and maybe Edmund Quincy), but they had refused; that he had consulted with "several persons," telling them the view he should take, and that they had told him to "*go on*"; that he had written "*carefully, deliberately, conscientiously*." Before he published, Parker had told what he would say to "one clergyman, who had no affinity with me, a man abler than any other, distinguished for good sense & piety" (Parker means Henry Ware Jr.) who had said, " '*You are right. Say it in God's name.*' " Parker also had read the article to another, "who had little theological affinity with me" (he means Quincy, no Transcendentalist despite his anticlerical bent), who had responded that " 'it ain't much for you to write, & I have but this criticism to make, that you have been too severe on . . . Mr. Pierpont, & not half severe enough on the Council.' "[213]

Gannett has heard enough. If, he says, Mr. Parker "can't disown what he has said," and as he is "no doubt" conscientious "we can't ask him to do so"— "I will say that I freely & from my heart forgive him, as I hope God Allmighty will forgive me—but I can never grasp him by the hand again cordially." After this declaration, everyone in the room stops addressing Parker as "Brother."[214]

Gannett turns from this painful subject back to the *Discourse of Religion*. He now gives the answer, obvious and unsurprising, to Parker's still-hanging question, as to what "quiddity" must be "added" to Absolute Religion and Morality to make it Christianity: "*Miracles*," says Gannett, and the "*authority of Christ*." Parker, all cuteness gone, gives a straightforward, logical reply: I make Christianity Love to Man and Love to God. Admitting miracles were performed, "for argument's sake," I do not see how they affect the case, making that true and a duty which was not so before. Moreover, I do "not believe the fact of [Jesus] working miracles as a general thing." It is "by no means certain that the 4 Gospels came from the men to whom they were ascribed," and if they did, I "cannot take their word in the circumstances of the case." Parker admits, as he had in the *Discourse*, that he had "no philosophical objection to a miracle," by his own definition of it, but he demands "more *evidence than for a common event*."[215] Then, cries someone, you are plainly no *Christian*, for Christianity was a *supernatural and miraculous revelation*. That "might be," answers Parker, "*but it had not been shown to be such*."

Dr. Frothingham at this point interrupts to challenge Parker's earlier definition of deism. There was, says Frothingham, a deist who believed in direct inspiration: Edward Lord Herbert of Cherbury. To this, Parker makes no reply (although a few weeks later, he will look up and read several works by the seventeenth-century thinker, whose life he will pronounce both "strong" and "heroic").

Continuing, he calls "preposterous" the attempt to make miracles the "*shibboleth* of Christianity," the way Trinitarians made a shibboleth of the Trinity, or Catholics of the Church. Nobody, he says, has accused me of preaching less than Absolute Morality and Religion, and if these can be had without Christianity, "what was the use of Christianity—?" It is a mistake, in Parker's view, to make Absolute Religion one thing and Christianity another.[216]

Parker's remarks prompt yet another member of the Association to announce that ministerial intercourse with him is impossible: "He denies the miracles." Parker answers that this was "only a *theological* matter at best." The theological line between us, Parker notes, was drawn immediately after the South Boston Sermon. He tells of his initial surprise that the "Transient and Permanent" had such an effect on the Unitarian ministers, of his opinion that the discourse was poor, of his illness when he was writing it. When the trouble started, recalls Parker, I looked around, to see who would stand by me, and I "have not been disappointed in general," for I "knew the ministers pretty well. But in two. . . ."[217]

Here Parker is interrupted, but Dr. Frothingham recalls him to the point: "Mr. P[arker] says there are *two* things. I want to hear that." Parker resumes his sentence: I have not been disappointed in general. But in two *"persons I have been disappointed*—grievously *disappointed."* Parker is thinking of Alvan Lamson and Convers Francis, but as he speaks he looks "full upon" Frothingham, and Frothingham's face falls. He recovers quickly, however, so Parker does not bother to correct the misapprehension.[218]

Meanwhile, Chandler Robbins is raising a new issue. As Mr. Parker finds "the feeling in respect to him so general," says Robbins, *"I think it is his duty to withdraw from the Association."* Others agree: You "hurt our usefulness" and "compromise our position."[219]

Parker's answers this challenge in the same way as when Dr. Parkman first had issued it, more than a year earlier. If his "personal feelings alone were concerned," he declares, I would "gladly" withdraw, but "as the right *of free inquiry*" is concerned, while "the *world standeth*" I will never do so.[220] Young again looks furious. Dr. Frothingham announces that if this were "a meeting *of free inquirers*" he would *"very soon withdraw."* Parker reminds him that theological agreement had never been required in the Association; the organization once had contained both Unitarians and Trinitarians. "The difference between Trinitarians and Unitarians is a difference *in* Christianity," answers Frothingham emphatically. "The difference between Mr. P[arker]. and the Ass[ociation]. is a difference between no Christianity & Christianity." Adds Gannett: we do not deny you are a Christian man, only that your book is not Christian, on account of its rejection of the miracles.

Someone else suggests that Parker would not be admitted to the Association now that his opinions are known, and that therefore he had either changed his opinions since he came or came with opinions not known to the Association, and that in either case he ought to withdraw. To this argument, Parker replies that he had not been examined as to his opinions on admission, nor asked to promise never to change them. If he had done the Association an injury, they had "had the remedy in their hands" and "could pass a vote of expulsion, any time." Parker in effect is daring them either to live up to their liberal professions and accept him, or break openly with these professions and expel him, but not to profess one thing and do another. Meanwhile, he continues to insist that it is "a new thing" for the "shibboleth" of Christianity among Unitarians to be miracles.[221]

The discussion has nowhere to go and degenerates into a series of attacks and recriminations. Parker tries to get Dr. Frothingham to admit his statement about Christianity not needing the Jachin and Boaz of prophecy and miracle, but Frothingham denies that he had said any such thing. George Ellis describes feeling *"shôcked"* on reading, in the *Discourse of Religion*, that Parker excused Jesus for "treating the Ph[arisees]. ill" on the grounds of his youth.

Parker tries to explain what he meant, which leads only to a testy exchange. Robert Waterston, the host of the meeting, tells Parker that he "*dipped his pen in Gall when he wrote, & his razor in oil.*" The lamp-lit room grows hotter and stuffier.[222]

At last, Cyrus Bartol decides to relieve the tension. The minister of the West Church speaks in praise of Parker's sincerity and high moral character. Then Gannett, perhaps to Parker's surprise, does the same, "at length, & with his usual earnestness." Chandler Robbins starts to follow in the same vein — but Parker bursts into tears. Rising quickly, he shakes hands with Waterston and hastens downstairs to the entry. He finds there Dr. Frothingham, who had stepped out a little before. Frothingham shakes his hand "with apparent cordiality" and hopes he will come by to visit. Parker, still moist-eyed, puts on his wrapper and steps out into the cold street. A clock bell tolls nine.[223]

PARKER REFUSED to renounce his formal affiliation with the Boston Association or the Unitarian denomination, yet savage storms of bitter feeling had toppled one by one his former idols among the liberal clergy. Eventually only two still stood on their pedestals — Dr. Channing and Henry Ware Jr. Parker continued to adulate Channing as a "great man & a good man" and love Ware as possessed of more "religious genius" than any other Unitarian clergyman.[224] Yet death stole even these icons from him, taking Channing in October 1842 and Ware the following September.

Channing had retired before the South Boston ordination, Ware in the midst of the controversy. The Federal Street pastor had ceased preaching in the spring of 1840, in part because he was increasingly feeble, and in part because he felt a growing distance from his congregation, which had failed to support his liberal stand on slavery. Thereafter he lived quietly, often at Newport or in the country, coming forward a few times to publish an article or letter. In August 1842, he mustered his strength to deliver what turned out to be his last address, and most unqualified declaration in favor of abolition, to an antislavery gathering at Lenox. Ware, meanwhile, had suffered what seems to have been a heart attack in January 1842. Much weakened, he decided to resign his position at the divinity school, effective in July, thereby creating the opening that Convers Francis filled. In April 1843 he was seized by "apoplexy" (probably a stroke), which left him bedridden, and in August had another seizure, which left him almost comatose until he "passed on." Until this final prostration, he kept planning good works.[225]

Parker knew neither Channing nor Ware wholly approved of his course, but neither publicly rebuked him, for which he was grateful. He privately turned to both men for advice and approval during his ordeal, and both gave him some of each. To Channing, he sent a copy of the *Transient and Permanent*, perhaps hoping for a benediction. This he did not receive; instead, in

July 1841 he got an assessment he thought "desultory" and "very queer." Yet Channing obviously intended to be kind. "The great idea of the discourse, the immutableness of Christian truth, I respond to entirely," Channing wrote. Although he "grieved" that Parker "did not give some clear, direct expression of his belief in Christian miracles," Channing insisted that his criticisms were those of a friend, and that Parker's "honest, earnest" spirit must speak out "fully and freely." As for Ware, Parker knew that his former teacher had "no affinity" with Transcendentalist innovations in theology or devotional practice, yet Parker sought and received his blessing before attacking the Hollis Street Council.[226]

When Channing died (peacefully in his bed, gazing out the window at a Berkshire sunset), Parker lamented in his journal that "so many are left when such are taken." He believed he carried on the great man's work better than most who eulogized him and preached a glowing eulogy of his own, which he later published at the solicitation of "hearers and friends." Since Washington, Parker here declared, "no man has died amongst us whose real influence was so wide, and so beneficent, both abroad and at home" as that of Dr. Channing. Parker praised Channing especially for doing "more to liberalize theology than any man now living," and for being a "rare instance of . . . a preacher that denounced the sins of his time." As for Ware, he died days after Parker sailed for Europe, so there was no possibility to preach a commemorative discourse. But Parker later judged Ware the last minister eminent for *religion* to die in Boston.[227]

In this assessment, Parker made an unfavorable judgment on Ware's Unitarian successors. The same harsh opinion runs through Parker's Channing sermon, in which he rather coolly referred to "a 'more liberal' sect called Unitarians" who disclaim "the most revolting doctrines of the old school," but halt "between life and death, between the liberty of the Spirit, and the thraldom of the letter." Parker also praised Channing for having gone in theology "farther than his former friends, to some [Transcendentalist] conclusions logically unavoidable, but now vehemently denied."[228]

While Parker exalted the memory of Ware and Channing in part to criticize his contemporaries, he also recognized that he was moving far beyond what either man would have endorsed, both in the radical nature of his ideas and in the confrontational, popular way he expressed them. Amid his encomiums for Channing, Parker identified one shortcoming: his subject had been "cautious and timid both in thought and action." Again, he particularly praised Channing for having refused to "quarrel with a theology because its circle was wider than his own"—in other words, as wide as Parker's own.[229]

PARKER LATER attributed his decision to leave for Europe to his "health becoming feeble, thro' excessive work & other causes perhaps"; the "other causes" he does not name, although he surely meant the emotional hardships he had endured. Meanwhile, the amount of work he did during the same period was indeed staggering. Between the South Boston ordination and his boarding a ship for New York 28 months later, he read at least 109 books (most of them scholarly tomes in languages other than English, and many of them multivolume), preached 221 times, lectured at least 64 times, wrote 194 sermons and 14 lectures, and published over 2,000 pages of material, including 3 pamphlets, 5 lengthy articles for the *Dial*, and 3 books: the *Discourse of Religion*, a collection of *Critical and Miscellaneous Writings*, and—at long last—his translation and expansion of *De Wette on the Old Testament*, in two massive quarto volumes.[230]

Parker had prepared the *Writings* in late 1842 (the preface is dated 28 December) and it went on sale early the following year, published by the respectable firm of James Monroe. In this little octavo, Parker gathered ten of what he considered his most important and enduring essays and sermons, as well as two inspirational parables, one about Paul, the other about Socrates. Everything in the book had been written since 1840 (earlier material Parker seems to have regarded as juvenilia) and all but the Socrates story had seen print before, in the *Dial*, the *Examiner*, or as a pamphlet.

The *Writings* indicates the varied public roles Parker had assumed as a reformer and intellectual. He makes recondite scholarship widely accessible and in the process challenges popular beliefs ("Strauss's Life of Jesus," "Primitive Christianity," "The Life of Saint Bernard," "German Literature," "Thoughts on Theology"); he assaults religious ideas and practices he finds false ("The Christianity of Christ, of the Church, of Society," "Transient and Permanent in Christianity," "The Pharisees"); he issues calls for general reform of society based on a recognition of individual worth and of human spiritual potential ("Thoughts on Labor," "Education of the Laboring Classes"). The two parables, meanwhile, show in brief compass his spiritual appeal—a mixture of sober, quiet self-culture that had sweeping social significance, and thrilling martyrdom that provided inner consolation. "How to Move the World" tells how the young Socrates learned that to reform everything, he must first reform himself. "Truth against the World," meanwhile, contrasts the "meek" young Paul with an arrogant, worldly Pharisee, who sneers at him for having taken up the cause of "the Nazarene," thereby relinquishing a life of "ease and fame" for one of "toil, infamy, and death." Paul replies that "I am ready to spend and be spent in the cause of Truth," whereupon the rabbi denounces him as a "fool" and an "unbelieving atheist." Years later, the rabbi learns with satisfaction that Paul lay in chains at Rome—but Paul himself was joyful, for the voice of God was in his heart, telling him, "In thee I am well pleased."[231]

The publication of the *Writings* showed how much Parker had "come to take his place among the more prominent writers of the country." As an anonymous reviewer of the book pointed out, the "gauntlet" Parker had run since 1841, being "denounced and persecuted" by the "narrower sort" and "extolled by the more liberal," had made a great many people curious to read whatever he wrote. Even those who thought him sometimes "extravagant" were attracted to his writings, with their "passages of brilliant and striking rhetoric," "beautiful and novel phrases," "sarcastic flings and denunciations," "bursts of pathos and indignation," and "heart stirring appeals." Even more, they were attracted to Parker himself, with his "pure and quick sensibilities," his strong "integrity of purpose," and lofty aims:

> The world is lying in wickedness before him, the State corrupt and the Church dying, and he burns to bring in higher modes of thought and life. With the impatient ardor of youth, he hurls his javelins and thunders at the abuses and men of the past. He pours out wild, furious, withering denunciations of the miserable chaunters [*sic*] of heartless hymns, and shrivelled changers of the temple-money. He can not away with the sleepy and droning dispensers of God's boundless grace. With the strong arm of a spiritual *Coeur de Lion*, he strikes his battle-axe into the rotten timbers of the church, till the welkin rings again. A brave, hearty, right noble young reformer is Mr. Parker.[232]

New opportunities were opening before Parker, but he did not see them; he had fixed his eyes not on what he was gaining, but on what he had lost. The future, after all, was but a shimmering unknown, while the present was both painfully tangible and problematic. He remained minister of a tiny parish and financially dependent on Aunt Lucy. His new audience was large, but of doubtful loyalty, and his new friends had not yet been able to replace his old ones. Then, too, he had not abandoned his original plan to make a mark on the world as a great religious scholar. As testament to this persistent ambition, he published his monumental *De Wette*.

Parker had built this 1,100-page edifice over seven years, penning the manuscript on hundreds of large quarto fascicles. Translating the German (rather freely) into English had been straightforward work, which Parker had largely completed by 1837 (although he had revised the text in 1840, when De Wette put out a new German edition). Much more demanding had been Parker's labor clarifying and expanding what De Wette had written. While the German had addressed fellow *Professoren*, Parker aimed at a broader readership of American clergymen and theological students, few of whom he anticipated having the languages or the library to make much sense of an unamplified text. Where De Wette provided quotations only in the original tongues, Parker provided translations; where De Wette indicated with citations that the reader should compare two biblical passages, Parker provided the full texts of each, often in translations of his own, placed in parallel columns to make the comparisons easier. He inserted (in brackets, to mark them off) translated excerpts from all relevant scholars and sources he could find, modern and ancient; he also added his own commentary and, in an appendix to the first volume, several original catalogues and essays. His own contributions were sometimes significant, and his opinions were generally more radical than those of the author. Parker added as well a long chapter, in the first volume, from De Wette's introduction to the Christian canon, which Parker considered prefatory to an *Introduction to the New Testament* that "I intend, at some future day, to prepare." He considered calling the final product an *Introduction on the basis of De Wette*, rather than a *Translation of De Wette's Introduction*, although in the end he settled on the latter title as "more modest."[233]

He actually would have had the book in press much earlier had not controversy engulfed him. Only a few weeks before he preached at the South Boston ordination, he had written to William Silsbee that he thought the work was ready for the printer. He was so preoccupied with other matters that year, especially writing the "Religion" lectures, that he did not mail off any part of the manuscript to the publisher, Little and Brown, until the middle of November. Six weeks later, Parker wrote to Silsbee that the book was "in press," and that it would come "out of the Press" in five or six months. But for the first five months of 1842 he was preoccupied with finishing the *Discourse*, after which he was too exhausted to work as hard as he would have liked. Nonetheless, by October 1842, three hundred pages of the book had been stereotyped, and by Christmas, Parker had brought to the printer everything but the introduction and the appendix, which he thought still required "a little looking over and rectification." Yet the introduction is dated fully eight months later—23 August 1843, the day before his thirty-third birthday. There are various possible reasons for the delay. For one thing, Parker had an impulse to revise. "What has often been hammered I take back to the anvil again," he wrote in a letter, "to file over the filed and linger over the [manuscript] with a superstitious regard for the accuracy of quotations, references, etc. etc." Then, too, he was busy with other work, including writing and delivering the "Six Plain Sermons." Also, he had agreed with Little and Brown to pay the stereotyping costs; he may have printed the book as quickly as he could afford to do so.[234]

The end result is remarkably straightforward to read, especially considering its vast scope and complex, often technical subject matter. More important, the *De Wette* provides a massive buttress of data to support Parker's skeptical position on the authority of Scripture. No one could peruse the book, or even parts of it, without developing an overwhelming sense that the Hebrew canon emerged from a long, contentious historical process; that the individual books composing it were themselves composites, being almost all the work of multiple, usually unknown, authors and editors; that the different books, and often different parts of the same book, stood at cross-purposes with one another. The Greek canon, meanwhile, as Parker's section on it indicates, had a similarly complex history. The unstated question hanging over the two volumes is, How can anyone who looks closely and honestly at the Bible regard it as having miraculous, infallible authority?

The *De Wette* received some notice (although never a long review in America), and it sold about as well as could have been expected, going through three editions in fifteen years. Parker thought of it as the first of many major scholarly efforts; besides planning a critical introduction to the New Testament, Parker began to envision writing a universal history of religion. Despite Parker's best intentions and extraordinary labors, he never completed either book. The *De Wette* stands as a giant, solitary marker indicating a road untaken.

PARKER BEGAN to think seriously of a European sabbatical in the fall or winter of 1842; by February or March 1843, he was writing out a Parker family genealogy in his journal, probably thinking of researching it further in England. By May, he had made definite plans for himself and Lydia to leave the country in September and had started searching for supply preachers to fill his pulpit. He could not finance the trip himself, but he had at least two offers of help. A generous one came from his church, but he declined it, because "a friend" supplied him the means. The surviving documents do not identify this patron, but as Parker generally avoided taking more money than he had to from Aunt Lucy, the most likely candidate is his confidante and neighbor, the wealthy George Russell. Parker also began gathering letters of introduction to use abroad (Emerson gave him one to Carlyle) and booked passage for two on a vessel leaving New York bound for Liverpool.[235]

After months of arranging and weeks of packing came time for him to take leave of the Spring Street Church. For the morning service that Sunday, 3 September, Parker delivered a discourse on Jesus, whom he imagined suffering most from the kind of sentimental agony he had himself endured. Jesus' external trials—his imprisonment, torture, death—Parker dismissed as "light things" to a man "filled with burning thought." No, Parker insisted, Jesus' worst pains were not physical and outward but spiritual and inward. They came from the lack of sympathy he received. They came from finding the Truth he preached met with "misunderstanding & scorn," while the false counsel of the Pharisee won acceptance: "To a young man, simple, unused to the world, enthusiastic, here must have been an exquisite disappointment." Similarly, Jesus' greatest joys were spiritual and inward, the knowledge that Truth and the Father were with him.[236]

From this implicit commentary on his own situation, Parker turned in the afternoon to an explicit one. A throng arrived to hear what he would say, many coming from Boston and surrounding towns. Among those present was a young Brook Farmer, Marianne Dwight, who found every "nook & corner" of the little meetinghouse filled, and faces looking in at the doors.[237] The preacher rose to the occasion. "The sermon was long, giving a full & faithful account of his ministry from the beginning," summarized Dwight in a letter written later that day. "How clear, how earnest & how eloquent! Never was he bolder! he has made a clean breast of it, and thrown the whole burden off his soul."

Parker's "Of My Own Stewardship" is both an autobiography and a Transcendentalist confession of faith. It was the first of several such works he would write over the course of his career, culminating sixteen years later in his famous *Experience as a Minister*.[238] "My Own Stewardship," which was never published, is more intimate and emotional than its successors.

After opening the sermon with the exciting warning that he would discuss himself and his doings "using great plainness of speech," Parker turns to a topic he often had treated before, the functions of a minister. The most obvious antecedent of this part of the discourse was his article on the Hollis Street Council, completed almost exactly a year earlier; the preacher even uses as one of his texts the same words of St. Paul that he had quoted in the essay: "I have not failed to declare unto you the whole counsel of God" (Acts 20:27). As before, Parker declares that a minister is to "teach Truth" and to "promote Goodness & Piety," and lays out a stark choice each clergyman must make: shall he teach all the Truth he can get and promote Religion in the highest possible degree? Or shall he teach only such Truth as is popularly believed and only promote Religion insofar as Religion is already popular?[239]

Strange as it may seem, says Parker, some men had "conscientious scruples" about teaching the whole Truth. He testifies that he has been told by more than one man, and more than once, that pure Truth is only for learned divines: the people "cannot bear it," and are not to be trusted with it, while a "little delusion in matters pertaining to Religion helps the world a great deal." There were also differences of opinion about teaching religion—"not *conscientious* differences of opinion," says Parker, but at any rate *practical* ones. Some say, "You must never contend with a popular sin, nor give judgment while an important matter is getting determined. The rage of a Sect—the rage of a Party—if powerful—must be left without rebuke because they are the rage of the Powerful. It is idle attempting to swim against the wind & tide." All that, Parker reports, "I have heard said & often."[240]

A minister's destiny "depends a good deal on the answer he gives to these questions." If he teaches only such Truth as has been accepted, and promotes Religion only so far as it is popular in his time and place, he has "a quite easy time of it." He is praised in all the churches, is called "sound" and "safe," is reckoned "orthodox," is hailed as a "great" man by the newspapers of his sect. Yet he is not a brave, free man, but only a trimmer and time server.[241]

By contrast, the minister who sets himself to teach Truth new and old, welcome and hated, to leave untouched no dangerous and popular error, and rebuke the sins of his time and place, will have "enough to say & enough to do." Behind one new truth he finds another, beneath one vice he finds still more sin, and his "work for life is laid out for him sooner than he is aware." Inevitably he must expose cherished false doctrines and chide the lowness of honorable men. "So from the very nature of the case he must offend men's prejudices & hurt their feelings—offend their dearest prejudices & hurt their tenderest feelings." He will not be reckoned "orthodox," nor called "sound" or "safe." The "champions of untruth & of Sin are banded against him." He is called "Heretic," "Unbeliever," "Infidel," "Atheist." Such "is the treatment which the churches have in store for a Prophet when he comes."[242]

In Parker's judgment, the most pressing danger a clergyman faces is to "succumb to things as they are around him," take popular opinion for Truth and the practice of his neighborhood for Religion. Then "the man becomes a mere thing,—with no independence, no self-respect, no power, a mockery set up in place of a man." There are such ministers, Parker tells his audience; "I have seen such—& so have you." Although born a giant, armed in the panoply of clerical mail, and master of the most crafty skill, "a single shepherd boy with a true heart can bring this boastful champion to the ground & smite off his giant head."[243]

Having laid down this paradigm of the prophet arrayed against the hypocrites, Parker describes his own career, starting with his ordination six years earlier. He then had "no considerable experience of the world, having lived an unobserved life," active and laborious yet "secluded, quiet & obscure." Parker reminds his listeners of the main themes of his preaching: how he had spoken in favor of "sound education for all—intellectual, moral & religious education," championed temperance, and denounced "our treatment of the Indians," "Negro Slavery," and the "Corruption of the Political Parties." These are exciting topics, Parker admits, and some men do not want to hear them in the pulpit. They say, " 'Preach us Religion, the Christian Religion, Christ & him crucified, but let Intemperance and Slavery alone.'" Yet "if I had forborne to speak to you my dearest convictions—you ought to have come & torn me down from this pulpit & trodden me in the dust."[244]

Parker considers his greatest work, however, to be the reform of theology. When he came to West Roxbury, Parker recalls, he "saw that common sense was applied to almost every thing here with us except to Religion." No one wholly trusted reason in this department of inquiry, not even the Unitarians and Universalists; what generally passed for Religion was nothing but "Theology, Formality, Superstition." After extensively investigating the subject of

Religion, he had found that it "is natural to man; that God is the Source of all religions as of all other Truth; that we learn . . . religious Truth as we learn other Truth—by the legitimate exercise of our faculties"; that there was only one kind of Religion, before Christ and after him, but various degrees of Religion; that theology was not Religion; that "Religion was a simple thing—, a natural thing; a reasonable thing"; that the only service God required was "being Good & doing Good." To distinguish this scheme from others, Parker continues, he called it Absolute Religion, "Religion with no limitations, free Goodness, free Piety; free Thought." Parker continues to insist that Jesus of Nazareth taught Absolute Religion and lived it, too, but that "his followers mingled many false doctrines with his pure truths—that some of these false doctrines were found even in the New Testament & many were popular in all the churches." To set forth the Absolute Religion, says Parker, became the main object of his teaching.[245]

He therefore proclaimed the "GREATNESS OF MAN'S NATURE, his vast powers, the capacity for unbounded growth; our duty to aim at Perfection." He aimed to show that there were laws of the soul as well as of the body, and that "man by the legitimate exercise of his powers can as naturally discover Truth, Justice & . . . Ideas relative to Religion with the same certainty that the eyes convers with Light & the ear with Sounds." There were sentiments, ideas, and actions related to Religion. Christian sentiments were to be expressed as ideas, and the ideas applied to life. These ideas must prevail, for they were of God, and God was immanent in both matter and spirit. The providence of God therefore created "a perfect System of Optimism," which we feel more than understand. "I have not taught these results," says Parker, "on the Authority of any Church, any Book, any Man. I have appealed only to Facts. . . . I have tried to teach Absolute Religion—on its own Authority."[246]

The great difficulty Parker says he found in teaching these doctrines was that "they were at variance with the common belief." He denounces this popular theology. It holds that "Religion is not natural to man"; that man is a fallen being; that his conscience and reason are unsafe guides; that God no longer makes revelations; that "the majority of men are born with the seal of eternal damnation burned into them"; that "no man's efforts can save him, but the imputed goodness of another being saves a few from the wrath of an offended God." This version of Christianity is not Absolute Religion, but a "ridiculous compound of superstitious feelings, formal observances, & abominable doctrines." It sends you for religious truth not to God, found through reason, conscience, and affections, but "to the Bible, as the word of God—who has now done speaking." It asks you to pray not in your own name, but that of another, "approaching God through an attorney." It tells you Christ was a miraculous person, a Mediator, through whom alone we can have access to God and eternal life. "It makes Belief more than Life, & by its terrible fear cuts out Love—Love of Men—& Love of God." I learned early, says Parker, "that the strength of the clergy was mainly devoted to keeping up this abominable system," and that the "so called 'liberal Christians' " were but a little less devoted than "the others who made no pretense to liberality."[247]

Parker recounts at some length the story of his hesitating thirteen months (from 1837 to 1839) before he dared preach the "Contradictions in Scripture." In this period of indecision, those he went to for advice counseled him to silence, some telling him he would lose his pulpit if he spoke; yet his only concern, he insists, was fear that he would "hinder the growth of true Religion in the hearts of men." He recalls finally delivering the discourses with a trembling heart, and joyfully discovering that "you were able to bear all that I had to say." He thanks his congregation for allowing him to preach what he thought.[248]

Finally, Parker turns to the "Transient and Permanent in Christianity" (which he rates a "poor" discourse, containing nothing he had not said before) and the controversy surrounding it. When the Orthodox started an outcry against it, Parker believes, the "controlling part" of the Unitarians only joined in the uproar because "they had long been hag-ridden by fear of the Orthodox"; most of his colleagues ceased ministerial fellowship with him because "[f]ear in the churches, like fire in the woods, runs fast & far leaving few spots unburned." Parker insists to his congregation that had they asked him to resign, he would have made a living with his hands and kept preaching: "The fact that a truth was unpopular was the reason why it should be spoken with a thousand tongues." Yet I learned again, Parker says, as in the case with "Contradictions in Scripture," that "I had underrated you . . .—that you could not only stand the Truth but could withstand abuse."[249]

Parker reminds his listeners that he stands "almost alone." What, he asks rhetorically, is the cause of this alienation? "Have I been false to the creed? The Unitarian creed has not yet been written. So far as my power went have I not taught Christian Goodness & Christian Piety? No one denies that." No, Parker asserts, the real evil is that he had "warred against the popular theology," commended "too plainly" Christian Goodness and Christian Piety, and "too openly exposed the Idolatry of the Churches & their sloth."[250]

Parker now issues the strongest public indictment he ever made against the Unitarian clergy. After declaring that most of them, in abandoning him, had behaved as he had expected (although some had shown "a degree of duplicity & malignity" he had not looked for), he takes up the controversy surrounding his denunciation of clerics who say one thing in their studies and preach the opposite in their pulpits. Parker reiterates, as he had in his meeting with the Boston Association, that he never "in any public speech meant to point at any particular person who did this"—that is, not in the "Transient and Permanent," nor in the sermon on the "Pharisees." He intended only to rebuke the evil wherever it existed; he never calumnated particular persons. But, he adds—with Dr. Frothingham, among others, evidently on his mind—"I say now that I have known men, Unitarian ministers, who did say one thing in the study, say it to me & then preach just the opposite in the pulpit—& not only so but warn the public against the doctrines which in private they professed to believe—denouncing to public odium such as believed or taught them. I say this publicly, advisedly, distinctly & with due deliberation well 'knowing' what it is I say & what it means." In the audience, Marianne Dwight sat shocked by this accusation. "Oh! . . ." she wrote a few hours later. "If those ministers have *any* feeling, must they not hide their heads!"[251]

The preacher now brings the discourse to an elegiac end:

> I will not pain you with a long farewell. I cannot trust my own feelings—
> I will not try yours. We have been friends together. The friends must
> part. We have discussed the loftiest themes. For six years our prayers
> have been mingled together. . . . I will not make parting sad; serious it
> must be. . . . I will not ask you to remember me. I know you will not for-
> get. I will only say that your affectionate remembrance of me may never
> blind you to my faults or infirmities; that no doctrine of mine may ever
> stand between you & the truth. Wherever I go the remembrance of
> your kindness will be fresh in my heart; the recollection of these mod-
> est walls, of these familiar faces while they bring tears to my eyes—will
> bring not less joy to my heart. May God bless you & keep you, & lift
> the light of His countenance upon you. May Reason guide you; may
> Religion be your daily Life, your Hope & your Portion forever & ever.
> Farewell.[252]

When Parker stepped down from the pulpit, reported Dwight, many in the audience were crying, and "sobs were heard even from *men*."[253]

TWO DAYS LATER, Theodore and Lydia set sail from a hot, sticky, and op-pressive Boston, bound for New York. He brought with him a number of books, a few sermon manuscripts in case he was asked to preach, and a large blank volume for a travel journal. On the flyleaf, he penciled a sketch of the Spring Street meetinghouse, for remembrance.[254]

The couple arrived on 7 September in Manhattan, where they waited a few days until their transoceanic vessel, the *Ashburton*, found a favorable breeze. Parker improved the time by practicing the mode of energetic, omnivorous gathering of people, sights, and information that he would pursue over the next eleven months. He called on Convers Francis's sister, the celebrated writer and abolitionist Lydia Maria Child, and made the acquaintance of two prominent Unitarian ministers, Isaac T. Hopper and his brother, John; with the latter, he made a snap moral inspection of the city, visiting a Broadway dive, the infamous slum at Five Points, and (as he had done once before, in 1840) the Tombs courthouse and prison. He also attended, with Lydia, a Thursday evening service at St. Paul's, which he predictably found "fussy."[255]

By Saturday, the wind had turned. The two travelers were seen to the ship by a few friends, who left their cabin fragrant with a parting gift of peaches and flowers. Finally, the gangplank was raised, the anchor hoisted, and the *Ashburton* sailed out of New York Harbor into the broad Atlantic. Parker's mind, like the prow of the ship, turned toward Europe.

I Can Stand Alone

Chapter Eight

Recovery, Observation, and Thought

Parker would look back on his year of "recovery, observation, and thought" as "the most profitable in my life, up to that time, in the acquisition of knowledge and in preparing for much that was to follow."[1] He confirmed old opinions, got new ideas, took stock, and even matured. The man who returned to the religious battlefields of Boston in the fall of 1844 was stronger than the one who had fled them the previous summer.

The trip had good effects even though not all parts of it were enjoyable. In Rome he endured a spell of "headache and feverishness," and almost all his ocean voyages, whether over the Atlantic or the Mediterranean, were marred by seasickness. He and Lydia had to endure all the predictable travelers' annoyances: unsatisfactory lodgings and food; lost luggage (a three-day search for a trunk cost them the chance to see Antwerp); failed connections (a missed train cost them the chance to see Edinburgh); and corrupt customs officials (passing from Naples to the Papal States, they had to pay the officers bribes to keep their luggage from being ransacked). Moreover, on the Continent few railroads had as yet been built, so the Parkers went overland almost entirely by public stage coach, often on overnight trips. This mode of transportation was uncomfortable even in the best of circumstances, and the circumstances were not always the best. Parker sometimes complained of miserable seating, bad-smelling travel companions, and coach offices with "an atmosphere that could generate onions."[2]

Parker discovered, too, that his extraordinary facility in reading other tongues was not matched by an ability to speak them. He had been teaching French since his schoolmaster days, but no one in Paris could understand him. He hired a tutor and kept his journal in the language for practice. Again, he had translated thousands of pages of De Wette, Ammon, Herder, Heine, and others, but could complain, after a conversation with a scholar in Berlin, that "I made worse work of German than usual, even."[3]

Despite such frustrations, Parker relished the break from routine. He performed no parish duties, published no essays, delivered no lectures, wrote no sermons, and preached only twice, once on board ship his first full day out from New York, and once, eleven months later, in Liverpool, just two days before he boarded ship back to Boston.

Meanwhile, all the new sights and acquaintances excited him. Observations fill his letters and travel journal. He wrote so much in the latter that well before the trip ended he filled the large book he brought with him and had to buy a second one. Together, the two volumes made up a manuscript of some 630 quarto pages.[4]

Most important, Parker delighted in having thousands of miles between himself and the Boston clergy, himself and Aunt Lucy. This was strong medicine for what ailed him. He became able to see his situation, which at home seemed so dark and parlous, with greater equanimity. He forgot nothing that had been done to him, but he found himself able to write amicable letters to those who in 1842 and 1843 had most disappointed and angered him. Silsbee and Lamson got mail from Parker, while Francis received seven long, jocose missives which together form a kind of humorous travelogue.

THE PARKERS pursued a partly improvised itinerary that took them on a great irregular loop through western and central Europe. They landed in Liverpool, after nearly four tiresome weeks at sea, on 4 October 1843. Over the next fortnight they worked their way southeast across England, making many stops, including at Oxford and Stratford. When they finally reached London, they stayed three weeks. In mid-November, they left for Paris, where they rented an elegantly fitted, if somewhat drafty, little *apartement* on the *rive gauche*, near Saint-Sulpice. After nearly a month and half in the French capital, they continued southeast to Lyons, where they spent Christmas. They passed New Year's Eve in a diligence rattling along the banks of the Rhone toward Avignon.

On 4 January, they sailed from Marseilles for Italy. After some weeks touring northern cities—Genoa, "Leghorn" (Livorno), Pisa, Florence—they sailed south to Naples. There they stayed a week, making an excursion to Pompeii, before taking a carriage up the peninsula into the Papal States.

They reached Rome on 17 February—the Sunday before the Shrove Tuesday festival—and took two cozy rooms in the quarter favored by foreigners, on the Via del Babuino near the Spanish Steps.[5] They tarried in the Holy City longer than in any other stop on their tour, not leaving until 11 April, when they drove north again, through the areas of Italy controlled by the Austrian Empire. Among them was Venice, where on 20 April they marked their seventh wedding anniversary. A week later, they crossed the Brenner pass to Innsbruck and, after passing an evening there, went on into Bavaria.

From Munich, the Parkers traveled by boat down the Danube to Vienna, then by diligence to Prague. Saxony came next, and finally, along the north-ernmost arc of their continental tour, Prussia. They stopped for nearly three weeks in Berlin, staying on the third floor of the British Hotel. Most of June they spent visiting the cities and towns of central and southwestern Germany, many of them lights that glittered brightly in Theodore's intellectual fir-mament (Wittenberg, Weimar, Heidelberg, Tübingen). The Parkers crossed into Basel, Switzerland, on 29 June.

After three weeks touring the Swiss cantons, they began the long trip toward home. They voyaged rapidly down the Rhine to Belgium, where they paused a week, before recrossing the Channel to London on 5 August. After another eight days there, they crossed England once more, this time in a northwesterly direction. Despite a stop in Cambridge, they took just three days to reach Liverpool. On 20 August 1844, they boarded a ship that brought them to Boston at the record-setting pace of twelve days.

THE PARKERS met a few Americans abroad who left behind vivid accounts of them. One of these compatriots was the twenty-year-old future historian Francis Parkman. The handsome son of Theodore Parker's foe Dr. Parkman was willing to overlook his father's animosities in choosing companionship on this, his first tour of the Continent.

He and the Parkers became acquainted at the Hotel de Rome in Naples. Parkman in his journal records a memorable few days spent with them, start-ing on the Sunday morning he and "Mr. Parker" climbed Vesuvius.[6]

Led to the top by local guides, they found a great crater, three or four miles around and a thousand feet deep, its bottom a crust of scarcely cooled lava, criss-crossed with glowing cracks. At the center stood a black cone spew-ing plumes of smoke and a fountain of magma high into the air. Everything was obscured by sulfurous fumes and the whole place echoed with great bel-lowing sounds and "an occasional shock like the report of cannon." Parker pronounced the scene a "lively picture of Hell."[7]

The two Yankees, like most visitors to the volcano in those days, now took a life-threatening closer look, clambering into the cavity with their guides. When they walked on the bottom, their shoes were scorched, and when they thrust their canes into the glowing cracks, the wood caught fire. They found that the smoke nearly choked them, and that ash and tiny fragments of melted rock dusted their shoulders. Encouraged by their guides, they dashed at the central cone with poles, detached small pieces of fresh lava, and carried them a short distance away to cool and have copper coins pressed into them as sou-venirs. Having completed this Sabbath forenoon excursion into the Inferno

("What stock in trade for an orthodox minister!" Parker exclaimed), they descended the mountain, stopping at a house halfway, as was the custom, to sample the Lachrymae Christi wine.[8]

That afternoon, Parker and Parkman rode in a carriage, now accompanied by Lydia and some other Americans, through Naples during the pre-Lenten carnival. It was the day of the grand masked procession. People packed the Toledo and filled the balconies and windows overlooking it. The Americans joined the long train of hackneys and carriages moving slowly up, then back down, the great street, protected from the crowd on either side by columns of motionless mounted dragoons. A huge dragon-shaped float carrying costumed nobles led the way, followed by other carriages full of "masquers," among them Ferdinand II, king of Naples and Sicily. Following custom, the physically massive monarch and his courtiers pelted each other and onlookers with sugar plums. His Royal Highness threw real ones; most of the others hurled pieces of lime or chalk. As the Parkers and Parkman were drawn past the royal party, they were greeted by a fusillade of sugared fruit; one struck Theodore's spectacles and broke a lens. Meanwhile, a formidable plum, thrown from a balcony, hit Lydia on the nose. "She was in great trouble," reports Parkman in his journal, "but there was no such thing as retreat." Theodore later dismissed the whole celebration as "worse than a sport for boys." Parkman noted, however, that there was method behind the madness; the king actually had discouraged the carnival for the past few years and only consented to it now to bring business to distressed tradesmen.[9]

The following Saturday, Parkman and the Parkers left Naples together for Rome. Their diligence, which Parkman thought "ponderous," was drawn by six horses he considered "consumptive."[10] They were too weak, he reports in his journal, to drag the machine up a little hill just a mile from the city. The "postillions spattered and swore *cazzo* and kicked their gigantic boots against the gaunt ribs of the miserable beasts, and lashed till they split their livery jackets"—all to no avail. A dozen "ragamuffins" joined in tugging the wheels, but in vain. Finally, a train of oxen was brought and the trip was resumed.

All at once, however, there was a "*crack*" from below, followed by a jounce. Lydia screamed. The carriage stopped again. A spring had been broken. After arguing for half an hour, the conductor and postillions decided to take the equipment back to Naples. Three hours later the passengers were refitted and on the road once more.

According to Parker's journal, he approached Rome with a copy of Horace in hand. Parkman records in his journal that as they drove within sight of St. Peter's and saw everywhere around them temples, aqueducts, and tombs, Parker "became inspired, and spouted Cicero and Virgil," while his wife grew "full of curiosity to know everything and see everything"; as they passed each ruin down the Via Appia, she studied it in her guidebook.[11]

Finally, the party reached the massive city walls. At the San Giovanni Gate, they were met by a mounted guard (Theodore called him a "centurion"), who escorted them in. "We passed through the grand and imposing streets of the new city," writes Parkman in his journal, "with the soldier following behind. Mrs. Parker made a sudden exclamation 'Oh, only do look here; *do* tell me what this is!' Her husband burst out with rather an untheological interjection, and caught me by the shoulder, 'The Coliseum!' But we had only time to look up at mountain of gigantic arches, piled one on the other, when we were buried in the streets below." [12]

Parkman soon left the Parkers in Rome as he went on with his adventures. But there were other Americans for them to meet—probably more than a hundred in the city that season. [13] Two that the Parkers befriended were Dr. Samuel Gridley Howe and his bride, the much younger Julia Ward Howe. Julia was not yet known as a poet or champion of women's education; she was then a celebrated belle from New York who had wed a famous Bostonian. In the winter of 1844, she was pregnant with their first child. Her dashing, bearded husband had made a name for himself more than twenty years earlier as a Philhellene, going overseas to fight with the Greek patriots in their war of independence against the Turks. Returning home a hero, he had gone on to win even greater fame as a pioneering educator of the blind and the first person successfully to educate a child both blind and deaf.

In January 1841, Parker had written in his journal on the character of this "wonderful child," a girl named Laura Bridgman, after reading a report Howe had published about her progress. Sometime, probably later, he and Howe had established a slight acquaintance; Parker respected Howe's philanthropy, while Howe liked Parker's theological independence and sympathy for reform. As for Julia, she and Parker were strangers. The first report of him she ever heard (she had been reared an Episcopalian) was as the Unitarian who had preached an impious and sacrilegious sermon at South Boston. When she actually read the *Transient and Permanent in Christianity*, however, she had been surprised to find it full of a "reverent and appreciative" spirit. [14]

Now, in Rome, her husband invited the Parkers to dinner. Many years later, Julia remembered the striking discrepancy between Parker's "youthful energy" and his "quite bald" head. She also considered the contrast between his combative countenance and Lydia's "mild" one to be greater even "than the usual [!] . . . between husband and wife." The two couples hit it off and saw each other frequently over the next few weeks. They even considered going to Greece together. Parker wrote in a letter that Dr. Howe was "the same man in Rome as at Boston, engaged in good works, looking out [for] the lame, the halt and the *blind*. I admire him more and more." [15]

After Julia went into confinement and was safely delivered of a daughter, the happy father asked his new friend (who also happened to be the only

American clergyman in the city) to christen her Julia Romana. Mrs. Howe's sisters—two of them traveled with her—were upset by this choice of a reputed infidel. One of them asked Parker in whose name her niece would be baptized. He replied, much to the new aunt's relief, that he knew of only one baptismal formula: "In the name of the Father, the Son, and Holy Spirit." According to Dr. Howe's account of the ceremony, written a few hours after it happened, Parker performed the service with "great earnestness, feeling, & beauty." Added Howe, "I shall ever love him for it." In fact, these weeks in the Eternal City mark the beginning of a lifelong friendship between Parker and both Howes.[16]

PARKER MAY be contrasted with the typical tourist of his day—the kind of person who was the intended audience of the standard English-language series of travel guides, the enormously popular *Murray's Handbooks*, published in London. One of these small, red-bound volumes, tucked under an arm, was the mark of a certain class of Briton abroad. Parker, although American, sometimes carried one tucked under an arm himself.[17] He must have found them useful because they were full of information about visas, exchange rates, lodging places, and sightseeing. But he was not the reader the *Murray* writers had in mind when they wrote.

This reader was assumed to be an Englishman of means. The *Murray* writers give much advice about servitors: how to hire them, how to keep them honest, and whether or not to bring them from home ("English servants taken for the first time to the Continent, and ignorant of every language but their own are worse than useless—they are an encumbrance").[18] Parker had no money for servants and would not have wanted them if he had. Among his baggage was a hearty republican dislike of aristocratic trappings.

The most important difference between Parker and an ordinary tourist, however, was why each traveled. For the latter, the motive was primarily pleasure and secondarily to develop more cosmopolitan tastes and habits. The *Murray* writers therefore dwell on the aesthetic experience of travel, providing especially detailed descriptions of art, architecture, and scenery.

Parker did gaze diligently upon paintings, buildings, and vistas. For that matter, he enjoyed plays, operas, and concerts—attending far more than he had ever done at home. Yet the scenery never impressed him. He found only one truly beautiful landscape in all of France (groves of olive trees, with the Mediterranean gleaming behind them, near Marseilles) and judged the Italian skies not so blue, the Italian countryside not so handsome as that of New England; even a panoramic view of the Alps failed to excite him (leading him self-critically to wonder if he were destitute of fancy). As for art, his judgments on the works he saw were neither profound nor, for the most part, original; he enthusiastically admired Raphael's *Transfiguration*, for example, which English-speakers generally considered the greatest painting of all time. Art remained for him a secondary concern. While in Italy, he remarked repeatedly on the contrast there between the magnificent paintings and sculptures, which he judged the "noblest . . . in the world," and the impoverished, "degraded" people. "I love beauty in nature and Art," he wrote to Silsbee, "but I would say *potatoes* first and *pictures* afterwards."[19]

Parker's strongest aesthetic interest was in literature. He paid homage to certain dead authors on his travels, plucking leaves from the grave of Shakespeare, gathering acorns from a ditch at Kenilworth, the estate of the late Sir Walter Scott, visiting the homes of Gibbon at Lausanne and of Voltaire at Geneva. At Weimar, Parker attempted to meet Frau von Goethe, but the widow was away (he later, however, had the satisfaction, at Leipzig, of sitting in Auerbach's Keller with thoughts of Dr. Faustus and Mephistopheles). Parker also made the acquaintance of a few literary lights. In London, he called on Charles Dickens, but the meeting seems not to have been memorable. Parker presented Emerson's letter of introduction to Thomas Carlyle, who found his American visitor "a most hardy, compact, clever little fellow, full of decisive utterance, with humor and good humor." Jane Carlyle, however, Thomas's sharp-tongued wife, recalled only a "little dreary snubnosed American with long hair over his coatneck . . . who always had a hand like a frog when you touched it." Parker, unlike Emerson, never became her husband's friend.[20]

Parker had no special interest, however, in meeting European "men of letters." Insofar as he did investigate literature or arts, it was only as a part of his longstanding, restless desire to gather knowledge of all sorts. This drive led him to seek out thinkers on every topic. In London, he breakfasted with Charles Babbage, the mathematician and inventor of the "calculating engine," whose machines left him wonderstruck. At the Jardin des Plantes in Paris, Parker heard the famous zoologist Étienne Geoffroy St. Hilaire lecture on "vultures." In Berlin, Parker listened to the eminent physiologist and anatomist Johannes Peter Müller explain "generation." At Heidelberg, Parker befriended Georg Gervinus, the liberal young historian of modern Europe. But if, as always, Parker was interested in many things, there was a clear theme in his choice of what to see and whom to meet: religion.

He concentrated his sightseeing on sacred places, such as churches and cathedrals (he visited them every place he stopped), and above all sites associated with prophets and dissenters. Parker carefully noted the spots where famous religious reformers had been martyred: Archbishop Cramner at Oxford; Savonarola at Florence; Servetus at Geneva.

In Rome, Parker was moved especially by the evidence of early Christian hardship and suffering. After a visit to Mamertine prison, where the Apostle Paul is supposed to have languished as a felon, Parker wrote to Francis that the experience "makes a man[']s heart beat a little": "It carries you back, over 1800 years to the time when [Christian] was a name of contempt, & cost a man his life." Parker had the same experience, with even greater force, when shown some recently excavated catacombs. No place in Rome filled him with greater emotion: "Here the persecuted when alive found refuge — when dead found repose for their ashes and bones long tortured."[21]

In Germany, Parker paid his respects to that greatest of Christian dissenters, Martin Luther. He and Lydia visited the church at Erfeurth where Luther took his monastic vows and said his first mass. They visited the castle at Wartburg, where they saw "the very room where Luther worked in translating the Bible, the table he wrote on!" Parker got to sit in Luther's own chair.[22]

Parker took Lydia on a special pilgrimage to Wittenberg. The *Murray's* guide for the region claims that "three or four hours" were sufficient to see the sights of this "dirty and ill-paved" little town, but the Parkers spent much of two days there in June 1844. They walked through the reverently preserved, memento-filled house that Luther shared with Catherine Bon (Parker purchased an impression made from Luther's seal and plucked leaves from a linden tree in his garden) and visited the churches where Luther preached. Among these was the *Schlosskirche*, where Luther was buried and where, according to tradition, he posted his ninety-five theses on the door (Parker bought a copy of them as well). The Parkers paused, too, at the spot outside the walls where Luther ensured his excommunication by burning the Papal Bull denouncing him. The night Parker passed in Wittenberg, he took a walk alone to the *Schlosskirche*. "The evening star looked down, a few persons went and came, the soft air fell upon my head," wrote Parker in his journal of the scene. "I felt the spirit of the great Reformer."[23]

Besides seeking inspiration in sacred places, Parker hunted for books on religion and philosophy. He delved into European libraries like the researcher he was, digging out the rare tomes and antique manuscripts. When he saw Scotus Erigena's *De Divisone Nature* at a library shortly after arriving in England, he stopped everything to read; later, when in Germany and Switzerland, he spent enough time in museums and archives to become familiar with the handwriting of Erasmus, Luther, Melancthon, and Zwingli.[24] Parker ransacked bookstores everywhere he went and established permanent relationships with booksellers in London and Paris. Ever with an eye for a bargain, he purchased not only for himself, but his friends, and even offered Francis to buy for the college library — a generous gesture, considering how Harvard had snubbed him over the previous two years. The zeal of Parker's bibliographic pursuit caught the fancy of his friend Christopher Cranch, who gently mocked it in a cartoon. "Theodore Parker's supposed delight on visiting a book store or library in Germany" shows its bespectacled subject in a parson's wide-brimmed hat, dashing in from the street toward a large case of formidable-looking folios, all multivolume works, his face gleeful, his arms stretched out in longing, and the tails of his frock coat flapping behind him, while the shopkeeper or librarian throws up his hands in alarm and two frantic *Spitze* bark at the madman.

Parker made a special effort to see philosophers and religious thinkers. In his two passes through England, he befriended James Martineau, the prominent English Unitarian from Liverpool, who had Parker preach for him, and who later would write significant articles introducing the American's work to the British public. Parker dined with Charles Hennell, whose unsettling book on the origins of Christianity he had reviewed for the *Dial*, and with the radical theologian Francis Newman. Parker tried, too, to meet Francis's older brother John Henry, well on his way to becoming a Catholic priest, who had resigned his Oxford position only weeks before Parker attempted to call on him there.

Parker was so anxious to meet Victor Cousin that on arriving in Paris he rushed to call on him before unpacking (unfortunately, Cousin was away). But it was to the scholars of Germany that Parker paid the most attention. At German universities he would audit lectures and appear on the doorstep of *Professoren* with the disarming declaration, "Sir, I am an American, have read your books, and want to see you."[25]

The German scholar who most interested him was David Strauss, but Strauss had retired from theology and was living privately in Heilbronn; Parker never met him. Parker asked almost every German scholar he did meet, however, about Strauss and his work. The assessments he received were as diverse as might be expected of so controversial a figure: Strauss was a Christian; he was a Christian only "if you make the definition wide enough"; he was not a Christian and was in fact growing "gar und gar unchristliche"; he had no influence any more; he had great influence still; he had little influence among the scholars but much among the people. Everyone agreed, however, that Strauss had an upright character, and Parker could not help identifying with and admiring this fellow theological outcast. When in Tübingen, Parker even tried to see the room where Strauss had written *Das Leben Jesu*, but only got to look at the outside of the cloister where it was located.[26]

Parker did meet or at least hear many other notables of German theology and philosophy. At Berlin, Parker listened to a sermon by Johann Neander, the great church historian, and audited several classes taught by various youthful Hegelians and one taught by E. W. Hengstenberg, the reactionary Lutheran confessionalist whom Parker had satirized in the *Register* in 1840.

At least twice, Parker sat in on Friedrich Schelling's "Philosophy of Revelation" class. Once dazzlingly charismatic, now dim-eyed and somewhat embittered, the famous Romantic recently had been invited to Berlin to counteract the skeptical tendencies of Hegelianism. In Parker's opinion the students did not take their white-haired teacher too seriously, but crowds of them came out of curiosity to hear what this still sharp-minded celebrity would say next. Parker summed up one talk:

> He found a good deal of fault with Kant, but praised Fichte, and said he had done great service to philosophy; thought his "Naturrecht" his best thing; praised the "Way towards a Blessed Life" for its *dialectic* skill, compared it with Hegel's works, which he said were merely mechanical, though he only alluded to Hegel and did not name him; some hissed at the allusion. Then he added that in his (Hegel's) case the work was mere mechanism, the grinding in a mill, and men paid much more attention to the noise of the *clapper* than to the meal that was alleged to be ground. Upon this all laughed.[27]

At Halle, Parker heard lectures by Johann Erdmann, the Hegelian historian of philosophy, paid his respects at the grave of the recently deceased Orientalist Wilhelm Gesenius, and had a long walk and conversation with Gesenius's successor, Friedrich Tholuck. Word had reached Tholuck, a prominent opponent of Rationalism, that some American Unitarians had become "Pantheists," and Parker had to spend some time explaining to him what Boston Transcendentalism was about. At Leipzig, Parker met Johann Hermann, the old philologist who had taught Edward Everett and George Bancroft. At Heidelberg, Parker called on half a dozen scholars, among them the pioneering New Testament critic Heinrich Paulus, now age eighty-two, whom Parker thought "eagle-eyed," "brave," and touched by "Genius." At Tübingen, Parker impressed the biblical historian Heinrich Ewald simply by being an American familiar with his works, and was impressed in turn by the historical theologian Friedrich Christian Baur. Not only had Baur's ideas about different "tendencies" in the New Testament shaped Parker's understanding of the conflicts in early Christianity, but when the American asked the German how many hours a day he studied, the big, bearlike Baur's apparently serious reply was, "*Ach! nur achtzehn!*"[28]

Parker's most poignant encounter came in Switzerland, in July 1844, with Wilhelm Leberecht De Wette. De Wette was now near the end of his career; exiled from Germany for his liberal political views, he taught at the tiny University of Basel, where the student population was no larger than Parker's congregation at home. Parker found the man whose opus he had labored on for so long to bring before the English-speaking public to be compact and small, "with a rather dry face."[29] To Parker's considerable dismay, he learned that De Wette had not yet received a copy of the translation from Little and Brown. Yet he greeted his translator warmly.

They went together to an exhibit of modern paintings and to the university library. De Wette showed him, among other things, the Codex from which Erasmus published his New Testament, a quarto copy of Erasmus's *Praise of Folly* with comic sketches in the margins by Holbein, and one of Holbein's portraits of Erasmus, which Parker thought "marvelously fine" — the best of the hundred or so images of the great humanist he had seen. De Wette held a reception for the Parkers at a friend's house, where the Americans enjoyed themselves despite the baffling Basel dialect spoken by the other guests ("[We] had a most mysterious time!" notes Parker in his journal). The next day, De Wette had the visitors over to his own house for dinner, where he and Parker talked about the state of German theology. Parker also heard De Wette lecture; when discussing the Harmony of the Gospels, "he cut left and right, & made no bones about saying such a passage was probably *Unächt*," reported Parker to Francis.[30]

Parker came away convinced De Wette was "great & noble," but "somewhat soured by his long disasters." He once had been "the leader of the enthusiastic young men," but only a year before Parker's visit he had given a speech at Jena in which he had enjoined the students "to go home & study their books & be silent!" Parker seems to have been somewhat disappointed that his estimate of the man had not been raised by their meeting. But it had not been lowered, either, and the two parted "tenderly."[31]

PARKER'S EXAMINATION of religion in Europe included many observations of Judaism, Catholicism, and Protestantism there. What he saw of the three faiths only confirmed his already critical opinion of them.

Parker had been thinking about Jews, the Jewish Scriptures, and the Jewish religion since his Watertown days, a dozen years earlier, when he wrote "A History of the Jews." He had become a champion of the idea that Christianity, as the Absolute Religion, had no essential connection to Judaism, a faith he thought based on the authority of myths and bypassed by history. Parker wanted Christianity purged of its Jewish elements. Yet Parker appears to have met just one Jew before coming to Europe: the Christian convert James Seixas, who had given him early lessons in Hebrew. Curiosity seems to have led him to look for other Jews in cities across the Continent.

Parker went to the gated ghetto at Rome, where the inhabitants were confined at night by guards, and the ungated one at Venice, the oldest in Italy. But he was impressed most by the ancient Jewish quarter of Prague, then the largest community of its kind in Europe, where he passed much of a day in May 1844.[32]

Parker visited none of the synagogues there, but he did stop at a bookstore. The elderly little owner "seemed pleased that a stranger took an interest in Hebrew literature," and Parker bought a few volumes from him. Parker was moved, too, by the *Alte Friedhof*, the first Jewish cemetery he had ever seen.

Elder trees, unusually large and old, shaded Hebrew-inscribed headstones so crowded together that they touched one another. Under one of the elders, Parker found a rabbinical grave supposedly dating from the ninth century. Reverent visitors had built a cairn by it; he placed a rock on the pile and from one of the branches overhead plucked an elder leaf as a keepsake. After he left the graveyard, he was moved in a different way when he saw, on the parapet of a bridge leading out of the *Judenstadt*, a crucifix of gilt bronze, erected with fines paid by Jews for "blaspheming the Christian religion." The monument disgusted Parker. "It stands there to insult them every time they pass the stream!" he wrote in his journal that night. "What would Jesus say of them who take his name in vain, could he come back."

In the same journal entry, Parker professed "inborn affection" for Jews, whom he refers to as a "mysterious people, for ages oppressed, yet green and living still." He thought of "the service they had done mankind—and the reward they got!" He thinks of "Abraham, Isaac and Jacob, Moses and Prophets." And of Jesus, whom Parker calls "the culmination of Hebrewdom, the blossom of the nation!"

Such love of Jews for the sake of Jesus could only go so far to counteract Parker's Transcendentalist hostility to the Jewish religion, or raise his generally low estimate of the Jewish character. A couple of weeks after leaving Prague, in a letter to Francis, Parker admitted never seeing a Jew without remembering "Noah & Baal & Balaam"—that is, the myths of the Old Testament that Parker considered absurd. He also joked that he always believed what Jews told him, even though they had "not lost their national peculiarity" to prevaricate: "In old time if a Hebrew was asked for a truth, *he told a story*. (At Venice, *now*, '*parola Ebrea*' means *a lie*.)"[33]

An incident that revealed much about Parker's attitudes occurred in Leipzig, where an American acquaintance of his, a promising young scholar named Charles Stearns Wheeler, recently had died of an illness. A dispute had arisen over the fees demanded by Wheeler's physician, a Jewish convert to Christianity named Lippert. Some thought Lippert's bill exorbitant. Lippert had married into a respectable local Protestant family, but Parker, after making inquiries, grew convinced that he was a "scoundrel" who had "plundered" his unfortunate patient.

Parker could not seem to help linking the doctor's alleged greed to his ancestry. "He was a Jew," explained Parker in another letter to Francis, "& now is like—some other Jews alleged to be converted—'twofold more the' &c &c." Parker in his journal, meanwhile, wrote that Lippert, despite his excellent connections, was nonetheless "a thankless and villainous Jew." He himself had "a great love for the Jews," Parker insisted, "but a great hate for Jewishness!"[34]

Parker had been quite critical of Roman Catholicism long before he set foot in a Catholic country. In the last section of his *Discourse of Religion*, which treated the various "parties" of Christiandom, he had discussed at some length the "Merits," "Defects," and "Vices" of the "Catholic Party." Although he here had praised Catholicism particularly for its historical achievements and for its "peculiar and distinctive doctrine" that "*God inspires mankind as much as ever*," he had lashed the church for claiming that inspiration exclusively for itself. Parker also had followed Protestant tradition that the Reformation was inevitable, because by the fifteenth century the church had become "a colossus of crime, with a thin veil of hypocrisy drawn over its face, and that only."[35]

The vitality and attractiveness of actual European Catholicism, especially as he saw it in Italy, surprised him.[36] Its churches had for him an unexpected appeal, which he evoked in a sermon preached shortly after his return to America:

> You go into some city at nightfall, you enter in the glowing of Evening, some great cathedral, which seems doubly vast from the obscure light that glows in its aisles. The Priest has retired, but the silent worshippers put up their prayers, kneeling before the altar or the shrine of some [Saint], perhaps |the| penitent Mary, or the Mary who needed no repentance. The labourer, weary with toil, retiring to his narrow home & homely supper, bends a moment . . . before the image of Peter the F[isherman] or Paul the tentmaker, thanking the Great father, for daily strength & daily bread. The mother left a widow, the Parent who is childless, bow them down before him who was a man of sorrows . . . & relief comes.[37]

Parker found himself admiring the "music, architecture, Paintings, Statues, &c." of the church and respecting its cultivation "of *Reverence*, . . . of *Gentleness*," which he conceded it did better than the Protestant churches. In Rome, he interviewed at length some priests and prelates from England; he came away impressed with their learning, asceticism, charity, and (as he explained in a letter to Francis) freedom from cant: "They don't draw down the corners of their mouths nor talk through their nose, nor roll up the whites of their eyes & say—ô—ô—ô!" Parker thought Pope Gregory XVI himself, with whom he (along with a party of other Americans) was granted a brief audience, had a "benevolent" face and "kind" look. Parker even conceded that Catholics had the better of Protestants in the old historical argument over the alleged "corruptions of Christianity": In the catacombs, Parker saw evidence that belief in Transubstantiation dated back to the beginning of the second century and worship of the Virgin nearly as far. "Of course," wrote Parker to Francis, "*I* should laugh at any argument built on such premises—even if I admitted the premises—but many would be overwhelmed by it."[38]

Qualifications like this one limit all of Parker's kind words for Catholicism. He may have lauded the Catholic art, but coming from him, this was damning with faint praise; he thought that only a "fop" would be converted to Christianity by beauty, and that no *real man* would be unable to preach "Humility, the Greatness of the Soul, the Nothingness of life's poor distinctions" in so gorgeous a temple as, say, Santa Croce in Florence. Again, although he held Reverence and Gentleness to be important qualities, they were not so important, in his view, as Reason and Conscience, which he thought developed better under Protestantism.[39]

Meanwhile, Parker dismissed much of the Catholic Church as corrupt or fraudulent. Despite his respect for a few priests, he remained suspicious of the priesthood. He was inclined to believe the Italian who told him only a tenth of the Catholic clergy were "pure, conscientious men," and he did not even reject out of hand a salacious tale told by an English opera musician, whom he met while voyaging on the Rhine, that Pope Gregory had an illegitimate son living in Milan. Parker regarded the biblical relics he saw in the basilicas, cathedrals, and churches as so many pious shams, and he regarded plenary indulgences, then commonly granted, as so much foolishness. When Parker learned, before he reached Rome, that all who went there during Holy Week and heard five sermons would receive an indulgence from the pope "for all sins, past, present & to come," his reaction was derisive. "I shall hear not only 5 but 50 if possible," he informed Francis, "& so shall be able to '*indulge*' you and eight others when I get home & save them by vicarious atonement!"[40]

What continued most to bother him, however, was the claim of the Catholic Church to have unique, miraculous authority and the right to enforce it. The church may have become more "prudent, it were to say cunning" than during the Counter-Reformation, but it had abandoned none of its "pretensions." The Inquisition, Parker frequently pointed out, still operated. He wrote Francis that the doctrines of the church, "its *rites*, & its general effect . . . *I hate* all the more in Europe than I hated at home."[41]

Parker's biases were obviously Protestant, in that he considered Protestantism a great advance over what had gone before. But he was a critic of Protestantism, too. In America, he had objected particularly to the Protestant reliance on the Bible as the miraculously inspired guide to faith and practice.[42] His principal objection to the European Protestant churches, by contrast, was that they were state-sponsored.

Puritan legend, Yankee pride, and reformist zeal all predisposed Parker to think of the Anglican church as venal and spiritually barren. These feelings came out in his reaction to the first Sunday service he saw in England. He and Lydia attended the Collegiate Church in Manchester, the oldest ecclesiastical building Parker had ever seen; it was already centuries old when Oliver

Cromwell's troops had destroyed some of the decorations. Although Parker felt "the natural emotions of reverence at treading such ancient aisles," they were dissipated by his impressions of the service: "The organ sounded out its beautiful tones; the sexton—arrayed in a surplice—showed *us* into a handsome pew, but sent an old, tottering, venerable man—into a little dirty box. Presently 'the Dean & Canons'—the D. has a salary of about £ 25,000 per an[num]—came in, in their *robes* preceded by an usher; a fat chough [*sic*] with a face like Geo. III. got into the reading desk, & 'galloped like a hunter over his prayers,' & another preached a most stupid & arrogant sermon. I could not but think Cromwell did only half his work."[43]

Parker's indictment of Anglicanism only lengthened as his weeks in England passed. He came to consider Anglican services a waste of time and wrote to a friend that the clergy of the country disappointed and vexed him: "It seems to me the mortality is like that to be read of in Egypt when all the first-born died—'there was not a House (Church) in which there was not one dead.'" Parker did find a "germ of spirituality" in the Oxford (or "Puseyite") movement, whose leaders he considered self-sacrificing and socially concerned. Yet he thought Anglo-Catholicism preposterous in its emphasis on ritual, sacrament, and Apostolic authority.[44]

In the Protestantism of Germany, Parker had a greater investment than in that of England. He owed much to German Protestant thinkers and had vigorously defended them from the charge of infidelity. Parker had pronounced German literature, in his 1841 *Dial* article on the subject, the most religious of modern times. Yet he seems to have been disappointed by the Germans he met. The theologians seemed not especially spiritual; they were "*sleek, well-fed*, & cosy as other men," and almost none of them went to church on Sunday.[45] There was, moreover, an undeniable skeptical tendency developing in German thought.

Parker blamed these spiritual shortcomings on state sponsorship of the German Protestant churches. In Prussia, he explained in a sermon preached shortly after his return home, "[t]he state declares that [at] a certain age *all be baptized*, [and at] about 14 months, *that all be confirmed & made members of the church*. Without a certificate of [Baptism] & Con[firmation] they cannot marry, or exercise a trade. Of course children are baptized, & made members of the church, just as they are enrolled in the army & the military service. Here too the Gov[ernment] determines what shall be believed in the Ch[urch]. The Parson cuts his cloth according to the Pattern, thinking one thing & preaching |or *seeming to Preach*| another thing." Under such circumstances, some amount of irreligion was unavoidable: "The government has taken a sure means of making Religion a Science with one class, & a ceremony with another." But his conviction that Protestant Germany was, despite everything, "the most religious part of continental Europe" had not been shaken.[46]

DESPITE ALL the attention Parker paid to religion in Europe, his sabbatical marks a shift in his thought toward politics and social reform. What he observed abroad inspired him with fresh insights on these subjects.

Parker saw certain political matters as falling naturally within his pastoral purview. Education was one of them, and he tried to get information about the educational system of every country he visited. Like other Massachusetts reformers, most famously Horace Mann, Parker admired the free schools of Prussia, with their thorough curriculum and professionally trained teachers who did not resort to the rod to keep order; Prussia, Parker thought, had done deeds in the education field "that may well make . . . [Americans] blush at not having done *worse*."[47] He made special arrangements to visit schools around Berlin, accompanied by the American chargé d'affaires,[48] and on returning to Boston allied himself publicly with Mann, who was trying to introduce Prussian-style innovations into the schools of Boston. Parker the educator was also inspired by the free public libraries and art galleries he found on his travels, neither of which yet existed in Boston.

Parker the moral reformer, meanwhile, came to appreciate the open air dances, outdoor music festivals, and cheap (often publicly funded) theaters of the Continent. Sobersided New England was mistaken, he decided, to discourage such "innocent" amusements. More of them would mean "less of money-making, less political violence, less sectarian bigotry, and less drinking oneself drunk."[49]

Parker saw moral value, too, in the free public parks, then common in Europe but largely unknown in the United States (Frederick Law Olmstead's landscaping career having not yet begun). The sight, Parker's first Sunday in Rome, of laborers relaxing on the grounds of the Villa Borghese left a deep impression. Later, after walking through the "fine gardens of fruits and flowers" that surrounded the German town of Gotha, he wondered in his journal, "Why have we nothing of this kind? Not even in Boston, for the Common is nothing in comparison with this. Shame on us republicans, with our short-sighted utilitarianism! Can't I (even I) do something to embellish our Spring Street?"[50]

Parker's observations and experiences startled him into thinking in new ways about problems of the poor, whose interests he thought of as a minister's special concern. Urban slums, in particular, came to him as a kind of horrific revelation. He had experienced nothing in Boston or New York to prepare him for the "low places" of European cities. He found "faces of men" in these slums "positively *frightening* . . . marked by *cunning, malice, lust, Rage, deceit.*"[51] He struggled with conflicting interpretations of this degradation.

On the one hand, he was inclined to see it as a lingering ill effect of "Feudalism," by which term he meant oppression by selfish aristocrats. Such an explanation fitted with his general tendency, which he shared with other American observers, to view Europe as a prisoner of its past. Slums were, from this perspective, among those things that gave the Old World its ancient aspect, like the ivy-festooned ruins. Slums were of a piece with the monarchs and nobles, who still wielded considerable power, and with the walls and fortifications that still surrounded so many urban centers. For an American, such an understanding of urban poverty was optimistic, because America had done away with the vestiges of feudalism during its revolution. Slums, in this view, were not in the American future.

On the other hand, Parker could not help but see that many slums, especially in England, were modern. They were a by-product of the social disruptions produced by the emergence of industrial capitalism, a force altogether new, which already was making itself felt at home in the mill towns of Lowell and Lawrence. Parker was enthusiastic about industrialization and the promise of prosperity it offered, but he now began to worry about what he called the "feudalism of Gold" or "Money"—that is, oppression by selfish plutocrats. He thought such "feudalism" was not so bad, on the whole, as the "feudalism" that went before, but was still "too bad to be born in a [Christian] land, it seems to me."[52]

As Parker considered poverty, public morality, and education in Europe, he began to link all three together in a new, political way. His thoughts were spurred by his observations of political oppression on the Continent. He saw soldiers patrolling the streets of every town and village square in Austria and most of Italy, their cannons trained on the citizenry. He saw chains strung across the streets of Munich to restrain possible unrest during a public festivity. He noted the aggressive censorship of the press practiced by the Holy Apostolic Government of Rome and the strict residency laws that prevented Germans from moving out of their native towns. He heard stories of police arresting suspected enemies of the state in the middle of the night and imprisoning them for years without trial. The power of politics over human life began to loom ever larger in his mind.[53]

THE DAY Parker sailed from New York, he wrote in his journal that "ONE is with me to whom my mortal weal and woe are united."[54] He frequently implies Lydia's presence in his journal by use of the pronoun "we." But he never notes how she reacted to sights or passed the time when he went off by himself; in the documents that survive, he does not even mention her by name. Aside from the few references in Francis Parkman's journal, already quoted, no record exists of her experience of the trip. There may have been relevant information in her husband's letters to her mother and Aunt Lucy (he catalogues letters to both women in his journal) but this correspondence is lost, nor has any letter survived that she wrote during the voyage. In letters by Theodore that survive, she is rarely mentioned.

Despite such paucity of sources, the historian must conclude that something important did happen between Theodore and Lydia on their trip. The dark cloud that had hovered over their marriage for seven years finally lifted.

The Parkers had made a deliberate decision to travel together. They were not forced by social convention to do so. Had Theodore left Boston alone, no stigma would have been attached to the separation. Many contemporary husbands went abroad without their wives; Ralph Waldo Emerson would do so in 1847–48. Also, Lydia, had she wanted to stay home, would have had the excellent excuse that Aunt Lucy needed her help.

Yet Lydia and Theodore, despite all the pain that had passed between them, elected to spend a year in close quarters, subjecting themselves to all the trials and annoyances of travel, which are known to cause strain between the most cordial of conjugal companions. Even assuming there had been a partial reconciliation in the fall of 1842, when Theodore had sided with his wife about taking Georgie Colburn as a ward, the couple must have set out with some trepidation and without either partner knowing the result. But the sabbatical held for them one hopeful attraction: they would be alone together. Lucy would not be standing between them, and Theodore would have no Anna Shaw to distract him from the handsome woman always by his side.

That things went remarkably well between them is suggested by the new, happier mood Parker evinced in his letters and journal from the moment he and Lydia landed in England. And from his letters and journal may be gleaned moments of romantic intimacy between him and his wife.

One such occurred in Innsbruck, Austria, where the couple arrived a week after their anniversary. They stopped two days in this pretty little baroque town, nestled in a green valley surrounded by mountains buried deep in snow; during this brief stay, the crown prince of Bavaria came through, escorting home to Munich his new, Italian wife, the daughter of the grand duke of Tuscany. The newlyweds happened to stay in the same inn as the Parkers, in the apartment below them. Theodore, although unimpressed by monarchy, was nonetheless charmed when an orchestra came to play outside the royal couple's window—and so outside his and Lydia's window as well. "Of course we enjoyed the music which was not meant for us, as much as the Bride and Bridegroom," he noted in a letter, "and were I doubt not *happy as a king*." [55]

Perhaps the most telling incident, however, occurred a few months later, at Berne, Switzerland. The Parkers were there only one day; judging only from Theodore's travel journal, and his letter to Convers Francis that touches on the visit, what was notable about the place were the view of the Alps, the local "lions" (among them the young Karl Vogt, later famous as a liberal revolutionary, a medical materialist, and the object of a massive polemic by Karl Marx), and especially the local bears, mascots of the town, which were kept in a section of its ditch. Parker mentions that he found the animals "quite interesting" and fed them bread. He does not mention that Lydia also found them quite interesting, but apparently she kept asking to go back to see them. Theodore playfully began calling her "Bear" or "Bearsie."[56]

Ever afterward, the "Bear" became for him a symbol of her and of their marriage. Over the coming years, he would collect bear figurines, until he had a whole shelf of them on display in his study. He took to wearing a gold shirt-stud with the impress of a bear. He gave Lydia bear-related gifts: one Christmas, it was a porcelain mug with the image of a bear glazed on it; another, it was a silver candlestick in the fanciful shape of a bear with a walking stick. And he developed a lifelong fascination with actual bears, going out of his way to see them in captivity. Once, he even planned to write a paper on them for the Boston Society of Natural History.[57]

After seven difficult years of marriage, Parker, in Berne, finally had found a pet name for his wife. That he did so suggests he felt a greater degree of affection for her and a greater willingness to display it than ever before.

Yet the name he gave her seems strange. More than one of the Parkers' friends were struck by the apparently comical contrast between Lydia, who impressed most people (Francis Parkman, for example) as "a pretty, timid, gentle little woman,"[58] and the large, ferocious animal with whom he had chosen to identify her. Most thought Parker was simply displaying a jocose sense of paradox. His motives were probably more complex.

Parker, after all, was a scholar of languages who liked wordplay. He knew that "bear" is not only a noun, but a verb with at least two relevant meanings. One is to "bring forth offspring," which he and Lydia were unable to do, to their common pain. A second meaning is to "carry a burden." In this sense, Parker had used the word in relation to his marriage during its dark periods. In his journal for February 1842, for example, scarcely a month after he had exploded that "my wife is a _DEVIL_," he wrote the following passage, later blotted out, on the warnings he had received as a young man about the trials of domestic life: "My sisters used to tell me of the world of woe appointed to try me. I know now all *that it means* & find their sad prediction more than verified. Well be it so. Let me *bear bear bear.*"[59]

The verb "bear" hints at all the problems Parker saw in his relationship with Lydia; the noun reminded him of a happy moment he and Lydia had spent together and of an animal he thought endearing. Of course, a bear could be fierce, but that, too, became a little joke between him and his wife. He knew, as very few others did, that Lydia had a temper.[60]

Lydia accepted the name Parker had given her, with all its complex shadings. On the most obvious level, she must have welcomed it as evidence of her husband's renewed affections. She also seems to have been ashamed of the secret, "bearish" aspects of her character (such as her temper). She struggled not to show them to the outside world and appreciated Parker for choosing to love her despite them.

Here is a rare instance in which Lydia's own testimony may be used as evidence. In one of the few letters by her that survives, written after her husband's death to one of his close friends, she lets slip her mask—or, more precisely, she reveals its existence. "Why are we not all willing to have our shortcomings known," she wonders, "& our innermost consciousness laid open to all. Perhaps most are, but I am not. I cannot make up my mind that others should know me as I am—Theodore did & he loved me, & now I oftener pray to him than to my God."[61]

This declaration may not be discounted as the sentimentality of a widow. Abundant testimony exists from contemporaries, who observed the Parkers' marriage in its later years, that she gave him attentive care, and he gave her the same. In 1845, around the time of their ninth anniversary, he wrote "To my wife"—his first poem dedicated to Lydia since the naive effusions composed during their long engagement. It is quite different from those, or from his abstract poetic evocations of the absent Anna Shaw. He considers his bond to Lydia as his strongest spiritual attachment, and wonders, somberly, about dying and leaving her behind (he assumed that he would die first). He assuages the pain of this meditation with the thought that they will be reunited in the afterlife. Once he had wondered if Lydia would even mourn him, but such doubts have been stilled:

> To part from thee—it is the only pang
> That Death can give—Sun moon & stars I can
> Forsake—And yet I love them too—& well.
> But not as I love thee. Thou art myself.
> And can I leave myself—I love the Sea.
> And every flower of spring is dear unto my heart.
> But I could live & never look upon a rose,
> nor hear the sounding of the joyous sea.
> But without thee existence were not Life.
> 'Twer double death—damnation infinite.
> With the Sea—the Heavens the flowers,
> I am alone—for they are not my counterpart.
> They help my solitary hour—& I
> Arise out of myself supported then.
> But then—sinkest me deeper still in self.
> Doubly I feel & truly live with thee
> Thou makest true eternity—a [Heaven] of life.

And yet some day, . . . I must leave thee here.
Thou wilt come & look upon my cold face
'Twill give no answering look—for I am gone.
Thou lay me gently in the ground—to rest.
Earth gives me little now—but then enough.
I will make ready for thy soul above,
Then we will live, eternally love on.[62]

The reconciliation of the Parkers was not perfect. For Theodore, at least, there remained a persistent gnawing sense that he and Lydia were not fully compatible, and that he was not therefore "fully married" (which may explain why he secretly cherished Anna Shaw's memory). From time to time, too, he and Lydia would suffer through a difficult stretch, and the alternate meanings of the pet name "bear" would again emerge. In 1855, after he returned home from a two-week lecture trip to Ohio, he lamented in his journal that "the old evil returns—often sadly chronicled in these volumes. I had hoped it was at an end—but the old curse has returned & sullied all my (outward) peace for now two months or more. I fondly thought a little absence would give the clouds time to clear up but they are thicker than ever. B e a r & F o r b e a r."[63]

This episode, whatever its exact nature and whatever had brought it about, seems to have been more cloudy than stormy and comparatively short-lived besides. By the following summer, which he spent with Lydia, he could happily report in his journal that "I never enjoyed a vacation more."[64] As for the lament in his journal, he seems to have scratched it out himself.

Among the reasons he and Lydia could now be reconciled more rapidly were that he had more realistic expectations of marriage than before. He also now had actual experience of happy times with Lydia, which would have given him grounds to hope for their return, and so not to retreat, as he had done so often during their early years together, into silent brooding.

PARTLY OWING to the marital reconciliation—and partly to finding so many major European thinkers taking him seriously—Parker grew more self-confident. In January 1844, while in Florence, he wrote to Convers Francis that after five months of leisure to consider his own position, "I feel all its melancholiness—the severity of the task that is laid on me—but I feel too that I must *on, on*; that the time of rest will never come in my day, & for me, but so long as I live that I must war against the false Gods—& their priests as false. . . . I have done wrong things no doubt, but the more I think of it, the more the general tendency of my path seems to me the true one, & the less do I feel an inclination to turn away, or to stand still."[65]

Along with this new assurance, Parker's temperament grew steadier. The extraordinary sensitivity to rebuff, the intense "agony of spirit," seemed to disappear. Before his European trip, he burst easily and often into tears; afterward, he almost never did so. He later would confront controversies far more severe, opponents far more dangerous, than any he had faced in 1841, 1842, and 1843, but none would so deeply affect him.

Again, because his present domestic situation had ceased to seem hopelessly miserable, he no longer felt so painfully the loss of his loving childhood home. Soon after his return to America, he visited the Parker farm in Lexington and remarked how much his perception of the place had changed. Just a few years earlier, he could look on it only with "heart ache"; it had seemed like "a spot in the forest—burnt and blasted by . . . fire." Now, by contrast, it seemed "like a garden green and smiling all the winter through," and the sight of the old brooks, trees, and stones gave him "pleasure."[66] Only after the trip to Europe did Parker begin to integrate stories of his happy early years into his Transcendentalist autobiography.

Having made peace with his past, he could put it behind him, and allow a profound change in self-perception to take place. When he left Boston, Parker referred to himself as a "young man." When he returned, he did not. As he later recalled, his "boyhood [had] continued long" into his adult years.[67] But the man who alighted from a carriage in West Roxbury on Sunday evening, 1 September 1844, eight days after his thirty-fourth birthday, finally had grown up.

A YEAR BEFORE Parker's trip, in his lecture on the "Education of the Laboring Classes," he had suggested in passing that there was an "American Idea," which he had associated vaguely with equal rights. In the fall of 1844, he began to organize his thoughts about what he had seen in Europe and articulate this idea and its implications more fully. In doing so, he started to develop his epochal definition of democracy as "government of the people, by the people, for the people."

Parker was thinking over the larger meaning of his tour well before it was over. In April 1844, he had written to a friend at home that "there are a great many things for us to learn which foreign nations may teach us"; in early August, during his second visit to London, he made notes in his journal toward a discourse on "Lessons which the Old World has to offer the New." He took this as the theme of his "Sermon of Travels," written within a week of his return. He delivered it as his homecoming homily at the newly renovated Spring Street meetinghouse (the high box pulpit had been lowered while he was away) on 8 September.[68]

Public interest in his pronouncements had not dimmed during his absence. So many came to the service that latecomers found no room to stand, while out in the churchyard was collected such a throng of "people, horses and carriages from far and near" that the scene reminded one witness of "an old-fashioned musterfield." Among those from Boston were Parker's self-anointed "disciple," Caroline Healey, soon to marry a young Unitarian minister from Baltimore, Charles Dall; her sister Marian; and their father, Mark. Caroline reports in her journal that the day was unpleasantly hot and the omnibus ride to Spring Street dirty, but for these inconveniences she was amply compensated by Parker's preaching and by "some minutes of delightful talk" with him.[69]

The travel sermon, fifty-six manuscript pages long, required two and three-quarter hours for Parker to deliver. He had to divvy up the time between the morning and afternoon services. The lengthy discourse shows him full of new ideas, but not yet able to discuss them systematically.[70]

In fact, the sermon barely processes the raw data of his European observations. He classifies them in a way that was conventional in his preaching, moving from the physical world "up" the scale of being to the human one, then "up" the scale of faculties, from the sensual to the spiritual, from the intellectual to the moral to, at last, the religious. Within this familiar, all-purpose framework, he arranges his evidence in the most obvious way possible: he follows his travel itinerary. The early part of the discourse draws its examples from England, the middle parts from the Continent, and toward the end from a mixture of the Continent and England.

The sermon shows Parker's trip had nurtured his interest in political and social problems. Although he had scoured Europe for information on theology and churches, he devotes less than a fifth of the discourse (ten pages near the end)[71] to such topics as the virtues and vices of the Catholic Church and the dangers of state sponsorship of religion. He has far more to say about other matters. His overall theme is that the institutions of Europe, in particular the social and political ones, are flawed because they fail to regard "*man as man.*"

England, for instance, values people according to their rank and wealth; Parker calls it the Paradise of the Noble and Rich, the Purgatory of the Wise and Good, and the Hell of the Poor and Weak. Despite the vast wealth of the kingdom, English laborers are the worst fed and clothed in Europe; they seem degraded as brutes, and no amount of toil and frugality can save them from "*pauperism or begging, or sheer & utter death.*" Parker blames this awful situation on both the old "aristocracy of birth, the Feudalism of descent," and the new "*aristocracy of wealth, the feudalism of Gold.*" The latter, he argues, has in some respects exacerbated the problem of serfdom left behind by the former. The old serf was at least sure of support, even in old age; the new "serf" has the liberty only to starve and steal, but no political rights. So "far as his physical welfare is concerned," Parker writes, ". . . he might pray for the condition of our negro slaves."[72]

If Parker uses the English example to show the evils of economic inequality, he uses the Continental one to show those of political despotism. In contrast to America, where "*all power is supposed to belong originally & of right to the people, who confer the faculty of exercising it on their Rep[resentatives] & prescribe how they shall exercise it*," in Europe, with few exceptions (parts of Switzerland, for example), "all is exactly the reverse."[73] As a consequence, the people and the government always are struggling against one another, a condition that "leads to jealousy, strife, conspiracies & persecution."

Poverty, oppression, and ignorance, Parker argues, together retard the moral development of a nation, and the corruption produced by these evils is compounded from generation to generation. The depravity that results can be found in European slums. He asserts (without fear of contradiction from his Yankee listeners) that this determination of character and appearance can be seen most obviously in the Jews, "[s]maller in stature, than other peoples, *cunning, sly, & ferocious, |& malignant[,]|* creeping stealthily |as cats| from city to city." But he finds the same debasement going on among millions "who have the same blood in their veins as you & I."[74]

Such abjection, he believes, inevitably leads to crime. Some crimes among the city poor "would make a villain turn black in the face." In the manuscript, Parker provides an example, but crosses it out, possibly thinking his audience would find it too shocking: "Parents murdering their children, & children their parents, by slow poison, for the sake of getting . . . from charitable societies, the fees paid for the burial!"[75] Seven-eighths of offenses in Europe, however, are not against persons but against property, which to Parker indicates how unjust the European system of property really is.

How can America avoid the evils of Europe? Parker approves of various ameliorative measures Europeans themselves have taken. He praises the systematic public schooling he has seen on the Continent; the institutions for public enlightenment there, such as free public galleries and libraries; the "innocent" popular amusements and public parks. More broadly, he argues that "we" Americans can save ourselves only if we make "*such a division . . . of the earth & its fruits that none consume themselves in luxury, none waste away in poverty*"; have our strong help our weak; promote "*the E[ducation,] intellectual, moral, & religious of all classes of men*"; abolish war, slavery, and "*all manner of monopolies.*"[76]

After Parker preached the "Lessons" sermon, he began planning a lecture with a similar theme. He wrote a four-page pencil outline, then began working up a version in pen. This manuscript, "Lessons Taught Us by the Example, History & Fate of Other Nations," was still incomplete, at twenty-nine pages, when he set it aside in early November. In his journal, Parker called it a "rude sketch" that "I don't like . . . altogether," but added that "some thoughts in it are dear to me." He planned to work on the lecture again after he had studied more political economy; he also wanted to add a large section on fine arts, music, and architecture.[77]

The lecture shows that in September and October Parker had developed a more theoretical and coherent understanding of the significance of his European experiences. He says even less here than in his travel sermon about specifically theological and ecclesiastical matters. He was coming to believe that the most important lessons he had learned abroad were about politics.

He organizes the lecture around a political idea. Implicitly adopting a concept from the German philosopher Herder (whose collected works he had bought in 1835) that each nation had a unique, divinely appointed project to perform, Parker argues that the American project is *"to organize the Rights of man*—not the privileges of a class."[78]

In light of this project, America must take special heed of *"the evils that come from legislating in favour of any one class of men—instead of legislating for man himself."* Parker finds as one of the clearest lessons of history that *"there is no permanent & real welfare for any one portion in Society except in connection with the welfare of all the rest of the nation."* Yet people have been slow to learn this truth. Those in power aim to provide themselves and their children with all the luxury and comfort of the world, and none of the work, while burdening the weak with all the work and giving them none of the luxury and comfort. Yet the world is made after another pattern, expressed, Parker thinks, in a Spanish proverb: " 'What you will have,' quoth God, 'pay for it and take it.' "[79]

To support his argument, Parker examines cases of disastrous elite selfishness: the patricians of the ancient Roman republic; the nobles of the *ancien régime* in France; the "capitalists" of contemporary England. The patricians thrust farmers off the Campagna to make room for the patricians' herds of cattle and sheep, and in this way turned a bountiful country barren and pestilential. The rich became haughty, licentious, and grasping, the poor licentious, indolent, bloodthirsty, yet unwarlike. Under these conditions, the republic could not be sustained and fell to a despot; ultimately, the despotism could not be sustained either, and the Roman Empire fell to barbarians. In the French case, the barons crushed the serfs, resulting in recurring famines and plagues. In the end, the evils of feudalism were swept away by the bloody but necessary deluge of the Revolution.

England, Parker thinks, gives America the most powerful warning of the dangers of partial legislation, because American institutions and political ideas were born there. He paints the same damning portrait of English inequality as in his travel sermon, but with new details: for example, that nearly one and a half million of its twenty million inhabitants are "indoor paupers," while three to five million eat nothing but potatoes. He claims that the hard maxims of the English political economists—for example, that capitalists can accumulate, but laborers only can make enough to prevent starvation—accurately reflect the English situation. Also, Parker notes that the depraved proletary "increase like rats & mice" (disproving the old belief that "rapid increase is proof of a sound state of things"). Some in England despair, says Parker, and seek relief only in famine and pestilence. He worries, as he had not in his travel sermon, that something like the English feudalism of gold is starting to appear in America.

The second lesson taught by other nations, Parker finds, is that "*the greatest possible freedom should be left to individual thought & action.*"[80] The difficult problem of government, he says (here articulating for the first time a theme that would often appear in his writings), is how to balance individual freedom, the "centrifugal" force in politics, with national unity of action, the "centripetal" one.

An example of excessive centripetal force are the state-supported Protestant churches of Europe (his only mention of ecclesiastic matters in the lecture). He criticizes European governments for imposing creeds and rites on the individual conscience.[81] In general, he argues that the stronger the central government, the more paralyzed is individual energy. In France, as the monarchy became more powerful, the barons and people grew weaker and less active. By contrast, during the French Revolution, the central government was nearly destroyed, "yet there was the greatest life & activity in the people—only misdirected—& there was no unity." This near anarchy was followed by the "violent centralization" of Napoleon, which again diminished both the liberty and the energy of the people.

The difference between the governments of Europe and that of the United States, Parker believes, is one of principle and idea. In Europe, "much is done *for* the people—little *through* the people, nothing . . . *by* the people directly."[82] Power there is deductive; it comes from a central point. By contrast, power in America is inductive; it comes from the whole circumference. Because "each man is left alone to rule himself," there is greater activity in America than anyplace else. The only check to our individuality, Parker thinks, is public opinion. This can become a real tyranny—one unknown in Europe; but Parker refuses to concede that the tyranny of public opinion was an "essential feature" of American democracy.

The third major lesson Parker discusses, one closely linked to the other two, is the necessity of educating "*all men of all classes.*" There are two major motives for education, he argues, one "*general & human,*" the other "*special & political.*" By the first, each person should have the best education, intellectual, moral, and religious, that society can afford. "If we are *to organize the Ri[gh]ts of Man,*" Parker believes, "this must be done." Then, too, when we look at the matter "merely" in a political light, we see plainly that if the people are to rule, they must be educated. Parker rejects the notion that stupid and immoral King Many is somehow superior to stupid and immoral King One, owing to some "Pythagorean magic in numbers." History teaches us instead, he asserts, that an ill-educated people will be the "tool & plaything of ambitious, crafty & tyrannical men."[83]

Parker's lecture remains a "rude sketch." In it are numerous notes to himself to check his facts, and the text breaks off in mid-argument. But Parker continued to turn over the ideas of the lecture in his mind. In early December 1844, he wrote in his journal further notes on the moral foundation of democracy: "Duty of a man—as self-conscious [being,] to rule himself—all else should but help to that—. So the duty of men *politically* considered [is] to govern themselves—*when the action of all results from the will of all*. All gov[ernment]. should be this, or help to it."[84]

Parker had brought back from Europe intellectual seeds that would yield for him a rich harvest of ideas about democracy and proposals for social and cultural reform. But before he could gather his crops, the controversy between him and Unitarians of Boston would explode with new and greater force, propelling him into the next phase of his career.

Chapter Nine

Shut In for My Own Good

In April 1844, while Parker was taking in the sights of Rome, Emerson published the last issue of the *Dial*. He had grown tired of losing "good time in my choosing & refusing & patching, that I want for more grateful work."[1] Besides, he thought the publication made headway too slowly with the public. Parker seems not to have missed the magazine much. Although it had been an important outlet for his articles, he always had thought it too callow in tone, too preoccupied with art and poetry, too uninterested in theology and reform. It was, however, the last remaining site of common Transcendentalist activity. Its disappearance signaled that one phase of the movement was at an end and another was beginning. The loose-knit "New School" coterie, woven in 1836, had been shedding threads for years, as the more conservative members of the group fell off in dissent. But in 1844 the unraveling accelerated rapidly. The lives of several key Transcendentalists changed, in ways that affected their relationships to reform and to each other. Yet their influence was to grow wider.

Emerson's decade of greatest intellectual fecundity was closing. Although some of his greatest writing was still ahead of him, including many of his best poems, new ideas came to him more slowly, and he spent more time elaborating earlier thoughts. In future, "he was to do proportionately less original writing and proportionately more editing of the rich materials he had already collected or written and stored up in his notebooks." Parker thought he perceived a loss of creative force in Emerson's new collection of *Essays*, published in October 1844. Parker started to read the *Second Series* shortly after it came out, but soon stopped. "It is not Emerson," he complained in his journal, "& I wish to have only his best. In many sentences you may insert the negative & it will be just as true & just as Emersonian as now. I dislike his *mannerisms*. He imitates himself. I think he has lost that wonderful sweetness & exquisite beauty he once possessed." The essay on "Manners," in particular, Parker complained was "carpentry & not growth—a patchwork from his journals & commonplace books."[2]

Parker wondered whether Emerson, or he himself, had fallen. In fact, Parker now responded differently to Emerson's work in part because his own interests had come to diverge more and more from those of his friend. Parker would continue to admire Emerson, praise him, and extol the virtues of his writing to others—but would never again be inspired by him.

Margaret Fuller, whom Parker never really understood or appreciated (any more than she understood or appreciated him), left New England and the Transcendentalist circle for new worlds. In the two years since she resigned as editor of the *Dial*, she had been searching restlessly for a field of action where she would be freed from the conventional and crushing social restraints imposed on women in Boston. In the winter of 1842–43, she had traveled to the West, a trip that resulted, a year later, in her first original book, the discursive travel narrative *Summer on the Lakes*. In July 1843, she had broken new intellectual ground with her *Dial* essay on women's rights, "The Great Lawsuit." She here rejected the idea of a restrictive women's "sphere," and dissented from the concept, which ran through much Transcendentalist thought, of a unitary mode of spiritual perfection, modeled on male accomplishment. She proposed a dual mode of spiritual perfection, in which both sexes partook of male and female characteristics. Most radically, she insisted that women must pursue spiritual growth on their own, without waiting for help from men, who too often were hopelessly prejudiced against female intellectual achievement. By the end of 1844, Fuller had expanded her essay into the book that would make her international reputation, *Woman in the 19th Century*. While completing this work, she moved to New York to become a correspondent and literary critic for the *New York Tribune*. There, a universe of opportunities opened for her.

Bronson Alcott's world, by contrast, nearly imploded in 1844. Since making a splash at the religious conventions of 1840, he continued to develop his austere vision of a perfected society. In 1842 he traveled to England (Emerson helped pay his way), where he met with admirers of his educational work who enthusiastically encouraged his emerging plan to establish a new Eden. A few of his English friends returned to Boston with him and one of them, Charles Lane, gave him the money to establish a community, to be called Fruitlands, on a small farm in the village of Harvard, thirty miles northwest of Boston.

In the summer of 1843, Alcott moved to this lovely hillside spot, along with his wife, Abba May, his four young daughters, among them the eleven-year-old future writer, Louisa May, his friend Lane, and a few others. Together they set out to free themselves from all corruption, worldliness, carnality, and cruelty. The Fruitlanders ate no meat, milk, or spices; drank no hot water;

took no hot baths; wore no cotton, wool, or silk (to avoid exploiting slaves, sheep, or worms); and attempted to farm their meager acres without forcing labor from draft animals. This severe experiment might have worked, had Alcott and his associates been as systematic, disciplined, and concordant as, say, Helen and Scott Nearing. But they were not. Alcott and Lane left to lecture in the fall, leaving Abba and the little girls to figure out how to harvest the grain. Then, in the winter, came bitter dissension, when Lane tried to persuade Alcott to renounce his family and become celibate. By January, the community had collapsed.

The crash of Alcott's millennial hopes plunged him into an acute depression. He lay in his bed for days without taking food or water. In the end he elected to live—he loved his family and could not leave them burdened with his many debts—but he never again took such a risk, and he left the public arena of reform altogether for many years.[3]

Knowledge of the Fruitlands catastrophe no doubt was one reason that Parker, despite his early admiration for Alcott, came in the end to judge him a failure. The two men remained personally cordial. In 1847, Parker invited Alcott to participate in a "convention of reformers" he was organizing; in the early 1850s they worked together against the Fugitive Slave Law; in 1857 and 1858, when Louisa May, now a shy young woman, was struggling to live on her own in Boston, Parker gave her help and encouragement. Yet in 1859, when Parker wrote his account of Transcendentalism in his *Experience as a Minister*, he deliberately made no mention of Bronson Alcott. As Parker explained to George Ripley, Alcott had "brought nothing to pass—so unsteady was his *punctum Stans*; so false his method; & so little his culture. He will be disappointed [at being passed over]. But he has affected only a few persons, them not well."[4]

Just as Alcott's Edenic dreams failed, Ripley remade his West Roxbury utopia along "associationist" (or "socialist") lines. In January 1844, a revised constitution for Brook Farm was issued, proclaiming the intention of transforming the community into a Fourierist Phalanx. The turn to Charles Fourier's ideas had been gradual. The Frenchman's ideas had been in circulation around Boston since 1840, when Ripley and Parker, among others, had read Albert Brisbane's *Social Destiny of Man*.[5] In the intervening years, Brisbane's relentless proselytizing had won many converts to the Fourierist program for making society and work conform to human nature. By adopting Fourierism, the Brook Farmers therefore were joining a national movement and winning wider influence; in 1845, they began publishing the national Fourierist newspaper, the *Harbinger*.

The gaily individualistic community now adopted Fourier's regimented plan of social organization, with all its peculiar terminology. Workers were separated into three "Series," Farming, Mechanical, and Domestic, which

Shut In for My Own Good

were in turn divided into "Groups" dedicated to particular tasks. The system eventually grew so elaborate that there were as many Groups as Brook Farmers.[6]

Parker could never warm to this development. He welcomed Fourierism only as a sign of the times—a protest against the "irrational" and "unchristian" state of society, in which the strong exploited the weak. Yet he questioned Fourier's "machinery," and thought that Fourier, like other socialists, had the right sentiment, but the wrong idea, and so took misdirected action. With Ripley's encouragement, Parker did read books by and about Fourier and in the spring of 1845 attended a Fourierist convention in Boston. Parker also continued to praise Brook Farm, even in its revamped form, as a "noble enterprise." But a cool tone nonetheless seeps into his comments about the place after 1844.[7]

In April 1845, when Brook Farm organized a large celebration of Fourier's birthday, Parker went, but admits in his journal that he left his own work "reluctantly." He liked the speeches, by Ripley and others, and took note of the elaborate decorations (including a bust of Fourier), but found only one truly "beautiful" thing about the whole affair: that the children were given whole oranges while the adults got only half ones. A week later, he visited Brook Farm again and commented in his journal, without explanation, that the community was "sad to look upon." Again, his lack of enthusiasm for Fourierism is suggested by his dealings, or lack of them, with the *Harbinger*. When it was launched, Parker dutifully wrote out in his journal a list of possible articles to write for the new publication, yet somehow never made the time to commit any of them to paper.[8]

While Ripley was becoming a Fourierist in 1844, his close friend Orestes Brownson was becoming a Catholic. On 20 October, the coadjutor bishop of Boston, John Bernard Fitzpatrick, heard Brownson's confession and received his abjuration of heretical opinions, then administered to him conditional baptism and the sacrament of Confirmation; the next day, Brownson, who had just turned forty-one, took his first communion from a priest. Brownson had been moving away from Transcendentalism for more than three years, and he had published his thoughts at every stage, making the whole process very public; as early as the spring of 1843, Parker knew Brownson was "tending towards" Rome. Brownson's move to a new religious home was accompanied by a sharp political turn to the right, as he became, in Parker's later, partisan opinion, "a powerful advocate of material and spiritual despotism, and perhaps the ablest writer in America against the Rights of Man and the Welfare of his race."[9]

Brownson, for his part, had come to believe that Parkerism was the ultimate expression of modern infidelity, so that refuting it would refute all contemporary theological errors. In 1845, with Parker much in the news,

Brownson decided to criticize Parkerism afresh, from the Catholic perspective. Brownson wrote three lengthy polemics that appeared, respectively, in the April, July, and October issues of *Brownson's Quarterly Review*, his new journal; the latter two pieces together made up a new, 82-page examination of the *Discourse of Religion* (bringing to 208 the total number of printed pages he had devoted to reviewing the book since it appeared).[10]

The object of Brownson's assaults, however, had ceased to take his assailant seriously. When Parker read the April polemic, he wrote in his journal that it "amuses me much" by being so "*ferociously abusive*." Parker was equally dismissive of Brownson's July effort: "Let him fire away till he has burnt all his powder & wasted his shot—me he will never hurt—one bit. Poor man—all the seven sacraments will not keep him cool."[11]

Parker once had admired Brownson, but now, looking over Brownson's stormy religious progress, with its conclusion that Parker found so eccentric, he decided that this pilgrim must have lost his way due to a spiritual defect. In a sermon from August 1845, Parker passed judgment on Brownson without naming him: "Who has not seen some men of unbalanced mind, intellectual always, but spiritual never, heady, not hearty, roving from church to church, now Trinitarian, then unbeliever, then Universalist, Unitarian, Catholic, everything by turns, but nothing long, seeking rest by turning perpetually over, and becoming at last a man having experienced many theologies, but never religion, not a Christian, but a verbal index of Christianity, a commonplace book of theology."[12]

Transcendentalism was hardly dead; its period of widest influence was just beginning. Yet in light of all the changes overtaking the original Transcendentalist circle, some conservative Unitarians began to hope that they had outlasted their opponents. One such optimist was Ezra Stiles Gannett. In an article for the April 1844 *Examiner*, Dr. Gannett (Harvard had awarded him the honorary degree in 1843) declared happily that the "transcendental movement" had "passed by," and that to mention it was "the making up of yesterday's journal."[13]

As for Theodore Parker, Gannett pronounced his hour over. Although Parker had done Unitarians "no slight harm," many who had been attracted to him by his "manifest earnestness and unimpeachable character," his "popular style of writing," and the "freshness and independence of his speculations" had recoiled once the true tendencies of his theological system became apparent. Gannett now found that "very little sympathy" remained with Parker, while the fear that he would precipitate "a serious breach" in the "integrity of . . . [the Unitarian] Communion" had "dissipated."[14]

Gannett's relief was premature. The denomination shortly would face an unprecedented crisis, as it divided over whether Parker was entitled to ministerial fellowship, and his supporters would begin to organize a new church for him, a development that inaugurated an epoch in his ministry.

PARKER HAD come back to Boston with a feeling of self-confidence, which old trials soon tested. Immediately and intimately, he still faced sharing a house with Aunt Lucy. A year of respite from one another's company had done little to soften their mutual antagonism. If anything, their having experienced life without the constant irritation of the other's presence made its renewal more difficult for either of them to tolerate.

Within six weeks of Parker's homecoming, the familiar, thinly veiled complaints begin to appear in his sermons and journals about "daily dealing with a sour, . . . peevish, morose person, whom God himself cannot please." A scratched out passage in Parker's journal from November observes that there are "some persons distinguished by their negatives & I have known one who likes few things except dollars & impossibilities. Cats she hates—so her neighbors. She only likes the past & the absent—she wishes lettuce in winter—& ice in summer. Her Heaven is to be disagreeable—Her atmosphere is peculiar —Few can breathe peacefully in its charmed circle." In a journal entry a few pages earlier, Parker notes that he had that day "seen a person who abuses— all good men & women indiscriminately unless they belong to her. She suspects bad motives—under good acts—& has a scoffing way of speech—which the devil might covet—. . . . Everlastingly she remembers an ill thing—But a good one—She never fails to forget—She hears a story—she understands part & imagines the rest—what she understood she forgets & remembers what she imagined—the[n] repeats it. If she says an ill thing of a man—not of her *ichor*—I always subtract half—& find commonly I have not taken away half enough. She is one thing good—that is good hater." Her "spiteful" quality was a trait, writes Parker, that "I felt the first time I ever saw her & only more strongly today."[15]

In October, Parker devoted an entire sermon to the problem of the "Evil Tongue." He here describes the case of a *man* with this "disease"—although he certainly did not have someone male in mind (he says women are more often afflicted). The friends of the evil-tongued man, Parker writes, "treat him as a *spoiled child*." They do not correct his mistakes, partly because they know "he prefers his own error to their truth," and partly because "they fear the Storm of fury . . . that will fall on their heads if the[y] offer to doubt" his words. His "Christian" friends try at first to argue with him, when he "suspects a base motive beneath an honorable act" or dwells with "diabolical delight" on the possibly suspicious acts of a good man. These Christian friends discover, however, that any attempt to correct the distortions of an evil tongue is met with "fresh indignation," and that they themselves are condemned as perpetrators or at least defenders of crime. They therefore give up their charitable efforts and are "silent & sad." But the evil-tongued man's "un-christian" acquaintances find pleasure in his company, as they would enjoy an exhibition of wild beasts. Parker quotes the words of "one of this sort," concerning an unnamed evil-tongued spinster: " 'I like to hear Miss ——['s] spiteful talk. It is good as a good cock fight, or a Bull-baiting.' "[16]

This discourse struck too close to home. A few days after Parker preached it, he noted in his journal that one of his "good friends" (meaning a member of his household) had objected that "it was a portrait of one—(a woman) [&] that it was *personal* & *abusive*."[17] The objector was no doubt either Lydia or, more likely, Lucy herself.

In the past, an incident like this would have been the occasion for matrimonial strife. Now, however, Theodore and Lydia trusted one another. If it was Lydia who did not like the sermon, she nonetheless seems to have been getting along with her husband very well. Only a few lines after Parker records the complaint in his journal, he notes that "my wife is kind as an angel."[18]

The improvement in Parker's relations with Lydia seems to have made him stronger and more secure when dealing with his difficult in-law. His complaints about her are no longer associated with rhetorical wailing and tearing of hair; declarations that his life is a veil of tears and his home a hell can no longer be found. Lucy, for her part, seems to have perceived the new balance of power in the household and not liked it. Such recognition may have prompted her to demand, in December, that the household be broken up—something she probably would not have wanted to do had she felt in control of the situation. As Parker records Lucy's "talk" with him (in a blotted out journal passage), she proposed that they separate their houses, announced her intention to sell the West Roxbury estate, and told Parker to "look out for another."[19] This plan was not acted on, however, possibly because Lucy changed her mind, or possibly because Parker refused to move until he could pay for a house himself.

Besides, he had nowhere to go. The prospect of ever leaving Spring Street appeared dim. No church besides his own wanted him; in only a handful was he even allowed to preach. Parker still was ambitious enough to feel trapped pastoring a tiny parish, but he attempted to meet the situation with a new, more mature attitude.

"*Frisch auf mein Herz, frisch auf*," wrote Parker in his journal in late November. "I am *shut in*—shut in *by God*—shut in *for my own good*." Parker elaborated the spiritual benefits of his situation a few weeks later, in a sermon for which he took as his text Genesis 7:16, "And the Lord shut them in." Suppose, Parker writes, "Our *sphere* seems . . . |narrow|. We feel the strength of a giant—while our task, so we fancy—demands only a pygmy's arm!" Suppose, again, a man "has *enemies* who watch him, suspect him—calumnate him." Such confined circumstances depend not on chance but on the infinite Wisdom and Love of God. From limitations, Parker writes, we learn the real virtue of patience and our own inner strength. So a man (like himself), confined in youth by poverty he had to struggle to overcome, looks back on this period of "mourning, . . . doubts—fear & struggles" as "the golden age of his life," because he now sees how overcoming obstacles has made him more powerful.[20]

Despite such exhortations to himself to be content, Parker inevitably felt restless at the prospect of preaching so much "at home," especially because he knew his sermons potentially had a huge audience in Boston. The muster-day turnout for his "Sermon of Travels" was no fluke. Not only did some Bostonians continue to come out every Sunday, by buggy or even on foot, to hear him, but when he was given an exchange in the city, he always found waiting a welcoming crowd. In October, for example, he preached in Boston for the first time since 1843, on exchange with his comrade-in-arms John Pierpont, and the attendance was so large that he cautioned himself against pride. In his journal that night, he reminded himself that "so many" had come to hear his "poor words" only because they were not getting the "proper bread" at home. He then wrote a prayer that he "not be down cast by success."[21]

Parker found other evidence for the size of his potential congregation in his growing success as a lecturer. "I am excluded from nearly all the pulpits in the Land," he noted in a journal entry from January 1845, "but [am] admitted to numerous *Lyceums*." The 1844–45 season marked the beginning of his mature career as an itinerant public speaker. He no longer delivered lecture courses in a few lyceums, but individual lectures in many. He did present, twice more, a revised version of the "Six Plain Sermons" (once at Marblehead and once at New Bedford), probably with an eye to their being published— which never happened. But his other twenty-eight appearances that winter, at twenty lyceums from Nantucket to Dover, New Hampshire, were to present a single lecture, such as "The Signs of the Times," "Education," or "Roman Slavery."[22]

Parker liked the listeners and income that lecturing provided, and the freedom it gave him to treat scholarly and political topics. But he found the lectern no substitute for the pulpit. Only in sermons, he thought, could he treat the highest and deepest themes and directly address spiritual and theological subjects.

Yet he was hard pressed to find preaching opportunities outside West Roxbury. A few small town or village churches did allow him in. In November 1844, he preached on exchange in Lincoln at the invitation of Samuel Ripley ("Mr. R. is very kind to exchange with me," noted Parker in his journal, "Heretic as I am reckoned");[23] in January 1845, he exchanged with the abolitionist Samuel J. May, who temporarily was filling the pulpit of Parker's boyhood church at Lexington; the following month, Parker exchanged with Samuel Robbins of Chelsea. In Boston, however, almost every church, aside from that of the embattled Pierpont, was closed to him.

One possible exception was the Suffolk Street Chapel, pastored by John Sargent. Sargent had swapped pulpits with Parker in December 1841 (after the South Boston controversy), but so much had happened since that Parker could not be sure Sargent would give him another chance. On 27 October 1844, he wrote Sargent a short, tentative note: "Would you like to exchange with me on the 3ᵈ Sunday in November? If you would please to [—] say *Aye* — if contrary-minded *Noe*."[24]

Sargent said "Aye." The exchange took place, as Parker had requested, on 17 November. Five days later, Sargent resigned. And so began a new season of controversy and discontent.

JOHN TURNER SARGENT, thirty-six years old, tall and handsome, reared a gentleman, educated at Harvard College and Harvard Divinity School, happily married to a wealthy woman with whom he had a large and growing family, had chosen to devote his life to helping the less fortunate. In 1837, he had been ordained a "Minister at Large" in Boston, his position sponsored by the Benevolent Fraternity of Churches.[25]

Unitarians had established the Fraternity in the 1820s to address the burgeoning problem of urban poverty. Interested churches established fund-raising auxiliaries and chose representatives to a central board, which in turn elected an executive committee; the committee submitted quarterly reports for the board to approve. The actual agents of Fraternity benevolence were the Ministers at Large. They visited the afflicted in their homes and helped them with money, references, information, counsel, and prayer; the ministers also ran Sunday schools and conducted marriages, baptisms, and funerals for the unchurched. Some ministers found that these pastoral duties, which involved countless claims on their time, day and night, consumed all their energy. Sargent, however, felt called also to preach. When he took up his work, the only Fraternity-controlled Unitarian pulpit, the Chapel for the Poor on Pitts Street, was occupied, so the Fraternity instructed him to gather his own church.[26]

Sargent moved to the South End, then a neighborhood of transient laborers wedged on the narrow isthmus between Boston Harbor and the polluted Mill Pond. He soon was operating a large Sunday school and had started holding services. The numbers coming to hear him preach increased so rapidly (despite the constant attrition of worshipers moving away) that the Fraternity authorized him to construct a new chapel. This rough stone structure, paid for in large part by Sargent family money, soon rose on Suffolk

Street and was dedicated in 1840. By 1844, around 136 families belonged to the congregation. Sargent's place in the community was much larger; he later calculated that of the 125 funerals he had conducted in the seven years of his ministry, only 50 were of persons connected with his chapel.[27]

The Fraternity was understandably pleased with Sargent's performance. They disapproved of only one thing about his course: his willingness to exchange pulpits with Theodore Parker.

Sargent had declared his inclusive vision of ministerial fellowship on 19 May 1841 at the very inception of the Parker controversy. At the South Boston ordination itself, just minutes after Parker had preached the "Transient and Permanent in Christianity," Sargent had offered Charles Shackford a Right Hand of Fellowship with a pointedly liberal message. The "distinctive and fundamental principle" of Unitarianism, he declared, was for "every man [to] be left unmolested, to analyze truth for himself, and to utter what he honestly *believes* to be truth." Unitarians were "never frightened by the progress of those who truly 'wait upon the Lord'": "We welcome as brother every teacher of the word, whose speculations, however wide from ours, are based upon a sincere faith in Christ, a love of truth, and care for souls."[28]

Sargent soon learned that his remarks were controversial—in particular, that Samuel K. Lothrop did not "approve or concur" with what he had said. In a public letter explaining himself (published in the *Boston Courier*), Sargent wondered whether his views were "more latitudinarian than even Unitarianism would allow" and whether he had been "mistaken in supposing that Unitarians *do*, or *will* welcome as a brother, any one whose views diverge from that something which they call the Unitarian creed." If so, Sargent concluded, he had misunderstood the Unitarian principles of faith and fellowship, and (he implied) now thought less of Unitarianism than before.[29]

Few seem to have noticed this letter, but in December 1841, when Sargent put his ideas into practice and actually gave Parker an exchange, some members of the Fraternity Central Board expressed their alarm. They told Sargent that fellowship with Parker was "inexpedient," because donors would be alienated if they thought someone with Parker's views were permitted to preach in a Fraternity pulpit. How Sargent replied to this concern later became a matter of dispute. Some board members remembered him offering them assurance that he would not exchange with Parker again. Sargent recalled saying only that *if he saw matters as they did*, he would not exchange with Parker again.[30]

The board seems to have believed, however, that the issue had been settled. If they had any doubts, these were allayed at Parker's conference with the Boston Association in January 1843, which Sargent attended along with several board members, including Lothrop and Ezra Stiles Gannett. Here, when

Parker was charged with holding "deistical" views, Sargent did not object. He in fact did not consider himself a Transcendentalist and later professed to have no sympathy with Parker's "peculiar and distinctive speculations" regarding inspiration and miracles. Yet Sargent also believed that "our dissent from a man's opinions is one thing, [while] our disposition to proscribe or excommunicate him in consequence of those opinions is quite another thing."[31]

Besides, Sargent admired Parker as a reformer. They were allies, for example, in the temperance movement, and both were friends of the Unitarian champion of temperance in Boston, John Pierpont. Although Sargent had served as a junior member of the Hollis Street Council and had signed its "Result," he afterward had continued to offer Pierpont ministerial fellowship—the only clerical signer to do so besides Dr. Gannett and the other Fraternity chaplain in Boston, Robert Cassie Waterston of Pitts Street (also a temperance man). Members of the pro-Pierpont faction at the divided Hollis Street Church, meanwhile, took up the cause of Sargent's ministry, even worshiping at Suffolk Street from time to time.[32] When Sargent accepted Parker's proffer of an exchange in November 1844, he seems to have expected no trouble, in part because Parker had conducted an uneventful—if unusually well-attended—service at Hollis Street just weeks earlier.

For Parker's visit to Suffolk Street on 17 November, enough people came to fill the aisles and even the pulpit stairs. In his sermons, Parker carefully avoided mention of his controversial theories. "On Strife & Peace in the Christian Churches" called for an end to sectarian warfare, while "Of Christian Advancement" envisioned the progress of religious ideas. His words were mild, yet his mere presence in a Fraternity pulpit triggered a reaction. The Executive Committee learned that "not a few of the best friends" of the Ministry at Large had been "much grieved" by the exchange and quickly convened to discuss the crisis.[33]

The five members of the Executive Committee included Parker's critic Samuel K. Lothrop and a prominent lawyer named Henry B. Rogers, who soon would lead a fight to keep Parker out of the pulpit of his own church. As a group, the committee took for granted that "the leading views of Mr. Parker are radically erroneous, and subversive of the authority of Scripture," and that this assessment was shared by "all the Pastors of those churches forming 'the Fraternity,' and a vast proportion of their congregations, if not all." The committee promptly prepared an order to Sargent and Waterston, drafted in part by Rogers, "that no exchange of pulpits with Mr. Parker ought again to be assented to."

The committee later claimed that they had not issued "an authoritative edict," but merely made a "friendly statement" of their "wishes and views."

Shut In for My Own Good

Yet their "communication" sounds like a ukase: "The general control of the ministrations of the Chapels rests, by the provisions of the Constitution, in the Executive Committee. . . . Under their responsibility . . . the Executive Committee will give assurances to the Fraternity, that . . . [Mr. Parker] shall not again occupy the pulpit in either of the Chapels, until they are otherwise instructed by some higher authority." The committee dated their order 22 November. Before the committee could make fair copies of the order and mail them, however, they received a letter from Sargent, also dated 22 November, resigning his office.[34]

Sargent had learned of the committee's displeasure when some "friends" of the chapel "admonished" him that he must resign his post unless he pledged to cease ministerial fellowship with Parker. Such a promise Sargent refused to make. He instead informed the committee that he would vacate his pulpit on 1 January.[35]

Sargent apparently calculated that the committee would yield on exchanges rather than lose him. He burnt no bridges in his resignation letter, which was not written in a confrontational tone. He said he must retire immediately because the Parker exchange apparently had so wounded the feelings of some Fraternity supporters, for reasons he professed not to understand, that his usefulness had been fatally compromised and "the real and spiritual interests of this ministry . . . absolutely put in jeopardy."[36] He seemed to want the committee to say that the exchange had been acceptable after all and to reject his offer.

The committee, however, did not withdraw their order. Instead, they sent it to him with an addendum, urging him, in effect, to come to his senses: "The Committee cannot but hope that Mr. Sargent will, on perusing this paper, readily acquiesce in the views of the Committee, and be not unwilling to be guided by them, and that he will consent to withdraw his letter of resignation."[37]

Sargent received this message with some shock. He now realized the committee considered him expendable. His resulting anger may have fueled his second letter of resignation, dated 29 November, which is very different from the first.

This time, Sargent did burn bridges. He emphatically reaffirmed his decision ("were I now to remain in this ministry, it could only be by a continued collision with a serious and weighty prejudice, which I could hardly hope to overcome"), and furiously attacked the committee's assumptions. How could it be, he asked, that the " 'vast proportion' " of the Fraternity congregations thought Parker's views " 'radically erroneous,' " yet "so many in those congregations are so athirst to hear those very views"? (Sargent apparently is referring to the crowds that came to hear Parker preach and lecture.) Sargent pointed out that some Fraternity pastors (meaning Pierpont and possibly James Freeman Clarke) in fact stood "ready to exchange with Mr. Parker any time he pleases," that others were willing to do so "*if their people consent*," and that still others were "said to hold views analogous or identical" with those of Parker, "though not publicly proclaimed" (Sargent here seemed to confirm Parker's claim that his opponents were hypocrites).[38]

As the committee read on, they must have grown more and more offended, as when Sargent accused Samuel Lothrop of inconsistency. Lothrop had allowed prominent Trinitarians to preach in his church, despite their theology being "irreconcilable and opposed" to his own. Sargent also raised hackles by criticizing how the Boston clergy had treated John Pierpont since the Hollis Street Council. Pierpont, Sargent noted, had been excluded from Fraternity pulpits just as effectively as Parker himself, although no one pretended that Pierpont was "*theologically* a heretic." Would not "the same rule which would exclude Mr. Parker from the Suffolk Street Chapel, because excluded from the pulpits of your Fraternity, . . . also close the door of that Chapel to Mr. Pierpont? If so, and the prejudice of the several pastors in your churches must be the criterion or condition of my fellowship and exchange with others, then I should prefer to vacate a pulpit so constrained."[39]

There could be no doubt how the Executive Committee would respond. They accepted Sargent's resignation on 7 December. The "character of your letter," they explained, ". . . is such as to preclude the hope of any different or useful result by any comment or answer we might make to it."[40]

Sargent could have chosen, at this point, to defy the Fraternity by setting up his own independent church in the South End. Some members of his Suffolk Street congregation urged him to take this course, as did Parker himself. But Sargent refused. He feared harming the chapel he had worked so hard to establish.[41]

Even taking into account Sargent's strong convictions about fellowship, his sacrifice seems extraordinary. He was, for one thing, surrendering a much-needed salary. Although he did have family money, he also had five children and many expenses stemming from a fire in June 1844 that had consumed his house.[42] But he also was giving up much more than money: a congregation he loved and, above all, a calling.

Sargent would try twice, later, to take up work as a regular parish pastor, but in both cases the experiment failed. At Somerville, he lasted less than two years; at the South Universalist Society of Boston, less than one. His professed reason for leaving in both cases was ill health. Yet the impression lingers that he could not be satisfied without the round-the-clock intensity and sense of mission that went with his former ministry. As a friend of his would say of him, many years later, Sargent "woke every morning to feel there was something wanting. He was what the French call *désoevré*; his work was not

Shut In for My Own Good

there. He occupied other positions; had definite duties; but . . . there was not a day to the end of his life when he did not feel the blow."[43]

By his act, Sargent transformed the three-year-old Parker controversy. It had been dominated by those who thought that Parker's theology made him obviously unfit to be recognized as a Christian teacher. The discussion had been so one-sided that Parker's opponents—Dr. Gannett, for example, and the members of the Executive Committee of the Benevolent Fraternity— could persuade themselves, despite much evidence to the contrary, that he had little or no support in the Boston churches. Many potential Parker supporters, meanwhile, felt intimidated into acquiescence. Sargent's resignation not only galvanized Parker's friends, it changed the terms of the debate. The key issue was no longer the value of Transcendentalist theology, but the obligations of liberal fellowship. This shift brought Parker new allies—people who fought less for him than for his right to be heard. The battle over how Unitarians should treat Parker finally was joined in earnest.

Sargent himself fired the first salvo when he resigned. He also fired the second. On Sunday, 8 December, the day after his resignation was accepted, he happened to be preaching on exchange at the Hollis Street Church. He used the occasion to justify his course before a sympathetic audience. His sermon was on the "Obstacles to Truth."

Two linked metaphors for suppressed freedom of religion frame the discourse. One is inspired by a text from the Hebrew Testament, "And a great stone was upon the well's mouth" (Genesis 29:2), the other by the Greek Testament story of a boulder sealing the tomb of Jesus. Sargent proclaims that prejudiced men always attempt to stopper "the well-spring of everlasting life," but in the end they always fail: "They bury truth in a sepulchre, and roll a great stone to the mouth of it, and set a big seal, and a snoring sentinel upon its grave, and think they have suppressed it; but *they*, even as the Saviour's foes, will find they are mistaken. Truth will rise again about midnight, and roll away the rocks of opposition, and go forth, with a troop of angel witnesses, for the confounding and amazement of her persecutors."[44]

Sargent attacks as foolish the tendency of ministers to "practice a too rigid exclusion towards one another." Clergy who place a veto on a brother entering their pulpits "because of his imagined heresy," and who say in effect to their people, "*you shall not hear him*," only excite their people to rise up "in a spirit of curiosity and of opposition, and say—'we *will* hear him, and you may help it if you can.'" Crowds rush to listen to the excommunicated man, and any church where he is admitted is taken "by storm." The heretic "is lifted at once into the position of a glorified outcast, an immortalized martyr; an amazement even to himself."[45]

Sargent vehemently denies that he encourages erroneous speculations by holding fellowship with someone who entertains and preaches them. I am not an infidel, he says, because I happen to hear one speak, nor a Methodist because I have had one preach in my pulpit: "I protest against such inferences. . . . I protest against such unreasonable conclusions." Instead, the

> more candor and generosity I show towards another's creed, the more do I manifest faith and stability in my own, and any conclusions to contrary are puerile and illegitimate; and it is equally puerile, to suppose that a Christian's faith is to be disturbed or stricken down like a puny fly by the feather-fan of some heterodox ingenuity. For one I can say, that, if *my* faith is such a bag of wind or wreath of smoke as to be so demolished, let it go, and I will go with it. But, so long as I live, I will remonstrate wholly and emphatically, now and forever, against the timid, slavish, and exclusive disposition which sees a ghost in every opinion different from our own, and trembles lest it carry us away in its cold arms.[46]

Sargent's sermon received an enthusiastic response from Pierpont's supporters in his audience, who asked him to publish it as a pamphlet. He did so a few weeks later, adding an appendix in which he printed his heated correspondence with the Executive Committee.

Contention grew over whether or not Sargent had done the right thing. At a meeting of the Boston Association at Sargent's house on 9 December, his resignation was the principal topic of discussion; of those present, only James Freeman Clarke unequivocally supported his position. Five days later, Sargent's congregation, at a special meeting, passed a resolution declaring that they "fully" supported the course he had pursued in support of "the liberty of the pulpit and right of free religious association." On 29 December, Sargent preached an emotional farewell sermon to his church, soon published as a pamphlet, in which he again defended the principle of liberal tolerance and explained that he could not stay without compromising it, "a thing which I know *you* would not ask, and which *you* know I could not grant."[47]

On 5 January, the Executive Committee of the Benevolent Fraternity offered its Fourth Quarterly Report for 1844 to the central board for approval. The committee presented their correspondence with Sargent and asserted they had acted "in no spirit other than becomes the guardians of a Christian enterprise." The board, led by Dr. Gannett, not only voted to accept the report, but singled out for approbation the "proceedings . . . in relation to the resignation of Rev. Mr. Sargent." Only two board members dissented—most likely John Pierpont and James Freeman Clarke. The report soon was published in the *Christian Register* and a new Unitarian weekly, the *Christian World*; the editors of both papers also strongly endorsed the Executive Committee's actions.[48]

Yet the report angered Sargent. Its first offense was to claim that he had assured "some members of the Fraternity," after his 1841 exchange with Parker, that no such exchange would happen again. Sargent fired off a letter to the *Boston Courier* (soon reprinted in the *Register* and the *World*), strongly denying that he had broken any promise.[49]

The report also included a provocative letter from the other minister of a Fraternity-sponsored chapel in Boston, Robert Cassie Waterston, approving of the committee's exclusionary order and agreeing to abide by it. Waterston and Sargent, as fellow pastors for the poor, had once labored together in a common cause. Now Waterston broke with his former colleague.

Waterston had hosted Parker's conference with the Boston Association in January 1843 and there had accused Parker of dipping his pen in acid and his razor in oil. Now Waterston denies that Unitarians, by advocating liberty of the pulpit, are "thereby bound to open the pulpit door to all persons who might be ready to speak, however crude or pernicious we might consider their views." Waterston sees Parker's views as an example. To show just how crude and pernicious they are, Waterston quotes proof texts from Parker's published writings: Parker says that the miracles of Jesus are "myths and fables," that Jesus himself was frequently "mistaken," that "the Evangelists have mingled with their story puerile notions, and tales which it is charitable to call absurd," that the Christianity of the church is "little better than heathenism," that those who revere the baptism and Lord's Supper are like children "pleased with a rattle, tickled with a straw." Waterston avers his own confidence in the miracles of Christ as "indissolubly" connected with the Christian revelation and concludes with the assertion that he was opposed not only to Parker's views, "but to taking any active steps (as I feel that I should do by opening my pulpit for them) to have them diffused through the community."[50]

Waterston wrote his letter shortly after the *Obstacles to Truth* was published, and he seemed to be assaulting a weak point in Sargent's sermon—its failure to refute the charge that Parker aimed to subvert Christianity. Sargent, recognizing the deficiency, by mid-February had produced a pamphlet (anonymously, although he soon confessed authorship) entitled *The True Position of Theodore Parker, Being a Review of Mr. R. C. Waterston's Letter*.[51] Here Sargent sets aside his theological disagreements with Parker to produce one of the warmest defenses of him ever written.

Sargent deprecates Waterston for "raking together all the exceptionable phrases and bolder expressions of a writer, and then parading them as a fair specimen of his actual or aggregate faith and opinions." To measure Parker's true "theological dimensions" by the passages Waterston quotes would no more be fair, Sargent believes, than to "judge of a man's bodily stature or physiognomy by some abscinded locks of his hair, the paring of his nails, or the number of humors we might count upon his face." To counter the impression Waterston has left, Sargent provides eight pages of excerpts from Parker's writings, all expressing reverence for Jesus, the Bible, Christianity, and Christian institutions.[52]

Sargent finds the secret of Parker's power and popularity—as well as his unpopularity—to be that he "cuts clear through the existing meshes and humanized forms of religion in his anxiety to realize the living spirit." He brings a battering ram to tear down the " 'rotten walls of the Church,' as it *is*, *under human organizations*." The outcry of "shrieking remonstrance" against him shows only that the fortress he assaults is weak. Time will reveal that "all Mr. Parker's battering is against the hypocritical formalities and human pretensions to religion, not religion itself; against make-believe Christianity, not real Christianity."[53]

Sargent sees no reason why the "doctrines of hope and duty, so fearlessly advocated by Mr. Parker," are not to be admitted into Unitarian pulpits; these are his predominating views, which he makes the burden of his preaching. Those who seek to exclude him, Sargent charges, are more attentive to opinions in religion than to practice; "lust, avarice, and fraud are often suffered to run riot almost up to the very altar of the sanctuary and lay hold of its horns with only a qualified rebuke, while meek heresy is waylaid at the porch . . . and put in irons without so much as a hearing."[54]

Sargent concludes his pamphlet by criticizing what he sees as Waterston's lack of charity and liberality. He accuses him of acting contrary to fundamental Unitarian principles. Turning seer, Sargent predicts that Parker will become like the ghost of Hamlet's father. He will "ever be rising up . . . as a retributive admonition to Unitarians—the spectre of their past offenses— telling of the wrong which a brother has done him . . . (not by pouring poison into his ears, but the ears of others), and calling on posterity to reverse and revenge, as they will, that wrong he has suffered."[55]

ON 26 DECEMBER 1844, just days before Sargent published *The Obstacles to Truth* and preached his farewell sermon to Suffolk Street, Parker came to Boston to deliver a Thursday Lecture. The timing was coincidental—Parker's turn had come up in the regular rotation of Boston Association members— but it could not have been more provocative. Many wondered at the inconsistency. The Fraternity of Churches, an organization effectively controlled by members of the Association, had barred Parker from the pulpits of the Chapels for the Poor, yet the Association as a whole now allowed him into one of the most prestigious pulpits in the city, that of the First Church, to preach the Thursday Lecture.

The typical audience at a Thursday Lecture was small and consisted disproportionately of Boston Association members. A very different audience greeted Parker. The morning after Christmas was one of the least convenient times imaginable, but so many people showed up (500, according to one observer, of whom 400 were women) that they filled the aisles and even crowded the singers in the choir.[56] Usually, some of the Brethren assisted the preacher. This time none did; most stayed away altogether, although Dr. Gannett, who considered Lecture attendance a solemn duty, hobbled in on his canes.

Parker preached on "The Relation of Jesus to His Age and the Ages." It was an obvious topic for the Christmas season,[57] but also the most contentious he could have chosen. His Christology had puzzled, upset, and outraged more people than any other aspect of his religious thought. Here Parker, as he has before, uses an account of the historical Jesus to discuss New England religious reform and his own story.

Parker opens with the claim that the greatest men are not recognized in their own time, because they are "in advance of men's conjectures, higher than their dreams": "They do not speak what you and I have been trying to say, and cannot; but what we shall one day, years hence, wish to say, after we have improved and grown up to a man's estate." The censors and guides of public opinion never welcome one of these great men, because he "disturbs their notions of order; he shows that the institutions of society are not perfect; that their imperfections are not of granite or marble, but only words written on soft wax, which may be erased and others written thereon anew." But if the censors hate him, others, "not half so well bred, nor well furnished with precedents," will welcome him, and say " 'Behold a prophet.' "[58]

Jesus was too great, according to Parker, to be recognized as such by the three religious "parties" of ancient Judea. These factions, as Parker imagines them, had obvious modern parallels. The Pharisees were the "Conservatives." They "represented the church, tradition, ecclesiastical or theocratical authority"; they believed that " 'Nobody but a Jew could be saved' "; they believed in Moses and the prophets, "at least in public." The Sadducees, who denied immortality, were wealthy cosmopolitans, "sleek respectable men," who lacked positive belief in anything they did not see or touch. The Essenes were the "Come-Outers." They despaired of state and church and withdrew from both to live ascetically and free from tyranny. The Pharisees and Sadducees had no ideas "which represented man, his hopes, wishes, affections, his aspirations and power of progress." The Essenes had faith in man, but were "imprisoned by their organization, and probably saw no good out of their own party lines."[59]

Parker thinks Jesus not the man any of these parties wanted: "The Sadducee expected no new great man unless it was a Roman quaestor, or procurator; the Pharisee looked for a Pharisee stricter than Gamaliel; the Essenes for an

Ascetic." So, Parker continues, the real Jesus was too independent-minded to be wanted by either Unitarians or Orthodox today.[60] Parker implies that modern prophets, such as himself, also are rejected for their independence.

Yet, says Parker (looking out over the packed house), there "were men not counted in the organized sects; men weary of absurdities; thirsting for the truth; sick, they knew not why or of what, yet none the less sick, and waiting for an angel who should heal them, though by troubled waters and remedies unknown."[61] These men had no need of theology, but they did need religion.

Parker devotes a large section of the sermon to the audience of Jesus. In an eloquent passage, drawing much of its power from familiar tropes of conversion, the preacher imagines the listeners of that greater preacher, long ago — and does so, in such a way that his own listeners readily could identify with them, and perhaps relive their own experience:

> It would be curious could we know the mingled emotions that swayed the crowd which rolled up around Jesus, following him, as the tides obey the moon, wherever he went . . . ; to see how this young Hebrew maid, deep-hearted, sensitive, enthusiastic, self-renouncing, intuitive of heavenly truth, rich as a young vine, with clustering affections just purpling into ripeness, — how she seized, first and all at once, the fair ideal, and with generous bosom confidingly embraced it too; how that old man, gray-bearded, with baldness on his head, full of precepts and precedents, the lore of his fathers, the experience of a hard life, logical, slow, calculating, distrustful, remembering much and fearing much, but hoping little, confiding only the fixed, his reverence for the old deepening as he himself became of less use, — to see how he received the glad inspirations of the joiner's son, and wondering felt his youth steal slowly back upon his heart, reviving aspirations, long ago forgot, and then the crimson tide of early hope come gushing, tingling on through every limb; to see how the young man halting between principle and passion, not yet petrified into worldliness, but struggling, uncertain, half reluctant, with those two serpents, Custom and Desire, that beautifully twined about his arms and breast and neck, their wormy folds, concealing underneath their burnished scales the dragon's awful strength, the viper's poison fang, the poor youth caressing their snaky crests, and toying with their tongues of flame — to see how he slowly, reluctantly, amid great questionings of heart, drank the words of truth, and then, obedient to the angel in his heart, shook off, as ropes of sand, that hideous coil and trod the serpents underneath his feet. All this, it were curious, ay, instructive too could we but see.[62]

Jesus spoke for no age or sect, but for eternity, and so "his words ride on the wings of time." He looked not back, "save for illustration and examples.

He looked forward for his direction. He looked around for his work. . . . He looked in, to God, for guidance, wisdom, strength." He met opposition. "It must be so." His existence was a reproach to the Pharisees; they "could not bear him"; his preaching was their trial; his life was their condemnation; the "man was their ruin." So they hung his body on a tree; "they hoped thereby to stifle that awful soul! they stifle only the body; that soul spoke with a thousand tongues." Now, he is worshiped as a God. "It is no wonder. Good men worship the best thing they know, and call it God."[63]

Toward the end of the discourse, Parker touches on some of his most controversial ideas concerning Jesus. Parker admits that Jesus may have taught some errors, but insists that "I care not if he did. It is by his truths that I know him, the absolute religion he taught and lived; by his highest sentiments that he is to be appreciated." Parker dismisses the New Testament miracles. People can believe them if they want, he says, but to himself, "they are not truth and fact, but mythic symbols and poetry; the psalm of praise with which the world's rude heart extols and magnifies its King." He admits as well the possibility of future, greater Christs: "To say this is not to detract from the majestic character of Christ, but to affirm the omnipotence of God." Parker concludes with a plea for his listeners to confer directly with God, as Jesus did.[64]

Parker predictably claimed to think little of his Lecture. Nonetheless, owing to the extraordinary circumstances surrounding its delivery and the controversial doctrines it expressed, "The Relation of Jesus" caused a sensation. Only days after he preached it, reports of what he had said had reached New York, where the *Herald* sneered that Parker probably regarded himself as a "future Christ": "In this his creed resembles a good deal that of the great Apostle of the Mormons, Joe Smith." By mid-January, Parker had printed the offending discourse as a pamphlet.[65]

AMONG THOSE offended was Dr. Gannett. In his diary, he described the Lecture as distressingly "radical," "addressed to the young & the people & denying the miracles of Jesus—making his inspiration only that of a great man."[66] Gannett worried less, however, over what Parker had said, than where he had said it—on a platform sponsored by the Boston Association.

Until this point, Gannett had opposed any suggestion that the Association take collective action, however mild, against Parker. In his April 1844 *Examiner* article, he had argued against those who wanted the Association to expel Parker or publish a disavowal of his opinions: "Expulsion of a member for not thinking with his brethren, however wrong his way of thinking, and however pernicious the influence of his teaching may be in their eyes, is not an act which that association contemplate among their privileges or their duties; nor do they come together to draw up statements of belief, either for their own benefit of for the satisfaction of others."[67] All they could do, continued Gannett, is what they had done: try to convince him, in "free and friendly conversation," that he could not consistently fulfill the function of a Christian minister while rejecting "the main facts of the Christian Scriptures."

Parker's Thursday Lecture roused such outrage among the Association membership, however, that sentiment shifted decidedly against Gannett's laissez-faire stand. Gannett apparently feared that if he did not take the lead, the Brethren might violate what he considered to be liberal principles. He therefore worked up a very carefully worded resolution of his own.

In its final form (more than one draft exists),[68] the resolution declares *both* that Parker, in his Lecture, had "advanced opinions which in the judgment of other members of this Association are subversive of faith the Divine mission & authority of our Lord Jesus Christ," *and* that "the constitution & well understood principles of this body preclude the exercise |on their part| of ecclesiastical power or the infliction of censure of opinions." The resolution expresses only a "disavowal of concurrence" with Parker's views, "so far as they involve a denial of the miraculous character of the Christian revelation, and of the supernatural facts of the New Testament history."

On 7 January 1845, Gannett wrote to Parker, informing him that the Brethren at their next meeting would discuss his Thursday Lecture and what action they would take in regard to it. Gannett urged Parker to attend: "I had much rather the discussion should proceed in your presence & with your participation than in your absence." Parker thought "it can't be a very pleasant evening we shall spend together," but he did plan to go. A winter storm, however, prevented him.[69]

Interest in the topic was so high that, despite the weather, fully thirty-one ministers showed up on 13 January at the house of James Freeman Clarke on Mount Vernon Street. A few of those present, Clarke and John Pierpont among them, spoke against repudiating Parker. The "inconveniences of liberality," they argued, must "be borne."[70] But they were in the minority.

Gannett offered his resolution—only for it to be lost in a forest of others. It was proposed that Parker be requested not to preach any Thursday Lecture again; that he formally be "excused" from preaching it; that the Thursday Lecture be abandoned altogether; that the Association request Parker (yet one more time) to resign his membership; that the Association be dissolved; that the Association expel him. All these actions found critics, however, who considered them either too weak or too illiberal. When the Brethren left Clarke's house late that night, they were still divided, and the debate had been laid over to the next meeting, two weeks hence.[71]

Meanwhile, Clarke himself had ignited a controversy over Parker in his own congregation—one far more furious and bitter than he had anticipated. The day before this Association meeting, on Sunday, 12 January, he had informed the Church of the Disciples that on the final Sabbath of the month, he and Theodore Parker would exchange pulpits.

CLARKE'S ONE previous exchange with Parker, three days after the South Boston ordination, had been marred by controversy; Clarke's slowness to repeat the painful experiment may have prompted some Parker sympathizers in his congregation to invite Parker to deliver the "Religion" course in 1841. The *Discourse of Religion* only increased Clarke's reluctance to swap pulpits. It convinced him that there was "no Unitarian . . . in the whole body, whose system of opinion stands more widely apart than mine from the views of Mr. Parker." Unlike Parker, Clarke believed that the New Testament miracles were historical facts, that the writers of the New Testament were miraculously inspired, that the Hebrew prophets had foretold the coming of Christ, that Christianity was a "peculiar manifestation of God, differing from all his other manifestations," that the message of Christianity was "pardon" for the "sinner," and that Christianity helped the sinner by providing, in Christ, a "Mediator" to God.[72]

Clarke did count himself a Transcendentalist, because he agreed with Coleridge that "though knowledge begins *with* experience it does not come *from* experience"; here Clarke and Parker were in agreement. Also, Clarke prized Margaret Fuller as one of his best friends and greatly admired Emerson. But he emphatically rejected what he called Parker's "negative Transcendentalism." *Positive* Transcendentalism, as Clarke defined it, asserts the reality of the spirit, and so "may well consist with Christianity." Negative Transcendentalism, by contrast, cannot; it denies all that is not spirit, and so "denies all means, all gradations, all steps; it tells us to *be* holy, it does not show us how we are to become holy; it ignores the fact of radical sin; . . . [i]t is at once . . . ignorant of the deep wants of human nature, [and] presumptuous in its contempt and self confidence. Such a system as this cannot of course stand the test of examination; it has too little in it to satisfy the needs of the soul; any progressive nature must soon outgrow it, and feel its emptiness." Put simply, Clarke objected that Parker left no possibility in his system for Christ to play a mediatorial role in human salvation.[73]

Clarke felt his disagreements with Parker so strongly that in early 1844 he publicly lauded a pamphlet (published anonymously by a Unitarian minister from New Hampshire) that denounced Parker as an "infidel." "In these days of smooth speech and gentlemanly Indifferentism," wrote Clarke in a newspaper notice, ". . . it is refreshing to meet with one who cannot tolerate error." Clarke here called Parker's theological system a "gospel of shallow naturalism," and denied that it was Christian. Yet even while Clarke attacked Parkerism as "sheer infidelity," he refused to call Parker *himself* an infidel: "A man may often advocate an infidel system of opinion, and yet have a real faith in his heart."[74]

If anyone noticed this demurral, few thought much of it; many Unitarians who excluded Parker from their pulpits conceded he was a Christian "in life." For them, however, his not being a Christian "in opinion" meant he obviously should not be recognized as a Christian teacher. That Clarke thought differently became apparent in the winter of 1844–45, when he took part in a multisided controversy in the *Christian World*. Clarke began to write in response to a challenge thrown down to Unitarians by a young Orthodox minister, pastor of a small church in the Connecticut River town of Springfield, Noah Porter.

Porter shortly would begin a life-long association with Yale University, first as a professor, eventually as president. He already was winning a reputation for theological polemics that were literate, philosophically informed, fair, and good humored. In 1844, he published two notable examples of his work in the *New Englander*, then establishing itself as the leading Orthodox journal. The first, appearing in the July issue, was a review of Parker's *Discourse of Religion*; the second, out in October, concerned "Theodore Parker and the Liberal Christians."[75]

In these two pieces, Porter advanced a thesis familiar in outline: Parker was an infidel, and his infidelity was the logical outgrowth of Unitarianism. Any number of Orthodox writers had said the same thing. But they had written as if to crow over the humiliation of enemies. Porter wrote as if to correct the failings of friends.

In his review of the *Discourse*, although clear that Parker was no Christian (Porter joked that he wore a turban, not a hat), he treated both author and work with uncommon generosity. Porter praised Parker's bravery and frankness, conceded that much of what he had to say was true and valuable, and (unlike almost every other critic) never accused him of sneering at sacred things. Parker himself liked the article enough that he wrote to Porter thanking him for its "spirit," one "so different from that generally displayed by theological writers, especially when they attack writers whom they call '*Deists*,' 'Infidels,' &c &c." The two men eventually met ("You see, Mr. Porter," Parker is supposed to have told him, "I do wear a hat after all!") and became lifelong friends. Parker never ceased to praise Porter's review as the only fair one the *Discourse* received in America.[76]

Meanwhile, Porter's article on "Parker and Liberal Christians," which sought to demonstrate how the former's ideas grew inevitably out of the beliefs of the latter, was welcomed in the Unitarian press for its "courteous and respectful spirit," and for appealing not to "prejudice," but to "the consent of reason." Hailed as "one of the weightiest attacks which have lately been made against us," the piece was judged worthy of serious and thoughtful responses.[77]

It received two. Samuel Lothrop and George Ellis, editors of the *Christian Register*, wrote a series of five lengthy replies, which ran in their paper in November and December 1844. Meanwhile, Clarke undertook to write and publish a series of lengthy replies of his own, five of which ran in the *Christian World* from November 1844 to January 1845. He planned to produce more, but became distracted when his answers to Porter unexpectedly embroiled him in the controversy over fellowship with Parker.[78]

Clarke took up the fellowship issue while responding to one of Porter's main points, that the Parker case showed liberal Christians to be wrong in their opposition to creeds. Porter argued, first, that liberal anti-creedalism had made Parker's infidelity inevitable. Unitarians thought that no doctrine could be the definitive expression of God's revelation, and that the "spirit of Christianity" was the only thing necessary to secure. Porter believed Parker simply put these opinions on a "philosophical basis" by making religion perpetually improve with human progress. When Parker's conceptions of the divine grow so "enlarged and elevated," however, "that he discovers that Christianity in no sense depends on the facts recorded in the gospels, or on the belief that Jesus wrought miracles, . . . and claims that he is still a Christian, and should be received as a Christian, [the Unitarians] know not what to do. They are all taken aback. On the one hand, they are posed with the fact that there is a Christian teacher among them with whom . . . the Bible, as a book of facts and history, is but little better than moonshine. On the other hand, they are driven to the wall, by the unquestioned fact that he claims to preach a high and pure Christianity in its principles and spirit."[79]

This dilemma has forced the Unitarians, Porter claims, to do in practice what they said they would never countenance in principle: adopt a creed. He points to Samuel Lothrop's 1842 sermons on *The Christian Name and Christian Liberty*, in which Lothrop had argued that the liberal Christian faith must rest on the authority of the New Testament. "So at last liberal Christianity has a creed," comments Porter wryly; "rather short, indeed, but very good so far as it goes."[80]

Lothrop himself responded in the *Register* of 23 November. He insisted that his sermon marked no departure from Unitarian principles, for liberal Christians always had held the "creed" of the Christian world to be the "Scriptures, individually interpreted." The difference between Parker and the Unitarians was "not a question of *interpretation*, . . . but a question of *fact*." Parker denied there existed genuine and reliable records of the origin of the Christian religion, and therefore he had gone "*off Christian ground*."[81]

Clarke's answer to Porter, published over two issues in the *World*, went in a very different direction. The first installment, appearing on 30 November, seems almost a rebuttal to Lothrop. After noting Porter's use of *The Christian Name and Christian Liberty*, Clarke protests "both on our own account, and that of MR. LOTHROP, to the supposition, that his sermon is to be taken as the expression of the Unitarian opinion on this subject, or that 'at last liberal Christianity has a creed,' because Mr. Lothrop has given his own."[82]

Clarke insists that there was "no authority in the New Testament" for creeds. The "basis of Union in the Christian Church as founded by Christ and his Apostles," Clarke asserts, "was not the belief and confession of a creed, but belief in *Christ himself*, and the confession of Christ as the son of God." To admit any other basis for union would be to establish "a new church, on a new foundation."[83]

Having reframed the problem of creeds to be one of Christian union, Clarke turned in his next installment specifically to the problem of union with Parker. Perhaps not coincidentally, this article appeared in the *World* on 7 December 1844, the day the Executive Committee of the Benevolent Fraternity accepted the resignation of Clarke's friend John Sargent.

Clarke argues that Parker must, under the New Testament standard of fellowship, be accepted "as a brother." Clarke admits that Parker's beliefs were not Christian, but holds that Parker could be personally Christian despite his theology; to think otherwise, in Clarke's view, was to "make the Christian life an intellectual, instead of a moral and spiritual state." Because Clarke feels "bound to love and have communion with all Christian hearts," and because Parker "claims to be a Christian, and desires to be in fellowship with Christians, and gives evidence of sincerity," he is worthy of love and communion.[84]

Clarke makes explicit that when he spoke of admitting Parker into Christian fellowship, he meant full ministerial fellowship. Clarke believes that to ban an "errorist" not only excited the curiosity of the community in his suppressed opinions, but made the errorist himself more intransigent and extreme in his views. "Excommunication and exclusion have never yet put down a single heresy," Clarke observes, "though they have set up a great many." He recommends that errorists like Parker be given unexceptionable treatment, but that their opinions should be shown "no mercy."[85]

Clarke's position was controversial and soon came under attack. The assailant was Richard Cecil Stone, pastor of the Unitarian Church in Sherborn; Stone had been reared a Baptist and now considered himself a nondenominational Christian. Like Clarke, he believed in fellowship on "the strong basis of Jesus," and therefore opened his pulpit to any preacher "who truly accepted Jesus Christ as a Redeemer and Saviour." Stone differed from Clarke, however, about what "accepting Jesus Christ" entailed, and therefore about opening pulpits to Parker. Stone undertook to critique the stand of "J. F. C."—

Clarke's pieces had appeared over his initials—in an article that appeared in the *World* on 21 December.[86]

Stone rejects the idea that Christianity was a life, not a belief. God, he writes, "has attempted to make himself known to man by a revelation, and has succeeded, so that candid men may know and agree upon what he has revealed." This revelation repeatedly enjoins, as essential to salvation, belief that Jesus is "the Christ of God." Although "J. F. C." himself says belief in Christ is essential to salvation, Stone notes, he writes as if this belief were a yoke he could accept for himself, but which he must not place on the neck of others. In Stone's opinion, Theodore Parker would not wear it: "He believes Jesus fell into some errors, pardonable, however, on account of his youth."[87]

Clarke considered this challenge by Stone important enough that he abandoned his series replying to Porter and started a new one replying to "R. C. S." In these articles, Clarke laid out in detail his controversial case for fellowship with Parker. He denies at the outset that there was *any* doctrine, belief in which was essential to salvation. *Truth*, he admits, was essential, but he makes a critical distinction between truth and doctrine: "Doctrine is of the head and lips, truth is of the heart and life. Doctrine is an attempt at a verbal statement of truth." Jesus and his Apostles "nowhere make belief in a doctrine essential to salvation." When they spoke of the necessity of faith, they always demanded "a faith of the heart rather than of the head."[88]

Turning to the theme of Christian union, Clarke argues that the principle of doctrines being essential to salvation "has been and is the cause of endless divisions in the Church, and therefore nullifies Christ's dying prayer for his disciples that they may be one." Different minds necessarily see different doctrines as essential. Those who accept one group of doctrines as essential are compelled by their principles to stand apart from those who do not agree with them, and thereby create a sect. Sectarians can only hope for Christian union by making all other sects agree with them, and therefore give their whole strength to building up their own party. To avoid these evils, Clarke writes, Unitarians historically have rejected the "Exclusive System"—which system Clarke accuses "R. C. S." of advocating.[89]

For Clarke, the problem is not whether Parker's views concerning Christ and the New Testament should be opposed as false and injurious—Clarke believes they should—but how they are to be opposed. To exclude Parker, Clarke finds neither right nor expedient. It is not right because it was opposed to the example and command of Christ: "Christ loves not to separate but to unite, to overcome evil by flooding it over with good, to come in contact with all error and overcome it with truth." Exclusion is inexpedient not only because it entrenched errorists in their mistakes, but because it deprived the exclusionists from "the benefit they would derive from those who are excluded, for there is always something which causes a new opinion to spring up."[90]

On 11 January, the *World* published a rejoinder by Stone.[91] He accuses "J. F. C." of advocating "external fellowship" without agreement of "internal spirit." He tries to demonstrate the absurdity of this position by imagining that, hypothetically, "T. PARKER PREACHES FOR 'J. F. C.'" Stone imagines Parker attempting to convince J. F. C.'s "flock" that "the *miracles of Christ were all a deception*," that "*Jesus never rose from the dead*, that the story grew out of the credulity of the age, or, was a cunningly devised fable," that "the New Testament is no more *inspired* than *any other book*; that the idea of a *Savior*, a *Mediator*, and the *forgiveness of sin are the vagaries* of a barbarous age." Surely, writes Stone, J. F. C. would not want false doctrines such as these to take hold in his congregation. Yet if Clarke really believed that no doctrines were essential to Christianity, he would be bound to maintain fellowship not only with Parker, but with "Emerson, saying 'there is no God but Nature,'—'man is Nature's highest exhibition,'—therefore man is God:—Alcott, placing himself several steps in advance of Jesus,—and VOLTAIRE, saying to his followers, 'crush the wretch,'—[for] all [these would] have a right to claim fellowship and the use of every Protestant pulpit."[92]

Had Stone intended to provoke Clarke, he could not have done better than to accuse him of foolishly inviting an old-fashioned Deist into his pulpit and to equate Emerson with Voltaire. Clarke confessed to having "half a mind to subject 'R. C. S.'s article to severe examination, from which process I am inclined to believe, it would have come out somewhat dismantled." Clarke probably had made the arrangement to exchange with Parker before he read Stone's rejoinder. The furor over fellowship had been mounting during December and early January, owing to the Sargent case and the hostility roused by Parker's Thursday Lecture; Clarke doubtless felt increasing pressure to act. He also seems to have corresponded with Parker during this time. Perhaps the final goad for Clarke was the decision of the Central Board of the Fraternity of Churches, on 5 January, to ratify the Executive Committee's report; Clarke was probably present, and if so he certainly cast one of the two dissenting votes. But he also must have realized an exchange was the best rebuttal possible to the kind of arguments Stone advanced. Clarke's announcement of the exchange must have looked to Stone like a rebuttal, coming as it did the day after his rejoinder was published.[93]

Clarke's announcement did not end his controversy with Stone, but their subsequent back-and-forth, which continued in the *World* for months, only detailed the already obvious differences between them (e.g., Stone professed to find incomprehensible Clarke's distinction between "truth" and "doctrine"). The "discussion" with Clarke, Stone later wrote, "opened my eyes in some degree to the tendencies of the liberal school in all its various shades"—and to the direction of these tendencies, which was, in his view, "downward." Within a few years, Stone had disassociated himself from Unitarianism and

Shut In for My Own Good

affiliated with the Wesleyan Methodists. He grew so alienated from liberalism that in his memoirs, written in the 1870s, he neglected even to mention that his church in Sherborn had been Unitarian.[94]

CLARKE EXPECTED some in the Church of the Disciples to dissent from his decision, although he did not anticipate how strong the dissent would be. The church, which at the time worshiped in the hall of the Masonic Temple on Tremont Street, was united in its affection for Clarke, its support of social reforms such as temperance and antislavery, and its commitment to the creation of a new, "democratic" kind of church organization. The Disciples collectively decided church business at a "social" meeting every Wednesday evening and Clarke was granted no special ministerial authority; he was supposed to take no pastoral action that the church had not authorized—an arrangement he embraced. (He always corrected outsiders who, following old New England custom, referred to "Clarke's church." The church was not "his" at all, he insisted. It belonged to its members.) The church was sharply divided, however, in its theological sensibilities. Some Disciples were self-styled "lovers of freedom" who found "liberal Christianity . . . not liberal enough for them," while others were "half orthodox in their belief, and quite orthodox in many of their most cherished opinions." The Parker exchange would inflame these differences.[95]

They were apparent as early as August 1842, when some Parker admirers introduced a resolution at one of the social meetings, "authorizing and requesting the Pastor to exchange with all persons professing to be Christian ministers." Everyone knew which particular "person" was meant. After some discussion, the meeting tabled the proposal as too divisive. All the different sides could agree on was their common confidence that Clarke would do the right thing; Clarke came away from the meeting with the clear understanding that the church had placed the matter of a Parker exchange entirely in his hands.[96]

This compromise, however, did not placate all Parker opponents. Among the most prominent to express their discontent were two brothers of William Ellery Channing: Walter, the distinguished surgeon and dean of the Harvard Medical School, and the somewhat callow George, editor and publisher of the *Christian World*—a paper founded to present the religious views of the Disciples to a wider public. Walter found even the theoretical possibility of a Parker exchange so troubling that he resigned his church membership. George, at first, was milder; he told Clarke only that he and his family would not attend services any Sunday Parker came to preach. Over the next two years, however, he came to regard this statement as too feeble an expression of his convictions. He therefore began to grow restive when publishing Clarke's controversy with Stone in the *World*. Channing privately thought his pastor's position "unscriptural, illogical, and therefore, to say the least, unwise." Yet he seems to have convinced himself that Clarke would not "dare" carry out his principles and risk exposing the Disciples to "the obloquy of every other branch of our denomination."[97]

Clarke thought he could blunt the protest of conservatives like Channing; he attempted to do so in the "carefully prepared" statement with which he announced the exchange. Clarke reiterated his own "entire dissent" from Parker's theology and said he would not have invited Parker to come if he thought that Parker would use the occasion to preach against miracles or the mediatorial role of Christ, or if he believed the Disciples were in such a state of mind that they could not listen to him profitably. Clarke, no doubt recalling what Channing had told him, reminded those who did not want to hear Parker that no one would object if they worshiped elsewhere that day.[98]

Clarke's reassuring words, however, did not have their desired effect. He learned almost immediately that "there were those who felt much conscientious disapprobation" of the exchange. The anti-Parker group included some who viewed the exchange as a "terrible wrong . . . inflicted upon the cause of Christ." These hard-liners startled Clarke by warning him that they might have to leave the church if the exchange went through. In this faction was Channing and the prominent lawyer Henry B. Rogers; as a member of the Executive Committee of the Benevolent Fraternity, Rogers had helped bar Parker from preaching in Fraternity chapels, only now to face the shocking prospect of Parker preaching at his own church. Others against Parker were less hostile to him and had no plans to leave the Disciples, but thought the exchange was ill advised because it would alienate co-worshipers like Channing and Rogers. Among these moderates was a twenty-seven-year-old, cherubic-faced lawyer who later would win fame as the Civil War governor of Massachusetts, John A. Andrew.[99]

The opposition attempted to persuade Clarke to abandon his plan. Five of them, including Andrew and Rogers, met with him at his house on 15 January. They spent hours endeavoring to convince him that the exchange was "wrong" and "dangerous." They "made every appeal, with the scope of language to offer," urging him to "retrace his steps . . . and thus restore peace to the Church." Clarke assured them the exchange was "right" and "necessary."[100]

Two days later, the opposition tried a tougher approach. They happened to dominate the Pastoral Committee, which supervised "the spiritual interests of the Church"; on Friday morning, the committee—led by hard-liners, but with Andrew among them—called on Clarke and accused him of exceeding his authority by arranging the exchange without consulting them. Clarke, however, refused to recognize the committee "as having anything to do with

Shut In for My Own Good

exchanges"; he argued that the church had ceded him the power to make decisions on this matter at the meeting of August 1842. The remonstrants were unpersuaded. One of them quoted the opinion of a lawyer in the congregation (Rogers?), that the committee could declare the pulpit vacant on the last Sunday of the month and supply it themselves. Clarke responded emphatically that if that expedient were tried, the pulpit would "probably *continue* vacant so far as I was concerned." [101]

He suggested that any who were worried that the exchange would put them in a position of seeming "to support and encourage Mr. Parker's opinions" could state their convictions in a public letter to himself, which could be published in the *World* and other papers: "Thus, it seemed to me, they might exonerate themselves from all responsibility, and put the whole of it on myself, who was not only willing but desirous of bearing it." But the committee thought the church as a whole should consider the issue. Clarke agreed to call a special church meeting on Sunday afternoon.[102]

Meanwhile, the opposition—evidently willing to try anything—attempted to persuade Parker to decline Clarke's invitation. On Friday afternoon, Andrew and another moderate called on him in West Roxbury. As politely as they could, they told him that there was "strong feeling" against him among the Disciples and that "some of the society would abandon the church" if he came. Could he possibly stay away?

A few years earlier, this appeal might have worked. Parker, after his painful exchange with Clarke in 1841, had told the Disciples he would not have preached to them had he known they did not want to hear him. Now, however, he had thicker skin. Besides, he increasingly saw himself as a prophet, who did not shy away when a fight was thrust upon him. So he promised only to "consider the matter anew & consult." But in truth he did not think withdrawal was a serious option. As he wrote in his journal, "the principle in which C[larke]. asked an exchange is true" and worth living out.[103]

With both Clarke and Parker standing firm, the opposition prepared for the church meeting, drawing up a set of resolutions that went well beyond what Clarke wanted. Instead of a simple declaration of dissent from Parker's beliefs, the opponents proposed that the church explicitly reject Clarke's theory of ministerial fellowship. As their key resolution declared, "We deny that any just principle of toleration or Christian love makes it obligatory on any minister to make an exchange of pulpits with one whose character or doctrines are such as to create conscientious scruples among his people as to their duty, in listening to him." [104]

Sunday morning, the day of the meeting, the opponents were caught off guard when Clarke chose to preach on "the true grounds of Christian Union." Although Clarke made no explicit reference to the resolutions (which he had not yet seen), he did explain again his idea of fellowship, and some opponents later accused him of unfairly trying to influence the action of the church, which they thought should have been "unbiased by any pastoral influence." After the sermon, Clarke announced the meeting would take place in the Masonic Temple that afternoon—but did so in a way that again upset the opposition. Contrary to their expectations, he invited not only church members to attend, but those who worshiped regularly with the church without having joined. Clarke here was following standard Disciples practice: nonmembers always had been invited to the church social meetings, where they could participate in the discussions but not vote. Yet the hard-liners considered this meeting a special case; to allow nonmembers to attend, they believed, especially when excitement over the Parker case in the general community was high, would be to risk flooding the meeting with "strangers."[105]

As it happened, almost four hundred people—more than twice the church membership—showed up. Rogers proposed the anti-Parker resolutions. He and others in the opposition, including Andrew, spoke at length. They variously recommended the resolutions, urged Clarke to change his mind, and decried Parker's heresies; one speaker read aloud Robert Waterston's letter to the Benevolent Fraternity "proving" Parker's infidelity. The resolves were about to be put to a vote, not a word having been said against them, when a Disciple named Samuel Brackett rose and urged with "great earnestness" that they should be defeated. This protest was met with a series of opposition replies. Before any conclusion was reached, the assembly decided to adjourn until Wednesday evening, 22 January. The meeting would take place not in the Tremont Temple but in the smaller Ritchie Hall nearby. The change of venue apparently was a concession to the hard-liners, intended to discourage members of the public from attending.[106]

Instead, Wednesday evening found many "strangers" present. The hard-liners, including Rogers and Channing, objected, insisting that only church members should take part in the discussion. Clarke disagreed—he argued that all regular worshipers, whether they were members or not, could participate. On this point, Andrew broke rank with the opposition and backed his pastor. Finally, Rogers, believing that church members would not talk freely in "the presence of a mixed company," and even fearing that nonmembers would try to vote undetected, withdrew his resolutions. Samuel Brackett then proposed a substitute resolution in line with what Clarke wanted: "Whereas, Our pastor may exchange with clergymen of various theological opinions, We, the Church of the Disciples, do hereby declare that by such exchanges we do not wish to be considered as approving their views of theology." Before a vote was taken, one more attempt was made to address hard-line concerns: the meeting was adjourned again, until the following evening, when it was to reassemble in a private residence with only church members present.[107]

On Thursday, about a hundred members (half the total) showed up for the climactic debate. Rogers, satisfied at last that strangers had been excluded, reintroduced his original resolutions. Again, he and several others defended them. Channing, for his part, argued that Clarke had no authority to make the exchange without the approval of the church or at least of the Pastoral Committee, which represented "the whole Church, as the Congress of the United States represents the whole nation." The committee was against the exchange, argued committee member Channing, and therefore the church was against the exchange.[108]

Channing must have believed at this moment that he was speaking for the "whole church." The opposition had predicated their strategy of excluding "strangers" on the belief that most actual members of the church agreed with them. The course of the debate so far had seemed to confirm their view. Those against Parker had controlled the discussion; few had contested their arguments. Yet in fact, most Disciples did not support the hard-line position; they had stayed silent only because, as one of them later explained, they wanted "to hear the full story of the sufferings" of their aggrieved brethren and give them a chance to "express their feelings."[109]

Andrew had enough political acumen to see the true situation. He had thought passage of the hard-line resolutions might reconcile the hard-line faction to the church, but now realizing they would never pass, he tried a different approach. In a dramatic reversal, he rose to speak against the resolutions and convince the opposition that Parker should be recognized as a Christian teacher.

Andrew held the floor for an hour. He admitted that Parker did not recognize the authority of Scripture, but pointed out that neither did the Roman Catholics, the Quakers, or the Swedenborgians, yet they were recognized as Christians. Besides, the Unitarian church was not founded on faith in Scripture, but on faith in Christ. Andrew echoed Clarke, that the right way to treat those in error was "not to go from them, but to go to them." Addressing his anti-Parker allies, Andrew argued that "to leave a church because the majority conscientiously differed from us" was also wrong; instead, we should "remain in it and convince them." He closed with an emotional plea: "Brethren! I do not believe in the principle of come-outer-ism. I am not a come-outer. I am a stay-iner. I shall not leave this church because the majority may differ from me on this or other questions. You may, indeed, turn me out; but you cannot make me go out of my own accord. If you turn me out of your meetings I will stand on the outside, and look in through the window, and see you. If I cannot do this, I will come the next day and sit in the place where you have been, and commune with you. I cannot be excommunicated, for I shall continue thus always to be in your communion."[110]

Clarke later judged this speech "as powerful in argument and persuasive in appeal as any I have ever heard."[111] Andrew sat down to enthusiastic applause; some in the room were crying. Yet the hard-liners were unmoved. To them, all Andrew had shown was that Parker "was not as bad as he had been represented to be, although bad enough."

The reaction to Andrew's speech, however, revealed to the opposition that they were in the minority. Some hard-liners were so shocked by this revelation that they could not accept it. One anti-Parker stalwart rose to dismiss as an illusion what he had just witnessed. These people are not giving their "*real* opinion," he claimed; they are only reacting to eloquence with a temporary rush of feeling. Similarly, he charged, the apparent approval of the majority for the pastor's course was "owing to the affection which they personally felt for him," rather than to actual agreement with his ideas about fellowship.[112]

Henry Rogers, however, now saw the writing on the wall: his resolutions would be voted down, and Parker would enter the Disciples' pulpit. He asked Clarke "if he knew of any way of averting the calamity." Clarke replied firmly he knew of none, unless the church should decide that he had no right to make such an exchange. A hard-liner immediately moved that the question be put to a vote, but there was such a general objection that the proposal was dropped.[113]

Clarke himself now spoke, defending himself at length. He declared the exchange with Parker to be a matter of principle. It was his pastoral duty to decide the question of exchanges, and he could not withdraw his offer to Parker, even if Parker himself should refuse it and the exchange resulted in trouble for the Disciples. "I cannot tell a lie," he said, "nor steal, though all the churches of the land should be destroyed in consequence of it—nor can I do wrong in this matter, though the results be ever so painful to myself and others." According to Channing's (decidedly biased) account, Clarke concluded with the following emphatic statement: "Romanism has tried *crushing* heresy, and Romanism is now a dry and barren tree. Protestantism has tried *excluding* heresy and excommunicating the heretic, and Protestantism is fast going to seed. I know of no other principle of union that can save the Church. I think in this question is involved the question, whether hereafter, there shall be any Church of Christ on earth."[114]

These uncompromising words still hanging in the air, one more opponent tried to "turn his pastor from his fatal purpose," making a pathetic appeal to be "spared the necessity of breaking the connexion which had been until now, one of unbroken peace." He met with no response.[115]

George Bond, a hard-line member of the Pastoral Committee, sensing that there was little more to be said, read a lengthy protest, which he apparently had prepared for just this emergency, asserting that "none but teachers of Christianity should be admitted to our pulpits," and that Parker was not such a teacher. Bond then resigned from the Pastoral Committee. He was followed by several other Pastoral Committee members, including Channing.

Shut In for My Own Good

Near midnight, with many no doubt hoarse and most exhausted, the meeting adjourned.[116]

Three days later, 26 January 1845—"Black Sunday," Clarke called it in his diary—Parker preached in the Tremont Temple. Although the audience was predictably large, the event was somewhat anticlimactic. Opponents of the exchange were absent, holding a service in another hall, and the sermons (by Parker's own estimate) were "inoffensive." They both concerned moral and spiritual growth: in the morning, "The Excellence of Goodness," at night "Christian Advancement" (one he had preached on his now infamous exchange with Sargent). The occasion nonetheless roused enough interest that "Excellence" was soon published as a pamphlet, which Margaret Fuller noticed in one of her reviews for the *New York Tribune*. As she correctly noted, the "discourse derives interest, not so much from intrinsic claims, as from the circumstances under which it was delivered, and the position occupied by the preacher in New England." The preacher himself did not think it one of his best efforts and later chose not to reprint it in collections of his writings.[117]

The final act of the Disciples drama opened a week later. On Monday, 3 February, the church held a special meeting to see if any way could be found to prevent a schism. The disaffected members, led by Rogers and Channing, explained that they would only be satisfied if the church passed a resolution that both disavowed Parker's views as destructive of "the very foundations of the Christian system" and committed both church and pastor never to invite Parker to preach again. Most Disciples rejected this proposal. Clarke and others tried to fashion a compromise that might be acceptable to both the majority and the minority, but none could be found. The meeting ended in failure.[118]

Soon afterward, the wave of resignations came in: thirteen Disciples, including Rogers, Channing, and Bond, asked that their names be "withdrawn from the church book." The total number of defections was small, but Clarke later called the loss like that of "a right arm," for "those who left us . . . were among the oldest, truest and most useful members." Gone were half the Pastoral Committee and the Sunday school superintendent; with George Channing went the special connection of the church to the *Christian World*.[119]

Clarke felt "personal bereavement" at this outcome, which he seems to have taken as a personal defeat. "Had I known," he wrote regretfully, "that there would have been such deep feeling and such extreme unwillingness as have since appeared, I might have been able, I certainly should have attempted, to carry out and make known my principles in some other way than by this exchange." One of the defectors, meanwhile, frustrated by the claim that those who supported inviting Parker had suffered for the cause of religious liberty, wondered "if *all* the sacrifices . . . have been on their part. Has there been no agony of mind among those who feel bound, in conscience, to oppose their pastor's principles while they truly loved the man, and was it an easy matter for them to decide upon a separation from a church which was dearer to their hearts than aught else on earth?"[120]

The defectors soon organized a religious society made up of themselves and their sympathizers, modeled closely on the Church of the Disciples, which they called the Church of the Saviour. Dr. Parkman and the conservative young minister of the South Congregational Church, Frederic Dan Huntington, helped lead services for the first few weeks. By March, the congregation had installed as its regular pastor Robert Cassie Waterston, who was on record as being of like mind with them on the matter of Theodore Parker.[121]

THE POSITION on fellowship advanced by Sargent and Clarke faced no small amount of ridicule in the Unitarian press. There is, for instance, this anonymous four-line fragment of rhymed anti-Parker sarcasm, which ran in the *Register* in early March, under the title, "New Way to Keep the Flock":

> What to do when unbelief
> Is trumpeting its views?
> Why put it in the pulpit, sir,
> To keep it from the pews.[122]

Clarke specifically was made a subject of satire in a short dialogue, which ran in the *Register* in February. Here a husband informs his wife that he has invited a young doctor to administer arsenic to their children. The doctor, explains the husband, "seems very pious and learned" and believes "that the old big wigs are all wrong; that arsenic is not a poison, but very good physic." The wife, aghast, says she will never allow any doctor to poison her children, and the children cry out in fear. The husband agrees with her that arsenic is poison, but believes that "we must encourage all physicians; if we don't agree with them, we ought not to refuse to take their medicine." The wife's protests that "I won't have such dangerous stuff in the house," but the husband lets in the young doctor anyway and tells him to prepare his arsenic. The husband blandly reassures his wife that "I will cure it with the greatest ease some time or other. I'll prove to the Doctor that he knows nothing at all. I say it's poison, and I'll prove it. I'll get my stomach pump, and get it all out of their stomachs one of these days. What will old Mr. Calvin say? Didn't I scold him because he would not take my physic? very good physic, too—not poison, like this. Give them some physic, Doctor. . . . Come, my little dears, I agree exactly with my wife. Open your mouth, now shut your eyes. . . ." At this point the wife alarms the neighbors (who all bear the names of Boston Unitarian churches: Chauncy, Brattle, Purchase, South), and the children are rescued.[123]

Shut In for My Own Good

This squib was answered two weeks later in the *Register* with "A Dialogue in an Orthodox Family." In the new scenario, the wife expresses alarm because her husband has brought home not arsenic, but the *Christian Register*. The husband admits that the paper is "very unsound in doctrine," but insists that it is worth reading, because "some of the articles breathe a real Christian spirit." The wife responds that she "would as soon give them a dose of arsenic" as suffer her children to read them a Unitarian paper. At this point her eye falls on the "Dialogue" about the arsenic doctor, which she reads intently. She points it out to her husband and suggests that an "evangelical minister" must have had it inserted. The husband reads the dialogue, acknowledges his error, and burns the *Register* in the fire. The column is signed "Prov. 26:5" ("Answer a fool according to his folly lest he be wise in his own conceit").[124]

Another anti-Parker piece, which apparently grew directly out of the events at the Church of the Disciples, and which received a pro-Parker response, appeared in late February when the *World* and the *Register* printed "Questions to the Rev. T. Parker and his Friends," soon after published as a pamphlet. The questioner is nowhere identified, but the style, tone, and attitude would seem to implicate George Channing. The reply was undertaken not by Clarke, but by John Sargent (writing under the pseudonym "A Friend Indeed"). Parker thought his answers "sharp & well put";[125] even a few samples of the thrust and counterthrust show the distance between the two sides:

> *Is . . . [a] man entitled, in his own eyes, to the name of a Christian, who rejects prophecy, who denies that a miracle is or ever was possible, and who holds the resurrection of our Lord to be only a pleasant legend? Who thinks the holy Jesus was not sinless, not without his weaknesses, not free from error?*

> Ans:—"Petitio principii"! "What is it to be a Christian"? The question here goes on the supposition, or assumption, that a belief in prophecy, the miracles, the resurrection, &c., constitutes a man's claims to be called a Christian, and that without this he is none. Whereas we maintain that a man may believe all these things and yet be no Christian at all, in any right sense. He, and he only, is a Christian, who lives, according to his ability, THE LIFE OF CHRIST. . . .

> *Why cling so tenaciously to a name out of which you take the peculiar and distinctive meaning?*

> Ans:—Ay! Sure enough! You may well ask that! Why call ourselves "LIBERAL CHRISTIANS," while we belie the title? . . .

> *Because Christianity bids mankind,—clergymen included,—love all their fellow men, must those clergymen go and exchange with Mormons, Mahometans, Millerites, Tartars, Idiots, Jews, Hindoos, Pantheists or Deists?*

Ans:—The Mormons, Mahometans, Tartars, Idiots, &c., might well teach a lesson of charity to some one who profess and call themselves "*liberal* Christians"; but what has inquiry to do with the main question at issue in regard to exchanges with Mr. Parker? He comes, rightly, under neither of the classes above enumerated. He professes to be and he is a UNITARIAN minister, and the question of fellowship is between him and *Unitarians* as such.[126]

ON 27 JANUARY 1845, the day after Clarke made his traumatic exchange, he joined eighteen other members of the Boston Association to resume the debate begun at their meeting two weeks earlier, over what they should do about Parker and the Thursday Lecture. That night, for the first and only time in American Unitarian history, a body of liberal Christian clerics seriously considered dismissing a colleague solely on the grounds of doctrine.

William Lunt of Quincy opened the evening, proposing that Parker be asked to resign his membership in the Association. A committee should be appointed "to make known to him, in an open & kind manner the reasons that have moved us to make the request." Lunt's resolution quickly was overshadowed, however, by an amendment, probably proposed by Samuel Lothrop, that Parker be expelled from the Association outright.[127]

The debate that followed was "earnest" and "long." Clarke no doubt spoke against the proposed action, but Lothrop did not rank him his most important opponent. The only reason the expulsion proposal failed, Lothrop later wrote, was "the opposition it received from the Rev. E. S. Gannett,—who differed '*toto coelo*' from Mr. Parker theologically, but had at the same time a very tender and very crotchety conscience."[128]

Gannett remained firm that "[i]t is not our way, to pass ecclesiastical censure." Instead, he supported a measure offered by Chandler Robbins, that the Association simply appoint a committee to confer with Parker "on the subject of his relation with the Association." Unlike Lunt's proposed committee, this one would not communicate to Parker the official request of the Association that he resign, but everyone understood that it would try, informally, to persuade him to do so, or at least to withdraw from preaching the Thursday Lecture. Robbins assured the Brethren that Parker would respond favorably to a "gentle & generous" approach. Some—Lothrop no doubt among them—derided the idea of talking with Parker as "utterly futile" and even "visionary" (in the bad sense of the word), but in the end the Brethren approved the plan 13-3 and appointed Robbins, Gannett, and Nathaniel Hall as their ambassadors.[129]

Robbins, who had conservative sensibilities but who liked Parker personally, promptly wrote him a confidential letter. The proposal for a commit-

Shut In for My Own Good

tee had been "warmly supported by all who feel most friendly towards you," Robbins assured him, and any conference would be nothing like the confrontational one of January 1843. This time, there would be no questioning—the committee only wished to offer "the offices of brotherly-kindness." Gannett, meanwhile, wrote to Parker inviting him to a meeting, so that "one or more or both of the parties who now seem to be in collision" might be brought "into more agreeable relation with one another." Parker doubted that a meeting would do "any good," but he appreciated the gesture and accepted the invitation.[130]

The little group met on a snowy Tuesday, 4 February, at a little past ten in the morning in the study of Gannett's rambling old wooden house at Bumstead Place. At two, still talking, they had dinner. They broke up finally at four, because Gannett had to supervise a Bible class and Parker had to catch the train for Salem, where he was to deliver a lecture. The long conversation had fallen into two parts. The committee first had allowed Parker to reply to some of the accusations made against him, then had tried to persuade him to withdraw from the Association or the Thursday Lecture.[131]

Parker's defense of himself was surprisingly nonconfrontational. To the charge that he had disparaged the professional integrity of his Brethren, he made a carefully worded reply to the effect that he "never in his *discourses, lectures*, or *Book* . . . intended to utter or convey any personality |(except in [sermon at] Sp[ring]. St[reet].)|."[132] In other words, his many attacks on clerical hypocrisy or Phariseeism had not meant to disparage the conduct of particular individuals—except in the case of his sermon taking leave of Spring Street in September 1843 (and that of his *article* on the Hollis Street Council, which, not wishing to start an argument with Gannett, Parker did not mention).

When asked about the passages in the *Discourse of Religion* that excused Jesus for making mistakes on account of his youth and that compared the Lord's Supper to a child's rattle, Parker denied he ever meant to speak "irreverently or lightly" of the character of Christ, which he insisted he held "in |the| highest veneration," or "scornfully or carelessly of the Christian ordinances," which he said he valued "as profitable . . . |& precious|." When asked about his claim to be a Christian, he explained that he accepted the truths of Christianity "with faith & gratitude," but differed from his colleagues "upon the grounds of faith." He did not base Christianity on miracles, for historical testimony he regarded "|only as a confirmation of faith|." Instead, he preferred "the facts of necessity, of consciousness |or intuition| & of demonstration."[133]

Parker, in his journal, assessed this part of the discussion as "frank & friendly," and thought it had produced, if nothing else, some "good feeling." Gannett confirmed this impression in an article he wrote for the March issue of the *Examiner*, "Mr. Parker and His Views." Gannett remained here quite critical of Parker, but he qualified each criticism in light of what Parker had told him on 4 February. After accusing Parker of having "uttered personalities" against his Brethren, Gannett added that, doubtless, "in the jealous state of feeling which has been awakened, a great deal has been imputed to him which was never in his mind or heart." After deprecating Parker's use of "language which must strike most readers as both light and sarcastic" in regard to Christ and the Lord's Supper, Gannett took pains to point out that Parker's most offensive passages run contrary both to the "prevalent spirit" of his writings and to his actual behavior as a minister (e.g., he still celebrated communion), and that therefore these passages must not be given "a stronger interpretation than they were intended by their author to bear." Most importantly, Gannett conceded that Parker did in fact "recognize and insist" on the truths of Christian religion, and that so "far as [these truths] are concerned, he whose course has given so much pain to his brethren, is a Christian believer; and so far as the inculcation of these truths is concerned, he is most certainly a Christian teacher."[134]

Gannett's limited concession did not go far enough for some, but went too far for others. Soon after his article was published, an anonymous Transcendentalist sympathizer put out a pamphlet, *Remarks on an Article from the Christian Examiner, entitled "Mr. Parker and his Views,"* endeavoring to show "the truth of the doctrines which the author of this article seeks to controvert." On the other side, a review of Gannett's article for the *Register* (probably by Lothrop) "dissented entirely" from any claim that Parker was in *any* sense a Christian believer. George Channing, meanwhile, in a notice of the article for the *World*, expressed his "grief and discomfort" that "so much good feeling as the writer [has] manifest[ed] throughout should have been so utterly wasted." To Channing, Gannett unwittingly had written "an indirect apology for Mr. Parker's peculiar views."[135]

If good feeling did not go far among Unitarians in the winter of 1845, promoting it was not the primary purpose of the 4 February conference, anyway. That was to persuade Parker either to leave the Association or to cease peaching the Thursday Lecture. Although Parker insisted, predictably, that if he remained a member, he would continue to preach the Lecture, he seems to have been unusually flexible on the question of membership itself (probably because, as shall be seen, there were new preaching opportunities opening up for him). The conferees seem to have discussed an arrangement that would have allowed Parker to sever his awkward connection with the Association while claiming a moral victory. Whether Parker himself proposed the compromise is unclear, but he certainly does seem to have considered it seriously.

According to notes taken by Gannett, Parker said he would withdraw from the Association "at once" if the Brethren made a "statement" that they had "no *right*" to expel him, then presented him with a formal list of reasons why

Shut In for My Own Good

he should go. Parker admitted that they currently *did* have the right of expulsion (had he not more than once dared them to exercise it?), but so long as they continued to claim it, he could not resign, for he then would "be admitting the justice of the censure" that the Association would "virtually be cast[ing] upon him by an act of expulsion."[136]

For Parker to resign, in other words, the Association needed only renounce the right to do what it had just voted not to do anyway and explain clearly why he should go. Yet the renunciation would also amount to a *de facto* acknowledgment that Parker had done nothing contrary to Unitarian principles—something some of the Brethren did not believe—and the explanation might sound to some too much like a creed. Gannett, Robbins, and Hall knew the proposal would be a hard sell, but they promised Parker to present it at the next Association meeting.[137]

The Association next met on 10 February at Robbins's house. Gannett presented the report of his committee. A long discussion followed. What exactly was said, and by whom, cannot be determined, for the minutes of the meeting show only that no "definite action" was taken and that the debate was rolled over for the third straight time.[138] One thing, however, seems clear: The Brethren must not have liked the proposed compromise. Although they had not explicitly rejected it, they had not accepted it, either, suggesting a general reluctance to grant Parker concessions.

By not acting they had in fact acted. Parker responded accordingly. On 17 February, he wrote to Gannett that after careful and serious consideration, he had decided not to resign his membership: "I can't see that it is my duty to move in this matter. I can't think that I am an injury to you—or that the Association is responsible for *my* opinions more than I for theirs. . . . If I were to expel myself from your body—it would be *unchurching myself of your fellowship* (to make a queer sort of expression) & avowing that there was a good case for my withdrawal. I can not therefore take the *onus damnandi* on my shoulders."[139]

Gannett presented Parker's decision to the next meeting of the Brethren, which convened at Waterston's house on 24 February. This was the fourth consecutive meeting the Association had devoted to the Parker problem. Desperation was doubtless setting in. Once more (according to the minutes), "[m]any propositions were offered by various members for the purpose of relieving the Association from its embarrassment." This time, however, the Brethren finally took action. They resolved that "care of the Thursday Lecture shall be relinquished by this Association, and restored to the Pastor of the First Church, to whom it originally belonged."[140]

Gannett may have suggested this ingenious maneuver (a draft of the resolution survives in his hand) but it seems more likely to have originated in the subtle mind of the pastor of the First Church himself, Dr. Frothingham.

Frothingham had written a history of the Thursday Lecture and so was well aware that before the Lecture became an obligation of Association membership, it was delivered by the invitation of his predecessors. The original system had not been used for 170 years, but by restoring it and putting him in charge, the Association could, in effect, exclude Parker from the Lecture while sidestepping the problem of how explicitly to censure him. As Frothingham himself later boasted, the Brethren had acted very "adroitly." [141]

THE DEBATE in the Association over the Thursday Lecture ran parallel to a wider Unitarian dispute that winter over creeds—defined as clear statements of acceptable belief. Parker's allies were unanimously against them, while his opponents were divided. Dr. Gannett always denied that liberals had or should have a creed, even as he declared that Unitarianism was a Christian faith and that Parker's views were subversive of Christianity. It was a position he could maintain only by making nice distinctions: between offering Parker *Christian* fellowship and denying him *ministerial* fellowship; between wanting the Association to declare that they dissented from Parker's *opinions*, and not wanting the Association to make any declaration or take any action that condemned Parker *himself* as no longer a Christian or a Unitarian; even, perhaps, between reassigning control of the Lecture to someone who would never invite Parker to deliver it, and directly barring him from delivering it.

Most Parker opponents seem to have been less fastidious than Gannett in their opposition to creeds, but none embraced creedalism wholeheartedly. The one who came closest to doing so was Samuel Lothrop. He believed that Unitarians had a creed—faith in the miraculous authority of Scripture—and that Parker had violated it; Lothrop was acting consistently with his convictions when he supported the expulsion of Parker from the Association. Yet even Lothrop denied that he favored creeds in the usual sense, because he refused to recognize the authority of anyone to interpret the Bible for others. While responding to Noah Porter, in November 1844, he appealed to the Protestant tradition as he understood it, declaring that there was "no middle ground between Luther appealing to Scripture and his right to interpret it, or the Pope and the Church crying out, 'submit to us; we are the authorized interpreters of the word of God; whatever we declare it to teach, you must receive.'" [142]

An even more ambiguous acceptance of creeds was that of Dr. Frothingham. In March 1845, he published four sermons in a single long pamphlet, *Deism or Christianity?* Here he argued not (like Lothrop) that Unitarianism already had a creed, but that it *ought* to have one. He denied that "religious opinions were matters of entire indifference; . . . as if to profess reverence for any conceivable thing that can be called sacred was to confess Christ." He rejected, too, the idea that liberals could not, consistently with their prin-

Shut In for My Own Good

ciples, "draw any lines of demarcation," as if "every degree of freedom" gave "allowance to anarchy." But his actual call for a creed was so vague and hedged with qualifications, it seemed little more than a sigh of longing for the un-attainable: "According to the view we are now taking of [a creed], there is nothing in it implying that it must be narrow, minute, rigorous; that it must be technical in its form, or abstruse and theological in its substance. It may leave all art to sectarian devisers, and all abstraction to the schools. Let it be as simple as it will, and as unencumbered, and as large in spirit. Only give it some existence." [143]

If some ministers reluctantly parted ways with Gannett on creeds, others reluctantly parted ways with him on the exclusion of Parker; in particular, there were those who rejected the distinction between Christian and min-isterial fellowship, although they were loath to accept the consequences of this rejection. An example is William Ware. Ware could hardly be counted a Parker ally; after the South Boston ordination, Ware, as editor of the *Chris-tian Examiner*, had ceased to accept Parker's submissions. But in early 1845 he preached a sermon to his church in West Cambridge, soon published, the point of which is epitomized in its title: *Righteousness Before Doctrine*. The church traditionally has placed doctrine before righteousness, Ware com-plained. It was an error that produced both sectarianism and unchecked sin. Ware considered the case of Parker to be an example of this baleful tra-dition showing itself among Unitarians. Parker "is not a Christian in *our* understanding of that term," Ware conceded. Nonetheless, "the same spirit breathes in his writings,—with, as far as I know, one or two exceptions only,— and the same aim elevates them which we witness in the writings of those who think very differently from himself, and as would commonly be thought, much more scripturally."

The logic of Ware's argument clearly points toward his asking Parker for an exchange—but Ware ducks this conclusion. "I should consider it my *duty* to exchange with no one," he reassures his parishioners. Yet, he tells them, if it were "convenient" and they would agree to it, he should "desire" an ex-change with Parker "because I should wish to be true to the principles I have advocated." This lukewarm manifesto did not inspire his congregation. No doubt to Ware's relief, the Parker exchange never became "convenient." [144]

A poignant example of an individual Unitarian being pulled in different directions by the controversy was a dialogue on "Ministerial Fellowship" that ran in the *World* in February and March 1845. Brother "Veritas" (Truth) holds that some preachers, if they advocate truly injurious opinions, should be ex-cluded from ministerial fellowship; Brother "Caritas" (Charity) denies this. The dialogue does not follow the ancient convention that one party in the argument clearly wins. Instead, and no doubt reflecting indecision on the part of the unknown author, both interlocutors are plausible and persuasive.

Neither can convince the other to change his mind. In the end, despite the hope of Caritas that "you and I can manage to continue one in love," Veritas simply breaks off the discussion: "There is too great a discrepancy here ever to be reconciled."[145]

Parker had been expecting the Association to expel him, or bar him from preaching the Thursday Lecture, or issue a repudiation of his views. When they relinquished the Lecture, he considered it a "circuitous" and dishonest attempt to censure him without admitting they were abandoning their liberal principles.[146] He would not let them escape so easily. In late March he published *A Letter to the Boston Association of Congregational Ministers, Touching Certain Matters of Their Theology*. In this many-layered, twenty-page polemic, Parker makes his only direct comment, in print, on the controversies raging around him.

The *Letter* had been germinating in Parker's mind for months. The seed was planted in late December 1844, when he wrote to Dr. Gannett protesting the Benevolent Fraternity's treatment of John Sargent. Gannett was probably the most influential member of the Central Board; the board, at its upcoming quarterly meeting on 5 January, was to decide whether to ratify the Executive Committee's treatment of Sargent. Parker wanted to persuade Gannett to oppose ratification.[147]

Parker frames his appeal around a series of overlapping rhetorical questions: are the Boston Unitarians, and Gannett himself, prepared to take the ground, "so new to the Unitarians," that "it is a matter of censure for a minister to exchange with one who agrees with the Unitarians in all matters of theology even, except this about . . . certain historical matters—which as I think have nothing to do with Religion?" Will Sargent, a noble and self-sacrificing pastor, be punished because he exchanges with "someone against whose moral & religious character you have nothing to object" ("I say this not boastingly") "solely because that one differed in theology—in historical theology, too?" Is Gannett "ready to make this issue before the world— *The Unitarians have a theological creed*—not patent but latent— *& if a man differs from that* (latent) *creed & another exchanges with him, he that so exchanges is worthy of censure; worthy of expulsion from a post he holds from the Fraternity of Churches, tho' no moral or religious blame attaches to the man who thus differs?*" Does Gannett suppose "that the Unitarians have attained *all* Truth— *all* Righteousness?"[148]

You have accused me, Parker reminds Gannett, of causing the Unitarians harm. But do you not see that you "are making me do more harm by thus identifying me with freedom in religious matters?" That you will give the enemies of Unitarianism grounds for charging it with inconsistency—"with show-

450 *Shut In for My Own Good*

ing the same spirit towards others they complained of when showed towards themselves?"[149]

Parker adds the explosive suggestion that the real issue between himself and the Boston clergy was not theological at all—that what the Brethren really resented was the attack Parker had made in 1842 on the Hollis Street Council. At his "memorable" conference with Boston Association in January 1843, Parker recalls, he was told (by Dr. Parkman) that his "'theological errors might be overlooked—but for that article on the . . . Council.'" So, Parker wonders, is Sargent in fact being punished because he exchanged with one who censured the council? Parker concludes by telling Gannett that if he allows the Central Board to ratify the action of the Executive Committee, then "I . . . |must| hang my head when your name is mentioned, & I . . . |must| say, *It was not Parker but Styles Gannett that did the Unitarians the most harm.*"[150]

Parker, no doubt wisely, chose not to send this letter; Gannett would only have been insulted by it. Yet Parker continued to think of questions for Gannett and the other Brethren. In mid-January, he filled six pages of his journal with numbered groups of these "Fraternal Queries."[151]

They all concern, in one way or another, historical theology. Having been accused so loudly of undermining the authority of Scripture, Parker here retorts *tu quoque*. He calculates that if his Unitarian critics were examined closely, their understanding of the Bible would be revealed as far less traditional than their attacks on him seemed to imply.

Parker first asks questions about the Old Testament, well aware that many of his colleagues, if honest, would have to answer them negatively: Do you believe the Old Testament came miraculously from God, "& are to be called His Words more than other Books equally filled with Truth & Goodness"? Do you believe that the ritual law of the ancient Hebrews, as contained in the Pentateuch, "is any more the work of divine INSPIRATION than the Revised Statutes of Massachusetts"? Do you believe that God commanded the sacrifice of Isaac, or that Balaam's Ass spoke the Hebrew words put in his mouth, or that Joshua made the sun stand still, or that Jonah composed the hymn ascribed to him in the belly of the fish? Do you believe the prophets of the Old Testament directly foretold the birth, life, death, and Resurrection of Jesus?

Parker grills the Brethren in the same manner about the New Testament: Do you believe the Epistles are the Word of God in any other sense than other works equally credible? Do you believe the Apostles were supernaturally inspired to teach, write, and act in any sense not given to other men equally good and pious? Do you believe the Apostles were right respecting the end of the world or the bodily resurrection of the dead?

Even when Parker asks about the miracles of Jesus, he could anticipate at least a few of his colleagues admitting some skepticism. For example, do you believe Jesus was miraculously born, as related in Mark and Luke, or tempted by the Devil? Do you believe Jesus never committed errors of deed or doctrine? Do you believe he turned water into wine, fed thousands with a few loaves, sent a demon into two thousand swine, cursed and destroyed a fig tree? Do you believe Jesus went from a state of entire and total death to entire and total life, did and said the things ascribed to him in the Gospels after the Resurrection, and ascended bodily and visibly into Heaven?

Parker most obviously tries to throw an accusation back in his enemies' teeth when he questions the Brethren about baptism and the Lord's Supper. In comparison with a Christian character and life, he asks, are the ordinances "but as straws & rattles & child's playthings"?

Parker's *Letter to the Boston Association* weaves together these "Fraternal Queries" with the arguments of his unsent letter to Gannett. From the latter, Parker takes his central thesis: In your efforts to sanction and censure me, he tells the Brethren, you have moved off traditional Unitarian ground. Unitarians, he asserts, have been until recently the "*Movement party in Theology*"; their greatest achievement has been to declare "either directly, or by implication, the right of each man to investigate for himself in matters pertaining to Religion, and his right also to the Christian name if he claimed it, and by his character seemed to deserve it." [152]

Parker reminds the Association that the Unitarians had complained of persecution when the Trinitarians denied them fellowship and called them infidels, "a term of great reproach in the theological world." Yet Parker thinks the Trinitarians were at least acting consistently, for they held that no one could be saved without belief in doctrines the Unitarians denied. You, by contrast, Parker tells the Brethren, are pursuing the same course in your treatment of me that you once complained of, and "if I rightly apprehend the Theology of your learned body . . . without the same consistency, having no warrant for it in your theological system." [153]

Before Parker develops this point, he pauses to consider the case of John Sargent. Parker's tone is calmer than in his Gannett letter, but his arguments are similar. Just as Parker told Gannett that Gannett, due to his influence on the Fraternity, would be responsible were Sargent's resignation accepted, Parker now tells the Association that they, through their influence on the Fraternity, had brought about Sargent's dismissal. Once again, Parker protests that Sargent did not deserve such treatment. Sargent was at most an "accessory after the fact in my alleged heresies," who was punished because he happened to pastor a "*Vassal Church*," and so was in your power, while I, the principal offender, who has no feudal lord, go unscathed. [154]

Returning to his main theme, Parker notes that the Unitarians "have no recognized and public creed." He recalls that at theological school, he assented to no symbolical books, and at his ordination to no form of doctrines.

Shut In for My Own Good

When he joined the Association, no one asked him his opinions—"No one even demanded a promise that I should never change an opinion or discover a new truth!" Therefore, Parker argues, "I do not know that I have transgressed the limits of Unitarianism, for I do not know what those limits are."[155]

He now bruits the theory, first recorded in the Gannett letter, that his real transgression was to criticize the Hollis Street Council. Parker notes (as had Sargent before him) that John Pierpont was excluded from fellowship as effectively as himself, despite being "guilty of no heresy,—*theological* and *speculative* heresy I mean, for in practical affairs it is well known that his course is the opposite of that pursued by most of his brethren in the city." Parker again recalls that at the 1843 conference with the Boston Association, Dr. Parkman had told him "that my main offense was not my theological heresies, they would have been forgiven and forgot, had it not been for an article I published on the Hollis-Street Council . . . in which, as he alleged, I 'poured scorn and contempt upon the Brethren.'"[156]

Ostensibly to clarify the "intricate confusion" of the issues between them, Parker asks a numbered list of questions—a revised version of the "Fraternal Queries." As in the original, the questions suggest that his opponents are far from traditional in belief. But Parker mutes the *tu quoque* implication; for example, he rephrases his question about baptism and the Lord's Supper, asking not if these are as straws and child's playthings, but if they are mere "*helps* and *means* for the formation of Christian character, and therefore valuable only so far as they help to form that character?"[157]

Parker's questions now imply that his critics differed among themselves so widely in theology that no Association orthodoxy could be said to exist, and therefore that no Association heterodoxy could be possible. To make this point, Parker adds questions to his original list—ones to which he knew there was no consensus answer. For example, "What do you mean by the word *Salvation*?" "What do you mean by a *Miracle*?" "What do you mean by *Inspiration*?" "What do you mean by *Revelation*?"

In addition, a few of the questions are designed to pin down the Association on whether or not they really were prepared to accept a creed and all that a creed implies. In some of these queries can be heard an echo of the Gannett letter:

> In questions of Theology, to what shall a man appeal, and what is the criterion whereby he is to test theological, moral, and religious doctrines; are there limits to theological inquiry,—and if so, what are those limits? is Truth to be accepted because it is true, and Right to be followed because it is right, or for some other reason?
> . . . Do you think it wrong or unchristian in another, to abandon and expose what he deems a popular error, or to embrace and proclaim

an unpopular truth; do you count yourselves, theoretically, to have attained all religious and theological truth, and to have retained no error in your own Creed, so that it is wholly unnecessary for you, on the one hand, to reëxamine your own opinions, or, on the other, to search further for Light and Truth, or do you think yourselves competent, without such search, or such examination, to pronounce a man an infidel, and no Christian, solely because he believes many things in Theology which you reject, and rejects some things which you believe?[158]

Parker concludes the *Letter* by urging the Brethren to give his questions serious consideration. He tells them that they have many "advantages" over him, being "men of leisure" (an unintentional Parkerian gibe?—a conscientious pastor would not like to be called a "man of leisure") and being "safe in your multitude of council." Yet he has not "feared to descend into the arena" and waits impatiently for their reply.

When the *Letter* was published, Parker asked James Freeman Clarke to answer it, but he declined; so, too, did John Pierpont (although he told Parker the pamphlet was welcome, because "[a]gitation is as necessary in the Theological as the aesthetical atmosphere"). Months later, a young, unordained divinity school graduate, George F. Ware, took up the challenge. In an anonymous pamphlet, *Answers to Questions Contained in Mr. Parker's Letter*, Ware made the obvious reply: Unitarians, although they differed widely in theology, did agree that the New Testament miracles were historical facts. But Ware's effort received little attention, and Parker's opponents in the Association remained silent. Parker concluded that he had won his argument by default.[159]

He did, however, receive a remonstrance from an Association member on one point. Dr. Parkman denied that he had said, at the January 1843 conference or any place else, that Parker's worst offense was his article on the Hollis Street Council. A few days after the *Letter* went on sale, Parkman wrote to Parker, accusing him of "fervor or carelessness, not uncommon to those who hasten into print, and print more than they well consider."[160]

Parker wrote back that he would overlook these "ungenerous remarks" and that his own recollection of Parkman's words was accurate. Parker claimed to have a "well-trained memory" and that he could recall Parkman's remark all the more readily because it had surprised him. Parkman answered this claim in another letter, insisting again that he had been misquoted. According to Parkman, he actually had said " 'that besides, or in addition to your theological opinions, we felt that there was just cause of complaint, in the contemptuous language you had used in regard to the brethren.' " Parkman summoned Chandler Robbins and George Ellis as witnesses in support his version of events. Parker refused to retract, however, and so the matter rested.[161]

Interestingly, Parker's own account of the January 1843 conference, in his journal, seems to support Parkman's account. Parker records Parkman as saying that the *Discourse of Religion* "was not the only offense, but the article on the Hollis Street Council was also bad for it reflected on members of the Ass[ociation]."

Parker viewed Dr. Parkman's role on the council with such suspicion that, in the "Hollis Street Council" article itself, he had misquoted a printed transcription of Parkman's words (Parker later had offered him an apology, which Parkman had accepted). Parker may well have misquoted him again, when there was no transcription. Parker had convinced himself that his real heresy had been political—a belief that fitted well with his growing interest in politics and social reform.[162]

After the *Letter* came out, Parker had few dealings with the Association. Over the next year, he attended only two or three meetings, and then (with one exception, which involved the Pierpont case) only to show that he was still a member. After one such demonstration in May, Parker noted in his journal that the Brethren had looked on him "much as the *Beni Elohim* looked on Satan as he came last of all." They shook Parker's hand "all the more tenderly because the heart was not in it," and then "turned the cold shoulder."[163]

THE FINAL word in the fellowship controversy went, perhaps fittingly, to Noah Porter. His October 1844 article in the *New Englander* on "Theodore Parker and Liberal Christianity" had helped open the debate. He now provided a final evaluation in the July 1845 *New Englander*, with an article on "Theodore Parker and the Boston Association."[164]

Porter had followed the crisis as closely as he could from Connecticut. In late May, Porter had traveled to Boston, where he met Parker for the first time; Parker apparently filled in his "critical foe—or friend" on many details. The opening assertion of Porter's article, therefore, if slightly waggish, is also well informed: "The winter of 1844–1845, will be a marked period in the history of Liberal Christianity in Boston and this country. It will be as the year of the Hegira to the followers of the prophet, whether with as happy an issue we do not presume to say."[165]

Porter reviews the events and polemics of that winter, paying particular attention to Parker's *Letter*, which he considers the "most remarkable publication, elicited by this discussion." It had, Porter thought, an air of "boyish roguery" about it, as "that of one who knows his advantage and means to use it, courteously, indeed, as becomes one who has been trained in a school in which courtesy is a prime virtue, and yet strongly, as we Calvinists should expect from him with our views of human nature."[166]

Parker, according to Porter, has maintained the advantage over his adversaries. Porter does not doubt that many Unitarians sincerely believe the Bible is their creed, yet their principles, he thinks, ride over this limit as all others. Besides, Porter wonders, what exactly does it mean for a liberal to "believe in the Bible"? Many liberals already have dispensed with the idea that Jesus was not the messiah predicted by the prophets; many already doubt almost everything the Old Testament says was a divine revelation given to Moses; many discount much of what is plainly written in the New Testament. In reality, then, the creed on which Parker's critics stand is merely "I believe Jesus is a messenger sent from God, who taught religious truth and wrought a miracle." This is "the *minimum* of faith which distinguishes the liberal Christian from the infidel; this the lowest mark in the *sliding scale* of their present creed." Yet Parker may ask "whether the difference between himself and such a believer is sufficient to justify his exclusion from Christian fellowship." [167] They both receive the same Christian truths; Parker merely puts them on a different, yet more apparently universal and obvious, foundation.

Parker's understanding of the Bible grows naturally out of the "principles of the liberal school." Liberal theology, argues Porter, because it rejects original sin, does not require a miraculous revelation to compensate for a fallen, hopelessly corrupted Reason; a Unitarian may think a miraculous revelation is historically useful, but there is no logical distinction between conservative Unitarians and Parker on this point. Liberals are in the position of the magician's apprentice in Goethe's poem, who turns an old broom into a servant to fetch him water, and then cannot stop it from bringing him more than he wants. Porter hopes his "liberal friends" do not make the mistake of the apprentice, who by throwing an axe at the spirit he has raised unintentionally doubles its power. [168] Porter wants instead that both Parker and his critics adopt "better," more Orthodox premises, which will lead them to "better," more Orthodox conclusions.

This article may have led Parker to recognize that, for all Porter's virtues, he was at bottom conventionally Orthodox in his outlook. Shortly after this article appeared, and after he had met with Porter a second time, Parker opined in his journal that his critic was "keen," and religious enough not to believe the "dead theology of his sect." But he lacked "great ability" or "wide culture." A few months later, Parker added that "Porter disappoints me in some things. I shall cease to expect much from him. I doubt that he will grapple with the great problems of theological science at this day & handle them as they require to be treated. Still, his liberality is worthy of all praise." [169]

IN MID-JANUARY 1845, a storm sheeted eastern Massachusetts with ice. Trees fifty feet tall were bent to the ground, and for more than a week the world was encased in glittering, cold crystal. During this spell of terrible but dazzling weather, on the evening of Wednesday, 22 January, a "company of gentlemen," styling themselves the "Friends of Theodore Parker," gathered at the Marlboro Chapel. There must have been a large attendance, to judge from the size of the hall (the site of Parker's lecturing triumphs in 1841 and 1842) and from the number of speeches delivered (at least six). The meeting unanimously resolved "that the Rev. Theodore Parker shall have a chance to be heard in Boston."[170]

This resolution was the product of a movement that had been building for some weeks, at least; the leadership of the Friends seems already to have conferred with one another several times "to consider how the cause of religious freedom could best be maintained amid the increasing bigotry and intolerance of the Unitarian clergy."[171] By the time of the Marlboro Chapel conclave, the fellowship crisis was coming to a head. Ten days earlier, the Boston Association had held its first meeting to decide whether to exclude Parker from the Thursday Lecture; five days earlier, the Unitarian papers had published the Fourth Quarterly Report of the Benevolent Fraternity and, with it, editorial endorsements of the Executive Committee decision to shut Parker out of Fraternity pulpits; the same night that the Friends passed their resolution, the Church of the Disciples, meeting over at Ritchie Hall, was debating whether to allow Parker to preach for them the following Sunday.

The Friends had a simple plan: they would hire a hall where Parker could preach on Sunday mornings. A similar, if less bold idea had been floated in 1842, when a group of young men had asked Parker to preach in Boston on Sunday evenings. At least one of those behind the earlier invitation, the lawyer Charles Mayo Ellis (who had grown up in the West Roxbury church), was behind the new one. Ellis himself proposed the "chance to be heard" resolution.[172]

Parker had declined the 1842 offer in favor of delivering the "Six Plain Sermons," but now the proposal was both more urgent and in some ways more attractive. In particular, the group inviting him was better financed than before, because the women and young men who had always backed him had been joined by a substantial number of prosperous, well-connected men. Among them was Caroline Healey Dall's father, the prominent merchant Mark Healey. Normally a contented member of the West Church, he seems to have joined the Friends to defend what he saw as fundamental Unitarian principles. Soon he was serving as chair of the Friends' Standing Committee.[173]

Another new source of influential support was the Suffolk Street Chapel. Although intended as a church for poor folk, some families of more substantial means worshiped there as a way of showing support for the Ministry at Large. Many of these felt discontented after the departure of John Sargent. That they should have seen Parker as an attractive alternative makes sense, especially in light of Sargent's frequently expressed admiration for him. Sargent himself later estimated that about a hundred members of his congregation eventually joined the Parker movement. Among them was the eminent physician John Flint, who was one of the speakers at the Friends' meeting of 22 January.[174]

A third large pool of potential benefactors, which became available within weeks of the Friends' meeting, was at the Hollis Street Church. On 18 February, John Pierpont met with some members of his congregation, allies in his eight-year-old struggle with the Hollis Street proprietors, and announced he soon would resign his pulpit.[175] The catalyst for his decision was a commitment from the proprietors to pay his long-withheld salary. He preached his last sermon at Hollis Street, closing a ministry that had lasted more than a quarter-century, on 4 May. Some five months later, the now sixty-year-old Pierpont left Boston altogether, to start anew with a pastorate in Troy, New York.

Pierpont's departure made sense for himself and his church, extricating both from a hopeless, paralyzing situation, but reformers around the city felt the loss keenly, and greatly resented his treatment. As Pierpont prepared to move, Parker wrote the older man a farewell letter in which he spoke for many: "I have always felt encouraged and strengthened by your example, and that long before I had any 'troubles' with my theological 'brethren.' If you had done as the other ministers, you had been as they are—you would not be leaving Boston. If you had flattered the follies and winked at the sins of the rich, you would have had, not *your* reward—that you have now—but *their* reward, I mean the reward of the ministers you leave behind. But you have chosen another part, and have your reward, a little different from theirs. You must go in triumph, for you have fought a good fight and a great one."[176]

In November, when Chandler Robbins presented a resolution to the Boston Association, offering Pierpont sympathy and good wishes in his new life, Parker made a point to attend, although he had not been to a meeting in months. But he deliberately skipped the tea. "I fear there is a drop or so of Arabian blood in my veins," he explained in his journal, "for I like not to eat bread with men that hate me."[177]

The debate over the Robbins resolutions fell along predictable lines. Dr. Parkman complained that Pierpont had "ruined" the Hollis Street Society and had "given *great pain* to his Brethren," and although he could be forgiven, for Christians "ought to remember ever charity," consistency should not be forgotten. "The public would say," Parkman complained, that "*if you feel so towards him, why did you treat him so—for . . . tho' perhaps there was no formal agreement, yet it was perfectly well understood how we were to treat him after the Council.*" Others among the Brethren, including Gannett, were less hostile. They thought Pierpont may have erred in judgment, but was at least a conscientious man.

Shut In for My Own Good

Parker, rising to speak, told the Brethren that Pierpont needed not charity, but justice. The Association could not keep Pierpont's light under a bushel, said Parker, for it shone out more and more. By passing the resolution, the Association would only help itself, by weakening the popular impression that they were hostile to Pierpont. Parker records that Gannett, Parkman, and Waterston "carped at" certain of his remarks, "which they twisted & perverted before they carped at them." Parker, disgusted, left before the meeting was over. He never again would attend an Association gathering. (Later, he learned that the Association had sent Pierpont a rather innocuous farewell letter. It was published as a pamphlet, along with Pierpont's predictably less innocuous reply, in early 1846.)[178]

Parker's strong sympathy for Pierpont resonated among Pierpont's supporters at Hollis Street. With their hero absent, they turned to Parker as a plausible substitute. A large number of former Pierpont parishioners joined the Parker movement in 1845; some of them had both money and many ties to the local reform community. Among these men were Francis Jackson, a land agent who helped bankroll William Lloyd Garrison's career (Garrison in gratitude named a son after him), and Samuel May, usually called "Deacon" because that had been his position at Hollis Street for many years, a successful merchant who was patriarch of a famous reforming family: the abolitionist Samuel May was his son, the women's rights crusader Abby May was his daughter, the abolitionist minister Samuel Joseph May was his nephew, and Abigail May Alcott, the wife of Bronson and the mother of Louisa May, was his niece.[179]

With such substantial characters backing them, the delegation that approached Parker in January 1845 must have seemed to him representative of a potentially viable congregation. Yet Parker responded to their suggestion that he preach on Sunday mornings with understandable caution. He must have been aware that the movement might fail. He knew he could draw listeners from time to time for a sermon preached on exchange, or for a weekday evening lecture; but he had no idea if worshipers would give up their regular Sabbath services, not temporarily or occasionally but permanently and routinely. Moreover, he must have worried that his parishioners in West Roxbury might feel, with reason, that he was abandoning them.

Parker suggested to the Friends that he would prefer the more conservative plan of 1842, of preaching on Sunday evenings.[180] This arrangement would have required no disruption of his connection with West Roxbury (he could still offer the usual two services there); it would require no listeners to leave their usual services to hear him; it would not even require him to write new sermons.

The Friends tried to accommodate him. They attempted to secure a Sunday evening space, checking at every large hall in the city and even with the Hollis Street Church. In each case, they found the space either already engaged or inaccessible to Parker "on account of existing prejudice against him." But they discovered that the Melodeon Theater could be had on Sunday mornings.[181]

In early February, the Friends told Parker the results of their investigation: Sunday morning at the Melodeon, or not at all. Forced to choose, he elected for Sunday mornings. He informed the Friends, however, that he could commit to just two Sundays. He would try to offer services for up to a year, but only if his parish consented and he could find preachers to substitute for him in West Roxbury.[182]

Arrangements were quickly made. The Friends hired the Melodeon, appointed a chorister, and designated someone to find "singing and other books." Parker enlisted John Sargent to help him for the first two weeks, filling in at Spring Street in the mornings and offering services at the Melodeon in the afternoon.[183]

On Sunday, 16 February 1845, a heavy snow fell, followed by a freezing rain; the streets were awash in slurry and lightning flashed in the grey sky. Still, hundreds of people—mostly men, Parker observed, "unlike most of my audiences"—braved the weather to hear the new prophet. He preached on "The Necessity of Religion for a State & an Individual." In the afternoon, after he had returned to Spring Street, Sargent preached to the new Melodeon congregation on the apposite topic of "Truth-tellers and Reformers, Their Fate and Fortune."[184]

"I felt the greatness of the occasion," wrote Parker in his journal that night, "but I felt it too much—to do justice perhaps to myself." He had been ill at ease, as "one that is with some friends, with some foes, with many strangers." Altogether, the day had been one of struggles: "I know not what will come of it."[185]

Shut In for My Own Good

Chapter Ten

The Ashes of My Success

The Sabbath sun now ascended over Parker's preaching in Boston and de-scended over his preaching in West Roxbury. The Melodeon, by all accounts, was a dingy, dirty, and bad-smelling place to worship, and rain seemed to fall every Sunday during Parker's first weeks there. Yet attendance soon grew to more than a thousand. Parker's opponents nonetheless expected the new con-gregation to disband within six months; in their view, it had sprung up like a toadstool in the wet weather and would wither as quickly. "Does Mr. Parker seriously suppose," asked the anonymous author of *Questions to the Rev. T. Parker and his Friends* (probably George Channing), "that his opinions will share any other fate . . . than to flourish showily a little while, and then mis-erably perish?"[1]

To make this prophecy self-fulfilling, some ministerial shepherds sought to dissuade their curious sheep from wandering over to his flock. One who insisted on straying was a Mrs. Bridge, who told Parker of her experience. A middle-age lady, Bridge was a member of the West Church, but by the sum-mer of 1845 she was attending the Melodeon services. She told Parker that although she did not accept everything he believed, or reject everything he denied, she coincided with him "in the main" and felt "fed."[2]

Her absence from her home pew was noted, however, and when the reason was discovered, she received cautionary visits from both her senior and junior pastors, Dr. Charles Lowell and Cyrus Bartol. Lowell warned her that "Mr. P. was himself unsettled; in 2 years he would change altogether; his doctrines were like those of Tom Paine—& every body knows how Tom Paine died [i.e., in poverty and dissipation]; his doctrines were like [David] Hume's, & H's mother—said to her son—'you have unsettled my Faith.' If you go to hear Mr. P. it is because you think we have not preached [Christianity]." "I am surprised," Lowell had told her, "that a woman of your respectability should countenance such preaching." Bridge had replied severely that it was better than Lowell's own, which made her sleepy and left her with nothing. Bartol called on her later. He had been a member of the Transcendentalist Club but had become a strong critic of Parker; she thought he seemed "really angry" that she had refused to take Lowell's advice.[3]

Although Bridge would not be moved, the same was not true of her sister, who belonged to the Charlestown church, pastored by Parker's former friend George Ellis. According to Bridge, Ellis was "quite angry" that any of his people wanted to hear Parker and often "showed ill-temper in the matter." Her sister, Bridge reported, could not "bear" Ellis, but dared "not venture out."[4]

Those who did venture out found at the Melodeon a sense of spiritual excitement unmatched at any other liberal church. A much-remarked upon instance of it occurred in September 1845, while Parker was preaching on "Forgiveness." His theme, exposited with characteristic intensity, was that all persons are redeemable and have redeeming traits. "Take the worst man in this assembly," he asserted at one point, "nay, the worst man in Boston, and doubtless there are moments when he *would* be better, when he *resolved* to be better, and perhaps *determined* on reformation." Suddenly, an agonized, male voice cried from the gallery: "Yes, yes, yes, I have *felt* it, I have *experienced* it!" Everyone was surprised and a little thrilled: no one had heard such an ejaculation from a Unitarian congregation. Parker calmly reassured the unknown penitent: "Yes, my friend . . . you cannot wander so far but God can call you back."[5]

If enthusiasm ran high at the Melodeon, at Spring Street it ebbed. Attendance at Parker's home church was off. No more "strangers" visited from Boston on Sundays (they now could hear Parker close to home), and even the regular parishioners were growing apathetic. On Thanksgiving 1845, a rainy day, so few people came to service that Parker decided, for the first time in his pastorate, not to preach a sermon. He offered only prayers and a Scripture reading.

Some locals stayed away because a day at church now meant having to listen to someone other than Parker in the morning. Even a good preacher would have been a disappointment by comparison, but stand-ins of even average ability were hard to find. Parker had a number of friends who could come for a morning or two—Convers Francis did so, as did Caleb Stetson of Medford, and, for the sake of old times, William Silsbee—but Parker needed preachers who could commit to several weeks at a stretch. This requirement limited the substitutes to ministers without parishes, and the pool was further restricted by the ill will of the fellowship crisis. Charles Dall, a young clergyman recently moved from Baltimore who had married Parker's "disciple" Caroline Healey, took Parker's place one morning at West Roxbury, but soon after accepted a temporary position in Portsmouth, New Hampshire. As he ex-

The Ashes of My Success

plained to his wife, he had to get out of Boston "to escape the Parker controversy": "If I stay, . . . I must take sides, and if I take sides it must be with Mr. Parker."[6] He did not need to tell her what doors would then be closed to him.

In the end, Parker did succeed in keeping his pulpit filled in 1845 and 1846, but the preachers he found for the work were a mixed lot. The best known was William Henry Channing, the mystically inclined nephew of Dr. Channing and prominent Associationist. In the fall of 1845, Channing left a church he had founded in New York to come live at Brook Farm; Parker seized the opportunity and arranged for him to preach seven Sunday mornings in succession. Most of the time, however, Parker had to rely on undistinguished supply preachers, such as Charles Chauncy Sewall. An obscure clergyman who had been settled briefly in Danvers in the 1820s and had never again held a regular pastorate, Sewall filled the Spring Street pulpit twelve mornings. However mediocre, he was at least reliable. Such was not the case with William Daniels Wiswall, another little-known clergyman who had been without a settlement for years. The morning he came to Spring Street, in January 1846, he for some reason declined to deliver a sermon. The details of the incident are lost, but Parker seems to have been angered by it. "No preaching," he notes disgustedly in his sermon record book. "*Wiswall* was present!"[7]

Although the quality of the morning service varied enough to discourage some parishioners from attending, they must have been more discouraged still by Parker's own attitude. His attention was shifting away from them. He inaugurated fewer and fewer sermons at West Roxbury. After mid-April 1845 (two months into the Boston experiment), he started delivering all his new discourses (with one exception) first at the Melodeon, and only later, sometimes weeks later, at "home." As home no longer seemed to be where his heart was, spirits at Spring Street sank.

BETWEEN FEBRUARY 1845 and February 1846, Parker worked harder even than usual on his preaching. His situation presented him with both a quantitative and qualitative challenge. Having two congregations and no exchanges compelled him to write some fifty sermons—more than he had ever written before or ever would write again in a comparable period.[8] He had to develop, too, a new sermon style for his larger, less intimate audience in Boston. His Spring Street sermons had read at times like pages from his journal. His Melodeon sermons are less personal and idiosyncratic. They read more like the lectures he had been giving since 1841.

Parker tried especially hard to convince the wary among his new listeners that he was not "a destroyer, a doubter, a denier of all truth, a scoffer, an enemy to man and God," as they had been told. He directly answered the charge of "infidelity" in one of the first sermons he preached in Boston. For five or six years, he said, there had been much talk of infidelity, some of it by pious persons, some by persons "not overburdened with love of God or man," who took special heed of Solomon's command to be not *righteous overmuch*. All their noise was but the predictable response to great thoughts arising, getting spoken and heard, and to theology becoming a science. Parker found no reason to fear changes in theology. The Trinity was gone from many churches in New England; the infallibility of church and pope from all Protestant lands; the old polytheism had passed from all Christiandom—and what had the world lost? Parker's answer: *Nothing, nothing, nothing.*[9]

Parker devoted many sermons to miracles, seeking to demonstrate that they could be dispensed with without loss of piety. He argued in more than one discourse, for example, that the early Christians did not triumph because they performed wonders ("Oh my Brethren, it was no *such miracle*, |believe it not|"), nor because they had been miraculously inspired with new doctrines (the Fatherhood of God, the religious nature of man, the immortality of the soul, future retribution—all had been taught by at least some Heathen philosophers), but because the Apostles and saints were in advance of the world in their moral and religious sentiments, in their characters, and in their actions.[10]

Parker lauded the first Christians as unmiraculous heroes. He praised St. Paul as the representative of the "intellectual & practical side" of Christianity, and held up St. John as the representative of the "contemplative & mystical side."[11] He more than once recalled his own awe when standing among the remains of the martyrs in the Roman catacombs.

Parker preached on Jesus repeatedly. On the one hand, Parker made no attempt to soften his thoroughly naturalistic Christology; on the other, he held up Jesus as a "model-man." Jesus was "the . . . |REDEEMER only| so far as you[,] like him[,] free yourself from the curse of Inst[itutions], Tradit[ion], lies & Sins that oppress the soul; the MEDIATOR—only so far as like him you come up to God—& at first hand receive Inspiration from the Father of Truth. He is the SAVIOUR only so far as you rescue yourself from Sin." While conceding that Jesus probably had taught a few false doctrines (e.g., about the existence of a personal Devil), Parker professed that "the more I learn of Rel[igion] and Piety—the more of Man & God—the more of life I live—Jesus becomes the less & less miraculous—but *greater—nearer—dearer* & more lovely to my soul."[12]

Parker's most immediate preaching challenge, however, was not to defend his reinterpretation of the Christian tradition, but to justify the existence of the Melodeon congregation itself. He had to persuade his listeners that a new, permanent organization was needed. His task was complicated because his own views about the church were in a state of transition.

Issues of church reform had interested Parker for years, and he finally was

The Ashes of My Success

in a position to put some of his theories into practice. He had long denied, for example, that the rites of the Lord's Supper and baptism were essential elements of Christianity, but at West Roxbury had continued to perform them because his parishioners were familiar with them and some found them spiritually useful. In October 1845, he even baptized a seventy-two-year-old woman who had just joined the Spring Street congregation; he felt "loathe" to sprinkle an adult, but thought himself obliged to honor her fervent request.[13] In Boston, however, where he was starting fresh, he abandoned both rituals as much as he could. There, Parker never offered the Lord's Supper, never baptized adults, and baptized babies only rarely, when the parents insisted.

Again, Parker had argued since the first Chardon Street Convention that the traditional, strict Puritan way of observing the Sabbath, which among other things required spending most of the day at church, lacked divine sanction. Yet Sundays at Spring Street continued to follow the old New England pattern, with two regular services. At the Melodeon, however, a significant innovation occurred: the afternoon service was dropped.

When Parker began preaching in Boston, he apparently thought his new congregation would want a second service and so arranged for John Sargent to offer one. This arrangement continued for two weeks. For week three, Parker offered a second service himself; the next week, he stayed in West Roxbury the whole day. After mid-March 1845, however, there were only morning services at the Melodeon.

The change may have been made because Parker could find no one else capable of conducting a sufficiently interesting afternoon service for this unusual congregation. But Parker also thought a single service was an improvement over the old system. People had more spiritually valuable ways to spend their Sunday afternoons, he believed, than listening to him preach. In April 1845, he encouraged members of the congregation to start regular Sunday afternoon meetings, which would open with a hymn and a chapter of the Bible being read, and would be followed by general spiritual conversation and perhaps a "serious" Bible class. By early 1846, his plan for these meetings had grown both looser and more ambitious. He wanted them to be informal and to be used "sometimes for the purpose of devotion, the practical work of making ourselves better Christians, nearer to one another, and sometimes that we might find means to help such as needed help, the poor, the ignorant, the intemperate and the wicked." By the time he finally left West Roxbury and could have resumed a second service, he had decided to give it up permanently.[14]

Changes in rites and Sunday observance still interested him, but they were no longer central to his reform program. In 1840, he had thought that reforming the church would by itself change the world, because ecclesiastical oppression was the foundation of political and economic oppression. By

1845, he still thought the church important, yet he had ceased to see existing churches as the linchpin of society.

He had been disillusioned by the treatment he had received after the South Boston ordination; his experience had convinced him that churches, as a group, would never be innovators. Then, too, the Hollis Street controversy helped change his mind. If John Pierpont could be driven from Boston, his defeat would seem an object lesson in how little power and independence the churches actually had. More broadly, Parker's new understanding of the church grew from insights he had gained during his sabbatical year.

Parker had returned from Europe in September 1844 with more to say about politics and political economy than churches and theology. In his "Sermon of Travels" and his unfinished lecture on the "Lessons Taught Us by the Example, History & Fate of Other Nations," which he set aside in early November 1844, he had begun to argue that there was an "American Idea," according to which, everyone had equal rights, that the purpose of America was to "organize the Rights of Man," and that, to achieve this purpose, national unity of action had to be balanced with individual variety of action.[15]

In early November, on the Sunday before the 1844 presidential election and just a week after putting the "Lessons" lecture away, Parker preached a sermon that indicates how important political reform had become for him.[16] In this discourse on "Politics," he evaluated the level of human achievement represented by a steamship, a library, a cathedral, and a city; he ranked the city far above the others, which he considered "child's toys" in comparison. He marveled that in Boston, so many, although possessed of all the normal human passions and driven by a thousand separate and hostile interests, could peacefully co-exist, without needing a single soldier in the streets to keep order. He especially praised the American system of government, which although far from perfect, had succeeded, to a degree never before seen, in balancing national unity of action with individual freedom.

Parker next preached on this theme the morning after Independence Day 1845, when he delivered "A Sermon of the State" at the Melodeon.[17] He here opened with the unequivocal assertion that the "greatest conscious achievement of the human race is a State—an organized government." As in the "Nation" sermon, he pronounced wonderful the social orderliness of Boston and praised the balance of liberty and order maintained by the American system of government. He added to his earlier argument an increasingly articulate vision of the "American Idea."

Parker now found this Idea expressed in the Declaration of Independence, the anniversary of which the nation had just celebrated. He presented the Idea schematically and in his own language: "1. that the *state is for the Man, not he for it. 2. that all right—like all power comes from the individual man. 3. that*

The Ashes of My Success

Right is born in us, is primitive—derived to us from no earthly source—but only from God. 4. that all are equal—not in Mights but in Rights."[18] The American state realizes this Idea about as well as the Christian church realizes the Idea of Christianity. Both, obviously, were much in need of improvement.

Parker did not here define the role of the church in organizing the American Idea, but he elsewhere made clear that, for the time being at least, it was a subordinate one. In December 1845, he noted in his journal that the "most important element in the education of a people is always the political action of a people"; however much Christianity was taught in American schools and churches, it would be overridden by the lessons of force and violence the nation taught by means of its political action.[19]

Parker elaborated this point in a sermon on "Education," preached in early February. Americans learned most, he here said, from the political action of the nation; next from its economic action, that is, trade; third, from the press; and last—and least—from the churches. Parker explicitly repudiated his hopes of 1840: "Once I looked to the Ch[urche]s—for the highest ed[ucational]. work—Some of you may have been as simple. But they are not organized for that; their servants are not hired for that, not paid for it. . . . The Ch[urch] . . . cannot show the living Genius for Rel[igion]—wh[ich] |shall| [Christianize] . . . the P[ress], Trade & Politics. Itself it is secularized, barbarized by these 3, & partitioned by them."[20]

Parker's reference was to the partition of Poland by Prussia, Russia, and Austria, which he later would call one of the worst political crimes of modern history. The partition of the church he plainly regarded as a similar atrocity. The goal of church reform for him was to regain for the church its independence, and with that, its power to shape history. For the church to become more independent meant for it to become more "American"; Parker had begun to dream of what he called an "Am[erican]. Ch[urch]" that "must at length rise up corresponding to the Am[erican]. thought" and help to "organize the great Am[erican] Idea."[21]

One of Parker's principal tasks at the Melodeon was to explain why such a church was desperately needed. In an announcement read at the start of his first service in Boston, he told his audience that they gathered in response to a religious crisis: unreasonable theology had been taught in the name of God; Absolute Religion had been denounced as infidelity; damnation had been pronounced against such as refuse to accept a theology that their reason rejects. We meet, Parker explained, to protest such narrowness, to mature Religion in our souls, and to apply that Religion to our lives. Although Parker insisted that the great religious work ahead was positive, he warned that "it may be needful to depart from much held sacred in the pop[ular]. belief"—adding, significantly, that destruction of the false had been a part of all great reformations, including those of Moses, Christ, and Luther. Parker clearly was suggesting that he and his audience were engaged in a reformation of similar significance.[22]

In the sermon preached immediately after this announcement (his first Melodeon discourse), Parker discussed the modern religious crisis at greater length.[23] When Religion fails to receive its "fair proportion" of public esteem, Parker argued, the human condition is "sad" and "dreary." No great ideas excite the public mind; the gates of the temple are gilded, the priests fat, the people convinced God was dead; corruption starts in high places and swiftly spreads to humble ones. Parker believed Athens passed through such a slough a century after Pericles, as did Judea at the time of Jesus; he implied that Boston was teetering on the brink of a similar depression.

To prevent it, Parker suggested in later discourses that a new church was needed. He threw down a gauntlet at the close of a sermon on the "Greatness of Man," preached at the Melodeon in early March: "What if *some church* felt . . . that man was great—god's child; his duties great, & great his Rights, & great his Powers—what a ch[urch] would that be, a ch[urch] of F[aith]. & works; that warred with Sin, & healed the woes of men, & loosed the chain! . . . One such ch[urch] is in this place . . . that work is for you."[24]

After blowing this bugle call, Parker used his next two sermons to advance his ecclesiastical vision. In the "Relation of Churches to Modern Science & Civilization," he lamented that because the churches feared science (which he considered always on the side of true Religion), they were intellectually behind the times. The clergy were generally less cultured than the better part of their flocks. Even worse, churches were behind the times morally. The great moral movements, such as antislavery and temperance, found no ecclesiastical home; they were held to be "exciting subjects" that "hurts men's feelings," and so were ignored or opposed. The cure for these evils was simple: put a prophet in the place "usurped" by the priest, and "make our church—the . . . |nurse| of great Ideas; the mother of Reforms."[25]

In "The Idea of a Church," Parker's next discourse, he held that a Christian church must teach absolute truths, help out its own members, and put down social evils. Had American churches been led by prophets, not "timid . . . & time serving" priests; had the churches "felt the greatness of man, the goodness & justice too of God; had they known the spirit of [Christianity]," they never would have "slumbered over" the evil of chattel slavery. There were battles to be fought against not only slavery, but intemperance, popular ignorance, pauperism, crime, and the "*terrible evils* of the old & corrupt civ[ilization] of Europe" (that is, social inequality) "coming already upon this young nation to contaminate, to wither, to curse & to ruin—our fair hopes." A church that did nothing about these things merely cumbered the ground. It did not belong in America, or in the nineteenth century.[26]

The Ashes of My Success

To believe everything in the New Testament, Parker insisted, was of less consequence than to follow the example of Christ and destroy these (metaphorical) "works of the Devil." Slavery, intemperance, ignorance, pauperism, crime were exactly the "works of the Devil" that Christ came to destroy, and a church possessed of Christ's spirit would war on these sins now and here. Yet such a spirit was at present sadly lacking: "I do believe that if [Christ] were to come to Boston—& proceed to destroy the works of the Devil—. . . in no recognized ch[urch]. would he be allowed to utter his voice."[27]

Parker closed the discourse by reiterating, in more vigorous language than he had used two weeks earlier, his call to action. What, he asked, "if we were to have such a ch[urch]? in Boston? Here? What Doctrines would be taught there! What Ideas would come! What Prayers be prayed! What works done." The creed of this congregation would be "all the Truth they could get"; their rites would be "all of Piety they could experience; all of the goodness they could practice"; their seven sacraments would be the seven days of the week, devoted to a holy life. They would commune with Christ, not only in bread and wine, but by having his spirit; they would commune with God by reason, conscience, and faith; they would "*commune with man*" by doing good deeds. Such a church "will come; must come. Yet God works no miracles; it will come through the works of men—You & I can do a little—a little for this great end. Let us do it!"

As POLITICS and the American Idea grew more important in Parker's thought, his circle of friends began to expand to include more politicians and political reformers. At the same time, he became more deeply and publicly involved with the antislavery movement.

Before Parker left for Europe, his friends had been ministers, scholars, and writers. A few of these were politically involved—Orestes Brownson was active in the Democratic Party, as was the historian George Bancroft, with whom Parker was acquainted. But Parker knew few practicing politicians. The only prominent political figure with whom he seems even to have had a private conversation was his congressman, John Quincy Adams, at this late point in his career, a Whig. The former president had been a delegate from the First Church, Quincy, to Parker's ordination; six years later, in the late summer of 1843, Parker and a few others spent a day fishing with him in Hingham.

Parker greatly admired Adams for his ongoing fight to overturn the congressional "gag rule," which mandated that all petitions sent to Congress on the subject of slavery be laid on the table without debate, but during the Hingham expedition, politics was not discussed. Adams, dressed in suitably shabby clothes, caught four or five good fish (one of the other anglers, to Parker's amazement, caught fifty-three), and confined his talk to geology. He expressed the view (which he shared with the seventeenth-century English divine Thomas Burnet) that the Earth was hollow and filled with water; he also denounced modern geologists as dishonest men who sought only to tear down respect for revealed religion by challenging the biblical account of Creation. When Parker and the rest of the party politely tried to persuade him that he might be mistaken about the geologists, the old man grew stubbornly silent.[28]

Parker's political contacts grew more substantial in 1844 and 1845, partly owing to his new friendship, begun in Rome, with Samuel Gridley Howe. Howe was active in the reform wing of the Massachusetts Whig Party and was especially intimate with Horace Mann and Charles Sumner. Partly with Howe's help, Parker made connections with both men.

Parker already thought highly of Mann, a shrewd but stern and principled Whig politician who since 1837 had served as the first secretary of the newly created Massachusetts Board of Education. Mann's energetic efforts had led to the building of more commodious schoolhouses, the lengthening of school terms, and the establishment of high schools and normal schools. In the fall of 1844, Mann was engaged in a bitter public dispute with the schoolmasters of Boston, whom he had angered by denouncing their methods as outdated, ineffective, and (in the case of corporal punishment) cruel. Howe, like Parker recently returned from Europe, organized a campaign to help his besieged friend. As part of this effort, he apparently suggested that Parker write something in Mann's defense.

In mid-September 1844, Parker offered Mann his services and within a month had composed a sermon on "Public Instruction" that strongly endorsed Mann's reforms. Subsequently Parker—possibly at Howe's urging—reworked this sermon into a lyceum lecture on "Education." He delivered it five times in the 1844–45 season and four more times the following year. With this experience he had formed a bond with Mann that became important as the years passed.[29]

The handsome Sumner was a socially well connected, learned young Whig lawyer, destined for greatness. He made his first run for political office in the fall 1844 elections, as part of a slate of reform candidates for the Boston School Committee—a ticket Howe had assembled as part of his pro-Mann campaign. Sumner seems to have met Parker at this time, no doubt introduced by Howe. Although Sumner lost his race, his efforts on Mann's behalf, during the campaign and afterward, earned him attention and respect. In 1845 he was invited to give the oration at the official Boston celebration of Independence Day, an honor reserved for "young men of promising genius."

Sumner surprised his audience on this occasion with an eloquent, sweeping, two-hour attack on all forms of war. "The True Grandeur of Nations" upset veterans and conservatives, but it impressed Parker, who wrote to Sumner thanking him "with all my heart" for the address. Thus opened what was to become a long correspondence and a close friendship.[30]

Parker's respect for Adams and for Whig reformers like Howe, Mann, and Sumner contributed to his decision of November 1844 to vote the straight Whig ticket, starting with Henry Clay for president.[31] That Parker voted at all is evidence of his growing sense that politics was important: in the previous presidential election, he had refused to cast a ballot. Although he retained many of the views that had led to that earlier abstention (in more than one sermon in 1844 and 1845, he decried the "Rage of Party"), his distaste for routine partisan politics was lessening.

In his journal, he noted that he made the decision to vote Whig "sadly," but with a "clear conscience." The Whigs represented property, while the Democrats represented working men. Parker himself professed to have "more sympathies with *men* than with *matter*," but he agreed with the Whigs that "property should be protected," and besides thought the Whigs "don't represent money alone." The Democrats, meanwhile, might be the "true friends of the people," but they did not represent men alone, or well, and Parker disliked their "political morals."[32]

These observations are interesting only because they are so ordinary. They show that despite his notoriety as a religious outsider and the often radical, prophetic quality of his social criticism, his thinking on actual politics remained, in late 1844, conventional. If he seemed slightly ill at ease with his own moderation, this discomfort had not yet produced exceptional political activity. In later years, Parker would advocate defiance of the law and eventually political violence, but the issue that would drive him to take these extreme positions had not yet moved to the center of his political thinking. In explaining his 1844 vote, Parker wrote nothing, either in his journal or elsewhere, about slavery.

The omission is striking not only because he often denounced slavery in his sermons, but because, for many voters, the election turned on slavery—or, more specifically, the issue of whether or not America should annex Texas. Ever since the Texans, led by emigrants from the American South, won their war of independence from Mexico in 1836, there had been a movement to incorporate their new republic into the United States. But annexation was controversial for two reasons: it was likely to produce a war with Mexico, and it would bring into the Union a new slave state. Annexation dominated the presidential race between Clay and his Democratic opponent, James K. Polk. Polk strongly favored immediate annexation, while Clay suggested that it be delayed.

Most abolitionists were disgusted with the candidates, who were both large slaveholders. A few abolitionists, notably William Lloyd Garrison, had years before concluded the political system was so corrupted by the "Slave Power," they would not vote. Others supported the antislavery Liberty Party: about 8 percent of Massachusetts voters chose Liberty candidates for president and governor. Parker's vote for the Whigs indicates that, despite his strong anti-slavery views, he was not yet really a part of the abolitionist movement.

Parker may have thought Clay the lesser of two evils on the annexation question, although he seems never to have recorded this opinion anywhere. Too, he may not have been much concerned about annexation because he thought it could not happen any time soon, no matter who won. In April 1844, the Senate had decisively defeated an annexation treaty, with Whigs casting most of the negative votes. Even if the Democrats won the presidency and submitted a new treaty, they seemed unlikely to muster the two-thirds majority necessary for ratification.

When Polk defeated Clay in a close contest, however, the political calculus changed. Many Whig members of Congress wanted to get rid of an issue that seemed to favor their opponents. In January 1845, the lame-duck Congress passed, now with Whig support, not a treaty, but a joint resolution in favor of annexation, which only required a simple majority for approval. In July, the Texas Congress agreed to annexation. Parker was appalled. "So we & T. are one," he wrote in his journal, "& there is no hope of escape!"[33] Texas became the twenty-eighth state that December. Although Parker continued to respect individual Whigs, like Adams, Howe, Mann, and Sumner, his limited faith in the Whig Party had been shattered.

Just as Parker's growing distrust of the major parties began to reach abolitionist levels of alienation, he started to lose his remaining Channingite reserve about associating with abolitionists. Parker's antislavery ties were growing rapidly stronger and more numerous.

He began to lecture in specifically abolitionist venues. In November 1844, he spoke on the "Signs of the Times" to the Adelphi Union, also called the "Negro Lyceum," which was presided over by Garrison's friend and ally, William Cooper Nell, a champion of integration who would later become the first African American historian of the African American experience and the first black federal employee. Nell introduced Parker as a "friend of mankind," and the black audience gave him an enthusiastic reception. Parker, surprised and gratified, seems to have decided to speak to more antislavery groups. Being already engaged in a study of Roman slavery, by the spring of 1845 he had produced two lectures on this topic, and by the end of the year had delivered one or the other of them to antislavery societies in Concord, Lynn, Fall River, and Salem.[34]

Parker also began befriending abolitionist leaders. Before 1844, the only important antislavery activist he knew well was the aristocratic Edmund Quincy. In November 1844, as has been mentioned, he met Nell, who in later years would become a faithful member of his church. Parker next got to know Samuel Joseph May, the sweet-tempered Unitarian minister and Garrisonian "disciple" who had helped persuade Dr. Channing to take a public antislavery stand. May, more than a decade Parker's senior, had admired the younger man's "ability" and "heroism" since the South Boston ordination and sympathized with his plight, having himself suffered social and ecclesiastical ostracism (and, in his case, repeated mobbings) for advocating immediate emancipation.[35] In January 1845, shortly after becoming the acting pastor of Parker's childhood parish in Lexington, May conducted a pulpit exchange with him. This act of ministerial fellowship led to a friendship that eventually became close. It was nurtured when May's uncle and aunt, "Deacon" May and his wife Mary Goddard May, with their family, transferred to Parker's new Boston congregation from the Hollis Street Church. Meanwhile, the deacon's friend and fellow Hollis Street refugee at the Melodeon, Francis Jackson, for whom Garrison named a son, provided Parker with yet another abolitionist connection.

This net of new acquaintances drew Parker ever closer to the arch-abolitionist, Garrison himself. For the time being they remained acquaintances, but increasingly respectful ones. In August 1845, Parker heard Garrison address one of the annual abolitionist-sponsored celebrations marking the anniversary of emancipation in the British West Indies and in his journal pronounced the speech "fine" and "full of instruction."[36] Garrison, for his part, began in 1846 to print friendly notices of Parker's activities and sermons in his newspaper, the *Liberator*.

Parker had yet to cross the psychological Rubicon of actually addressing an abolitionist gathering, but he came close at a clerical antislavery convention in Boston in May 1845. Many of the speakers, among them John Pierpont, were not intimately associated with the abolitionists, which probably put Parker at ease. According to his journal, he "intended to have spoken & defined the position of the [churches]—in relation to Reform."[37] Something, probably a scheduling conflict, prevented him. Just a few weeks later, however, he would issue his most radical public attack on slavery to date, in "Another Sermon of Slavery."

"Another Sermon of Slavery" was the only new sermon Parker preached at Spring Street after March 1844; he delivered it there in mid-June, but held off presenting it to the Melodeon congregation until November. Parker evidently considered the views he expressed as potentially incendiary, especially during an election year, and wanted to wait until after the election before presenting them to his new Boston audience.

This second "Slavery" discourse differs markedly from the first. The 1841 sermon discussed slavery almost entirely in abstract moral terms and diluted its message with a section on "slavery to sin." The 1845 sermon is concerned entirely with chattel slavery. In Parker's discussion of the topic, he does not neglect the moral and religious dimension—he takes as his text the Golden Rule (Matthew 7:12: "All things whatsoever ye would that men should do unto you—do ye ever so unto them")—but his approach is far more explicitly political than it had been before.

Parker denies that slavery is the "*peculiar* Inst[itution]. of the South." The government "has adopted it—made it federal & national." Sounding almost Garrisonian, he repeatedly attacks the Constitution for binding all the states, Massachusetts included, to support slavery. At different points in the sermon he explicitly condemns the various proslavery constitutional provisions: the so-called "fugitive slave clause" (in Article 4, Section 2), which requires states to "deliver up" fugitives from "Service or Labor" who have escaped from another state; the requirement to send state militia to put down domestic insurrections (such as a slave revolt) in another state (Article 1, Section 8); and the "three-fifths clause," by which slaves are recognized as three-fifths of a person for the apportionment of representation and direct taxation (Article 1, Section 2).[38]

Parker develops the argument that starting with the compromises of the Constitution, United States policy has favored slavery. He calls attention to the decision of the constitutional convention to allow the international slave trade to continue until 1808; the 1819 admission of Missouri into the Union as a slave state; and the campaign to annex Texas. Parker notes that all but three of the eleven presidents had owned slaves,[39] and that one of the largest slave markets in the world operated within sight of the Capitol. The question now, declares Parker ominously, seems to be not *shall slavery exist*, but "*shall there be any Freedom*."

Parker condemns both the Whig and Democratic Parties for upholding slavery. For the first time in a sermon, he attacks political leaders by name. In earlier years, Parker sometimes had expressed a certain respect for John C. Calhoun, the champion of states rights from South Carolina. But Calhoun, in 1844, when serving as secretary of state, had championed annexation of Texas and issued a well-publicized letter defending enslavement of Africans; Parker now regards him as the "Patriarch of Slavery." Parker also attacks the family of Henry Clay, who just months before had received his endorsement for president; Parker condemns Clay's son-in-law as a slave trader.[40]

Finally, Parker offers a program for removing slavery; something so specific he had never proposed before. First, he says, we must form true ideas of the subject. We must recognize that slavery is wrong by nature and by Christianity; that there is no excuse for it in the nineteenth century in a Christian land; that slavery is also inexpedient, as demonstrated by both history (slavery destroyed ancient Rome) and by current events, which show slavery to be the greatest cause of quarrel in the government and the corrupter of the nation.

The next step is to *"speak Right"* about slavery in legislatures and newspapers, and from pulpits. Slavery exists only because the apathy of the North allows it to exist. A public opinion must be created that will not bear slavery. Finally comes right action. We must send *"men* to legislate," abolish slavery in the territories and the District of Columbia, and change the Constitution. Parker concludes the sermon with a parable of the genius of the Old World, hoary and huge, sitting on the Alps, warning the proud and foolish young genius of the New World, atop the Alleghenies, to learn a lesson from the fate of great kingdoms that fell because they were unjust.[41]

Parker's program seems to moderate between that of the antipolitical abolitionists, like Garrison, who held the Constitution to be proslavery and therefore unusable, and that of the political opponents of slavery, among them his new Whig friends, who sought to work within a legal, constitutional framework. The sermon foreshadows Parker's later role as a conciliator between these two frequently hostile antislavery factions.

When Parker delivered this discourse to the Melodeon in November 1845, it was well received.[42] He now set aside whatever reservations he still had about associating with the antislavery movement. A few months later, when the annexation of Texas led, as many had feared, to war with Mexico, Parker was ready to step from the wings and join the agitators and politicians at the front of the antislavery stage.

THE FRIENDS of Theodore Parker judged his preaching experiment in Boston a success after just eight months. Over a series of meetings in November 1845, the Friends' Standing Committee, chaired by Mark Healey, discussed whether to give Parker a permanent call. The consensus was in favor. As a final test of support, the committee took up a subscription for funds. The response was impressive: pledges for $3,000 were received in just eleven days.[43]

The committee proceeded methodically, making sure they fulfilled every legal formality. On Saturday, 22 November, fourteen qualified voters in the Melodeon congregation (the required number was five) applied to a justice of the peace for the County of Suffolk, requesting a warrant to hold a meeting of the worshipers at the Melodeon, at which a vote would be taken on whether to invite Parker as their pastor. The application was filed with a justice of the peace who himself sat on the Standing Committee, a counselor named John King, who granted it immediately.[44]

The following day, the Melodeon service was particularly interesting. Not only did Parker preach his radical sermon on slavery, but the audience found printed notices in their seats, asking those who considered themselves regular worshipers to stay after the benediction. Almost the whole congregation did so. They were asked to elect a clerk and a moderator as the first step to organizing a society; the young lawyer Charles Mayo Ellis was chosen clerk, and King, the older lawyer, moderator. The meeting then was adjourned until the following Thursday morning, again at the Melodeon.

When it reconvened, those present elected a treasurer and a new Standing Committee—King was chosen its chair—and unanimously passed a resolution to give Parker a permanent call. There was some debate over how much money to offer him, but this question was deferred, as was the problem of what to call the new church. On 28 November, the committee sent Parker a letter, officially informing him that "a Society has been organized according to law" and asking him to be its minister.[45]

Parker did not hesitate. He already had decided that "I shall go to B[oston]. & work, if they need me—& wish me." He wrote to the West Roxbury Standing Committee on 6 December, telling them he was "constrained" to accept the invitation and therefore to resign his connection with "the church & society in this place." His resignation was not formally accepted until a parish meeting on 26 December, but Parker treated this outcome as a foregone conclusion. He had started to plan his installation service by 9 December and wrote to the Boston committee agreeing to their offer on 12 December. At the Melodeon the following Sunday, after the service, King read Parker's acceptance letter aloud to the congregation.[46]

The issues of what Parker should be paid and what the new church should be called were quickly resolved. On 20 December, the new Standing Committee voted Parker $2,000 a year—a handsome salary, especially when compared to his $600 annual compensation in West Roxbury. As for the church name, Parker himself chose it. He did not want the new organization named after an "old hero or saint," for "we call nothing else after the old names"; nor, apparently, did he want a name that suggested any specific theological commitment, however broad (such as Orestes Brownson's old "Society for Christian Union and Progress," or the "Church of the Disciples"). Instead, Parker wrote to Dr. Parkman to find out how many congregational churches were in Boston (Parker evidently regarded Parkman, the senior minister in the city, as an authority on such matters, if not on others of more importance). Parkman replied with a rather chilly note, explaining that if Parker looked in the Massachusetts Annual Register, he would find the total number was twenty-seven. On the basis of this information, Parker designated his new church the "Twenty-Eighth Congregational Society of Boston."[47]

The form of the installation service took somewhat longer to determine. Installations were generally less elaborate than ordinations, but customarily a committee of clergy participated. Collectively, they would endorse the choice of the church. Also, one minister would preach a sermon, another would present a Charge to the pastor, a third would offer the Right Hand of Fellowship, and a fourth would deliver an address to the congregation. Parker initially hoped for something resembling a typical installation ceremony, with colleagues helping. In early December, he approached the obvious choice for such work, his most conspicuous ally remaining among the city clergy, James Freeman Clarke.

Clarke balked. He was reluctant to make another grand gesture on Parker's behalf when the pain caused by the last one was still fresh. In a letter, he replied that although he would be "happy" to help Parker, "there is probably no Unitarian minister in the city who agrees less with *a part* of your theology than I do"—particularly the rejection of Christ's mediatorial role. Clarke explained that were he to participate in the installation, "multitudes" would get the false impression that he did not think the points on which they differed were very important. To prevent such misapprehension, he would have to declare his dissent from Parker's positions. "I can not say precisely what I shall wish to say," Clarke wrote, "but it will place me in an attitude of opposition not very pleasant on such an occasion." He therefore suggested that others would better take his place.[48]

Parker briefly tried to convince Clarke that he would not be compromised by participating (no more so than by "buying a barrel of apples out of my garden"). Parker even drafted for him a jocular disclaimer: "Here Parker is coming to Boston—There is a mess of his theology that I don't believe in—but that is his affair—mine is in general to take care of my own—& now in special to help put the creature in his stall—'*The ox knoweth his* MASTER'S *crib*' so here goes."[49]

Soon, however, Parker decided against having the help of Clarke or any other cleric. Maybe he did not want the offices of anyone reluctant; maybe, too, he realized that by going it alone, he would emphasize his isolation in a dramatic way. Besides, assistants were required neither by law nor New England church tradition; a congregation needed no outside approval to put a pastor in place. At a meeting with members of the new Standing Committee on 23 December, Parker suggested the "simplest form" of installation possible: "The whole to be done by ourselves." The proposal received "warm approval." The service was scheduled for the first Sunday of the new year.[50]

SUNDAY, 4 JANUARY 1846, dawned clear and mild. Encouraged by the fine weather, a throng turned out to see the big event at the Melodeon. The audience filled every seat, sat on stools in the aisles, and stood packed against the back walls of the house and gallery. Perhaps two thousand people were present—nearly 3 percent of the entire Protestant population of Boston.[51] The Standing Committee and Parker sat behind a desk on the stage.

The installation began with a hymn. Parker offered a prayer, which was followed by a voluntary on the organ. Then he and the committee rose, and John King spoke.[52] He rehearsed the history of the congregation: it had been formed to counteract "certain influences which seemed hostile to the cause of religious freedom" and to give "a minister of the Gospel, truly worthy of that name," who had been "proscribed on account of his opinions," a " 'chance to be heard.' " The well-attended services over the previous months had shown that "though our friend was shut out from the temples, yet 'the people heard him gladly.' " Meanwhile, the "warm feelings of gratitude and respect expressed on every side, are the best evidences of the efficacy of his words, and of his life." The congregation, therefore, was convinced that Parker's "settlement in Boston would not only be important for ourselves, but also for the cause of liberal Christianity and religious freedom," and so had decided to give him a permanent call.

King explained the unusually simple installation ceremony:

As to our Choice, we are, upon mature reflection, and after a year's trial, fully persuaded that we have found our minister, and we ask no ecclesiastical council to ratify our decision.

As to the Charge usually given on such occasions, we prefer to do without it, and trust the conscience of our minister for his faithfulness.

As to the Right Hand of Fellowship, there are plenty of us ready and willing to give that, and warm hearts with it.

As for such of the other ceremonies usual on such occasions, as Mr. Parker chooses to perform, we gladly accept the substitution of his services for those of any stranger.[53]

King asked all who wanted Parker to be their pastor to rise. Most in the hall stood. Those sitting were discounted as curious onlookers, and the vote was declared unanimous. King now turned to Parker and asked him if he would accept the offer. Parker (perhaps momentarily unable to speak) nodded. King pronounced the installation complete.

After a hymn, Parker stepped to the desk. For the scriptural lesson for the day, he recited the parable of the sower (from Matthew 13), but announced no biblical text for the sermon. He had never before delivered a discourse without one and did not explain the striking omission; possibly he wished to indicate that modern saints need not take their inspiration from the past. Obviously excited, with his delivery unusually rapid, he proceeded to preach on "The True Idea of a Christian Church." Parker built on his thinking over the previous year about the role of a church in modern America, while projecting for himself and his listeners a lifetime of work.[54]

We are here, he begins, to establish a Christian church, which he defines broadly as "a body of men and women united together in a common desire of religious excellence" and with a "common regard" for Jesus of Nazareth as the model of morality and religion. With this definition, Parker can dismiss the controversy of the previous year, for if neither ritual nor doctrine constitute a Christian church, then neither can be used as a test of Christianity. "In our day," he notes, "it has strangely come to pass that a little sect, themselves hooted at and called 'Infidels' by the rest of Christiandom, deny the name of Christian to such as publicly reject the miracles of the Bible. Time will doubtless correct this error." [55]

The word "publicly" here hints at much, but Parker does not elaborate, swiftly moving instead to examine the action of the church on its members and on those "out of its pale." For the former, a church should help them help themselves "become Christians"—that is, help them develop their mind, conscience, heart, and soul without destroying "the sacred peculiarities of individual character." [56]

Christianity, however, is not only the Absolute Religion; it also has an "ideal-man" in Jesus of Nazareth. Parker here presents his latest thinking on Jesus—that he is the "model of religious excellence" only "in a certain sense." If "Jesus were ever mistaken, as the Evangelists make it appear, then it is a part of Christianity to avoid his mistakes as well as to accept his truths." But we can regard Jesus as a model in that "he stands in a true relation to men, that of forgiveness for their ill-treatment, service for their needs, trust in their nature, and constant love towards them,—towards even the wicked and the hypocritical; in a true relation to God, that of entire obedience to Him, of perfect trust in Him, of love towards Him with the whole mind, heart and soul; and love of God is also love of truth, goodness, usefulness, love of Love itself." [57] If Jesus is the model-man, Parker continues, then a Christian church should teach its members to have the same relation to God that Jesus had, and reject the limitations of any book, or any teacher.

To attain such a relation to God requires entire freedom; as "much freedom as you shut out, so much falsehood do you shut in." The great problem of both church and state is "to produce unity of action and yet leave individual freedom not disturbed"; in their state, Americans have accomplished this "more wisely than any nation heretofore," but in their churches, the balance leans too heavily in favor of unity. Yet if freedom is allowed, there will be truth, and all truths are of God. [58]

After touching on certain practical provisions a church should make for its members (instruction for the young, moral counsel, direct material help), Parker turns to the problem of how a church should act on those "out of its pale"—that is, how it could help reform the world. He fashions for the church a prophetic role: it should bring up the sentiments, ideas, and actions of the times, and judge them by the "universal standard." We expect, says Parker, that the sins of commerce will be winked at on the street, and the sins of the state applauded on election days, in Congress, or on the Fourth of July; but in a church, public sins are to be measured by conscience and reason, with reference to the laws of God. Parker wants no false idea or action to pass without rebuke, but he also wants no "noble heroism of the times" to pass without due honor; Parker says he knows a few "saints of to-day," and "I will not wait until they are dead and classic before I call them so."

A church should not only promote true sentiments and ideas, but good works. Every ignorant person, every beggar, drunkard, and criminal amongst us is a reproach; they need education, charity, and justice. Every almshouse and jail in Massachusetts shows, Parker believes, that the churches have not done what they ought to be doing. We must also resist war, which America is always so reckless to provoke. Then, too, there is slavery. Three million of our brethren are "hopeless sufferers of a savage doom"; it is the mightiest sin of the age, yet there is no outcry: "The church is dumb, while the state is only silent; while the servants of the people are only asleep, 'God's ministers' are dead!"[59] A church that dares call itself Christian must be a "church militant" if it ever is to become a "church triumphant."

Parker presents his characteristic model of religiousness when he extols the reformers of Boston as saints and martyrs. In keeping with his general preference for the modern, he finds them more heroic even than the saints and martyrs of the past, whose fate was bloodier:

> I love and venerate the saints of old; men who dared step in front of their age; accepted Christianity when it cost something to be a Christian, because it meant something; they applied Christianity, so far as they knew it, to the lies and sins of their times, and won a sudden and fiery death. But the saints and the heroes of this day . . . who burn in no fires of wood or sulphur, nor languish briefly on the hasty cross; the saints and heroes who, in a worldly world, dare to be men; in an age of conformity and selfishness, speak for Truth and Man, living for noble aims; . . . these men I honor far more than the saints of old. I know their trials, I see their dangers, I appreciate their sufferings, and since the day when the man on Calvary bowed his head, bidding persecution farewell with his "Father, forgive them, for they know not what they do," I find no such saints and heroes as live now! They win hard fare, and hard toil. They lay up shame and obloquy. Theirs is the most painful of martyrdoms. Racks and fagots soon waft the soul to God, stern messengers but swift. A boy could bear that passage, the martyrdom of death. But the temptation of a long life of neglect, and scorn, and obloquy, and shame, and want, and desertion by false friends; to live blameless though blamed, cut off from human sympathy, that is the martyrdom of to-day. I shed no tears for such martyrs. I shout when I see one; I take courage and thank God for the real saints, prophets and heroes of to-day. In another age, men shall be proud of these puritans and pilgrims of this day. Churches shall glory in their names and cele-

The Ashes of My Success

brate their praise in sermon and in song. Yea, though now men would steal the rusty sword from underneath the bones of a saint or hero long deceased, to smite off therewith the head of a new prophet, that ancient hero's son; though they would gladly crush the heart out of him with the tombstones they piled up for the great men, dead and honored now, yet in some future day, that mob, penitent, baptized with a new spirit, like drunken men returned to sanity once more, shall search through all this land for marble white enough to build a monument to that prophet whom their fathers slew; they shall seek through all the world for gold of fineness to chronicle such names! I cannot wait; but I will honor such men now, not adjourn the warning of their voice, the glory of their example, till another age! The church may cast out such men; burn them with the torments of an age too refined in its cruelty to use coarse fagots and vulgar axe! It is no less to these men; but the ruin of the church.[60]

Parker accuses the churches in Boston, as he has before, of being behind the times, and an obstacle to reform. Look, says Parker, at what happened to Dr. Channing; when he began applying religion to life, "he lost favor in his own little sect!" Now Unitarians hope to make "sectarian capital" out of his great name, and so he is praised; "perhaps praised loudest by the very men who then cursed him by their gods!" Look, too, at John Pierpont, who was "driven out of this city, and out of this state" because he was a conspicuous reformer! "You know it is so," Parker tells his audience, many of whom were Pierpont's parishioners, "and you know how and by whom he is thus driven out!"[61]

The churches do not lead, Parker believes, because they lack Christ's spirit. There are many ways to deny Christ. That of the bold blasphemer does little harm, for no scoffing word can silence religion. But "to call him Lord, and never do his bidding; to stifle free minds with his words; and with the authority of his name to cloak, to mantle, screen and consecrate the follies, errors, and sins of men"—from this, Parker believes, "we have much to fear."[62]

Parker argues, as he has so often before, that a church that is to lead must not always look backward for truth, appeal to old books, or be "antiquarian" in its habits. There have been great advances in commerce, manufactures, and "all the arts of life," and religion needs a corresponding development. In the middle ages the church led the world; its idea of religion is embodied in the cloister, minister, dome, and cathedral—"the prayers of a pious age done in stone, a psalm petrified as it rose from the world's mouth; a poor sacrifice, no doubt, but the best they knew how to offer." Now, if we were to engage in religion as in politics, commerce, and arts, we should build up the "noblest monument to Christ, the fairest trophy of religion, . . . a noble people, where all are well fed and clad, industrious, free, educated, manly, pious, wise and good."[63]

Parker closes the discourse with a long exhortation, aimed at the young men and women before him, to have the reality of Christianity, though people deny them the name. Despite his insistence on being modern, he uses archaic rhetoric for dramatic effect when, in his final sentences, he enjoins his listeners to stay away from the "dirty, fetid pools of worldliness and sin" and go to the "stream of life," fed by dews from God: "Fill there thine urn, oh, brother-man, and thou shalt thirst no more for selfishness and crime, and faint no more amid the toil and heat of day; wash there, and the leprosy of sin, its scales of blindness, shall fall off, and thou be clean for ever. Kneel there and pray; God shall inspire thy heart with truth and love, and fill thy cup with never-ending joy!"[64]

The sermon was followed by an anthem. Then Parker gave a benediction. Then the service was over. Parker no doubt felt drained, but he had more to do that day: in the afternoon he conducted his usual service in West Roxbury. When he finally got to bed, exhausted but exhilarated, he instantly fell asleep, but woke at midnight. Not till daybreak could he doze again. Around nine on Monday morning, he rose and started writing new sermons.[65]

THE DAY before the installation, Parker had written to the Parish Committee of his old church to inform them, "with great grief," that he had set the second Sunday in February as the date of his resignation.[66] He thereby fulfilled, in an unexpected way, the promise he had made when the Boston experiment began, to preach at both Spring Street and the Melodeon for a year. The twelve months originally had been a probation period for Boston. They ended as a grace period for the Second Parish of Roxbury.

In his letter to the committee, Parker was anxious that they understand he parted from them only under duress: "Circumstances I could neither prevent nor foresee constrain me to leave a place which has become dearer to me each year I have filled it—a place in which I had fondly hoped to live long & usefully, & die as I had lived amongst you." Parker denied that any "personal ambition" lead him to this step ("I think you all know the circumstances of this case too well & me too well, to believe for a moment it is so").[67] He was going to Boston only because his Brethren had refused him ministerial fellowship.

Parker took pains to document this claim in a special manuscript volume of the "Church Records of the Second Parish in Roxbury." The parish already had a record book that had been kept since the eighteenth century, but in January and February 1846 Parker prepared a fresh one, covering just the period of his pastorate. The old and new volumes both contain lists of marriages, baptisms, and deaths, as well as a copy of the 1838 church cove-

The Ashes of My Success

nant, which Parker had helped to write. To these, Parker's book adds two key supplements. The first is a sixteen-page chronicle of the previous eight and a half years, in which he emphasizes that after the South Boston ordination, "I . . . found myself standing almost alone." The other is a fifty-one-page "List of my Preachings, Exchangings, etc.," copied from his sermon record book, in which he calculates for each year since his settlement the ratio of his exchanges to his preachings; his purpose is to demonstrate how sharply this ratio fell after May 1841 (e.g., 45/105 in 1840 compared to 14/108 in 1843–44).[68]

Despite these interesting numbers, ambition surely contributed to Parker's move. Not only was he exchanging a post that paid $600 a year for one that paid more than three times as much, and a congregation of sixty adults for one of more than a thousand, he was escaping a place where he had long felt trapped. Moreover, he had exhorted his Boston audience to create a new church for him and was thrilled with his new position.

No doubt, Parker's denial of worldly motives was partly conventional. Ministers were not supposed to think about such things as money and fame (although everyone knew they did), and the traditional New England ideal was for a pastor to be wedded to a single parish till death or retirement (although this norm was crumbling for the younger generation of clergy).[69] Again, Parker himself regularly preached down preoccupation with wealth and reputation, and he did not want to appear inconsistent.

More particularly, Parker seems to have worried that his old congregation would consider him ungrateful. Was he not leaving them with no prospect of a replacement after they had sustained him in his hour of need? In Parker's January letter to the Parish Committee, he assured them that he would "never forget" how they stood by him when his "personal friends" forsook him and "shrunk off," and that it was not his desire, but his duty that commanded him elsewhere.[70]

Parker need not have been so concerned. Although Spring Street was sorry to lose the most talented and famous minister they ever had or were likely to have again, few of his neighbors seemed to begrudge him his success. Some West Roxbury families had shown their approval of his move by going to hear him at the Melodeon, and a parish meeting, held in late January 1846, passed a resolution declaring themselves "cheered with the hope that the loss of the few will be the gain of the many, & that more extended fields for . . . [Rev. Theodore Parker's] labours will promote the cause of free inquiry & of truth."[71]

The deepest reason, however, that Parker denied his ambition related not to how others perceived him, but to how he perceived himself. Seeing himself as a prophet and martyr, he could not accept the move to Boston as anything other than a sacrifice. In a journal entry, he called the necessity of leaving

West Roxbury a "calamity": "How can I bear to stand in the dear old familiar Pulpit for the last time & look on the dear old faces for the last time out of that Pulpit! God help me! I know not." A few days later, he wrote that to "part from my old friends" was "sad & bitter to my heart—but I will not dwell on that!" Again, the day his resignation from Spring Street took effect, he noted in his sermon book, "Here sorrowfully I end my connection with the Parish in Roxbury! Alas me!"[72]

Similarly, his self-image compelled him to think of his triumph in Boston as a perilous trial of character. On the last day of 1845, as he considered the challenges of the new year, he penned a prayer in his journal that expressed this outlook. "*Oh Father of wisdom guide me,*" he writes. "*If defeated—may I not despair: if successful—may I toil all the more—a noble idea rising from the ashes of my success!*"[73]

Parker expanded on this martyrological interpretation of his departure most fully in his "Final Sermon for the Second Parish." He preached it, the first new discourse delivered to his old church since his "Slavery" sermon six months earlier, on the cold, blustery afternoon of Sunday, 8 February 1846.[74]

The occasion was less dramatic than his leavetaking for Europe in 1843. No one reports a crowd at the little meetinghouse. Those from the city who wanted to hear him had already done so that morning at the Melodeon, where he had spoken (fittingly enough) on "Seeking the Praise of Men." Few, apparently, thought they needed to see him say his goodbye to old friends.[75]

Nor does anyone report any weeping among those present. His congregation seems to have found this farewell less poignant than the previous one. Then, he was to disappear from their lives for at least a year. Now, he would still be preaching nearby. Besides, Parker repeatedly reassured them that he intended to continue living in West Roxbury. In January, he had written to the Parish Committee that he hoped "long to be your neighbor & fellow citizen," and in his "Final Sermon," he reiterates the point: "I do not come today to bid farewell to *you*. I am not to leave you. We shall often meet as Friends & neighbors I trust for many a year. I am to bid farewell to this Pulpit—."[76]

Parker took his scriptural "lesson for the day" from Jeremiah and the Gospels, but his discourse, like his installation sermon five weeks earlier, lacked a biblical text. The sacred Scripture on which he preached was, in effect, the story of his own life and work; this sermon was to be his second major autobiographical confession of faith. His duty on the present occasion, he announces, is "to say something of the *plan of my ministry* & *something of its results*—at least to myself."[77]

He looks back on himself almost nine years earlier, freshly ordained and settled. He came to Spring Street "little knowing what was before" him. He already was aware, however, that the more ably he taught Truth, the more powerfully he would have to come into contact with error, and the more

The Ashes of My Success

he promoted Goodness and Piety, the more powerfully, practically, and minutely he would have to war on the actual sins of the day. "Then I saw the acorn—now the Oak."[78]

Parker remembers that he had "no very distinct conception of the work to be done," yet he recreates his younger self, with some exaggeration, as already feeling deeply alienated from the conventional ecclesiastical world. I saw, Parker says, that Theology was mistaken for Religion; that all sects worshiped the Bible although few understood it; that all sects worshiped Christ although few took pains to imitate his spirit and none "would tolerate such a person as Jesus—living such a life."

Parker grounds his own theological ideas in the spontaneous religious feelings he had in childhood. He once had avoided direct public discussion of his early years. But the pain of his boyhood losses had grown less sharp after his reconciliation with Lydia in Europe, and Parker at last could use the story of his youth for homiletic purposes.

He recalls that as "far back" as he could look in life, religion was the "uppermost thing" in his character. "I could as easily believe the Truths of Rel[igion] . . . ," he says, "as the things I saw with my eye & felt with my hand." Prayer was never a duty to him: "When a boy I wondered to hear men preach it as such—To me it was a *desire*—& a *delight*. . . . I prayed as the . . . |thrush| sings—because it cannot help it, not in words always—but in the joyful lifting up of the Heart towards the Great Father—." Again, there was no historical figure he knew so well, or loved so much, as Jesus. As for the Bible, he loved its *"grand figures,"* "hearty faith," and "trust." As for its "stories of wonders &c," they seemed to him "as natural as the stories of Homer, & Plutarch." He says he never doubted either.[79]

Parker assures his listeners that he does not "mention these things to boast of them" ("You see by the frankness of the disclosure that I feel I am among friends"); rather, he credits his religiousness entirely to his mother. Hannah Parker, whom he had never before mentioned in the pulpit, he now uses as a model of maternal spiritual mentorship: "Many men have been better born than I—few have had so good a Mother—|I never heard of Rel[igion]. as something *unnatural* &c. at home—. . . Much pain was taken with my Ed[ucation]. but more than all with . . . my moral & rel[igious]. Ed[ucation]. Rel[igion]. has always taken the lead—.|"[80]

Parker implicitly rebuts the many critics who attacked his theology as a German import, by arguing that his views sprang naturally from his childhood faith. He denies that religion with him is "*carpentry*—something built up—of dry wood—from without—by hard hands." Rather, it is "*growth*, growth of a germ in my soul—wh[ich] found food—wherever it turned itself."[81]

He describes himself (surely to the surprise of some listening to him) as "more speculative than practical; more contemplative & mystic than rational & speculative." He reports needing "a long time to express in words & make clear to others—what flashes on me . . . |all at| once, clear as the sunrise." He says that if he had lived centuries earlier, he would have told of his experiences just as Paul and Isaiah tell of theirs: "When I came to *study* & develope [*sic*] the power of reasoning, & ascertain the Laws of things—& to separate between *fact* & *fancy*, do you wonder—that I saw how men constantly mistake the dress of a Truth—for the Truth itself?"[82]

His studies before he came to West Roxbury, he reminds his audience, were "wide ranged." The best writings of Greece and Rome "were early familiar to me." At Harvard, he had worked mightily to learn more about religion, philosophy, theology, and above all the Bible. "You need not wonder," he says, "I saw that much of the O[ld]. T[estament]. & some of the N[ew]. T[estament]. is [*sic*] no part of [Christianity]—is even hostile to [Christianity]." Yet he was told, by the precept or example of his elders, that it would "*not do*" to inform others of his discovery. Probably referring to the criticism he received for his 1836 *Scriptural Interpreter* article on the "suffering servant" passage of Isaiah, Parker recalls that "before I left the Sem[inary], I was reproved more often than once for *infidel* opinions."[83]

After his settlement, Parker continues, he discovered that "men were not [*Christians*]—in my sense of the word." He found that "some worshipped *Mammon*—i.e., Money, Honors, Ease, Fame &c" and that to accomplish their idolatry, "they would poison a nation with *Rum*, or hold . . . men in [Slavery], Blacks at the S[outh], whites at the North." He found that others worshiped the Bible to point of silencing conscience, reason, "Rel[igion] itself almost"; the Bible was the idol of the sects. He saw that the churches said nothing against public sins, such as slavery and war—in fact, apologized for them. Yet he believed Christianity condemned such sins—not the Christianity of the street, which was worship of Mammon, nor the Christianity of the church, which was worship of the Bible, but the Christianity of Christ, which was not getting preached.[84]

Parker remembers consulting with clergy older than himself. He relates that one of these ministers, "quite conservative—but truly pious & a [Christian]" (Henry Ware Jr.) "confessed it all." Another (Dr. Frothingham?) told Parker that the problem could not be helped: "I only aim to keep men where they are. Sunday is only a break in the worldliness of the week!" When Parker confessed to this same colleague feeling troubled about the Lord's Supper, the older man admitted there was nothing in the rite, but "it was useful for old women—& did them good." Parker says he turned away from this minister, a good man corrupted by his profession, "in horror." Not until years later did he understand that there was a weight "on the neck of every minister of this neighborhood who separates with his [brothers]!"[85]

Parker relates his discovery that few of his Brethren thought independently or made original investigations. He tells of his growing disappointment with the Boston Association of Congregational Ministers. He would walk, he recalls, "in mud & storm to attend their meetings, & came away with a bursting heart, pained at the silliness—& wordy trifling that I found when I looked for [Christianity]." Parker says that by 1839 he was "distinctly conscious" that he differed from most of his brothers in first principles, ideas, "*Purpose, Aims & Expectations*." He realized that each step he took would separate him from them more and more. Yet he could still find counsel from "one great man" (Dr. Channing), "pious by nature, careful by experience, slow & hesitating, but never turning back."[86]

At length, says Parker, he found that in pursuing Christianity in the spirit of its founder, he was compelled to reject the fundamental principle of Protestantism, that the Bible was the Word of God and a sufficient guide in all matters of faith and practice. He had learned that war, intemperance, and slavery could be justified out of the Bible; that the New Testament "destroyed" the Old; that the principle of biblical infallibility worked "hideous woe . . . among men."[87]

Parker therefore differed from the "*public* words of all the sects." Some of the Unitarian clergy, he notes accusingly, had less respect for the Bible than himself, for he always had it; the truths of Scripture always seemed to him nobler when God was not made answerable for the "false Phil[osophy] or bad grammar of the Bible." But those Unitarians who doubted Scripture "*did not say so in their pulpits*." Parker recalls (again with some exaggeration) his own foresight and determination: "I knew from the past what the future was like to be—. |I knew most of my friends would desert me at the first fire &c &c| I did not hesitate—nor resolve to be true—I went on without a word of resolving—I had confidence in Truth."[88]

Parker now relates the tale of his martyrdom. He starts with his Thursday Lecture of January 1840, on "Inspiration," in response to which Dr. Parkman had told him that "I can't beâr ye" and Parker had wept. Parker recalls that his arguments in the sermon were answered with "ill temper—& hard words," which "came from a man who never investigates anything—[and] therefore is always ready to condemn." This was the first time "theological invective ever drew a tear from my eye."[89] Parker goes on to mention the growing alienation of his colleagues after the articles he wrote for the *Dial* in 1840 and his participation in the Chardon Street Convention. Finally, he comes to the ordination at South Boston.

He reviews ensuing events at some length: the newspaper controversy; the "Religion" lectures; the *Discourse of Religion*; the article on the Hollis Street Council (which his Brethren thought "the unkindest cut of all"); the "Six Plain Sermons for the Times"; the overwork and exhaustion that led to his trip to Europe; the furor over the Sargent and Clarke exchanges and over his final Thursday Lecture. Parker pronounces the failure of the Brethren to answer his *Letter to the Boston Association*, or publicly to admit they could not answer it, "equal to a *confession of dishonesty* — & a *confession of defeat*." During this long "period of trial," he became "unavoidably identified" with the cause of religious freedom. The invective, hard names, and secret calumny against him, and his exclusion from pulpits, led "[Christian] men" to fear that the freedom of religion was in danger. This fear led them to invite him to Boston.[90]

Repeatedly, Parker denies the desire for worldly success. In discussing the *Discourse of Religion*, for example, he notes that the book received "no favor from the press" but claims he does not care because he lacks "literary ambition": "I think . . . feeble as I am |I| could get *fame* if I would pay the price & that with little toil. |I have never *sought honor of Men* &c. I can't understand the def[erence]. to P[opular]. O[pinion]. &c It is *unmanly*, [*unchristian*].|" Parker reiterates that he is going to Boston only because he is obligated to do so. He insists (like Luther) that "I could have done no otherwise." He calls the move a "duty": "They were many, & you few; they were oppressed, & found nowhere what they sought after. . . . I *sacrifice* my ease & comfort. I go to double labor—to unknown trials & difficulties. . . . I leave a Pulpit—I need not tell *you* how dear to me."[91]

Parker protests too much; his ambition is obviously apparent in his resentment over how he has been treated. "That Persecution &c was intended to ruin me!" he announces at one point. Later he asks, "*Why* have I been opposed, &c. not because [I] said what [was] not *true*, &c. not *honest*, not friendly to the *interests of Man* &c. . . . *With what intention* opposed? To ruin me, to give me no chance." Here can be heard the voice of the pump maker's son, who had worked so hard to make something of himself, only to see his dreams snatched from him.[92]

Parker thanks his congregation for their "perpetual kindness," for never having chided him for his freedom, and for the "wise counsel & kind counsel" some of them had given him. He asks them to forgive him if he has ever been "*arrogant*" or "wantonly unjust." He urges them to keep the truths he has taught—"keep them in Heart, keep them in Hand." His final exhortation is poignant:

Let me beg you—to remember that it is a very little thing to reject the errors—that I have pointed out—but a very great thing to accept, welcome & live the Truths I have told you. . . . Let my truths remain with you forever. Add now to these—You will respect me most—by outgoing me soon as possible. . . . I speak now as for the last time—. . . Remember there is something besides money & power & lands—something worth more than to stand well in the eyes of your acquaintance. Remember that you are an immortal soul & have duties to do—a C[onscience]. to obey, R[eason] to follow—Rel[igion] to live. Remember God sees you—& will bless your faithfulness forever & ever.[93]

The sermon over, Parker administered, for the last time, the Lord's Supper. With bread and wine, an epoch in his life quietly came to a close.

PARKER HAD been documenting his persecution for posterity since at least January 1843, when he spent weeks writing and annotating the account of his conference with the Boston Association, with the intention that it be "*printed in 1899.*" Some months later he collected the letters he had received about the controversies surrounding him, catalogued them by author and date, and placed them in a special folder. A few months after that, when he left for Europe, he presented his version of the controversy surrounding him in his "Sermon of My Own Stewardship." On returning to America in 1844, he made a fair copy of this discourse and added two appendixes. One contained annotated newspaper clippings from the South Boston ordination controversy, an extract from his journal about his lack of exchanges, and copies of the two letters Convers Francis wrote in 1842, in which he first offered Parker an exchange, then canceled it. The other appendix was a copy of the first edition of the *Transient and Permanent*, which he had carefully annotated to show that the changes he had made from preaching text to publication were in fact, and contrary to the charges of his critics, minor.[94]

In early 1846, Parker made the special copy of Second Parish "Church Records," which seems to have been written as much as for the future as for his parishioners. He also placed the manuscript of his farewell sermon in a folder with his "Stewardship" sermon, and left instructions for the two discourses to be published after his death.[95]

Finally, in March 1846, Parker wrote to the scribe of the Boston Association, an office now held by his former friend George Ellis, requesting a copy of all references to himself in the Association records. Ellis replied with ten pages of excerpts. They conclude with the deceptively bland statement that Parker's "membership in the Association, according to usage, ceased on his resigning his Pastoral charge of his Church & Society."[96] In other words, when he left the Spring Street pulpit, the long-vexed question of his connection to the Association became moot. Parker filed this manuscript away, confident that history would vindicate him.

GEORGE ELLIS and the Brethren may have thought themselves finished with Parker in February 1846, but his feud with Boston Unitarianism was not in fact over. It had merely entered a new stage, one characterized not by hot words but by the cold shoulder. In the coming years, Parker would continue to be shut out of pulpits and parlors, the *Register*, the *Examiner*, and Harvard. Only occasionally would the smoldering animosity flare up into a pamphlet or article. Most of the time, Parker's colleagues tried to act as if he did not exist.

Parker himself, however, refused to be ignored. Each year he attended the annual convention of the American Unitarian Association and the annual conference of Unitarian ministers at Berry Street. He went only to prove a point; he did not in fact like the proceedings. He complained to Dr. Gannett, for example, that nowhere was there "such & so much bitter sectarianism" as at these supposedly liberal gatherings.[97]

With no Boston Unitarian was Parker's relationship more complex and conflicted than with Gannett, who already was well on his way to becoming the revered dean of the local clergy. He and Parker continued to respect each other's sincerity, piety, and faithfulness to duty. At the 1847 AUA meeting, Parker even voted with the majority for Gannett to become Association president. "You will excuse me," Parker wrote to him afterward, "for thinking you are the only minister in the denomination who ought to be thought of for *that* place."[98]

Yet, partly owing to this mutual respect, each found all the more exasperating the other's seemingly pernicious wrongheadedness on so many subjects. Neither could forget or wholly forgive the other's position on the Hollis Street Council. In 1846, Parker preached one of his most celebrated sermons, concerning the "Perishing Classes" of Boston, in which he mentioned in passing that John Pierpont, for his temperance work, had been driven out of the city by "rum and the Unitarian clergy." When this discourse received a hostile notice in the *Register*, Parker wrote to Gannett asking if he had been the reviewer. Gannett replied that he had not, but took the opportunity to reprimand Parker severely for "some of the sentences" in the sermon (meaning those on Pierpont). These statements are, Gannett writes, "unworthy of you," "are taken as indications of a soured & irritated mind," and "are thought to betray a meanness to which you were believed to be superior": "You do not seem to me so high minded a man as I deemed you to be."[99]

This rebuke prompted Parker to write an emotional, confessional reply that he labeled "*Private*" ("I beg you not to show this . . . to anyone—no not to your wife").[100] After thanking Gannett for being "the only one of the ministers who ever came & told me of a wrong doing in my course," Parker insisted that "*I have never printed or preached one line which any feeling of ill-nature or sourness has sullied in the faintest degree.*" Many misunderstand this, admitted Parker, but he himself knew the truth, as did God and "the *few noblest Hearts*" whose approval Parker found far more important than "a world's applause— or world's scorn." He himself used to think, when a boy, that Christ was angry with persons "when he said those dreadful things in the Gospels," but now knew otherwise. Those who heard Jesus, however, thought *he had a Devil*. "Now I don't say I am comparing myself with [Christ]," Parker added. "I only mean to say that it was unavoidable *he* should be mistaken, & if HE, why not so little a man as I am?" Parker sometimes had suspected Gannett of "saying things in ill-temper, yes of saying them against me," yet was inclined to believe any denial Gannett made.

As Parker's letter continued, he once again self-consciously assumed the thorny crown of a martyr:

> The things which sound so hard when I . . . say them, or print them — are said *wholly in sorrow*; not *at all in anger*. I weep when I write them. I wrestle with myself afterwards, & say *I can't say them*. I *won't*, but the awful voice of conscience says, *who art thou, that darest to disobey thy Duty!* So I say them — tho it rends my heart. Trust me I feel no *sourness* — no *disappointed ambition*. I saw long ago what my course was to be — & submitted cheerfully, joyfully. . . . When my tears flow no longer — ; when the grass grows over my grave — |When my name has perished from among men| the hearts of men shall flame with the truths that I have tried to teach. Others shall reap where I have only mown down the thorns & that with lacerated arms — men calling me DESTROYER — ILL-TEMPERED & all that. These things count nothing. . . . If I have hard things to say I MUST say them — not that I would.[101]

MORE THAN a few of Parker's contemporaries, even those who recognized his claim to be a prophet, thought the martyr's crown fit awkwardly on his brow. James Freeman Clarke, in a review for the *World* of the just-published *True Idea of a Christian Church*, noted skeptically Parker's claim that modern martyrs, who face ostracism and poverty, suffer far worse than did the martyrs of old, who faced torture and death. Parker seems to forget, writes Clarke, that "the ancient martyr had *also* the neglect, and scorn, and obloquy, and want, *besides* having a cross or stake to look forward to at the end of it." Turning to Parker himself, "as much a martyr as we can easily find," Clarke wonders what his persecution amounts to: "A few grave attacks made against his views — many ministers refusing to exchange with him, and other many continuing to do so — a few sermons and newspaper articles to prove him a deist, accompanied by other sermons and articles to prove the contrary — . . . an unsuccessful attempt to expel him from the Boston Association, it being voted down by a large majority — ." In compensation for such suffering, Parker has won "a congregation of two thousand persons to hear him preach every Sunday, enthusiastic reverence and love from hosts of friends, large audiences in other places wherever he goes." This kind of martyrdom, writes Clarke wryly, "is rather bearable."[102]

Clarke could not see the world through Parker's eyes and so missed the peculiar tint that his vision cast on all events. For Parker, his public troubles had been made more extreme and painful by his domestic sufferings and his loss of friendships and dreams. He felt he had endured martyrdom, despite his having achieved, by many objective measures, a comfortable success. Moreover, most of his followers accepted him as a prophet and a martyr figure.

Parker's support drew from more than one source. Many loved him for the causes he championed: social and cultural reform, rational theology, and above all freedom of the pulpit, which was widely seen as a prerequisite of free thought and speech generally. The famous Boston journalist "Warrington" (William S. Robinson) expressed a widely held view when he wrote, at Parker's death, that Parker, as the great champion of pulpit freedom, had been the most influential person in America: "To him more than to any other man, — I had almost said, more than to all other men, — are we indebted for the privilege we have of thinking and speaking pretty much what we please to think and speak."[103]

Yet there was another, more specifically spiritual strain in Parker's appeal. The role he had assumed, of the prophet-martyr, belonged to a generally accepted typology of sainthood in mid-nineteenth-century New England, one derived primarily from biblical and Puritan traditions. Other Transcendentalists may be seen as having taken on, in modernized form, traditional sacred roles: Emerson as the man who works in the world while maintaining the inner light; Alcott as the Come-Outer; Thoreau as the ascetic in the wilderness. Part of the attraction of these writers sprang (and to an extent continues to spring) from the cultural resonance of the sacred roles they played. In Parker's case, the resonance of the prophet-martyr role ran deep. His admirers routinely compared him to Paul ("in our modern Athens") and Luther.

The apparent contradiction Clarke finds in Parker's case — that he rose to accomplishment, prosperity, and fame while becoming a martyr for his convictions — in fact made his example more useful for many, particularly for those like himself who were driven to rise in the world. At a time when this drive was both nearly universal and spiritually troubling for many, with fears of "materialism" rampant, Parker showed a way one could get ahead without losing one's soul. "Parkerites" could be confident of salvation if they were "persecuted" by the powerful, the rich, and the respectable. As Jesus is reported to have said in Luke 6:22–23 — a scriptural passage that, significantly, Parker himself read as part of the lesson during his final service at West Roxbury:

> Blessed are ye, when men shall hate you, and when they shall separate you *from their company*, and shall reproach *you*, and cast out your name as evil, for the Son of man's sake.

Rejoice ye in that day, and leap for joy: for, behold, your reward *is* great in heaven: for in the like manner did their fathers unto the prophets.

The experience of persecution became an essential part of "Parkerism." When young Caroline Healey had her "Transcendentalist conversion experience," declaring herself a Parker "disciple," critical to the process was her sense that by this declaration she had "struck her own death blow." Too, when certain female members of the Twenty-Eighth Congregational Society, following a common devotional practice of middle-class Victorian women, compiled scrapbook albums devoted to their pastor, they pasted into them not only the usual laudatory notices of him, but also (and less typically) editorials, sermons, and speeches denouncing him as an infidel, a traitor, and a fraud. These attacks were mounted onto beautiful colored paper with calligraphic page headings—carefully, even lovingly, preserved as proof that Parker was a holy man and that his devotees were engaged in a holy cause.[104]

A good example of how Parker's model of salvation worked is that of a young farmer named Henry Wilcox, who lived in a frontier town in western Illinois. In the winter of 1854–55, when Wilcox was struggling to find a respectable career, he read Parker's *Discourse of Religion*. He immediately ordered more of Parker's books from back east. In 1856, he wrote their author an enthusiastic letter: "I feel like one that has just awoke from a horrid dream. I have found there is something to live for, and that instead of my pocket I have a mind to cultivate."[105]

In other words, Wilcox could now satisfy himself that he could be a self-made man without being a man on the make. He improved his mind. In his letters to Parker, not only does he start to standardize his spelling and punctuation, but his prose, which at the beginning of the correspondence was plain, grows self-consciously literary, as when he waxes lyrical about, for example, agriculture. Even more strikingly, Wilcox transformed his life into a kind of *imitatio Parkeri*. He gave a lecture declaring opposition to slavery to be a religious duty (a controversial stand in his neighborhood) and started theological arguments with local evangelicals. He thereby gained a local reputation as an infidel, which made him a social outcast. He resolved to be a preacher who would work to tear down the "dreadful theology" around him.

His new faith was put to the ultimate test in September 1858, when he became gravely ill. In a letter to Parker, he described his ordeal:

Frequently while discussing religious subjects with others, they have said that my belief would do to *live* by, but it would not do to die by. The day of trial came. On the evening of the 26th of September, I felt that I could not live till morning. My stand being close to the bedside, while my friends were absent for a few minutes, I with great effort wrote these words on a piece of paper: "I die in the belief in which I live," dated and signed it, and placed it with my other papers. When my friends returned, I told them I thought I was going to die; and I settled up my worldly affairs. The physician and my friends conversed with me, and tried to shake my belief, but in vain: . . . there was no doubt, no fear, but a peaceful happiness came over me. Gradually I lost all consciousness, my body lost its feeling, my pulse was gone. I lay in that state for several hours, when, contrary to expectation, I rallied; for a week life hung in the balance. . . . Part of the time I was conscious, and conversed freely with those that came to see me; my bed was besieged daily by church members and ministers; daily I was urged to renounce my belief, but daily that belief grew stronger, and the contrast between natural and ecclesiastical religion grew wider and more distinct. At the end of the week, my youth and excellent constitution triumphed.[106]

Wilcox, by his own lights, had achieved a kind of sanctification.

Respectable enemy inquisitors, such as those who surrounded Wilcox's bed, were the key to Parker's religion. His followers would find them plentiful in the years after his installation in Boston. In February 1846, his controversial career was just beginning.

A Long, Long Warfare
Opens before Me

When Parker resigned from the West Roxbury pulpit, he said many times he would continue to live in the neighborhood. Not eleven months later, he and Lydia moved to Boston. Their new home was a pleasant, four-story townhouse on Rowe Place, a quiet, dead-end extension off Rowe Street, just south of the Public Garden and southeast of the Melodeon; shortly after they arrived, their cul-de-sac was renamed Exeter Place. On New Year's Day 1847, Parker recorded in his journal that he was now a citizen of the city.[1]

Moving into his new "parish" was more convenient for Parker as a pastor, but he and Lydia probably elected to leave Spring Street for another, more personal reason. He and Aunt Lucy at last could live apart. Lucy had wanted them to separate their houses since 1844, and now she enabled the separation to take place by purchasing the Parkers' new house for them. She even offered to give Theodore the mortgage, worth $7,000, perhaps out of generosity to Lydia or perhaps as an added incentive for him to leave. He declined, however, to take it.[2]

Pride must have been involved in his insistence on paying. With his new salary, supplemented by lecture fees and royalties, he no longer needed to be what he had never wanted to be, Lucy's dependent. He doubtless was delighted that he and Lydia had a place to call their own; as for Lydia, she doubtless was relieved to be released from the constant tension of having to live with these two strong, warring personalities. Another advantage for Lydia was that Georgie Colburn could at last move in with her, something that seems to have not been possible in Lucy's house. Georgie, at any rate, could not continue boarding at Brook Farm, which was failing.

By late 1845, the financial anemia of Brook Farm had grown so severe that the residents did not always have enough food. Defying their indebtedness, they launched an ambitious, Fourierist project to centralize their scattered living arrangements into a single large building designed for communal living. They invested their thin resources into raising this "Phalanstery." But during the night of Sunday, 1 March 1846—exactly three weeks after Parker preached his "Final Sermon" to the Second Parish—a spark from a carpenter's stove ignited the nearly completed structure, which was completely destroyed in a terrific blaze. The community could not absorb such a blow to its finances or morale and rapidly disintegrated.

Parker nowhere records witnessing the Phalanstery fire (although he probably did—the glow was visible for miles), but as a creditor of Brook Farm and a friend of George Ripley, he helped oversee the formal dissolution of the enterprise in 1847. In March, he took part in a meeting of creditors and stockholders that authorized Ripley to rent out his fields; in August, when the property of the community was transferred to a board of trustees, Parker was one of them; again, when Ripley auctioned off his library to pay some of his obligations (selling his books, he said, felt like attending his own funeral), Parker was the principal purchaser.

In September 1847, George and Sophia Ripley, defeated and all but bankrupt, left West Roxbury for New York City. George for a short time continued to edit the *Harbinger*, until it too, folded. Desperate for income, he joined the staff of the *New York Tribune* writing literary notices for eight dollars a week. Years would pass before he regained prosperity. He and Parker remained friends, but they now had less in common; Ripley had quit the crusades for theological and social reform. As for Sophia, she showed her disappointment with Transcendentalism and Associationism by becoming a Roman Catholic.

Parker no doubt found these events in West Roxbury sad; what happened there the following year he found traumatic. In August 1848, while he and Lydia were back in the old place for the summer, staying with Aunt Lucy, dysentery struck the household. The formidable Lucy died of the disease on 18 August. Next, Lydia grew violently sick, followed by a female domestic; fortunately, the two women recovered, although Parker, in nursing them, passed six days with just sixteen hours sleep.[3]

Once the crisis had passed, Parker had to deal with a new shock: the terms of Lucy's will. The original document had been drawn up in February 1846, with a codicil added two days before Lucy's death. Its provisions divided her sizable fortune, most of it derived from investments in railroads and banks, in half. From one half, $20,000 were taken to establish a trust fund for Lydia; the unspecified remainder of this half, which turned out to be $30,000, was used to establish a similar fund for Lydia's brother George Dodge Cabot. The rest of Lucy's money, some $50,000, was given outright (not in trust) to the six children, all adults, of her sister, Frances Cabot Jackson, the wife of the distinguished lawyer and jurist Charles Jackson (among these children was Amelia Lee Jackson Holmes, wife of the elder Oliver Wendell Holmes and mother of the younger). Lucy's codicil added $10,000 to Lydia's fund.[4]

Parker was named the executor, and he seems to have fulfilled his obligations faithfully. Yet he was appalled by the terms of the will. Whether he was aware of them before Lucy's death is unclear, but his reaction afterward was strong. He became convinced that Lucy had intended to give Lydia the bulk of her estate. That Lydia received such a comparatively small portion he blamed on the machinations of Charles Jackson. Not only were Jackson's offspring the principal beneficiaries of the will, he was also the lawyer who had drawn up the document; he even had signed the codicil in Lucy's stead, as she was then too ill to sign it for herself.

Why did Parker think Lucy's intentions had been thwarted? Did he know of some unrecorded promise that she had made to Lydia or to Lydia's parents? Were his perceptions skewed by the thought that he and Lydia should have been better rewarded, in consideration of all that they suffered on Lucy's account? Unfortunately, Parker's journal for 1847–51 is lost. Notes Lydia made on it in the 1860s, however, indicate that two days after Lucy's death, Parker wrote four pages about her; that soon afterward he wrote a "letter to Hon. Charles Jackson"; and that soon after that, Parker wrote a long "letter to the Heir."[5]

These letters, too, are lost, but their content is suggested by a passage from Parker's missing journal, which Lydia copied into her notes. In 1850, he read an article by Charles Jackson in the *Daily Advertiser* defending the new Fugitive Slave Law—legislation that Parker considered abominable. "This is a worthy sequel to his robbing my wife of some $30,000 or $40,000," Parker fumed, "which I think he did by taking advantage of" Aunt Lucy ". . . & making her will." In 1851, in another passage from the missing journal that Lydia copied, Parker complained that even "those Relations of Lydia's who shared in the plunder of Aunt Lucy thro' Judge Jacksons *legal* actions—never paid us the smallest civility."[6]

Parker's perception of events must have been shared by Lydia; that Lucy died "leaving a will which did not embody the intentions she had plainly in mind" eventually became part of Parker family lore. Whether the story is accurate cannot be determined. Perhaps Lucy really was manipulated into lessening Lydia's inheritance; then again, Lucy plausibly could have lessened it of her own free will, because she could not bear Lydia's husband. Or, perhaps, more innocently, she simply thought that the claims on her money of her other nieces and nephews were as great or greater than that of Lydia, who, unlike most of them, was childless. Besides, one of Charles Jackson's daughters was named "Lucy Cabot," which may indicate this branch of the family was closer to her and meant more to her than Parker thought. Lucy's codicil, signed by Charles Jackson, adding $10,000 to Lydia's trust fund (thereby giving her the largest of Lucy's bequests to any one person), would seem to belie the charge that either Lucy or her brother-in-law wanted to deny Lydia her fair share.[7]

Yet Parker firmly believed, perhaps with reason, that he and Lydia had been swindled by her relations, and the thought cast a final pall over his memory of West Roxbury. Years after he left Spring Street, shortly before his death, he recalled that the house he had shared with Lucy and Lydia, although "associated with some of the pleasantest scenes of my life," was "also connected with some of the most bitter and cruel experiences I ever lived through."[8]

In 1846, Parker completed the shift from the first phase of his career, when he was deeply involved in the Transcendentalist movement and challenged how people thought about religious truth, to the second phase, when he became deeply involved in the events leading to the Civil War and challenged how people thought about American democracy. Events propelled him forward. In April 1846, two months after his installation in Boston, fighting broke out between American and Mexican troops in the disputed Texas territory. Within weeks, Congress had declared war. In June, Parker denounced the war in his first speech to an abolitionist gathering, the annual meeting of the New England Anti-Slavery Society. A few days later, he attacked the war again in his first political sermon to be published.[9]

Meanwhile, his ideas about politics and society were maturing rapidly. In August 1846, he delivered a celebrated sermon on the "Perishing Classes," in which he analyzed poverty in Boston and proposed measures to relieve it; five months later he delivered a notable discourse on the "Dangerous Classes," about the social causes of crime. In a sermon preached just before the 1846 elections, he finally articulated what he considered a satisfactory definition of democracy: government of, for, and by all the people. He put this definition into what was, for him, its canonical form — "Government of all, by all, and for all" — a few weeks later in one of his most important sermons, soon published, on "Merchants." He here argued that the "merchant class" was to take the lead in creating American democracy.[10]

"A long — long — warfare opens before me," Parker had predicted in his journal in February 1845, the day he first preached at the Melodeon.[11] He was girding himself to attack the "popular theology." Yet the battle ahead would be less about religious doctrine than politics and would be waged not only with words but with bullets.

The era of the American Civil War is commonly remembered as a time of struggle between the North and the South, but it was marked just as much by strife within each section. At the center of the fight for the heart, mind, and soul of the North would be Theodore Parker.

Notes

Sources

I cite original manuscripts, with a few exceptions. Parker's Journals F and C (November 1835–June 1838) are lost, as are the journal that I call "K" (September 1843–July 1844) and Parker's second Journal N (December 1848–April 1851). I have been able to reconstruct partially F, C, and "2N" from the notes Lydia Cabot Parker took on these journals in the 1860s and from quotations in the Weiss and Frothingham biographies (although Weiss and Frothingham sometimes transcribe the same passage very differently). Especially useful in making these reconstructions has been a copy of the Weiss biography (actually, the page proofs of the British edition) in the Boston Public Library, with annotations in the margin by Lydia Cabot Parker and Joseph Lyman that provide the journal page number of many of Weiss's quotations. No notes by Lydia Cabot Parker survive for Journal K, but it is extensively quoted in Weiss and Frothingham and some of it was transcribed in the 1880s by Franklin Sanborn; a fragment of this transcription is at the Houghton Library.

The manuscript of Parker's sermon on the "Transient and Permanent in Christianity" is lost; I have relied on Philip F. Gura's plausible reconstruction of the preached text. I cite from the manuscript of Parker's Journal N (1838–40), except for the last six months of 1840, when I generally rely on the late Carol Johnston's transcription. (I consider Johnston's decision to omit from her transcription any letter of the alphabet not clearly visible to be arbitrary. Parker's handwriting has the character of speedwriting; whether or not he intended to write a particular letter in a given word is impossible to determine. Unlike Johnston, I therefore give Parker the benefit of the doubt. What I would transcribe as "from," for example, she transcribes as "frm." My quotations follow my readings.) I also rely on Gary Collison's edition of Parker's correspondence with Convers Francis. Unfortunately, I have been forced to rely on heavily edited nineteenth-century transcriptions of some of Parker's most important correspondence—for example, his letters to Lydia Cabot Parker, William Silsbee, and Elizabeth Palmer Peabody.

I use many anonymous published writings by Parker that have never before been attributed to him. For explanations of these attributions, see the bibliography, under "Theodore Parker's Published Writings, 1832–1846."

Citations of Parker's Sermons

I use the following form when citing Parker's manuscript sermons: "The State of the Church" (#94, 5 August 1838), in which the title of the sermon is followed in parentheses by its number in Parker's sermon record book and the date on which the sermon was first preached. Note that some sermons were written months before they were first preached, and many were preached more than once. Some sermons also have two titles, because Parker wrote one on the manuscript but listed it under another in his sermon record book. Both titles are provided, with the one on the manuscript listed first: for example, "Duty of Citizens/Patriotism, Man to Men" (#134, 28 March 1839). All sermon manuscripts, unless otherwise noted, are located at the Andover-Harvard Theological Library.

Abbreviations

Short titles are used throughout, with complete citations given in the bibliography. The exception are pieces published in periodicals of the time (e.g., the *Christian Examiner*, the *Christian Register*, the *Christian World*); for these, I provide the complete citation in the notes. Unless otherwise noted, manuscripts cited from the Andover-Harvard Theological Library, the Boston Public Library, or the Massachusetts Historical Society are in the respective Theodore Parker Papers of each library.

A-H	Andover-Harvard Theological Library, Harvard Divinity School, Cambridge, Mass.
"Anecdotes"	Columbus Greene, "Anecdotes in the Life of Theodore Parker" (ca. 1862), Andover-Harvard Theological Library, Harvard Divinity School, Cambridge, Mass.
ASAOS	Theodore Parker, *Additional Speeches, Addresses, and Occasional Sermons*, 2 vols. (Boston: Little, Brown, 1855)
BA Records	Boston Association of Congregational Ministers Records, Theodore Parker Papers, Massachusetts Historical Society, Boston, Mass.
BPL	Boston Public Library, Boston, Mass.
BSP	"The Book of the Sermons and the Preachings of T[heodore]. P[arker].," Boston Public Library (a copy made by Lydia Parker is at Andover-Harvard, titled "Sermon Record Book")
CE	*Christian Examiner*
CMW	Theodore Parker, *Critical and Miscellaneous Writings* (Boston: James Munroe, 1843)
CR	*Christian Register*
CTPCF	Gary Collison, "A Critical Edition of the Correspondence of Theodore Parker and Convers Francis, 1836–1859," Ph.D. dissertation, Pennsylvania State University, 1979
CW	*Christian World*
CWRWE	Ralph Waldo Emerson, *The Collected Works of Ralph Waldo Emerson*, 5 vols. to date, edited by Alfred Furguson et al. (Cambridge: Harvard University Press, 1971–)

DR	Theodore Parker, *A Discourse of Matters Pertaining to Religion* (Boston: Charles C. Little and James Brown, 1842)
DW	Theodore Parker, *A Critical and Historical Introduction to the Canonical Scriptures of the Old Testament. From the German of Wilhelm Martin Leberecht De Wette* (Boston: Charles C. Little and James Brown, 1843)
EPJC	Lydia C. Parker, list of erased pieces from Parker's Journal C, Theodore Parker Papers, Library of Congress, Washington, D.C.
EPJ2N	Lydia C. Parker, list of erased pieces from Parker's second Journal N, Theodore Parker Papers, Library of Congress, Washington, D.C.
JC	Theodore Parker, Journal C (1836–38) [reconstructed]
JF	Theodore Parker, Journal F (1835–36) [reconstructed]
JI	Theodore Parker, Journal I (1841–44), Andover-Harvard Theological Library, Harvard Divinity School, Cambridge, Mass.
JK	Theodore Parker, Journal K (1844–45) [reconstructed]
JL	Theodore Parker, Journal L (1844), Massachusetts Historical Society, Boston, Mass.
JM	Theodore Parker, Journal M (1844–47), Massachusetts Historical Society, Boston, Mass.
JMNE	Ralph Waldo Emerson, *The Journals and Miscellaneous Notebooks of Ralph Waldo Emerson*, 16 vols., edited by Ralph H. Orth et al. (Cambridge: Harvard University Press, 1971–87)
JN	Theodore Parker, Journal N (1838–40), Andover-Harvard Theological Library, Harvard Divinity School, Cambridge, Mass.
J2N	Theodore Parker, second Journal N (1847–51) [reconstructed]
JO	Theodore Parker, Journal O (1851–56), Andover-Harvard Theological Library, Harvard Divinity School, Cambridge, Mass.
JTP	Carol Johnston, "The Journals of Theodore Parker: July–December, 1840," Ph.D. dissertation, University of South Carolina, 1980
LCP	Lydia Dodge Cabot Parker
LCTP	John Weiss, *The Life and Correspondence of Theodore Parker*, 2 vols. (New York: D. Appleton, 1864)
LE	Ralph Waldo Emerson, *The Letters of Ralph Waldo Emerson*, 8 vols. to date, edited by Ralph Rusk and Eleanor M. Tilton (New York: Columbia University Press, 1939–)
Lexington Records	"Records of the First Parish Church, Lexington, Massachusetts, 1690–1845" (1854 copy), Lexington Historical Society, Lexington, Mass.

LOC	Library of Congress, Washington, D.C.
MHS	Massachusetts Historical Society, Boston, Mass.
"Mr. Greene"	Lydia Cabot Parker, "Recollections of Mr. Greene," notes of an interview with Columbus Greene (ca. 1862), Library of Congress, Washington, D.C.
"Recollections"	Columbus Greene, "Recollections of the Early Life of Theodore Parker" (ca. 1862), Andover-Harvard Theological Library, Harvard Divinity School, Cambridge, Mass.
Roxbury Records	Theodore Parker, "Church Records of the Second Parish in Roxbury" (1837–40), Theodore Parker Church, West Roxbury, Mass.
Sanborn JK	Franklin Sanborn, notes on Parker's Journal K, Houghton Library, Harvard University, Cambridge, Mass.
Sanborn Memoir	Franklin Sanborn, notes for a memoir of Theodore Parker, Houghton Library, Harvard University, Cambridge, Mass.
SAOS	Theodore Parker, *Speeches, Addresses, and Occasional Sermons* (Boston: Crosby and Nichols, 1852)
SBO	*The South-Boston Unitarian Ordination* (Boston: Saxton and Pierce, 1841)
SI	*Scriptural Interpreter*
338 Appendix	Theodore Parker, Scrapbook Appendix to "A Sermon of My Stewardship" (#338, 3 September 1843), Boston Public Library, Boston, Mass.
TP	Theodore Parker
TPAB	Octavius Brooks Frothingham, *Theodore Parker: A Biography* (Boston: James R. Osgood, 1874)
28CS Papers	Twenty-Eighth Congregational Society Papers, Andover-Harvard Theological Library, Harvard Divinity School, Cambridge, Mass.
WRS	Theodore Parker, *West Roxbury Sermons, 1837–1848*, edited by Franklin Sanborn (Boston: Roberts Brothers, 1892)
WTP	Theodore Parker, *Works of Theodore Parker*, Centennial Edition, 15 vols. (Boston: American Unitarian Association, 1907–13)

Chapter One

1. "Autobiography," in *LCTP*, 1:24; the precise time of birth, according to his father's record book, was five minutes before three (see Parker [TP's great-nephew], *Genealogy*, 154). For a description of Kite's End, see *Proceedings of the Lexington Historical Society*, 2:101–2; for the population of Lexington, see *Calendar History of Lexington Massachusetts*. For the ages of the Parker family members, see Parker, *Genealogy*, 80, 150–54; Hudson, *History of the Town of Lexington*, 2:515–17. Note that *LCTP*, 1:15, incorrectly gives the ages of TP's parents as 50 and 47, and the error is followed by his other biographers. Note, too, that TP incorrectly remembers his grandmother as being "over 80 at my birth," "Autobiography," in *LCTP*, 1:21. The date of her bap-

tism in Lexington Records (p. 90) confirms Parker and Hudson in placing her birth in January 1731, but even the minister recorded that she was ninety-two at her death on 15 December 1822 (p. 353), which shows that her age was commonly overestimated.

2. "Autobiography," in *LCTP*, 1:24–25. For a description of the house, see "Autobiography," in *LCTP*, 1:18; for a picture of it, see *LCTP*, 1:26. It was torn down in 1843 by TP's brother Isaac, who built beside it another house which is still occupied. The original foundations were destroyed in 1967 to build a water main. The site today is beside a highway exit ramp, and much of the surrounding area of Lexington has been developed, but the hill behind where the house once stood is now wooded. A visitor may climb it, stand on one of the rocky outcrops that TP knew, look out over the valley, block out the sounds of traffic, and imagine an earlier time.

3. "Autobiography," in *LCTP*, 1:17–21, 24–25.

4. Capt. John Parker's estate records and account book survive at the Lexington Historical Society. Hudson, *History of the Town of Lexington*, 2:512–13, 535–36; "Autobiography," in *LCTP*, 1:21; since Ephraim did not die until 1790 (Hudson, *History of the Town of Lexington*, 2:535), this statement raises a few questions. Did Ephraim also need help? Were he and Lydia separated? Did John Parker in fact not move back to the homestead until 1790?

5. In "Recollections," Greene says he comes to Lexington in the "winter of 1818 & 19"; in "Mr. Greene," 1, he says 1819. For an account of Greene's life and a portrait, see Parker, *Genealogy*, 240–42. Regarding TP's woodworking: as of 1899, there survived a cradle he had made as young man; Chadwick, *Theodore Parker*, 10. "Mr. Greene," 5, 11; "Autobiography," in *LCTP*, 1:22.

6. "Experience as a Minister," *WTP*, 13:292; Autobiographical Sketch (1854), 3, A-H. This autobiographical sketch, which covers TP's life until 1846, was written to George Ripley, apparently as a source for an article on TP that Ripley wrote for the *Phrenological Journal* (10 January 1855), 324–43. A clipping of the article is at A-H.

7. The estate records are in the Parker family papers, Lexington Historical Society; Autobiographical Sketch (1854), 2; "Autobiography," in *LCTP*, 1:22. In the Lexington Records, "Mr." is rarely used; that John Parker was the oldest son of a Revolutionary War hero probably increased his chances of being "mistered." Autobiographical Sketch (1854), 3–4; "Autobiography," in *LCTP*, 22–23; "Mr. Greene," 9, 12; see also LCP's notes of the "Recollection of J. Bowers Simons," 3, LOC. Note that LCP may have misspelled "Simons's" name; it may be "Simonds." "Mr. Greene," 2.

8. Autobiographical Sketch (1854), 2; J. Hastings to LCP, 3 January 1861, LOC. "Mr. Greene," 3; Autobiographical Sketch (1854), 2; "Autobiography," in *LCTP*, 1:23.

9. "Mr. Greene," 12; JM, 14 (19 November 1844).

10. "Mr. Greene," 12; see TP to LCP, 30 October 1833, Sanborn Memoir, 1.

11. "Mr. Greene," 2, 12; Autobiographical Sketch (1854), 2–3, 2. Note that Paley's natural theology was well respected, but his ethical theory was severely criticized; see Howe, *Unitarian Conscience*, 64–67, 73–74.

12. "Recollections of J. Bowers Simons," LOC; "Finis/Farewell Sermon to West Roxbury" (#413, 8 February 1846), 6, BPL.

13. "Autobiography," in *LCTP*, 1:23; "Recollections of J. Bowers Simons," 3, LOC; Autobiographical Sketch (1854), 2, 3; "Mr. Greene," 2.

14. *LCTP*, 1:30; "Autobiography," in *LCTP*, 1:24.

15. Autobiographical Sketch (1854), 2–3; "Autobiography," in *LCTP*, 1:24; "Experience as a Minister," *WTP*, 13:291; "Of Theology & Religion" (#275, 13 February 1842), 12.

16. Chadwick, *Theodore Parker*, 186.

17. "Autobiography," in *LCTP*, 1:25–26.

18. Hudson, *History of the Town of Lexington*, 2:667–68; Lexington Records, 263; *LCTP*, 1:29.

19. I side with those historians of New England Puritanism who question the famous "declension" thesis of Perry Miller—that is, that Puritans were growing more secular; see, for example, Foster, *Long Argument*, and Peterson, *Price of Redemption*.

20. *Proceedings of the Lexington Historical Society*, 1:337; 3:83.

21. See Hall, *Worlds of Wonder, Days of Judgment*, 152–62.

22. Orville Dewey, "The Rite of the Lord's Supper," *CE* 5 (November 1832), 261. See also Henry Ware Jr., *On the Formation of the Christian Character*, chap. 4, pt. 5, in Henry Ware Jr., *Works*, 4:367–74.

23. For TP's childhood struggle with belief in Hell, see JN, 99 (January 1839); "Finis/Farewell Sermon to West Roxbury" (#413, 8 February 1846), 6, BPL; "Experience as a Minister," *WTP*, 13:295–96. For the reference to the *New England Primer*, see *WTP*, 2:170. Note that well into the nineteenth century, many even in Unitarian families continued to fear that unbaptized children risked damnation, despite all their ministers said against original sin. In 1852, TP—by this time a notorious Transcendentalist—baptized the children of one Mr. Stacy, a Unitarian from West Newton; he describes the incident in "A Record of the Marriages and Deaths among the Members of the XXVIIIth Congregational Society," a document found in the Theodore Parker Church: "The little Boy *Walter* was dangerously ill, & some of the Relations had the old notions of Baptism & feared that an angry God would damn the babe unbaptized. Mr. S had no such opinions. Mr. Knapp the Unit.n Minister was sick. Mr. Gilled the Orthodox [Minister] refused to perform the ritual."

24. For Hannah Parker deciding the religious reading of the family, see Autobiographical Sketch (1854), 3. TP's different accounts differ as to when he abandoned belief in Hell: in JN, he says his fear of Hell went away before he was nine years old; in the "Farewell Sermon" (#413), he says he "trod" the doctrine of eternal damnation "under foot" when he was six years and three months old; in the "Experience as a Minister," *WTP*, 13:295–96, he says he abandoned it by the age of seven. Yet he seems not to have rejected Hell until he was at Harvard Divinity School. See chap. 2.

25. John Parker told the story of 19 April to Eli Simonds, *Proceedings of the Lexington Historical Society*, 2:102. For the Sunday dinner breaks, see "Mr. Greene," 5; in the *Proceedings of the Lexington Historical Society*, 1:79–80, appears the following note on Dudley's tavern, which closed in 1835 and is no longer standing: "On Sundays, the women and children would eat their lunch in the parlor, and the men would go to the bar room, for gingerbread and cheese. The old men would sit in a circle before the peat fire, passing a great mug of flip, and talking of the French and Indian War." Note that the Simonds family claimed that one of their ancestors captured the musket

from a drunken Irish dragoon and gave it to Captain Parker; see Brown, *Beneath Old Roof Trees*, 32–36.

26. *Trial of Theodore Parker*, 220. This monument still stands.

27. *Proceedings of the Lexington Historical Society*, 1:30–31; TP to Bancroft, 10 September 1858, in *LCTP*, 1:11–12. In a deposition taken six days after the battle, Captain Parker testified only that he and his men had decided "not to meddle or make with said Regular Troops (if they should approach) unless they should insult us" (Tourtellot, *Lexington and Concord*, 123). For TP being an ensign, see "Recollections of J. Bowers Simons," 4–5, LOC. As for the state of the militia, the following story is of note. One Lexington resident recalled showing up for militia drill in 1832 without a musket or cartridge box; as the militiamen mustered on the common, it began to rain, so they suspended the drill and retired to Dudley's tavern. There a regimental officer from Concord demanded they elect a captain. The men, "noisy and ungovernable," proceeded to elect a woman "who was an inmate of the almshouse." The officer left in disgust, and the militia company disbanded permanently. See *Proceedings of the Lexington Historical Society*, 2:87–89.

28. *Trial of Theodore Parker*, 221.

29. TP also grew up hearing sermons in which religious and national mythology were mixed. He later recalled, as a boy, hearing a sermon along the following lines: "The British government oppressing the Puritans is the 'great red dragon' of the Revelation." See *CMW*, 300, 300n.

30. "Experience as a Minister," *WTP*, 13:293. There are two Unitarian churches in Lexington. TP attended what is now called the First Parish Church (then it was simply the Lexington Church), which at that time had a meetinghouse that stood on the Lexington Common where the Minuteman Monument now stands; the contemporary First Parish Church building is diagonally opposite from the monument. The Second Church, also called the Follen Church, is in east Lexington. Organized in the early 1830s and incorporated in 1845, it is named after the Rev. Dr. Karl Follen (1796–1840), who was its minister from 1835 to 1840.

31. Ibid., 296.

32. For biographical sketches, see *Sibley's Harvard Graduates*. Hancock was class of 1689, Clarke class of 1752. See also Hudson, *History of the Town of Lexington*, 1: chaps. 13–14. Hancock was the grandfather of the patriot.

33. *Sibley's Harvard Graduates*, 3:433; different versions of the surveying story appear in *Sibley's Harvard Graduates* and Hudson.

34. There is a voluminous literature on this subject; in preparing the following section, I have found most useful Conrad Wright, *Beginnings of Unitarianism*, and the first part of Kuklick, *Churchmen and Philosophers*.

35. Arminianism is named after the Dutch theologian Jacobus Arminius (1560–1609), who broke with orthodox Calvinism when he argued that although God offered us grace, we were free to accept or reject it (of course God knew beforehand what we would decide). His followers emphasized even more strongly human rationality and free will.

36. By "religious experience," I refer not to a specific spiritual event, but to the gen-

eral way in which religion is experienced, as for instance the "healthy minded" and "sick souled" types of religious experience that William James identified. I assume both that religious experience is "shaped by" psychology and ideas, and that religious language is an "expression of" religious experience.

37. John Hancock, *Gaining of Souls*, 14, 19; Hancock's opinion of the Awakening may be indicated by that of his eldest son, the Rev. John Hancock of Braintree, wrote several anti-revival pamphlets. For Mayhew, see Conrad Wright, *Beginnings of Unitarianism*, 66.

38. The inscription is taken almost word for word from various passages of two of his sermons; see Clarke, *Fate of Bloodthirsty Oppressors*, 20n, and his Election Sermon for 1781, 42.

39. *Sibley's Harvard Graduates*, 13:211. For Clarke's orthodox theological position, see *Christ's Mission of the Seventy*.

40. Hudson, *History of the Town of Lexington*, 1:319; Clarke, *Use and Excellency of Vocal Music*, 27.

41. "Mr. Greene," 9; Hudson, *History of the Town of Lexington*, 1:334. Briggs, who was ordained in Lexington the Sunday before Channing preached "Unitarian Christianity," retired in 1835 to become secretary of the American Unitarian Association; see Lexington Records, 288. There is also evidence that Briggs and TP were personally friendly. In 1828, Briggs wrote a letter in which he "cheerfully" recommends TP as qualified to be a teacher in the Lexington common schools (Charles Briggs, 27 October 1828, BPL), and in 1832 it was he who introduced TP to Convers Francis, a classmate of Briggs's at Harvard who was to become TP's intellectual mentor (*LCTP*, 1:59). See chap. 2, below.

42. Hudson, *History of the Town of Lexington*, 1:334; "Mr. Greene," 9.

43. Briggs, *Sermon Delivered at the Installation of the Rev. Artemas B. Muzzey*.

44. Lexington Records, 172, 186.

45. "Autobiography," in *LCTP*, 1:22 (Lydia Parker may have been among the quarter of the church members who voted against introducing the new hymnbook in 1766); Hudson, *History of the Town of Lexington*, 1:349; Spevack, *Charles Follen's Search*.

46. TP to Greene, 29 August 1834, 18 November 1834, MHS.

47. TP to Greene, 18 November 1834, 21 December 1834, MHS. TP also urged Greene to read Jacob Abbott's *Young Christian*; Abbot was Orthodox, but his writings were so doctrinally loose that he was suspected of being a Unitarian.

48. See Howe, *Unitarian Conscience*, 165 and chap. 6, and Howe, "The Cambridge Platonists of Old England and the Cambridge Platonists of New England," in Conrad Edwick Wright, ed., *American Unitarianism*, 87–119. Note that Clarke, after he became minister in Lexington, married one of Hancock's granddaughters.

49. "Mr. Greene," 3. The exception was one Mary Ann Smith, but she had fewer opportunities than did Theodore; she married, had four children, and died in 1859.

50. Autobiographical Sketch (1854), 3 (see also Dall Journal, 15 March 1856, MHS); "Anecdotes," 9.

51. "Education of Spirit/Spiritual Culture" (#83, 29 April 1838); Brown, *Beneath Old Roof Trees*, 48.

52. All these stories appear in the Autobiographical Sketch (1854).

53. Until the 1830s, women commonly taught only in the summer and men in the winter, because older girls went to the summer classes while older boys went to the winter ones. Women were considered unfit to prepare boys for college, and it was considered inappropriate for young women to teach young men nearly their own age. Of course, the women were paid less than the men. See Cott, *Bonds of Womanhood*, 30–35.

54. The book was *Theism, Atheism and the Popular Theology*, *WTP*, vol. 2.

55. See *Statement of the Course of Instruction, Terms of Admission, Expenses, &c at Harvard University*.

56. "Mr. Greene," 7; a letter exists from TP to this principal, William P. Huntington, that indicates friendly relations between them: 23 August 1832, MHS.

57. See LCP's notes of "The Recollections of Dr. Oliver Hastings Wellington," LOC; TP to S. G. Howe, 23 March 1860, quoted in *LCTP*, 1:50; "Anecdotes," 3–4.

58. Among those who criticized TP's teaching was the minister at Concord, old Dr. Ezra Ripley, who was also Emerson's step-grandfather. See "Recollections of Dr. Oliver Hastings Wellington," LOC. Note that schoolmastering to pay for college remained a practice in some parts of the country until the late nineteenth century, at least; see W. E. B. Du Bois's recollections in *Souls of Black Folk*, chap. 4.

59. There is a tradition that while at Concord, TP taught little "David Henry" Thoreau. I have been unable to confirm this story.

60. J2N, 469 (23 August 1850), quoted in *LCTP*, 1:47; see also JM, 326 (23 August 1846) and JO, 486 (23 August 1854). A different version of these events appears in Cushing, *Memorials of the Class of 1834*, 107. According to Cushing, TP had borrowed the family horse, ridden into Cambridge, and came back in time to inform his father over the evening meal. Cushing says he got this story from TP himself, but it contradicts TP's repeated written testimony. The account of an entrance examination at Harvard in the early 1830s is based on files in the Harvard Archives; apparently in the later 1830s, the exams became two-day affairs.

61. *LCTP*, 1:46–47; *TPAB*, 26–27.

62. "Anecdotes," 11. Note that in one of TP's ordination sermons in 1837, he attacks the idea, which "we all know," that only the exchange and the bar require intellect, study, and genius, "while innocent dullness will suffice for the Pulpit." See "The Christian Ministry" (#39, 25 June 1837), 24.

63. TP to S. P. Andrews, 15 February 1837, MHS; TP to LCP, 17 June 1835, Sanborn Memoir, 34; "Experience as a Minister," *WTP*, 13:294.

64. On "Poems by a Young Man," see TP to F. B. Sanborn, 13 May 1859, MHS. Another literary project of TP's youth was to edit a volume of Shakespeare's sonnets; see TP to Francis, 23 June 1840, in CTPCF, 190. On the epic poem, see TP to S. P. Andrews, 20 October 1836, MHS; JN, 7 (July 1838).

65. "Experience as a Minister," *WTP* 13:290; JN, 295 (January 1840).

66. TP to George T. Bigelow, 14 May 1833, MHS; TP to S. G. Howe, 23 March 1860, in *LCTP*, 1:50. Poland was a topic of popular interest owing to the anti-Russian insurrection there in 1830.

67. Francis, *Historical Sketch of Watertown*, 148–49. See also LCP's Watertown recollections, LOC.

68. TP to William Huntington, 23 August 1832, MHS.

69. The manuscript is in the BPL. The form of TP's "History of the Jews," at least in its opening chapters, is suggested in another book that TP admired, Abbot's *Young Christian*. In chap. 8, Abbot says that young students of Scripture should retell the sacred stories in their own words and prepare lists of questions about each story. In the first chapters of TP's "History of the Jews," he retells Jewish biblical history and lists of questions run along the bottom of each page.

70. TP to LCP, 20 February 1834, Sanborn Memoir, 16–17.

71. *WTP*, 6:167–70.

72. JI, 334 (11 October 1844).

73. "My Childhood's Home," *CR*, 14 November 1835.

74. Hudson, *History of the Town of Lexington*, 2:513–17; TP to D. Huntington, 24 August 1832, MHS. TP, in TP to Bowditch, 12 October 1858, in *LCTP*, 2:514, says eight of the Parker children had consumption—not including himself, who also was to die of the disease. Parker, *Genealogy*, 153, mistakenly lists Mary's ("Polly's") death as 1831 (TP refers to her as alive in a letter, quoted below, from 1832); Lydia's death is noted in JC, 194 (she is referred to as "L. P. H.," for Lydia Parker Herrick). Hiram's drinking problem is strongly implied in TP to Henry A. Miles, 9 February 1842, Myerson Collection, Thomas Cooper Library. To Miles, a Unitarian minister in Lowell, where Hiram lived, TP wrote: "I thank you exceedingly . . . for the interest you take in my poor brother. . . . I think he will persevere though he lacks *firmness*. . . . I suspect his wife is not of the *kindest* character originally. The blame of his course is in some measure hers, for I suspect the outside of the house was sometimes the pleasantest *before* his habits became |very| bad." I generalize about TP's relationship to his brother John and to Greene on the basis of his letters to them in MHS.

75. JM, 315–16 (22 July 1846); TP to D. Huntington, 24 August 1832, MHS.

76. Stevenson, "Theodore Parker: A Biographical Sketch," in *Discourse of Matters Pertaining to Religion* (1876 edition), lxvi.

77. TP to LCP, 10 November 1836, Sanborn Memoir, 81–82.

78. He comments on the exchange between Andrews Norton and George Ripley, prompted by Ripley's review of Martineau's *Rationale of Religious Enquiry*. See chap. 3, below.

79. "My Childhood's Home," *CR*, 14 November 1835.

80. TP to Frances Power Cobbe, 5 May 1848, Huntington Library.

81. "Life as it *is*," JN, 249 (October 1839).

82. James, *Varieties of Religious Experience*, 79–81 (James mistakenly says the passage he cites comes from a "letter"; it comes from the sermon cited at the opening of this section); *CWRWE*, 1:10; *DR*, 16. TP took the term "sense of dependence" in part from Schleiermacher (*DR*, 18n).

Chapter Two

1. For chaps. 14–16, TP relied heavily on Flavius Josephus's *History of the Jewish War* and he drew from a variety of sources, including the Babylonian Talmud and "the Weimar statement," to write the last four chapters, which cover Jewish history from the Diaspora to the nineteenth century.

2. "History of the Jews," 1, BPL.

3. Ibid., 240.

4. Palfrey, while discussing Mosaic health laws in his *Academical Lectures*, adds the following note (1:263n): "If there be anything in national tendencies, the filth one sees in the lanes of the Jewish *Ghetto* in cities of Europe, is an intimation that the fathers of the race needed to be subjects of a rigid legislation of this kind." TP's book is wholly free of such remarks. As TP became more of a Transcendentalist, his dislike of Judaism increased.

5. I believe the opinions TP expressed in this book were his own (i.e., he was not condescending to his presumed audience of Sunday school students) because he goes further than he must to support the actuality of miracles. He even accepts as valid a few nonscriptural miracles. For example, he thinks it was "certain" that "supernatural agency" caused the earthquake that prevented the Jews from rebuilding their Temple on Moriah, in defiance of Jesus' "stern decree" for the ruin of Jerusalem, during the reign of the Roman emperor Julian the Apostate ("History of the Jews," 213, BPL). See also "History of the Jews," 25 (Red Sea), 48 (Joshua). When TP describes Isaiah's miracle of making the shadow "retrograde 15 degrees upon the dial" (2 Kings 20:9–11), he adds the comment that the question of whether "the sun actually retrograded, or a shadow was produced by *direct*, supernatural agency," is a question for schoolmen, "since he, who is able to produce it by the latter, is equally competent to effect the same by the former method" ("History of the Jews," 95–96).

6. Weiss, *Discourse Occasioned by the Death of Convers Francis*, 67.

7. TP to Francis, 3 February 1859, in CTPCF, 582; *Record of Church Members, Deaths, Marriages, &c in Watertown, Commenced June, 1819*, 8, Watertown Free Public Library.

8. Francis, "The Value of Enlightened Views of Religion," 73–74.

9. In the Harvard Archives.

10. William Ellery Channing, *Works*, 368.

11. The chair was actually established in 1811. Brown, *Rise of Biblical Criticism in America*, 10–11.

12. "On the Account of the Creation of Man" (#704, 2 February 1834), "On the Longevity of the Antediluvians" (#711, 30 March 1834), "On the Deluge" (#714, 20 April 1834); all manuscripts in the Convers Francis Papers, Watertown Free Public Library.

13. TP to LCP, 27 February 1834, Sanborn Memoir, 15.

14. "History of the Jews," 66; TP to LCP, 13 March 1834, Sanborn Memoir, 19, 20–21; TP to Greene, 2 April 1834, MHS.

15. TP to Greene, 11 July 1834, MHS.

16. Three decades later, Bigelow would become chief justice of the state supreme court.

17. TP to Bigelow, 4 June 1833, MHS.

18. Bigelow to TP, 5 June 1833, MHS.

19. TP to Charles Miller, 1 November 1833, MHS; TP to LCP, 30 October 1833, Sanborn Memoir, 1.

20. In November 1833, TP wrote that he and LCP had been acquainted "nearly two

years" (TP to Charles Miller, 1 November 1833, MHS). This is a slight exaggeration; TP had moved to Watertown in April 1832 and probably met her either then or shortly thereafter.

21. For information about the LCP's family, see Briggs, *History and Genealogy of the Cabot Family*, 118, 266–68, 642–44; for LCP's residence, see TP to Charles Miller, 1 November 1833, MHS, in which he says that LCP lived with Lucy at 10 Essex Street, Boston. TP to LCP, 22 and 23 August 1836, Sanborn Memoir, indicates that LCP was living in Brookline. Did Lucy have a summer house there?

22. JF, 178 (April 1836). For Lucy being mistaken for LCP's foster mother, see Mackintosh, *Some Recollections*, 7.

23. For Peabody being LCP's teacher, see E. P. Peabody to Brownson, n.d. (ca. summer 1842), Brownson Papers, Notre Dame; I thank Philip Gura for bringing this letter to my attention. LCP's surviving letters almost all date from 1858 and after; the only document in her hand from the 1830s is the "Memoir of Henry Martyn," apparently a copy of a Sunday school tract, in LOC. For LCP's knowledge of French, see TP to Greene, 29 August 1834, 11 July 1834, MHS. After LCP and TP were married, he would sometimes use Latin when writing things in his journal that he did not want her to read. In February 1834, he offered her a German dictionary (TP to LCP, 20 February 1834, Sanborn Memoir, 18), but she could not have known much of that language, because several months later he had to explain to her what "Kindergesang" ("children's songs") meant (TP to LCP, 24 September 1834, Sanborn Memoir, 30).

24. The "Commonplace Book" is at A-H. See "Hints to Sunday School Teachers," *Sunday School Teacher, and Children's Friend* 2:(3?) (March? 1837), 142–49, etc.; EPJC, 12, originally JC, 244 (May 1838); "The Memoir of Henry Martyn, Missionary to India," LOC.

25. See LCP's recollections of his Watertown years in LOC. Although these recollections are unsigned and are written impersonally (there is no "I"), they are in her handwriting and describe details of the Broad household (e.g., that the Broads did not scrimp on lamp oil) that only she would have been in a position to know.

26. For TP's reading in Watertown, see Autobiographical Sketch (1854), 5–6. The teacher with whom he studied Hebrew, Siexas, had written a well-received Hebrew grammar; he taught Hebrew not only to TP, but later to the Mormon prophet Joseph Smith. TP's Cuba lecture is at A-H. When TP was preparing for college, he asked his sister Mary if he could live off two crackers a day; her answer is not recorded ("Recollections," 11). TP to LCP, 25 January 1836, quoted in *LCTP*, 1:84.

27. TP to LCP, 14 August 1833, Sanborn Memoir, 5; TP to E. P. Peabody, 30 August 1839, MHS.

28. He says in his letter to Greene of 2 April 1834 (MHS), a Monday, that he "came last Saturday, or rather Sunday night," which suggests that he moved in to his room past midnight. In his letter to Greene of 4 June 1834 (MHS), he says he lives in room 40; he must have lived in the second-floor room that used to be labeled as his in Divinity Hall (before the recent reconstruction) at a later time.

29. Samuel Eliot Morison, *Three Centuries of Harvard*, 242.

30. See Story, *Forging of an Aristocracy*, and Dalzell, *Enterprising Elite*.

31. Silsbee, "Abercrombie on the Intellectual Powers," *CE* 14 (March 1833), 49–53. See also Rosa, " 'Aesthetic Culture.' "

32. For a description of his schedule, see TP to Greene, 11 July 1834, MHS; the knots are mentioned by C. A. Bartol, quoted in *TPAB*, 42. Some of these student discussions are described in TP's "Commonplace Book," A-H.

33. Gannett gave up editing the *SI* because he had too many other pressing projects. See Gannett to Ellis, 16 June 1835, Ellis Papers, MHS.

34. Quoted in *TPAB*, 45–46. The complete Cranch recollections are in the first volume of the second set of Thayer Albums (unpaginated), BPL.

35. In *LCTP*, 1:66. The discussion may have been prompted by Margaret Fuller's article on *Artevelde*, which appeared in the *Western Messenger* in 1835.

36. Quoted in Orvis, "First Parish, West Roxbury," 182–83.

37. C. A. Bartol and Christopher Cranch, quoted in *TPAB*, 42–46.

38. TP to Greene, 2 April 1834, MHS.

39. Ibid., 4 June 1834, MHS.

40. See Palfrey, *Discourse on the Life and Character of Rev. Henry Ware, D.D.*; Henry Ware, *Inquiry*, 1:91; TP to Silsbee, 14 September 1839, MHS; TP et al to Henry Ware, 15 May 1836, MHS.

41. See especially Conrad Wright, "Rational Religion in Eighteenth Century America," in Conrad Wright, *Liberal Christians*, 1–21.

42. Henry Ware, *Inquiry*, 2:1–2; Palfrey conceded that God may have given revelations to other nations than the Jews and cites Rammohon Roy's claims that the Vedas were monotheistic. Other revelations had become so corrupted, however, that they were lost—as the Christian revelation itself was almost lost, Palfrey believed, during the Middle Ages. See Palfrey, *Academical Lectures on Jewish Scriptures*, 1:96–97, 96n.

43. Henry Ware, *Inquiry*, 2:46–54, 255, 256.

44. Ibid., 166, 197, 202.

45. "Retribution" (#5, Theological School Exercise).

46. Gatell, *John Gorham Palfrey*, the best available biography, says nothing about Palfrey's theology and scarcely more about his biblical criticism; TP to Palfrey, 23 January 1836, Palfrey Family Papers, Houghton Library.

47. See Gatell, *John Gorham Palfrey*, 73; Gary L. Collison, " 'A True Toleration': Harvard Divinity School Students and Unitarianism, 1830–1859," in Conrad Edick Wright, *American Unitarianism*, 213–14; *DR*, 331n.

48. William Ellery Channing, *Works*, 367; "How ought the Bible to be Read?," *SI* 6, no. 5 (15 May 1836): 230–31.

49. Perhaps his most radical position, however, was on the Canon; he believed the Canon had been set quite late—several centuries after Christ.

50. Sometimes it was argued that without dramatic miracles, a primitive, sensual people like the early Jews would never have believed that Moses or Jesus were messengers from God. The implication of this argument is that miracles were once needed to confirm a revelation, but can be dispensed with among modern, civilized people. Few Unitarians appear to have drawn this conclusion, which appears in De Wette, *Theodore* (Clarke), 1:99.

51. "The Book of Job," *SI* 5, no. 4 (1 November 1835): 229.

52. "Translation and Exposition of Isaiah LII:13–LIII:12," *SI* 6, no. 4 (15 April 1836): 174–90. TP also makes the point that the second half of the book (chaps. 40–66) is so different in style and content from the first half (1–39) that it was probably not written by the same person, and in passing cites Gesenius, that the prophecy of Daniel 11 was written after the events it describes.

53. JF, 186 (May 1836), quoted in *LCTP*, 1:83.

54. Quoted in *LCTP*, 1:77.

55. *SI* 6, no. 5 (15 May 1836): 240. Perhaps because the letter writer was a woman, and it would have been too great a violation of propriety for her to reveal her name?

56. See also Brown, *Rise of Biblical Criticism in America*, 156.

57. For an editorial in defense of Noyes, see the *CR*, 2 August 1834; for a copy of Norton's attack, see TP Letterbooks, 12:51–56, MHS; Palfrey, *Diary*, 15 July 1834, Palfrey Family Papers, Houghton Library.

58. Norton to Joseph Blanco White, 12 July 1836, printed in Thom, *Life of the Reverend Joseph Blanco White*, 2:250; Palfrey, *Academical Lectures on Jewish Scriptures*, 2: Lecture 34.

59. JF, 190–91 (May 1836), quoted in *LCTP*, 1:82.

60. Norton to Joseph Blanco White, 12 July 1836, printed in Thom, *Life of the Reverend Joseph Blanco White*, 2:250–51. Norton worked seventeen years before the first volume appeared; others followed.

61. "The Alleged Mistake of the Apostles," *SI* 5, no. 4 (1 October 1835): 161.

62. TP to Greene, 11 July 1834, MHS; TP to John Ware, 2 January 1846, quoted in *LCTP*, 1:262.

63. TP to LCP, 11 September 1834, Sanborn Memoir; see John Ware, *Memoir of the Life of Henry Ware, Jr.*, and Emerson's comments in *JMNE*, 9:29 (1843); TP to Ellis, 3 January 1839, MHS.

64. John Hopkins Morison, "Divinity School of Harvard University," 704.

65. TP to John Ware, 2 January 1846, quoted in *LCTP*, 1:262; "Idolatry" (#1, Theological School Exercise).

66. "Mistakes and Faults of Preaching," Harvard Archives. Ware's lecture notes are full of contractions, which I have expanded for reasons of clarity.

67. *On the Formation of the Christian Character*, in Henry Ware Jr., *Works*, 4:290–94.

68. "Mistakes and Faults of Preaching," Harvard Archives.

69. "Speech of Rev. Theodore Parker," *Liberator*, 2 November 1855.

70. "Records of the Philanthropic Society," 53 (9 July 1834), 55 (24 September 1834), Harvard Archives.

71. Quoted in Collison, " 'A True Toleration' . . . ," in Conrad Edick Wright, *American Unitarianism*, 218; "Records of the Philanthropic Society," 2–3 (13 June 1831), Harvard Archives.

72. A recent, vivid account of this famous incident is in Mayer, *All on Fire*, 199–208.

73. Howe, *Unitarian Conscience*, 270.

74. The society adopted Ware's platform without the reference to colonization, but with a proposal urging the melioration of the condition of free blacks. See Stange, *Patterns of Antislavery among American Unitarians*, 84–90 (Stange does not make use of the

Philanthropic Society records) and Conrad Wright, "Minister as Reformer: Profiles of Unitarian Ministers in the Anti-Slavery Reform," in Conrad Wright, *Liberal Christians*, 62–80; Henry Ware to Samuel May, 15 October 1834, in John Ware, *Memoir of the Life of Henry Ware, Jr.*, 2:152–53.

75. John Ware, *Memoir of the Life of Henry Ware, Jr.*, 2:150; *CWRWE*, 3:59–60.

76. Channing to Karl Follen, 7 July 1834, in William Henry Channing, *Life of William Ellery Channing*, 531.

77. William Henry Channing, *Life of William Ellery Channing*, 529–30. See also Mumford, *Memoir of Samuel Joseph May*, 154–56.

78. William Henry Channing, *Life of William Ellery Channing*, 533–36.

79. William Ellery Channing, *Works*, 688–743.

80. "Records of the Philanthropic Society," 69–70 (28 October 1835), Harvard Archives.

81. John Ware, *Memoir of the Life of Henry Ware, Jr.*, 2:154.

82. "Records of the Philanthropic Society," 71 (4 November, 11 November 1835), Harvard Archives.

83. "Speech of Rev. Theodore Parker," *Liberator*, 2 November 1855.

84. TP to LCP, 13 April 1836, Sanborn Memoir, 44.

85. The charging records are in the Harvard Archives; JF, 318ff.? (list of books read), cited in *LCTP*, 1:95.

86. Emerson quoted in Wellek, *Confrontations*, 190–91; "Library Charging Records," Harvard Archives: Spinoza, 2 June 1835; Voltaire, 25 August 1834; Irving, 17 August 1835; Scott, 18 August 1834; Newton, 9 June 1835; Kirby and Spence, vol. 1, 30 March 1835, vol. 2, 6 May 1835, vols. 3–4, 20 July 1835; Boccaccio, 20 April 1835; Boswell, 24 November 1834; Bullock, 18 December 1834; Gibbon, 12, 22, 26 January 1835; Cuvier, 16 September 1834; Buckland, 8 September 1834; System of Anatomy, 3 March 1835.

87. See Francis, "The Journals of Convers Francis," 249 (Francis commented, "A gigantic project; but he is young and ardent"); JF, 17, 27, 28 (November/December 1835); Autobiographical Sketch (1854), 5–6; TP to LCP, 20 February 1837, Sanborn Memoir, 101. For TP's limitations in German, see TP to [Heinrich Wolf], 5 June 1847, MHS: "I would write this letter in your own language, but though I can read German easily enough, it is quite difficult to *write*—for I *think* in English." (Wolf was an archdeacon from Kiel who had offered to translate TP's *DR*; the following year he produced *Theodor Parker's Untersuchen über Religion*). For an example of a letter in Latin, see TP to Silsbee ("Gulielmo Silsbeo"), 14 August 1836, A-H.

88. Dwight quoted in Orvis, "First Parish, West Roxbury," 183–84.

89. "Idolatry" (#1, Theological School Exercise); "The Godly Student of Theology, and How He Deporteth Himself," *CR*, 22 October 1836.

90. Gatell, *John Gorham Palfrey*, 73; "The Laws of Moses," *SI* 7:1 & 2 (15 July/ 15 August 1836), 63n.

91. Ripley, *Philosophical Miscellanies*, 1:37.

92. Howe, *Unitarian Conscience*, 29.

93. See for Coleridge, TP to Silsbee, 30 November 1836, MHS, and *DR*, 236; for Cousin, see TP to Silsbee, 27 March 1837, MHS, and "The Extent of Moral Obliga-

tion" (#15, 7 November 1836), 28, where he cites "Cousin, Int. 281" for confirmation of the statement that "a man's thoughts are of more consequence to him than his actions."

94. In TP's early writings, he describes Reason, Conscience, and Soul; "Heart," or affections, he added later, perhaps to give emphasis to a quality he believed to be especially prominent in women. See also "Experience as a Minister," *WTP* 13:309–10; 301 and TP to Silsbee, 23 February 1842 (misdated 1841), MHS.

95. TP told this story to Caroline Healey Dall. Dall Diary, 8 March 1856, MHS (TP here refers to Francis only as "my Father in the Lord" and Silsbee as "my most intimate friend"); see also Jackson, "Social Construction of Thomas Carlyle's New England Reputation, 1834–36."

96. "Einlieben," *American Monthly Magazine* 8, no. 5 (November 1836): 459–60.

97. "Library Charging Records," 22 September 1834, Harvard Archives.

98. The proposal is in the "Records of the Philanthropic Society," 66, Harvard Archives. The "Report" was supposedly prepared by a committee, which included TP and his fellow classmates and editors of the *Scriptural Interpreter*, George Ellis and William Silsbee, but the manuscript is entirely in TP's hand and bears throughout the marks of his style; after the introduction, he drops the pretext of the "we," and begins to use "I." In preparing the "Report," TP doubtless borrowed books from Convers Francis and George Ripley, among others.

99. Autobiographical Sketch (1854), 6; TP to LCP, 30 January 1834, Sanborn Memoir; "Library Charging Records," 22 January 1835, 23 February 1835, Harvard Archives; JF, 51, 54 (November 1835–January 1836); JM, 52 (26 March 1845).

100. John Hopkins Morison, "Divinity School of Harvard University," 704–5.

101. JF, 36 (December 1835), quoted in *LCTP*, 1:72.

102. TP to S. P. Andrews, 3 January 1837, MHS; "Library Charging Records," 18 March 1835, Harvard Archives. Note that the work TP charged was probably a single volume and not in German; had there been more than one volume, the librarian would have listed the volume numbers; had the volume been in German, he normally would have listed it as "Kant's Werke." The mysterious book may have been *Philosophie Transcendentale; ou Systeme d'Emmanuel Kant* (1831) by L. F. Schön, "a Frenchified German," which years later TP remembered reading while at Harvard (see TP to E. P. Peabody, 15 July 1841, MHS).

103. "Report on German Theology," 32, Harvard Archives.

104. The standard English-language edition of *Die Religion* is *Religion within the Limits of Reason Alone* (1960); the note TP refers to is on 74–75. See also "Report on German Theology," 77, Harvard Archives.

105. For purposes of my own exposition, I do not present these in the same order as does TP; he puts the Supernaturalists after the Rationalists.

106. "Report on German Theology," 28, 58, 86, Harvard Archives.

107. Ibid., 82.

108. See notes 35, 49, 56, 60, 62, 63, 69, 70, ibid. De Wette's name is mentioned, without a work of his being cited, on p. 32. See also JF, 139, 144–45 (January–March 1836); "Translation and Exposition of Isaiah LII:13–LIII:12," *SI* 6, no. 4 (15 April 1836): 174–90; "The Laws of Moses," *SI* 7, nos. 1 & 2 (15 July/15 August 1836): 1–23, 60–80, etc.

109. Rogerson, *Old Testament Criticism in the Nineteenth Century*, 28–29; Rogerson, *W. M. L. De Wette*, 60.

110. Samuel Osgood, "De Wette's Views of Religion and Theology," *CE* 24 (May 1838), 137, 139. For a study of De Wette's theology and its influence, see Howard, *Religion and the Rise of Historicism*. In chap. 2, Howard presents Schleiermacher and De Wette as having significant philosophical differences and a complex, if friendly rivalry. See TP to De Wette, 19 November 1839, A-H; Norton, *Tracts Concerning Christianity*, 278.

111. TP mentions the novel in JF, 180–82 (April/May 1836); he apparently read the second edition, which was published in 1828. This edition was translated into English by James Freeman Clarke and published in 1841 as volumes 10 and 11 of George Ripley's Specimens of Foreign Standard Literature series. My citations will be to this translation. The translation reprints, as "The Author's Preface to the American Edition," a valuable letter that De Wette wrote to Clarke, explaining the meaning of his novel and comparing his own intellectual development to that of the novel's hero (De Wette also here frankly admits his limitations as novelist). Other characters represent various types of orthodoxy, others neology, and one, called Hartling, is modeled on the nationalist educational reformer and "father of gymnastics," Friedrich Jahn. De Wette's aesthetics deserve attention, if for no other reason than that one of his students at Basle was Jakob Burckhardt. For a valuable study of De Wette's influence on Burckhardt, which, however, does not focus on its aesthetic aspect, see Howard, *Religion and the Rise of Historicism*.

112. De Wette, *Theodore* (Clarke), 1:15, 17–18. Note that De Wette uses the term "rationalism" in the book in a different way than TP uses it in his "Report"; TP describes De Wette as a Rationalist, but this is not how De Wette would describe himself.

113. At this point, a fellow student introduces him to the writings of Schelling. Theodor finds in Schelling a "dim inkling" of a higher religion than pure morality, but his Naturphilosophie is ultimately unsatisfying: "A God who, in order to become acquainted with himself, sheds himself abroad in creation, and in eternal change is destroyed and produced anew, though more real and living than Kant's thought of God, is also more earthly and unholy, and, in fact is not God, but only the constantly renewed life of nature, brooded over by a dark necessity." (De Wette, *Theodore* [Clarke], 1:58.) He criticizes Schelling's philosophy for absorbing the individual soul into the All and vitiating morality; if all is of God, how can anything be wrong?

114. De Wette, *Theodore* (Clarke), 1:98. De Wette describes A. as mediating between Kant and Schelling. In TP's "Report on German Theology," he does not name the person who discovered that religion originates in the feelings. Was he trying to identify Professor A.?

115. JF, 223 (July 1836), quoted in *LCTP*, 1:86, *TPAB*, 65–66. The manuscript of the Gnosticism piece is in the Harvard Archives; see "The Gnostic Philosophy, and Allusions to it in the New Testament," *SI* 7, no. 3 (15 September 1836): 136–44; no. 4 (15 October 1836): 145–252.

116. JF, 223 (July 1836), quoted in *TPAB*, 66.

117. "Report on German Theology," 80, Harvard Archives.

118. JF, 188, quoted in *LCTP*, 1:82.

1. TP does not refer to tremors until a few weeks later, in Barnstable, but he implies that he has had them since he began preaching. *LCTP*, 1:88; TP to LCP, 22 August 1836, Sanborn Memoir, 63; 23 August 36, Sanborn Memoir, 72; JF, 225 (1 August 1836), quoted in *TPAB*, 67, 68 (see also *LCTP*, 1:88).

2. JF, 81 (January 1836), quoted in *TPAB*, 63; TP to Greene, 22 May 1836, MHS.

3. See Cabot, *Memoir of Ralph Waldo Emerson*; Rusk, *Life of Ralph Waldo Emerson*; Allen, *Waldo Emerson*; Richardson, *Emerson*; TP to LCP, 13 February 1837, Sanborn Memoir, 97; TP to Dwight, 15 February 1837, BPL.

4. TP to Silsbee, 16 September 1836, MHS; Francis Bowen, "Transcendentalism," *CE* 68, no. 9 (January 1837): 372, 375–76; *CWRWE*, 1:7–45.

5. TP to SP Andrews, 3 January 1837, MHS. TP had hoped Frost would settle at Northfield, TP to LCP, 20 October 36, Sanborn Memoir, 77. *LCTP*, 1:98, says that TP did receive a call from Concord; I have found no evidence for this. The only way it could be true is if Frost did not at first accept the Concord call, so the church turned to TP, who by that time had already accepted the call to West Roxbury and so had to turn it down. At any rate, Frost did become the Concord minister. See also Sanborn, *Recollections*, 2:540.

6. JC, 228–29 (4 August 1836), quoted in *TPAB*, 69–70 (another version of this passage appears in *LCTP*, 1:89–90); TP to LCP, 22 August 1836, Sanborn Memoir, 62. The overheated pastoral expectations of the divinity school students are indicated in TP's "Commonplace Book," 14 (April 1835?), A-H, in which he reported a student discussion on the question of "whether personal religion should be made the subject of familiar conversation." Most of the students thought so—"That ministers, when they are settled over parishes, do not meet the wants of the people in this respect—in their visits they will talk about almost anything except religion—this disappoints the people very much."

7. TP to LCP, 10 August 1836, Sanborn Memoir, 50. He had written seventeen sermons by 21 August (see BSP).

8. TP to LCP, 18 August 1836, 22 August 1836, Sanborn Memoir, 59, 62.

9. Ibid., 22 August 1836, Sanborn Memoir, 63–66.

10. TP to Silsbee, 21 August 1836, MHS; JF, 273 (29 August 1836), quoted in *TPAB*, 73.

11. TP to LCP, 18 August 1836, 23 & 26 August 1836, Sanborn Memoir, 61, 70; JF, 265 (ca. 24 August 1836), quoted in *LCTP*, 1:93–94.

12. TP to LCP, 18 August 1836, 22 August 1836, Sanborn Memoir, 61, 63; JF, [page unknown], quoted in *LCTP*, 1:93; *DW*, 1:vii. TP finished the draft 20 May 1837 (JC, 138, quoted in *LCTP* 1:98).

13. LCP much later wrote that TP might have settled in Barnstable, "but in his great love & care for me, he thought it best to be settled near Boston, & so he never went." LCP to Edouard Desor, 24 August 1867, Neuchâtel State Archives.

14. TP to Ellis, 15 October 1838, Ellis Papers, MHS; TP to LCP, 18 August 1836, Sanborn Memoir, 60 (the name of the parish has been deleted from the only copy of this letter, but from the description of the congregation as comprising only 40–50

people and from the reference to Aunt Lucy wanting him to settle there, TP must be referring to West Roxbury).

15. On 12 September he preached three times, in Boston and Watertown; TP to LCP, 20 October 36, Sanborn Memoir, 76; TP to S. P. Andrews, 20 October 1836, MHS; JF, 288 (November 1836). In February, TP wrote to LCP that, "[b]ating one or two things," he "should prefer Northfield to Concord," because the salary was "far better" (10 February 1837, Sanborn Memoir, 95); this remark seems to contradict the story I am piecing together here, but in context, he appears to be remarking on the decision of Barzillai Frost to decline the Northfield pulpit, which Frost was offered, in favor of the Concord one. See TP to LCP, 20 October 1836, Sanborn Memoir, 77.

16. TP to LCP, 6 November 1836, Sanborn Memoir, 80; TP to Francis, 12 November 1836, in CTPCF, 102; "Experience as a Minister," WTP, 13:307.

17. Myerson, "A Calendar of Transcendental Club Meetings," 200. See Hedge's remarks in Cabot, Memoir of Ralph Waldo Emerson, 1:245.

18. My description of Ripley is based partly on that of Octavius Frothingham, George Ripley, 45; in Hutchison, Transcendentalist Ministers, 60, is a picture of Ripley with a beard, but I suspect this is how he looked in later life. Might he have grown the beard at Brook Farm? Crowe, George Ripley, although a good discussion of Ripley's Utopian Socialism, contains many small inaccuracies in his discussion of the Transcendentalist group. For Ripley's praise of the SI, see CR, 19 December 1835.

19. James Martineau, Rationale of Religious Enquiry; SI 7:1 & 2 (15 July/15 August 1836), 94–96; TP to LCP, 10 November 1836, Sanborn Memoir, 83. For different interpretations of Ripley's article and the controversy it engendered, see Miller, Transcendentalists, 129–32, 157–63, and Hutchison, Transcendentalist Ministers, 52–64.

20. "Martineau's Rationale of Religious Enquiry," CE 21 (November 1836), 246.

21. The Norton-Ripley exchange is reprinted in CR 15:11 (12 November 1836), 182.

22. Heralds of a Liberal Faith, 2:198; Ellis to TP, 26 September 1838, Ellis Papers, MHS (some theological students also reportedly referred to Norton's handsome daughters as "the Evidences of Christianity"); Norton to John Gorham Palfrey, 1819, Norton Papers, Houghton Library; JF, 186, quoted in LCTP, 1:82 (compare this comment to TP's description of Norton twenty-three years later, in the "Experience as a Minister," WTP, 13:312–13).

23. JN, 91 (2 January 1839).

24. "The Laws of Moses," SI 7:1 & 2 (15 July/15 August 1836), 6.

25. Ibid., 21–22n.

26. "Necessity & Use of a Heavenly Life" (#6, Theological School Exercise), 11; "Dominion of God" (#8, 14 August 1836), 2; "Self-Denial" (#16, 23 October 1836), 18.

27. "Concluding Remarks," by "Eds.," SI 7:5 & 6 (15 November/15 December 1836), 288.

28. "The Greatness of Christ's Character, its Sources & its Uses" (#17, 21 August 1836), 9–10.

29. TP to LCP, 10 November 1836, Sanborn Memoir, 82.

30. "The Object of the Creation of Man" (#20, 18 December 1836), 20; "The Office of Jesus Christ" (#21, 25 December 1836), 15.

31. JC, 86–87 (January/March 1837), quoted in *LCTP*, 1:95–96, *TPAB*, 81.

32. TP to LCP, 6 February 1837, Sanborn Memoir, 92; 13 February 1837, Sanborn Memoir, 97; 10 February 1837, 13 February 1837, Sanborn Memoir, 94, 95, 97; 23–24 February 1837, Sanborn Memoir, 99; TP to Ellis, 20 February [1837], Ellis Papers, MHS; TP to LCP, 26 February 1837, Sanborn Memoir 101–2 (refers only to "Mr. Davis"; Charles Capper suggested to me it might be George T. Davis); TP to Silsbee, 15 March 1837, MHS. In JF, 288 (November 1836), is the note: "Received call from Greenfield, declined." Why did TP get a call from Greenfield before he ever preached there? Also, why would he suggest Greenfield to LCP in February when he had already declined it four months earlier? Without the actual journal, these questions cannot be answered.

33. TP to Silsbee, 21 April 1837, MHS. A wedding notice is in *CR* 16:17 (29 April 1837), 67.

34. Mackintosh, *Some Recollections*, 8; JN, 344 (April 1840).

35. Shortly after moving to Roxbury, TP wrote to Silsbee (27 June 1837, MHS) that he was head of a household of "seven souls." He was evidently joking, however, by including in the number the two horses. For Lucy being the actual owner of the Parkers' house, see LCP's notes on erasures from JM, LOC; originally JM, 25 (11 December 1844), MHS. See also the assessment of Lucy Cabot's estate in the Norfolk County probate records.

36. See Myerson, "Calendar of Transcendentalist Club Meetings"; John Pierpont and J. S. Dwight offered hymns. A notice of the ordination appears in *CR*, 24 June 1837. See also "Experience as a Minister," *WTP*, 13:306; TP to Silsbee, 27 June 1837, MHS; Orvis, "First Parish, West Roxbury," 173–74; the "Record of the Second Church in Roxbury," Theodore Parker Church, West Roxbury. Ripley's "Right Hand" is at A-H.

37. See Drake, *Town of Roxbury*, 441, 447; TP to Sarah and Caroline Whitney, 21 June 1859, MHS.

38. EPJC, 5; originally JC, 183 (14 October 1837).

39. JN, 344 (17 April 1840). See also "The Fruitful Tree" (#89, 17 June 1838), 19: "Sometimes the success [of] . . . a minister is estimated by a visible standard, the number who have visited themselves to the church. Of this alas there is nothing to be said. We are but a handful."

40. See Drake, *Town of Roxbury*; Appleby, "The First Parish, West Roxbury." A plan of the pews, with the rental cost of each and the names of the renters, appears in the Roxbury Records. This plan evidently dates from after TP's time—probably the 1850s.

41. TP to Silsbee, 10 August 1838, MHS. See TP's kinder portrayal of him in "A Discourse Occasioned by the Death of [the] Rev. [Mr.] George Whitney" (#285, 7 April 1842). For a portrait, see Mackintosh, *Some Recollections*.

42. See the "Parish Membership Book," Theodore Parker Church, West Roxbury.

43. See *Earliest Meeting Houses in West Roxbury*; JN, 199 (August 1839).

44. Mary Whiting helped organize the Evangelical Society; other Whitings show up in TP's records. For a member of Marsh's congregation attending Unitarian temperance lectures, see the "Diaries of Hannah Davis Richards," 27 March 1838, 7 April 1842, West Roxbury Historical Society.

45. See Mackintosh, *Some Recollections*, 33, 46–47.

46. Ibid., 38–39 (also contains a photograph of Billings); TP to Silsbee, 10 August 1838, MHS.

47. They witnessed both versions. See *LCTP*, 2:446–47. See also Briggs, *History and Genealogy of the Cabot Family*, which contains a portrait of Frederick Cabot; Mackintosh, *Some Recollections*, 42–43.

48. JN, 392 (June 1840). See Mackintosh, *Some Recollections*, 52–54; also contains a photograph.

49. For an account of the Shaw family, see Shaw, "Robert Gould Shaw [1776–1853]." See too, Mackintosh, *Some Recollections*, 54–55; also contains a photograph of Francis Shaw.

50. JC, 119 (20 April 1837), quoted in *TPAB*, 87; translated by Frothingham. The Latin does not survive.

51. "Certain rules to observe with L.C."; the second rule indicates the rules refer to LCP, not Lucy Cabot. EPJC, 2; originally JC, 158 (21 June–3 July 1837). Translated by Bruce Venarde; 2. and 4. include my conjectures as to the meaning of TP's sometimes idiosyncratic Latin. The original reads: "Regulae quaedam observandae apud L.C. I. Nunquam contradicere. II. illam[:] Virginem frequenta laudare. III. Prae-judicia sua nunquam tangire. IV. Feritatem illae nullibi opprimere. V. Silentium magis colloquio exercere. VI. Vituperationes suas negligere."

52. EPJC, 3; originally JC, 158 (21 June–3 July 1837).

53. The Sanborn Memoir dates from the 1880s. The largest collections of LCP's letters are in the Edouard Desor Papers at the State Archives of Neuchâtel, Switzerland (nineteen letters), and the TP Papers, LOC (ten letters); all letters in both collections date from after TP's death. There are some letters and notes at the BPL (most from 1856–59) and in various collections at MHS—the TP Papers, the Caroline Healey Dall Papers, and the Ripley Papers. Other letters are scattered among various collections, such as the Emerson Papers at Houghton Library and the Harriet Beecher Stowe Papers at the University of Virginia. The letters at the LOC all concern the dispute over whether LCP alone controlled the publication of TP's works and first biography; see Broderick, "Problems of the Literary Executor."

54. EPJC, 13; originally JC, 273 (June 1838).

55. Ibid., 4; originally JC, 181 (October 1837).

56. Ibid., 9–10; originally JC, 236 (March 1838).

57. "The Uses of Sufferings" (#99, 23 September 1838), 9–10. TP's audience likely thought that the vine was female and the tree male; see TP's own metaphor, below.

58. JN, 118 (February/April 1839). Why TP writes of two ravens instead of one is unclear; but if his imagery is somewhat obscure, his unhappiness is obvious.

59. TP to LCP, 9 December 1836, Sanborn Memoir, 91; TP to E. P. Peabody, 26 June 1841, MHS.

60. TP to S. P. Andrews, 12 December 1837, MHS; TP to E. P. Peabody, 30 August 1839, MHS.

61. "A Sermon of Married Life" (#242, 26 September 1841).

62. "Education of Spirit" (#83, 29 April 1838); TP to LCP, 23 & 24 February 1837, Sanborn Memoir, 100.

63. TP to Silsbee, 27 June 1839, MHS; JN, 155 (17 June 1839); "Sorrows & their

Meaning" (#169, 29 December 1839). In early 1839, at the bottom of one of the inked-over pages in his journal, on which TP apparently had written an extended lament about his home life, there is a sentence that seems to read: "Yet . . . [illegible] . . . what I wish, that I am about to be father, & then, Farewell, you disturbers of my Peace!" (JN, 114 (January/April 1839). This suggests TP thought LCP was pregnant. If she was, then the child was miscarried; more likely, the diagnosis was wrong, for there is no surviving evidence of an event so traumatic as a miscarriage in 1839.

64. TP to Silsbee, 21 April 1837, 10 August 1838, MHS; JM, 320 (August 1846); JN, 440 (15–23 August 1840). "Nothing" is "0" in the original.

65. JI, 73 (April 1841).

66. Ibid., 70 (April 1841); See, for example, "Human Culture: Pt. II Means/Education[:] Means" (#113, 16 December 1838), 7; "Home" (#115, 5 January 1839), 11.

67. JN, 136 (May 1839).

68. Ibid., 53 (September 1838).

69. "Pride" (#148, 16 June 1839), 12–13.

70. "Execution of the Law, pt. II/Law & its Execution" (#180, 8 March 1840); "A Sermon of Peevishness" (#214, 22 November 1840).

71. JN, 55 (September 1838).

72. Ibid., 177 (July 1839).

73. Ibid., 114 (January/April 1839).

74. Ibid., 69 (13 November 1838).

75. Ibid., 408 (June 40). Note that TP paraphrases this passage is "A Sermon of Married Life" (#242, 26 September 1841), quoted above.

76. JI, 66 (April 1841).

77. JN, 292 (January 1840). See also JN, 495 (December 1840), in JTP, 152: "Is a man ever made richer by marrying a wife . . . More wealthy than himself? Perhaps there is no need to query the matter. The result of my own observation agrees with that of Siracides." Siracides, a character in a play by Anaxandrides, observes that "a poor man who marries a wealthy woman gets a ruler and not a wife" (JTP, 220, 39n).

78. On motherhood: "Home" (#115, 5 January 1839); "Duty of Citizens/Patriotism, Man to Men" (#134, 28 March 1839). On the condition of women: "Silent Growth in Christianity/The K[ingdom of God]" (#188, 10 May 1840); "Influence of Religion on Thought: A Sermon of Optimism" (#193, 13 September 1840).

79. TP to E. P. Peabody, 30 August 1839, MHS; Capper, "Margaret Fuller as Cultural Reformer," 511; December 1839 (JN, 263).

80. TP to Silsbee, 9 December 1837, MHS.

81. "Charity" (#69, 28 January 1838). I have surmised these lines are by Lucy, although I cannot prove it.

82. In *Collection of Psalms and Hymns for Christian Worship*. See the pulpit copy in the records of the Theodore Parker Church; according to a note on the flyleaf of this copy, it was in use at Spring Street from August 1833 to September 1855.

83. EPJC, 6–7; originally JC, 203 (January 1838).

84. See Myerson, "A Calendar of Transcendental Club Meetings." TP had been proposed for the club during his candidacy; see Alcott, *Journals of Bronson Alcott*, 91–92 (May 1837).

85. "The Tongue" (#138, 19 May 1839); "False Witness" (#158, 27 October 1839); JN, 253 (October/December 1839); "The Tongue" (#138, 19 May 1839).

86. See Emerson to Fuller, 17 August 1837, *LE*, 3:95. The inaccurate but widely repeated claim that it was called "Hedge's Club" seems to stem from Dall, *Transcendentalism in New England*.

87. Hedge to Emerson, 14 June 1836, quoted in Myerson, "Frederic Henry Hedge," 400–401; Emerson to Hedge, 20 July 1836, *LE*, 2:29.

88. Emerson, "Historic Notes of Life and Letters in New England," *Complete Works*, 10:323; Bowen, "Transcendentalism," *CE* 21 (January 1837), 371–85; see also Bowen, "Locke and the Transcendentalists," *CE* 23 (November 1837), 170–94. Different interpretations of the emergence of Transcendentalism in New England are found in Miller, *Transcendentalists*; Rose, *Transcendentalism as a Social Movement*; Parker, "Transcendentalists"; and Robinson, "Theological Emergence of Transcendentalism."

89. See Myerson, "Calendar of Transcendental Club Meetings."

90. Francis to TP, 7 May 1838, in CTPCF, 106; TP to Francis, 18 December 1840, in CTPCF, 203; JN, 264. This JN entry was begun in December 1839, but TP added to it over the next year. See TP to Francis, 21 November 1840, in CTPCF 191: "I have a page in my journal entitled 'Questions to ask Dr. Francis' & the list grows fearfully long."

91. Ronda, *Elizabeth Palmer Peabody*; JN, 477 (November 1840), in JTP, 109–10; JN, 492–93 (December 1840), in JTP, 148–49; E. P. Peabody to John Sullivan Dwight, [1836], in *Letters of Elizabeth Palmer Peabody*, 187; TP to E. P. Peabody, [23 April] 1837, [1840–41], MHS.

92. JN, 462 (October 1840), in JTP, 100; TP to E. P. Peabody, 21 June 1841, MHS; in TP to E. P. Peabody, "Sat. Morning" [October/November 1840], MHS, he mentions sending her volumes of Lessing.

93. E. P. Peabody to Dwight, 20 September 1840, in *Letters of Elizabeth Palmer Peabody*, 246–47; JN, 210 (23 August 1839); TP to E. P. Peabody, 30 August 1839, MHS; TP to E. P. Peabody, [1840–41], MHS.

94. JN, 181 (19 July 1839); see Ripley to TP, 25 October 1858; TP to Ripley, 1 November 1858, Ripley Papers, MHS. What TP-Ripley correspondence does survive is in the George Ripley collection at MHS; the letters date from the mid-1840s and later.

95. Ripley, *Philosophical Miscellanies*, 1:ix.

96. Schlesinger, *Orestes Brownson*; Brownson, *Convert*; Brownson, *Early Works*; TP to Silsbee, 27 March 1837, MHS; the manuscript of Ripley's "Right Hand" in George Ripley Papers, MHS; Hutchison, *Transcendentalist Ministers*, 157–58; "Mr. Brownson," *CR* 16:17 (29 April 1837), 67.

97. TP to Ellis, 1 August 1838, Ellis Papers, MHS; JN, 239 (25 September 1839). "Christian" is "Xn" in the original.

98. "Introductory Remarks," *Boston Quarterly Review* 1, no. 1 (January 1838): 3; JN, 331 (14 March 1840).

99. Shepard, *Pedlar's Progress*; Dahlstrand, *Bronson Alcott*; Harriet Martineau, *Society in America*, 2:277–78, for her comments on Alcott, and 2:358, 358n, 402–15 (Appendix E) for her comments on Brownson (she did, however, bring copies of Peabody's

Record of Mr. Alcott's School and Alcott's *Conversations with Children on the Gospels* to England and give them to Alcott supporters there); Emerson to F. H. Hedge, 20 July 1836, *LE*, 2:29.

100. Dahlstrand, *Bronson Alcott*, 116, says Alcott came on 17 September. The society passed its resolution on the sixteenth; see "Records of the Philanthropic Society," 66, Harvard Archives.

101. JN, 467 (9 September 1840), in JTP, 72; *JMNE*, 7:347; Peabody, *Record of Mr. Alcott's School*, 31.

102. Alcott, *Journals of Bronson Alcott*, 134 (3 August 1839); see also p. 105 (October 1838), where Alcott classifies TP among the few "living" and "philosophical" men. JC, 219 (February 1838), in *LCTP*, 1:106, *TPAB*, 98; JN, 74, 75 (November 1838). TP's view of Alcott's ideas was shared by Ripley. Alcott, in his journal, describes this conversation with Ripley: "He asked for an explanation of my theory of God. This I gave as clearly as I could. In reply to my views, he said that, so far as he apprehended their character, they classed with the doctrines of atheism. They virtually denied the being of God. They abolished all else but the human soul. Nature, Providence, God, were nonentities. The soul was all. Yet he admitted that occasional statements of mine implied a belief in a superior Nature which found no place in my philosophical theory." *Journals of Bronson Alcott*, 101.

103. Fuller to Emerson, 11 April 1837, in *Letters of Margaret Fuller*, 1:269, 272; Myerson, "Caroline Dall's Reminiscences of Margaret Fuller."

104. See Capper, *Margaret Fuller*; until Capper's biography is completed, see also Blanchard, *Margaret Fuller*, and the introduction by Hudspeth to *Letters of Margaret Fuller*.

105. TP to E. P. Peabody, 30 August 1839, MHS; JN, 232–33 (September 1839).

106. JN, 430 (August 1840), in JTP, 33; JI, 23 (January/February 1841); JN, 187 (July 1839).

107. JN, 155 (June 1839).

108. Ibid., 187 (July 1839). "Nothing" is "0" in the original.

109. Ibid., 446 (7 September 1840), in JTP, 60–61. "Character" is "Xtr" in the original. The word I read as "marked" Johnston reads as "naked."

110. Emerson to Fuller, 24 April 1840, 8 May 1840, *LE*, 2:292–94.

111. Myerson, "Caroline Dall's Reminiscences," 416, 419–20, 420n.

112. Emerson to Moncure Conway, 6 June 1860, *LE*, 5:221; article pasted into JN, 35 (August 1838).

113. "Appearances" (#100, 7 October 1838). See *CWRWE*, 1:10.

114. *LE*, 2:147; JN, 4 (July 1838); *CWRWE*, 1:84–85. Note that the class of 1838 was one of the most politically radical in the history of the theological school; the Philanthropic Society had that year defied their professors and the Harvard administration and resolved that laws supporting slavery were null and void. See Gary Collison, "'A True Toleration' . . . ," in Conrad Edick Wright, *American Unitarianism*, 223–25.

115. *CWRWE*, 1:77–78.

116. Ibid., 81.

117. Ibid., 88–89, 89.

118. Ibid., 90, 92, 92–93.

119. JN, 2 (15 July 1838). Marianne Cabot Jackson (1820–46) was one of various young women—Anna Shaw was another—whom TP idealized. See TP's comments, JN, 64 (16–26 October 1838): "Mary anne is a charming girl /—as beautiful as sweet / And young as sweet, soft as young / & good as soft, / and happy (if aught happy *here*) as good." Her older sister Amelia Lee Jackson would marry the elder Oliver Wendell Holmes in 1840.

120. These sermons will be discussed in chap. 4.

121. TP to Ellis, 1 August 1838, Ellis Papers, MHS; TP to Silsbee, 10 August 1838, MHS; JN, 6 (July 1838).

122. "State of the Church" (#95, 5 August 1838), 8, 19.

123. See Robinson, *Apostle of Culture*, 131–34; *Early Lectures of Ralph Waldo Emerson*, 2:340–56; JC, 217, quoted in *TPAB*, 97; TP to E. P. Peabody, 8 January 1839, MHS.

124. "Mr. Emerson's *Address*," *Boston Quarterly Review* 1:2 (October 1840): 500–514; JN, 304 (February 1840).

125. JC, 218, quoted in *LCTP*, 1:105–6 (see also *TPAB*, 97); *LE*, 2:165–66; TP to E. P. Peabody, 8 January 1839, MHS.

126. *CWRWE*, 1:85–86.

127. TP to Ellis, 1 August 1838, Ellis Papers, MHS. The copy in the Parker Papers, MHS, has Seiders's name removed. Seiders's name was at some point changed to Richard Thomas Austin.

128. See Conrad Wright, "Emerson, Barzillai Frost, and the Divinity School Address," in Conrad Wright, *Liberal Christians*, 41–61.

129. JN, 211 (24 August 1839), 344 (17 April 1840).

130. Francis, "Journals of Convers Francis," 246.

131. JC, 217 (8 February 1838), quoted in *LCTP*, 1:105–6, *TPAB*, 96–98; JN, 2 (13 July 1838).

132. See entry for 20 September 1838, *JMNE*, 5:194–95.

133. For a report, see "Transcendentalism," *CR*, 24 February 1838; TP to Ellis, 3 January 1839, MHS (not in Ellis Papers).

134. Robbins attended twice in 1837 and once in 1839 (see Myerson, "Calendar of Transcendental Club Meetings"); "Editorial Notice," *CE* 22 (March 1837), 135–36; "Introductory Remarks," *Boston Quarterly Review* 1:1 (January 1838): 3.

135. TP to S. P. Andrews, 3 January 1837, MHS.

136. *CR*, 2 June 1838.

137. Ibid., 24 September 1836; ibid., 3 December 1836; *CE* 21 (January 1837), 402–3; *CR*, 10 December 1836.

138. Alcott, *Conversations with Children on the Gospels*, 1:222–23.

139. *CR*, 4 March 1837, 29 April 1837; *CE* 23, no. 2 (November 1837): 252–61.

140. Emerson to Silsbee, 4[?] October 1838, *LRWE*, 2:165–66; TP to E. P. Peabody, 3 January 1839, MHS.

141. TP to Silsbee, 27 November 1838, MHS.

142. J. H. Morison, "Mr. Parker's *Discourse*," *CE* 32 (July 1842), 348. Note that this comes from a review *attacking* TP's *DR*.

143. *CR*, 10 December 1836.

144. JN, 4 (July 1838); see also TP to Silsbee, 10 August 1838, MHS, where TP reports Palfrey's remark as "that part of it which is not *folly*, I apprehend, will be found to be *Atheism*."

145. Inserted into JN, 33 (August 1838).

146. Henry Ware Jr., *Personality of the Deity*, in *Works*, 3:26–39.

147. "Three Ways to the Name of Atheist," *CR*, 21 November 1838.

148. TP to Ellis, 15 October 1838, Ellis Papers, MHS.

149. *CR*, 19 January 1839; TP, "Ralph Waldo Emerson," *Massachusetts Quarterly Review* 3:2 (March 1850): 215; TP to Ellis, 3 January 1839, MHS (not in Ellis Papers).

150. JN, 129 (19 April 1839) ("Christianity" is "Xy," "Christ" is "X," and "character" is "xtr" in the original); JN, 343 (11 April 1840).

151. Ibid., 323 (February/March 1840). "Christian" is "Xn" in the original.

Chapter Four

1. An order of services, dated 2 March 1834, is written into the pulpit copy of *Collection of Psalms and Hymns for Christian Worship*, at the Theodore Parker Church. There is no reason to believe TP changed the order of services when he became pastor.

2. *LCTP*, 1:103.

3. "A Discourse Occasioned by the Death of [the] Rev. [Mr.] George Whitney" (#285, 10 April 1842), 6; Buell, *Literary Transcendentalism*, 106–12; "On the Application of Good Sense to Rel[igion]/On the Application of Common Sense to Religion" (#207, 25 October 1840); "On the Application of Religion to Life" (#208, 25 October 1840), printed in *WRS*, 72–88; for examples of sermons with a section of "applications," see "The Spirituality of Man" (#42, 29 April 1838), 19, and "A Sermon of Idols" (#223, 21 March 1841), 14; examples of sermons devoted to exegesis include "The Sermon on the Mount" (#109, 30 December 1838) and "The Lord's Prayer" (#110, 24 February 1839). For an example of TP explicitly using words of Scripture in a sense very different from what he believes in their original sense, see "A Sermon of Revivals" (#183, 2 April 1840). TP takes as his text Galatians 4:18: "But it is good to be zealously affected . . . and not only when I am with you." TP explains that the Apostle wrote to rebuke and instruct, but "I have chosen these words as a suitable motto for a discourse on Revivals of Rel[igion]."

4. "A Sermon of Contentment," #190 (12 July 1840), 2. Compare "The Christian Ministry" (#39) and "Duties of Parishioners/Duties of Worshippers" (#40) with XXVIII and XXIX in *Complete Sermons of Ralph Waldo Emerson*, 231–43. Emerson preached on Romans 1:16 for his first sermon and II Corinthians 4:5 for his second. TP preached on II Corinthians 2:16 and Malachi 2:7 for his first sermon and Romans 12:1–2 for his second.

5. See TP to G. D. Cabot, 27 March 1844, MHS, on the excellent schools in the parish. For examples of TP writing letters of recommendation for a schoolteacher, see TP to Francis, 28 February 1840, 9 March 1840, in CTPCF, 169, 177. For private student lesson plans, see JI, 274 (February/April 1843).

6. JN, 9 (27 July 1838). Three hundred dollars for the renovations were appropriated by September 1838; another $300 was borrowed in December; the renovations

were completed by January. The story of the organist is a reconstruction of events. An organ was purchased in 1838, presumably as part of the renovations of that year, and George G. North became the long-tenured organist. I consider it likely that he was the one who threatened to quit the church; who else would be so concerned about an organ? See Mackintosh, *Some Recollections*.

7. "Boston Thursday Lecture," *Monthly Miscellany* 4 (January 1841), 172–74.

8. TP to LCP, 15 February 1836, Sanborn Memoir, 98; JN, 354 (April/May 1840); TP to Isaac Parker, 22 January 1840, MHS.

9. *DW*, 1:ix; TP to Silsbee, 19 May 1838, MHS.

10. Ripley, *Philosophical Miscellanies*, 1:ix; TP's manuscript is at A-H.

11. Hedge to TP, 9 August 1838, A-H.

12. "Morality & Religion/God Love & Man Love" (#101, 14 October 1838), 8. There is no direct evidence TP yet had read Schleiermacher's renowned early work, *Speeches on Religion to Its Cultured Despisers*; TP did later own a copy of it.

13. JI, 55 (March 1841); TP to Silsbee, 23 April 1841, MHS.

14. J2P, 7 (13 March 1859).

15. Useful accounts of Strauss include: Harris, *David Friedrich Strauss and His Theology*, the best biography of Strauss in English despite Harris's conclusion, which he unwittingly shares with Andrews Norton, that if you deny that the miracles happened you cannot logically sustain Christianity; Schweitzer, *Quest of the Historical Jesus*, chaps. 7–9; Hodgson's introduction to the Fortress Press edition of George Eliot's 1846 translation of Strauss's *Life of Jesus Critically Examined*.

16. "Reasons Why a Clergyman Should Not Study Scripture Carefully and Critically," *CR*, 4 November 1837.

17. "A Sermon of Faith" (#128, 7 July 1839).

18. TP to Silsbee, 10 August 1838, MHS; "Human Nature (Part I)" (#120, 3 March 1839).

19. "Man's Relation to God" (#59, 25 February 1838); "Character of Paul" (#26, 20 February 1837); "Man's Relation to God" (#59, 25 February 1838); JN, 286 (January 1840).

20. "The Object of the Creation of Man/Object of Man's Life" (#20, 21 November 1836); JN, 199 (August 1839); "Duties of Parishioners/Duties of Worshippers" (#40, 25 June 1837), 23; "Influence of Religion on Thought: A Sermon of Optimism" (#193, 13 September 1840), 14; JN, 202 (August 1839); "Influence of Religion on Thought" (#193, 13 September 1840), 17.

21. "The Ideal of Perfection" (#24, 13 August 1837); "The Rule of Right Within/The Foundation of Morality" (#44, 20 August 1837), 14–16; "The God Witnesses/Three Testimonies to God's Power &c" (#91, 2 September 1838); "Man's Relation to God & the Duties Resulting from that Relation" (#59, 25 February 1838). "Christianity" is "Xty" in the original.

22. "Education" (#170, 19 January 1840).

23. JC, 49 (December 1836). First published as "Jesus" in *CR*, 6 May 1837, over the signature "T. P." Printed with many modifications, 60–61 (whether these modifications were made by TP or by Frothingham is unclear), in *TPAB*. The later version is printed in *LCTP*, 1:95, and *WTP*, 13:421–22.

24. "Human Culture: Pt. II Means/Education[:] Means" (#113, 16 December 1838), 17.

25. "A Sermon of Symbols/Natural Symbols" (#133, 4 August 1839), 5.

26. JN, 95 (15 January 1839).

27. "Extravagance vs. Moderation" (#171, 26 January 1840), 17; TP to Silsbee, 10 August 1838, MHS; JN, 286 (January 1840); "God's Common Law" (#119, 10 February 1839); "The Rule of Right Within" (#44, 20 August 1837).

28. "A Sermon of Symbols/Natural Symbols" (#133, 4 August 1839).

29. JN, 6–7 (July 1838), 122 (January–April 1839), 400 (June 1840); "Influence of Religion on Thought: A Sermon of Optimism" (#193, 13 September 1840).

30. "Sowers & Reapers" (#70, 28 January 1838), 24; "Education" (#170, 19 January 1840), 12ff.; "Education of Spirit/Spiritual Culture" (#83, 29 April 1838); "Human Culture Pt. II: Means/Education[:] Means" (#113, 16 December 1838).

31. "Human Culture Pt. II: Means/Education[:] Means" (#113, 16 December 1838); "Home" (#115, 6 January 1839).

32. "Hidden Treasure" (#70, 25 February 1838); "Home" (#115, 6 January 1839).

33. "Human Culture Pt. II: Means/Education[:] Means" (#113, 16 December 1838), 5; "Labour" (#107, 31 March 1839); "A Sermon of Work" (#192, 21 June 1840); "The Charms of True Religion" (#206, 4 October 1840), 7.

34. "Duties of these Irreligious Times" (#95, 5 August 1838), 8–9.

35. TP to Silsbee, 10 August 1838, MHS; "Godlikeness" (#165, 17 November 1839); "Power of Christianity" (#173, 5 January 1840) [see also "Morality and Religion" (#101, 14 October 1838), 22]; "Being & Seeming; Christianity & Phariseeism; Spiritual Life & the Formal Life" (#72, 18 February 1838).

36. "Self-Renewal" (#48, 3 September 1837); JN, 96–97 (10 January 1839).

37. "Duty of Citizens/Patriotism, Man to Men" (#134, 28 March 1839), 9; "Independence of Character" (#149, 9 June 1839), 16; "Sin" (#85, 20 May 1838).

38. TP to Silsbee, 22 September 1837, MHS; "Being & Seeming; Christianity & Phariseeism; Spiritual Life & the Formal Life" (#72, 18 February 1838); "Advantages and Disadvantages of the Present Times" (#73, 20 May 1838); "A Sermon of Evil/Sermon of Sin (part 2)" (#219, 20 December 1840).

39. "Gnow [sic] Thyself" (#43, 6 August 1837); "Influence of Religion upon Thought" (#193, 13 September 1840); "A Small Sermon of Small Things" (#181, 29 March 1840) (the biblical reference is to Ecclesiaticus 19:1).

40. "Morality and Religion" (#101, 14 October 1838).

41. "The Privilege of Prayer" (#18, 21 November 1836); "Prayer" (#77, 1 April 1838).

42. "Prayer" (#77, 1 April 1838); "The Idea of Prayer" (#156, 15 September 1839).

43. "Parable of the Talents" (#33, 16 April 1837); printed in WR, 1–14.

44. Compare "The Laborers in the Vineyard/A Penny a Day" (#53, 1 October 1837), 14, and "Uses of Suffering" (#99, 23 September 1838), 8–9; "A Sermon of Burthens" (#216, 6 December 1840); "Sorrows & their Meaning" (#169, 29 December 1839).

45. JN, 196–97 (August 1839); "Sorrows & their Meaning" (#169, 29 December 1839).

46. "The Spirituality of Man" (#42, 29 April 1838); "Parable of the Talents" (#33, 16 April 1837).

47. "The Labourers in the Vineyard/Penny a Day" (#53, October 1837); "A Sermon of Sects" (#185, 19 April 1840; second edition), 29, 30; "Parable of the Talents" (#33, 16 April 1837).

48. "Morality and Religion" (#101, 14 October 1838); "The Laborers in the Vineyard/A Penny a Day" (#54, 1 October 1837); "Parable of the Talents" (#33, 16 April 1837); see JN, 266 (December 1839); "A Sermon of Divine Love" (#186, 19 April 1840), 10–12.

49. "Godlikeness" (#165, 17 November 1839).

50. TP to Silsbee, 22 September 1837, 10 August 1838, MHS.

51. "Duties of Parishioners/Duties of Worshippers" (#40, 25 June 1837), 26.

52. Ibid., 9.

53. TP to Silsbee, 13 November 1837, MHS.

54. "The Rule of Right within/Foundations of Morality" (#44, 20 August 1837), 6; "The Importance of Truth/The Duty of Veracity" (#47, 25 March 1838); "Meaning of the Ordinance of the Lord's Supper" (#46, 6 August 1837), 24–25.

55. JC, 172 (July–October 1837); quoted in *LCTP* 1:101–2, *TPAB*, 91–92.

56. "Reasons Why a Clergyman Should not Study the Scriptures Carefully and Critically," *CR*, 4 November 1837.

57. W. mentions he has doubts about prophecy and miraculous births, "which I dare not communicate." This is his only oblique reference to having problems with the New Testament accounts.

58. "A Word in Reply to W.," *CR*, 11 November 1837.

59. TP to Silsbee, 14 November 1837, MHS; "My Dear Brother," *CR*, 18 November 1837.

60. Overall, TP's favorite sources of texts were, in order, Matthew, John, Psalms, Proverbs, and Luke. More than half the texts he used in his first 300 sermons came from these five books.

61. "Experience as a Minister," *WTP*, 13:321–22; TP to Francis, 9 February 1839, in CTPCF, 130; "Palfrey on the Pentateuch," *CE* 25 (September 1838), 106.

62. "Contradictions in Scripture" (#61, #62, 13 January 1839).

63. TP does not specify the source of his figure that Canaan had three million inhabitants, but probably he got it from biblical historians of the day. The sanguinary Mosaic laws TP refers to are probably those in Deuteronomy 7:1–5 and 20:16–18.

64. "Character" is "Xtr.," and "Christianity" is "Xy" or "Xty" in the original.

65. Francis, "On the Account of the Creation of Man" (#704, 2 February 1834), Watertown Free Public Library.

66. "Palfrey on the Pentateuch," *CE* 25 (September 1838), 119.

67. "A Sermon of My Own Stewardship" (#338, 3 September 1843; second edition), 33 ("Christianity" is "Xty" in original); "Experience as a Minister," *WTP*, 13:321–22.

68. Ibid., 38.

69. TP to Francis, 9 February 1839, in CTPCF, 129 (note that this was written only a few weeks after TP finally preached "The Contradictions in Scripture"); Francis to TP, 6 March 1839, in CTPCF, 133–34.

70. TP to Silsbee, 19 May 1838, MHS; "Palfrey on the Pentateuch," *CE* 25 (September 1838), 128.

71. TP to Ellis, 27 May 1840, MHS; "Palfrey's Lectures on Jewish Scriptures and Antiquities," *Boston Quarterly Review* 1:3 (July 1838): 261–310.

72. "Palfrey's Lectures on Jewish Scriptures and Antiquities," *Boston Quarterly Review* 1:3 (July 1838): 269, 270.

73. Ibid., 297.

74. Ibid., 306.

75. "The Miracles of J. C." (#80, 15 April 1838), 8; TP to Silsbee, 27 November 1838, MHS.

76. "The Life of Jesus/The Life of J. C." (#67, 21 January 1838); TP comments on preaching this series on communion days in "The Sermon on the Mount" (#109, 30 December 1838), 2; TP to Silsbee, 27 November 1838, MHS. But see "Christianity—Past, Present, & Future" (#65, 24 December 1837), 11, where TP says that it was "quite doubtful" the Apostles wrought miracles, "except immediately after the ascension of Jesus." He evidently had doubts about this assertion, however, because the sentence has a pencil line through it and was probably not preached.

77. "The Miracles of Jesus Christ/Miracles" (#80, 15 April 1838), 7, 8. "Character" is "xtr." in the original.

78. TP to Silsbee, 10 August 1838, 27 November 1838, MHS; "Life of Jesus/Life of J. C." (#67, 21 January 1838).

79. "The Miracles of Jesus Christ/Miracles" (#80, 15 April 1838), 11–12.

80. JN, 190–91 (4 August 1839).

81. Furness believed that a true Christian had to appreciate the greatness of Christ's character, which was impossible without recognizing that Jesus had miraculous powers, but never used them to benefit himself. See Furness, *Remarks on the Four Gospels*.

82. "The Miracles of J. C./Miracles" (#80, 15 April 1838), 14–15.

83. "The Three Primal Duties of Man" (#75, 2 December 1838), 2–3.

84. "Christianity as Old as Creation & even Older" (#78, 22 July 1838), 7, 10, 17. The title is provocative, being the same as that of a famous deist tract of the previous century, Matthew Tindal's *Christianity as Old as the Creation, or the Gospel a Republication of the Religion of Nature* (1730).

85. "Ackermann's Christian in Plato," *CE* 25 (January 1839), 367–84. Daniel Walker Howe, "The Cambridge Platonists of Old England and the Cambridge Platonists of New England," in Conrad Edick Wright, *American Unitarianism*, 107–8, discusses another important example of TP's Platonism, his review of Cudworth's *Intellectual System*.

86. "Peculiarities of the Christian Religion" (#93, 22 July 1838). "Character" is "xtr" in the original; "reward or punishment" is supplied by me.

87. JN, 7 (July 1838); "Ackermann's Christian in Plato," 383.

88. "Xy as Tradition & as Truth/Xy as a Tradition & a Truth" (#88, 17 June 1838), 17.

89. "Life of Jesus/Life of J. C." (#67, 21 January 1838), 7–8.

90. "Christianity as Old as Creation & even Older" (#78, 22 July 1838), 22. "Character" is "xtr." in the original.

91. "Ackermann's Christian in Plato," 379.

92. See the "Parish Membership Book," Theodore Parker Church, and the Roxbury Records. The third covenant itself is undated, as are most of the signatures on the membership list; but the twenty-ninth signature on the list is dated 8 July 1838, which is therefore the *terminus ante quom*. Conceivably, this covenant could have been written before TP was settled in West Roxbury; his own signature is nineteenth on the list, and those of LCP and Lucy are even further down. On the other hand, the name of George Whitney, his predecessor, does not appear on the list, which probably means it was not in effect when he was minister (although Whitney's name also is absent from the list of the 1834 covenant). The best evidence that TP wrote the third covenant is that it matches his views and even uses his language (TP often claimed that religion consisted of goodness and piety).

93. "A Sermon of My Own Stewardship" (#338, 3 September 1843; second edition), 35. Among the hymns TP chose that day was #256, which seems in keeping with his effort to separate the New Testament and Old: "The Law by Moses came: / But peace and truth and love / were brought by Christ, a nobler name / Descending from above." See *Collection of Psalms and Hymns for Christian Worship*.

94. "A Sermon of My Own Stewardship" (#338, 3 September 1843; second edition), 38–39. TP does not say these specific remarks by Farrington and Arnold were made in response to the "Contradictions in Scripture," but their reaction was probably along the lines indicated.

95. Ibid., 35; "Experience as a Minister," *WTP*, 13:313; "A Sermon of My Own Stewardship" (#338, 3 September 1843; second edition), 36.

96. TP to Francis, 9 February 1839, in CTPCF, 130.

97. Ibid., 22 March 1839, in CTPCF, 141. "Christianity" is "Xy" and "Abraham" is "Abm." in the original.

98. The intervening Sunday was when he preached "Christianity as Old as Creation" and "The Peculiarity of Christianity."

99. For a discussion of the traditions behind this distinction, see Stout, *New England Soul*, esp. 27–49 and elsewhere.

100. "The Birthright: A Sermon of Esau" (#202, 6 September 1840), 8; "The Signs of the Times" (#31, 6 April 1837), 2; JN, 335 (2 April 1840); "The Christian Ministry" (#39, 25 June 1837), 22.

101. "The Signs of the Times" (#31, 6 April 1837). Normally, two sermons were preached on Fast Day; but on this day, TP preached in different towns in the morning and the afternoon, and so used the same sermon.

102. "Dominion of God" (#8, 14 August 1836); TP later used this as his Thanksgiving sermon for 1836.

103. "Peace" (#81, 5 April 1838). He also preached a sermon he had written during his candidacy, "The Intellectual Character of Jesus" (#32, 5 April 1838). In "Peace," TP identifies two other world religions, "Idolatry" and "Mohammedism"; having ceased to grow, these two will, he predicts, soon "die & crumble to dust" and new and better religions will rise in their ashes. TP does not mention Judaism.

104. "A Sermon of My Own Stewardship" (#338, 3 September 1843; second edition), 14; the intemperate couple is also referred to in JN, 13 (31 July 1838); for Reed Taft, see Mackintosh, *Some Recollections*, 55–56; in "A Sermon of My Own Steward-

ship," TP refers to delivering a "temperance sermon" in the fall of 1837, but as I have found no sermon devoted entirely to this topic until 1838, I assume he is referring to a lecture; for TP's views of beer and wine, see "A Sermon of Travels, or the Lessons wh[ich] the Old World Offers the New" (#339–#340, 8 September 1844), 35–36.

105. "Christianity—Past, Present & Future" (#65, 24 December 1837), 20–21.

106. TP to Silsbee, 22 September 1837, MHS.

107. "State of the Church" (#94, 5 August 1838), 13.

108. Ibid.

109. Ibid., 16.

110. Ibid., 18.

111. Ibid., 20, 21, 23, 24. "Heaven" is "Hn" in the original. I have supplied "what of the night" and silently added punctuation.

112. "Duties of These Irreligious Times" (#95, 5 August 1838), 5.

113. Ibid., 18–20.

114. JN, 13 (31 July 1838). The two of them were accompanied on their fishing trip by Cowing's son.

115. "What our People Need/Things of a Bad Tendency & Their Remedy" (#98, 2 September 1838.)

116. "Labour" (#107, 31 March 1839), 12–13.

117. "Temperance" (#108, 18 November 1838).

118. *Emerson's Antislavery Writings*, 2, 3; "Thanksgiving" (#111, 29 November 1838).

119. Senex also learns that everyone the world over speaks English and that the "Spanish race" has "failed before the Anglo-Saxon."

120. "Boston in the Year of Grace 3839. A Dream by a Very Old Man," *CR*, 30 March 1839.

Chapter Five

1. A copy of the degree, with a citation, is at MHS; see also TP's letter of thanks to Josiah Quincy, 3 October 1840, MHS; Chadwick, *Theodore Parker*, 150.

2. E. P. Peabody to John Sullivan Dwight, 18 June 1840, [10 June 1841], in *Letters of Elizabeth Palmer Peabody*, 253, 246. See also G. W. Curtis in Myerson, *Brook Farm Book*, 98.

3. Sermons #9, #16, #26, #51, #101, #56. "The Fall of Man," which from its title sounds possibly controversial, was not: TP argued that the story of the Fall was not literally true, but was meant to convey the "beautiful doctrine" that we are born without sin, know good from evil, have the ability to choose between them, and that if we choose evil, our conscience will prevent us from attaining spiritual peace.

4. JN, 295 (12 January 1840); JN, 331 (14 March 1840); TP to Isaac Parker, 22 January 1840, MHS.

5. JN, 344–45 (17 April 1840).

6. Clarke quoted in JTP, 158 n. 12; Shaw's letters are at the Houghton and the Boston Public Libraries; for Greene, see Gura, "Beyond Transcendentalism" and Greene, *Equality*; for Shaw and the conversations, see Simmons, "Margaret Fuller's Boston Conversations"; Buell, *Literary Transcendentalism*, 83–84.

7. JN, 204 (18 August 1839).

8. Ibid., 369 (17 April 1840). See also Simmons, "Margaret Fuller's Boston Conversations," 221; I thank Megan Marshall for calling this passage to my attention.

9. JN, 375 (20 May 1840).

10. Ibid.

11. For Anna Shaw walking in the woods, see TP to E. P. Peabody, n.d. (ca. March 1842), MHS, and the poems he wrote about Shaw after 1842, discussed in chap. 7; JN, 391 (June 1840).

12. JI, 8 (January 1841); JN, 460 (26 September 1840). Johnston, who worked from microfilms, could not see this writing and describes only the mutilation of the page (see JTP, 98).

13. JN, 463 (October 1840), in JTP, 102.

14. TP to Fuller, late June 1841, quoted in *LCTP*, 1:303; *Dial* 2, no. 1 (July 1841): 77.

15. JI, 70 (April 1841).

16. Ibid., 73 (April 1841).

17. TP to Silsbee, 16 July 1839, MHS; JN, 180 (19 July 1839).

18. Norton, *Discourse on the Latest Form of Infidelity*.

19. *The Latest Form of Infidelity Examined: A Letter to Mr. Andrews Norton*; TP to Silsbee, 14 September 1839, 15 October 1839, MHS.

20. This part of the *Letter* resembles Ripley's reply to Norton's attack on his Martineau review three years earlier. He even cites some of the same writers and biblical passages.

21. "Evidences of Christianity" (#157, 15 September 1839); TP here also argues against the argument from prophecy.

22. TP to E. P. Peabody, 30 August 1839, MHS. For TP's thinking at the time he wrote this sermon, see TP to Francis, 8 January 1839; Francis to TP, 21 January 1839; TP to Francis, 9 February 1839; Francis to TP, 6 March 1839, in CTPCF, 117–18, 124–25, 129, 133.

23. "The Relation of the Bible to the Soul" (#131, 21 April 1839), 6, 10. "Christianity" is "Xy" in the original.

24. Ibid., 14.

25. Ibid., 16. In the original, "Kingdom" is "Km" and "Heaven" is "Hn."

26. "Inspiration" (#163, 10 November 1839). Quotations come principally from the second edition.

27. JN, 285 (2 January 1840). See also TP's recollection of this event in "Finis/Farewell Sermon to West Roxbury" (#413, 8 February 1846), 13.

28. Norton, *Remarks on a Pamphlet entitled "The Latest Form of Infidelity Examined"*; Ripley, *Defence of "The Latest Form of Infidelity Examined." A Second Letter to Mr. Andrews Norton* and *Defence of "The Latest Form of Infidelity Examined." A Third Letter to Mr. Andrews Norton*.

29. *Previous Question*, reprinted in Dirks, *Critical Theology of Theodore Parker*, 149. See *CR*, 4 January 1840, 18 January 1840, 25 January 1840.

30. JN, 320 (February 1840). "Christianity" is "Xy" in the original.

31. Ibid., 235 (September 1839); see also JN, 329 (February 1840).

32. Norton, *Discourse on the Latest Form of Infidelity*, 45–47; JN, 129 (19 April 1839).

33. JN, 335 (1 April 1840).

34. *CMW*, 305.

35. TP to Francis, 9 February 1839, in CTPCF, 128 ("Christian" is "Xn" in the original); for TP's doubts about the New Testament, see, besides his letters to Francis, "Casting Out Devils/The Demoniaks" (#123, 17 March 1839), and JN, 126 (ca. March/April 1839), and 190–91 (4 August 1839); see JN, 129 (ca. March/April 1839), 191–92 (4 August 1839).

36. JN, 344 (13–15 April 1840); *CMW*, 248–308.

37. CMW, 248–52.

38. Ibid., 306.

39. Ibid., 248, 303.

40. Ibid., 266, 267, 269, 276, 281.

41. For an interesting comparison between Strauss and TP, see James Martineau, "Strauss and Parker."

42. *CMW*, 299.

43. Ibid., 298.

44. Ibid., 304.

45. JN, 335 (3–4 April 1840). "Manuscript" is "M.S." in the original.

46. Myerson, "Frederic Henry Hedge," 403; JN, 337 (7 April 1840), 341, 342 (9, 10 April 1840).

47. Norton to Palfrey, 13 April 1840; Norton to W. Ware, [March?] 1840, Norton Papers, Houghton Library.

48. See *CR*, 21 March 1840.

49. JN, 342 (10 April 1840).

50. "Transcendentalism," *CR*, 25 April 1840.

51. Ibid.

52. "A Desultory Notice of a Recent Pamphlet, entitled 'Two Articles from the Princeton Review . . . ,'" *CR*, 16 May 1840.

53. TP does not actually know the names of any of the writers and assumes the Alexander and Dod article is by one author. My copy of the pamphlet was once owned by one Ezra Abbot Jr., who notes in the margins that Alexander wrote the "historical survey" (that is, the part of the article dealing with German philosophy), while Dod wrote the critique of Cousin.

54. TP has in mind Heine and "Young Germany."

55. "A Desultory Notice," 78. The allusion is to Numbers 13:17–14:10.

56. *The Previous Question*, in Dirks, *Critical Theology of Theodore Parker*, 137.

57. Ibid., 140.

58. Ibid., 140–41.

59. Ibid., 141–44.

60. Ibid., 145.

61. Ibid., 145–47.

62. Ibid., 147–48.

63. Ibid., 148–49.

64. Ibid., 149–50.

65. Ibid.

66. Ibid., 151.

67. Ibid., 152–53.

68. Ibid., 154.

69. Ibid., 155–57.

70. Ibid., 157.

71. Ibid., 157–59.

72. *CE* 32 (July 1842), 388; Francis to TP, 22 June 1840, in CTPCF, 187.

73. "The Previous Question . . . ," *CE* 28 (July 1840), 400–402.

74. "Mr. Damon's *Address. Miracles as an Evidence of Christianity*," *CE* 29 (September 1840), 1–19. Damon also attacks the views advanced by Brownson in his autobiographical novel, *Charles Elwood*.

75. JN, 381 (ca. 27 May 1840). "Christian" is "Xn" in the original.

76. Ibid., 344 (14–16 April 1840), 381 (ca. 27 May 1840).

77. Peabody to Dwight, 20 September 1840, in *Letters of Elizabeth Palmer Peabody*, 246. "Fervant" is a conjectured reading by the editors.

78. "The Divine Presence in Nature and the Soul," *Dial* 1, no. 1 (July 1840): 58–70; "The Relation of the Bible to the Soul," *Western Messenger* 8:8 (December 1840): 337–40; 9 (January 1841): 388–96.

79. JN, 235 (September 1839); JN, 469 (ca. 9 November 1840), in JTP, 113.

80. *CMW*, 25, 27.

81. Ibid., 28, 30, 32.

82. Ibid., 32.

83. Ibid., 33–34.

84. Francis to TP, 18 January 1841, in CTPCF, 209.

85. *CMW*, 35–36.

86. Ibid., 36–37, 38.

87. Ibid., 41–42.

88. JN, 466 (September 1840), in JTP, 93–94.

89. *CMW*, 66–68, 72–75, 81–82, 101–2 (quotation on 82); *DR*, 274–75 (TP cites his own Bernard article, 275n). When TP discusses how Bernard's agitation for the First Crusade was confirmed by miracles (*CMW*, 102), he may have been trying to show that miracles can be used to justify murder—something David Damon, criticizing the Levi Blodgett pamphlet, denied had ever happened.

90. *CMW*, 86–87.

91. "On the Application of Religion to Life" (#208, 25 October 1840); printed in *WRS*, 72–88 ("Christianity" is "Xty" in the original); JN, 333 (March 1840).

92. JN, 401 (June 1840). "Christianity" is "Xy" in the original.

93. Ibid., 400, 401 (June 1840).

94. Ibid., 441 (August 1840), in JTP, 50–51. "Christian" is "Xn" in the original.

95. Ibid., 333–34 (March 1840).

96. For discussions on this theme, see Walters, *American Reformers*, and Blumin, *Emergence of the Middle Class*.

97. TP to Silsbee, 21 April 1837, MHS; TP to S. P. Andrews, 2 May 1837, MHS.

98. "A Letter Addressed to the Congregational Church in Purchase Street," re-

printed in Octavius Frothingham, *George Ripley*, 74; William Henry Channing, *Life of William Ellery Channing*, 481; Schlesinger, *Orestes Brownson*, 66–68.

99. "Thanksgiving" (#111, 29 November 1838), "National Prosperity" (#168, 28 November 1839); "What Makes a People Happy" (#215, 26 November 1840), 5; "National Prosperity" (#168, 28 November 1839).

100. For a recent account of this election, sympathetic to the Whigs, see Michael F. Holt, *Rise and Fall of the American Whig Party*, 108–13.

101. TP to Francis, 6 December 1839, in CTPCF, 152 (see *Early Lectures of Ralph Waldo Emerson*, 3:185–201); Emerson to William Emerson, 9 November 1840, *LE*, 2:357; JN, 468 (9 November 1840), in JTP, 111; JN, 308 (14 February 1840).

102. "On the Application of Religion to Life" (#208, 25 October 1840); printed in *WRS*, 72–88.

103. JI, 64 (7 April 1841).

104. "Mechanical Tendency of the Times" (#233, 8 April 1841).

105. "On the Application of Religion to Life" (#208, 25 October 1840), printed in *WRS*, 72–88.

106. JN, 402 (June 1840).

107. Ibid., 403 (June 1840).

108. Ibid., 400 (June 1840).

109. *CMW*, 1–2.

110. Ibid., 3. Emerson, in the Address, twice calls Jesus a "true man" (see *CWRWE*, 1:81) and says that people today "have come to speak of the revelation as somewhat long ago given and done, as if God were dead" (*CWRWE*, 1:84). See "State of the Church" (#94, 5 August 1838), 3–4.

111. *CMW*, 8. Compare to "State of the Church" (#94, 5 August 1838), 7–8.

112. *CMW*, 9, 10.

113. Ibid., 11–12. TP began developing these arguments in JN, 185 (July 1839).

114. *CMW*, 13.

115. Ibid., 14.

116. Ibid., 18–20.

117. Ibid., 17–18, 20.

118. Ibid., 21.

119. Ibid., 22.

120. Ibid., 24.

121. JN, 144 (9 May 1839).

122. Ibid., 400 (June 1840).

123. "The Laboring Classes," *Boston Quarterly Review* 3:3 (July 1840): 394–95.

124. JN, 422 (July 1840), in JTP, 18; JN, 400 (June 1840); JN, 423 (July 1840), in JTP, 19–20; Brownson, "The Laboring Classes," *Boston Quarterly Review* 3:4 (October 1840): 506–8. Note that both TP and Brownson thought the violence would be initiated by the property holders, not the laborers.

125. JN, 401, 400 (June 1840).

126. *CWRWE*, 1:9; "The World Belongs to Each Man/All things yours" (#86, 15 July 1838), printed in *WRS*, 45–57.

127. "A Sermon of Property" (#198, 23 August 1840).

128. JN, 333 (March 1840).

129. Ibid., 334 (ca. 22 March 1840).

130. "The Laboring Classes," *Boston Quarterly Review* 3, no. 3 (July 1840): 367, 371, 372, 367.

131. JN, 422, in JTP, 18. See also *CMW*, 120–21.

132. JN, 400 (June 1840).

133. *CMW*, 111 (see JN, 278 [December 1839]), 112–13.

134. *CMW*, 123.

135. Ripley to Emerson, 9 November 1840, quoted in Octavius Frothingham, *George Ripley*, 307–8. For TP's comment on the analogy of the Apostles, see his remarks to the Groton Convention, copied in the TP Letterbooks, 7:185, MHS.

136. *CMW*, 110.

137. "Labour" (#107, 31 March 1839); JN, 442 (September 1840).

138. Brisbane, *Social Destiny of Man*, vi; *CMW*, 114.

139. JN, 442 (September 1840), in JTP, 52.

140. *CMW*, 117–18. Compare to "Labour" (#107, 31 March 1839), 11–13; this sermon was written in November 1838, but not preached until March.

141. *CMW*, 126–27.

142. Ibid., 127.

143. Ibid., 125, 128.

144. Ibid., 124.

145. Ibid., 119, 121.

146. Ibid., 122, 124.

147. Ibid., 130; JN, 489, in JTP, 143–46.

148. TP uses a similar argument in "Thoughts on Labor," *CMW*, 120–21.

149. See Rousseau, *Social Contract*, bk. 2, chap. 7.

150. JN, 423 (July 1840), in JTP, 20.

151. Myerson, "Calendar of Transcendental Club Meetings."

152. "On the Application of Religion to Life" (#208, 25 October 1840), printed in *WRS*, 72–88; "The Laboring Classes," *Boston Quarterly Review* 3:3 (July 1840): 373–75.

153. After TP's "Lesson for the Day" and "Thoughts on Labor" were published, Orestes Brownson apparently told E. P. Peabody that TP's ideas had been stolen from the "Laboring Classes"; see Peabody to Brownson, n.d. (ca. summer 1842), Brownson Papers, Notre Dame. The charge is an odd one—the Transcendentalists were not as a group proprietary about their ideas—yet it has been repeated by recent historians, who accuse TP of presenting Brownson's ideas in "diluted" form (see Schlesinger, *Orestes Brownson*, 104; Miller, *Transcendentalists*, 449–50). There are two obvious rebuttals. First, TP wrote the original drafts of both the "Lesson" and the "Thoughts" in June, before Brownson's first article appeared. Second, and as I have tried to show, TP's social reform ideas had grown out of his thinking over the previous two years, and his starting point was not "The Laboring Classes," but Emerson's Divinity School Address.

154. He probably took this idea from the French novelist and historian Benjamin Constant; see Ripley, *Philosophical Miscellanies*, 2:292–319. TP disagrees with this view; in the *DR*, 73n, he calls Constant "one-sided."

155. "The Laboring Classes," *Boston Quarterly Review* 3, no. 3 (July 1840): 386, 387.

156. JN, 403 (June 1840); JN, 430 (August 1840), in JTP, 32; JN, 403 (June 1840).

157. The following account is based largely on that in JN, 431–38, in JTP, 34–47; see also the "Christian Union Convention," *Liberator*, 21 August 1840; and the speeches of TP, Ripley, and Mrs. Bearse copied in the TP Letterbooks, 7:168–89, MHS. The materials from JN, and the speech by TP, are in *LCTP*, 1:125–35.

158. Ahlstrom, *Religious History of the American People*, 479.

159. TP Letterbooks, 7:175, 181, MHS.

160. "A Sermon of Sects (first edition)" (#185, 19 April 1840); "Causes of Error in Matters Pertaining to Religion" (#187, 3 May 1840). "Character" is "xtr" in the original.

161. Henry Jones, "Groton Convocation: Without Martha's neat Serving," *Liberator*, 2 October 1840. Interestingly, TP's speeches to the convention, in the TP Letterbooks, MHS, depart somewhat from his usual style: he tends to use "Christ" instead of "Jesus" and frequently quotes biblical texts. He was probably adapting to his audience by imitating the style of the other speakers.

162. TP Letterbooks, 7:168, 174, MHS.

163. TP's picture of the conflicts of the early church, which he here announces publicly for the first time, are parallel to those of F. C. Baur and the Tübingen School. TP may have been influenced by Baur's early writings on Paul. See Hodgson, *Formation of Historical Theology*, 202–12.

164. TP Letterbooks, 7:169–71, MHS.

165. TP to Silsbee, 15 September 1840, MHS.

166. TP Letterbooks, 7:184–85, MHS; JN, 436 (August 1840), in JTP, 44. Olive Bearse's husband, Austin Bearse, was later a prominent figure in the Boston Vigilence Committee; see Bearse, *Reminiscences*. The Bearses also became members of TP's Twenty-Eighth Congregational Society.

167. "Come Outers," *Monthly Miscellany* 4 (May 1841), 297–300.

168. TP Letterbooks, 7:188–89, MHS; "A Sermon of Old Bottles" (#203, 23 August 1840); JN, 424 (July 1840), 440–41 (15–23 August 1840), in JTP, 21–22, 48.

169. See JN, 467 (23 September 1840) in JTP, 94–95; the letter from Edmund Quincy prefacing the call to the convention in the *Liberator*, 16, 23, or 30 October 1840; Edmund Quincy, "History of the Church, Ministry and Sabbath Convention," *Liberator*, 14 March 1841.

170. See the *Liberator*, 30 October 1840; this is just one example of many printings of the call in various papers.

171. It has been widely assumed, following Emerson's famous report in the *Dial* in 1842, that Channing was at the November convention as a delegate. He does not appear in the roll of members, however, nor in the reports of the debates (the roll is admittedly incomplete; it leaves out Alcott, for example, even though he addressed the convention more than once).

172. For examples of the hostile reaction to the convention, see the *Liberator*, 6 and 13 November 1840; TP to Francis, 21 November 1840, in CTPCF, 191; JN, 469 (November 1840), in JTP, 113–14.

173. "Finis/Farewell Sermon to West Roxbury" (#413, 8 February 1846), BPL. The

gathering was also sometimes called the "Sabbath, Ministry and Church Convention," because that was the order in which they discussed the topics.

174. Emerson, *Essays and Lectures*, 1210–11.

175. In the March convention, the delegates did pass a resolution, proposed by Garrison, explaining why they voted down an earlier resolution to receive the "Scriptures of the Old and New Testaments as the paramount and only authoritative tale of faith and duty." See *Liberator*, 9 April 1841, 58–59.

176. "Church, Ministry and Sabbath Convention," *Liberator*, 27 November 1841.

177. Ibid.; Francis to TP, 23 November 1840, in CTPCF, 194.

178. The *Observer* article is reprinted in the *Liberator*, 4 December 1840; Phelps, *Argument*, 18, 19. I thank Joel Myerson for finding a copy of this pamphlet for me.

179. "A Sermon of Sunday/A Sermon of the Sabbath" (#212, 15 November 1840).

180. "A Sermon of the Church/A Sermon of the Church & Ministry" (#213, 22 November 1840).

181. "A Letter Addressed to the Congregational Church in Purchase Street," reprinted in Octavius Frothingham, *George Ripley*, 81.

182. Ibid., 71–73; Margaret Fuller to W. H. Channing, 3 April 1841, in *Letters of Margaret Fuller*, 2:206; E. P. Peabody to J. S. Dwight, 10 June 1841, in *Letters of Elizabeth Palmer Peabody*, 252.

183. Frothingham to TP, 3 January 1843, MHS; Quincy to Caroline Westin, 9 February 1841, Westin Papers, BPL; see also Quincy to Westin, 25 February 1841 [misdated 1840], Westin Papers, BPL.

184. JN, 465 (3 November 1840), in JTP, 105–7; BSP. In the BSP, just above this resolve, TP records that on 27 December he preached at Jamaica Plain and adds (the passage has been scratched out but can still be read), "where I intend never to preach again, for reasons too obvious to need mention." What had happened there is unclear; Jamaica Plain was the neighboring parish, and its minister was his predecessor at Spring Street.

185. See *Liberator*, 12 March 1841, 2 April 1841; *SBO*, 7, 11; Phelps, *Argument*, 18–19.

186. JN, 453 (9 September 1840), in JTP, 72 (I would correct Myerson, "A Calendar of Transcendental Club Meetings," 206, who places the last meeting around 20 September); JN, 467 (23 September 1840), JTP, 95–96.

187. Myerson suggests Emerson and Fuller were forced to make the *Dial* a literary magazine because they could not find enough contributors to write on religious subjects. See Myerson, *New England Transcendentalists and the* Dial, 43.

188. Ibid., 49–53; JN, 410–11 (July 1840), in JTP, 1–3; JN, 431 (10 August 1840), in JTP, 35.

189. TP to Francis, 18 December 1840, in CTPCF, 203–4. Claud Halero is a poet in Walter Scott's novel *The Pirate*; the "organs of combativeness" are phrenological.

190. Emerson to Ripley, 15 December 1840, *LE* 2:368–71.

191. JN, 467 (23 September 1840), in JTP, 95–96; Rose, *Transcendentalism as a Social Movement*, 117.

192. JN, 442, in JTP, 53.

193. A detailed description of the service appears in John Pierce, "Memoirs of John Pierce," 9:86–89, MHS; Chadwick, *Theodore Parker*, 95–96; *SBO*; for the story of Dea-

con Arnold's chaise, see Mackintosh, *Some Recollections*; for Peabody's presence, see Peabody to J. S. Dwight, 10 June 1841, in *Letters of Elizabeth Palmer Peabody*, 254.

The text of the sermon used here is in Gura, "Theodore Parker," 162–78, except as noted. I would divide the sermon into sections as follows: I. The claims of the conservatives and the radicals (Gura, "Theodore Parker," 162: "In this sentence . . ." to ". . . calls us together"); II. Evocation of the Permanent and Transient (ibid., 162–64: "Nothing seems more fleeting . . ." to ". . . shall always stand"); III. Address to the claims of the conservatives (ibid., 164–71: "Let us look at the matter more closely . . ." to ". . . but not the sea"); IV. Address to claims of the radicals (ibid., 171–74: "To leave all the disputes . . ." to ". . . so high and pure"); V. Exhortation to let the Transient pass away (ibid., 174–75: "Let then the Transient pass . . ." to ". . . he cannot for another"); VI. Closing exhortation to Shackford and the Congregation (ibid., 175–76: "My friends . . ." to "depends upon your choice").

194. Silsbee's ordination took place on 1 July 1840 (see JN, 408 [29 June 1840]); Convers Francis delivered the Charge. See *CR*, 19:28 (11 July 1840), 110; Francis to TP, 22 June 1840, TP to Francis, 23 June 1840, in CTPCF, 186–90; JN, 407, 408 (June 1840). TP's "Right Hand of Fellowship" for Silsbee is in A-H.

195. JI, 248 (23 January 1843).

196. TP to Francis, 5 June 1841, in CTPCF, 215; "Church, Ministry and Sabbath Convention," *Liberator*, 9 April 1841; JI, 59 (30 March, 1 April 1841); BSP, October 1840, May 1841, BPL (copy A-H); "A Sermon of Post-Mortem ⟨Predictions⟩ Prophecies" (#239, 14 May 1841) [note that the National Fast Day was observed a month after the regular Massachusetts Fast Day]; TP to Silsbee, 23 April 1841, MHS. Gura, "Theodore Parker," 150, mistakenly claims that Parker first preached the "Transient and Permanent" to his congregation in West Roxbury on 2 May 1841, in which case he would have written the sermon in April; I explain why I think Gura is mistaken in the bibliography, under "Published Writings of Theodore Parker," 1841.

197. JI, 21 (January 1841); JN, 470 (November 1840), in JTP, 114–16.

198. Dall Journal, 4 April 1841, MHS; Fuller to W. H. Channing, 5 April 1841, in *Letters of Margaret Fuller*, 2:206.

199. "Sermon of Idols/Sermon of Idolatry" (#223, 21 March 1841), 7–8. "Nothing" is "0" and "Christianity" is "Xy" in the original.

200. Ibid., 14.

201. Fuller to W. H. Channing, 5 April 1841, in *Letters of Margaret Fuller*, 2: 206.

202. JI, 51 (March 1841). "Christianity" is "Xty" and "nothing" is "0" in the original.

203. See JN, 188 (3 August 1839). "Christianity" is "Xy" and "Christ" is "X" in the original. For an account of this meeting from Alcott's point of view, see *Journals of Bronson Alcott*, 134.

204. See TP to Ellis, 1 August 1838, Ellis to TP, 26 September 1838, Ellis Papers, MHS. "New Works Recently Published in Germany," *CE* 26 (May 1839): 267–68. I believe the first historian to note that TP took his title from Strauss was Octavius Frothingham, in *George Ripley*, 60–61.

205. *CMW*, 302–3; see Strauss, "Über Vergängliches und Bleibendes im Christenthum." The English translation is *Soliloquies on the Christian Religion: Its Errors and Its*

Everlasting Truth (London, 1845). It was printed as part of the Catholic series, which had earlier introduced TP's *Transient and Permanent in Christianity* to English readers. Strauss's piece probably was retitled so as to distinguish it from TP's sermon.

206. *CMW*, 281. I am indebted to Barbara Packer for calling this quotation to my attention.

207. Gura, "Theodore Parker," 162.

208. Ibid., 163.

209. Ibid., 166–67, 168.

210. In the published version of the "Transient and Permanent," TP added a long excerpt from "Idolatry"—the two pages on Jesus that follow "Doubtless the time will come when men shall see Christ also as he is." This passage does not appear in the Gura text, because TP may not have preached it (or if he did, he delivered it from memory). See Gura, "Theodore Parker," 170, 176 (19n); *CMW*, 156–58; *WTP*, 4:24–26; Conrad Wright, *Three Prophets*, 135–37; "Sermon of Idols/Sermon of Idolatry" (#223, 21 March 1841), 18–19.2.

211. Gura, "Theodore Parker," 166–67.

212. Ibid., 168–69.

213. Ibid., 169.

214. Ibid., 171.

215. Ibid., 173.

216. Ibid., 175.

217. "A Sermon of My Own Stewardship" (#338, 3 September 1843; second edition); Peabody to J. S. Dwight, 10 June 1841, in *Letters of Elizabeth Palmer Peabody*, 254.

Chapter Six

1. The report appears in *SBO*, 3–6; 338 Appendix, 1–2. The abstract is reprinted in Gura, "Theodore Parker," 177–78.

2. The pieces selected in *SBO* are almost all hostile to TP and to the Unitarians' claim that they were not responsible for TP's views, while some of those TP himself collected in his 338 Appendix and JI are more sympathetic.

3. TP later recalled that the only press he could find even to print his sermon was a Swedenborgian one. "Experience as a Minister," *WTP*, 13:324; E. P. Peabody to Dwight, 24 June 1841, in *Letters of Elizabeth Palmer Peabody*, 258.

4. See *SBO*, 4, 60.

5. Compare the preaching text in Gura with the published version in *CMW*: Gura, "Theodore Parker," 167 vs. *CMW*, 148; Gura, "Theodore Parker," 170 vs. *CMW* 156–58. For the relation of this latter passage to the sermon on "Sermon of Idols/Sermon of Idolatry" (#223, 21 March 1841), see above, chap. 5, note 21, and Grodzins, "Transient and Permanent in Theodore Parker's Christianity," 17 n. 37.

6. *SBO*, 18–19, 35–36; 338 Appendix, 5; see also Gura, "Theodore Parker," 156. TP had been urged to do something by at least one friend in the Unitarian ministry, Caleb Stetson of Medford, who wrote to him that if he could satisfy Fairchild "about certain alterations in your printed discourse something might be gained" (Stetson to TP, 29 June 1841, MHS). Charles Robinson of Medfield, who canceled an exchange with

TP in July, told him that many people in his congregation believed the false rumors and reports of TP's sermon, and that even if they were shown the printed discourse, they would respond that "it has been altered. The most objectionable parts have been suppressed" (see Robinson to TP, 21 July 1841, MHS). A copy of the first edition of the *Transient and Permanent*, on which TP marked every change from the preaching text, is at Meadville/Lombard Theological School. He used this copy to construct the appendix to the second edition. Later he labeled the marked-up copy "Codex B," evidently intending it as a second appendix to Sermon #338 (the first is 338 Appendix). I thank Rosemary Frances for finding this document and bringing it to my attention.

7. Noah Porter, "Theodore Parker," *New Englander* 2, no. 3 (July 1844): 373; TP to Horace Seaver, 14 January 1843, quoted in *TPAB*, 179. The full clause reads: "With what I *understand* to be the spirit of his writings on theology and religion, I have not the smallest sympathy"; this statement seems to imply that TP had not yet read Paine's deistic works.

8. Copies of the Fairchild, Driver, and Dunham report can be found in 338 Appendix, *SBO*, and Gura, "Theodore Parker." The order of the paraphrases generally follows that in which the original passages and statements appeared in the sermon, but does not always do so.

9. Gura, "Theodore Parker," 167. At least one member of his audience remembered TP's version. See also "One of the Laity" in 338 Appendix, 10.

10. Gura, "Theodore Parker," 172.

11. *SBO*, 19.

12. Dall Journal, 11 June 1841, MHS.

13. Gura, "Theodore Parker," 167. Gura (176, n.7) accepts TP's recollection that he did not preach the phrase "and to degrade the infinite God to the same level as Neptune and Jupiter." I think TP was mistaken, because John Pierce remembered the allusion and was offended by it (see below). The words do not appear in the published versions.

14. E. P. Peabody to Dwight, 24 June 1841, in *Letters of Elizabeth Palmer Peabody*, 240.

15. Dall Journal, 4 July 1841, MHS.

16. Gura, "Theodore Parker," 177–78; *SBO*, 62n, 63n; *SBO*, 18–19. E. P. Peabody, in a draft reply to TP's critics that was never published (tipped into JI, 94), comments quite correctly on TP's allusion that he himself had made no application of it. Other minds, however, taking "the literal & vulgar view of the fables of antiquity," had "committed the double indelicacy of putting a gross interpretation on them, & then associating them with a passage in the New Testament of which *they* were reminded." Note that Emerson, in the Divinity School Address, had made a similar comparison: The "language that describes Christ to England and America . . . paints a demigod, as the Orientals or the Greeks would describe Osiris or Apollo" (*CWRWE*, 1:82).

17. John Pierce, "Memoirs of John Pierce," 9:81, MHS.

18. *SBO*, 64, 61.

19. JI, 101 (August 1841). In the days immediately following 19 May, TP worried that—as he wrote to Convers Francis—the "cause of Freedom" would be attacked at Berry Street (TP to Francis, 24 May 1841, in *CTPCF*, 213). But the gathering proved surprisingly peaceable. Robert C. Waterston, one of the two ministers-at-large in Bos-

ton, gave an address declaring that "what we *believe* to be Christianity" was "Christianity itself." (*Boston Semi-weekly Courier*, 27 May 1841.) In 1844–45, as shall be seen below, Waterston would be less tolerant.

20. E.g., *SBO*, 31–32.

21. "J. T.," 5 June 1841, in *SBO*, 11–13.

22. Ibid., 6–7 (also in 338 Appendix, 3). Folsom's letter appalled TP's friends. E. P. Peabody, writing privately to John Sullivan Dwight, thought Folsom's "meanness . . . surpasses anything—not one word is said to express indignation at the garbled extract but he delivers Parker over to the *dogs*!" (E. P. Peabody to Dwight, [10 June 1841], in *Letters of Elizabeth Palmer Peabody*, 255. See also the letter of "One of the Laity," 338 Appendix, 10).

23. *SBO*, 7–8.

24. "A Sermon of My Own Stewardship" (#338, 3 September 1843; second edition), 40.

25. 338 Appendix, 11.

26. John Pierce, "Memoirs of John Pierce," 9:81–83, MHS. David Johnson informs me that Pierce's "Memoirs" is a transcription of his original journal, and that Pierce appears occasionally to have altered his first impressions when copying them. The entry on the South Boston ordination appears, however, to have not been much edited, if at all; Pierce did not modify his opinion of TP here to reflect his later views, nor does he bother to delete a repeated comment.

27. For references by Fairchild to a meeting or meetings with Pierce, see *SBO*, 18–19, 22, 45. Although Pierce probably said this at their meeting of 26 May, he may have said it at another meeting with Fairchild, prior to 25 June.

28. *Boston Semi-Weekly Courier*, 16 June 1841, in 338 Appendix, 10. The most influential Whig paper was the *Boston Daily Advertiser*, but the pronouncements of the *Courier* received wide attention.

29. 338 Appendix, 11.

30. *Puritan*, 24 June 1841, in *SBO*, 33.

31. For information on Lothrop, see his *Reminiscences* and the account of him in Octavius Frothingham, *Boston Unitarianism*, 181–84.

32. *CR* (12 June), in 338 Appendix, 4. See also Lothrop to Fairchild, 19 June, in *SBO*, 13–17; Fairchild to Lothrop, 25 June, *SBO*, 17–25; Lothrop to Fairchild, 30 June, in *SBO*, 36–43; Fairchild to Lothrop, 8 July, *SBO*, 43–52.

33. *SBO*, 48.

34. Ibid., 48–49, 14, 20, 22, 23.

35. See, e.g., ibid., 25–26.

36. Ibid., 49.

37. See Dexter, *Biographical Sketches of Graduates of Yale College*, and Fairchild, *Objections to the Deity of Christ Considered* (1832). For information on the Fairchild sexual misconduct case, see *Celebrated Trial of Joy Hamlet Fairchild* (1844), a neutral account of the ministerial inquiry; Fairchild, *Iniquity unfolded!* (1844), Fairchild's first published effort to defend himself; *The Truth Revealed* (1845), in which the deacons present their case; *Correspondence between Rev. Nehemiah Adams and Rev. J. H. Fairchild* (1846), in which Fairchild confronts a prominent Boston minister who believed him guilty; Fair-

child, *The New Doctrine of Clerical Privilege* (1852), in which Fairchild again defends himself; and finally, Fairchild's memoirs, *Remarkable Incidents in the Life of Rev. J. H. Fairchild* (several editions), in which he elaborates his defense. His memoirs do not mention the South Boston ordination.

38. Preface to the third edition of the *Transient and Permanent in Christianity* (1841); *Unitarianism Identified with Deism*; *CE* (September 1841), 114. I thank Joel Myerson for bringing the *Unitarianism* pamphlet to my attention. A more substantive notice, in the Baptist *Christian Review*, makes a similar argument, except that the reviewer seeks to link TP's heresy not only to the Unitarians but to all heirs of the Puritans who champion infant baptism. See the *Christian Review* 7, no. 21 (June 1842): 161–81. The review contains an extended comparison between TP and Tom Paine, which disgusted TP when he read it. See JI, 179 (16 June 1842).

39. *JMNE*, 8:262. The comment is dryly ironic, as it compares TP to a lion in the Coliseum; his "victims," by inference, are Christians.

40. For a discussion of Emerson's life in this period, see Richardson, *Emerson*.

41. 338 Appendix, 13; *Boston Quarterly Review* 4, no. 4 (October 1841): 436–74. Both sermon and review essay defend TP's view of the inspiration and authority of Scripture; the review essay also includes a partial defense of TP's view of the nature and authority of Christ.

42. 338 Appendix, 10, 7.

43. TP to the *CR*, 21 June 1841, in 338 Appendix, 7. The editorial to which TP is responding is dated Friday, 26 June. Either the date on the letter is incorrect or the *CR* was published on Mondays, but dated for Fridays.

44. 338 Appendix, 10; JI, 94 (July 1841); TP to E. P. Peabody, 1841, MHS.

45. E. P. Peabody to Dwight, [10 June 1841], 253.

46. William Larned, S. E. Brackett, Charles L. Thayer, and Charles Ellis to TP, 21 June 1841, MHS.

47. E. P. Peabody to Dwight, [10 June 1841], in *Letters of Elizabeth Palmer Peabody*, 253.

48. JI, 242 (23 January 1843).

49. See, e.g., *CR* and *CE*.

50. JI, 91 (June 1841). If word of the course did reach him before the formal invitation of 21 June, it probably came via Peabody or from Charles Ellis, a Boston merchant, signer of the invitation, and pillar of the Spring Street Church. Peabody mentions that one of the four signers of the letter was acquainted with TP (see E. P. Peabody to Dwight, 24 June 1841, in *Letters of Elizabeth Palmer Peabody*, 259). This was almost surely Ellis. He had been on the ordination committee that had invited TP to Spring Street; he and his family were enthusiastic TP supporters. His son, Charles Mayo Ellis, who became a lawyer only after consulting with TP, and whose son TP baptized in 1845, helped invite TP to Boston in 1845–46, joined TP's Twenty-Eighth Congregational Society, and became his lawyer in the Anthony Burns case. He is also the likely author of the thoughtful *Essay on Transcendentalism*. TP dedicates *The Trial of Theodore Parker* to him. See Roxbury Records and Mackintosh, *Personal Recollections*, 46.

51. Charles Thayer to TP, 10 August 1841, MHS; a copy of the advertisement in TP's hand is in the first Thayer Album at the BPL; JI, 109–10 (August 1841) (only

the first lecture and part of the second, on "Inspiration," are sketched); TP to Francis, 26 August 1841, in CTPCF, 219–20.

52. Many of the points of the *DR* appear in the "Levi Blodgett" letter, for example, while in "The Divine Presence in Nature and in the Soul," from the July 1840 *Dial*, TP already had presented all his basic arguments about inspiration.

53. The scraps, the envelope (postmarked 5 September 1841), and the first draft are in A-H.

54. See *CWRWE*, 1:161–216; JI, 103 (August 1841).

55. Gannett, "Intelligence" for TP's "Lectures on Religion," Gannett Papers, Houghton Library; Brownson, "Parker's Discourse," *Boston Quarterly Review* 5, no. 4 (October 1842): 49 (among other commentators on the audience); Myerson, *Brook Farm Book*, 134; Grodzins, "Theodore Parker's 'Conference,'" 83.

56. Deese, "Tending the 'Sacred Fires,'" 27; Dall Journal, 14 October 1841, 6 October 1841, 4 November 1841, Dall Papers, MHS.

57. Ibid., 27 October 1841.

58. Ibid., 28 October 1841, 27 October 1841.

59. "Mr. Parker and the Unitarians," *Boston Quarterly Review* 5, no. 2 (April 1842): 198–220. The essay has two parts. The second (209–20), which Peabody wrote in the summer of 1841, is a defense of TP's arguments for immortality; she could not, however, get this essay published in 1841. When she wrote her refutation of TP's "errors," she did so in the form of a letter to Brownson, which she submitted to him as a preface to her earlier essay (201–9).

60. E. P. Peabody to TP, 20 October 1841 (TP used the back of this uncatalogued letter to make notes for his last lecture; the letter is found among his other "Religion" lecture notes in A-H); "Mr. Parker and the Unitarians," *Boston Quarterly Review*, 206–7, 206, 207, 208.

61. Brownson, *Convert*, 152.

62. JI, 124 (18 November 1841); also, JI, list of books read.

63. See TP to Ware, 29 May 1841, MHS; JI, 124 (18 November 1841).

64. *CMW*, 330–60; see esp. 334n, 338–40, and 357–58.

65. Ibid., 324, 324n. For TP's explicit contrast between them, see *DR*, 106n.

66. Parker was in the habit of writing the date he purchased the book on the flyleaf. His copies of works by Comte are in the Boston Public Library.

67. Whewell, *History*, 1: introduction, esp. 12–16.

68. *CMW*, 313.

69. Naturally, he must also have a "good, pious, loving heart." Ibid., 314.

70. Ibid., 317, 318.

71. Ibid., 320–21.

72. Ibid., 328.

73. Ibid., 359–60. TP cites Leibniz, *Opera Omnia*, 5:344.

74. The omissions are marked on the manuscripts, at A-H; "Experience as a Minister," *WTP* 13:326.

75. TP to Silsbee, 1 January 1842, MHS; TP not only chose all the typefaces and the running headers (there is no index), but determined the placement of all the footnotes; JI, 178 (June 1842); JI, 179 (16 June 1842); JI, 180 (18 June 1842); JI, 187 (28 June

1842). See also TP to Increase Smith, 10 October 1842, MHS: "After the last M.S. went to the press, the excitement that sustained me in the work failed."

76. *DR*, 2, 10, 158, 488.

77. *CMW*, 36.

78. *DR*, 23n.

79. Ibid., 23.

80. Ibid., 164n, 20n, 263 (see also 246–47).

81. Deguise, "La religion de Benjamin Constant et l'Unitarianisme américain"; Ripley, *Philosophical Miscellanies*, 2:251–91; Fontana, *Benjamin Constant and the Post-Revolutionary Mind*; J. H. Morison, "Parker's Discourse," *CE* 32 (1842) 338n.

82. See the flyleaf notation on TP's copies of these books, BPL; JI, 133 [A] (December 1841), 480.

83. JI, 133 [A] (December 1841).

84. Meiners, in his *Allgemeine kritische Geschichte der Religionen* (General critical history of religion), provides a "Geschichte des Fetishismus" in 1:142–289. TP cites Meiners in *DR*, 34n, 52n, 56n, 68n, 71n, 80n, 97–98n, 124–25n, and 390n, but is hardly uncritical of Meiners's book, which he calls "passionate," "one-sided," "altogether unworthy of the subject, and 'behind the times' of its composition" (*DR*, 97–98n); presumably, TP disliked how Meiners refers to all nonmonotheistic religions as "false" and "polluted." The term "Fetishism" apparently was coined by Charles de Brosses, *Du Culte des Dieux Fétiches.* . . . (1760). TP did at some point read Brosses (at TP's death, he owned the book), but does not cite him in the *DR*. For TP's judgment of Constant, see JI, 133 [A] (December 1841); *DR*, 73n, 118n. TP also rejected Constant's "sensualist" epistemology; like Locke, Constant admitted only sensation and reflection as sources of knowledge, whereas TP insisted on adding intuition as a third source. See Ripley, *Philosophical Miscellanies*, 2:348–49.

85. Cashdollar, *Transformation of Theology*, 96.

86. List of books read, in JI (TP also notes reading volume 4); the booklet with notes on volume 5 is in A-H.

87. Cashdollar, *Transformation of Theology*, 97; Pickering, *Auguste Comte*, 274.

88. *DR*, 70n, 106n.

89. As TP revised the lectures, he jotted references to Comte in the margins; see also, *DR*, 56n, 62n, 419n, 424n; for TP's comment on Comte's religiousness, see ibid., 32n. See also the comments of Pickering, *Auguste Comte*, who argues that there was much continuity between the early and late phases of Comte's intellectual career.

90. J. H. Morison, "Parker's Discourse," *CE*, 389; *DR*, 393. TP heard that Morison had not finished reading the *DR* only ten days before the review appeared in print, and the review itself contains no mention of Book V or the Conclusion (see JI, 179 [16 June 1842]). TP was so disgusted by this review that he considered breaking his own rule and writing a "Polemick" in reply, which he sketched in his journal (JI, 187–88 [28 June 1842]). But before he had the chance to work up anything publishable, Morison wrote a public letter protesting that the editor of the *CE*, William Ware, had "mutilated" his conclusion by deleting several critical sentences. In them, Morison had said that he did not feel called on to "cast [TP] off" or "deny to him the Christian

name," for although TP was "sadly mistaken" on "the most important subjects connected to our religion," he nonetheless adhered earnestly to the "two essential truths" of Christianity—the existence of God and the immortality of the soul. TP, evidently mollified by this public acknowledgment from an avowed opponent that he was still a Christian, clipped the letter from the newspaper, pasted it into his journal, and left his "Polemick" in outline (*Daily Evening Bulletin*, 1 July 1842, in JI, 190).

91. *DR*, 261.

92. *DR*, 1847 ed., 244–45.

93. Besides the evidence presented below, TP favors the early state of Monotheism in "Idolatry" (#147, 16 June 1839).

94. TP to Francis, 26 August 1841, in CTPCF, 219–20; "Religion" Lecture I (draft), 26–28, A-H; "Religion" Lecture I, 48–51, A-H.

95. "Religion" Lecture I (draft), A-H; TP to Francis, 9 December 1841, in CTPCF, 229.

96. "A Sermon of Sin & Death/Death & Sin" (#273, 6 February 1842), 7–8.

97. *DR*, 114n, 116. See also TP to Francis, 9 December 1841, in CTPCF, 229–30.

98. *DR*, 115.

99. Ibid., 324–25.

100. Ibid., 256; see also 294.

101. On Peter as a liar, see ibid., 223, 292, 309, 312; on Peter trying to keep Christianity Jewish, see ibid., 355–56, 386.

102. Ibid., 269–70, 272, 274. TP does admit that miracles, defined as a "transgression of all law known or knowable by man, but yet in conformity with some law out of our reach," are possible: "The world is a perpetual miracle of this sort" (*DR*, 270–71). When Noah Porter accused him in a review of denying that miracles were possible, TP responded by indicating this passage (TP to Porter, 1 October 1844, MHS). Note that TP doubts the genuineness of the Gospels (that is, he doubts that they were written by their reputed authors and that we have them in their original form), but he does not discuss the problem at any length, perhaps because his mind is not yet decided. See *DR*, 357, 357n.

103. *DR*, 256–57 (see also Book III, chap. 5; 400); *DR*, 294, 300.

104. "Religion" Lecture III, 16, A-H; *DR*, 251n.

105. Roxbury Records; "Religion" Lecture III, 25, A-H.

106. "Religion" Lecture III (draft), 15, A-H. "Nothing" and "Nothingness" are "0" in the original.

107. *DR*, 260; "Religion" Lecture III (draft), 15–16, A-H.

108. "Religion" Lecture III, 25, A-H.

109. *DR*, 260.

110. "Religion" Lecture III (draft), A-H.

111. *DR*, 291; Grodzins, "Theodore Parker's 'Conference,'" 93.

112. "Religion" Lecture III, 55–56, A-H; *DR*, 290.

113. JN 130–31 (April 1839); "Hennel" [*sic*] appears on TP's list of "Books Read" in JI; "Hennell on the Origin of Christianity," *Dial* (October 1843), 155.

114. JI, 29 (January/April 1841); "Religion" Lecture III, 19, 55–56, A-H.

115. *DR*, 291n, 255, 278, 255n.

116. Ibid., 291, 257n.

117. Ibid., 11–18.

118. Ibid., 20, 21; ibid., Book I, chap. 5.

119. See, e.g., "Transcendentalism," *WTP* 6.

120. *DR*, 114n. TP also discusses race on pp. 35–37.

121. Grodzins, "Theodore Parker's 'Conference,' " 83.

122. Whipple, *Chapter of Theological and Religious Experience*, 22. That Whipple was a printer I have determined from references in TP's correspondence.

123. Cobbe, *Life of Frances Power Cobbe*, 1:97–98.

124. See, e.g., *DR*, 105–7, 148–49, 223–26, 442–43.

125. Porter, "Theodore Parker," *New Englander* 2:3 (July 1844), 387. Porter specifically is referring is Book III, chap. 7.

126. JI, 181 (22 June 1841). About this same time, Ripley turned down an offer to preach in TP's church because "with my present feelings, & convictions, I could not go through the routine of our pulpit services, without self-inconsistency, & of course, self-reproach." By 1851, he admitted to TP that he had "long since" lost his "immediate interest" in theological speculation; this comment may have some bearing on his feelings in 1842 (Ripley to TP, [n.d.; probably 1841–43], and 24 August 1851, Ripley Papers, MHS). After Ripley, TP's hopes next turned to Dr. Channing's nephew, William Henry Channing, an eloquent young Unitarian minister and Transcendentalist reformer whom TP long had admired. Channing promised a review of the *Discourse* both to TP and to Emerson, who now edited the *Dial*. Unfortunately, Channing was a man whose brave intentions were all too often undercut by indecisiveness and irresolution. By August, after three failed attempts to write the essay, he gave up. His problem, as he explained apologetically to TP, was that his opinion of the *Discourse* kept changing as he wrote. See W. H. Channing to TP, 11 August 1842, Emerson Papers, Houghton Library.

127. Brownson to Horace Greeley, 31 May 1842, in *New York Tribune*, 3 June 1842.

128. Brownson, "Parker's Discourse," *Boston Quarterly Review*, 445, 512. Brownson was not yet ready, however, to abandon all his Transcendentalist friends. To emphasize that he still respected TP, he conducted a special pulpit "exchange" with him immediately after the review was published (the exchange took place on 2 October 1842); Brownson's disbanded congregation had to be called back together for the purpose.

129. TP to Brownson, 2 December 1842, in H. F. Brownson, *Brownson's Early Life*, 238–39. TP (who had not responded sooner because he had been preoccupied with writing and delivering the "Six Plain Sermons for the Times") does say that he may try over the winter to write a review of all Brownson's writings in the *Quarterly*, including his essay on the *Discourse*, but this proposal died aborning; perhaps TP grew alienated by Brownson's ever more anti-Transcendentalist views.

Chapter Seven

1. JI, 89 (June 1841). See JI, 101–2 (August 1841): "I do not suffer for lack of sympathy, & am beside able to stand alone." See also JI, 163 (13 February 1842): "I feel in

the general way quite able to stand alone. I rejoice in the sympathy of the good & true, few men more so, but I do not expect it, nor rely much upon it."

2. See Clarke to TP, 29 May 1841, MHS; copy in the Church of the Disciples Papers, A-H.

3. This was E. P. Peabody's opinion. See E. P. Peabody to Dwight, [10 June 1841], in *Letters of Elizabeth Palmer Peabody*, 252. These rumors had started immediately after the sermon was preached. See *SBO*, 6.

4. E. P. Peabody to Dwight, [10 June 1841], in *Letters of Elizabeth Palmer Peabody*, 253.

5. TP to Clarke, 29 May 1841, MHS; TP to Church of the Disciples, 29 May 1841, MHS.

6. TP to Church of the Disciples, 29 May 1841, MHS. "Christian" is "Xn" in the original.

7. Clarke's notes in the Church of the Disciples Records, A-H; E. P. Peabody to Dwight, 10 June 1841, *Letters of Elizabeth Palmer Peabody*, 253 (Peabody indicates there was only one meeting of the Disciples, but Clarke's notes seem to indicate more than one meeting); TP to E. P. Peabody, 26 June 1841, MHS; JI, 152 (January 1842); E. P. Peabody to Clarke, [1841], in *Letters of Elizabeth Palmer Peabody*, 257.

8. Gannett, *Ezra Stiles Gannett*, 207; E. S. Gannett Diary, 21 April 1841, Gannett Papers, MHS.

9. Gannett's notes on the "Transient and Permanent" are found enclosed in TP to Gannett, 17 June 1841, Gannett Papers, Houghton Library; "Ordination at South Boston, Mass.," *Monthly Miscellany* 4 (June 1841), 351–52 (see also 5 [July 1841], 45); Gannett to TP, 18 June 1841, in JI, 87–88.

10. TP to Gannett, 17 June 1841, Gannett Papers, Houghton Library; Gura, "Theodore Parker," 171; "Ordination at South Boston, Mass.," *Monthly Miscellany* 4 (June 1841), 351–52.

11. TP to Gannett, 17 June 1841, Gannett Papers, Houghton Library. "Unchristian" is "unXn" in the original.

12. "A Discourse on the Transient and Permanent in Christianity," *Monthly Miscellany* 5 (July 1841), 46. TP opens the letter of 17 June with a statement that it is the first Gannett had ever received from him; for Gannett's visit, see E. S. Gannett Diary, 18 June 1841, Gannett Papers, MHS; Gannett to TP, 18 June 1841, tipped into JI, 87–88. Gannett's diary indicates that he missed TP's first lecture, but attended at least parts of the other four (see 13, 20, 27 October, 4 November, 1841). See "Lectures on Religion," *Monthly Miscellany* 5 (December 1841), 352–53; Gannett's manuscript for this article in Houghton Library. For Gannett's "pleasant call" on TP to show him "the notice of the Lectures I had written for the Miscellany," see E. S. Gannett Diary, 27 November 1841, Gannett Papers, MHS.

13. E. P. Peabody to Clarke, [1841], in *Letters of Elizabeth Palmer Peabody*, 256.

14. Rev. Leonard Withington, D.D., proposed prosecuting TP. See "A Sermon of My Own Stewardship" (#338, 3 September 1843; second edition), 41n; 338 Appendix.

15. JI, 294 (13 April 1843). I have added commas after TP's two "good mornings" and after "object."

16. "A Layman" to TP, 21 August 1841, MHS. The letter evidently was written by

a Unitarian, because the author facetiously expresses the fear that "that all accommodating Sect would . . . manage to fasten upon the world for many long centuries to come the Religion of that illbegotten imposture," Christ.

17. JI, 197 (11 July 1842). An invitation to TP for 1841 is among the scraps of paper on which he took notes while writing the *DR* in 1841–42, at A-H.

18. E. P. Peabody to Dwight, [10 June] 1841, in *Letters of Elizabeth Palmer Peabody*, 252. Ripley was of the opinion that had TP come, the church would not have allowed him to stay more than a few years anyway.

19. JI, 101 (August 1841).

20. Grodzins and Myerson, "Theodore Parker's Preaching Record."

21. JI, 89 (June 1841); TP to Francis, 24 June 1842, in CTPCF, 251–52.

22. JI, 177 (12 June 1842); TP to Francis, 24 June 1842, in CTPCF, 252; "A Sermon of My Own Stewardship" (#338, 3 September 1843; second edition), 43–44.

23. There is also the unusual case of Melish Motte of the South Congregational Church in Boston; in June 1842, TP preached in his church, but Motte never preached in TP's church. The circumstances involved Convers Francis's canceled exchange with TP, which will be discussed below. For TP preaching one old sermon each Sunday, see JI, 197 (10 July 1842).

24. JI, 102 (TP comments: "See how these Xns love one another! How much candor and freedom flourish!!!"); "Finis/Last sermon for the Second Parish" (#413, 6 February 1846), 16–17, BPL.

25. "A Sermon of My Own Stewardship" (#338, 3 September 1843), 44–45; Roxbury Records.

26. See, for example, the efforts to go hear TP that are recorded in the Child Diary, MHS.

27. Stetson to TP, 27 July 1842, MHS.

28. JI, 135 (2 December 1841); see also TP to Silsbee, 1 January 1842, MHS.

29. Robinson to TP, 21 July 1841, MHS.

30. For Hall being on the ordaining council, see John Pierce, "Memoirs of John Pierce," 9:89, MHS; Nathaniel Hall to TP, 30 June 1841, MHS; for TP's support at First Dorchester, see his letters to Patience Ford, MHS.

31. Hall to TP, 14 October 1841, MHS.

32. Lothrop, *Christian Name and Christian Liberty*, 19–20.

33. Ibid., 35, 37.

34. TP to Ellis, 1 August 1838, MHS; JN, 408 (29 June 1840); *CR*, 11 July 1840; TP's "Right Hand of Fellowship" for Silsbee, A-H.

35. JN 387 (5 June 1840).

36. TP to Silsbee, 23 February 1842 [misdated 1841], MHS; JI, 179 (16 June 1842), 181 (23 June 1842), 234 (December 1842). See also TP to Silsbee, 23 March 1844 [misdated 1843], MHS: "I know that you don't approve the course I have pursued for some years past, and have perhaps felt a certain coldness towards me as a consequence." For some idea of Silsbee's theological disagreements with TP, see his criticisms of the "Transcendental Doctrine of Self-Reliance," *CE* 37:3 (November 1844), 331–49. Silsbee gave TP labors of love in October 1841, July 1843, and December 1845 (although TP may have paid for this last preaching).

37. "A Sermon of My Own Stewardship" (#338, 3 September 1843; second edition), 50–52.

38. Andrew Peabody, "Memoir of Alvan Lamson"; JN, 182 (July/August 1839); JI, 101 (August 1841).

39. Conrad Wright, "The Dedham Case Revisited." For TP's impression of Lamson's congregation, see JN, 335 (5 April 1840): "These rogues have the sleekest looks I have ever seen. They take their ease in their pews. Soon as the minister rises, they seek out for themselves quiet seats, & look up as he proceeds . . . & nod approval or at least acquiescence. I never saw a congregation more contented than they."

40. JM, 5 (9 November 1844). Interestingly, this is not far from what actually was said of Lamson when he died.

41. Francis to TP, 10 June 1842, in CTPCF, 249–50 (mistakenly dated 9 June).

42. Francis, "Journals of Convers Francis," 252 (22 April 1838); see letters #5–44 in CTPCF.

43. TP to Francis, 22 March 1839, in CTPCF, 141; Francis to TP, 24 May 1839, in CTPCF, 144–45; Francis to TP, 23 November 1840, in CTPCF, 194. See also TP to Francis, 21 November 1840, in CTPCF, 191.

44. Francis, "Journals of Convers Francis," 255 (13 June 1841); Francis to TP, 30 June 1841, in CTPCF, 216–17; Francis, "Journals of Convers Francis," 256 (11 December 1841).

45. JI, 157 (February 1842).

46. TP to Ripley, 13 May 1859, Ripley Papers, MHS (the question of dedicating the DR does not appear in the correspondence or journals of Francis or TP from 1841 or 1842, so TP's offer is impossible to date exactly); TP to Francis, 5 May 1842, in CTPCF, 246; Francis to TP, 13 May 1842, in CTPCF, 248.

47. Francis to TP, 21 December 1839, in CTPCF, 122 (note that Francis evidently does not think the doctorate he was awarded by Harvard in 1837 to have been an adequate "token of confidence or esteem"); Francis to TP, 25 December 1838, in CTPCF, 113–14.

48. Ibid., 10 June 1842, in CTPCF, 249.

49. BSP, 12 June 1842. The Boston minister was Melish Motte of the New South Church, who would shortly retire for health reasons; the minister who filled in for TP was F. A. Whitney, pastor at Brighton, the older brother of George Whitney, who had unexpectedly died a few months earlier. For the fib, see JI, 182 (25 June 1842). That Mrs. Francis spoke to LCP is a conjecture; she certainly would not have told this story directly to TP himself, as Francis had told him the true circumstances.

50. JI, 176 (12 June 1842), 177 (15 June 1842), 180 (18 June 1842).

51. TP to Francis, 24 June 1842, in CTPCF, 251–53. The statement that no one who took part in TP's ordination would exchange with him turned out not to be strictly accurate. Caleb Stetson of Medford, the sometime member of the Transcendentalist's little club who had given the Charge to the Congregation, would give TP an exchange in April 1843.

52. Francis to TP, 19 August 1842, in CTPCF, 269; Francis, "Journals of Convers Francis," 256 (25 June 1842); JI, 182 (27 June 1842).

53. Francis, "Journals of Convers Francis," 257 (23 July 1842); 281 n. 857 (the ser-

mon title was "Afar Off—and made Nigh by the Blood of Christ"); Conway, *Autobiography*, 1:163.

54. TP to Francis, 3 July 1842, 25 July 1842, in CTPCF, 254, 260.

55. Ibid., 9 August 1842, in CTPCF, 266-67.

56. Francis to TP, 19 August 1842, in CTPCF, 269, 270.

57. "Of Expediency & Morality, or the LAW OF THE LORD" (#305, delivered as a lecture 24 October 1842, preached as a sermon 4 December 1842), 64; JI, 210 (October 1842); TP to Francis, 23 September 1842, in CTPCF, 271-72; JI, 234 (22 December 1842).

58. Hedge quoted in CTPCF, 282 n. 11; Francis to TP, 22 February 1843, in CTPCF, 280.

59. TP to Francis, 18 February 1843, in CTPCF, 274; Francis to TP, 22 February 1843, in CTPCF, 281. The Latin reads: "Shall I always be a writer? Will you never reply!!" and is a play on Juvenal, *Satires*, 1.1: "Shall I be a mere listener and never reply?" "Adyta" means inner sanctum (CTPCF, 276n).

60. See CTPCF, letters #55-60.

61. JI, 302 (18 May 1843). "Edition" is "Ed." in the original. I have supplied a question mark after "[there]."

62. TP to Gannett, 19 December 1846, Gannett Papers, Houghton Library; TP to Ripley, 13 May 1859, Ripley Papers, MHS. In 1845, TP visited Francis in Cambridge, and commented in his journal that Francis, "as is usual now-a-days," had much to talk about but nothing to say: "Poor old gentleman, he is dead! but he smiles benevolently as a corpse." JM, 60 (8 April 1845). In early 1857, when the senior class at the divinity school would vote that TP be its speaker (the role Emerson had filled nineteen years earlier), Francis would join the other faculty members in voting to prevent TP from coming. TP was very sick when this vote was taken, and he felt deeply offended by it: "They saw fit to offer me the greatest ecclesiastical, academical, and personal insult in their professional power, in the most public manner, and that, too, at a time when I was just recovering from a severe illness, and fluttering 'twixt life and death. . . . Others might have expected such treatment from these men; I confess . . . that I did not" ("Experience as a Minister," *WTP* 13:391). Francis and TP seem not to have seen each other for a year thereafter, until Francis wrote TP a letter asking to visit (Francis to TP, 20 February 1858, in CTPCF, 566-67); then their friendly sounding correspondence resumed. But the incident certainly contributed to TP's decision to leave Francis's name out of the "Experience as a Minister" (the only mention of him is as one of the faculty members who delivered the 1857 insult).

63. JI, 143 (December 1841/January 1842).

64. Ibid., 163 (February 1842).

65. Ibid., 200 (21 July 1842).

66. Ibid., 70 (April 1841). See chap. 5.

67. E. P. Peabody to Orestes Brownson, n.d. [summer 1842], Brownson Papers, Notre Dame. The letter is incomplete and undated, but it evidently was written after TP's "Religion" lectures of 1841-42, to which Peabody refers, and during the summer, as she records a conversation with Anna Shaw's sister and TP's neighbor, Sarah Russell, who remarks that "now" her family is in West Roxbury "all summer." This letter also

seems to be related to another written by William Batchelder Greene to Brownson, 15 August 1842, Brownson Papers, Notre Dame. I am indebted to Philip Gura for calling both these letters to my attention, although I date and interpret the Peabody letter somewhat differently than he does. See Gura, "Beyond Transcendentalism: The Radical Individualism of William B. Greene," 482–83.

68. See Gura, "Beyond Transcendentalism"; Pierce, *Batchelder, Batcheller Genealogy*, 455–57; Thomas Wentworth Higginson describes Greene as "ruthlessly opinionated" in *Cheerful Yesterdays*, 106.

69. Peabody, *Reminiscences*, 435, does not give a date, but TP, in TP to E. P. Peabody, 15 July 1841, MHS, seems to be helping her find the translation for Greene: "I saw at Little and Brown's, a short time ago, a french version of the critique of Pure Reason which may be just what your friend wants."

70. E. P. Peabody to Brownson, n.d. [summer 1842], Brownson Papers, Notre Dame.

71. Ibid.

72. Ibid. Peabody does not date Greene's change of plan, but it must have occurred sometime after TP delivered his "Religion" lectures in October/November 1841 (Peabody associates Greene's low opinion of TP with Greene's negative reaction to the lectures) and April 1842, when Greene met with Emerson, apparently seeking advice about whether or not to become a minister. Moreover, Peabody mentions that for the first four months she knew Greene (assuming she met him in October 1841, this would be until January 1842), he was living with his parents. After this, he seems to have lived on his own. Could his decision to leave his parents' house be associated with his decision to stay in Boston? The link is plausible (e.g., that he felt he could live at home only if he were expecting to leave soon), although it cannot be proven. Greene's preaching in Methuen is mentioned in none of his biographies, but is strongly implied in his letter to Brownson, 24 August 1842, Notre Dame: "I am getting along famously with the people here: I am very popular with them, and can do pretty much as I please. The *Doctrine of Life* takes well. I have only spoken two or three times in public, but have laid a pretty good foundation in private conversation. The leading men in the Church are nearly all friendly to me; and generally back me up even though I am upon rather 'tall' doctrine." There had been a Baptist church in Methuen since the late eighteenth century; see Joseph S. Howe, *Historical Sketch of the Town of Methuen*, 42–43. Note that in the Baptist tradition, unlike the Unitarian, a minister commonly started preaching before he attended seminary.

73. E. P. Peabody to Brownson, n.d. [summer 1842], Brownson Papers, Notre Dame. Peabody seems to date Greene's learning of the charges about the time he made his change of plans. She indicates that there was a gap in time—how long is unclear—between when she herself learned that there were charges, and when she learned the nature of the charges.

74. TP to E. P. Peabody, n.d. (ca. March 1842), MHS. Peabody uses the word "ludicrous" more than once, E. P. Peabody to Brownson, n.d., Brownson Papers, Notre Dame.

75. In E. P. Peabody to TP, 20 October 1841, A-H (uncatalogued; in folder of "Religion" lecture notes), makes clear her abhorrence of infidelity. She calls dismissal of

Jesus the "worse [*sic*] Cant of all"—as opposed to the "worst," which is " 'the corrupter of the Bed.' "

76. See Mary T. Peabody to S. A. Hawthorne (ca. September 1842), Berg Collection, New York Public Library: "Anna & W[illiam]. are pretty well found out by the world—but their affairs are not *officially* known. . . . W. still lives at Newton when he is not in Boston." I thank Megan Marshall for bringing this letter to my attention. Greene would have had many opportunities to meet Anna Shaw, whose family was well known to both Brownson and Peabody; besides, Greene took an interest in Brook Farm and paid many visits to West Roxbury ("William Batchelder Greene," in Myerson, *New England Transcendentalists and the* Dial, 155, says Greene stayed at Brook Farm, but Sterling Delano informs me that there seems to be no evidence of his stay in the Brook Farm records). Greene apparently told Peabody more than once, when he first met her in the fall of 1841, that he was "*too old* to fall in love," but such convictions, especially when held by someone twenty-two years old, are known to give way. See E. P. Peabody to Brownson, n.d. [summer 1842], Brownson Papers, Notre Dame.

77. Greene to Brownson, 24 August 1842, Brownson Papers, Notre Dame.

78. JI, 181 (24 June 1842).

79. TP to E. P. Peabody, n.d. (ca. March 1842), 3 June 1842, MHS.

80. Ibid., 234 (22 December 1842).

81. TP to E. P. Peabody, 5 February 1859, Antiochiana, Antioch College; TP to E. P. Peabody, April 1845, MHS.

82. JI, 231 (5–19 December 1842).

83. Ibid., 332 (September/October 1844).

84. JM, 360 (January 1847).

85. Ibid., 397 (March 1847).

86. Notebook A/B, A-H.

87. JO, 699, 700 (30 August 1856).

88. JM, 530 (September/December 1847).

89. JO, 330 (September 1852).

90. JM, 497 (June/August 1847).

91. Other poems include JM, 499 (June/August 1847).

92. JO, 13 (7 June 1851).

93. George Dodge Cabot to Jos. F. Clarke, 9 August 1856, George Dodge Cabot Papers, MHS. That this was the story TP had heard is strongly implied in George Cabot's letters and in TP's Notebook K, A-H, which both lay much emphasis on another version of events: that Sarah Jane Goodhue was a prostitute; that although she had a child by John Cabot, it had died in infancy; that George Colburn was in fact the legitimate child of Sarah Jane's sister Charlotte Hubbard; Sarah Jane had taken the boy in. He was therefore unrelated to John Cabot.

94. Will of Jane Colburn, 16 May 1842, Suffolk County Probate Records; statement of John Hayden, 27 November 1842, Suffolk County Probate Records.

95. George Dodge Cabot to Joseph F. Clarke, 9 August 1856, George Dodge Cabot Papers, MHS.

96. Howe, *Reminiscences*, 160. The girl's name was Julia Frances Redlon. For her

story, see LCP to Edouard Desor, 24 August 1868, Desor Papers, Neuchâtel State Archives, Neuchâtel, Switzerland, in which LCP reports the girl is eleven years old and had been living with LCP for four years; Will of LCP, 1879, Suffolk County Probate Records.

97. See George Dodge Cabot's attempt in 1856 to cajole, browbeat, or legally force Georgie to drop the Cabot name: George L. Cabot to George Colburn Cabot, 4 August 1856; George Dodge Cabot to Jos. F. Clarke, 9 August 1856; George Dodge Cabot to George Colburn Cabot, 20 October 1856, George Dodge Cabot Papers, MHS.

98. Swift, *Brook Farm*, 57.

99. George William Curtis, "Hawthorne, Brook Farm and Transcendentalism," in Myerson, *Brook Farm Book*, 98; Notebook I, 107, A-H. Curtis in another recollection asserts that TP, although a "friendly neighbor," "seldom came to the Farm," but this assertion seems mistaken (see George William Curtis, "Brook Farm and Transcendentalism," in Myerson, *Brook Farm Book*, 178).

100. In Myerson, *Brook Farm Book*, 273.

101. Swift, *Brook Farm*, 20.

102. "Covetousness" (#319, 2 April 1843).

103. The issue of state debt repudiation receives thorough treatment, from a conservative Whig point of view, in Curtis, *Article on the Debts of the States*. The quotation, a characterization by Curtis of a pro-repudiation argument, appears on p. 30. Another common argument in favor of repudiation was that at least some of the debt a state owned had been contracted fraudulently.

104. "A Sermon for the Times" (#283, 7 April 1842). I have deleted a comma between "rob" and "the few."

105. "A Discourse of Freedom" (#293, 3 July 1842), 20; "Of Expediency & Morality, or the LAW OF THE LORD" (#305, delivered as lecture 24 October 1842; first preached as a sermon 4 December 1842), 53.

106. The lecture, delivered before the American Institute for Instruction, is partly based on "A Sermon of Education" (#227, 7 February 1841).

107. *CMW*, 192–94.

108. Ibid., 196.

109. Ibid., 198, 199, 200.

110. Ibid., 202, 202–3.

111. Ibid., 205.

112. Ibid., 206, 208, 211.

113. Ibid., 212, 213.

114. Ibid., 214.

115. Ibid., 216, 218–19.

116. Ibid., 206–7.

117. He did make occasional references to slavery in sermons. In "God's Common Law" (#119, 10 February 1839), 14–15, he argued that slave rebellions are one of the "Laws of Nature." In "Execution of the Law/Law & its Execution, Part II" (#180, 8 March 1840), he made the disgusted observation that if people discovered they could make much more money by freeing slaves than keeping them, eloquent speeches would

be heard all over the land, including in the South, proclaiming the rights of man and wrongs of slavery.

118. "A Sermon of Slavery" (#226, 31 January 1841). I quote from the text as it appears in *WTP* 11; Edmund Quincy to Caroline Westin, 9 February 1841, 25 February 1841 [misdated 1840], Westin Papers, BPL.

119. See in particular Channing, *Works*, "The Abolitionists: A Letter to James G. Birney," "Remarks on the Slavery Question, in a Letter to Jonathan Phillips, Esq.," "Remarks on Associations."

120. Cabot, *Memoir of Ralph Waldo Emerson*, 2:425–26. See also Len Gougeon's introduction to Emerson, *Emerson's Antislavery Writings*, xvi–xvii.

121. Quincy to Caroline Westin, 25 February 1841, Westin Papers, BPL; *WTP* 11: 10–11.

122. Quincy to Caroline Westin, 25 February 1841, Westin Papers, BPL; *WTP* 11: 12–13.

123. *WTP*, 11:13–14.

124. "The Life and Character of Dr. Follen," *WTP* 8:449.

125. "Socrates in Boston: A Dialogue between the Philosopher and a Yankee," *Liberty Bell* (1843), 117–45. This piece is interesting, too, because in it TP introduces (he is mentioned as Jonathan's pastor) the "very learned" proslavery clergyman, the Rev. Dr. "Banbaby"—so called, presumably, because he believes in infant damnation and so would "ban babies" from Heaven. In later years, TP would make frequent use of the Banbaby character to satirize what he saw as the moral failings of the Boston clergy.

126. Perhaps, too, TP intended the section on sin to complement the discourse he had written immediately preceding this one, "Freedom & its Limitations," in which he had said nothing about politics but much about the will and the circumstances that constrain it. See "A Sermon of Freedom and its Limitations" (#225, 21 February 1841).

127. Quincy to Caroline Westin, 12 August 1842, Westin Papers, BPL.

128. See Campbell, *Slave Catchers*, 13–14; Garrison and Garrison, *Garrison*, 3:66–67n.

129. "A Sermon of Laws the Foundation of a Divine Life" (#268, 16 January 1842).

130. TP to George Adams, 5 December 1842, MHS; "A Sermon of the Application of Religion to Life, or the Objective Influence of Religion" (#310, delivered as a lecture 21 November 1842, preached as a sermon 22 January 1843).

131. TP to George Adams, 5 December 1842, MHS.

132. TP to Healey, 5 October 1842, Dall Papers, MHS.

133. "Of Expediency & Morality, or the LAW OF THE LORD" (#305, delivered as a lecture 24 October 1842, preached as a sermon 4 December 1842), 60.

134. "A Sermon of the Application of Religion to Life, or the Objective Influence of Religion" (#310, delivered as a lecture 21 November 1842, preached as a sermon 22 January 1843).

135. Emeline A. H. Smith to Caroline Westin, 11 March 1842, Westin Papers.

136. Emerson to Hedge, 25 November 1842, in *LE*, 3:99. After Boston, TP delivered the "Sermons" in Charlestown, West Roxbury, Roxbury, Salem, Dorchester, and Hingham.

137. JI, 243 (23 January 1843). Two outlines appear on JI, 189. One evidently was

written around 28 June 1842, the other sometime later; conceivably, these outlines, or at least the first of them, could have been written before the young men approached TP. The arguments of "Of Expediency & Morality, or the LAW OF THE LORD" (#305, delivered as a lecture 24 October 1842, preached as a sermon 4 December 1842) were partly worked out in "A Sermon of Laws the Foundation of a Divine Life" (#268, 16 January 1842); "Of Religion & Theology, or of . . . the doctrines of God & Man's commands" (#307, delivered as a lecture 7 November 1842, preached as a sermon 25 December 1842) were largely worked out in "A Sermon of Theology and Religion, Part I" (#275, 13 February 1842) and "Part II" (#276, 19 March 1842).

138. TP also, as with the earlier lectures, planned to publish them. In his journal in 1842, he plans to flesh them out with "a wide study of the Hist[ory] of Phil[osophy], Ethics & Theol[ogy] among Pagans and Christians"—in other words, to match the scholarly labor he had put into transforming the "Religion" lectures into the *DR* (JI, 262 [25 February 1842]). His journal indicates that he considered pursuing this project as late as 1845 (see JI, 349 [19 October 1844], and JM, 84 [June 1845]). In 1844–45, he did make some revisions on the "Sermons," bringing them up to date, and rewrote the conclusion of sermon #310. But the work seems to have gone no further and the "Six Sermons" remain unpublished.

139. "Of Expediency & Morality, or the LAW OF THE LORD" (#305, delivered as a lecture 24 October 1842, preached as a sermon 4 December 1842); "Of Morality & Religion, or of the . . . LOVE OF GOD & MAN" (#306, delivered as a lecture, 31 October 1842, preached as a sermon, 18 December 1842); "Of Religion & Theology, or of . . . the doctrines of God & Man's commands" (#307, delivered as a lecture 7 November 1842, preached as a sermon 25 December 1842); "Of Morality & Religion"; "Of Religion & Theology."

140. "Of Religion as a Subjective Matter or the development of Rel[igion] in the Soul" (#309, delivered as lecture 21 November 1842, preached as a sermon, 15 January 1843).

141. "A Sermon of the Application of Religion to Life, or the Objective Influence of Religion" (#310, delivered as a lecture 21 November 1842, preached as a sermon 22 January 1843).

142. "Of Expediency & Morality, or the LAW OF THE LORD" (#305, delivered as a lecture 24 October 1842; preached as a sermon 4 December 1842), 2; "A Sermon of the Application of Religion to Life, or the Objective Influence of Religion" (#310, delivered as a lecture 21 November 1842, preached as a sermon 22 January 1843), 99. This statement may come from the 1844–45 revisions of the sermon. The original version of the statement may be this: "I have spoken as I could not help speaking—plain, right on" (#310, 67).

143. "Of Applying Good Sense to Theology, or of *Confusion & Peace*" (#308, delivered as a lecture 14 November 1842, preached as a sermon 8 January 1843), 63.

144. Ibid., 63–64

145. Stanton gives two accounts, which differ in various details, of attending the lectures. The quotations in this paragraph are taken from the first, dated 1886, which appears in the *Index*, the newspaper of the Free Religious Association; a clipping is found in the first volume of the second set of Thayer Albums (unpaginated), BPL

(another copy, as reprinted in the spiritualist newspaper *Banner of Light*, is in the second volume). The second account, better known, appeared eleven years later in Stanton's memoir, *Eighty Years and More*, chap. 7. The later version contains information the earlier one does not, but also contains errors. She there says she heard TP's "Religion" lectures at the Marlboro Chapel. This was impossible, however, because, as she notes in the 1886 article, she did not move to Cheslea until the winter of 1842–43. Also in *Eighty Years*, she remembers going to hear the lectures a second time at Cambridge-port, but TP did not deliver the course there. Yet she recalls that her second hearing came immediately after her first; if this memory is right, she almost certainly heard the sermons a second time in Charlestown, where TP next delivered them. See also Eliza-beth Cady Stanton to Elizabeth J. Neall, 3 February 1843, in Stanton and Anthony, *Selected Papers of Elizabeth Cady Stanton and Susan B. Anthony*, 1:40.

146. *Proceedings of the Hollis Street Council*, 136, 138.

147. "A Sermon of Infidelity" (#243, 20 June 1841).

148. "The Pharisees," *CMW*, 188–89.

149. JI, 127 (November 1841). "Christianity" is "Xty" in the original. See also "Hollis Street Council," *Dial* 3:2 (October 1842): 210.

150. TP, "Hollis Street Council," *Dial*, 219; see also Boston Association and John Pierpont, *Letter of the Boston Association*, 9–10; Pierpont to TP, 22 March 1845, MHS.

151. "Hollis Street Council," *Dial*, 215–16; the speakers are identified in JI, 255 (January/February 1843).

152. Emerson to Fuller, 21 March 1842, *LE*, 3:35; TP to Emerson, 7 April 1842, Houghton.

153. Emerson to TP, 22 May 1842, 17 July 1842, 8 September 1842, *LE*, 3:54–55, 71, 86.

154. "Theodore Parker," in Emerson, *Complete Works*, 11:271. Reflecting these dif-ferences, Emerson and TP had dissimilar assessments not only of Pierpont, but of other ministers. TP thought Henry Ware Jr., was a religious genius; Emerson was skep-tical. TP again had great admiration for late Karl Follen, as his essay on Follen for *Dial* indicates. Emerson responded to TP's proposal to write the Follen essay by remark-ing that although the German had been a "brave erect man," he had been possessed of "a singularly barren & uninteresting intellect, who always baulked any inquiry for an opinion or a spiritual fact, by a quotation." See Emerson to TP, 17 July 1842, *LE*, 3:71.

155. TP to Emerson, 16 May 1842, 3 September 1842, Houghton.

156. TP to Emerson, 8 July 1842, Houghton; Emerson to TP, 8 September 1842, *LE*, 3:86.

157. "Hollis Street Council," *Dial*, 201–2, 204–10. See also TP to Emerson, 3 Sep-tember 1842, in which TP says he has tried to make the piece about "things in general."

158. "Hollis Street Council," *Dial*, 209, 212–13.

159. Ibid., 218.

160. Ibid., 210–12, 216, 215, 220, 220–21.

161. TP to Emerson, 3 September 1842, Houghton.

162. Fuller to Emerson, 16 October 1842, in Fuller, *Letters of Margaret Fuller*, 3:97 (the semicolon is a comma in the original). Emerson probably was recalling the "Hollis Street Council" furor when he later wrote that "some numbers [of the *Dial*] had an

instant sale, because of papers by Theodore Parker." See "Historic Notes of Life and Letters in New England," *Complete Works of Ralph Waldo Emerson*, 10:324.

163. JI, 157 (14 February 1842).

164. "A Sermon of My Own Stewardship" (#338, 3 September 1843; second edition), 37.

165. *CMW*, 168, 188.

166. See Lothrop in the *CR*, 26 June 1841: "We are no friends to concealment, much less to hypocrisy of any kind. Nor do we approve of thinking one thing in the closet and another in the pulpit. We do not believe any man consents to do this, though Mr. Parker seems to insinuate that it is, or may be the case. Because a man preaches an old-fashioned Christianity, a Christianity which rests upon the genuineness and authenticity of the New Testament records, and the authority of Jesus Christ as the mediator between God and man, we should be loth to write him down a hypocrite." Octavius Frothingham, *Boston Unitarianism*, is the only biography of Nathaniel Frothingham.

167. JI, 100 (August 1841); N. Frothingham to TP, 3 January 1843, MHS.

168. JI, 100 (August 1841).

169. See Grodzins, "Theodore Parker's 'Conference,'" 89–90, 92; also, see variations of quotations about Strauss and the Resurrection stories at JI, 100–101 (August 1841). The emphases are all those of TP.

170. See Norton to N. Frothingham, 11 April 1837 and [no date], Norton Papers, Houghton.

171. N. Frothingham to TP, 3 January 1843, MHS.

172. Octavius Frothingham, *Boston Unitarianism*, 67.

173. JM, 87 (13 June 1845); Grodzins, "Theodore Parker's 'Conference,'" 89–90. I have expanded the contractions.

174. In this passage, TP identifies the Pharisees with the Boston clergy (who summered by the sea). The rabbi just quoted goes on to profess worry about "Simon Peter, James and John, those poor unlettered fishermen, on the lake of Galilee, to whom we gave a farthing and priestly blessing in our summer excursion, what will become of them when told that every word of the Law did not come straight out of the mouth of Jehovah, and ritual is nothing! They will go over to the Flesh and the Devil, and be lost. It is true, that the Law and the Prophets are well summed up in one word, Love God and man. But never let *us* sanction the saying, it would ruin the seed of Abraham; keep back the kingdom of God, and 'destroy our usefulness.'" See *DR*, 306–7.

175. JI, 107 (September 1841) ("character" is "xtr" in the original); JI, 157 (14 February 1842). See Octavius Frothingham, *Boston Unitarianism*, 161–66, and *Francis Parkman*, 5–7. Jacobs, *Francis Parkman, Historian as Hero*, 3–4, 6–7, mentions that Dr. Parkman was also, privately, subject to depressions.

176. JI, 152–53 (January 1842).

177. JN, 405 (ca. June 1840); TP to Silsbee, 1 January 1842, MHS. See also JI, 133 (2 December 1841).

178. JI, 107 (July/August 1841).

179. "Hollis Street Council," *Dial*, 213; *Proceedings of the Hollis Street Council*, 104; Parkman to TP, 25 March 1845, and 31 March 1845, MHS.

180. *SBO*, 31.

181. *CR*, June 1841; Frothingham to TP, 3 January 1843, MHS.

182. TP to Silsbee, 1 January 1842, MHS.

183. BA Records, 10 October 1842 [misdated 9 October], 28 November 1842. Note that the cycle for delivering the lecture was about nine months long (there were twenty-nine members, although some were excused from duty on various grounds). As TP preached the Lecture in June 1841, he ought to have preached it again around March 1842, but at that time he was writing the *DR* and probably did not want to be bothered.

184. Ibid. The nature of Lothrop's arguments are inferred from Ezra Stiles Gannett's response.

185. See "A Discourse on the Transient and Permanent in Christianity," *Monthly Miscellany* 5 (July 1841), 46; "Lectures on Religion," *Monthly Miscellany* 5 (December 1841), 352; E. S. Gannett Diary, 27 October 1841, Gannett Papers, MHS; "Grounds of Religious Belief," *Monthly Miscellany* 6 (June 1842), 310, 310–11 (this exchange is not explicitly given as being between Gannett and TP, but in context it almost certainly was so); "A Discourse on the Transient and Permanent in Christianity," *Monthly Miscellany* 5 (July 1841), 47; "Grounds of Religious Belief," *Monthly Miscellany*, 311.

186. "Lectures on Religion," *Monthly Miscellany*, 353; "Grounds of Religious Belief," *Monthly Miscellany*, 310.

187. See Gannett's draft resolutions, Gannett Papers, Houghton Library; BA Records, 14 November 1842 [misdated 13 November]; E. S. Gannett Diary, 14 November 1842, Gannett Papers, MHS.

188. BA Records, 14 November 1842 [misdated 13 November]. More precisely, Gannett proposed appointing a committee; it seems to have been understood that he would have charge of it and be principally responsible for its final report.

189. Ibid., 28 November 1842, copy MHS; Grodzins, "Theodore Parker's 'Conference,'" 82.

190. JI, 223 (5 December 1842); BA Records, 12 December 1841.

191. Frothingham to TP, 3 January 1843, MHS.

192. JI, 218 (ca. October 1842); John Pierce, "Memoirs of John Pierce," vol. 1 New Series, 110 (July 1843), MHS (I thank the Rev. Tim Jensen for calling this anecdote to my attention); JI, 218 (ca. October 1842). In December 1841, Putnam had said at an Association meeting that the members were responsible for one another's opinions—and for this reason the Association should be broken up (JI, 135 [2 December 1841]).

193. Putnam was certainly present at the 10 October meeting, which was held at his house; he was probably present at the later ones.

194. JI, 233 (19 December 1842). TP and Putnam exchanged some cold, awkward letters after this, but nothing more.

195. Ibid.

196. Grodzins, "Theodore Parker's 'Conference,'" 94. Much of the following section was first presented in this article.

197. Volume 14 of the TP Papers, MHS collection. The table of contents, written in TP's hand, lists three "curious letters" by E. P. Peabody, but, according to a note, TP removed them on 19 August 1843, and sent them back to her; the volume must have

been put together, therefore, before that date, probably around March 1843. All but a few of the letters were written before March. The volume of clippings constitutes the 338 Appendix.

198. JI, 241 (January/February 1843). See also Grodzins, "Theodore Parker's 'Conference,'" 95, n. 3.

199. E. S. Gannett Journal, 23 January 1843, Gannett Papers, MHS; BA Records, 23 January 1843 [misdated 25 January] ("Avowing" is "avowed" in the original).

200. Grodzins, "Theodore Parker's 'Conference,'" 82. Here and elsewhere, I change the verb tenses from past to present.

201. Ibid.

202. Ibid., 83, 82–83.

203. Ibid., 83.

204. Ibid., 84.

205. Ibid., 83, 88.

206. Ibid., 84.

207. Ibid.

208. Ibid., 84–85.

209. Ibid., 85. TP reports that another voiced complained that "you treated the writers of the New Testament about the same way and said the Apostle James '*roars like a fanatic radical!*'" In fact, the quotation comes from *DR*, 312: "James roars like a fanatic radical at the rich man." In "Hollis Street Council," *Dial*, 217, TP points out that Pierpont's harsh language has a precedent in James 5:1–6: "Go to now ye rich men, weep and howl for your miseries that shall come upon you."

210. Grodzins, "Theodore Parker's 'Conference,'" 85.

211. Ibid.

212. Ibid., 88. For a description of Young, see Octavius Frothingham, *Boston Unitarianism*, 166–71. See also TP's satire of Young (by this time deceased) in TP to Francis, [November 1855], in CTPCF, 548–49.

213. Grodzins, "Theodore Parker's 'Conference,'" 85, 92; I have added punctuation to the Quincy quotation. TP also notes in his account that three of those he spoke with before writing in fact were present; he does not name them, but they were probably Sargent, Hall, and Shackford.

214. Ibid., 85, 86. See also JI, 246 (January/February 1843).

215. Ibid., 86.

216. Ibid., 86; JI, 272–73, 275 (January/February 1843); Grodzins, "Theodore Parker's 'Conference,'" 86.

217. Grodzins, "Theodore Parker's 'Conference,'" 86; the account says TP again here mentions the letters.

218. Ibid., 86–87.

219. Ibid., 87.

220. Ibid.

221. Ibid., 87, 88.

222. Ibid., 87, 88, 92. I place the statements of Ellis and Waterston here, although TP does not specify when in the conversation they were uttered; this seems, however, the most likely place for them.

223. Ibid., 87–88. That TP was wearing a wrapper is a conjecture; he reports wearing one a month earlier, during his confrontation with Putnam.

224. JI, 173 (May 1842), 246 (23 January 1843).

225. See John Ware, *Memoir of Henry Ware*, chaps. 21–22.

226. TP to E. P. Peabody, 15 July 1841, MHS; W. E. Channing to E. P. Peabody, 18 July 1840, 6 July 1841, August 1841, in W. H. Channing, *Life of William Ellery Channing*, 449–51, 453 (W. E. Channing had written Peabody because she had written him in defense of TP); Grodzins, "Theodore Parker's 'Conference,'" 85. Note that W. E. Channing also approved of Pierpont's course, dissenting only from his denunciatory language. W. H. Channing, *Memoir of Channing*, 507–8.

227. JI, 208 (5 October 1842); "A Sermon on the Death of Dr. Channing" (#301, 9 October 1842), published as *An Humble Tribute to the Memory of William Ellery Channing, D.D.* (1842), 8, 9, 11, 33. Although TP preached no sermon for H. Ware, see his praise for Ware in TP to John Ware, 2 January 1846, in *LCTP* 1:261–62.

228. TP, *Humble Tribute* (1842), 22, 25.

229. Ibid., 11, 25.

230. Roxbury Records, 7. For the books, see the JI "books read" list. For his preaching, see Grodzins and Myerson, "Preaching Record of Theodore Parker." For the number of TP's lectures, I drew off TP's Lecture Book in A-H; JI; notes on the lecture manuscripts themselves; and the Child Diary, Child Papers, MHS. I calculated as follows: TP delivered the five "Religion" lectures in five towns and the six "Sermons for the Times" in five towns (not including, in both cases, West Roxbury, where he delivered each series as part of his regular preaching); he also delivered his lecture on the "Education of the Laboring Classes" and gave other lectures on "Pythagoras" and "Temperance." In calculating the number of lectures and sermons TP wrote, I count the "Sermons for the Times" as lectures. Note that one of the articles TP wrote, his review of Hennell's "Origin of Christianity," actually appeared in the October 1843 *Dial*, a month after TP left the country.

231. *CMW*, 107–8, 220–21.

232. Review of *CMW*, "The Literary Pathfinder," tipped into JI, 290 (February/April 1843).

233. Some fascicles of *DW* (parts of volume 2) can be found at Brown University Library. In a letter to Ripley, 19 November 1858 [in *LCTP*, 1:401–3], TP says he translated the book "word for word," but in the introduction (*DW*, 1:x), he gives a more accurate picture: "In translating, I have aimed to give the sense of the author than to render his language word for word. I have not hesitated, therefore, to condense or to expand the original, as the case seemed to require. I have removed notes into the text, or placed the text in the notes, as I found it convenient for my purpose." The other quotations in the paragraph are from *DW*, 1:x, xn. See also the comments of *LCTP*, 1:195. See also Brown, *Rise of Biblical Criticism in America*, 163–69.

234. TP to Silsbee, 23 April 1841, MHS; JI, 124 (18 November 1841); TP to Silsbee, 1 January 1842, MHS; TP to Increase J. Smith, 10 October 1842, MHS; JI, 236 (23 December 1842); TP to Increase J. Smith, 10 October 1842, MHS ("Manuscript" is "M.S." in the original); JI, 124 (18 November 1841).

235. JI, 279, 281 (February/April 1843); for the offer from the church, see Roxbury Records; JK, 1 (in *LCTP*, 1:199).

236. "A Sermon of the Joys of Jesus" (#337, 3 September 1843).

237. Marianne ("Mary Anne") Dwight to Anna Q. T. Parsons, 3–5 September 1843, Brook Farm Records, MHS. I thank Joel Myerson for calling this letter to my attention.

238. "A Sermon of My Own Stewardship" (#338, 3 September 1843). There are two manuscripts, both at A-H; the first is the manuscript he preached from, the second a fair copy he made later, probably in 1845 or 1846. I have drawn quotations from the latter version because it contains obvious corrections and fills out sections that TP marked to be extemporized in the first manuscript. Some of the wording is altered from the first version, but never the sense. Excerpts from the second edition of "Of My Own Stewardship" are published in *LCTP* 1:197–99.

239. "A Sermon of My Own Stewardship" (#338, 3 September 1843; 2nd ed.), 1–4.

240. Ibid., 4–5. TP here replies to something Gannett had said to him. Shortly after the "conference" with the Boston Association, TP met Gannett on the street. He describes the encounter as follows: "[I] assured him I felt no ill nature towards the Ass[ociation]. He said I had *written* ill-natured things viz. about the H[ollis]. S[treet]. C[ouncil]. which I had called *Jesuitical*. He said 'You say the Result in council was a most Jesuitical document. I say it was a most *Christian* document.' 'Then there,' said I [, ']is an honest difference of opinion between [us].' 'Not an *hónést* difference of opinion'! was the reply." Grodzins, "Theodore Parker's 'Conference,'" 91.

241. "A Sermon of My Own Stewardship" (#338, 3 September 1843; 2nd ed.), 5–7.

242. Ibid., 8, 9.

243. Ibid., 10, 11, 12.

244. Ibid., 13–17.

245. Ibid., 17–21.

246. Ibid., 22–26.

247. Ibid., 26–28.

248. Ibid., 31–35.

249. Ibid., 39–45.

250. Ibid., 45–49.

251. Ibid., 49, 51, 52; Marianne ("Mary Anne") Dwight to Ann Q. T. Parsons, 3–5 September 1843.

252. "A Sermon of My Own Stewardship" (#338, 3 September 1843; 2nd ed.), 57–58.

253. Marianne ("Mary Anne") Dwight to Ann Q. T. Parsons, 3–5 September 1843.

254. For the weather, see E. S. Gannett Diary, 5 September 1843, Gannett Papers, MHS; JK flyleaf, described in *TPAB*, 183.

255. JK, [page undetermined], in *TPAB*, 184.

Chapter Eight

1. "Experience as a Minister," *WTP*, 13:326–27.

2. JK, 318 (25 February 1844), in *LCTP* 1:209; the only sea trip in which TP was not sick was one over the English Channel (see JL, 53 [5 August 1844]); JL, 42, 50–52,

58 (30 July, 1 August, 10 August 1844); Parkman, *Journals of Francis Parkman*, 1:174; JK, 212–14 (3 January 1844), in *LCTP*, 1:204.

3. JK, [454?] (24 May 1844), in Sanborn JK, 6–7.

4. JK and JL.

5. The date of the Parkers' arrival in Rome is difficult to determine from the surviving excerpts of TP's journal; *TPAB*, 190, says they arrived in March. Parkman, *Journals of Francis Parkman*, 173–75, indicates 17 February.

6. See also TP to Isaac Parker, 12 February 1844, MHS.

7. Parkman, *Journals of Francis Parkman*, 1:167.

8. Baker, *Fortunate Pilgrims*, 71–72; Parkman, *Journals of Francis Parkman*, 1:167–68; TP to Isaac Parker, 12 February 1844, MHS.

9. Parkman, *Journals of Francis Parkman*, 1:168–69; TP to Isaac Parker, 12 February 1844, MHS.

10. Parkman, *Journals of Francis Parkman*, 1:173–75.

11. JK, 300 (18 February 1844) in *LCTP* 1:207; Parkman, *Journals of Francis Parkman*, 1:175.

12. Parkman, *Journals of Francis Parkman*, 1:175.

13. This is an educated guess based on the numbers provided in Baker, *Fortunate Pilgrims*, 20.

14. JI, 25 (January 1841); Howe, *Reminiscences*, 159. Note that in the MSS of "Expediency and Morality," the first of the "Six Plain Sermons," when TP gives examples of heroically moral behavior, he interlines "(Story of S. G. H.)" ("Of Expediency & Morality or the LAW OF THE LORD" [#305], 29). Whether he added this note in 1842, when he wrote the discourse, or in 1844, when he revised it, is unclear.

15. Howe, *Reminiscences*, 160; TP to G. D. Cabot, 27 March 1844, MHS.

16. Samuel Gridley Howe to Charles Sumner, 28 March 1844; Howe Papers, Houghton; for the friendship of Samuel Gridley Howe and TP, see Grodzins, " 'Dear Chev.' "

17. See JL, 52 (24 July 1844), when TP mentions "the English like ourselves with a Murray in red under their arm." A *Guide de Florence* (Florence, 1839) appears in the catalogue of TP's library.

18. *Handbook for Travellers on the Continent*, xxii.

19. JK, 215 (4 January 1844); JL, 4 (3 July 1844); Baker, *Fortunate Pilgrims*, 142; TP to Silsbee, 24 March 1844, MHS.

20. Carlyle to Emerson, 31 October 1843, Jane Welsh Carlyle to Thomas Carlyle, 14 August 1845, *Letters of Thomas and Jane Welsh Carlyle*, 16:164, 19:144. Note that Dickens had been to Boston in February 1842, and TP had been to a dinner given for him, but Dickens was ill and could not attend; TP recorded in his journal that he was "not a bit disappointed" to have missed the famous novelist (JI, 157 (2 February 1842). TP liked Dickens's books, but did not love them, being himself no great fan of fiction.

21. TP to Francis, 18 March 1844, in *CTPCF*, 352; see JK, 316 (ca. 23 February 1844), in *LCTP* 1:209; JK, 348 (6–8 March 1844), in *LCTP* 1:210.

22. For Erfeurth, see JK [page undetermined] (13 June 1844), in Sanborn JK, 19; the Parkers wanted to visit the cloister, but their schedule did not permit them. For Wartburg, see JK [page undetermined] (14 June 1844), in Sanborn JK, 20.

23. *Handbook for Travellers on the Continent*, 359; JK, ca. 486 (5–6 June 1844), in Sanborn JK, 10–13.

24. *LCTP* 1:202; TP to Francis, 17 July 1844, in CTPCF, 422–24.

25. TP to Francis, 17 July 1844, in CTPCF, 419.

26. F. C. Baur, who had been Strauss's professor, thought he was a Christian and his influence was great; W. M. L. De Wette thought that Strauss was a Christian only by a broad definition and that his influence was mainly popular; Heinrich Ewald, Karl Ullman, and Karl Nitzsch all denied Strauss was a Christian (to the last belongs the "gar und gar unchristliche" remark); Ewald added that Strauss's influence was over. See JK [page undetermined] (19 June 1844), Sanborn JK, 22 [Ullman]; ca. 535 (24 June 1844), in Sanborn JK, 33 [Ewald]; ca. 525 (25 June 1844), in Sanborn JK, 38 [Baur]; JL, 3 (2 July 1844) [De Wette]; JL, 35 (26 July 1844) [Nitzsch]. For TP and Strauss's room, see JK (25 June 1844), in Sanborn JK, 35.

27. JK, [440?] (ca. 18–24 May 1844), in *LCTP* 1:215–16. Schelling was not actually a professor at Berlin, but a member of the Academy of Sciences, and so had a right to lecture.

28. *TPAB*, 205.

29. TP to Francis, 17 July 1844, in CTPCF, 420.

30. JL, 2 (3 July 1844); TP to Francis, 17 July 1844, in CTPCF, 420.

31. TP to Francis, 17 July 1844, in CTPCF, 420; JL, 4 (3 July 1844). Note that TP ran into De Wette again some weeks later at the German spa of Weisbaden (JL, 32 [24 July 1844]).

32. JK, 429–[432?] (13 May 1844), in *LCTP* 1:214–15. I do not discuss the events of the day in sequence. TP first visited the graveyard, then the bridge, then the bookstore.

33. TP to Francis, 26 May 1844, in CTPCF, 383.

34. Ibid., 20 June 1844, in CTPCF, 397; JK [page undetermined] (8 June 1844) in Sanborn JK, 16.

35. *DR*, 408–35, 410, 416, 431.

36. In this, he was similar to other tourists from New England. See Franchot, *Roads to Rome*, chap. 2.

37. "A Sermon of Travels, or the Lessons which the Old World Offers the New/Of Travels, or the Impressions which the Old World Makes and the Lessons it Offers to the New" (#339–40, 8 September 1844), 44.

38. TP to Francis, 18 March 1844, in CTPCF, 353–54 (two of those he spoke with were Bishop Charles Baggs and a Father Glover, SJ; see JK, 328ff. [1 March 1844], in *LCTP* 1:211–13; JK, 365ff. [9 March 1844], in *LCTP* 1:212); JK, 333 (3 March 1844) in *LCTP* 1:210; TP to Francis, 18 March 1844, in CTPCF, 353 (see also TP to Francis, 18 March 1844, in CTPCF, 354, and TP to Francis, 28 January 1844, in CTPCF, 333).

39. TP to Francis, 28 January 1844, in CTPCF, 335; ibid., 18 March 1844, in CTPCF, 354.

40. Ibid., 18 March 1844, in CTPCF, 355; JL, 37 (17 July 1844); TP to Francis, 28 January 1844, in CTPCF, 333.

41. "A Sermon of Travels, or the Lessons which the Old World Offers the New/Of Travels, or the Impressions which the Old World Makes and the Lessons it Offers to

the New" (#339–40, 8 September 1844), 46; JL, 46 (1 August 1844); TP to Francis, 18 January 1844, in CTPCF, 333.

42. See, e.g., *DR*, 439–47.

43. TP to Francis, 18 and 23 October 1843, in CTPCF, 295–96.

44. TP to Hannah Stevenson, 31 October 1843, Houghton; TP to Francis, 18 and 23 October 1843, in CTPCF, 294–95.

45. TP to Francis, 26 May 1844, in CTPCF, 380; 12 June 1844, 395.

46. "A Sermon of Travels, or the Lessons which the Old World Offers the New/Of Travels, or the Impressions which the Old World Makes and the Lessons it Offers to the New" (#339–40, 8 September 1844), 48. "Baptism" is "Bp" in the original.

47. Ibid., 39.

48. JK [page undetermined] (May/June 1844) in *LCTP* 1:126.

49. TP to Cornelius Cowing, 19 November 1843, in *LCTP* 1:324.

50. JK, ca. 319, in *LCTP* 1:209; "A Sermon of Travels, or the Lessons which the Old World Offers the New/Of Travels, or the Impressions which the Old World Makes and the Lessons it Offers to the New" (#339–40, 8 September 1844), 37; JK, [page undetermined] (13 June 1844) in Sanborn JK, 20.

51. "A Sermon of Travels, or the Lessons which the Old World Offers the New/Of Travels, or the Impressions which the Old World Makes and the Lessons it Offers to the New" (#339–40, 8 September 1844), 33.

52. TP to Francis, 18 March 1844, in CTPCF, 350.

53. Ibid., 355; "A Sermon of Travels, or the Lessons which the Old World Offers the New/Of Travels, or the Impressions which the Old World Makes and the Lessons it Offers to the New" (#339–40, 8 September 1844), 23–25; *Trial of Theodore Parker*, 4.

54. JK, quoted in *TPAB*, 184.

55. TP to Mary and Anna North, 27 April 1844, MHS.

56. JL, 4 (4–5 July 1844); TP to Francis, 17 July 1844, in CTPCF, 423. Note that TP specifically went to see Vogt's father, a professor at Berne (as Vogt would be later), who had married a sister of Karl Follen; Follen's wife was a relative of LCP, and she had written a letter of introduction to her sister-in-law.

57. Howe, *Reminiscences*, 162; see JO, 459–60 (5 August 1854), about two captive bears, whose habits he describes in detail; in JO, 530 (November 1854), TP proposes the paper for the Boston Society of Natural History.

58. Parkman, *Journals of Francis Parkman*, 175.

59. JI, 165 (20 February 1842). See also his New Year's resolutions for 1840, the first three of which are: "1. Bear outrage better 2. Reply not to wicked words 3. Forgive wrongs and forget them." JN, 286 (January 1840).

60. Caroline Healey Dall, for example, who became acquainted with LCP in the early 1840s, never saw her angry until 1864, and then was very surprised by LCP's mood. Dall Diary, 5 February 1864, Dall Papers, MHS.

61. LCP to Edouard Desor, 24 August 1863, State Archives of Neuchâtel.

62. JM, 85 (May/Jun 1845). "Heaven" is "Hn." in the original.

63. Ibid., 320 (August 1846); JO, 630 (November 1855).

64. Ibid., 686 (16 August 1856).

65. TP to Francis, 28 January 1844, in CTPCF, 336.

66. JI, 334 (11 October 1844).

67. TP to EPP, 5 February 1859, Antiochiana, Antioch College Library.

68. TP to Sarah Clarke, 28 April 1844, MHS; JL, 73 (August 1844); Mackintosh, *Personal Recollections*, 10.

69. Mackintosh, *Personal Recollections*, 11; Dall Diary, 8 September 1844, MHS.

70. Dall Diary, 8 September 1844, Dall Papers, MHS; "A Sermon of Travels, or the Lessons which the Old World Offers the New/Of Travels, or the Impressions which the Old World Makes and the Lessons it Offers to the New" (#339–40, 8 September 1844). Note that in summarizing this sermon, I do not discuss TP's arguments in the same order he presents them.

71. "A Sermon of Travels, or the Lessons which the Old World Offers the New/Of Travels, or the Impressions which the Old World Makes and the Lessons it Offers to the New" (#339–40, 8 September 1844), 42–52.

72. Ibid., 16, 19.

73. Ibid., 22, 23.

74. Ibid., 32.

75. Ibid., 34.

76. Ibid., 29, 37, 54, 55.

77. The outline and pen versions are at A-H; see also JM, 1 (4 November 1844), 6 (10 November 1844). Note that both the outline and pen version contain notes toward the section he did not write. TP evidently planned to argue that Americans had been right to neglect the arts until they had developed the country economically, that they now needed to refine their taste and sensibilities, but that they must not expect the American government to sponsor art for them, as the European governments did for their peoples.

78. "Lessons Taught Us by the Example, History & Fate of Other Nations," 5, A-H.

79. Ibid., 6, 7.

80. Ibid., 16.

81. Ibid., 19.

82. Ibid., 21. "Nothing" is "0" in the original.

83. Ibid., 24, 27–28, 28.

84. JM, 19 (3 December 1844).

Chapter Nine

1. Quoted in Myerson, *Transcendentalists and the Dial*, 98.

2. Richardson, *Emerson*, 380 (Richardson dates this shift to 1842); JM, 4 (9 November 1844).

3. Shepard, *Alcott*, 357–80; Packer, "Transcendentalists," 478–79.

4. JM, 421 (April 1847); see also the *Diaries of Louisa May Alcott* for 1857–58, and her novel, *Work*, in which TP appears, thinly disguised, as the minister "Thomas Power"; TP to Ripley, 13 May 1859, Ripley Papers, MHS.

5. See chap. 5.

6. Walters, *American Reformers*, 53; Packer, "Transcendentalists," 485–88.

7. TP to Francis, 18 March 1844, in CTPCF, 350; JM, 26 (December 1844), 59 (7 April 1845), 91 (May 1845).

8. JM, 59 (7 April 1845); compare TP's descriptions of the decorations, which make them sound homemade and threadbare, with the glowing account of Marianne Dwight, in Dwight, *Letters*, 88–93; JM, 64 (19 April 1845); 76 (May 1845). I so far have found only one possible piece by TP for the *Harbinger*, a review of "Plato Contra Athens" in the first issue—1, no. 1 (14 June 1845): 7. Judged by subject matter, content, and style, this seems by TP, but I have no independent evidence confirming this attribution.

9. Ryan, *Orestes A. Brownson*, 300; TP to Healey [Dall], 4 April 1843; "Experience as a Minister," in *WTP* 13:314.

10. "Parkerism, or Infidelity," *Brownson's Quarterly Review* 2:2 (April 1845): 222–49; "Transcendentalism, or the Latest Form of Infidelity," *Brownson's Quarterly Review* 2:4 (July 1845): 273–323; no. 5 (October 1845): 409–41.

11. JM, 60 (9 April 1845), 118 (4 July 1845).

12. "Of Religious Rest" in *WTP* 3:311–12; originally "Of Restlessness & Rest" (#392, 31 August 1845), 10. See also TP's conversation with Clarke, recorded in JM, 60 (9 April 1845): "JF Clark thinks Brownson never felt a religious truth—but as only thought thereon—& therefore changes so often. This seems nearly true."

13. "The Present Position of Unitarianism," *CE* 36:3 (May 1844), 407.

14. Ibid., 406–9. Interestingly, Gannett distinguishes between the "transcendental movement," which he dismisses as a "foolish, pert, and troublesome" philosophical system, and the more dangerous "assailant movement," that is, the "attack upon the common foundations of faith"—of which the *DR* was the prominent example. Gannett was surely right that not all Transcendentalists rejected the authority of historical Christianity. Yet Transcendentalist assumptions did tend logically to undermine the distinction between natural and miraculous inspiration on which that authority rested.

15. "Of Overcoming Evil" (#347, 27 October 1844), 1; JM, 14 (ca. 19 November 1844), 8 (ca. 6 November 1844).

16. "A Sermon of the Evil Tongue" (#349, 20 October 1844).

17. JI, 354 (25 October 1844).

18. Ibid.

19. JM, 25 (11 December 1844).

20. Ibid., 16 (23 November 1844); "A Sermon of the Lord's Ark" (#355, 9 December 1844). Two other sermons which touch on the theme of being trapped in a small village are "A Sermon of Prayer & Walk with God" (#346, 6 October 1844) and "The Power of a Central Idea, for the New Year 1845" (#359, 5 January 1845).

21. Hannah Stevenson, who would later join TP's household, and her sister, Margaret Stevenson McKean, would walk out from Boston every week (see the memorial notices of her by Samuel Longfellow in the *Unity*, 16 July 1889, clipping in the first volume of the second set of Thayer Albums [unpaginated], BPL); JI, 335 (13 October 1844).

22. JM, 31 (16 January 1845); I have reconstructed TP's lecture schedule principally from JM, 42 and his Lecture Book at A-H.

23. JM, 16 (23 November 1844).

24. TP to Sargent, 27 October 1844, Dr. Williams's Library, London.

25. For an account of Sargent's life, and a portrait, see Sargent and Sargent, *Epes Sargent of Gloucester and His Descendants*, 162–65; some information can also be gleaned from *In Memoriam: John Turner Sargent*.

26. There was also a famous Unitarian Chapel for the Poor on Warren Street, which operated independently of the Fraternity, and various chapels sponsored by evangelical denominations.

27. John Turner Sargent, *Ministry at Suffolk St. Chapel*, 14.

28. Sargent to *Boston Courier*, 23 June 1841 (published 24 June 1841).

29. Ibid.

30. "Report of Executive Committee," 5 January 1845, in *CR* and *CW*, 18 January 1845; Sargent to *Boston Courier*, 14 January 1845, reprinted in *CR* and *CW*, 18 January 1845.

31. Sargent to *Boston Courier*, 23 June 1841 (published 24 June 1841); John Turner Sargent, *Ministry at Suffolk St. Chapel*, 4; Sargent to *Boston Courier*, 14 January 1845, reprinted in *CR* and *CW*, 18 January 1845.

32. See Diary of Daniel and Mary Child, Daniel F. Child Papers, MHS.

33. John Turner Sargent, *Obstacles to Truth*, 9; "On Strife & Peace in the Christian Churches" (#343, 27 October 1844); "Of Christian Advancement" (#350, 27 October 1844), published in *WRS*; "Order of the Executive Committee," 22 November 1844, in *CR* and *CW*, 18 January 1845.

34. "Report of the Executive Committee," 5 January 1845, in *CR* and *CW*, 18 January 1845; Order of the Executive Committee, 22 November 1844; in *CR* and *CW*, 18 January 1845.

35. Sargent to the Executive Committee, 22 November 1844, in *CR* and *CW*, 18 January 1845.

36. Ibid.

37. J. I. T. Coolidge et al. to Sargent, 25 November 1844, in *CR* and *CW*, 18 January 1845.

38. Sargent to the Executive Committee, 29 November 1844, in *CR* and *CW*, 18 January 1845.

39. Ibid.

40. J. I. T. Coolidge et al. to Sargent, 7 December 1844, in *CR* and *CW*, 18 January 1845.

41. TP to Sargent, 18 December 1844, A–H; *Ministry at Suffolk Street Chapel*, 19.

42. Sargent to the Executive Committee, 5 October 1844, in *CR*, 23 November 1844.

43. Thomas Wentworth Higginson, in *In Memoriam: John Turner Sargent*, 10–11.

44. John Turner Sargent, *Obstacles to Truth*, 4.

45. Ibid., 8, 9.

46. Ibid., 10–11.

47. Clarke Journal, 9 December 1844, Perry-Clarke Collection, MHS; John Turner Sargent, *Ministry at Suffolk St. Chapel*, 38–39, 12.

48. *CR* and *CW*, 18 January 1845.

49. Sargent to *Boston Courier*, 14 January 1845, reprinted in *CR* and *CW*, 18 January 1845.

50. Waterston to the Executive Committee, 3 January 1845, in *CR* and *CW*.

51. Sargent confessed authorship in letters to the *CR* and *CW*, 1 March 1845.

52. [John Turner Sargent,] *True Position of Theodore Parker*, 5-13.

53. Ibid., 14, 15.

54. Ibid., 16, 19.

55. Ibid., 22. Note that years later, Sargent again uses the ghost of Hamlet's father to indicate that his prophecy was fulfilled; see [John Turner Sargent,] *Crisis of Unitarianism*, 5, 13-14.

56. *TPAB*, 213-14; *Boston Post*, reprinted in the *New York Herald*, tipped into JI, 377 (ca. January 1845).

57. TP first had delivered the sermon ten days earlier for a communion service in West Roxbury.

58. *SAOS*, 1:2, 2-3.

59. Ibid., 1:4-5.

60. Ibid., 1:6.

61. Ibid., 1:7.

62. Ibid., 1:9-10.

63. Ibid., 1:11, 12, 13, 14.

64. Ibid., 1:12, 15.

65. JM, 21 (17 January 1845); *New York Herald*, 29 December 1844, pasted into JI, 377 (ca. January 1845).

66. E. S. Gannett Diary, 26 December 1844, Gannett Papers, MHS.

67. Gannett, "The Present Position of Unitarianism," *CE* 36:3 (May 1844), 408n.

68. In the Gannett Papers, Houghton Library; I thank Guy Litton for calling these documents to my attention. One draft is in pencil; a longer one is in pen. I judge the latter to be the final version. There are differences in content between the two. The first protests against TP for abusing the Thursday Lecture by using it to promote views "subversive of all confidence in Scripture, as well as of faith in our [Lord Jesus Christ] as a specially commissioned messenger of God to the world." TP is asked to assure the Association that he will not use the Lecture again "for such a purpose"; if he declines to give such assurance, the protest of the Association is to be published in the Unitarian newspapers.

69. Gannett to TP, 7 January 1845, Gannett Papers, MHS; TP to ESG, 15 January 1845, MHS.

70. Clarke Journal, 13 January 1845, Perry-Clarke Collection, MHS. The speaker of these words is listed as "Bellows"; this may have been the well-known Henry Whitney Bellows, but he was not a member of the Association, being settled in New York City. Yet I know of no minister named Bellows settled in or near Boston.

71. BA Records, 13 January 1845; Clarke Journal, 13 January 1845, Perry-Clarke Collection, MHS.

72. "J. F. C." [Clarke], "Article in the 'New Englander' on Liberal Christianity," *CW*, 7 December 1844; "Shall Unitarians Adopt the Exclusive System? A Reply to 'R. C. S.,'" *CW*, 11 January 1845.

73. Hale, *James Freeman Clarke*, 39; "J. F. C." [Clarke], Review of [Thomas], *A Rejected Article, in Reply to Parker's Review of 'Hennell on the origin of Christianity,'* *CW*,

3 February 1844 (pasted into JI, 320). Thomas is identified as the author on the presentation copy he gave to the Harvard library, now found at A-H (the item is catalogued as being by E. S. Gannett, but the style is nothing like his). Thomas wrote the piece in reply to TP's laudatory *Dial* article on Hennell, whom Thomas dismissed as a deist. Thomas rather naively submitted his polemic to the *Dial*, where Emerson predictably rejected it, then to the *CE*, where it was also rejected, before publishing it as a pamphlet.

74. "J. F. C." [Clarke], Review of [Thomas], *A Rejected Article, in Reply to Parker's Review of 'Hennell on the origin of Christianity,'* *CW*, 3 February 1844 (pasted into JI, 320).

75. Merriam, *Noah Porter*, 57–58, 124–25; [Porter], "Theodore Parker," *New Englander* 2:3 (July 1844); [Porter], "Theodore Parker and the Liberal Christians," *New Englander* 2:4 (October 1844).

76. TP to "the writer of the article in the New Englander" [Porter], 1 October 1844, MHS; JM, 91 (30 May 1845); Merriam, *Noah Porter*, 121–22; "Experience as a Minister," *WTP*, 13:328.

77. *CR*, 16 November 1844; "J. F. C." [Clarke], "Article in the New Englander on 'Liberal Christianity,'" *CW*, 30 November 1844.

78. *CR*, 16 November 1844, 23 November 1844, 30 November 1844, 7 December 1844, 21 December 1844 (on the basis of style and content alone, I would guess that the first four were written by Lothrop, the fifth by Ellis); "J. F. C." [Clarke], in *CW*, 30 November 1844, 7 December 1844, 14 December 1844, 21 December 1844, 4 January 1845.

79. Porter, "Theodore Parker and Liberal Christianity," 530, 531.

80. Ibid., 530–31.

81. [Lothrop], "The Tendencies of Liberal Christianity," *CR*, 23 November 1844.

82. "J. F. C." [Clarke], "Article in the 'New Englander' on Liberal Christianity," *CW*, 7 December 1844.

83. Ibid., 30 November 1844.

84. Ibid., 7 December 1844.

85. Ibid.

86. Stone, *Life Incidents*, 57, 79–81, 91–92, 131. See also Frederick Lewis Weiss, "List of the Unitarian Churches and Their Ministers in the United States and Canada," which notes that the Sherborn Church had become Unitarian under Stone's immediate predecessors.

87. "R. C. S." [Stone], "The 'New Englander' and 'J. F. C.,'" *CW*, 21 December 1844.

88. "J. F. C." [Clarke], "Shall Unitarians Adopt the Exclusive System? A Reply to 'R. C. S.,'" *CW*, 4 January 1845. Clarke's last piece on Porter appeared on 4 January 1845.

89. Ibid.

90. "J. F. C." [Clarke], "Expediency of the Exclusive System: Reply to R. C. S.," *CW*, 18 January 1845.

91. A rejoinder to Clarke's first reply.

92. "R. C. S." [Stone], "The Fellowship of Theodore Parker," *CW*, 11 January 1845.

93. "J. F. C." [Clarke], "Expediency of the Exclusive System: Reply to R. C. S.,"

CW, 18 January 1845; see TP, Roxbury Records, 8: "Some correspondence had taken place between [Clarke] & me."

94. "R. C. S." [Stone], "Fellowship with Theodore Parker, Reply to 'J. F. C.,'" *CW*, 1 February 1845; see also the letters and columns of R. C. S. and J. F. C. in *CW*, 8 March 1845, 15 March 1845, 22 March 1845, 29 March 1845, 12 April 1845; Stone, *Life Incidents*, 142–43, 160–61.

95. Hale, *James Freeman Clarke*, 146; Clarke, *Church of the Disciples*, 31.

96. Church Journal, Church of the Disciples Records, MHS; Clarke in *CW*, 8 February 1845.

97. Clarke in *CW*, 8 February 1845; George Channing in *CW*, 15 February 1845; [George Channing], "Church of the Disciples," *CW*, 1 February 1845 (see also Hale, *James Freeman Clarke*, 150); [George Channing], [editorial], *CW*, 15 February 1845; [George Channing], "Church of the Disciples," *CW*, 1 February 1845; Clarke, "Church of the Disciples," *CW*, 22 February 1845; [George Channing], [editorial], *CW*, 15 February 1845. See also [George Channing], "Our own position—Parkerism," *CR*, 11 January 1845.

98. [George Channing], "Church of the Disciples," *CW*, 1 February 1845.

99. Clarke, "Church of the Disciples," *CW*, 8 February 1845 (see also Clarke Journal, 12 January 1845, Perry-Clarke Papers, MHS); [George Channing], "Church of the Disciples," *CW*, 1 February 1845.

100. Clarke Journal, 15 January 1845, Perry-Clarke Papers, MHS; [George Channing], "Church of the Disciples," *CW*, 1 February 1845; Clarke, "Church of the Disciples," *CW*, 8 February 1845.

101. [George Channing], "Church of the Disciples," *CW*, 1 February 1845; Clarke Journal, 17 January 1845, Perry-Clarke Collection, MHS.

102. Annals of the Church [of the Disciples], week of 12 January, Perry-Clarke Collection, MHS; Clarke, "Church of the Disciples," *CW*, 8 February 1845; [George Channing], "Church of the Disciples," *CW*, 1 February 1845.

103. JM, 32 (17 January 1845). Clarke's supporters, for their part, apparently wrote TP, urging him to accept the invitation; see Roxbury Records, 9.

104. See [George Channing], "Church of the Disciples," *CW*, 1 February 1845.

105. Clarke Journal, 19 January 1845, Perry-Clarke Collection, MHS; [George Channing], [editorial], *CW*, 15 February 1845; Clarke, "Church of the Disciples," *CW*, 22 February 1845; [George Channing], "Church of the Disciples," 1 February 1845; Clarke, "Church of the Disciples," *CW*, 8 February 1845.

106. Clarke, "Church of the Disciples," *CW*, 8 February 1845; Annals of the Church [of the Disciples], 19 January 1845, Perry-Clarke Collection, MHS; Clarke Journal, 19 January 1845, Perry-Clarke Collection, MHS; [George Channing], "Church of the Disciples," *CW*, 1 February 1845.

107. Annals of the Church [of the Disciples], 22 January 1845, Perry-Clarke Collection, MHS; [George Channing], "Church of the Disciples," *CW*, 1 February 1845.

108. Annals of the Church [of the Disciples], 23 January 1845, Perry-Clarke Collection, MHS; [George Channing], "Church of the Disciples," *CW*, 1 February 1845. Channing only identifies himself as "one of the earliest members of the Church"; but see Clarke, "Church of the Disciples," *CW*, 8 February 1845.

109. "W. F. C." [William F. Channing], "The Church of the Disciples," *CW*, 8 February 1845.

110. See [George Channing], "Church of the Disciples," *CW*, 1 February 1845; Browne, *Sketch of the Life of Governor Andrew*, 19–21. The account in Browne evidently draws from Clarke's report of Andrew's speech.

111. Browne, *Sketch of the Life of Governor Andrew*, 19. See also Julia Ward Howe, *Reminiscences*, 262; [George Channing], "Church of the Disciples," *CW*, 1 February 1845.

112. [George Channing], "Church of the Disciples," *CW*, 1 February 1845.

113. Ibid.; see also Clarke, "Church of the Disciples," *CW*, 8 February 1845.

114. I attempt a plausible reconstruction of Clarke's remarks from the two variant accounts of them in [George Channing], "Church of the Disciples," *CW*, 1 February 1845, and Clarke, "Church of the Disciples," *CW*, 8 February 1845.

115. [George Channing], "Church of the Disciples," *CW*, 1 February 1845.

116. Ibid.; see also Annals of the Church [of the Disciples], 23 January 1845, Perry-Clarke Collection, MHS.

117. Hale, *James Freeman Clarke*, 152n; Roxbury Records, 9; "Of the Excellency of Goodness" (#351, 10 November 1844), published as *The Excellence of Goodness, A Sermon Preached in the Church of the Disciples*; "A Sermon of Xn Advancement" (#350, 27 October 1844), was published forty-eight years later as "Christian Advancement" in *WRS*, 130–44 (the text, edited by Frank Sanborn, is not always reliable); Fuller, "The Excellence of Goodness," in *Essays on American Life and Letters*, 284.

118. Annals of the Church [of the Disciples], 3 February 1845, Perry-Clarke Collection, MHS. Originals of the resolutions presented at this meeting are found in the Church of the Disciples Papers, A-H.

119. Henry B. Rogers et. al. to the Church of the Disciples, 15 February 1845, in Church of the Disciples Papers, A-H; Clarke, *Church of the Disciples*, 31–32.

120. Clarke to Henry B. Rogers et al. [draft], 22 February 1845, Church of the Disciples Papers, A-H; Clarke, "Church of the Disciples," *CW*, 8 February 1845; [Anon.], "Church of the Disciples," *CW*, 1 March 1845.

121. Waterston, *True Position of the Christian Church in Relation to the Age*, 35–40. Note how the title of Waterston's sermon plays off the title of John Turner Sargent's pamphlet, *True Position of Theodore Parker*.

122. *CR*, 1 March 1845.

123. "A Dialogue," *CR*, 8 February 1845.

124. *CR*, 22 February 1845.

125. *CW*, 22, 29 February 1845; *CR*, 22 February 1845; *Questions Addressed to Rev. T. Parker and His Friends*. As the two papers do not mention a pamphlet, I assume the pamphlet was published later. The provenance of the *Questions* pamphlet also implicates George Channing: it seems to have originated in the *CW*. [John Turner Sargent], *Answer to "Questions."* TP, in his letters, sometimes refers to Sargent "as friend in Deed." JM, 118 (July 1845).

126. [John Turner Sargent], *Answer to "Questions,"* 7, 8, 23. I have italicized the questions, capitalized words italicized in the original questions, and taken the questions out of quotation marks. The small capitals are in the original.

127. BA Records, 27 January 1845, MHS; Clarke, Diary, 27 January 1845, in Hale, *James Freeman Clarke*, 152n; Lothrop, *Reminiscences*, 201. The proposal to expel TP is not mentioned in the BA Records, which only notes that "many amendments" were offered to Lunt's resolution.

128. Lothrop, *Reminiscences*, 201.

129. "Mr. Parker and his Views," *CE* (March 1845), 271–72; BA Records, 27 January 1845, MHS; Chandler Robbins to TP, [29 January 1845], MHS.

130. Chandler Robbins to TP, [29 January 1845], MHS; Gannett to TP, 29 January 1845, Gannett Papers, Houghton; TP to Gannett, 30 January 1845, Gannett Papers, Houghton Library; see also TP to Sargent, 30 January 1845, MHS.

131. TP to Sargent, 30 January 1845, MHS; Gannett to TP, 1 February 1845, Houghton; E. S. Gannett Diary, 4 February 1845, Gannett Papers, MHS; JM, 44 (7 February 1845); William Gannett, *Ezra Stiles Gannett*, 204–5; Gannett notes (4 February 1845), Gannett Papers, Houghton Library. (I thank Guy Litton for calling this document to my attention, which I interpret slightly differently. I infer the questions TP was asked from the answers Gannett records that he gave.)

132. Gannett notes (4 February 1845), Gannett Papers, Houghton Library (italics mine).

133. Ibid.

134. JM, 44 (7 February 1845); Gannett, "Mr. Parker and His Views," *CE* 38, no. 2 (March 1845): 251–74, 256n, 255, 253–54.

135. *Remarks on an Article*, 5; "The Christian Examiner and Religious Miscellany, March, 1845," *CR*, 1 March 1845 (see also [Lothrop], "The Christian Examiner and Rev. Theodore Parker," *CR*, 8 March 1845); [George Channing], "Christian Examiner for March, 1845," *CW*, 8 March 1845.

136. Gannett notes (4 February 1845), Gannett Papers, Houghton Library.

137. JM, 44 (7 February 1845).

138. BA Records, 10 February 1845, MHS.

139. TP to Gannett, 15 February 1845.

140. BA Records, 24 February 1845, MHS.

141. The draft resolution is in the Gannett Papers, Houghton Library; see Nathaniel Frothingham, *Shade of the Past*; JM, 47 (1 March, 2 April 1845). There was another advantage to changing the lecture. As the "Whereas" section of Gannett's draft resolution complains, the Lecture not only had "recently presented the difficulty of . . . a virtual implication of the whole body [of this Association] in . . . opin[ion]s . . . there delivered," its connection to the Association, as an obligation of membership, had "long been a source of inconvenience" (on the back of TP to Gannett, 15 January 1845, Gannett Papers, Houghton). This concession must have been a hard one for Gannett to make; he venerated the Lecture tradition. So, too, did the grand old men of the Association. For years, Dr. Parkman had sternly informed each new member, "You, sir, shall preach the Lecture." Although most Association members were willing to defer to Parkman and Gannett on the matter, they actually resented the Lecture as a disagreeable chore. This dislike cut across all factions: TP's enemy Samuel Lothrop had tried to abolish the Lecture in 1842, while TP's ally John Pierpont considered

the Lecture "a sacrifice more costly than any profit to be derived from it would justify" (Pierpont to TP, 22 March 1845, MHS). The enemies of the Lecture seized the opportunity to get rid of it; even Pierpont voted in favor of the supposedly anti-TP measure.

142. "Tendencies of Liberal Christianity," *CR*, 23 November 1844.

143. Nathaniel Frothingham, *Deism or Christianity*, 27, 29, 33.

144. William Ware, *Righteousness before Doctrine*, 26, 27, 27–28.

145. "P.," "Ministerial Fellowship," *CW*, 22 February, 8 March 1845. Other pamphlets published that had relevance to this debate were Furness, *Exclusive Principle Considered*, and Muzzey, *Plea for Christian Spirit*. Muzzey, who came from an old Lexington family and had known TP for decades, exchanged with him on 29 June 1845.

146. *Letter to the Boston Association* (1845); JM, 47 (1 March, 2 April 1845).

147. TP to Gannett, 28 December 1845, MHS. TP recognized that it was an awkward letter for him to write, owing to the "delicacy" of his discussing a case in which he had a direct personal interest and the strains in his relationship with Gannett ("You have misunderstood my motives & intentions, even my *words* sometimes").

148. Ibid.

149. Ibid.

150. Ibid.

151. JM, 34–39 (ca. 17–24 January 1845). TP may have started this list in mid-January and finished it over the next several weeks, but it appears to have been written in one sitting.

152. *Letter to the Boston Association* (1845), 4–5.

153. Ibid., 5, 5–7.

154. Ibid., 7, 8, 9. I am slightly rearranging TP's points to give a clearer exposition.

155. Ibid., 8.

156. *Letter to the Boston Association* (1845), 10. Note that TP believed that only three members of the Boston clergy exchanged with himself (Pierpont, Sargent, and Clarke), while only three exchanged with Pierpont (Gannett, Sargent, and Clarke). According to Pierpont himself, however, this was a mistake. Pierpont still received fellowship from five Boston ministers (Gannett, Sargent, Clarke, Waterston, and Cyrus Bartol of the West Church), although from only three ministers who were on the Hollis Street Council (Gannett, Sargent, and Waterston). Pierpont to TP, 22 March 1845, MHS.

157. *Letter to the Boston Association* (1845), 18.

158. Ibid., 12–13, 18–19.

159. TP to Clarke, 8 April 1845, Clarke Family Papers, Houghton Library; Pierpont to TP, 22 March 1845, MHS; [George F. Ware], *Answers to Questions*. For Ware's identity, see the copy of this pamphlet at the Meadville/Lombard Theological School.

160. Parkman to TP, 24 March 1845, MHS.

161. TP to Parkman, 24 March 1845, MHS; Parkman to TP, 31 March 1845, MHS.

162. Grodzins, "Theodore Parker's 'Conference,' " 82; Parkman alludes to this previous mistake in Parkman to TP, 24 March 1845, MHS.

163. JM, 87 (20 May 1845). TP later heard (JM, 108 [June 45]) that his attendance at this meeting upset William Lunt, who threatened to withdraw if TP came again;

Lunt, Alexander Young, and Samuel Barrett tried to think of some way of excluding TP from the meetings, but evidently could think of none.

164. Porter also used this article to respond to some of the answers given to his earlier article, especially by Lothrop.

165. JM, 91 (30 May 1845); "Theodore Parker and the Boston Association," *New Englander* 3:2 (July 1845): 450.

166. "Theodore Parker and the Boston Association," *New Englander* 3:2 (July 1845): 453.

167. Ibid., 461.

168. Ibid., 467n.

169. JM, 133 (29 July 1845.), 161 (September 1845).

170. TP to Samuel Gridley Howe, 24 January 1845, in Grodzins, "'Dear Chev'"; JM, 40 (24 January 1845); Society Book, 28CS Papers.

171. TP's account in Roxbury Records, 11.

172. Ellis's father was among the group who invited TP to deliver the "Religion" lectures in 1841 (see chap. 6, n. 50); he was almost certainly among the "young men" who made the 1842 invitation. For his relationship to the West Roxbury church, see Mackintosh, *Personal Recollections*, 46; Society Book, 22 January 1845, 28CS Papers.

173. Society Book, 31 January 1845 ff., 28CS Papers.

174. See [John Turner Sargent], *Crisis of Unitarianism*; for wealthier families worshiping at the chapels, see Sargent to the Executive Committee of the Benevolent Fraternity, 1844.

175. Diary of Daniel and Mary Child, Daniel F. Child Papers, MHS.

176. TP to Pierpont, 15 October 1845, in *LCTP* 1:256.

177. JM, 199 (10 November 1845).

178. Ibid., 199–202 (10 November 1845); Boston Association and John Pierpont, *Letter of the Boston Association*.

179. Grodzins, "Theodore Parker and the 28th Congregational Society," 85–86.

180. Society Book, 28 January 1845, 28CS Papers.

181. Ibid., 31 January 1845, 10 February 1845, 7 February 1845, 28CS Papers.

182. JM, 45 (ca. 8–9 February 1845).

183. Society Book, 10 February 1845, 28CS Papers; TP to Sargent, 8 February 1845, MHS. TP and Sargent apparently also talked about Sargent possibly becoming a copastor with Parker, but the arrangement was never made; Sargent probably did not want the position. See John Turner Sargent, "Sympathies of Theodore Parker," *National Standard*, 12 August 1871. I thank David Pettee for calling this article to my attention.

184. JM, 46 (16 February 1845); "A Sermon of the necessity of the Religion for a State & an Individual" (#363, 16 February 1845); John Turner Sargent, *Crisis of Unitarianism*, 21.

185. JM, 46 (16 February 1845).

Chapter Ten

1. *ASAOS*, 2:335–36; *SAOS*, 1:39; [John Turner Sargent], *Answer to "Questions,"* 13; *ASAOS*, 2:325–26; quoted in [Sargent], *Answer to "Questions,"* 14.

2. JM, 122 (July 1845).

3. Ibid. "Christianity" is "Xty" in the original.

4. Ibid.

5. Two versions of this story survive. See Diary of Daniel and Mary Child, 15 September 1845, Daniel F. Child Papers, MHS; [Cheney] in *LCTP*, 1:416. See also "Of Forgiveness" (#394, 14 September 1845).

6. Dall Diary, 19 February 1846, Dall Papers, MHS.

7. BSP, 18 January 1846.

8. Some of these are rewrites of favorites from the past. Compare "A Sermon of Infidelity" (#243, 20 June 1841) with "A Discourse of Infidelity" (#366, 23 February 1843) (with note on the cover that it is "In part rewritten from 243"); "A Sermon of the Fact of Life, the Idea of Life & the Reconciliation thereof" (#279, 12 March 1842, printed in WRS, 58–71), with "A Sermon of the Idea of Life, the Fact of Life, & their Reconciliation, 2nd Edition" (#370, 7 April 1845); "Influence of Religion on Thought: A Sermon of Optimism" (#193, 13 September 1840) with "Influence of Rel[igion]. on Thought. A Sermon of Optimism" (#373, 14 April 1845) (with note to "see 198"); "A Sermon for the Strong" (#204, 6 September 1840) with "A Sermon for the Strong" (#400, 2 November 1845) (with note in BSP to "see 204"). Several other sermons have similar or identical titles as earlier sermons, but they do not seem to have been direct rewrites.

9. *SAOS* 1:40; "A Discourse of Infidelity" (#366, 23 February 1845).

10. "Christianity in contest with Heathenism/Christianity in contrast with heathenism" (#384, 29 June 1845), published in WRS, 161–77, as "Christianity in contact with Heathenism"; "Christianity as Old as the Creation, and the points it has in common with other forms of Rel[igion]" (5 October 1845); "Of the Relation of the Churches to Modern Science & Civilization" (#361, 19 January 1845; preached at the Melodeon 16 March 1845).

11. "A Sermon of Paul—Considered as a Representative of the intellectual & practical side of Xty" (#398, 19 October 1845); "Of John as representing the contemplative & mystic side of Xty" (#399, 19 October 1845).

12. "A Sermon of the Relation of Jesus of Naz[areth] to Mankind" (#381, 15 June 1845); "Of Christ as the Model-Man" (#390, 17 August 1845); "Design of the Mission of Jesus of Nazareth" (#368, 9 March 1845; preached at the Melodeon 21 September 1845).

13. JM, 181 (6 October 1845).

14. Ibid., 61 (9 April 1845); *SAOS*, 1:31; see also the *Liberator*, 9 January 1846, and JM, 227 (4 January 1846).

15. See chap. 8.

16. "A sermon of the nation/Of politics" (#357, 10 November 1844).

17. "A Sermon of the State" (#385, 5 July 1845).

18. Ibid.

19. JM, 215 (December 1845).

20. "A Sermon of Education" (#412, 1 February 1846); "Christianize" is "Xtianize" in the original. Parts of this paragraph and the next draw on Grodzins, "Theodore Parker and the 28th Congregational Society."

21. "The Mexican War," *Massachusetts Quarterly Review* 1 (1847), 47; "Of the Relation of the Churches to Modern Science & Civilization" (#361, 19 January 1845; preached at the Melodeon 16 March 1845).

22. Announcement inserted with "A Sermon of the necessity of Religion for a State & an Individual" (#363, 16 February 1845). I would guess that this announcement preceded the service, because it seems to preface the sermon.

23. "A Sermon of the Necessity of Religion for a State & an Individual" (#363, 16 February 1845).

24. "A Sermon of the Nature & Greatness of Man" (#364, 23 February 1845; preached at the Melodeon 2 March 1845).

25. "Of the Relation of the Churches to Modern Science & Civilization" (#361, 19 January 1845; preached at the Melodeon 16 March 1845).

26. "A Discourse of the Idea of a Church" (#367, 16 March 1845; preached at the Melodeon 23 March 1845). "Christianity" is "Xty" in the original.

27. "Christ" is "X" in the original.

28. JI, 315–17 (17 August 1843). For Adams being TP's congressman, see TP to J. Q. Adams, 26 January 1845, BPL.

29. TP to Mann, 17 September 1844, Mann Papers, MHS; "Of Public Instruction" (#348, 20 October 1844); JM, 21 (December 1844); TP to Samuel Gridley Howe, 24 January 1845, in Grodzins, " 'Dear Chev,' " 62.

30. TP to Sumner, 17 August 1845, Houghton. Donald, *Charles Sumner and the Coming of the Civil War*, 106–17.

31. JM, 9 (12 November 1844).

32. TP adds: "The Foreigners—I am sorry to see having so great an Influence here—will trouble come of it?" To this remark is added a note, evidently written later: "This is a mistake—the Foreigners have no more influence than is just—that of their votes & their xtr!"

33. JM, 123 (6 July 1845).

34. Ibid., 14 (19 November 1844), 4 (9 November 1844), 104 (18 June 1845); TP to Jules Michelet, 25 September 1845, MHS. The two lectures were on "Roman Slavery" and "Influence of Christianity on Roman Law and Slavery."

35. Parker Pillsbury in May, *Memoir of Samuel Joseph May*, 167.

36. JM, 137 (1 August 1845).

37. Ibid., 89 (27 May 1844).

38. "Another Sermon of Slavery" (#382, 15 June 1845; preached at the Melodeon 23 November 1845), 6 7, 13–14. TP may not have delivered the attack on the three-fifths clause at least one of the times he preached it; the passage is marked "Omit" in the manuscript.

39. TP evidently counts William Henry Harrison among the slaveholders; although Harrison had lived many years in Ohio, he grew up in Virginia.

40. "Another Sermon of Slavery" (#382, 15 June 1845; preached at the Melodeon 23 November 1845), 12, 10.

41. TP seems to have first used this parable in his Fast Day sermon for 1845, "The moral condition of our country considered with reference to a Xn standard/Moral condition of the U.S." (#371, 3 April 1845).

42. Diary of Daniel and Mary Child, 23 November 1845, Daniel F. Child Papers, MHS.

43. Society Book, 28CS Papers.

44. The following account is drawn from the Society Book, 28CS Papers; "Report of the Committee on Finding the Best and Proper Method of Forming a Society for Mr Parker," found in the Society Book, 28CS Papers; Diary of Daniel and Mary Child, 23 November 1845, Daniel F. Child Papers, MHS.

45. *SAOS*, 1:439.

46. JM, 205 (27 November 1845; I suspect this entry was misdated and was actually written on 23 November, because it starts with "Today—my friends meet in Boston—to organize more fully—with a view to my settling with them"); TP to Healey et al., in *SAOS*, 1:439–40 (original in 28CS Papers); Diary of Daniel and Mary Child, 14 December 1845, Daniel F. Child Papers, MHS.

47. *SAOS*, 1:37; Parkman to TP, 26 December 1845, MHS.

48. Clarke to TP, 9 December 1845, Clarke Family Papers, Houghton Library.

49. TP to Clarke, 14 December 1845, Clarke Family Papers, Houghton Library.

50. JM, 217 (23 December 1845); Society Book, 23 December 1845, 28CS Papers; *SAOS*, 1:441.

51. Accounts of the service appear in Diary of Daniel and Mary Child, 4 January 1846, Daniel F. Child Papers, MHS; *Liberator*, 9 January 1846. The estimate of 2,000 people comes from "J. F. C." [Clarke], Review of TP's *True Idea of a Christian Church*, *CW*, February 1846.

52. King's remarks are reported in *SAOS*, 1:440–42.

53. *SAOS*, 1:441.

54. "Idea of Christian Church" (#408, 4 January 1846); the citations come from *SAOS*.

55. *SAOS*, 1:18.

56. Ibid., 1:19.

57. Ibid., 20–21.

58. Ibid., 21–23.

59. Ibid., 30.

60. Ibid., 32–33.

61. Ibid., 35.

62. Ibid., 36.

63. Ibid., 39.

64. Ibid., 45.

65. JM, 228 (5 January 1846).

66. TP to Committee of the Second Parish, 3 January 1846, in Roxbury Records.

67. Ibid.

68. Roxbury Records. In TP's opening chronicle of his ministry, he twice indicates the date at which he was writing: on page 12, he mentions that his *Letter to the Boston Association* has not been answered as of 27 January 1846; the later part of the chronicle, meanwhile, seems to have been written after he delivered his Farewell Sermon on 8 February, as he refers to this as a past event.

69. Douglas, *Feminization of American Culture*, 28–30.

70. TP to Parish Committee, 3 January 1846.

71. Parish resolutions, 30 January 1845, in Roxbury Records. The resolutions were offered by Parker's friend and neighbor George Russell.

72. JM, 223 (27 December 1845), 226 (31 December 1845); BSP, 8 February 1846.

73. JM, 226 (31 December 1845).

74. For the weather, see Diary of Daniel and Mary Child, 8 February 1846, Daniel F. Child Papers, MHS.

75. "Sermon of Seeking the Praise of Men" (#414, 8 February 1846); Diary of Daniel and Mary Child, 8 February 1846, Daniel F. Child Papers, MHS, indicates the Child family was not present: "We learn Mr. Parker preached his farewell sermon at West Roxbury this afternoon."

76. TP to Parish Committee, 3 January 1845; "Finis/Last Sermon for the Second Parish" (8 February 1846), 2, BPL.

77. "Finis/Last Sermon for the Second Parish" (8 February 1846), 2, BPL. The mss. reads "some *thing.*"

78. Ibid., 4.

79. Ibid., 5, 6, 7.

80. Ibid., 6, 7.

81. Ibid, 7.

82. Ibid., 7, 8.

83. Ibid., 8 ("Christianity" is "Xty" in the original), 8–9.

84. Ibid., 9.

85. Ibid., 9–10. "Christian" and "Brothers" are "Xn" and "Brs" in the original.

86. Ibid., 11–12. "Christianity" is "Xty" in the original.

87. Ibid., 12.

88. Ibid., 12–13.

89. Ibid., 13.

90. Ibid., 20. "Christian" is "Xn" in the original.

91. Ibid., 16 ("unchristian" is "unxn" in the original), 21.

92. Ibid., 15; note inserted into the sermon on separate sheet.

93. Ibid., 23–24.

94. The folder is at MHS. There are two manuscripts of "A Sermon of My Own Stewardship," both at A-H; one is obviously a fair copy of the other. The fair copy includes notes that refer to an "Appendix," which is missing. The appendix apparently contains both newspaper articles and correspondence. A microfilm copy of the booklet of newspaper clippings and copied correspondence is at BPL (the original is apparently lost); the booklet is labeled "A," so I assume it was originally the "Stewardship" appendix. As I have mentioned before, I believe TP intended the marked-up copy of the first printing of the *Transient and Permanent*, which he labeled "Codex B" and which is now at Meadville/Lombard, to be the second "Stewardship" appendix.

95. The sermons have been separated (the folder, containing only the farewell sermon, is at BPL). The instructions, which were not followed, appear in BSP, p. 137.

96. Ellis to TP, 10 March, 11 March 1845, MHS.

97. TP to the President of the Unitarian Association [Gannett], 1 June 1847, A-H.

98. Ibid.

99. *SAOS*, 1:151; Gannett to TP, 18 December 1846, Gannett Papers, Houghton Library.

100. TP to Gannett, 19 December 1846, Gannett Papers, Houghton Library. Ironically, considering TP's injunction, Gannett's wife died within a week of his receiving this letter. See William Gannett, *Ezra Stiles Gannett*, 240.

101. TP to Gannett, 19 December 1846, Gannett Papers, Houghton Library.

102. "J. F. C." [Clarke], Review of TP's *True Idea of a Christian Church*, *CW*, February 1846.

103. *"Warrington" Pen-Portraits*, 506.

104. See the albums compiled by Matilda Goddard and especially those compiled by Caroline Thayer, BPL.

105. *LCTP*, 1:439–40. This paragraph and the next two draw from Grodzins, "Theodore Parker and the 28th Congregational Society: The Reform Church and the Spirituality of Reformers in Boston, 1845–1859."

106. *LCTP*, 1:444.

Afterword

1. JM, 358 (1 January 1847).

2. Chadwick, *Theodore Parker*, 160n. See also Lucy Cabot's estate records in the Norfolk County archives.

3. TP to Emerson, 31 August 1848, *LE*. That Lucy succumbed to dysentery is not stated, but this seems a reasonable inference from the timing of her death.

4. The will and codicil are in the Norfolk County Probate Records.

5. J2N, 161, 163–65 (20 August 1848); 176 (August–October 1848); 180–82 (August–October 1848); see also "more about Aunt L," J2N, 184.

6. J2N, 530 (25 October 1850), quoted in EPJ2N; J2N, 629 (27[?] March 1851), quoted in EPJ2N.

7. The lore is recorded in Chadwick, *Theodore Parker*, 160n; for the Jackson family, see Putnam and Putnam, *Hon. Jonathan Jackson*.

8. TP to F. Jackson, 17 December 1859, MHS.

9. *Liberator*, 5 June 1846; "A Sermon of War" (#429, 7 June 1846), in *SAOS* 1:46–80 (the manuscript for this sermon is missing from the A-H collection).

10. "A sermon of not letting the little ones perish" (#435, 30 August 1845), published as "A Sermon of the Perishing Classes of Boston" (*SAOS*, 1:133–62); "Treating offenders &c" (#454, 31 January 1847), published as "A Sermon of the Dangerous Classes in Society" (*SAOS*, 1:201–38; the manuscript for this sermon is missing from the A-H collection); "A Sermon of the One and the Many" (#443, 8 November 1846), 2: "The Gov[ernment] *of* all—*for* all & *by* all is the essential element wh[ich] makes it a *Democ[racy]*.,—not an Arist[ocracy]., nor a Monarchy"; "A Sermon of Merchants and their Calling/A sermon of Merchants and their Position" (#445, 22 November 1846), published as "A Sermon of Merchants." See *SAOS*, 1:163–200; on p. 186, TP writes, "The Government of all, by all, and for all, is a democracy."

11. JM, 46 (16 February 1845).

Bibliography

Manuscript Collections

Andover-Harvard Theological Library, Harvard Divinity School, Cambridge, Massa-
    chusetts
    Church of the Disciples Papers
    Theodore Parker Papers
    Twenty-Eighth Congregational Society Papers
Antiochana, Antioch College, Antioch, Ohio
    Peabody Papers
Boston Public Library, Boston, Massachusetts
    John Sullivan Dwight Papers
    Theodore Parker Papers
    Westin Family Papers
British Library, London, United Kingdom
    Charles Babbage Papers
Chapin Library, Williams College, Williamstown, Massachusetts
    Howe Papers
Dr. Williams Library, London, United Kingdom
    Unitarian Manuscripts
Harvard Archives, Harvard University, Cambridge, Massachusetts
    "Library Charging Records"
    Andrews Norton, "Lectures on Biblical Criticism"
    TP's "On the Gnostic Philosophy . . ." (Visitation Day exercise, 20 July 1836)
    TP's "Report on German Theology" (31 May 1836)
    "Records of the Philanthropic Society"
    "Records of the Theological School" (also called "Manuscript History" or "Student
        History")
    Henry Ware Jr., "Mistakes and Faults of Preaching"
Hay Library, Brown University, Providence, Rhode Island
    W. M. L. De Wette, *Critical and Historical Introduction to the Canonical Scriptures of
        the Old Testament* (manuscript of TP's translation, 1836–43)
Henry D. Huntington Library, San Marino, California

Frances Power Cobbe Papers
Thomas Wentworth Higginson Papers
Houghton Library, Harvard University, Cambridge, Massachusetts
Alcott Family Papers
Autograph File
Clarke Family Papers
Emerson Family Papers
Ezra Stiles Gannett Papers
Howe Family Papers
Andrews Norton Papers
Palfrey Family Papers
Franklin Benjamin Sanborn, "Memoir of Theodore Parker"
Franklin Benjamin Sanborn, notes on Parker's Journal K
Charles Sumner Papers
Lexington Historical Society, Lexington, Massachusetts
Parker Family Papers
"Records of the First Parish Church, 1690–1845" (1854 copy)
Library of Congress, Washington, D.C.
Theodore Parker Papers
Massachusetts Historical Society, Boston, Massachusetts
Brook Farm Records
George Dodge Cabot Papers
Daniel F. Child Papers
Caroline Wells Healey Dall Papers
George Edward Ellis Papers
Ezra Stiles Gannett Papers
Horace Mann Papers
Theodore Parker Papers
Perry-Clarke Collection
John Pierce, "Memoirs of John Pierce"
George Ripley Papers
Massachusetts State Archives, Boston, Massachusetts
Suffolk County Probate Records
Meadville/Lombard Theological School, Chicago, Illinois
Pamphlet File
New York Public Library, New York, New York
Berg Collection
Norfolk County Courthouse, Dedham, Massachusetts
Norfolk County Probate Records
State Archives of Neuchâtel, Neuchâtel, Switzerland
Edouard Desor Papers
Theodore Parker Church, West Roxbury, Massachusetts
A Collection of Psalms and Hymns for Christian Worship (with TP's marginalia)
Daguerreotype of "Theodore Parker as a Young Man"
Letters from Parker to his parishioners in West Roxbury

"Parish Membership Book" (1713–)
TP's "Record of the Second Church in Roxbury, 1837–1846"
Pew Rental Records
Thomas Cooper Library, University of South Carolina, Columbia, South Carolina
Joel Myerson Collection
University of Notre Dame Archives, Notre Dame, Indiana
Orestes A. Brownson Papers
Watertown Free Public Library, Watertown, Massachusetts
Convers Francis Papers
"Record of Church Members, Deaths, Marriages &c in Watertown (commenced
June 1819)"
West Roxbury Historical Society, West Roxbury, Massachusetts
"Diaries of Hannah Davis Richards"

Theodore Parker's Journal

Note: Parker kept a journal before November 1835, but there seems to be no surviving record of its contents. Why he assigned nonconsecutive letters to the consecutive
volumes of his journal is unclear. I have distinguished between his first and second
volume N by referring to the second as "2N" and his first and second volume P by
referring to the second as "2P"; Parker himself did not use the labels "2N" and "2P."
I also have assigned the letter "K" to the missing volume chronicling Parker's sabbatical in Europe. How Parker designated it is unknown, but he designated its companion
volume, which survives, "L."

Volume F (November 1835–November 1836)
    Missing. Can be partially reconstructed from Lydia Cabot Parker's notes, at the
    Library of Congress, and from quotations in John Weiss's *Life and Correspondence
    of Theodore Parker* (see especially the annotated page proofs of the London edition,
    at the Boston Public Library) and Octavius Brooks Frothingham's *Theodore Parker*.
Volume C (December 1836–June 1838)
    Missing. Can be partially reconstructed from Lydia Cabot Parker's notes, at the
    Library of Congress, and from quotations in John Weiss's *Life and Correspondence
    of Theodore Parker* (see especially the annotated page proofs of the London edition,
    at the Boston Public Library) and Octavius Brooks Frothingham's *Theodore Parker*.
Volume N (July 1838–December 1840)
    At Andover-Harvard; catalogued as Journal Volume 1.
Volume I (January 1841–September 1843 and fall 1844–ca. January 1845)
    At Andover-Harvard; catalogued as Journal Volume 2.
Volume K (September 1843–July 1844)
    Missing. Can be partially reconstructed from Franklin Sanborn's notes, at the
    Houghton Library, Harvard University, and quotations in John Weiss's *Life and
    Correspondence of Theodore Parker* (see especially the annotated page proofs of the
    London edition, at the Boston Public Library) and Octavius Brooks Frothingham's
    Theodore Parker.

Volume L (July 1844–September 1844)

At the Massachusetts Historical Society; catalogued as Volume 1 of the Theodore Parker Papers.

Volume M (November 1844–October/November 1847)

At the Massachusetts Historical Society; catalogued as Volume 2 of the Theodore Parker Papers.

Volume 2N (December 1847–March 1851)

Missing. Can be partially reconstructed from Lydia Cabot Parker's notes, at the Library of Congress, and from quotations in John Weiss's *Life and Correspondence of Theodore Parker* (see especially the annotated page proofs of the London edition, at the Boston Public Library) and Octavius Brooks Frothingham's *Theodore Parker*. Two additional quotations appear in Franklin Sanborn, *Dr. S. G. Howe*.

Volume O (May 1851–October 1856)

At Andover-Harvard; catalogued as Journal Volume 3.

Volume P (November 1856–January 1859)

Missing. Can be partially reconstructed from Lydia Cabot Parker's notes, at the Library of Congress, and from quotations in John Weiss's *Life and Correspondence of Theodore Parker* (see especially the annotated page proofs of the London edition, at the Boston Public Library) and Octavius Brooks Frothingham's *Theodore Parker*.

Volume 2P (March 1859–January/February 1860).

At Andover-Harvard; catalogued as Journal Volume 4.

Theodore Parker's Published Writings, 1832–1846

Note: Periodical pieces (i.e., articles, poems), books, and nonsermon pamphlets are listed by when they were printed. Sermons are listed by when they were preached. I have identified many anonymous or pseudonymous pieces; these attributions have never been made on stylistic grounds alone. Either I have located a manuscript or found evidence of Parker's authorship in Parker's journal or correspondence. I provide the location of the manuscript or the evidence with the entry for each item, except in the case of the pseudonymous pieces Parker wrote for the *CR*. I base my attribution of these, in part, on Parker's list of the pseudonymns he used for his *CR* publications; the list appears in Lydia C. Parker's notes to Parker's lost Journal C. An asterisk by the title indicates that a complete citation cannot be provided.

1834

"Shall I Seek to Please Men, or God?," by "T. P.," *CR* 14, no. 30 (26 July): 118.

"Prayer ('God of the night, thy sun has set')" [poem], by "T. P.," *CR* 14, no. 13 (8 November): 52.

1835

"A King's Return ('' T was night,—a glorious eastern summer night')" [poem], by "T. P.," *CR* 14, no. 25 (31 January): 100.

"Morning Hymn ('Great God, who giv'st the morning light')" [poem], by "T. P.," *CR* 14, no. 32 (21 March): 128.

"God ('Thou viewless spirit! where is thy secret home')" [poem], by "T. P.," *CR* 14, no. 41 (23 May): 164.

"Translation and Exposition. Matthew XV.1–20. *Traditions of the Elders*," *SI* 5, no. 3 (August): 97–100. This issue of the *SI* is undated, and the magazine had been published irregularly for some time previously; a notice of this issue appears, however, in *CR* 14, no. 52 (8 August): 207. See Ezra Stiles Gannett to George Ellis, 16 June 1835, Ellis Papers, MHS, in which Gannett transfers editorship of the *SI* to a committee of theological school students (TP, Ellis, and William Silsbee).

"Translation and Exposition. Matthew XV.21–28. *The Canaantish Woman*," *SI* 5, no. 3 (August): 101–3.

"Traditions of the Elders," *SI* 5, no. 3 (August): 103–7.

"The Alleged Mistake of the Apostles," *SI* 5, no. 4 (1 October): 161–70. There was no issue of the *SI* for September 1835. According to an announcement in the August issue, the issues for October, November, and December were to appear on the first of each month.

"The Book of Job," *SI* 5, no. 4 (1 October): 180–90; no. 5 (1 November): 226–40; no. 6 (December): 247–51.

" 'Where Heaven is Found' ('Is there a step the soul can take')" [poem], by "T. P.," *CR* 14, no. 60 (3 October): 234.

"Evening Skies ('Those evening skies, those evening skies')" [poem], by "T. P.," *CR* 14, no. 61 (10 October): 244.

"My Childhood's Home ('My childhood's home! where art thou now?')" [poem], by "T. P.," *CR* 14, no. 66 (14 November): 264.

"Sabbath ('Hail, holy Sabbath day!')" [poem], by "T. P.," *CR* 14, no. 66 (14 November): 264.

"Translation and Exposition. Matthew XVII.1–13," *SI* 5, no. 6 (1 December): 241–47.

"The Forest ('Purple daylight is fading')" [poem], by "T. P.," *CR*, 14, no. 69 (5 December): 276. See JF, 19 (November 1835).

"The Shipwreck of Sin," by "T. P.," *CR* 14, no. 70 (12 December): 280.

1836

"Epistle to the Thessalonians," *SI* 6, no. 1 (15 January): 33–40.

"Introduction to the Second Epistle to the Thessalonians," *SI* 6, no. 1 (15 January): 64–66.

"A Vision ('A vision came upon me, and behold!')" [poem], by "T. P.," *CR* 15, no. 6 (6 February): 24. See JF, 82 (ca. January 1836).

"The Meaning of the Word Angel in the New Testament," *SI* 6, no. 2 (15 February): 58–64; no. 3 (March): 111–20. The first part of this article is reprinted in the *CR* for 27 February 1836.

"The Song of Deborah and Barak (Translated from the German of John Gottfried von Herder)," *SI* 6, no. 2 (15 February): 67–77.

"Exposition of I Peter III.17–20," *SI* 6, no. 2 (15 February): 77–80.

"The Temptation of Jesus (Translated from the German of Dr. Christopher Frederick Ammon)," *SI* 6, no. 2 (15 February): 80–84.

"The Snow ('How beautiful the snow, the spotless snow!')" [poem], by "Agapa," *CR* 15, no. 11 (12 March): 44.

"Translation and Exposition. Matthew XVIII.21–35," *SI* 6, no. 3 (15 March): 97–101.

"The Epistle to the Galations," *SI* 6, no. 3 (15 March): 101–11.

"Introduction to the First Epistle to the Corinthians," *SI* 6, no. 4 (15 April): 160–70; no. 5 (May): 209–17.

"Remarks upon John IV.13,14, and VI.35 (Translated from the German of Christopher Ullman, Professor in the University of Heidelberg)," *SI* 6, no. 4 (15 April): 170–73.

"Translation and Exposition of Isaiah LII.13–LII.12," *SI* 6, no. 4 (15 April): 174–90.

"A Symbol ('I saw a tree of giant trunk')" [poem], by "Agapa," *CR* 15, no. 16 (16 April): 64.

"A Prayer ('Great God! thy servant fain would bow')" [poem], by "Agapa," *CR* 15, no. 17 (23 April): 68. See JF, 168 (April 1836).

"A Prayer ('Help me, my God, to lift mine eye')" [poem], by "Agapa," *CR* 15, no. 19 (7 May): 76. See JF, 178 (April 1836).

"Remarks upon Several Passages in Isaiah LII.13–LII.12," *SI* 6, no. 5 (15 May): 203–8.

"Conjectures upon the Original Memoirs which Moses Made Use of to Compose the Book of Genesis (Translated from the French of [Jean] Astruc)," *SI* 6, no. 5 (15 May): 218–26; 7, nos. 1 and 2 (15 July/15 August): 23–31, 80–94. The July and August 1836 issues of the *SI* were published together. See JF, 185 (6 May 1836).

"How Ought the Bible to be Read?," *SI* 6, no. 5 (15 May): 226–34.

"Spring ('Once more the fields are gaily green')" [poem], by "T. P.," *CR* 15, no. 21 (21 May): 84. See JF, 151 (ca. March 1836).

"Fellow Students ('I saw two Students: arm in arm')" [poem], by "Agapa," *CR* 15, no. 22 (28 May): 88. See JF, 152 (ca. March 1836).

"A Report on German Theology read before the Philanthropic Society in Divinity College, Harvard University" (31 May). Manuscript in Harvard Archives. Printed in Kenneth Cameron, *Transcendentalist Epilogue*, 2:706–20.

"Translation and Exposition, Matthew XX.17–24," *SI* 6, no. 6 (15 June): 241–47.

"Hug's Introduction to the New Testament (Translated from the third German edition, by D. Fosdick)," *SI* 6, no. 6 (15 June): 261–73.

"On the Beauties of the Old Testament. (From the French of [J. E.] Cellerier)," *SI* 6, no. 6 (15 June): 280–82.

"The Voice of a Flower ('I bow before thee, little Flower')" [poem], by "Agapa," *CR* 15, no. 26 (25 June): 104.

"Evening ('How sweetly from the western sky')" [poem], by "T. P.," *CR* 15, no. 27 (2 July): 108. See JF, 183 (April/May 1836). Reprinted in *LCTP*, 1:83; *WTP*, vol. 13.

"The Laws of Moses," *SI* 7, nos. 1 and 2 (15 July/15 August): 1–23, 60–80; no. 3 (15 September): 103–14; no. 4 (15 October): 159–78; nos. 5 and 6 (15 November/15 December): 210–27, 258–71. The November and December 1836 issues of the *SI* were published together.

"The Rationale of Religious Enquiry, or the question stated of Reason, the Bible and the Church, by James Martineau," *SI* 7, nos. 1 and 2 (15 July/15 August): 94–96.

"Has Every Man a Soul?" [parable], by "Z.," *CR* 15, no. 29 (16 July): 116.

"To Prayer ('To prayer, to prayer,—'Tis break of day')" [poem], by "Agapa," *CR* 15, no. 30 (23 July): 120.

"Translation and Exposition, Matthew XXII.1–22," *SI* 7, no. 3 (15 September): 97–103.

"The Gnostic Philosophy, and Allusions to it in the New Testament," *SI* 7, no. 3

(15 September): 136–44; no. 4 (15 October): 145–51. Manuscript in the Harvard Archives; this was TP's Visitation Day exercise (20 July 1836).

" 'The humble pile our fathers raised' " [poem], *CR* 15, no. 38 (17 September): 151. See Francis to TP, 18 August 1836, in CTPCF, 100. This hymn, one of the few early poems published over TP's name, was sung at the dedication of Convers Francis's new church in Watertown, 7 September 1836.

"Evangelical History, or the Books of the New Testament, with a General Introduction, a Preface to Each Book, and Notes Explanatory and Critical. By Alden Bradford," *SI* 7, no. 4 (15 October): 151–56. TP wrote to his fellow *SI* editor William Silsbee that he had been obliged to write all the material for the October number of the *SI*. See TP to Silsbee, 16 September 1836, MHS.

"Translation and Exposition. Matth. XXII.23–46," *SI* 7, no. 4 (15 October): 178–86.

"Translation and Exposition. Matth. XXIII.1–39. *Jesus rebukes the hypocrisy of the Pharisees, and Fortells the destruction of Jerusalem*," *SI* 7, no. 4 (15 October): 201–4; nos. 5 and 6 (November/December): 205–10.

"The Godly Student of Theology, and How He Deporteth Himself," by "Agapa," *CR* 15, no. 42 (15 October): 166; no. 43 (22 October): 168. A clipping of the part of this piece published on 15 October is pasted into JI, 321.

"Einlieben. Ein Märchen, von das nacht-buch [*sic*] Gottesgabe von Thiergarten, (a Romantic Tale, from the night-book of Gottesgabe Von Thiergarten)," *American Monthly Magazine* 8, no. 5 (November): 458–61. See list of publications, JC. See also JF, 289–94, noted in *TPAL*, 80–81: "History and Spirit of Coxcombry or Puppyism, in its Origins and Development, from the Night-Book of Gottesgute [*sic*] von Thiergarten" (probably a mistranscription of "gute" for "gabe").

"History of the Creation of Woman (From the German of H. E. G. Paulus)," *SI* 7, nos. 5 and 6 (15 November/15 December): 227–30.

"Exposition of Ecclesiastes XI.7–XII.7," *SI* 7, nos. 5 and 6 (15 November/15 December): 230–36.

"Translation and Exposition, Matthew XXIV.1–51," *SI* 7, nos. 5 and 6 (15 November/15 December): 271–82.

"Concluding Remarks," by "Eds.," *SI* 7, nos. 5 and 6 (15 November/15 December): 285–88. The editors were TP, William Silsbee, and George Ellis. But Silsbee had contributed nothing since August, and Ellis very little; TP had written all of issue 4 and almost three-quarters of issues 5 and 6. There is every reason to suspect that he wrote the "Concluding Remarks," which are in his style. See TP to Silsbee, 16 September 1836, MHS.

1837

"To a Star ('Spirit of night! why shines yon star')" [poem], by "T. P.," *CR* 16, no. 4 (28 January): 18.

"The Trial and Condemnation of Jesus of Nazareth (Translated from the French of M. Dupin, Attorney and Doctor of Laws. [From the Gazette des Tribunaux])," by "T. P.," *CR* 16, no. 5 (4 February): 12; no. 6 (11 February): 21; no. 7 (18 February): 26; no. 9 (4 March): 34. See list of publications in JC.

*"Hints to Sunday School Teachers, nos. I–V," *Sunday School Teacher, and Children's Friend* 2, no. 3? (March?): 142–49; no. 6? (June?): 245–51; 3, no. 1 (July): 1–13; no. 5

(November): 217–23; no. 6 (December): 298–306. See list of publications in JC: "5 Pieces in Sunday School &c; no signet." TP here, as elsewhere (e.g., his Senex pieces), takes on the persona of an old minister.

"Robinson's Greek and English Lexicon," *CE* 22 (March): 124–27.

"Parable of Talents" (16 April). Manuscript in A-H: Sermon #33. Written ca. April 1837. Printed in *WRS*, 1–14.

"Gesenius's Hebrew and English Lexicon," *CE* 22 (May): 265–68.

"Jesus ('Jesus, there is no dearer name than thine')" [poem], by "T. P.," *CR* 18, no. 17 (6 May): 72. See JC, 49. See 1846. Reprinted in *LCTP*, 1:95; the 1846 version of this poem (the last eight lines are new) is printed in *TPAL*, 60–61, and *WTP*, vol. 13.

"Miriam, A Dramatic Poem" [notice], by "T. P.," *CR* 16, no. 19 (13 May): 75.

"Olhausen's Proof of the Genuineness of the New Testament," *CE* 22 (July): 406–8.

"Spiritual Indifference" (3 September). Manuscript in A-H: Sermon #49. Written ca. August/September 1837. Printed in *WRS*, 15–29.

"Tranquillity" (24 September). Manuscript in A-H: Sermon #51. Written ca. September 1837. Printed in *WRS*, 30–44.

"Reasons Why a Clergyman Should Not Study Scripture Carefully and Critically," by "W.," *CR* 16, no. 44 (4 November): 174. See TP to Silsbee, 14 November 1837, MHS.

"The Spirit of Prayer" [parable], by "T. P.," *CR* 16, no. 46 (18 November): 180.

" 'My Dear Brother' " [letter, dated 11 November], by "W.," *CR* 16, no. 46 (18 November): 183.

"A Vision ('I lay in a green meadow')" [poem], by "T. P.," *CR* 16, no. 46 (18 November): 184.

1838

"Matter's History of Gnosticism," *CE* 24 (March): 112–30.

"German Parables," [unsigned], *CR* 17, no. 26 (30 June): 101; no. 27 (7 July): 105; no. 28 (14 July): 109; no. 29 (21 July): 113; no. 30 (28 July): 117; no. 31 (4 August): 122; no. 32 (11 August): 125; no. 35 (1 September): 137. See the list of "extra-curricular" publications in JN.

"Palfrey's Lectures on Jewish Scriptures and Antiquities," *Boston Quarterly Review* 1, no. 3 (July): 261–310. See TP to George Ellis, 27 May 1838, MHS.

"The World Belongs to Each Man" (15 July). Manuscript in A-H: Sermon #86. Also titled "All things yours." Written ca. May/June 1838. Printed in *WRS*, 45–57.

"Roy's Hebrew and English Dictionary," *CE* 25 (September): 129–31.

"The Alehouses of England. A Parody" [unsigned poem], *CR* 17, no. 38 (22 September): 152. Manuscript in A-H: JN, 49.

"Tranquillity," by "T.," *CR* 17, no. 46 (14 November): 182. See the list of "extra-curricular" publications in JN.

"The Three Ways to the Name of Atheist," by "Senex Who Hath Crept Out of His Cave," *CR* 17, no. 47 (21 November): 186–87. See the list of "extra-curricular" publications in JN.

"Dr. Channing's Lecture on Self-Culture before the Franklin Lyceum," [unsigned], *CR* 17, no. 47 (21 November): 186–87. See TP to Silsbee, 27 November 1838, MHS.

1839

"Ackerman's Christian in Plato," *CE* 25 (January): 367–84.

"A Parable (Solomon's ring)," by "T. P.," *CR* 18, no. 1 (5 January): 4. Manuscript in A-H: JN, 81.

"Dr. Henry More," *CE* 26 (March): 1–17.

"A Law Case. *Duty vs. Appetite*. Report of an abridged case in the High Chancery of Justice, his Honor, Universal Reason, on the Bench," by "T. P.," *CR* 18, no. 10 (9 March): 37–38. See JC, 139 (ca. May/June 1837).

"Boston in the Year of Grace 3839. A Dream by a Very Old Man," by "Senex," *CR* 18, no. 13 (30 March): 49. Style, content, and pseudonymn indicate that this is by TP; besides, the editor of the *CR*, Chandler Robbins, comments on this piece (p. 50) that "if there are a few mistakes in the typography of the worthy old gentleman's article (which we did not revise) we trust that they will be attributed to the difficulty which the compositors found in deciphering the characters traced by his trembling hand." TP, over his career, received many such tongue-in-cheek rebukes for his poor handwriting.

"Specimens of Foreign Standard Literature, edited by George Ripley, vol. III — Containing Select Minor Poems, from the German of Goethe and Schiller" [translated by J. S. Dwight], *Boston Quarterly Review* 2, no. 2 (April): 187–205. See JN, 3, and list of "extra-curricular" publications in JN. See TP to J. S. Dwight, 10 January 1839, BPL.

"New Works Recently Published in Germany," *CE* 26 (May): 267–70. Among the pieces TP lists is "The Transient and Permanent in Christianity," by David Strauss.

"The Origin of Writing in Greece and Egypt," *American Biblical Repository*, 2d ser., 2 (July): 71–90. See TP to Convers Francis, 17 May 1838, BPL (in CTPCF, 107–10).

"More's Works," *CE* 27 (September): 48–71.

"A Letter from Dr. J. G. Buttner, A German Preacher at St. Louis, to the Editor of the Kritische Predigen Bibiolthek. (Translated for the Register)," [unsigned], *CR* 18, no. 42 (19 October): 165; no. 43 (26 October): 196. See the list of "extra-curricular" publications in JN.

1840

"Cudworth's Intellectual System," *CE* 27 (January): 289–319. Reprinted in *WTP*, vol. 14.

"A Brief Treatise of Interior and Exterior Worship," by "T. P.," *CR* 19, no. 5 (1 February): 17.

"German Literary Intelligence," *CE* 28 (March): 135–36.

"Charles Elwood, or an Infidel Converted. By O. A. Brownson," by "G. G.," *CR* 19, no. 16 (18 April): 62. TP notes that he sent this piece to the *CR* in JN, 345.

"Academical Lectures on the Jewish Scriptures and Antiquities, by John Gorham Palfrey, D.D. L.L.D., vol. 2, Genesis and Prophets," [unsigned], *CR* 19, no. 17 (25 April): 66. TP notes that he sent a review of the Academical Lectures, signed "Juvenisulus," in JN, 345. This may be that piece; some of the opinions expressed are similar to those of TP (see JN, 342). On the other hand, (1) it is unsigned; (2) it is published among the editorials, not the correspondence, and is written as if by the editor of the *CR* ("We have read the volume before us") and not by a correspondent (who would tend to use "I"); and (3) the reviewer remarks that "the views and arguments . . . [Palfrey] presents are not satisfactory to ourselves, nor do we see reasons from his book to change the opinions, in which we were educated." As Palfrey's views on the Old Testament were radical for the day (he argued that almost none of the writings was inspired and that the prophets did not predict the coming of Christ), the reviewer seems to be suggesting that he holds a more conservative view of the Old Testament than Palfrey. But TP's view of the Old Testament was more radical than Palfrey's, as his review of Palfrey's first volume (in the *Boston Quarterly Review* of July 1838) made clear. The reviewer's apparently conservative stance may be just a rhetorical pose, however; TP sometimes tried to appear more conservative than he was (e.g., in his review of Strauss's *Life of Jesus*; see July 1840).

"Transcendentalism," by "Senex," *CR* 19, no. 17 (25 April): 66–67. TP notes that he sent this piece to the *CR* in JN, 345.

The Previous Question Between Mr. Andrews Norton and His Alumni Moved and Handled in a Letter to all Those Gentlemen, by "Levi Blodgett." Completed 9 April; published 27 April. Boston: Freeman and Bowles. See JN, 335, 342. Reprinted in Dirks, *The Critical Theology of Theodore Parker*.

"A Desultory Notice of a Recent Pamphlet, entitled 'Two Articles from the Princeton Review . . . ,'" by "T. P.," *CR* 19, no. 20 (16 May): 77–78. See JN, 342.

"Strauss's Life of Jesus," *CE* 28 (July): 273–317. Written 1 April 1840. See JN, 335; *TPAL*, 121, reprints this passage, but misdates it 1839. Reprinted in *CM*, 248–308 (where it is mistakenly listed as having been published in April 1840), with modifications described in *CM*, "Preface."

"The Book of Jasher," *CE* 28 (July): 390–95.

"The Divine Presence in Nature and in the Soul," *Dial* 1, no. 1 (July): 58–70. Manuscript in A-H: Sermon #163, "Inspiration." Three manuscript versions: #1: Written ca. November 1839; preached 10 November 1839. #2: Written ca. December 1839/January 1840; first preached 3 January 1840 (Thursday Lecture). #3: Retitled "The Divine Presence in Nature and the Soul"; written May/June 1840.

"Two Old Sayings of Old Times ('All is God')," by "****," *CR* 19, no. 36 (8 September): 142. See the list of "extra-curricular" publications in JN.

"The Influence of Religion Upon the Feelings" (27 September). Manuscript in A-H: Sermon #194. Written ca. June 40. Printed in *WRS*, 58–71. "Parable of Nathan Ben Elim" is part of this sermon. See *WRS*, 69–70; reprinted separately in *WTP*, vol. 13.

"A Lesson for the Day, or the Christianity of Christ, of the Church, and of Society," *Dial* 1, no. 2 (October): 196–216. Manuscript in A-H: Sermon #197: "The Lesson for the Day: The Christianity of Christ and that of the Church" (on the manuscript) or "The Christianity of Christ and the Church" (in the "Sermon Record Book"). Written late June 1840 (see JN, 407). First preached 28 June 1840. Partly drafted in Sermon #94: "State of the Church," written July–August 1838 in response to Emerson's Divinity School Address. See JN, 2 (15 July 1838). First preached 5 August 1838. Reprinted in *CM*, 1–24; in *WTP*, vol. 9.

"Truth Against the World. A Parable of Paul," *Dial* 1, no. 2 (October): 218–19. Manuscript in A-H: First draft in JN, 7 (late July 1838). Second draft in Sermon #179, "Conscience: Its Relations False and True." Written ca. March 1840. First preached 16 August 1840. Reprinted in *CM*, 107–8; in *WTP*, vol. 13.

"The Ecclesiastical and Political History of the Popes of Rome . . . by Leopold Ranke . . . ," *Dial* 1, no. 2 (October): 266.

"Geschichte des Urchristenthums durch A. Fr. Gfrörer," *Dial* 1, no. 2 (October): 272.

"The Application of Religion to Life" (24 October). Manuscript in A-H: Sermon #208. Written ca. October 1840. Printed in *WRS*, 72–78.

"The Relation of the Bible to the Soul," *Western Messenger* 8, no. 8 (December): 337–40; no. 9 (January 1841): 388–96. Manuscript in A-H: Sermon #131. Written ca. February 1839. First preached 21 April 1839. Reprinted in *WTP*, vol. 4.

1841

"German Literature," *Dial* 1, no. 3 (January): 315–39. Finished 9 November 1840. See JN, 235 (September 1839); JN, 329 (March 1840); JN, 360 (May 1840); JN, 429 (July 1840), in Johnston, "Journals," 30; JN, 469 (9 November 1840), in Johnston, "Journals," 113. Reprinted in *CM*, 25–54; *WTP*, vol. 8.

"A Sermon of Man" (28 February). Manuscript in A-H: Sermon #228. Written ca. February 1841. Printed in *WRS*, 89–104.

"The Life of Saint Bernard of Clairvaux," *CE* 30 (March): 1–56. See JN, 466 (September 1840), in Johnston, "Journals," 93–94; JN, 462 (October 1840) [*sic*], in Johnston, "Journals," 101. Reprinted in *CM*, 55–106; *WTP*, vol. 14.

"Thoughts on Labor," *Dial* 1, no. 4 (April): 497–519. Manuscript in A-H: Sermon #192, "A Sermon of Work." Written June 1840. First preached 21 June 1840. See JN, 404. Reprinted in *CM*, 109–35; *WTP*, vol. 10.

"Come Outers," [unsigned], *Monthly Miscellany* 4 (May 1841): 297–300. Manuscript in BPL. See also JN, 433–35 (August 1840), printed in *LCTP*, 1:126–28.

A Discourse on the Transient and Permanent in Christianity (19 May). First edition on sale ca. 17 June. Boston: printed for the author. Sermon #238, "A Discourse of [*sic*] the Transient and Permanent in Christianity." Manuscript unlocated, although the preaching text has been plausibly reconstructed by Gura, "Theodore Parker and the South Boston Ordination," 162–78. Note that there are hundreds of changes between the published version of the sermon and the preaching text. Written ca. early May 1841. First preached 19 May 1841, at the ordination of Charles C. Shackford in South Boston. Gura asserts (p. 150) that TP first preached this sermon to his congregation in West Roxbury on 2 May. I believe this is a mistake that derives from an error in TP's "Book of Sermons and Preachings," the original of which is at BPL, and a copy of which is at A-H. According to the "Book," TP did indeed preach sermon #238 to his West Roxbury congregation on 2 May; the "Book" also indicates, however, that he preached it to them again on 23 May—the Sunday after the South Boston ordination. Surely he would not have preached the same sermon to the same people twice in three weeks. I believe the sermon he preached on 2 May was #235, "A Sermon of Gentleness." According to notes on the manuscript for #235 (at A-H), TP preached it twice, but the "Book" lists only a single preaching, in 1844—some three years after the sermon was written. Evidently #235 was first preached on 2 May or 23 May, and TP either wrote the number incorrectly into the "Book," or made his "5" look like an "8" (he makes both kinds of mistakes elsewhere in the "Book"). Given the choice between the two dates, I am inclined to pick

2 May for two reasons: (1) #238 was written to be an ordination sermon—TP's first; it would make sense that he would have inaugurated it at the occasion for which it was written; (2) the traditions about #238 (see JI, 248) nowhere indicate that TP had preached it without incident before the South Boston ordination. Reprinted in *CM*, 136–69; *WTP*, vol. 4; Conrad Wright, *Three Prophets of Religious Liberalism*. Second edition on sale ca. 10 July. Boston: Freeman and Bowles. It includes an appendix showing the alterations TP made in the original manuscript when preparing it for publication. Subsequent editions lack the appendix. A copy of the first edition that TP marked up in preparing this appendix is at Meadville/Lombard Theological School. TP labeled this copy "Codex B," evidently intending it to be an appendix to Sermon #338, "Of My Own Stewardship."

"A Letter to the Editors of the Register touching their strictures on my late discourse [dated 21 June]," *CR* 20, no. 27 (3 July): 106.

"The Pharisees," *Dial* 2, no. 1 (July): 59–76. Manuscript in A-H: Sermon #222, "A Sermon of Pharisees" (on the manuscript) or "of the Pharisees" (in the "Book of Sermons and Preachings"). Written December 1840 (See JI, 245). First preached 24 January 1841. Reprinted in *CM*, 170–91; *WTP*, vol. 4.

"Protean Wishes ('I would I were the Grass')" [poem], *Dial* 2, no. 1 (July): 77. Original "To A. S. [Anna Shaw]" in JN, 375 (20, 21 May 1840); JN, 463 (October 40), in Johnston, "Journals," 102. See TP to Margaret Fuller, late June 1841; partially reprinted in *LCTP*, 1:303. To date this letter, compare the comments on LCP's trip to New Jersey in E. P. Peabody to John Sullivan Dwight, 10 June 1841, in *Letters of Elizabeth Palmer Peabody*, 254.

1842

Lecture on the Education of the Laboring Classes. Probably on sale in early 1842. Boston: William D. Ticknor. Manuscript in A-H: Sermon #227, "A Sermon of Education." Written January/February 1841. Preached 7 February 1841. Extensively revised and delivered as a lecture in August 1841 (revised manuscript unlocated); see JI, 97 (July 1841). TP sent manuscript to American Institute of Instruction for publication 17 November 1841 (see JI, 124). Also printed in *The Lectures Delivered before the American Institute of Instruction at Boston, August 1841* (Boston, 1842), 65–90. Reprinted in *CM*, 192–219; *WTP*, vol. 10.

"Primitive Christianity," *Dial* 2, no. 3 (January): 292–313. Based on manuscript in A-H: Sermons #245, "A Sermon of Paul," written June/July 1841, first preached 4 July 1841, and #246, "A Sermon of Primitive Christianity," written June/July 1841, preached 26 December 1841. Revised manuscript unlocated. Sent to *Dial* 22 November 1841 (see JI, 124). See also JI, 97 (July 1841). Reprinted in *CM*, 222–47; *WTP*, vol. 4.

"The Fact of Life and the Idea of Life" (12 March). Manuscript in A-H: Sermon #279, "A Sermon of the Fact of Life, the Idea of Life, & the Reconciliation Thereof" (on the manuscript) or "The Idea of Life, the Fact of Life, & their Reconciliation" (in the "Book of Sermons and Preachings"). Written ca. March 1842. Printed in *WRS*, 105–18.

"Thoughts on Theology: Dorner's Christology," *Dial* 2, no. 4 (April): 458–528. TP sends to *CE* for publication, 19 November 1841 (JI, 124). Rejected by *CE*, submitted to *Dial*. Reprinted in *CM*, 309–60.

"The Philosophy of the Inductive Sciences . . . By William Whewell," *Dial* 2, no. 4 (April): 529–30.

"On the Foundation of Morals . . . By the Reverend William Whewell &c.," *Dial* 2, no. 4 (April): 530–31.

"Institutes of Ecclesiastical History . . . By John Lawrence von Mosheim" (translated by Murdock with additions by Soames), *Dial* 2, no. 4 (April): 531–35.

"German Anti-Supernaturalism, by Philip Harwood," *Dial* 2, no. 4 (April): 535–39.

[Introduction], *Dial* 2, no. 4 (April): 539–40.

"Milman's History of Christianity," *Dial* 2, no. 4 (April): 540–42.

"The History of the Decline and Fall of the Roman Empire, by Edward Gibbon," *Dial* 2, no. 4 (April): 542–44.

A Discourse of Matters Pertaining to Religion. On sale May. Boston: Charles Little and James Brown. See JI, 91–171 passim, esp. 109–11. Manuscript in A-H. Three drafts: first draft (1–16 September 1841); second draft (delivered as lectures in Boston, 6 October–3 November 1841, and in West Roxbury, Duxbury, Providence, Plymouth, and New Bedford, November 1841–February 1842); final copy (as returned from printer, 6 May 1842). This edition is not reprinted in *WTP*, vol. 1; *WTP*, vol. 1, is the fourth edition (1855). There are substantial differences between the two editions, especially in how they present Jesus and Christianity; compare, in the two editions, Book III, chaps. 3–5.

"Hollis Street Council," *Dial* 3, no. 2 (October): 201–21.

"Lectures on Modern History . . . by William Smyth," *Dial* 3, no. 2 (October): 277–78.

"The Crucifixion" (9 October). Manuscript in A-H: Sermon #300. Written ca. October 1842. Printed in *WRS*, 119–29.

An Humble Tribute to the Memory of William Ellery Channing, D.D. (9 October). On sale October–December 1842. Boston: Charles Little and James Brown. Manuscript in A-H: Sermon #301, "A Sermon on the Death of Dr. Channing." Written 2–9 October 1842.

"A Dream," by "A. A. A.," *Latimer Journal*, 18 November. Reprints of this piece, which bear strong marks of TP's style, are included in Caroline Coddington Thayer's collection of TP's writings, Boston Public Library.

1843

Critical and Miscellaneous Writings. On sale early 1843. Boston: James Munroe.

"Preface." Dated 28 December 1842.

"A Lesson for the Day," 1–24. See October 1840.

"German Literature," 25–54. See January 1841.

"The Life of St. Bernard of Clairvaux," 55–106. See March 1841.

"Truth Against the World," 107–8. See October 1840.

"Thoughts on Labor," 109–35. See April 1841.

"A Discourse of the Transient and Permanent in Christianity," 136–69. See May 1841.

"The Pharisees," 170–91. See July 1841.

"On the Education of the Laboring Classes," 192–219. See 1842.

"How to Move the World," 220–21. Manuscript in A-H: See Sermon #204, "A Sermon of the Strong," 3–4. Written 4 September 1840 (JN, 442). First preached 6 September 1840. Reprinted in *WTP*, vol. 13.

"Primitive Christianity," 222–47. See January 1842.

"Strauss's Life of Jesus," 248–308. See June 1840.

"Thoughts on Theology," 309–60. See April 1842.

"Life and Character of Dr. Follen," *Dial* 3, no. 3 (Jan.): 343–62. Reprinted in *WTP*, vol. 8.

"Conference with the Boston Association" (23 January). Manuscript in JI, 241–61. Printed in Dean Grodzins, "Theodore Parker's 'Conference with the Boston Association,'" 81–94.

A Sermon of Slavery (4 June). On sale ca. 19 June. Boston: Thurston and Torrey. Manuscript in A-H: Sermon #226. Written ca. January 1841. First preached 31 January 1841. Reprinted in *WTP*, vol. 11.

*"Home Considered in Relation to its Moral Influence," *Notion*. A copy of the printed version pasted into JI, 312–14 (ca. August 43). Manuscript in A-H: Sermon #329. First draft: "A Sermon of Home Considered as a Spiritual Influence." Written ca. June 1843. Preached 18 June 1843. Second draft as published. On the second draft manuscript is written: "As printed in Notion." Reprinted in *WTP*, vol. 9.

A Critical and Historical Introduction to the Canonical Scriptures of the Old Testament. From the German of Wilhelm Martin Leberecht De Wette. Translated and Enlarged, 2 vols. On sale ca. September. Boston: Charles C. Little and James Brown. Manuscript fragments (parts of volume 2) at the Hay Library, Brown University.

"Hennell on the Origin of Christianity," *Dial* 4, no. 2 (October): 137–65.

"Socrates in Boston," *Liberty Bell*, 117–44.

1844

"Christian Advancement" (27 October). Ms. in A-H: #350. Printed in *WRS*, 130–44.

The Relation of Jesus to His Age and the Ages (26 December; published 1845). Boston: Charles C. Little and James Brown. Manuscript in A-H: #356. Reprinted in *SAOS*, vol. 1; *WTP*, vol. 4.

1845

The Excellence of Goodness: A sermon preached in the Church of the Disciples (26 January). Boston: Benjamin H. Greene. Manuscript in A-H: #351. Reprinted in *WTP*, vol. 4.

A Letter to the Boston Association of Congregational Ministers, Touching Certain Matters of their Theology (dated 20 March). Boston: Charles C. Little and James Brown. See TP to Ezra Stiles Gannett, 28 December 1844; JM, 34–39 (ca. 17–24 January 1845). Some revisions between first and second editions. For example, TP corrects the list of those who have offered Rev. John Pierpont an exchange (p. 10). Reprinted in *WTP*, vol. 14.

"Prayer and Intercourse with God" (11 May). Manuscript in A-H: #376. Printed in *WRS*, 145–60.

"Christianity in Contrast with Heathenism" (19 June) (or "in Contact" or "in Contest"). Manuscript in A-H: #384. Printed in *WRS*, 161–77.

"Low Aims and Lofty" (22 June). Manuscript in A-H: #383. Printed in *WRS*, 178–96.

"Of Restlessness and Rest" (31 August). Manuscript in A-H: #392. *WTP*, vol. 3, "Of Religious Rest." Notes in *WTP* 3 indicate this sermon was preached 2 April 1848; it was, but this was not the earliest date it was preached.

1846

The True Idea of a Christian Church (4 January). Manuscript in A-H: #408. Boston: Benjamin H. Greene. Reprinted in *SAOS*, vol. 1; *WTP*, vol. 13.

A Sermon of War (7 June). Manuscript in A-H: #429. Boston: Charles C. Little and James Brown. Reprinted in *SAOS*, vol. 1; *WTP*, vol. 9.

A Sermon of the Perishing Classes in Boston (30 August). Manuscript in A-H: #435 ("Sermon of not letting the little ones perish"). Boston: Published by request. Second edition, 1847. Reprinted in *SAOS*, vol. 1; *WTP*, vol. 10.

A Sermon of Immortal Life (20 September). Manuscript in A-H: #437. Boston: Published by request. Reprinted in *SAOS*, vol. 1; *WTP*, vol. 3, where it is mistakenly listed as 2 September.

"God's Income to Man" (11 October). Manuscript in A-H: #440. Printed in *WRS*, 197–215.

A Sermon of Merchants (22 November). Manuscript in A-H: #445 ("Merchants and Their Calling"). Boston: Published by request (ca. 10 March 47). Reprinted in *SAOS*, vol. 1; *WTP*, vol. 10.

A Discourse of Matters Pertaining to Religion (third edition). Second edition published in London in the fall of 1846 by Chapman Brothers. Preface dated 25 December 1846. Boston: Charles C. Little and James Brown, 1847.

"A Parable" ("Parable of Ishmael"), *Liberty Bell*, 21–24. Reprinted in *WTP*, vol. 13.

"Jesus There Is No Name So Dear as Thine" [poem], *Liberty Bell*, 54–55. See 1836. Reprinted in *WTP*, vol. 13.

"O Thou Great Friend to All the Sons of Men" [poem], *Liberty Bell*, 55–56. Reprinted in *WTP*, vol. 13.

"Dear Jesus Were Thy Spirit Now on Earth" [poem], *Liberty Bell*, 56–57. Reprinted in *WTP*, vol. 13.

Newspapers and Periodicals

American Monthly Magazine, 1836
Biblical Repository, 1839
Boston Daily Advertiser, 1836–41
Boston Quarterly Review, 1838–42
Boston Semi-Weekly Courier, 1840–41
Brownson's Quarterly Review, 1844–59
Christian Examiner, 1831–46
Christian Register, 1831–46
Christian World, 1844–46
The Dial, 1840–44
The Liberator, 1840–60
The Liberty Bell, 1842–46
Monthly Miscellany of Religion and Letters, 1841–42

National Standard, 1871
New Englander, 1844–45
New York Tribune, 1841–42
North American Review, 1835–46
Scriptural Interpreter, 1831–36
Sunday School Teacher, and Children's Friend, 1836–37
Western Messenger, 1840–41

Other Works

Abbott, Jacob. *The Young Christian: or a Familiar Illustration of the Principles of Christian Duty*. New York: John P. Haven, 1833.

Ahlstrom, Sydney E. *A Religious History of the American People*. New Haven: Yale University Press, 1972.

Albrecht, Robert C. *Theodore Parker*. New York: Twayne, 1971.

Alcott, Bronson. *Conversations with Children on the Gospels*. 2 vols. Boston: James Munroe, 1836–37.

———. *The Journals of Bronson Alcott*. Edited by Odell Shepard. Boston: Little, Brown, 1938.

Alcott, Louisa May. *The Journals of Louisa May Alcott*. Edited by Joel Myerson and Daniel Shealy. Boston: Little, Brown, 1989.

———. *Work: A Story of Experience*. Boston: Roberts Brothers, 1875.

Allen, Gay Wilson. *Waldo Emerson: A Biography*. New York: Viking, 1981.

Altherr, Alfred. *Theodor Parker in seinem Leben und Wirken*. St. Gassen: Thomas Wirth, 1894.

Appleby, John H. "The First Parish, West Roxbury. An Historic Sketch." *West Roxbury Magazine* (1900): 5–29.

Baker, Paul R. *The Fortunate Pilgrims: Americans in Italy, 1800–1860*. Cambridge, Mass.: Harvard University Press, 1964.

Bearse, Austin. *Reminiscences of Fugitive Slave Law Days in Boston*. Boston: Warren Richardson, 1880.

Blanchard, Paula. *Margaret Fuller: From Transcendentalist to Revolutionary*. New York: Merloyd Lawrence, 1978.

Blumin, Stuart M. *The Emergence of the Middle Class: Social Experience in the American City, 1760–1900*. Cambridge: Cambridge University Press, 1989.

Boston Association and John Pierpont. *Letter of the Boston Association of Congregational Ministers to Rev. John Pierpont, with His Reply*. Boston: Benjamin H. Greene, 1846.

Briggs, Charles. *A Sermon Delivered at the Installation of the Rev. Artemas B. Muzzey*. Cambridge, Mass.: Charles Folsom, 1834.

Briggs, Vernon L. *History and Genealogy of the Cabot Family, 1475–1927*. 2 vols. Boston: Charles E. Goodspeed, 1927.

Brisbane, Albert. *Social Destiny of Man, or Association and Reorganization of Industry*. Philadelphia: C. F. Stollmeyer, 1840. Reprint, New York: Augustus M. Kelley, 1969.

Broderick, John C. "Problems of the Literary Executor: The Case of Theodore Parker." *Quarterly Journal of the Library of Congress* 23 (October 1966): 260–73.

Brosses, Charles de. *Du Culte des Dieux Fétiches: ou Parellèle de l'ancienne Religion de l'Egypte avec la Religion actuelle de Nigritie*. 1760. Reprint, Paris: Fayard, 1988.

Brown, Abram English. *Beneath Old Roof Trees*. Boston: Lee and Shepard, 1896.

Brown, Jerry Wayne. *The Rise of Biblical Criticism in America, 1800–1870: The New England Scholars*. Middletown, Conn.: Wesleyan University Press, 1969.

Browne, A. G., *Sketch of the Official Life of John A. Andrew*. New York: Hurd and Houghton, 1868.

Brownson, Henry F. *Brownson's Early Life*. Vol. 1 of *Orestes A. Brownson's Life*. 3 vols. Detroit: Henry F. Brownson, 1898–1900.

Brownson, Orestes A. *The Convert, or, Leaves from My Experience*. New York: Dunigan and Brother, 1857.

———. *The Early Works of Orestes A. Brownson*. 2 vols. to date. Edited by Patrick N. Carey. Milwaukee: Marquette University Press, 2000–.

———. *The Works of Orestes A. Brownson*. 20 vols. Edited by Henry F. Brownson. Detroit: Thorndike Norse, 1882–87.

Buell, Lawrence. *Literary Transcendentalism: Style and Vision in the American Renaissance*. Ithaca: Cornell University Press, 1973.

Cabot, James Elliot. *A Memoir of Ralph Waldo Emerson*. 2 vols. Boston: Houghton, Mifflin, 1887.

Cameron, Kenneth. *Transcendentalist Epilogue*. Hartford: Transcendental Books, 1982.

Campbell, Stanley W. *The Slave Catchers: Enforcement of the Fugitive Slave Law, 1850–1860*. Chapel Hill: University of North Carolina Press, 1970.

Capper, Charles. *Margaret Fuller, an American Romantic Life: The Private Years*. New York: Oxford Univesity Press, 1992.

———. "Margaret Fuller as Cultural Reformer: The Conversations in Boston." *American Quarterly* 39, no. 4 (Winter 1987): 509–28.

Capper, Charles, and Conrad Edick Wright, eds. *Transient and Permanent: The Transcendentalist Movement and Its Contexts*. Boston: Massachusetts Historical Society, 1999.

Carlyle, Thomas. *Sartor Resartus*. 1836. Reprint, New York: Chelsea House, 1983.

Carlyle, Thomas, and Jane Welsh Carlyle. *The Collected Letters of Thomas and Jane Welsh Carlyle*. Vol. 17. Durham, N.C.: Duke University Press, 1990.

Cashdollar, Charles D. *The Transformation of Theology, 1830–1890: Positivism and Protestant Thought in Britain and America*. Princeton: Princeton University Press, 1989.

The Celebrated Trial of Joy Hamlet Fairchild for the Seduction of Miss Rhoda Davidson. N.p.: Daily Mail, 1844.

Chadwick, John White. *Theodore Parker: Preacher and Reformer*. Boston and New York: Houghton, Mifflin, 1900.

Channing, William Ellery. *The Works of William E. Channing, D.D.* Boston: American Unitarian Association, 1875.

Channing, William Henry. *The Life of William Ellery Channing, D.D.* Centenary Memorial Edition. Boston: American Unitarian Association, 1880. Reprint with an introduction by Conrad Wright. Hicksville, N.Y.: Regina, 1975.

Clarke, James Freeman. *The Church of the Disciples in Boston: A Sermon on the Principles and Methods of the Church of the Disciples*. Boston: Benjamin H. Greene, 1846.

———. *Memorial and Biographical Sketches*. Boston: Houghton, Osgood, and Company, 1878.

Clarke, Jonas. *Christ's Mission of the Seventy*. Boston: Edes and Gill, 1761.

———. *The Fate of Bloodthirsty Oppressors*. Boston: Power and Willis, 1776.

———. *Sermon Preached before His Excellency John Hancock* (Election sermon). Boston: Gill, Edes and Sons, 1781.

———. *The Use and Excellency of Vocal Music*. Boston: Nicholas Bowes, 1770.

Cobbe, Frances Power. *Life of Frances Power Cobbe*. 2 vols. London: Richard Bentley and Son, 1894.

Coleridge, Samuel Taylor. *Aids to Reflection*. New York: Chelsea House, 1983.

A Collection of Psalms and Hymns for Christian Worship. 10th edition. Boston: Carter, Hendee, 1833.

Collison, Gary L., ed. "A Critical Edition of the Correspondence of Theodore Parker and Convers Francis, 1836–1859." Ph.D. dissertation, Pennsylvania State University, 1979.

Commager, Henry Steele. "The Dilemma of Theodore Parker." *New England Quarterly* 6 (1933): 257–77.

———. *Theodore Parker: Yankee Crusader*. Boston: Little, Brown, 1936.

Comte, Auguste. *Course de la philosophie positive*. 6 vols. Paris: Bachelier, 1830–42.

Constant, Benjamin. *De la religion: considere'e dans sa source, ses formes et ses developpments*. Paris: A. Leroux et C. Chantpie, 1826–31.

Conway, Moncure Daniel. *Autobiography, Memories and Experiences*. 2 vols. Boston: Houghton, Mifflin, 1904.

Cooke, George Willis. *John Sullivan Dwight: Brook-Farmer, Editor, and Critic of Music*. 1898. Reprint, New York: Da Capo, 1969.

Copleston, Frederick. *A History of Philosophy*. 9 vols. in 3. Image edition. New York: Doubleday, 1985.

Correspondence Between Rev. Nehemiah Adams and Rev. J. H. Fairchild. Boston: Dutton and Wentworth, 1846.

Cott, Nancy F. *The Bonds of Womanhood: "Woman's Sphere" in New England, 1780–1835*. New Haven: Yale University Press, 1977.

Crowe, Charles. *George Ripley: Transcendentalist and Utopian Socialist*. Athens: University of Georgia Press, 1967.

[Curtis, Benjamin R.] *An Article on the Debts of the States, from the North American Review, for January, 1844*. Boston: T. R. Marvin, 1844.

Cushing, Thomas. *Memorials of the Class of 1834 of Harvard College*. Boston: D. Clapp and Sons, 1884.

Dahlstrand, Frederick C. *Bronson Alcott: An Intellectual Biography*. Rutherford, N.J.: Fairleigh Dickinson University Press, 1982.

Dall, Caroline. *Transcendentalism in New England: A Lecture*. Boston: Roberts Brothers, 1897.

Dalzell, Robert F. *Enterprising Elite: The Boston Associates and the World They Made*. Cambridge, Mass.: Harvard University Press, 1987.

Dean, Peter. *The Life and Teachings of Theodore Parker*. London: Williams and Norgate, 1877.

Deese, Helen. "Tending the 'Sacred Fires': Theodore Parker and Caroline Healey Dall." *Proceedings of the Unitarian Universalist Historical Society* 23 (1995): 22–38.

Deguise, Pierre. "La religion de Benjamin Constant et l'Unitarianisme américain." *Annales Benjamin Constant* 12 (1991): 19–27

De Wette, Wilhelm Leberecht. *Theodore; or a Skeptic's Conversion. History of the Culture of a Protestant Clergyman.* 2 vols. Translated by James Freeman Clarke. Specimens of Foreign Standard Literature, nos. 10, 11. Boston: Hilliard, Grey, 1841. Originally published as *Theodor oder des Zweiflers Weihe: Bildungsgeschichte eines evangelischen Geistlichen.* 2 vols. Berlin: G. Reimer, 1822.

Dewey, Orville. *Works.* Boston: American Unitarian Association, 1899.

Dexter, Franklin Bowditch. *Biographical Sketches of Graduates of Yale College with Annals of the College History.* 6 vols. New York: H. Holt and Company, 1885–1912.

Dirks, John Edward. *The Critical Theology of Theodore Parker.* New York: Columbia University Press, 1948.

Donald, David. *Charles Sumner and the Coming of the Civil War.* New York: Alfred A. Knopf, 1960.

Douglas, Ann. *The Feminization of American Culture.* 1977. Reprint, New York: Anchor Books, 1988.

Drake, Francis S. *The Town of Roxbury.* Boston: Registry Department of the City of Boston, 1905.

Du Bois, W. E. B. *The Souls of Black Folk. 1903.* With introductions by Nathan Hare and Alvin F. Poussant. New York: New American Library, Signet, 1982.

Dwight, Marianne. *Letters from Brook Farm, 1844–1847.* Edited by Amy L. Reed. Poughkeepsie, N.Y.: Vassar College, 1928.

The Earliest Meeting Houses in West Roxbury. West Roxbury Historical Society, n.d.

[Ellis, Charles Mayo (attributed).] *An Essay on Transcendentalism.* 1842. Introduction by Walter Harding. Gainesville, Fla.: Scholars' Facsimiles & Reprints, 1954.

Emerson, Ralph Waldo. *The Collected Works of Ralph Waldo Emerson.* 5 vols. to date. Edited by Alfred R. Furguson et al. Cambridge, Mass.: Harvard University Press, 1971–.

———. *The Complete Sermons of Ralph Waldo Emerson.* 4 vols. Edited by Albert J. Von Frank. Columbia: University of Missouri Press, 1989.

———. *The Complete Works of Ralph Waldo Emerson.* 12 vols. Edited by Edward Waldo Emerson. Centenary Edition. Boston: Houghton Mifflin, 1903–4.

———. *The Early Lectures of Ralph Waldo Emerson.* 3 vols. Edited by Robert E. Spiller, Stephen E. Wicher, and Wallace E. Williams. Cambridge, Mass.: Harvard University Press, 1972.

———. *Emerson's Antislavery Writings.* Edited by Len Gougeon and Joel Myerson. New Haven: Yale University Press, 1995.

———. *Essays and Lectures.* Edited by Joel Porte. New York: Library of America, 1983.

———. *The Journals and Miscellaneous Notebooks of Ralph Waldo Emerson.* 16 vols. Edited by Ralph H. Orth et al. Cambridge, Mass.: Harvard University Press, 1960–82.

———. *The Letters of Ralph Waldo Emerson.* 8 vols. to date. Edited by Ralph L. Rusk (vols. 1–6) and Eleanor M. Tilton (vols. 7–8). New York: Columbia University Press, 1939–.

The Encyclopedia of Philosophy. 8 vols. Edited by Paul Edwards. New York and London: Macmillan and the Free Press, 1967.

Fairchild, Joy Hamlet. *Iniquity Unfolded! An Account of the Treatment of Mr. Fairchild by the Deacons of South Boston, and Others.* Exeter, N.H.: privately printed, 1844.

———. *The New Doctrine of Clerical Privilege.* Boston: Redding and Company, 1852.

———. *Objections to the Deity of Christ Considered.* Boston: Pierce and Parker, 1832.

———. *Remarkable Incidents in the Life of Rev. J. H. Fairchild.* Boston: the author, 1855.

Fellman, Michael. "Theodore Parker and the Abolitionist Role in the 1850's." *Journal of American History* 61 (1974): 666–84.

Fontana, Biancamaria. *Benjamin Constant and the Post-Revolutionary Mind.* New Haven: Yale University Press, 1991.

Foster, Stephen. *The Long Argument: English Puritanism and the Shaping of New England Culture, 1570–1700.* Chapel Hill: University of North Carolina Press, 1991.

Franchot, Jenny. *Roads to Rome: The Antebellum Protestant Encounter with Catholicism.* Berkeley: University of California Press, 1994.

Francis, Convers. *Christianity as a Purely Internal Principle.* Boston: American Unitarian Association, 1836.

———. *Historical Sketch of Watertown.* Cambridge, Mass.: W. Metcalf, 1830.

———. "The Journals of Convers Francis." Edited by Guy R. Woodall. *Studies in the American Renaissance* (1981): 265–343; (1982): 227–84.

———. "The Value of Enlightened Views of Religion." *Liberal Preacher* 2:5 (1831).

Frothingham, Nathaniel Langdon. *Deism or Christianity? Four Discourses.* Boston: William Crosby and H. P. Nichols, 1845.

———. *The Shade of the Past: for the Celebration of the Close of the Second Century since the Establishment of the Thursday Lecture.* Boston: Russell, Odiorne, and Metcalf, 1833.

Frothingham, Octavius Brooks. *Boston Unitarianism, 1820–1850: A Study of the Life and Work of Nathaniel Langdon Frothingham.* 1890. Reprint, Hicksville, N.Y.: Regina Press, 1975.

———. *Francis Parkman: A Sketch.* Boston: John Wilson and Son, 1894.

———. *George Ripley.* Boston: 1882. Reprint, New York: AMS, 1970.

———. *Theodore Parker: A Biography.* Boston: James R. Osgood, 1874.

———. *Transcendentalism in New England: A History.* New York: G. P. Putnam and Sons, 1876. Reprint, with an introduction by Sydney Ahlstrom, Gloucester, Mass.: Peter Smith, 1965.

Fuller, Margaret. *Essays on American Life and Letters.* Edited by Joel Myerson. New Haven: Yale University Press, 1978.

———. *The Letters of Margaret Fuller.* 6 vols. Edited by Robert M. Hudspeth. Ithaca: Cornell University Press, 1983–94.

———. *Woman in the Nineteenth Century.* With an introduction by Bernard Rosenthal. New York: W. W. Norton, 1971.

Furness, William Henry. *The Exclusive Principle Considered: Two Discourses on Christian Union and Truth in the Gospels.* Boston: B. H. Greene, 1845.

———. *Remarks on the Four Gospels.* Philadelphia: Carey, Lea, and Blanchard, 1836.

Gannett, William C. *Ezra Stiles Gannett: Unitarian Minister in Boston, 1824–1871.* 1875. Reprint, Port Washington, N.Y.: Kennikat Press, 1971.

Garrison, Wendell Phillips, and Francis Jackson Garrison. *William Lloyd Garrison, 1805–1879: The Story of His Life.* 4 vols. 1889. Reprint, New York: Negro Universities Press, 1969.

Gatell, Otto Frank. *John Gorham Palfrey and the New England Conscience.* Cambridge, Mass.: Harvard University Press, 1963.

General Catalogue of the Divinity School of Harvard University. Cambridge, Mass.: Harvard University Press, 1905.

Ghodes, Clarence L. F. *The Periodicals of American Transcendentalism.* Durham, N.C.: Duke University Press, 1931.

Greene, William Batchelder. *Equality.* 1849. Reprinted with Greene's *Transcendentalism* (1849) and an introduction by Martin K. Doudna. Delmar, N.Y.: Scholars' Facsimiles and Reprints, 1981.

———. *Transcendentalism.* 1849. Reprinted with Greene's *Equality* (1849) and an introduction by Martin K. Doudna. Delmar, N.Y.: Scholars' Facsimiles and Reprints, 1981.

Grodzins, Dean. "Theodore Parker and the 28th Congregational Society: The Reform Church and the Spirituality of Reformers in Boston, 1845–1859." In *Transient and Permanent: The Transcendentalist Movement and Its Contexts.* Edited by Charles Capper and Conrad Edick Wright. Boston: Massachusetts Historical Society, 1999.

———. "Theodore Parker and Transcendentalism." Ph.D. dissertation, Harvard University, 1993.

———. "The Transient and Permanent in Theodore Parker's Christianity." *Proceedings of the Unitarian Universalist Historical Society* 22, pt. 1 (1990–91): 1–18.

———, ed. " 'Dear Chev . . . O, Julia': A Critical Edition of the Theodore Parker Letters in the Howe Papers at the Chapin Library." Unpublished undergraduate thesis, William College, 1983.

———. "Theodore Parker's 'Conference with the Boston Association,' January 23, 1843." *Proceedings of the Unitarian Universalist Historical Society* 23 (1995): 66–101.

Grodzins, Dean, and Joel Myerson. "The Preaching Record of Theodore Parker." *Studies in the American Renaissance* (1994): 55–122.

Gura, Philip F. "Beyond Transcendentalism: The Radical Individualism of William B. Greene." In *Transient and Permanent: The Transcendentalist Movement and Its Contexts,* edited by Charles Capper and Conrad Edick Wright. Boston: Massachusetts Historical Society, 1999.

———. "Theodore Parker and the South Boston Ordination: The Textual Tangle of *A Discourse of the Transient and the Permanent in Christianity.*" *Studies in the American Renaissance* (1988): 149–78.

Habich, Robert D. "Emerson's Reluctant Foe: Andrews Norton and the Transcendentalist Controversy." *New England Quarterly* 65 (June 1992): 208–37.

Hale, Edward Everett, ed. *James Freeman Clarke: Autobiography, Diary and Correspondence.* Boston: Houghton, Mifflin, 1899.

Hall, David D. *Worlds of Wonder, Days of Judgment: Popular Religious Belief in Early New England.* Cambridge, Mass.: Harvard University Press, 1990.

Hancock, John. *The Gaining of Souls.* Boston: Rogers and Fowle, 1748.

Handbook for Travellers in Central Italy, Including the Papal States, Rome, and the Cities of Etruria. London: John Murray, 1843.

Handbook for Travellers on the Continent: Being a Guide through Holland, Belgium, Prussia, and Northern Germany, and along the Rhine, from Holland to Switzerland. London: John Murray, 1845.

Harris, Horton. *David Friedrich Strauss and His Theology.* Cambridge: Cambridge University Press, 1973.

Heralds of a Liberal Faith. 4 vols. Edited by Samuel A. Eliot. Vols. 1–3, Boston: American Unitarian Association, 1910. Vol. 4, Boston: Beacon, 1952.

Higginson, Thomas Wentworth. *Cheerful Yesterdays.* Boston: Houghton, Mifflin, 1898.

Hodgson, Peter C. *The Formation of Historical Theology: A Study of Ferdinand Christian Baur.* New York: Harper and Row, 1966.

Holt, Michael F. *The Rise and Fall of the American Whig Party: Jacksonian Politics and the Onset of the Civil War.* New York: Oxford University Press, 1999.

Howard, Thomas Albert. *Religion and the Rise of Historicism: W. M. L. De Wette, Jacob Burckhardt, and the Theological Origins of Nineteenth-Century Historical Consciousness.* Cambridge: Cambridge University Press, 2000.

Howe, Daniel Walker. *The Unitarian Conscience: Harvard Moral Philosophy, 1805–1861.* 2nd ed. Middletown, Conn.: Wesleyan University Press, 1988.

Howe, Joseph S. *Historical Sketch of the Town of Methuen, from Its Settlement to the Year 1876.* Methuen, Mass.: E. L. Houghton and Company, 1876.

Howe, Julia Ward. *Reminiscences, 1819–1899.* Boston: Houghton, Mifflin, 1899.

Hudson, Charles. *History of the Town of Lexington, Middlesex County, Massachusetts; from its first settlement to 1868. Revised and continued to 1912 by the Lexington Historical Society.* 2 vols. Bicentennial ed. Boston: Houghton, Mifflin, 1913.

Hutchison, William R. *The Transcendentalist Ministers: Church Reform in the New England Renaissance.* New Haven: Yale University Press, 1959.

In Memoriam: John Turner Sargent. Boston: William F. Gill, 1877.

Jackson, Leon. "The Social Construction of Thomas Carlyle's New England Reputation, 1834–1836." *Proceedings of the American Antiquarian Society* 106 (1996): 165–89.

Jacobs, Wilbur R. *Francis Parkman, Historian as Hero: The Formative Years.* Austin: University of Texas Press, 1991.

James, William. *The Varieties of Religious Experience: A Study in Human Nature.* Introduction by Reinhold Neibuhr. New York: Collier, Macmillan, 1961.

Johnston, Carol L., ed. "The Journals of Theodore Parker, July–December 1840." Ph.D. dissertation, University of South Carolina, 1980.

Kant, Immanuel. *Critique of Pure Reason.* Translated by Norman Kemp Smith. New York: St. Martin's, 1965.

———. *Groundwork of the Metaphysic of Morals.* Translated and edited by H. J. Paton. New York: Harper and Row, 1964.

———. *Religion within the Limits of Reason Alone.* Translated and edited by Theodore M. Greene and Hoyt H. Hudson. With an essay by John R. Silber. New York: Harper and Row, 1960.

Kuklick, Bruce. *Churchmen and Philosophers: From Jonathan Edwards to John Dewey.* New Haven: Yale University Press, 1985.

Kümmel, Georg Werner. *Introduction to the New Testament.* Translated by Howard Clark Lee. Nashville: Abington, 1975.

Leibniz, Gottfried Wilhelm von. *Opera Omnia.* 6 vols. Edited by Louis Duten. Geneva: Apud Fratres de Tournes, 1768.

Lothrop, Samuel K. *The Christian Name and Christian Liberty.* Boston: Published by request, 1843.

———. *Some Reminiscences of the Life of Samuel Kirkland Lothrop.* Cambridge, Mass.: J. Wilson, 1888.

Mackintosh, Charles G. *Some Recollections of the Pastors and People of the Second Church of Old Roxbury.* Salem: Newcomb and Gauss, 1901.

Mann, Mary Peabody. *Life of Horace Mann.* Boston: Walker, Fuller, and Company, 1865.

Martineau, Harriet. *Society in America,* 2 vols. New York: Saunders and Otley, 1837.

Martineau, James. *The Rationale of Religious Enquiry: or the Question Stated of Reason, the Bible and the Church.* London: Wittaker, 1836.

———. "Strauss and Parker." *Westminster and Foreign Quarterly Review* 47 (1847): 136–74.

May, Samuel Joseph. *Memoir of Samuel Joseph May.* Boston: Roberts Brothers, 1873.

Mayer, Henry. *All on Fire: William Lloyd Garrison and the Abolition of Slavery.* New York: St. Martin's Press, 1998.

Meiners, Christoph. *Allgemeine kritische Geschichte der Religionen.* 2 vols. Hanover: Helwig, 1806–7.

Merriam, George S., ed. *Noah Porter: A Memorial by His Friends.* New York: Charles Scribner's Sons, 1890.

Merrill, Walter M., ed. *The Letters of William Lloyd Garrison.* Vol. 3, *No Union with Slaveholders, 1841–1849.* Cambridge, Mass.: Belknap Press of Harvard University Press, 1973.

Miller, Perry. "Theodore Parker: Apostasy within Liberalism." *Harvard Theological Review* 54 (October 1961): 275–95. Reprinted in *Nature's Nation.* Cambridge, Mass.: Harvard University Press, 1967.

———. *The Transcendentalists: An Anthology.* Cambridge, Mass.: Harvard University Press, 1950.

Morison, John Hopkins. "Divinity School at Harvard University." In *Transcendental Epilogue,* vol. 2, edited by Kenneth Walker Cameron. Hartford: Transcendental Books, 1982.

Morison, Samuel Eliot. *Three Centuries of Harvard, 1636–1936.* Cambridge, Mass.: Harvard University Press, 1936.

Mumford, Thomas James. *Memoir of Samuel Joseph May.* Boston: American Unitarian Association, 1890.

Muzzey, Artemas. *A Plea for the Christian Spirit.* Boston: William Crosby and H. P. Nichols, 1845.

Myerson, Joel. "An Annotated List of Contributions to the Boston *Dial.*" *Studies in Bibliography* 26 (1973): 133–66.

———. "A Calendar of Transcendental Club Meetings." *American Literature* 44 (May 1972): 197–207.

———. "Carolyn Dall's Reminiscences of Margaret Fuller." *Harvard Library Bulletin* 22 (October 1974): 414–28.

———. "Frederic Henry Hedge and the Failure of Transcendentalism." *Harvard Library Bulletin* 23 (October 1975): 396–410.

———. *The New England Transcendentalists and the* Dial: *A History of the Magazine and Its Contributors*. London: Associated University Presses, 1980.

———. *Theodore Parker: A Descriptive Bibliography*. New York: Garland, 1981.

———. *The Transcendentalists: A Review of Research and Criticism*. New York: Modern Language Association, 1984.

———, ed. *The Brook Farm Book: A Collection of First Hand Accounts of the Community*. New York: Garland, 1987.

Newell, William. *Memoir of the Rev. Convers Francis, D.D.* Cambridge, Mass.: John Wilson and Sons, 1866.

Norton, Andrews. *A Discourse on the Latest Form of Infidelity, delivered at the request of the "Association of the Alumni of the Cambridge Theological School," on the 19th of July, 1839, with notes*. Cambridge, Mass.: John Owen, 1839.

———. *The Evidences of the Genuineness of the Gospels*. 3 vols. Vol. 1, Boston: John B. Russell, 1837; vols. 2–3, Cambridge, Mass.: John Owen, 1844.

———. *Remarks on a Pamphlet entitled " 'The Latest Form of Infidelity' Examined."* Cambridge, Mass.: John Owen, 1839.

———. *Tracts Concerning Christianity*. Cambridge, Mass.: John Bartlett, 1852.

———, ed. *Two Articles from the Princeton Review, concerning the Transcendental Philosophy of the Germans and of Cousin, and its Influence on the Opinion of this Country*. Cambridge, Mass.: John Owen, 1840.

Orvis, Helen D. "First Parish, West Roxbury." In *Sketches of Some Historic Churches of Greater Boston*. Boston: Beacon, 1918.

Packer, Barbara L. "The Transcendentalists." In *The Cambridge History of American Literature*, vol. 2, *1820–1860*, edited by Sacvan Berkovitch. Cambridge: Cambridge University Press, 1995.

Palfrey, John Gorham. *Academical Lectures on the Jewish Scriptures and Antiquities*. 4 vols. Vols. 1–2, Boston: James Munroe, 1838–40. Vols. 3–4, Boston: William Crosby and H. P. Nichols, 1852.

———. *Discourse on the Life and Character of the Rev. Henry Ware, D.D.* Cambridge, Mass.: John Owen, 1845.

———. *Lowell Lectures on the Evidences of Christianity*. 2 vols. Boston: James Munroe, 1843.

Parker, Theodore. *Additional Speeches, Addresses, and Occasional Sermons*, 2 vols. Boston: Little, Brown, 1855.

———. *The Collected Works of Theodore Parker*. 14 vols. Edited by Frances Power Cobbe. London: Trübner, 1863–64.

———. *Speeches, Addresses, and Occasional Sermons*, 2 vols. Boston: William Crosby and H. P. Nichols, 1852.

———. *Theodor Parkers Saemmtliche Werke*. 5 vols. Translated by Johannes Ziethen. Leipzig: Voigt and Günther, 1854–61.

——. *Theodore Parker: An Anthology*. Edited by Henry Steele Commager. Boston: Beacon, 1960.

——. *The Trial of Theodore Parker, for the "Misdemeanor" of A Speech in Fanueil Hall against Kidnapping, before the Circuit Court of the United States, at Boston, April 3, 1855. With the Defence.* 1855. Reprint, New York: Negro University Press, 1970.

——. *Untersuchen über Religion.* Translated by Heinrich Wolf. Kiel: Carl Schröder, 1848.

——. *West Roxbury Sermons, 1837–1848.* Edited by F. B. Sanborn. Boston: Roberts Brothers, 1892.

——. *The Works of Theodore Parker.* 15 vols. Centennial Edition. Boston: American Unitarian Association, 1907–13.

Parker, Theodore. *Genealogy and Biographical Notes of John Parker of Lexington and his Descendants, Showing his Earlier Ancestry in America from Dea. Thomas Parker of Reading, Mass.: From 1635 to 1893.* Worcester: Charles Hamilton, 1893.

Parkman, Francis, Jr. *The Journals of Francis Parkman.* Edited by Mason Wade. 2 vols. New York: Harper and Brothers, 1947.

Parrington, Vernon. "Theodore Parker." In *The Main Currents of American Thought: Interpretation of American Literature from the Beginning to 1920*, vol. 2, pt. 3, chap. 4. New York: Harcourt, Brace, 1930.

Peabody, Andrew. "Memoir of Alvan Lamson." *Proceedings of the Massachusetts Historical Society* 11 (1869–70): 258–62.

Peabody, Elizabeth Palmer. *The Letters of Elizabeth Palmer Peabody, American Renaissance Woman.* Edited by Bruce A. Ronda. Middletown, Conn.: Wesleyan University Press, 1984.

——. *Record of Mr. Alcott's School, Exemplifying the Principles and Methods of Moral Culture.* 3rd ed. Boston: Roberts Brothers, 1974.

——. *Reminiscences of Rev. Wm. Ellery Channing, D.D.* Boston: Roberts Brothers, 1880.

Pearson, Henry Greenleaf. *The Life of John A. Andrew, Governor of Massachusetts, 1861–1865.* Boston: Houghton, Mifflin and Company, 1904.

Peterson, Mark A. *The Price of Redemption: The Spiritual Economy of Puritan New England.* Stanford: Stanford University Press, 1997.

Phelps, Amos A. *An Argument for the Perpetuity of the Sabbath.* Boston: D. S. King, 1841.

Pickering, Mary. *Auguste Comte: An Intellectual Biography.* Vol. 1. Cambridge: Cambridge University Press, 1993.

Pierce, Frederic Clifton. *Batchelder, Batcheller Genealogy.* Chicago: W. B. Conkey, 1898.

Proceedings of an Ecclesiastical Council, in the Case of the Proprietors of Hollis Street Meeting House and the Rev. John Pierpont, their Pastor. Samuel K. Lothrop, scribe. Boston: W. W. Clapp and Son, 1841.

Proceedings of the Lexington Historical Society and Papers Relating to the History of the Town. 4 vols. Lexington: Lexington Historical Society, 1890–1912.

Puknat, Siegfried B. "De Wette in New England." *Proceedings of the American Philosophical Society* 102, no. 4 (August 1958): 376–95.

Putnam, Elizabeth Cabot, and James Jackson Putnam. *The Hon. Jonathan Jackson and Hannah (Tracy) Jackson, their Ancestors and Descendents.* Boston [?]: privately printed, 1907.

Questions Addressed to Rev. T. Parker and His Friends. Boston: Halliburton and Dudley, 1845.

Remarks on an Article from the Christian Examiner, entitled "Mr. Parker and his Views." Boston: William Crosby and H. P. Nichols, 1845.

Réville, Albert. *Théodore Parker, sa vie et ses oevres: un chapitre de l'histoire de l'abolition de l'esclavage aux états-unis.* Paris: Reinwald, Cherbuliez, 1865.

Richardson, Robert D., Jr. *Emerson: The Mind on Fire.* Berkeley: University of California Press, 1995.

Ripley, George. *Defence of the "The Latest Form of Infidelity" Examined. A Second Letter to Mr. Andrews Norton, occasioned by his defence of a Discourse on "The Latest Form of Infidelity."* Boston: James Munroe, 1840.

———. *Defence of the "The Latest Form of Infidelity" Examined. A Third Letter to Mr. Andrews Norton, occasioned by his defence of a Discourse on "The Latest Form of Infidelity."* Boston: James Munroe, 1840.

———. *"The Latest Form of Infidelity" Examined. A Letter to Mr. Andrews Norton, occasioned by his "Discourse Before the Association of the Alumni of the Cambridge Theological School," on the 19th of July, 1839.* By "An Alumnus of that School." Boston: James Munroe, 1839.

———. *A Letter Addressed to the Congregational Church at Purchase Street.* Boston: Freeman and Bowles, 1840.

———, ed. and trans. *Philosophical Miscellanies. Translated from the French of Cousin, Jouffroy, and B. Constant. With Introductory and Critical Notices.* 2 vols. Specimens of Foreign Standard Literature. Boston: Hilliard, Grey, 1838.

Robinson, David. *Apostle of Culture: Emerson as Preacher and Reformer.* Philadelphia: University of Pennsylvania Press, 1982.

———. "The Theological Emergence of Transcendentalism." In *Transient and Permanent: The Transcendentalist Movement and Its Contexts.* Edited by Charles Capper and Conrad Edick Wright. Boston: Massachusetts Historical Society, 1999.

———. *The Unitarians and the Universalists.* Westport, Conn.: Greenwood Press, 1985.

Robinson, William S. *"Warrington" Pen Portraits: A Collection of Personal and Political Reminiscences from 1848 to 1876.* Boston: Mrs. William S. Robinson, 1877.

Rogerson, John W. *Old Testament Biblical Criticism in the Nineteenth Century: England and Germany.* London: Society for Promoting Christian Knowledge, 1984.

———. *W. M. L. de Wette, Founder of Modern Biblical Criticism: An Intellectual Biography.* Sheffield: Journal for the Study of the Old Testament Press, 1992.

Ronda, Bruce A. *Elizabeth Palmer Peabody: A Reformer on Her Own Terms.* Cambridge, Mass.: Harvard University Press, 1999.

Rosa, Alfred F. "'Aesthetic Culture': A Lyceum Lecture by William Silsbee." *Essex Institute Collections,* 107 (1971): 35–61.

Rose, Anne C. *Transcendentalism as a Social Movement, 1830–1850.* New Haven: Yale University Press, 1981.

Rousseau, Jean-Jacques. *Of the Social Contract.* Translated and edited by Richard W. Crosby. Brunswick, Ohio: King's Court Communications, 1978.

Rusk, Ralph. *The Life of Ralph Waldo Emerson*. New York: Charles Scribner and Sons, 1949.

Ryan, Thomas Richard. *Orestes A. Brownson: A Definitive Biography*. Huntington, Ind.: Our Sunday Visitor, 1976.

Sanborn, Franklin Benjamin. *Dr. S. G. Howe: The Philanthropist*. New York: Funk and Wagnalls, 1891.

———, ed. "Parker's Ecclesiastical Relations (1842–1843)." *West Roxbury Magazine* (1900): 41–46.

———. *Recollections of Seventy Years*. 2 vols. Boston: Gorham Press, 1909.

Sargent, Emma Worcester, and Charles Sprague Sargent. *Epes Sargent of Gloucester and His Descendents*. Boston: Houghton, Mifflin, 1922.

[Sargent, John Turner.] *An Answer to "Questions Addressed to Rev. T. Parker and his Friends."* By "A Friend Indeed." Boston: Andrews, Prentiss and Studley, 1845.

[———.] *The Crisis of Unitarianism in Boston, as Connected with the Twenty Eighth Congregational Society; with Some Account of the Origin and Decline of that Organization*. By "Bronze Beethoven, 'A Looker On.'" Boston: Walker, Wise, 1859.

———. *Ministry at Suffolk Street Chapel; its Origin, Progress and Experience*. Boston: Benjamin R. Greene, 1845.

———. *The Obstacles to Truth*. Boston: Samuel N. Dickenson, 1845.

[———.] *The True Position of Rev. Theodore Parker, being a Review of Rev. R. C. Waterston's Letter, in the Fourth Quarterly Report of the Benevolent Fraternity of Churches*. Boston: Andrews, Prentiss and Studley, 1845.

Schleiermacher, Friedrich. *On Religion: Speeches to Its Cultured Despisers*. Translated by John Oman. Introduction by Rudolf Otto. New York: Harper and Row, 1958.

Schlesinger, Arthur M., Jr. *Orestes A. Brownson: A Pilgrim's Progress*. Boston: Little, Brown, 1939. 2nd ed., *A Pilgrim's Progress: Orestes A. Brownson*. Boston: Little, Brown, 1966.

Schwartz, Harold. *Samuel Gridley Howe: Social Reformer, 1801–1876*. Cambridge, Mass.: Harvard University Press, 1956.

Schweitzer, Albert. *The Quest of the Historical Jesus: A Critical Study of Its Progress from Reimarus to Wrede*. Translated by W. Montgomery. Introduction by James M. Robinson. New York: Collier Books, Macmillan, 1968. Originally published as *Von Reimarus zu Wrede*. 1906.

Shaw, Francis George. "Robert Gould Shaw [1776–1853]." *Memorial Biographies of the New England Geneological Society* 2 (1853–55): 38–61.

Shepard, Odell. *Pedlar's Progress: The Life of Bronson Alcott*. Boston: Little, Brown, 1937.

Sibley's Harvard Graduates. 18 vols. Vols. 1–17, Cambridge, Mass.: Harvard University Press, 1873–1975; vol. 18, Boston: Massachussetts Historical Society, 2000.

Simmons, Nancy Craig. "Margaret Fuller's Boston Conversations: The 1839–1840 Series." *Studies in the American Renaissance* (1994): 195–226.

Smith, H. Shelton. "Was Theodore Parker a Transcendentalist?" *New England Quarterly* 23 (1950): 351–64.

The South-Boston Unitarian Ordination. Boston: Saxton and Pierce, 1841.

Spevack, Edmund. *Charles Follen's Search for Nationality and Freedom: Germany and America, 1796–1840*. Cambridge, Mass.: Harvard University Press, 1997.

Staehelm, Ernst. *Dewettiana: Forsuchen und Texte zu Wilhelm Martin Leberecht de Wettes Leben und Werke*. Basel: Helbing and Lichtenhahn, 1956.

Stange, Douglas C. *Patterns of Antislavery among American Unitarians, 1831–1860*. Cranbury, N.J.: Associated University Presses, 1977.

Stanton, Elizabeth Cady. *Eighty Years and More: Reminiscences, 1815–1897*. 1898. Reprint, Boston: Northeastern University Press, 1993.

Stanton, Elizabeth Cady, and Susan B. Anthony. *The Collected Papers of Elizabeth Cady Stanton and Susan B. Anthony*. 2 vols. to date. Edited by Ann D. Gordon. New Brunswick, N.J.: Rutgers University Press, 1997.

A Statement of the Course of Instruction, Terms of Admission, Expenses, &c at Harvard University. Cambridge, Mass.: Harvard University Press, 1823.

Stevenson, Hannah. "Theodore Parker: A Biographical Sketch." In *A Discourse of Matters Pertaining to Religion*, by Theodore Parker. New York: G. Putnam and Sons, 1876.

Stone, Richard Cecil. *Life Incidents of Home, School and Church*. St. Louis: Southwestern Book and Publishing Company, 1874.

Story, Ronald. *The Forging of an Aristocracy: Harvard and the Boston Upper Class, 1800–1870*. Middletown, Conn.: Wesleyan University Press, 1980.

Stout, Harry S. *The New England Soul: Preaching and Religious Culture in Colonial New England*. Oxford: Oxford University Press, 1986.

Strauss, David Friedrich. *The Life of Jesus Critically Examined*. Translated by George Eliot. Introduction by Peter C. Hodgson. Philadelphia: Fortress Press, 1972. Originally published as *Das Leben Jesu, kritisch bearbeitet*. 2 vols. 1836.

———. *Soliloquies on the Christian Religion*. London: John Chapman, 1845. Originally published as "Über Vergängliches un Bleibendes im Christianthum." *Die Freihaven* 3 (1838): 1–48. Reprinted in *Zwei Friedliche Blätter*. Altona, 1839.

Swift, Lindsay. *Brook Farm: Its Members, Scholars and Visitors*. New York: Macmillan, 1904.

Teed, Paul. "'A Very Excellent Fanatic, a Very Good Infidel and a First-Rate Traitor': Theodore Parker and the Search for Perfection in Antebellum America." Ph.D. dissertation, University of Connecticut, 1994.

Thom, John Hamilton, ed. *The Life of the Reverend Joseph Blanco White*. 2 vols. London: John Chapman, 1845.

Thomas, George Moses. *A Rejected Article in Reply to Parker's Review of "Hennell on the Origin of Christianity."* By "A Unitarian Minister." Boston: Benjamin H. Greene, 1844.

Tourtellot, Arthur B. *Lexington and Concord: The Beginning of the War of the American Revolution*. New York: W. W. Norton, 1963.

The Truth Revealed. STATEMENT and Review of the Whole Case of the Reverend J. H. Fairchild, from its Commencement to its Termination, Compiled from Original Documents. Boston: Wright's Stream Press, 1845.

Unitarianism Identified with Deism; Exhibited in a Review of a Discourse Lately Delivered by the Rev. Mr. Parker, in Boston. By "Junius." New York: Charles R. Moore, 1842.

Walters, Ronald G. *American Reformers, 1815–1860*. New York: Hill and Wang, 1978. Rev. ed., 1997.

Ware, George F. *Answer to Questions Contained in Mr. Parker's Letter to the Boston Association of Congregational Ministers*. Boston: Andrews, Prentiss and Studley, 1845.

Ware, Henry. *An Inquiry into the Foundation, Evidences, and Truths of Religion*. 2 vols. Cambridge, Mass.: John Owen; Boston: James Munroe, 1842.

Ware, Henry, Jr. *The Life of the Saviour*. 7th ed. Boston: American Unitarian Association, 1873.

———. *Works*. 4 vols. Boston: James Munroe, 1846–47.

Ware, John. *Memoir of the Life of Henry Ware, Jr.* 2 vols. Boston: American Unitarian Association, 1874.

Ware, William. *Righteousness before Doctrine*. Boston: Freeman and Bowles, 1845.

Waterston, Robert Cassie. *The True Position of the Christian Church in Relation to the Age*. Boston: William Crosby and H. P. Nichols, 1847.

Weiss, Fredrick Lewis, compiler. "List of the Unitarian Churches and Their Ministers in the United States and Canada." Unpublished typescript, Meadville/Lombard Theological School, ca. 1960. Copy Andover-Harvard Theological Library.

Weiss, John. *Discourse Occasioned by the Death of Convers Francis, D.D.* Cambridge, Mass.: Welch, Bigelow, 1863.

———. *The Life and Correspondence of Theodore Parker, Minister of the Twenty-eighth Congregational Society, Boston*. 2 vols. Boston: D. Appleton, 1864. Reprint, New York: Negro University Press, 1969.

Welch, Claude. *Protestant Thought in the Nineteenth Century*. 2 vols. New Haven: Yale University Press, 1972.

Wellek, René. *Confrontations: Studies in the Intellectual and Literary Relations between Germany, England and the United States during the Nineteenth Century*. Princeton: Princeton University Press, 1965.

Wendte, Charles G. *Bibliography and Index to the Works of Theodore Parker*. Boston: American Unitarian Association, 1913.

Whewell, William. *History of the Inductive Sciences, from the Earliest to the Present Times*. London: J. W. Parker, 1837.

Whipple, Charles K. *A Chapter of Theological and Religious Experience*. Boston: R. F. Wallcut, 1858.

Williams, Avery. *A Discourse, Delivered at Lexington, March 31st, 1813, the Day which Completed a Century from the Incorperation of the Town*. Boston: Samuel T. Armstrong, 1813.

Williams, George Hunston, ed. *The Harvard Divinity School: Its Place in Harvard University and in American Culture*. Boston: Beacon, 1954.

Woodhall, Guy R. "A Calendar of the Preaching Appointments of the Rev. Convers Francis with a List of His Manuscript Sermons." Unpublished research guide.

Worthen, Edward Burrough. *A Calendar History of Lexington, Massachusetts*. Lexington: The Bank, 1946.

Wright, Conrad. *The Beginnings of Unitarianism in America*. Boston: Starr King, 1955.

———. "The Dedham Case Revisited." In *The Unitarian Controversy: Essays in American Unitarian History*. Boston: Skinner House Books, 1994.

———. *The Liberal Christians: Essays on American Unitarian History*. Boston: American Unitarian Association, 1970.

————, ed. *A Stream of Light: A Short History of American Unitarianism*. Boston: Unitarian Universalist Association, 1975.

————. *Three Prophets of Religious Liberalism: Channing, Emerson, Parker*. Boston: Beacon, 1961.

Wright, Conrad Edick, ed. *American Unitarianism, 1805–1865*. Boston: Massachusetts Historical Society and Northeastern University Press, 1989.

Index

Boston and South Boston, Mass., ix, xi, 1,
3, 11, 12, 13, 24, 47, 53, 56, 57, 58, 76,
77, 80, 81, 86, 87, 88, 90, 103, 107, 119,
176, 197, 238, 248, 251, 252, 253, 255,
259, 260, 261, 264, 266–70, 291, 292,
312, 323, 324, 326, 335–39, 341, 343,
353, 379, 381, 382, 383, 385, 390, 396,
402, 411, 416, 418, 420, 424, 458, 462,
463, 466, 468, 473, 476, 477, 483, 489,
494, 495, 498
Boston Association of Congregational
Ministers, 127, 141, 182, 297, 378, 422,
458–59; and TP, 132, 253, 257, 267,
304, 352, 355–69, 417–18, 423, 424,
427–29, 444–48, 487, 489, 491, 573
(n. 163). *See also* Fellowship, ministerial;
Thursday Lecture
Boston Daily Advertiser, 83, 121, 124, 497,
541 (n. 28)
Boston Quarterly Review, 108, 116, 120,
134, 156, 214, 237, 261, 262, 293, 319,
322, 546 (n. 129). *See also* Brownson,
Orestes Augustus
Boston Recorder, 248
Boston Semi-Weekly Courier, 121, 256, 258,
417, 423, 541 (n. 28)
Boston Society of Natural History, 399
Bowen, Francis, 103, 120, 121, 125
Brackett, Samuel, 438
Bradford, John, 89
Brattle Square Church (Boston, Mass.),
246, 306, 442
Bridge (member of West Church, Boston),
461–62
Bridgman, Laura, 385
Briggs, Charles, 16, 17, 18, 132, 506
(n. 41)
Brisbane, Albert, 218, 219, 410
Broad, Nathaniel, and Broad family, 25,
36–37, 38
Brook Farm, 91, 218, 222, 235, 238,
261, 292–93, 302, 306, 328–31, 375,
463, 495–96; and TP, 222, 302, 327–31,
410–11, 495–96, 553 (n. 99). *See also*
Fourier, Charles/Fourierism/Associa-
tionism
Brookline, Mass., 115, 246
Brooks, Charles, 311
Brosses, Charles de, 544 (n. 84)

Brown, James (TP's publisher). *See* Little
and Brown
Brown, William, 24
Brownson, Orestes Augustus, 64, 104,
107, 109, 116, 117, 120, 123, 134, 207,
318, 469, 476, 521 (n. 99), 550 (n. 67),
551 (n. 72); described, 107, 321; and TP,
107–8, 156, 237, 261–62, 268, 270–71,
293–94, 320–22, 411–12, 535 (n. 153),
542 (n. 41), 546 (nn. 128, 129); *New
Views of Christianity, Society, and the
Church*, 118; "The Laboring Classes,"
214–17, 222–24, 534 (n. 124), 535
(n. 153); converts to Catholicism, 271,
293, 411
Brownson's Quarterly Review, 412
Buckingham, Joseph, 256
Burkhardt, Jacob, 515 (n. 111)
Burlington, Vt., 27
Burnet, Thomas, 470
Burns, Anthony, ix
Byron, George Gordon, Lord, 79

Cabot, Follen, 90
Cabot, Frederick, 80, 90, 339
Cabot, George (LCP's brother), 327, 496,
552 (n. 93)
Cabot, George (senator), 37, 97
Cabot, George Colburn ("Georgie," TP's
ward), 326, 327, 398, 552 (n. 93); at
Brook Farm, 327, 328, 495
Cabot, John (LCP's father), 37, 98, 178
Cabot, John Lee (LCP's brother), 101,
167, 326, 327, 552 (n. 93)
Cabot, Lucy ("Aunt Lucy"), 37, 59, 91,
149, 327, 329, 529 (n. 92); and TP, 37,
79, 86–89, 96–99, 102, 113, 167–68,
176, 179, 302, 317, 318, 321, 366, 372,
374, 382, 397–98, 413–14, 495; and
LCP, 37, 96, 98, 102, 176, 320, 327,
398, 414, 495, 497–98; lack of surviving
papers of, 92; only surviving sentences
in hand of, 101; death of, 496; terms of
will, 496–98
Cabot, Lydia Dodge (LCP). *See* Parker,
Lydia Dodge Cabot
Cabot, Lydia Dodge (LCP's mother), 37
Calhoun, John C., 59, 474
Calvin, John, 442

Flagg, John, 89
Flint, John, 458
Florence, Italy, 382, 387, 394, 401
Florida, 318
Follen, Karl, 17, 54, 90, 119, 335, 556 (n. 154), 564 (n. 56)
Folsom, Nathaniel, 247, 254, 255, 256, 257, 541 (n. 22)
Ford, Patience, 305
Fourier, Charles (Françoise Marie)/ Fourierism/Associationism, 91, 134, 495–96; and TP, 218–19, 329, 333, 410–11. *See also* Brook Farm; Property/ social inequality/pauperism/labor/work
Fox, George, 219
France, 62, 64, 166, 278, 323, 386. *See also* Revolution, French
Francis, Abby B. Allyn ("Mrs. Francis"), 312, 549 (n. 49)
Francis, Convers, 32, 55, 75, 104, 118, 119, 127, 164, 184, 187, 237, 281, 379, 387, 388, 391, 392, 393, 394, 401; and TP, 32–35, 65, 80, 88, 104–5, 134, 175, 198, 201, 232, 238, 264, 462, 489, 506 (n. 41); and views of Bible, 33–35, 154, 155–56, 313, 354; TP's disappointment with, 309–16, 322, 368, 382, 550 (n. 62); as professor at Harvard Divinity School, 310–11, 313–15
"Friends of Theodore Parker." *See* Melodeon Theater/Melodeon Congregation; Twenty-Eighth Congregational Society
Fries, J. F., 72
Frost, Barzillai, 77, 118, 213, 516 (n. 5), 517 (n. 15)
Frothingham, Nathaniel Langdon ("Dr. Frothingham"), 47, 48, 119, 132, 235, 345, 357, 360, 363–65, 367–69, 447–49, 486; TP regards as hypocrite, 352–55, 368, 379
Frothingham, Octavius Brooks, ix
Fruitlands, 238, 409–10
Fugitive slaves/Fugitive Slave Law, ix, 11, 497. *See also* Latimer, George
Fuller, Margaret (Sarah), 100, 104, 127, 177, 190, 238, 240, 261, 296, 319, 429, 511 (n. 35); *Eckermann's Conversations with Goethe*, 110; edits *Dial*, 110, 179, 236, 347, 409; described, 110–11; and

TP, 110–13, 241, 352, 441; *Woman in the 19th Century*, 409
Fuller, Timothy, 110
Furness, William Henry, 159, 198, 280

Galileo Galilei, 273
Gannett, Ezra Stiles ("Dr. Gannett"), 41, 132, 253, 267, 268, 345, 417, 418, 422, 425, 453, 458–59, 573 (n. 156), 579 (n. 100); described, 297; and TP, 297–99, 358–60, 365–67, 369, 412–13, 427–28, 444–48, 450–51, 459, 490–91, 547 (n. 12), 561 (n. 240), 566 (n. 14), 568 (n. 68), 572 (n. 141)
Garrison, William Lloyd, ix, 53, 54, 173, 230, 233, 335, 459, 471, 473, 475, 537 (n. 175)
Geneva, Switzerland, 387
George III (king of Great Britain), 395
Georgia, 172
Germany/German culture/German states, 63, 64, 166, 188, 192, 200–202, 381–83, 388, 395–97, 398, 485
Gervinius, Georg, 387
Gesenius, Wilhelm, 68, 390
Gibbon, Edward, 387
God: arguments for, 62, 63, 64, 72, 173, 277, 289–90; personality of, 110, 116, 125–26, 137; theodicy and TP's conceptions of, 6, 29, 110, 115, 117, 139, 140, 142, 153
Goethe, Christiane Vulpius (Frau von Goethe), 387
Goethe, Johann Wolfgang von, 38, 67, 80, 134, 136, 202, 319, 387
Goodhue, Sarah Jane. *See* Colburn, Sarah Jane Goodhue
Goodwin, Hersey, 75
Gospels. *See* Bible/biblical criticism
Government/state, 173, 209, 406–7, 466–67
"Government of all, by all, for all," x, 402, 405–7, 498, 579 (n. 10). *See also* "American Idea"/"American project"
Graham, Sylvester, 206
Great Awakening, 13
Great Britain, 58, 62, 64. *See also* England; Scotland
Greece, 385

Greene, Columbus (TP's nephew), 35, 42, 43, 76; joins Parker household, 2; recollections of TP's childhood and youth by, 4, 5, 10, 18, 19, 21, 22, 23; relationship of to Lexington Church, 16–17; ordination of as Baptist minister, 17; and later relations with TP, 27

Greene, Hannah Parker (TP's sister), 7; death of, 27

Greene, Mary Parker (TP's sister), 510 (n. 26); baptized, 7; death of, 27

Greene, Nathaniel, 318

Greene, Samuel (TP's brother-in-law): death of, 27

Greene, William Batchelder, 177, 318–23, 551 (nn. 67, 72); described, 177, 318; and marriage to Anna Blake Shaw, 177, 321, 323, 326, 552 (n. 76)

Greenfield, Mass., 86, 87, 518 (n. 32)

Greenwood, F. W. P., 120

Gregory XVI (pope), 393, 394

Grimké, Sarah and Angelina, 206

Groton, Mass. *See* Christian Union Convention

Grund, Francis, 24

Half-Way Covenant, 8, 9

Hall, Nathaniel, 304–5, 356, 363, 364, 444, 447

Halle, Germany, 390

Hamlet, 311, 424

Hancock, John ("Bishop Hancock"), 12–14, 16, 18

Hancock, John (of Braintree), 506 (n. 37)

Hanover Street Church (Boston, Mass.), 12

Harbinger, 91, 410, 411, 496, 566 (n. 8)

Harris, Thaddeus Mason, 305

Harrison, William Henry, 208, 239, 576 (n. 39)

Hartford Convention, 37

Harvard, Mass., 409

Harvard College and University, 13, 17, 22, 32, 33, 113, 119, 157, 292, 301, 318, 388, 412, 416; and Unitarianism, 15, 39–40; bicentennial of, 80–81, 103

Harvard Divinity School, 25, 42, 113, 180, 311, 313, 321, 416, 486, 550 (n. 62); described, 39–40

Harvard Medical School, 435

Hastings, John, 20

Haverill, Mass., 247

Hawes Place Church (South Boston, Mass.), 238, 255, 260

Hawley, Silas, 225, 226, 228

Hawthorne, Nathaniel, 87, 328

Hayden, John, 326–27

Healey, Caroline Wells. *See* Dall, Caroline Wells Healey

Healey, Marian, 403

Healey, Mark, 269, 403, 457

Hedge, Frederick Henry, 54, 81, 102, 103, 104, 110, 116, 119, 120, 135, 190, 191, 199, 214, 238, 314, 315

Hegel, Georg Wilhelm Friedrich/ Hegelianism, 64, 135, 136, 137, 191, 192, 193, 389, 390

Heidelberg, Germany, 383

Hell. *See* Damnation/devils/Hell

Hengstenberg, E. W., 68, 135, 189, 191, 192, 193; TP hears lecture by, 389

Hennel, Charles Christian, 287

Hennell, Charles, 287, 389

Herbert, Edward Lord, of Cherbury, 367

Herder, Johann Gottfried, 64, 68, 81, 82, 136, 202, 381, 405; TP purchases *Werke*, 67

Hermann, Johann, 390

Herndon, William ("Billy"), x

Higginson, Thomas Wentworth, ix

Himes, Joshua, 230, 231

Hingham, Mass., 469

Hodge, Charles, 191, 193, 204

Holbein, Hans (the Younger), 391

Hollis Street Church/Hollis Street Council (Boston, Mass.), 232, 344–52, 356, 357, 359, 418, 420, 451, 453, 454–55, 458–60, 473, 490. *See also* Parker, Theodore: writings: "Hollis Street Council"; Pierpont, John

Holmes, Oliver Wendell, 37, 497

Holmes, Oliver Wendell, Jr., 37, 497

Home: religious role of, 142–43

Homer, 135, 178, 179

Homosexuality, 135

Hopper, Isaac T., 379

Hopper, John, 379

Howe, Julia Romana: TP baptizes, 385–86

Labor. *See* Property/social inequality/
pauperism/labor/work
Lamennais, Hughes de, 293
Lamson, Alvan, 134, 231, 264, 316, 382;
TP's disappointment with, 308–9, 368
Lane, Charles, 409–10
Latimer, George: and Latimer fugitive
slave case, 336–40. *See also* Antislavery/
abolitionism; Fugitive slaves/Fugitive
Slave Law
Latimer Journal and North Star, 337
Lawrence, Mass., 397
Leibniz, Gottfried Wilhelm von, 36, 275
Leipzig, Germany, 387, 390, 392
Lenox, Mass., 369
Leominster, Mass., 227
Leonardus de Unterio, 315
Lessing, G. E., 68, 202, 521 (n. 92)
Lexington, Battle of, 10–12
Lexington, Mass./Lexington Church, 1, 7,
8, 21, 24, 27, 36, 118, 176, 402, 415–16,
504 (n. 25), 505 (n. 30), 573 (n. 145);
sacred geography of, 12
Liberal Christianity. *See* Unitarianism
Liberator, 53, 54, 473
Liberty Bell, 335
Liberty Party, 472
Lincoln, Abraham, x. *See also* "Govern-
ment of all, by all, for all"
Lincoln, Mass., 415
Lippert (Jewish physician), 392
Little and Brown (publishers), 275, 315,
373, 390
Liverpool, England, 374, 382, 383, 389
Locke, John, 36, 62, 83, 193, 276
Loco Foco. *See* Democratic Party
London, England, x, 382, 383, 386, 387,
388, 402
Lord's Supper, 8–9, 76, 228, 411, 486; TP
administers, 131, 465, 489; TP's views
on, 149, 174, 224, 225; controversy over
TP's comparison of to child's rattle,
280–81, 423, 445–46, 452–53
Lothrop, Samuel Kirkland, 246, 248, 256,
345, 417, 418, 420, 432, 572 (n. 141);
and debate with Fairchild, 257–59; and
TP, 258, 262–63, 306–7, 356, 357–58,
431, 444, 445, 448
Louisville, Ky., 122

Lovejoy, Elijah, 334
Lowell, Charles, 461–62
Lowell, Josephine Shaw: TP baptizes, 91
Lowell, Mass., 27, 87, 397
Lunt, William, 357, 444, 573 (n. 163)
Luther, Martin, 66, 315, 350; TP's identifi-
cation with, 343, 388, 468, 492

Manchester, England, 394–95
Mann, Horace, ix, 171, 206, 396, 470, 472
Marblehead, Mass., 415
Marseilles, France, 382, 386
Marsh, Christopher, 90
Martineau, Harriet, 108, 521 (n. 99)
Martineau, James: *Rationale of Religious
Enquiry*, 81, 82, 263; and TP, 389
Marx, Karl/Marxism, 209, 216, 219, 399
Massachusetts Evangelical Missionary
Society, 120
Massachusetts Quarterly Review, 111
Matthiessen, F. O., xi
May, Abigail Williams ("Abby"), 459
May, Mary Goddard, 473
May, Samuel (abolitionist), 459
May, Samuel ("Deacon May"), 459, 473
May, Samuel Joseph, 55, 56, 415–16, 459,
473
Mayhew, Jonathan, 14
McKean, Hannah Stevenson, 566 (n. 21)
Medfield, Mass., 304
Medford, Mass., 88, 304
Meiners, Christoph, 278, 544 (n. 84)
Melodeon Theater/Melodeon congrega-
tion (Boston, Mass.), 460–67, 473, 475,
477, 483, 484, 498
Methodism/Methodists, 248, 435
Methuen, Mass., 319, 551 (n. 72)
Mexico/Mexican War, 471–72, 475, 498
Michaelis, Johann, 67, 68, 135
Middle Ages, 201, 203–4. *See also*
Feudalism
Middle class, 206, 493
Milan, Italy, 394
Militia, 11, 505 (n. 27)
Millerism/Millerites, 225–26, 443
Miracles, 5, 43–49, 62, 81–83, 114, 121,
123, 124, 127, 138, 180–82, 185, 191,
198–99, 251–53, 268, 280, 304, 308,
313, 353–54, 364, 367, 368, 418, 423,

428, 429, 431, 434, 436, 443, 456, 511
(n. 50); TP's views on, 31–32, 35, 36,
42–43, 46–49, 69, 73–74, 84–86, 123,
138, 148–51, 153, 157–60, 187–88,
195–98, 203–4, 211–12, 245, 251–53,
269, 284, 290–91, 364, 367, 368, 427,
445, 451–52, 464, 479, 528 (n. 76), 533
(n. 89), 545 (n. 102). *See also* Authority,
religious; Bible/biblical criticism; Christianity and religious truth; Inspiration,
divine; Jesus/Christology; Norton-
Ripley debates; Prophecy; Strauss, David
Friedrich; Supernatural rationalism
Missouri, 474
Mohammed ("Mohamet"), the Prophet,
146, 236
Monopolies, 404
Monroe, William, 11
Monthly Miscellany, 229, 253, 297, 299,
358–59
More, Henry, 134, 160, 175, 203
Morison, J. H., 280, 544 (n. 90)
Mormonism/Mormons, 299, 427, 443, 510
(n. 26)
Morse, Jedidiah, 15
Moses, Mary Ann, 326
Moses/Mosaic Law, 44, 84, 153, 154,
156–57, 168–70, 183, 232–33, 284, 425,
468
Motte, Melish, 548 (n. 23), 549 (n. 49)
Munich, Germany, 192, 397, 398
Muzzey, Artemas, 573 (n. 145)
Muzzey, John, 4
Myths. *See* Bible/biblical criticism; De
Wette, Wilhelm Martin Leberecht;
Jesus/Christology; Miracles; Strauss,
David Friedrich

Nantucket, Mass., 415
Naples, 381, 383–85
Napoleon I (emperor of France), 406
Nature/natural world, 77, 434; TP's views
on, 1–2, 86–87, 141–42, 162
Neander, Johann, 389
Nearing, Helen Knothe and Scott, 410
Nell, William Cooper, 472
Neo-Orthodoxy, xi
New Bedford, Mass., 268, 415
New Divinity, 13

New England Anti-Slavery Society, 55,
498
New Englander, 292, 430, 455
New England Primer, 10
New Jersey, 191
New Lights, 13
Newman, Francis, 389
Newman, John Henry, 389
New North Church (Boston, Mass.), 355
Newport, R.I., 57, 369
New Testament. *See* Bible/biblical
criticism
Newton, Mass., 37, 87, 295, 319, 321
New York, 343
New York City, 55, 205–6, 374, 379–80,
382, 385, 396, 463, 496
New York Herald, 427
New York Observer, 232, 253
New York Tribune, 409, 441, 496
Niagara Falls, 59
North, George G., 524 (n. 6)
North American Review, 45, 119
Northampton, Mass., 306
Northfield, Mass., 80, 517 (n. 15)
Norton, Andrews, 33, 45, 48, 49, 82,
121, 123, 152, 154, 193, 204, 239, 254,
255, 354, 517 (n. 22); *Genuineness of the
Gospels*, 49, 189, 512 (n. 60); and TP,
83–84, 180, 276; on Divinity School
Address, 125; *Latest Form of Infidelity*,
128, 180–81, 186. *See also* Norton-
Ripley debates
Norton-Ripley debates, 83–84, 85, 120,
180–82, 184–86, 190–94, 198–200, 203,
214. *See also* Inspiration, divine: debates
over; Miracles; Norton, Andrews; Ripley, George
Noyes, George Rapall, 47, 48, 122, 353

Ohio, 401, 576 (n. 39)
Old Testament. *See* Bible/biblical criticism
"Old World." *See* Europe
Original sin, 13, 14, 42, 44
Orthodox Congregationalism. *See* Calvin-
ism/Orthodox Congregationalism
Owen, Robert, 177
Oxford, England/Oxford University, 382,
387, 389
Oxford Movement, 257, 395

Paine, Thomas ("Tom Paine"), 250, 253, 300, 303, 360, 461, 540 (n. 7), 542 (n. 38)

Paley, William, 5

Palfrey, John Gorham ("Dean Palfrey"), 25, 41, 45–46, 48, 49, 50, 61, 67, 82, 124, 134, 152, 154, 190; *Academical Lectures on Jewish Scriptures*, 156–57, 509 (n. 4), 511 (nn. 42, 49)

Palmer, Edward, 206

Palmer, Joseph, 227

Panic of 1837, 88, 207

Pantheism, 109–10, 121, 125, 191, 193, 390, 443

Papacy. *See* Catholics/Catholicism/papacy/pope

Paris, France, 323, 381, 382, 387, 388, 389

Parker, Emily (TP's sister): as TP's playmate, 6; baptized, 7; death of, 27

Parker, Hannah. *See* Greene, Hannah Parker

Parker, Hannah Stearns (TP's mother), 1, 2; described, 5–6; TP's relationship with, 6–7, 10; and religious training of TP, 6–10, 485; religious beliefs of, 7–10, 17; death of, 27; age of at TP's birth, 502 (n. 1)

Parker, Hiram (TP's brother): baptized, 7; intemperance of, 27, 167, 508 (n. 74)

Parker, Isaac (TP's brother), 27, 176; baptized, 7

Parker, John ("Captain John," TP's grandfather), 2, 10, 11

Parker, John (TP's brother), 7; death of, 27

Parker, John (TP's father), 1, 10, 15, 18, 19, 502 (n. 3); occupation of, 2; described, 3–4; and TP, 4, 20, 22, 36; rationality of religiousness of, 4–5, 17; studious habits of, 5, 18; death of, 27–28, 85; age of at TP's birth, 502 (n. 1)

Parker, Jonas, 11

Parker, Lydia (TP's sister): baptized, 7; death of, 27, 101

Parker, Lydia Dodge Cabot (LCP), 59, 60, 67, 79, 85–87, 132, 312, 323, 326, 510 (n. 23), 529 (n. 92); description and character of, 37–38, 320–21, 327, 384–85, 399–400, 564 (n. 60); and Lucy Cabot ("Aunt Lucy"), 37, 96, 98, 102, 176, 320, 327, 398, 414, 495, 497–98; scarcity of surviving papers of, 92, 94, 519 (n. 53); attends Margaret Fuller's conversations, 100, 110

—and TP, 4, 36, 38–39, 75, 302, 379–81, 384–85, 388, 394, 495–98; wedding and anniversaries of, 87, 382–83; marriage problems of, 91–96, 99–102, 106, 167–68, 176, 177, 179–80, 316–18, 320–21, 366, 520 (n. 77); literary executor of, 92; childlessness of and willingness to take in children, 95, 327, 519 (n. 63), 552 (n. 96); and improvements in marriage, 327–28, 397–401, 414, 485; and nickname "Bear," 399–401, 564 (n. 59)

Parker, Mary. *See* Greene, Mary Parker

Parker, Rebecca (TP's sister): baptized, 7; death of, 7, 27

Parker, Ruth (TP's sister): baptized, 7; death of, 27

Parker, Theodore (TP): described, x, 1, 20–21, 41–42, 102, 175, 321, 385, 387

CHARACTER/CHARACTERISTICS

—aesthetic sense of, 386–87, 394

—ambition of, 18, 25–26, 60, 88–89, 118, 132–33, 175, 176, 265, 266, 372, 483–84, 488, 491

—criticism and conflict, ability to deal with, 41–42, 98–99, 101–2, 182, 184, 262–63, 295–99, 437, 458–59, 537 (n. 184), 544 (n. 90)

—humor, sarcasm, and satire of, 21, 35–36, 41, 43, 65–66, 96–97, 191–92, 203–4, 208–9, 237, 297, 300, 312–13, 315, 328, 335–36, 383–84

—as martyr and prophet: self-conception of, 292, 299–300, 340, 342–43, 351, 362, 401, 437, 483–84, 487–88, 491–92; self-documentation as, 361–62, 364, 482–83, 489; and interest in/praise for martyrs and prophets, 387–88, 480–81

—maturity or immaturity of, 401–2

—public appeal of, ix, x, 290–92, 340, 371–72, 461–62, 492–94

—remarkable memory of, 19

—social skills of, 132, 321

—weeping, tendency toward and instances

of, 21, 39, 50, 184, 352, 361, 369, 402, 487

PERSONAL LIFE

—birth and birthdays of, 1, 21, 22, 78, 146, 177, 266, 373, 402
—childhood and youth of: early joys of, 1–2; home of, 1–2, 12, 22, 503 (n. 2); early sorrows of, 26–30; and recollections of early sorrows, 95, 402, 485
—marriage and household: engagement of, 36–39; wedding of, 87, 105; household of, 88, 326–27, 518 (n. 35); problems in marriage of, 91–102, 106, 143, 167–68, 177, 179–80, 206, 316–18, 320–21, 366, 520 (n. 77); childlessness of, 95, 118, 317, 327, 519 (n. 63); craving for "sympathy" in, 96; improvements in marriage of, 327–28, 397–401, 414

EDUCATION/LEARNEDNESS

—languages, knowledge of, ix, 60; Latin, 20, 38, 41, 60; Greek, 20, 38, 60; French, 21, 37, 41, 60, 381; German, 24, 38, 41, 60, 381–82, 513 (n. 87); Hebrew, 24, 38, 41, 60; Anglo-Saxon, 60; Danish, 60; Dutch, 60; Italian, 60; Portuguese, 60; Swedish, 60; Æthiopic, 60, 61; Arabic, 60, 61; Chaldic, 60, 61; Coptic, 60, 61; Icelandish, 60; Persian, 60, 61
—reading/study by, 5, 18–19, 21, 22, 24, 25, 32–33, 38–39, 59–62, 64–70, 78–79, 80, 132–36, 201, 240, 276, 379–80, 387, 388, 472; and purchase of books and personal library, 20, 24, 25, 67, 132, 388–89, 496, 543 (n. 66)
—schools: primary, 19–26; Harvard College, 21–22, 507 (n. 60); Harvard Divinity School, 39–74 passim, 486, 510 (n. 28); and Visitation Day, 73, 83; and master's degree, 175

CAREER

—audiences of, ix, 77–78, 163–64, 175, 267–68, 340–41, 344, 375, 402–3, 415, 418, 425, 426, 461, 472, 477
—lectures at lyceums, ix, 24, 38, 267–68, 302, 338–41, 371, 401, 415, 445, 472
—literary activity of (not including sermons or lectures), ix, 23, 41, 133–34, 237, 371, 374, 507 (n. 64). *See also* writings

—as schoolmaster, 20–21, 24–25, 38, 39, 507 (n. 58); school committeeman, 131

MINISTRY

—baptisms performed by, 91, 131, 303, 385–86, 465, 504 (n. 23)
—Boston, ix, 457–62; moves to, 323, 495; vision of, 464–69, 478–82; and installation, 476–82
—early: and decision to become minister, 22–24; and Harvard Divinity School, 39–74 passim, 486, 510 (n. 28); candidacy of, 75–88, 517 (n. 15), 518 (n. 32), 520 (n. 84)
—funerals performed by, 78, 131
—Lord's Supper administered by, 131, 465, 489
—prophetic conception of, 348–51, 354, 375–76, 468–69, 479–80
—sabbatical, European, 315–16, 370–71, 374; travel experiences during, 379–402; intellectual effects of, 391–97, 402–7; personal effects of, 397–402
—sermons/preaching: first student exercise sermon, 50; first sermons to "real" audiences, 75; sermonic and preaching style, 75, 77–78, 175, 264, 343–44, 378–79, 462, 463, 536 (n. 161); habits of sermon writing, 130–31; first two sermons after ordination, 131, 148–49, 150, 165, 524 (n. 4); Thanksgiving sermons, 165, 172–73, 333, 462; Fast Day sermons, 165–66, 330, 576 (n. 41); on civil and political sins, 165–73; number of sermons and preachings (1841–43), 371, 560 (n. 230); during sabbatical, 382; first time preaching at Melodeon, 460; themes of preaching at Melodeon (1845–46), 463–69, 575 (n. 8). *See also* Fellowship, ministerial
—West Roxbury: reluctance to settle in, 79, 80, 86, 87; and ordination, 88; discontentment with smallness of parish in, 88–89, 118, 176–77, 301–2, 414–15; relationship with church and congregation in, 90, 163–64, 171, 234, 257, 291, 302–3, 374–79, 402–3, 459–60, 462–63, 473, 483; pastoral activities in, 129–32, 285, 396; recurring themes in weekly

described, 344; TP's sympathy with and admiration for, 346–52, 458–59, 481. *See also* Hollis Street Church/Hollis Street Council

Pitts Street Chapel (Boston, Mass.), 418

Plato/Platonism/Neo-Platonism, 104, 134, 136, 137, 138, 142, 160–62, 175, 203, 279

Plymouth, Mass., 268

Poland, 38, 507 (n. 66); partition of, 467

Politics, party, 208–9, 375, 376, 396, 469–72. *See also* Elections; *names of specific parties*

Polk, James Knox, 471–72

Pope, Alexander, 3, 19, 280

Popular opinion, 166, 350–51, 406

Porter, Noah, 292, 430, 431, 432, 448, 455–56, 545 (n. 102); friendship of with TP, 430, 456

Portsmouth, N.H., 462–63

Prague, Austrian Empire, 383; TP visits Jewish quarter in, 391–92

Prayer/prayers, 24, 78, 101, 129–30, 145–47, 171

Predestination, 13, 14

Presbyterianism, 107, 343

Prichard, James, 290

"Primitive state of mankind," 281–83, 290

Princeton Review, 191, 200

Princeton University, 191, 193

Property/social inequality/pauperism/ labor/work, 51, 171–72, 205, 206, 207, 214–22, 329–33, 396–97, 403–4, 468–69, 534 (n. 124); TP's views on, 52, 143, 171, 205, 214–22, 302, 329–33, 396–97, 403–4, 468–69. *See also* Brook Farm; Fourier, Charles/Fourierism/ Associationism

Prophecy, 46–48, 353–54; TP's views on, 46–48, 74, 512 (n. 52)

Protestantism, 394–96

Proudhon, Pierre-Joseph, 177

Providence, R.I., 110

Prussia. *See* Berlin, Germany; Germany/ German culture/German states

Publishers, TP's. *See* Little and Brown; Peabody, Elizabeth Palmer

Pulpit, freedom of, 269–70, 345, 492

Purchase Street Church (Boston, Mass.),

81, 207, 234, 251, 442; considers inviting TP as minister, 235, 240, 301

Puritan, 248, 254, 255, 257, 299

Puritanism/Puritans, 8, 130, 185, 320, 323, 338, 394, 492, 505 (n. 29). *See also* Great Awakening

Putnam, George, 81, 102, 103, 119, 246, 256, 558 (nn. 192, 193, 194); and confrontation with TP, 360–61

Quakerism, 185, 231, 439

Quincy, Edmund, 231; and TP, 235, 334–35, 339, 347, 351, 366, 472

Quincy, Josiah, 22, 40, 80

Quincy, Mass./Quincy churches, 88, 357, 444, 469

Race, 290, 530 (n. 119)

Raphael Sanzio, 386

Rationalism, German, 69, 70, 72, 138, 515 (n. 112)

Redlon, Julia Francis (LCP's adopted daughter), 552 (n. 96)

Reid, Thomas, 63

Reimarus, Hermann Samuel, 68, 69, 297, 298

Religion: nature of, and religious experience, 14, 72–73, 289, 505 (n. 36); and TP on religious sentiment or element, 29, 85, 194–95, 289–90; TP on origin of in feelings, 70, 73–74; TP on progressive development of, 265–67. *See also* Inspiration, divine; "Sense of dependence"

Revelation. *See* Inspiration, divine

Revivals, religious, 12, 17–18, 78

Revolution, American, 10, 11, 12, 14–15, 89, 338

Revolution, French, 405, 406. *See also* France

Right Hand of Fellowship, 88, 239, 246–47, 303, 307, 308, 417, 476, 478

Ripley, Ezra, 507 (n. 58)

Ripley, George, 62, 64, 86, 103, 104, 116, 119, 120, 159, 180, 191, 199, 207, 214, 215, 225, 232, 301, 316, 353, 522 (n. 102), 546 (n. 126); described, 81, 517 (n. 18); and TP, 81–82, 88, 107, 134, 181, 218, 222, 224, 239, 292–93, 306,

Shaw, Elizabeth Willard, 177
Shaw, Francis George, 90, 178, 329
Shaw, Robert Gould (colonel), 90
Shaw, Robert Gould (merchant), 178
Shaw, Sarah Blake Sturgis, 90
Shelley, Percy Bysshe, 318
Sherborn, Mass., 432, 435
Siexas, James, 38, 391, 510 (n. 26)
Silsbee, William, 41, 65, 76, 78, 95, 105,
    116, 122, 123, 133, 137, 148, 149, 151,
    158, 167, 180, 227, 275, 297, 316, 373,
    387; and TP, 40, 239, 307–8, 322, 382,
    462, 548 (n. 36)
Simonds family, 504 (n. 25)
Sin, 101, 147, 320; original sin, 13, 14, 42,
    44
Slavery. See Antislavery/abolitionism;
    Latimer, George; Fugitive slaves/Fugi-
    tive Slave Law
Smith, Joseph, 427, 510 (n. 26)
Smith, Mary Ann, 506 (n. 49)
Smith, Samuel, 290
Society for Christian Union and Prog-
    ress (Boston, Mass.), 107–8, 476, 546
    (n. 128). See also Brownson, Orestes
    Augustus
Society of the Friends of Progress, 119
Socrates, 86, 119, 335–36, 371
Somerville, Mass., 420
Sorrows/afflictions: religious significance
    of, 146
South Boston ordination. See Parker,
    Theodore: writings: Discourse on the
    Transient and Permanent in Christianity
South Carolina, 474
South Congregational Church (Boston,
    Mass.), 303, 442
South Universalist Society (Boston, Mass.),
    420
Sparks, Jared, 37
Specimens of Foreign Standard Literature. See
    Ripley, George
Spinoza, Benedictus de, 59, 185, 186, 188
Springfield, Conn., 430
Spring Street Church. See West Roxbury,
    Mass./West Roxbury Church
Staël, Madame de (Anne-Louis-Germaine
    Necker), 66, 111, 278
Standing Order of Massachusetts, 13, 23

Stanton, Elizabeth Cady, ix, 343–44, 555
    (n. 145)
Stetson, Caleb, 88, 104, 199, 238, 304,
    462, 549 (n. 51)
Stevenson, Hannah, 566 (n. 21)
Stone, Richard Cecil, 432–35
Stratford, England, 382
Strauss, David Friedrich, 35, 150, 157,
    185, 197; Life of Jesus, Critically Exam-
    ined [Das Leben Jesu], 137, 138, 164,
    186–90, 200, 242, 287, 353; Transiency
    and Permanency in Christianity, 242–43;
    and inquiries in Germany, 389, 563
    (n. 26)
Stuart, Moses, 79, 134
Sturgis, Caroline, 91
Suffolk Street Chapel (Boston, Mass.),
    246, 356, 416–18, 420, 457–58
Sumner, Charles, ix, 470–72
Sunday, observance of, 214, 224, 231–33,
    383–84, 395; TP's views on, 214, 224,
    232–33, 383–84, 395. See also Chardon
    Street Conventions; Church: and reli-
    gious reform
Sunday schools, 37, 38
Sunday School Teacher, and Children's Friend,
    38
Supernaturalism, German, 69, 72, 138
Supernatural rationalism, 43–44, 74, 82,
    123, 157, 177; and TP, 44–49, 73–74,
    86, 157. See also Unitarianism
Swedenborgianism, 439
Switzerland, 383, 390, 404

Taft, Reed, 167
Taylor, Henry, Philip Van Artevelde, 42
Temperance, 52, 166–67, 205, 344–47,
    351, 396, 418, 468, 529 (n. 104); TP's
    views on, 166–67, 205, 346, 351, 396,
    468, 480, 486, 529 (n. 104). See also Hol-
    lis Street Church/Hollis Street Council;
    Pierpont, John
Texas: annexation of, 471–72, 474, 475
Thanksgiving, 131, 165
Theodicy. See God
Theology: science of, 138, 272–75,
    289–90, 464
Tholuck, Friedrich, 390
Thompson, George, 53, 57, 58

TP, 49–51, 60, 80, 88, 347, 369–70, 486, 556 (n. 154); and antislavery, 53–54, 55, 57, 58, 78, 512 (n. 74); "Personality of the Deity," 125; on Hollis Street Council, 347, 351, 366, 370; death of, 369–70

Ware, William, 127, 128, 134, 187, 189, 190, 191, 198, 199, 203, 271, 301, 449, 544 (n. 90)

Warren Street Chapel (Boston, Mass.), 567 (n. 26)

"Warrington," 492

Wartburg, Germany, 388

Washington, D.C./Capitol, 59, 474, 475

Waterston, Robert Cassie, 362–63, 369, 418, 423, 424, 438, 442, 447, 459, 540 (n. 19), 573 (n. 156)

Watertown, Mass., 24, 31, 34, 64, 75, 80, 104, 154, 189, 311, 391

Watts, Isaac, 15

Wayland, Mass., 117

Webber, Samuel, 15

Webster, Daniel, 130, 208

Wegscheider, J. A. L., 69, 202

Weimar, Germany, 383

Weld family, 90

West Church (Boston, Mass.), 457

West Brookfield, Mass., 321

Western Messenger, 119, 120, 200

West Roxbury, Mass./West Roxbury Church, 75, 79, 80, 86, 87, 88, 105, 115, 118, 130, 148, 157, 159, 176–77, 234, 235, 257, 260, 268, 271, 285, 291, 295, 300, 301, 306, 307, 311, 314–17, 324, 326, 374–75, 376, 396, 401–2, 414, 457, 459–60, 462–63, 465, 473, 476, 482–89, 486, 496, 524 (n. 6); described,

89–91, 129, 402, 492, 498; and church covenants, 89, 149–50, 163, 529 (n. 92); church services of, 129; intemperance in, 167, 529 (n. 104); becomes pariah church, 302–3. *See also* Brook Farm

Wheeler, Charles Stearns, 392

Whewell, William, 272–73

Whig Party, 108, 208, 215, 256, 318, 330, 469–72, 474, 475

Whipple, Charles K., 291

White, William Hoar, 20, 21

Whitney, George, 75, 89, 317, 529 (n. 92)

Whittemore family, 90; names son after TP, 303

Wilcox, Henry, 493–94

Willard, Sidney, 120

Williams, Avery, 7, 16

Wiswall, William Daniels, 463

Wittenberg, Germany, 383, 388

Wolf, Heinrich, 513 (n. 87)

Wolfenbüttel Fragments, 68, 69, 135, 188, 287. *See also* Reimarus, Hermann Samuel

Women's rights, 206, 343–44; TP's views on, 100–101, 113, 179, 205. *See also* Fuller, Margaret

Woods, Leonard, 43

Wordsworth, William, 140

Work. *See* Property/social inequality/pauperism/labor/work

Workingmen's Party, 107, 108

Yale University, 13, 259, 430

Young, Alexander: marries TP and LCP, 87; as hostile to TP, 236, 366, 368, 573 (n. 163)